CORNISH
ARCHAEOLOGY

50   HENDHYSCANS KERNOW   2011

Golden Jubilee Volume

SERIES EDITORS

GRAEME KIRKHAM AND PETER HERRING

EDITOR FOR VOLUME 50

PETER ROSE

ISSN 0070 024X
ISBN 978-0-9500308-7-6

Publisher: Cornwall Archaeological Society

Printing and binding by 4Word Ltd, Bristol, England
Design and layout by Donna Anton and John Bennett

Contents

CONSERVING THE PAST

PRESENTING THE PAST

25 YEARS OF DISCOVERY AND RESEARCH

Contributors

Eric Berry	Historic buildings consultant
Tony Blackman	President, Cornwall Archaeological Society
Pamela Bousfield	Wadebridge
Nick Cahill	Historic Environment, Cornwall Council
Ainsley Cocks	World Heritage Site office, Cornwall Council
James Gossip	Historic Environment, Cornwall Council
Steve Hartgroves	Historic Environment, Cornwall Council
Peter Herring	Characterisation Inspector, English Heritage
Margaret Hunt	St Keverne
Charles Johns	Historic Environment, Cornwall Council
Nicholas Johnson	Former County Archaeologist and Historic Environment Manager, Cornwall Council
Andy M Jones	Historic Environment, Cornwall Council
Graeme Kirkham	Historic Environment, Cornwall Council
Andrew Langdon	Truro
Jane Marley	Curator of Archaeology and World Cultures, Royal Cornwall Museum
Jeremy Milnn	The National Trust (West Midlands)
Jacqueline Nowakowski	Historic Environment, Cornwall Council
Hilary Orange	UCL Institute of Archaeology
Caradoc Peters	Truro College, University of Plymouth
Ann Preston-Jones	Historic Environment, Cornwall Council; and English Heritage
Henrietta Quinnell	Exeter
Ann Reynolds	Historic Environment, Cornwall Council
Adrian Rodda	Editor, CAS Newsletter
Peter Rose	Historic Environment, Cornwall Council
Adam Sharpe	Historic Environment, Cornwall Council
Cheryl Straffon	St Just; Cornwall Earth Mysteries Group; Cornwall Ancient Sites Protection Network
Vanessa Straker	Regional Science Adviser, English Heritage, Bristol
Professor Charles Thomas	Lambessow, Truro
Nigel Thomas	Historic Environment, Cornwall Council
Carl Thorpe	Historic Environment, Cornwall Council
Anna Tyacke	Finds Liaison Officer for Cornwall, Portable Antiquities Scheme
Imogen Wood	University of Exeter
Andrew Young	Historic Environment, Cornwall Council

Cornwall Archaeological Society 1961-2011

Presidents

C A Ralegh Radford 1961-1964
Professor Martyn M Jope 1965-1967
Andrew D Saunders 1968-1972
Patricia M Christie 1973-1975
Paul Ashbee 1976-1979
Geoffrey W Wainwright 1980-1983
Professor Charles Thomas 1984-1987
Cynthia Gaskell-Brown 1988-1990
Norman V Quinnell 1991-1993
Martin Fletcher 1994-1996
Peter Gathercole 1997-1999
Nicholas Thomas 2000-2003
Henrietta Quinnell 2004-2006
Tony Blackman 2007-2011

Hon Treasurers

Peter A S Pool 1961-1966
J R Cory 1967-1968
T P F Trudgian 1969-1977
P G Pearce 1978-1984
Ursula M Davey 1985-2001
Konstanze Rahn 2002-2005
John Bennett 2006-

Hon Membership Secretaries

Patricia M Carlyon 1969-1974
Daphne Harris 1975-1992
David Donohue 1993-1998
Barbara Tripp 1998-1999
Dorothy Cudlipp 2000-2001
Jennifer Beale 2001-

Hon Secretaries

Florence Nankivell 1961-1969
Betty Greene 1970-1973
Mary M Irwin 1974-1986
Anita F Cooke 1987-1992
Brian Hammond and Sheila Hammond 1993-1997
Polly Fryer 1998
Imogen Wood 1999-2001
Hilary Orange 2002-2004
Sally Ealey 2005-2009
Roger Smith 2010-

Hon Editors

Professor Charles Thomas 1961-1975
Henrietta Quinnell (Miles) 1976-1981
Professor Malcolm Todd 1982-1984
Rowan P Whimster 1985-1986
Daphne Harris 1987-1991
Sarnia A Butcher 1992-1994
Christopher Dunn and Margaret Dunn 1995
Peter Gathercole and Conn Murphy 1996
Peter Gathercole and Peter Herring 1997-1999
Peter Herring and Graeme Kirkham 2000-2004
Graeme Kirkham and Peter Herring 2005-

Newsletter Editors

Edith Dowson 1969-1973
Sheila de Burlet 1973-1977
Margaret Hunt 1977-1979
Les Douch 1979-2003
Konstanze Rahn 2003-2006
Adrian Rodda 2007-

Note: Dates of office have generally been rounded to the nearest year, based on information in editions of *Cornish Archaeology*. Not included in the table are site directors, walks and talks organisers and one-off posts such as Hon Photographic Editor (held by Charles Woolf, 1963-1984) and Hon Legal Adviser (Peter Pool, 1967-1974).

Boscawen-un stone circle, St Buryan. Photograph by Paul Chrome, CAS member.

MARKING 50 YEARS OF THE CORNWALL ARCHAEOLOGICAL SOCIETY

A look back from the members' perspectives.

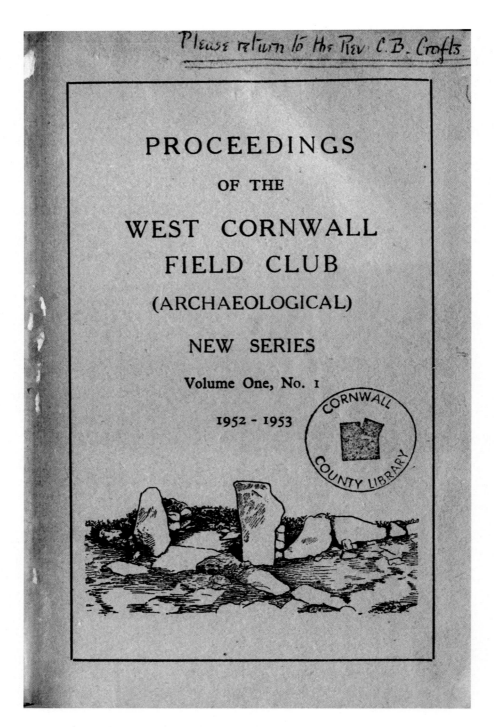

PROCEEDINGS

OF THE

WEST CORNWALL

FIELD CLUB

(ARCHAEOLOGICAL)

NEW SERIES

Volume One, No. 1

1952 - 1953

The Proceedings of the West Cornwall Field Club *preceded* Cornish Archaeology, *Volume I of which was published in 1962. Charles Thomas was the editor of both journals from 1952 to 1975.*

Cornish Archaeology 50, 2011, 3–5

How it all began?
A personal viewpoint

CHARLES THOMAS

So this year, 2011, marks our half-centenary. What can 50 years mean to an archaeologist? One might suppose very little indeed, in a discipline concerned with millennia. At a personal level, the context in which I now write, it can mean a great deal though with the proviso that the succession of events, the rate of progress, can make that half-century seem more like a rapid-motion decade. Looking back, it's far from easy to define the significance of our Cornwall Archaeological Society, CAS, with its annual journal *Cornish Archaeology, CA,* but here goes. This is the testimony of an Original Member.

My life as an archaeologist began in the 1940s when, as a bicycling teenager obsessed with the 1840 Tithe Apportionment Map of Camborne, my native parish, I scoured dozens of lanes and by-ways – Camborne's a large parish – trying to find and plan rounds, hut circles, field systems, holy wells, and the rest. You name it, I looked for it, and by the age 14 I had learnt enough Cornish to work out what place- and field-names meant. It had been assumed that my career would be as a solicitor in the family law firm, Daniel and Thomas, Camborne. Even then I suspect that, like dear Peter Pool in later life, the idea of spending sunny days stuck in a dark office instead of being out in the field had become distasteful. It became more so when, as a young soldier, I spent two years in Egypt, examining native villages, picking up flints (cherts?) on the hills west of the Canal Zone, and playing chess with the Afrika Korps veterans who manned the laundries. Home

again, it was three years at Oxford reading law or Honours Jurisprudence; I failed at the first try, got 3rd-class Honours at a re-sit, and devoted most of my time to home-centred history, archaeology and folklore. I had discovered the books of V Gordon Childe, who seemed to me as important as Charles Darwin; I wrote to the great man, and after Oxford was allowed to enter the Institute of Archaeology for its two-year postgraduate Diploma in Prehistoric Archaeology. This was, in its prime (with Childe, Wheeler, Zeuner, Mallowan, Kenyon, *et al)* 'The Institute' to which a galaxy of CAS stars (kick off with Paul Ashbee, Paddy Christie, Nicholas Thomas) has been linked.

It was far from easy in the mid-1950s to get any kind of paid job in archaeology either in a British university or the Ministry of (Public Buildings and) Works, unless you happened to be a Cambridge person inside the J G D Clarke empire. Incredibly, back in 1957 outside Cambridge, there were only seven lectureships. None became available unless a lecturer moved on to a chair, as Richard Atkinson did to Cardiff in 1958, when I was appointed without interview to his post at Edinburgh. A year on, my salary having risen from £600 to £700, I could afford to marry and also to buy a New Town apartment for £1500 immediately below that of my boss Stuart Piggott. The Edinburgh degree course, spawning endless future professors, took four years; apart from departmental digs elsewhere, vacations were spent in Cornwall at our Gwithian house. This was the pre-motorway age and the two-day drives from Edinburgh to Cornwall in the old Bedford van were necessary nightmares. But when at home I could re-connect with my interval years (1955-58) as a WEA Tutor in Archaeology, Cornwall's first-ever in that line, and with dozens of friends headed by my mentor R Morton Nance, Grand Bard. In all those seasons in the field at Gwithian from 1953 onwards, aided by three other future professors, West Cornwall Field Club (WCFC) and then CAS members (Peter Fowler, J V S Megaw and Bernard Wailes), I had no more idea than any of them where I might find myself in the year 2011.

Well, now that we're here, most of us pensioner archaeologists and still loyal CAS members, what has happened? To some extent, any distinctions do tend to come up with the rations, as one used to say of the army's Long Service medals. I find that, in common with a CAS ex-president Nicholas Thomas at Newlyn, 50 years as a Fellow of the Society of Antiquaries of London, an FSA, means one no longer has to pay the (vast) annual subscription! In Scotland my 50 years as an FSA (Scot) turned me into an Hon FSA (Scot); and more like 65 years with the Royal Institution of Cornwall including a spell as president and a long period as Hon Courtney Librarian has left me as an Hon Vice-President and Jenner Medallist. Ought we to consider presenting 50-year certificates to surviving members of CAS – and there are some – who joined in 1961? I was made a Bard, *Gwas Godhyan,* of the Gorsedd of Cornwall in 1953 on the top of Trencrom, and in 2003 was given an ornate sheet to that effect. At home we have a downstairs convenience resembling those of a great many retired academics; between the coats and umbrellas are any number of framed certificates. Where else is one supposed to hang them?

What has all this to do with the formation of our Society? Answer: everything, because during that long professional career my concern was only secondarily with Cornwall's (and Scilly's) recent and remote past. It was with people young and old, friends and colleagues, mostly within Cornwall and also from further afield if they were interested in us. I never met Lt Col Frederick C Hirst, our real Founder, but after my time at the Institute I did spend six months at the Wayside Museum, Zennor, as resident curator doing my best to catalogue a mass of finds from saddle-querns to arrowheads. Hirst, to me, underlay all that we'd done post-War

and intended to do next. In 1952-3 the small but active West Cornwall Field Club wanted to revive its 1936-37 *Proceedings.* I was made editor, and saw through nine annual issues, I, 1-4, II, 1-5, up to 1961. We started a Cumulative Index of Cornish Archaeology and, inspired by Vivien Russell, Parochial Check-lists; foundation-stones of what would become one of Britain's largest county-based Sites and Monuments Records.

By 1960 the idea of a 'Cornwall Archaeological Society' came to the fore. Among prime movers were C A R Ralegh Radford, self-employed, and myself, only recently employed, as the professionals; and Florence Patchett, Bret Guthrie, Vivien Russell, Florence Nankivell with, as a lawyer skilled in preparing societies' constitutions, Peter Pool. Various factors urged us onwards. First, whatever exactly '*West* (Cornwall)' had meant in 1936, it hardly covered past or future work at Tintagel, Castle Dore, Bodmin Moor, The Rumps, and so on. Second, since most other counties had long possessed their own archaeological societies, why shouldn't we? and a modern one, inspired by Wheeler, Fox, Piggott, Clark and the like, quite separate from a Royal Institution of Cornwall that still held believers in Phoenicians and Druids. Third, we plainly needed a new and larger annual journal and, though it was early days for such, one able to attract grants and several hundred subscribers. Fourth, and Radford was insistent here, the last thing we wanted was any kind of intra-Cornwall fission, formation of other little societies digging (but not publishing) as was happening in Somerset.

So we went ahead; in 1961-62 our society came into being, embracing Cornwall from the Tamar to Lands End (and Scilly), soon tripling its membership. I was induced to edit *Cornish Archaeology* 1 (1962), designed for us by Ian Mackenzie-Kerr of Thames and Hudson, where Vincent Megaw was on their archaeological staff. The verso of the cover of *CA* 1 lists all the officers, headed by Radford, and committee members (Fig 1). Eighteen people were named. Today only two of those, Margaret Y Morgan and myself, are still around.

If pressed to say what, in 2011, I regard as my most useful contributions to Cornish archaeology, early history and place-names, I would have to be selective and brief. Faced in childhood as I was with the 'Dark Ages' and all that Arthurian nonsense, I would like to think that from Gwithian and elsewhere it has been possible to make better sense of a post-Roman Cornwall, say fifth to eighth-ninth centuries; to compose the story of how and when Christianity came, with its sites and inscriptions; and again mainly from Gwithian and Tintagel, more or less to invent a pottery sequence and to identify and describe post-Roman imports (Radford had invented imported pottery classes A to D; I invented Class E at Gwithian!). After my 10 years at Edinburgh, which I loved, and five at Leicester, which I didn't, came two decades directing the new Institute of Cornish Studies. This had to be interspersed with service on national bodies like the Council for British Archaeology, RESCUE, and the former Royal Commission, always making sure Cornwall's voice was heard. Here the Institute, strongly tapping the Manpower Services Commission for funds, could not only train a new generation of archaeologists; it underlay formation of the Cornwall Committee for Rescue Archaeology, later Cornwall Archaeological Unit, and the start of proper archaeological work in Scilly.

And now, thanks to so many hard-working friends, I can look forward to a prolonged reading of *CA* 50 (for 2011). What happened to all those early CA cover drawings, editorially commissioned at a fiver a time from Cornish artists like Peter Lanyon, Roger Penhallurick, Michael Tangye? Well, they're not in my downstairs convenience alongside documents signed by HM the Queen and John Major, nor will they appear in local salerooms. Finally, to whom apart from a long-suffering family do I owe the most for my lifetime in Cornish archaeology? I can't list all their names; some are no longer with us; most, fellow-workers, close and dear friends for a great many years, continue to protect and interpret our past, and also to underpin our Society and its splendid journal. My gratitude goes to them all. Enough; that's the end of reminiscing, and now read the real archaeology brought together to celebrate our half century.

CHARLES THOMAS
CBE DL MA DLitt HonDLitt FBA Hon MRIA FSA FRHistS
President of the Cornwall Archaeological Society 1984-1987

Fig 1. List of officers from Cornish Archaeology, *Vol 1, 1962, cover verso.*

CORNWALL ARCHAEOLOGICAL SOCIETY

newsletter

NEWSLETTER No.58   OCTOBER 1988

Congratulations to our new President, Cynthia Gaskell-Brown, on her recent promotion to Assistant Curator in Plymouth Museum. We also hear that Win Scutt is moving to 'the Dome' on the Hoe where he will be setting up a historical interpretation unit. We are assured that the pedestrianisation of the city-centre and the new florabundance there are coincidental.

Your Hon. Secretary, Anita Cooke, is off to New Zealand for 2 months, from October 7th to December 10th and during that time Pat Carlyon has very kindly and generously offered to act as Temporary Secretary. Her address is: Miss P.M. Carlyon, Penwinnick, Barrack Lane, Truro. Telephone Truro 72023.

We have had a very good response to our questionnaire which we will summarise in the next newsletter, so if anyone still wishes to send theirs in, it will be very welcome.

PROGRAMME OF WINTER LECTURES

Our series of winter lectures will be held as usual at the County Museum, Truro, starting at 7.30 p.m. These are open to the public as well as members of the Society so do bring along anyone who might be interested in the subject. PLEASE NOTE the first lecture will be held at PENAIR SCHOOL which is on the St Clement Road leaving Trafalgar Roundabout past the Police Station. There is plenty of parking at the BACK of the school, the front park is for lecturers only, and you may be asked to move your car in the middle of the lecture.

Friday 14th October – Penair School
"Tombs for the Ancestors; Neolithic Burial in Britain by Dr Timothy Darvill.

Thursday 24th November
"Conservation of the Heritage, or, do you want to live in a Museum" by Professor John Wacher.

Friday 2nd December
The Holbeche Corfield Lecture
"Dartmoor Prehistory and the Wider World" by Mr Andrew Fleming who is Senior Lecturer in Pre-History at Sheffield University. He has been involved in field work on Dartmoor since the 70s and put reaves and prehistoric land boundaries on the map.

Friday 20th January 1989
"The once and future monument; Tintagel, Retrospect and Prospect" by Professor Charles Thomas.

Thursday 23rd February
"The Castles of the South West" by Dr Robert Higham.

WINTER LECTURE SERIES AT PENZANCE, LISKEARD AND BUDE

In the past there have been any number of requests for more lectures at centres other than at Truro. This winter the CAS and the Cornwall Archaeological Unit are jointly organising a series of five monthly talks at each of three venues, Penzance, Liskeard, and Marhamchurch, Bude, between late October and late March/early April. The talks will be given by members of the CAU and will look at the results of some of the Unit's recent projects.

For details see the enclosed poster which gives the winter programme in full.

Peter Rose

EXETER UNIVERSITY CLASSES IN ARCHAEOLOGY WINTER 1988/9

A sheet with full details is included with this Newsletter. Please retain for future reference. Weekly courses are planned for Truro and hopefully Liskeard; the Bude class has progressed from archaeology to the geology of the Cornish landscape. There are also classes in Plymouth which may be accessible to some in East Cornwall. Planning regular classes in Cornwall is now restricted by the few archaeologists with time to teach. If there is anyone in Cornwall who might be interested in taking classes in any branch of archaeology, with whom I have not been in touch, I would be pleased to hear from them.

A Service of Secretaries, who span the history of the Cornwall Archaeological Society: from left to right, Florence Nankivell, Anita Cooke and Mary Irwin. Thank you ladies!

This 1988 edition of the CAS Newsletter, edited by Les Douch, was the first to include a photograph. It shows three honorary secretaries of the Society – Florence Nankivell, Anita Cooke and Mary Irwin.

Cornish Archaeology 50, 2011, 7–24

MARKING 50 YEARS

Why bother?
Some clues from the Newsletters

ADRIAN RODDA

The Cornwall Archaeological Society's first Newsletter was published in December 1969. Its editor, Edith Dowson, of Mawnan, set out her purpose: 'We aim to establish close contact not only between the Society and its scattered members, but between members themselves.'

The excitement of members being actively involved in researching, recording and preserving their heritage is reflected in the report on the CAS Symposium, 'Cornish Archaeology – the next five years.' A Steering Committee to plan the Centre or Institute for Cornish Studies had been set up by Exeter University and the County Council, with Charles Thomas, who was to become its first Professor of Cornish Studies, putting archaeology high on its agenda.

Less prominent or influential members were encouraged to play their part by three appeals for help. Dorothy Dudley asked members to keep an 'open eye' for damage to listed or unlisted monuments. John Stengelhofen wanted a watch kept on industrial sites and reports sent to the Industrial Archaeology Sub-Committee. Mary Henderson invited members to contribute to her listing of Cornish Crosses.

Fig 1. The CAS excavations at Carn Brea, 1971. Director Roger Mercer is standing at the left of the trench. With his colleague Joyce Greenham, Charles Woolf created a magnificent photographic record of Cornish archaeology. He was the CAS Hon Photographic Editor to 1984. (Photograph: Charles Woolf Collection, reproduced with the kind permission of the Royal Institution of Cornwall, RIC)

Fig 2. Volunteers at Carn Brea (1971) included Margaret Morgan (with drawing board), then and now a CAS stalwart.
(Photograph: Charles Woolf Collection, reproduced with the kind permission of the Royal Institution of Cornwall, RIC)

Members' local knowledge was again evoked in Issue 2 (February 1970) when Dorothy Dudley of the 'Open Eye' suggested where to look for cross bases - in field gateways, by stiles or bridges or where hedges had been scrubbed out. Michael Tangye asked for reports of subterranean tunnels cut into soft marl, which Charles Thomas named 'tatie hulls' (potato holes). Another special interest group, the Cornwall Water Wheel Preservation Society, was formed.

Members were not only exhorted to get out on their feet with an 'open eye'; they were encouraged to grovel on their knees at excavations at Carn Brea (CAS's own dig), Carvossa, Halangy on the Isles of Scilly, Launceston Castle, Piran Round, or Carn Euny, where professionals welcomed volunteers at what were generally research driven excavations.

For members who wanted to follow up fieldwork or to find where to look for sites, Les Douch, Curator of Royal Cornwall Museum, wrote an article in Issue 3 (June 1970) describing the books and source material available at the Royal Institution of Cornwall to compilers of the Parochial Checklists, begun by Vivien Russell and other members of the West Cornwall Field Club, which were to become such a feature of the Society's research and formed the foundation of the county's Sites and Monuments Register when it was established by the Cornwall Committee for Rescue Archaeology. By June 1971 a meeting of the Parochial Checklist Compilers reported that there were 17 people working on 23 lists and a further 18 workers planned to start on an extra 16 lists. Eleven would 'make an attack

on Trigg Major', but more people were needed for Truro, Stratton and the east of the county. Ironically the current Area Representatives Committee has been recruiting members to cover every parish in the county and its appeals in Newsletters 124 and 125 (Oct 2010 and Feb 2011) have been successful. The nature of the work may have changed with new planning laws to protect the heritage and with more professional archaeologists to carry them through, but there always seems to be a place for the amateur with time and local knowledge.

Another feature of fieldwork is revealed in two extracts from early Newsletters – the value of what is now termed Oral History. Michael Tangye, who only retired as an Area Representative in 2010, wrote in Issue 5 (February 1971).

The regrettable destruction of a legend

In a field at Lizerea Farm, Burhos, Wendron, bordering the main Helston – Redruth road stands a huge menhir. At one time fallen, it has been recorded that it was re-erected by the three brothers Pearce in the early 1900s. One of them, John, a man of great strength and an accomplished wrestler, was known as "the Sampson of Wendron". Stories of this great feat made the brothers legends in their own lifetime in the locality.

Some years ago while doing fieldwork in the area I talked with an old farmer who remembered the occasion well. I here record it with much regret! The Pearce brothers arranged to re-erect the menhir in the presence of Sir George Smith, the owner of the land. A large pit was dug and on the appointed day the small group gathered and waited silently – not for the spirit of some long departed Celtic warrior who would endow their brawny arms with added strength – but for the clanging, hissing and puffing of a steam engine which, passing the farm on the road each week, had been solicited to help in erecting the mighty stone. With the combined efforts of the three men of Wendron and the engine the task was completed to the applause of Sir George, who then threw some coins into the pit around the base of the erect menhir. "How much?" I asked the old man. He smiled, squinting in the afternoon sunlight, "Dunnow. But whatever 'twas, theese could be sure 'twadn wery much!"

This story illustrates the value of re-investigating local features which may have previously been recorded and published. Very often the initial survey would have been of necessity hurried and conducted in territory strange to the writer. The local field worker however has the advantage of visiting and re-visiting sites and recording in great detail.

It is here that the value of the oldest inhabitant often proves itself. Time spent in giving a lead and patiently listening to much rambling and uninteresting information is often rewarded by some gem of authentic material. It should be remembered that an octogenarian who recounts something told to him by a grandparent could take us back to the 1830s! This was well illustrated to the writer recently when such a conversation revealed the original site of a Stithians cross, not as recorded by Langdon, in Sewrah Mill, but in Sewrah Farm, out of the valley, where it had been found by the old man's grandfather, lying in croft land and brought down to Sewrah Mill by cart. The Tithe Apportionment list and map proved the validity of the old man's story. Near the point indicated was a field named "Well Crow", obviously a form of "Gwell crouse" and "Churchway field".

Daphne Harris recorded a much more frustrating encounter with another ancient informant in Newsletter 31 (September 1979).

A brief and tantalising glimpse of the past

One cold sunny day around midsummer 1979, Mary Irwin and I drove westwards to investigate a suggestion in the Sites and Monuments Register that a possible beaker burial in a cist had been discovered in West Penwith. Our information was scanty, but the discovery seemed to have been reported to the local headmaster, and so we started at the village school. There the master was extremely kind and ready to spend time on our problem, but not prepared to betray any confidences. He did not himself know of a cist being discovered on any farm nearby. We were invited into the classroom to ask the pupils, who were mostly local farmers' children, whether they had heard of a stone box being found, but the result was polite but complete silence. However it was suggested to us that a certain local worthy was interested in antiquities and might be able to help us, though we were warned that he was getting on in life and was apt to mix fact with fancy. Our next call was therefore on this gentleman.

We were again received with great courtesy and kindness, and were shown a collection of flints. Our informant had collaborated over archaeology in the past with the vicar, but had parted from him over a difference of opinion. After an apology for the personal nature of the question, we were asked why elderly ladies like ourselves were interested in these old things. When we had explained our interest as eloquently as we could, and recovered from the slight shock of being described as elderly by someone 15 years our senior, we found that to him the fascination of archaeology lay in discovering something that nobody else knew about – and then keeping the secret to himself. Then he told us about his most exciting discovery.

One bright moonlight night he had set out, guided by a little reading but mostly by intuition. With the aid of an entrenching tool and a child's metal spade he scraped away a shallow depth of soil, and came across a stone. When the top stone was removed, he found a stone cist, just as he had seen it beforehand in his mind's eye. It was hollow, except for a very slight filtering of the earth. Its floor was cobbled with smooth round stones. On this lay the skeleton, in an extended position. The earth was smoothed hard under the skull. On the right hand side of the body was a stone spearhead. On the left was a pot, lying on its side, and unbroken. The pot was not shaped at all like a beaker, but more like the teacup that was in my hand at the time. It was decorated with two or three rows of cord impression round its fattest part near the top.

After its discovery the grave was covered

Fig 3. CAS field trip to the Men an Tol, 5 May 1974, led by Professor Charles Thomas. Those to his right include (from left) Mary Irwin, Lindy Stengelhofen (then Voisey), John Stengelhofen, Sheila de Burlet, Joyce Greenham, Pam and Michael Tangye and daughters; amongst those to his left are Peter Trudgian, Justin Brooke, Bret Guthrie and Florence Nankivell. (Photograph: Charles Woolf Collection, reproduced with the kind permission of the Royal Institution of Cornwall, RIC)

again. The finder swore an oath to himself that he would never reveal its whereabouts to a living soul. He has, however, made notes about the burial which could go to an Old Cornwall Society or some such similar organisation on his death. And so the position and date of the burial may one day be known to posterity.

The mixture of fact and fiction which passes as folklore is revealed by another long serving Area Representative, Richard Heard, in Issue 24 (June 1977).

In the parish of Jacobstowe there is a large tumulus on high ground called Beacon, in a field known as Burrow Moor. This was used as the parish beacon. At the end of the last century school children still knew the folk-tale surrounding it:

"A giant lived at Beacon and quarrelled with another living at Warbstow Burrow. There was a scrap, the Warbstow giant was killed, and his grave can be seen at the centre of Warbstow earthwork."

Another folk-tale is attached to the Holy Well of St James but a short distance from Beacon Barrow: "Under the well lies a crock of gold; if ever man so much as cleans it out there will be thunder and lightning, the Almighty showing his disapproval."

I feel it worth relating these, the only folk-tales attached to ancient monuments that I know in the Stratton area, though stories of ancient battles are common enough.

The passion for preservation is reflected in John Stengelhofen's whimsical use of the folk lore style to make a political message in issue 7 (February 1971).

Mine waste...or monument to generations of Cornish miners

Once upon a time, and it was not so very long ago, there stood upon the hill a most curious old chimney stack, watching over one of the county's old mining towns... just like a castle... The mineral landlords had said it should be, and the miners had built it... just like a castle. So it stood, for a hundred years and more; all the townsfolk (or nearly all) agreed it was a fine monument to the generations of Cornish miners – the best Cornish miners, who had come from the town at the foot of the hill.

But what had fate in store for this curious stack? The miners all departed for places like Burra Burra .. Who owned the stack? All was well for a time.... It belonged to a most respected business man, a proud citizen of the town. And when he was old he gave the stack to his local council..... years later, one spring when he was very old he died.... No doubt happy in the thought that the stack would stand on the hill for ever.

But in the summer an estate agent auctioned some land for the council... it included "an area of mine waste" the agent said, but as it was "a valuable area of residential land" a builder paid the council many many pounds and bought the land... and a spokesman for the council assured everyone that "the stack was not scheduled as an ancient monument and the developer will be quite at liberty to pull it down". Then some people said it must be scheduled, but before the man from Whitehall could get here to look at it there was a big big bang and "the blast brought the local residents running from their homes thinking it was Concorde".

The townsfolk were angry, and they blamed their elected representatives for allowing the destruction, but all they would say was this council is in no way responsible for the demolition... it would have cost a considerable amount to renovate the stack". And to show they really were concerned about such things the council voted £10 for the preservation of Cornish mine buildings.... But then maybe the curious stack was just mine waste.... Like the agent said.... And we just dreamt the history.

Could this be in your parish? Make sure that your industrial monuments get scheduled and don't get treated like mine waste.

Edith Dowson died in February 1973 and Sheila de Burlet, of Polperro, took over as editor. Number 12 (June 1973) introduced the Lanyon Quoit logo to a strap line similar to today's editions. The newsletter was still being typed onto stencils and their pages stapled at the corner. Members' addresses were handwritten onto envelopes. Number 14 (February 1974) reported that the production of the Journal had been disrupted by the shortage of wood-pulp for paper and the energy shortage caused by the 3-day week, since printing presses were electrically powered. However, there was no shortage of energy from the volunteers who turned the Roneo for the newsletter, still produced in Foolscap size. Postage was only 2.5 pence in 1972.

Another 'quaint' aspect of the CAS activities in the 1970s was the need to take tea after field

MARKING 50 YEARS

Fig 4. Watch Hill Barrow, 1973. Henrietta Quinnell's (then Miles') rescue excavations in the St Austell china-clay area involved many members of the Society. (Photograph: Charles Woolf Collection, reproduced with the kind permission of the Royal Institution of Cornwall, RIC)

Fig 5. CAS and Lizard Field Club at the Dry Tree menhir, 15 June 1974, led by Margaret Hunt.
(Photograph: Charles Woolf Collection, reproduced with the kind permission of the Royal Institution of Cornwall, RIC)

trips. Issue 11 (February 1973) records a Field Meeting on Bodmin Moor shared with Devon Archaeological Society members. More than 100 members and friends finished their tour with tea at St Neot, which was quite an invasion for such a small village. I wonder if they felt, like Trigg Major, that they were being attacked by CAS?

Despite the 3-day week and economic problems, road works and clay quarrying were a recurring feature of the Newsletters in the 1970s. In October 1972 Peter Trudgian asked for volunteers to watch the road works alongside Tichbarrow, near Camelford, sponsored by the Department of Environment. Volunteers were needed for Henrietta Quinnell's rescue excavations on Caerloggas Downs. Another rescue dig was on a square earthwork enclosure at Grambla, Wendron, threatened by the clearance of woodland. The extension of by-pass schemes, which occupied our members in often unproductive field walking in all weathers, moved Daphne Harris to lament in Newsletter 20 (February 1976).

Ballad of the by-pass

The graders and the diggers are driving us silly
From Bodmin Great Ditch to the Henge of Castilly;
The JCBs shock St. Ingunger, who frowns
At the mess they are making along Innis Downs.
At Callywith, Carminow Cross and Treffry
There are deep excavations, and no-one knows why
We find paleolithic axe-hammers, and flint,
Even oil-jars; of settlement sites not a hint!

Digging could be a dangerous experience as Les Douch, Colin Edwards, Pat Best and Pat Carlyon recounted in Issue 19 (October 1975).

Les Douch had been called up to a farm at Kilhallon, in the parish of Tywardreath, where Mr Richard Kittow was levelling an area to make a tennis court. His JCB had revealed a midden of cockle-shells and some pottery. Les recruited at very short notice more intrepid CAS members, who located a ditch and attempted to follow its course, collecting sherds of Romano-British pottery and even some Samian ware and glass, thought to be from the second century AD.

The tennis-court area was mechanically scraped of its top soil, revealing an outlined circle filled with a yellower earth than that surrounding it. The red-blackness of the outline warned of a pit in which there had been intense burning. Understandably, we had high hopes of our pit: it was measured, drawn, photographed in irreproachably archaeological fashion before being sectioned. Removal of the top fill disclosed charcoal and comminuted bone; lower down there was charred wood and coal which, in turn, overlay the whole bones of a bullock and even part of its hide and hair. By this time the spectators and the diggers were expressing some concern both at the modernity and the nature of what had been found. Mr Kittow assured us that there had been no cases of anthrax on the farm in his day or that of his father, so the animal had evidently been buried more than 30 years ago. The fact of a single burial declared it not to have been a case of "official" foot-and-mouth, and the facts of an attempted cremation in a pit showed it to have been something more than a sudden death when the animal would almost certainly have been taken to the knacker-yard.

It was thought best to contact the Ministry of Agriculture where we spoke to a Mr Lamb who was most intent on telling Les Douch that it was an offence to resurrect a carcase!!! He was sure that the cremation was not "official", the pit being so shallow and the burning so inefficiently incomplete. We were left with the suspicion that we had excavated a case of "unofficial" anthrax. On enquiring of Mr Lamb what precautions those involved should take, we were informed that the Ministry dealt only with animals, evidently not human animals, and that we should consult our doctors. Finally, we were told by the Public Health Authority that we had two alternatives – to have six massive doses of penicillin in our tender backsides immediately or wait until the symptoms appear and then have them. Needless to say, we preferred the latter course. You will be pleased to know, as we have been pleased to observe, that no black blood pustules have appeared on our hands or forearms.

Although money was tight in the 1970s the Carnegie Trust awarded a grant of £70 in 1974 to purchase a Dumpy Level and CAS bought a Sopwith Staff to go with it. Members learned how to use these tools by surveying sites on Bodmin Moor. Now we are learning how to use electromagnetic and geophysical location and surveying equipment. The term Dumpy Level sounds very earthbound compared with our use of satellite signals today. Fieldwork techniques move on apace. A register of members who could help at short notice on rescue excavations in February 1975 brought 50 responders. Issue 18 (June 1975) described the formation of the Cornwall Committee for Rescue Archaeology. In 1976 Peter Sheppard was supervising a new register of Sites and Monuments for the CCRA.

But members were not only learning about archaeology and prehistory in the field. The Extra-Mural Department of the University of Exeter advertised 17 courses and day schools, some lasting 20 weeks, for the winter of 1976/77, along with two weekend courses in Exeter. They were distributed around the county at a time when it was not assumed that everyone had a motor car. Indeed some of the CAS fieldtrips were organised by coach and if there were not enough members to book a coach a programme of car sharing was encouraged.

Other technology that we take for granted was not available to most people in this period. If you look at your family photograph albums you will be disappointed to see how badly faded are your early colour photographs. In the decades when few people had good quality cameras, the Society was fortunate to have a professional photographer, Charles Woolf, to record its excavations. In February 1972 he mounted an exhibition of his photographs of Cornish Antiquities. His archives are today treasured by the Royal Cornwall Museum.

Margaret Hunt took over to edit number 23 and numbers 25-29.

A close look at Issue 24 (June 1977), edited by Les Douch and Daphne Harris while Margaret Hunt was recovering from a road accident, shows a very active society. The President, Paul Ashbee, commented at the AGM: *'CAS has been active at Harlyn Bay, Launceston, Rough Tor, The Lizard, Trencrom, the Royal Cornwall Show, day-schools, surveys, excavations, trench watching, conferences, seminars and lectures – all showing clearly that the Society is fortunate in having so many members willing to work for it.'*

Members had helped with Nicholas Johnson's exhibition themed 'Agriculture and Archaeology' at the Royal Cornwall Show. Johnson had explained that, *'The walls, lynchets, ridge and furrow, huts and other remains of our agricultural past are being rapidly eroded by modern agricultural processes. ….. the exhibition will show which modern farming activities are doing the damage …. (and) ways in which the destruction can be minimised.'*

As if to illustrate Johnson's point, reports from Area Representatives included how a *'well built cist... containing soil, human skeletal remains and a large number of beach pebbles'* had been discovered through deep ploughing. Charles Woolf had called on Peter Trudgian and Daphne Harris to help excavate and record the feature on a cliff near Porthcothan. Michael Tangye noted that one of the five stones of the Nine Maidens Circle, Wendron, *'had been removed by a mechanical digger because it hindered ploughing'*. He quoted Dr Borlase in 1758, *'two incomplete circles … most of the rest fallen'* and added ruefully, *'Of these two circles there remains only four stones erect.'*

Peter Trudgian undertook a watching brief over a trench for a water pipe in North Cornwall. Twenty CAS members helped Peter record 17 graves along

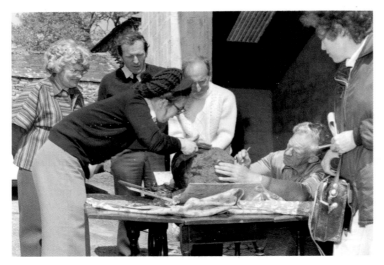

Fig 6. Excavations at Stannon Pit, St Breward, 1977. The excavations were directed, undertaken and written up by members of the Society. An urn is examined by (from the left) Daphne Harris, 'Capt' Welch (of Stannon Pit), Henrietta Quinnell (then Miles), unidentified person, and Peter Trudgian. (Photograph: Charles Woolf Collection, reproduced with the kind permission of the Royal Institution of Cornwall, RIC)

the line of the trench near St Endellion. He also directed a rescue dig on a third barrow on Stannon Downs in advance of china clay waste tipping. Diggers and their plans and tools sheltered from the elements in a caravan donated by Mrs S Lanyon (Carbis Bay), which was to become a permanent feature of CAS excavations.

If we move on to Issue 35 (February 1981) we find CAS members still active in organised fieldwork. CAS and Exeter University Extra-Mural Department launched a scheme to compile a record of old farm buildings with a brief description and photographs or sketches. A study weekend was held at Launceston and a Briefing Day for volunteers at St Austell, while the CAS/DAS Joint Symposium at Saltash concentrated on smaller domestic buildings in the region, with presentations on Totnes and Penryn.

Another centre of field activity was the Lizard Peninsula with excavations at Carngoon Bank, a Roman period salt production site and a Bronze Age house and field system at Poldowrian. The main project was known as the Lizard Project. It involved widespread fieldwalking to attempt to discover a site where gabbroic clays were fired and to settle the question of whether clay or finished pots were exported from the St Keverne area. No pottery was found, but the scatter of chipped flint and nearby settlements should have indicated its presence. It was concluded that what pottery there was had been destroyed by ploughing. At least two flint tool manufactories were identified. Centuries of ploughing over the thin topsoil of the serpentine

area and over the more fertile gabbroic area had gone into the subsoil and confused archaeological horizons as well as destroying barrows and other features. Taking its responsibilities seriously CAS published a Guide to Fieldwalking Methods and ran a practical course in field survey techniques.

Threats to sites came not only from farmers and developers; Issue 38 (February 1982) alerted members to the fact that it had become illegal to use a metal detector on a Scheduled Ancient Monument. Dr Wainwright provided guidance to CAS members

Fig 7. CAS field trip at Rough Tor, June 1982, led by Nicholas Johnson. Right is Gwynneth King, then CAS walks organiser.

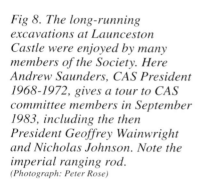

Fig 8. The long-running excavations at Launceston Castle were enjoyed by many members of the Society. Here Andrew Saunders, CAS President 1968-1972, gives a tour to CAS committee members in September 1983, including the then President Geoffrey Wainwright and Nicholas Johnson. Note the imperial ranging rod.
(Photograph: Peter Rose)

MARKING 50 YEARS

who might be *'confronted by someone using a metal detector on a protected site'*. He ended his advice – *'No attempt should be made to restrain anyone physically and no approach should be made to anyone if it is thought he might resort to violence or threats of violence.'* Nicholas Johnson brought home to members that the problem was *'right here in our own backyard'* by explaining that *'the second church of Perranzabuloe lying close to the now buried oratory may have to be buried as well due to the damage by vandals and extensive diggings by treasure hunters.'* This, of course, is the medieval church abandoned in 1820 and dug out in 2005 and made accessible to the public with new interpretation boards. It is encouraging to think that we are now in the business of revealing rather than hiding our heritage from the public.

Lectures and courses were not always centred in Truro. Exeter University Extra-Mural Department ran five weekly lectures and two field days with Henrietta Quinnell. Local interest was evoked by Nicholas Johnson and Peter Rose describing 'The Archaeology of Bodmin Moor' to an audience in Liskeard, while George Smith and Daphne Harris updated 'The Lizard Project' in Helston. In 1984 Exeter University sponsored courses in Newquay and St Ives as well as Truro and Exeter. The popularity of archaeology was shown when in 1986 Sandy Gerrard's lecture on his excavations at Colliford Reservoir was attended by 90 people, with standing room only for late-comers to Webb's Hotel, Liskeard. Extra-mural classes were available in St. Ives, Truro, Penzance, and day schools and courses at Bodmin, Exeter and Truro.

Issue 44 (February 1984) reported from CCRA that Stephen Hartgroves had been appointed Sites and Monuments Officer to organise the Record for computerisation. This has been achieved and Issue 123 (June 2010) explained how it has been made available to the public through a website, www. heritagegateway.org.uk. His appointment freed up the two (only) existing Field Officers, Nicholas Johnson and Peter Rose, to continue their surveys of Bodmin Moor, supported by Norman Quinnell and Martin Fletcher (Royal Commission on the Historical Monuments of England) and Peter Herring. No wonder support was welcomed from CAS members.

Issue 47 (February 1985) launched 'The Megalithic Project' to follow Charles Thomas's excavation at Bosiliack in August 1984. Teams of volunteers were recruited to 'adopt' monuments classed as Penwith Chamber Tombs and Land's End Entrance Graves along with similar sites in other regions of Cornwall and to prepare a dossier of documentary and fieldwork evidence relating to each site. The aim was to identify sites where excavation could most likely answer questions about their construction, purpose and date.

Social events became learning experiences. Sunday 21 June 1987 found members assembled at Park Farm, St Clements, with wild foods and milk products thought to have been available in Iron Age times, together with a range of meats and fish, all to be cooked in pits with heated stones. The organisers were particularly insistent that beverages should be confined to beer, mead and cider. One assumes that water was acceptable, but not recommended on health and hygiene grounds. These health considerations led Henrietta Quinnell to cut open each joint of meat to inspect that it was fully cooked before allowing it to be tasted. Henrietta herself learned from this experience that hot stones are best handled with long tongs and that most of the meat was overcooked.

The themes of cooking and megaliths were tastefully combined when Ann Preston-Jones presented Mary Irwin, the retiring secretary, with a farewell cake baked in the form of a megalithic monument. Archie Mercer, who appeared frequently as a reporter in Newsletters of the day and who was an indefatigable organiser of field activities, commented, *'I'd never before realised how tasty the contents of a cremation-urn could be.'*

Issue 55 (October 1987) highlighted the problems arising from amateurs not being allowed on developer sponsored professional excavations, but there were still plenty of sites where they could dig, including the ditch at Killhallon, where no more anthrax pits were reported. Indeed members were greeted to the open day on the site with scones, cake and tea. There is much to be said for amateurism, it tastes better.

Issue 57 (June 1988) described how the CCRA evolved into the Cornwall Archaeological Unit. But there were still not enough professional archaeologists to watch over all the trenches in the county. In the next newsletter, Geoff Walford's regular 'Notes from East Wivelshire' complained that the Gas Board was laying a trench unknown

Fig 9. Iron Age picnic, 1987. Centre – Norman Quinnell and Archie Mercer at the cooking pit.
(*Photograph: Henrietta Quinnell*)

Fig 10. Iron Age picnic, 1987. Preparing the cooking pit – Ursula Davey (left), Henrietta Quinnell (centre), Carole Vivian (left, rear)

to CAU. Road schemes promoted field walking in advance of the bulldozers at Indian Queens, Penryn, and Carland Cross to Truro.

Les Douch included the first photograph in Issue 58 (October 1988). It was a delightful photograph of the three honorary secretaries of the Society, who between them spanned its life to that date – Florence Nankivell, Anita Cooke and Mary Irwin. From then on we were treated to pictures of members digging, surveying, being guided around sites and, being CAS, picnicking!

Opportunities to become actively engaged in excavation reduced during the 1990s, but volunteers were still welcomed at Porthcollum and Penhale Round. Issue 75 (June 1994) reported that by-pass walking was no longer allowed. However, CAS members had set up training programmes within more formally organised groups, such as Tony Blackman's Young Archaeologists' Club, the experimental archaeology at Trewortha Farm and Geoff Walford's Caradon Archaeological Group in 1994. Attempts to enthuse young people about archaeology led the society to organise a day in August 1993 for 60 scouts and guides from a jamboree at Wadebridge Showground. Field walking turned up a few flints at Tregurtha Farm, St Wenn, home of Vercoe and Val Benallick. The youngsters cooked in Iron Age style and tasted the savouries and sweets they produced, made and fired clay pots and wove reed mats. Vercoe allowed them to grind corn on querns from his farm and conducted all of them through his private collection of flints found on his land.

Fig 11. Iron Age picnic, 1987. Charles Thomas and Anita Cooke, then President and Hon Secretary.

Adult members' interests were appreciated through a competition for photographs on archaeological themes, which had been promoted by Archie Mercer, and in 1993 Morwen Morris launched an appeal for arts and crafts to display at the forthcoming AGM. As part of our 50th Anniversary Celebrations similar competitions were advertised in Issue 124 (October 2010) to populate an exhibition being held at Trerice in September 2011. To further encourage its adult members the Society began a programme of training projects and courses in June 1994, known as PAST – Practical Archaeological Skills Training. The aim of these was to train people in post excavation skills, recording and surveying techniques and to give practice in field walking.

However, we must not assume that the society

was becoming parochial in its activities. In Issue 77 (February 1995) Geoff Walford promoted the idea of a Brittany link to host exchanges and meetings with like-minded folk from a similar 'Celtic' area. A small group visited Vannes to meet the Societe Polymathique and to tour its museum and to plan the exchange. The four day programme for the Breton visitors in June 1997 began with a tour of the Royal Cornwall Museum and Jacqui Wood's Cornwall Celtic Village, then a day each was devoted to Penwith, the Lizard and the Bodmin area. All talks were in French, at which Anna Tyacke proved fluent, while other guides had to have translators. But the linguistic laurels must have been won by Prof Charles Thomas, who gave the final farewell speech in Breton.

Archie Mercer had handed over the organisation of field trips to Chris Riding and CAS members enjoyed a two day visit to the Isles of Scilly in addition to their monthly walks in the county.

Les Douch, the Curator of the Royal Cornwall Museum, had taken over editing the newsletter with Issue 30 in 1979 and continued until his sudden death in 2003, producing 69 issues. It was now professionally printed and included photographs of sites and groups of members. His humour and erudition illuminated the editorial and news items. One example came in Issue 80 (February 1996).

The diary had not forecast anything out of the ordinary for this particular day. In mid-morning the phone rang and an unidentified man asked if I were the Curator. There was desperation in his voice when he pleaded for my help. "What advice can

Fig 12. Iron Age picnic, 1987. Preparing the greens – Henrietta Quinnell (centre) and Nancy Reed (standing, right)

Fig 13. CAS field trip to Tintagel, 1988, led by Professor Charles Thomas, using CAS members to mark the outline of a post-Roman building
(HE, Cornwall Council)

MARKING 50 YEARS

you give," he asked, "to the caterpillars in central Africa who are in danger of being cremated in forest fires?" After an interval which I hope did not betray my disbelief, I asked if his communication with these sufferers was telepathic and two-way. After replying that it was, he went on to say that the danger of fire rose from the broken bottles which littered the forest floor. His concern was so real and his anxiety so fraught that I had to make some suggestion. "Advise your friends," I said, "to pull the heaviest of the leaves over the glass and so obscure it from the sun's rays." He replied, "What an obvious and simple answer. I will tell them immediately.

I replaced the phone, paid the experience into my memory bank and went about more routine affairs. Some days later, the man rang again to express his own and the caterpillars' profuse thanks for my advice. The danger had been averted.

On two more occasions I was asked to help moths and caterpillars in difficulties, once for those in South America and once for some nearer home, on the Lizard.

My final contact with this still anonymous enquirer came in his last phone-call when he announced in utter despair and misery that his flat-mate had thrown on the open fire a collection of friendly slugs which he kept in his wardrobe. My friend left me with the graphic pictures which they had projected to him during their death agonies.

One of the supreme privileges of being a museum curator, especially at the toe-end of the world, is that you are always there as a fixed point of contact for all sorts of people who ask you to join in all sorts of experiences, and share an endless variety of theories and beliefs. Ultimately you feel enriched by all the information, argument and colour which you have received through academics, "ordinary" people with extra-ordinary ideas, and the brilliantly barmy.

Being editor of the CAS newsletter is in some ways a comparable occupation; it keeps me in touch with the inspired and the obsessed. Without further comment, I report a letter addressed to CAS by a Len Fulton of Warrnambool in Victoria, Australia. He introduces himself as a great grandson of Richard Johns and Margaret Nancarrow who married in Phillack in 1833. He writes: "I have located a name N. McElgurrn and a date 1010 on a large rock, and a map of Australia on another rock, and steps cut into a rock face.

All the stone mason work and engraving has been done by expert tradesmen. The name McElgurrn is not known in Australia. I believe Irish, Scotch or Celtic Monks used the area here, plus Pirates.

"There is a lot of ships here covered with silt near an old river bed.

"A hill is covered with sunken holes resembling a mine field. They are buried artefact sites. I believe one object is a large Porcelain cross…. The history books of Australia will have to be rewritten."

Welcome to the Club, Mr Fulton.

Eccentrics who caused concern and surprise, not to mention confusion, were not confined to the twentieth century, as this tale by Michael Tangye, published in Issue 61 (October 1989) will witness.

All that glitters Is not gold!

In 1977 this writer was granted access to the library of the Dorrien Smith family within the Abbey on Tresco. In a drawer was noted a small bronze, 65mm in height, depicting a nude couple perched on a column, in the most intimate of positions. The hairstyles and appearance of the object suggested it was possibly Roman. Furthermore, an old label attached to it read:-

'Found in the Kist Vain on the highest part of the northern half of the island of Samson. Opened about 1871 by Augustus Smith.'

The reference could well refer to the well known barrow opened in 1862 by labourers under the direction of Augustus Smith in the presence of the visiting Cambrian Archaeological Society. A sketch was made and shown to Professor Charles Thomas who forwarded it to a colleague in the Roman Antiquities Department of the British Museum for identification. Back came the reply that it was not Roman – but a naughty Victorian pipe-stopper!

It would perhaps indicate that it had been dropped by one of the Cambrian Society, composed mainly of elderly and respectable Welsh clergy, when stooping low to inspect the tongue and groove cist. No doubt when Augustus held the object aloft and enquired as to whom it belonged its owner was too embarrassed to step forward! As the Society members were afterwards entertained in the "Abbey" it must have been placed in the drawer to await its owner – and there it has remained for 127 years!

Occasionally the newsletter published letters from its members who challenged the academics, sometimes in very strong language. One such was from Pat Brierley, who challenged the ideas of Professor Chris Tilley, which he was to formulate in the study of phenomenology and which he illustrated by reference to his work on Bodmin Moor, especially at Leskernick. In the same newsletter Issue 81 (June 1996) Theresa Lowndes summarised his arguments presented in a lecture to the society:

... to examine the role of the landscape and recognise how the interaction and our perceptions are based around interpretations of its beauty and its role in our lives as something to be used to enhance our leisure time. The experience of landscape in prehistory was, however, totally different. The landscape was both used and lived in, and as such it represented a set of relationships between different places. The entire landscape was of great significance and the symbolism of place existed alongside the practical daily existence.

Dr Tilley suggested that the nature of the symbolic landscape is probably best expressed by the monuments of prehistory that serve to both impose a cultural form on the landscape and highlight the significance of rocky outcrops on the tops of tors. During the Neolithic this relationship was expressed from a distance and the rocks were referenced and signposted by the various monuments, whereas in the Bronze Age the interaction of natural outcrop and monument was much closer.

..... Leskernick is the ideal place in which to put these theories to the test as it represents both the late Neolithic and the Bronze Age. .... (the site) did serve to highlight some intriguing features in the landscape. On top of Leskernick Hill lies a propped up granite boulder through which, on the summer solstice, the dying rays of the sun shine. On the surrounding hilltops lie an array of enclosures, cairns etc. As one follows the course of the stone row down the slope Rough Tor comes into view just as a wet area is crossed. It may be all coincidence of course but Dr Tilley feels that this is how the symbolic landscape would have been highlighted and brought into the day-to-day experience of place.

Within the settlement itself the survey work suggested a significance in the orientation of hut doorways with those on the south side of the hill showing a view out across the plain toward the ceremonial monuments of the past and those on the west oriented toward certain features in the landscape. There are also indications that the entire site was systematically destroyed at the end of the Bronze Age, possibly a symbolic decommissioning of the site as it was abandoned.

Pat Brierley's letter criticised any attempt to get into the minds of prehistoric peoples.

It was suggested that the rocks represented a "Power Source" and that they would have held enormous significance for those peoples. Slides were shown of crags and tors "redolent with power" to support this. ... The direction in which (the huts) faced was considered to be of great importance and we were treated to a slide of the investigators sitting inside the ruined hut holding a door frame (of remarkably modern dimensions) and making notes of what could be seen through it in terms of the "power sources". This for me put the whole lecture into perspective!

Pat complained that it was a waste of time and money trying to get inside the minds of the ancestors

...one only has to look at modern anthropological variations or indeed at one's nearest neighbour, to see that this is impossible.

In the following issue Archie Mercer joined the debate,

much discussed amongst members of late. Modern man can simply use his intelligence - reputedly the equal of prehistoric man's - to try to reconstruct the "best fit" for the prehistoric mentality, on the basis of the physical remains that our predecessors have left us. ... Why, one asks, is the doorway in that position? It may well be because it overlooks some particular feature – whether terrestrial or astronomical – which the builders considered important. Or, again, possibly it could be in the precise spot because it did not overlook a certain feature: or something else that we would consider so trivial that no-one has ever thought of it, since it went out with the Romans, or someone. Enough, I think, of that.

But another comment on the same topic, made in free verse some three years earlier, seems to me to express best the attraction of imaginative recreation of the past for amateurs.

Evening walk into the past

We stood around – our archaeology group –
Scanning the ring of tumbled granite stones
In the serene sunlight of a summer's eve
On one of Fowey Moor's vast rock-strewn shoulders.
"It is," said the speaker, "a good example
Of a Bronze Age hut circle." His practised eye
Skipped briefly round the stony jumble
Then away across the slope as he went on
To indicate where tiny fields once served
To feed and clothe an ancient farming folk
Whose work was done three thousand years ago.
We stepped inside across the hut's low wall,
Some, at least, aware that although unbidden
We had entered no mere study object
But the cherished spot that someone knew as home.
However wide and deep the gulf of years
That separates their simple world from ours,
We cannot doubt our linked humanity,
That here within this crude and humble space
Beat hearts as full of passion, love and fear,
Minds as calculating, wise or foolish
As any modern casual strangers' there.
We may not bridge the cultural gulf between us
But as we left their ancient hearth and floor
To the moor's deep solitude and emptiness
We spared a fond thought for those whose comfort,
Shelter and security resided there,
This, at least, as fellow men we owed them.

Mike Dundrow Issue 73 (October 1993)

Margaret Hunt wrote a personal piece for issue 83 (February 1997) about her work as the Area representative for the Lizard, where so much excavation (Poldowrian) and field - walking had taken place (The Lizard Gabbro Project). She reminded readers of how the Area Reps were set up by Professor Martin Jope, the then president, writing in the 1966 Journal:

The Committee would like to explore the possibility of actual area representatives, not necessarily burdened with committee duties, but as representatives or spokespersons of the Society to deal with such matters as chance discoveries. It is hoped to offer a scheme such as this in the future.

Margaret paid tribute to the work of Edith Dowson, her mentor and first Area Representative, as well as the originator of the Newsletter. In a later talk Margaret introduced us to this poem, attributed to Edith.

Gone to pot

The modern sage may scratch his head
And ponder on the ancient dead,
But doubtless couldn't care a cuss
What early man may think of us.

For surely our behaviour's what he
Might well consider to be "potty".
Could he understand us gloating
With an attitude quite doting
Over what – to him- was just a common pot?

The sort of kitchen jar that got kicked around the floor,
Till its fragments joined the garbage in the pit!
Women made them by the dozen
And fired them in the oven.

Each mother taught her daughter how to do the
* patterned bit;*
Till one day a stubborn daughter
Made some shapes she shouldn't oughter!
(Teenage – problem-child, of bygone age.)

Now scholars sweep like vultures
On the remnants of these cultures,
Argue fiercely with each other
And smash their teeth with rage
As they bandy heated words
Over simple homely sherds,
In elucidating what
Has, long since, gone to pot.

Margaret herself ruminated on the reasons for putting so much effort into exploring her past, not only in the field but also in libraries and the County Record Office. Her comments will surely echo with us all, they certainly recall the poem and sentiments of Mike Dundrow, quoted above.

I had plenty of time to think not only about what was driving me to do it, but also to think of those whose steps I was retracing so many hundreds of years later. Their loves, their hates: were they worried about what they were to have for tea: did they appreciate the song of the skylarks over the moors, or the busy-ness of the bees in the heather? Who knows, but I guess that their lives were too hard for this sort of romancing. It is too easy for us, going back to a warm home with food on the table, to romanticise about it all.

Field-walking was always a most important part of my duties as an Area Correspondent. Today I cannot see a ploughed field without getting an almost irresistible urge to go and have a look. Between 1973 and 1993 over 200 fields have been walked. The chances of finding prehistoric artefacts on plough-ridges were high. ... One of my favourite finds was one of 26 small flint scrapers all lying close to each other. There was perhaps a hint of something in the name of a nearby field, Carworgy.

Any of us who have walked fields or excavated can appreciate the great feeling of comradeship when working with a group of like-minded people in the pouring rain or standing ankle-deep in a muddy trench. Sometimes one wonders, "Why, oh why, am I doing this?" But the feeling of satisfaction is still there. As for those warm sunny days, well they are the ultimate.

By the late nineties it was taken for granted that members would not need coaches for fieldtrips but would have their own cars. In October 1997 (Issue 86) 20 members met at Pendeen fogou, drove on to Carn Euny, visited the ice-house at Trengwainton Gardens, and paused to picnic at Marazion beach, while their leader, Dave Smart, took a dip in the sea! Then they drove to Halligye fogou on the Trelowarren estate and finished at the Loscombe 'hull' near Four Lanes. But such breathless expeditions were outpaced in 2007 and 2008 when Graeme Kirkham and Nigel Thomas led two excursions across the channel to explore sites in Brittany (Issues 114 and 118).

An interesting and perceptive letter from Maurice Smelt in Issue 89 (February 1999) raised the problem of the use of 'formulaic' scientific language and expression in the reports included in the CAS journals, which had become almost exclusively the outlets for professionals describing excavations and sometimes theorising from their discoveries. He argued:

I see this issue as important not only because I think obscurity is always wrong, but because it is a special sin in the CAS. Our objective is to

foster knowledge (Constitution Clause 2). We can't disseminate if our reports are written in a style that freezes out the layman and reinforces the professional closed shop...

To this we might add the complaint that so much excavation within the county, developer led and often performed by professional groups or universities from outside the county, is not published at all, but remains as 'grey literature', so it is vital that newsletters should keep up with all the Cornish discoveries, hence the regular features, 'News from the Historic Environment Service' and 'News from Royal Cornwall Museum' as well as occasional essays from Anna Tyacke when a spectacular find has been reported to the Portable Antiquities Scheme. Our own county planning authorities are to be congratulated when they write into a developer's permission the need to publish any archaeological discoveries, but the Coalition Government's cuts in spending and their encouragement of development by the private sector with less 'red tape' is surely going to lead to more secrecy, let alone obscurity of expression. Recent discussions in *Current Archaeology* (Issue 250 January 2011) have challenged amateur societies to be more watchful and challenged professional archaeologists, academics and field-workers, to make more effort to include the public and to encourage amateurs in order to have more support in their corner when they argue again the challenges of the 60s and 70s to keep an open eye and to attempt to educate and capture the interest of people in archaeology.

Issue 95 (February 2001) set out the rationale for Practical Archaeological Skills Training courses to be organised by CAS for its members. The same edition reminded members of the hut building at Trewortha Bronze Age Village by Graham Lawrence and Tony Blackman. That was a shining example of a practical skill, attempting to replicate Bronze Age living conditions. However, issue 96 (June 2001) ruefully observed that most of the PAST sessions had to be suspended because of the foot and mouth restrictions on movement which also closed footpaths in the countryside.

These activities were in part to compensate for the loss of the Extra-Mural Department of Exeter University short courses and day schools distributed through the county. What courses there are, seem to be at degree level, designed to prepare more professionals and are expensive to follow. As Ursula Davey pointed out in a letter (Issue 105 June 2004): 'The local colleges offer some good courses but not everyone wishes to take examinations.'

Dr Oliver Creighton, the Programme Coordinator for the Department of Lifelong Learning Archaeological Studies, replied to Ursula's letter and to concerns expressed by other members in Issue 106 October 2004.

We are keen to stress the Department's continuing intention to offer modules in Cornwall in the future. The School of Education and Lifelong Learning is currently carrying out a full review of its part-time provision beyond Exeter, and a feasibility study into which subject areas can be offered in Tremough is ongoing.

The review decided to offer only distance learning courses in archaeology, which required individual study through the internet. When we recall Margaret Hunt's comments about making friends with people with shared interests, we may wonder how many friends we can make on the internet. Best leave that to Facebook and concentrate on our CAS lectures which do at least get some of its members into the same room together.

Non-examination evening courses and subsidised courses for mature students have disappeared with new rules on Further Education funding. However, while they were running many new members had been recruited through Hilary Orange's A level evening classes at Truro College and Geoff Walford described the adult education classes held at Liskeard and Saltash by Sallyann Couch. These were very practical in nature and became the foundation of the Tamarside Group, whose geophysical surveys were to become so valuable in extending our knowledge of Cornish archaeology (Issue 107 February 2005).

In Issue 106 October 2004 the PAST courses were revived and Henrietta Quinnell, as President, introduced Day Schools planned to cover all the cultural periods from the Paleolithic and Mesolithic (Issue 111June 2006) to Early Medieval. Some of these gave us news hot from the press. Professor Tim Darvill explained to us his latest theories on the reason why the bluestones were brought from Pembrokeshire to Stonehenge. Professor Mike Parker Pearson had barely shaken the mud of Stonehenge off his boots

when he excited us again with his discoveries as part of the Riverside Project (Issue 121 October 2009). You do not get that kind of excitement on a computer screen!

For the sake of our out-of-county members and those who do not enjoy driving on winter nights the Newsletter has attempted to summarise every lecture and describe every walk in a way that it can be replicated by other walkers. Konstanze Rahn, taking over on the sudden death of Les Douch to edit Issue 102 (June 2003), set this as her goal, so that the Newsletter has become a publication of record as well as comment and news. Another initiative by Henrietta Quinnell was to set up bi-annual 'Archaeology in Cornwall Day Conferences'. Here working archaeologists could update us on excavations and discoveries often waiting in a long queue to be published. The first one, on May 12 2007, needed to be reported across two newsletters, Issues 115 and 116. Indeed Issue 116, February 2008, had to be expanded to 12 pages to cover the lectures from the Cornwall and Devon Archaeological Joint Symposium in October 2007.

In an effort to get more interplay between readers and writers, Konstanze encouraged letters and introduced a front page quiz to identify sites photographed from the air (February 2004). The use of personal computers allowed her and the current editor to lay out the pages and make them print-ready on a disc to save on printing costs. Indeed we are faced with the conundrum that our newsletter costs more to post than it does to print.

Under a new President, Tony Blackman, CAS began to organise its own research excavations after a gap of 25 years. Hay Close at St Newlyn East turned out not to be a Neolithic henge hoped for from an air photograph (Issue 114 June 2007). However, Dr Andy Jones intrigued us all at a lecture by suggesting that it was some kind of special ritual site through the Iron Age and later, which promoted the choice of the village as an especially potent Christian settlement (Issue 121 October 2009). To confirm the latent interest in archaeology amongst the public the Open Day brought more than 200 'pilgrims' to St Newlyn East (Issue 116 February 2008).

The season at Boden, when a Bronze Age house revealed some of the biggest pots in Britain, was amongst the happiest of digs under the genial leadership of James Gossip.

Issue 119 February 2009 recorded the comments of several members. Sandra Thomas, who farmed near the site, remarked on unearthing one piece of pot, 'You never know, one of my ancestors may have handled this.'

Chris Verran wrote,

My first find was a small piece of Iron Age pottery; even though Trevisker ware and cord decorated sherds were being found all around me, I couldn't be more pleased. Jacky Nowakowski, in the next trench, must have thought I looked dejected, for she said, "Don't worry, you will find plenty more." How right she was!

Phil Tizzard echoed how encouraging the professionals were to first time volunteers.

I learnt how to record and catalogue finds, but also I discovered a great deal about round houses of the period and I began to understand just how much work goes into excavations, both at the planning stage and the processing of finds followed by the final report. Perhaps more importantly I discovered how enjoyable a time could be had with several like minded amateurs and a scattering of willing and able professionals.

Andy got his chance with the genuine Neolithic at Carn Galver and Bosporthennis Entrance Tomb. The later site gave work for our geophysical survey team, who have been so active on several sites across the county, but most noteworthy in Peter Nicholas's pursuit of Roman sites. Issue 115 October 2007 proudly proclaimed 'Second Roman Fort Confirmed in Cornwall'. Restormel might prove to be an oppidum in addition to a fortified camp and in January 2008 Chris Smart of Exeter Archaeology excavated part of another fort overlooking the Tamar at Calstock (Issue 117 June 2008).

Our members have been active surveyors or diggers at all these sites and some were able to help on developer financed digs by HES at Richard Lander School's new site, Truro College, Tremough and the clay country. The newsletter has covered them all, now supplemented by our colourful Website, which even includes videos from YouTube and the BBC. The website is able to bring up-to-date information to members and has space to publish longer reports to complement the summaries published in the Newsletter. This has

Fig 14. Set up in 2002, the CAS web site has been looked after by Simon Thorpe, John Bennett and Ryan Smith.

worked well with recent excavations, such as Carn Galver (Issue 122 February 2010) and Gunwalloe (Issue 124 October 2010). Newsletters are now available through the website and members can enjoy photographs in colour!

Community digs financed in part by the Heritage Lottery Fund have occurred at Glasney College and St Piran's second church. We have become involved in the CBA Festival of Archaeology and been acknowledged as one of the most active and diverse societies visited by the Council for British Archaeology. (Issue 119 February 2009).

Activities have sometimes been inspired and part financed by the renewal of interest in protecting the local heritage amongst regional groups. In 1997 the Cornish Ancient Sites Protection Network brought together people with any interest at all in protecting our ancient monuments and its members regularly visit and monitor sites, mostly to begin with in West Penwith. It has a website with guided walks and directions to the sites, which can be downloaded, and its associate organisation, FOCAS, has a weekend of walks and talks and a regular programme of site clearances (Issue 111 June 2006). Its expertise and enthusiasm has helped to form Lizard Ancient Sites Network (Issue 120 June 2009). CAS and CASPN are now working on extending its protection and monitoring to sites on Bodmin Moor. These activities are Dorothy Dudley's 'Open Eye' on a really organised and committed basis. The Bodmin Moor Monitoring

Group was partly stimulated by letters to the newsletter from Roger Farnworth, who found that people had been making their own cairns of stones from the platform cairn of Showery Tor (Issue 116 February 2008) and from the walls of Stowe's Pound (Issue 122 February 2010).

Even more locally focused is the Meneage Archaeological Group which promoted and part financed the excavations at Boden. St Piran's Trust is dedicated to digging out the oratory on the sand dunes above Perranporth after restoring the medieval second church of St Piran. The Tamarside Group, based around Saltash, has shown us what can be done with a magnetometer and a lot of patient walking to and fro. Indeed its members have made us think very deeply about the Roman army's interest in Cornwall as a source for iron. All this has been flagged up and reported in the newsletters.

Unfortunately when a society has been active for 50 years it has outlived many of its founders. The newsletters have included obituaries to our most active members and regrettably in the last three years has recorded the deaths of valued and revered past presidents: Norman Quinnell (Issue 117 June 2008), Andrew Saunders (Issue 120 June 2009), Paul Ashbee (Issue 122 February 2010) and Peter Gathercole (Issue 125 February 2011).

It would be tedious to list the range of distinguished lecturers and their topics over 50 years. Suffice it to say that academics and field archaeologists have taken us to sites on all continents – Belize to New Zealand, Sri Lanka, Greenland, Siberia, Benin and most European countries. Every corner of Cornwall has been covered and often followed up with field trips. Some members have been 'hands on' diggers and many more have been 'foot on' field walkers, visitors to sites and often 'open eye' custodians of the heritage. All these activities have been recorded in the Newsletters and this article is an attempt to present a montage of an active society carrying out a range of regular and special activities when like - minded people can indulge their imaginations and wonder at the achievements and lifestyle of our ancestors. To quote Mike Dundrow again:

'This, at least, as fellow men we owed them.'

Cornish Archaeology 50, 2011, 25–26

Members remember

JEREMY MILNN, MARGARET HUNT, PAMELA BOUSFIELD

Working with CAS in the early days; a brief recollection

Jeremy Milln

I was 13 when, in 1969, I applied for membership of CAS encouraged by Peter Sheppard, and under whose guidance I prepared the 'check-list' for the parish of Ladock. These lists were the fore-runner of today's Historic Environment Records which most county authorities began to set up in the mid-1970s, so the combination of desk-top and field survey with CAS, proved an immensely valuable experience later on for entry to professional life as an archaeologist.

Too young to be allowed to participate in the 1970 season, opportunity in 1971 to join Roger Mercer's research excavation at Carn Brea near Redruth, proved irresistible. This I owe very much to the kindly support of Pat Carlyon, as she then was, and in that year and in 1972 travelled down to the excavation with her. For those staying overnight, the accommodation was basic – the floor of a local school-room - and the catering, for which we contributed the princely sum of £4 per week, rudimentary. My memories as a boy were of the joy of working on one of the county's greatest sites, with its fabulous views, and with people of like enthusiasm. The acid soil of the site, darkened by the charcoal of ancient fires, seeped into every pore, literally and metaphorically. I was hooked. The number of flint arrowhead finds, suggestive of violent assault, was so great that everyone got to

share the buzz and I was rewarded also by finding one of the rare greenstone axes amidst the collapse of the rudimentary granite walls of the Neolithic settlement. It is salutary to reflect that the Carn Brea dig was closer in time to Wheeler's set piece pre-World War Two excavation at Maiden Castle, than today, and that in many respects its organisation and techniques were Wheeler's too. We recorded meticulously, we discussed earnestly and we socialised heartily. I secretly admired a girl on the dig and the fruit cake provided at lunch. I don't think the girl ever knew, but Roger did spot that I had sneaked an extra cake one day. Years later I was to see Roger in Scotland and mentioned the cake incident as though seeking absolution. Fortunately he had entirely forgotten.

Around the same time, CAS members were involved in the first excavations by Henrietta Miles (later Quinnell), then a young, and immensely inspiring, graduate from Cardiff University. Technically I cut my trowel with her on Longstone Down above St Austell on an early rescue dig of one of the few surviving barrows of the china clay district, but substantive involvement with Henrietta's archaeology awaited until her 1973 excavation of the Trethurgy Round. We stayed at Vounder Farm, roughing it on the floors, and walked in daily. Excavation by area, rather than by baulked trench, rewarded us with a much more joined-up picture of the lay-out of the site with its amazingly well-preserved round houses. There were thousands of stones to draw and I remember building a planning frame for the dig while at home one weekend. I enjoyed the digging and was thrilled to have found a substantial piece of one of Trethurgy's distinctive lugged elvan-stone grinding mortars, but it was to be the recording I would do for digs thereafter.

My supervisor there was Keith Ray, now County Archaeologist for Herefordshire, and – as it happens – now a close professional colleague. However, unlike Roger, he does remember my peccadilloes, but seems to have forgiven them!

How Edith Dowson changed my life
Margaret Hunt

It was in the early days of CAS that Edith came into my life. History had always been my focus of interest. But nothing came of that until she knocked on my front door early one spring morning in 1962 or 1963.

There at the door stood an elderly lady. One of the most notable things about her was the orange-yellow stain on her light grey hair, caused by a lot of smoking. Her first words were to ask could she go and see the burial mounds on our land. I took her immediately to see them. On returning to the house I put the kettle on for the inevitable cup of tea and for the next two hours Edith told me all about the many sites of prehistory she had been going to see on the Lizard peninsula.

Edith had been spending a lot of time walking across the moors and fields and along the cliff paths, checking up on the visible evidence for these sites as recorded on the OS maps or that people had told her about. For instance there are 35 recorded burial mounds in St Keverne parish. She was doing this for the establishment of the future Parochial Checklists. I immediately became highly intrigued by what she

was doing and I volunteered to go with her.

Edith and I became very good friends and she actually changed the focus of my life. Archaeology was to become the focus point of everything in my life and this continues to be so to this day.

Pamela Bousfield writes …

After my husband and I bought Hantergantick in St Breward in 1966 we attended Veronica Cheshers's wonderful lectures on local history. She taught us to look around us to descry 'the effects of man on the landscape and the effects of the landscape on man'. She also encouraged us to join the Cornwall Archaeological Society. We knew little of the subject, but who could live on Bodmin Moor and not develop an interest in archaeology?

Nicholas Johnson and his team were so generous with their time and so inspiring with their expertise. We enjoyed the educational walks on the Moor and elsewhere, the Day Schools in Bodmin, the Discovery Holidays in Brittany and Ireland and the Isles of Scilly, When I gathered a group together to write 'A history of St Breward', it was through my membership of CAS that Nicholas helped me write my chapter on the prehistory of St Breward. He gave me a table and a chair in his office and allowed me to copy everything to do with St Breward from the new and as yet unpublished aerial survey of Bodmin Moor.

What amazing privileges and pleasures the CAS has given us over the years! And the St Breward History Group has recently taken on a new lease of life to give the village archive a proper name and to continue to foster interest in local history.

Fig 1. Bodmin Moor roundhouse – Garrow, St Breward.

ARCHAEOLOGY IN CORNWALL: RECORDING, CONSERVING AND RECONSTRUCTING THE PAST

The principles and practice of archaeology in Cornwall over the last 25 years

Cornish Archaeology 50, 2011, 29–33

The changing archaeological scene in Cornwall, 1985-2010

NICHOLAS JOHNSON

There has been a strong archaeological tradition in Cornwall, supported since 1818 by the Royal Institution of Cornwall, the Penzance Natural History and Antiquarian Society (1845-55 and 1880-98), Cornwall Excavations Committee (1931-1939), the West Cornwall Field Club (1933-1961), and since 1961 the Cornwall Archaeological Society. Of the seven councils created in the 1974 reformation of local authorities none had an officer qualified to advise on historic buildings or archaeology. Excavation, field survey and archaeological documentation was carried out by a mixture of university researchers, local independent researchers, set piece excavations with professional directors on Ministry of Public Buildings and Works/Department of the Environment properties, 'rescue' excavations supported by the above but directed variously by freelance archaeologists and 'expert amateurs' with links to the Society. The Society ran training excavations and supported field surveys and parish surveys.

Looking back it seems like a different world, with no calculators, desktop computers, photocopiers, faxes, mobile phones, electronic theodolites, GPS or digital mapping. There were 50% fewer Scheduled Monuments than today, 83% fewer Conservation Areas, and 85% fewer Listed Buildings. There were no Registers of Parks and Gardens or Battlefields,

no Designated Wrecks or Designated War Graves and no World Heritage Site. Heritage legislation was only partial, there was no Planning Guidance on the historic environment, no professional institutes, or any special interest groups dealing with archaeology or historic buildings within the Local Government Association.

Much of this anniversary volume is devoted to documenting the advances that have been made in archaeological knowledge and the new historical narratives that are emerging. The section 'Archaeological Protection' (Johnson, below) outlines the legislative and statutory framework that has emerged over the last 25 years. This section explores how and why archaeological research and field work (principally archaeological assessment and excavation, landscape survey, industrial survey, air survey, buildings survey, and maritime survey) has developed as it has over the same period. The interplay between threats to the archaeological resource, the changes to the planning system, availability of public funding, political direction and varying research agendas is complex but the results, in terms of the protection, conservation, management, access and understanding of our archaeological heritage, are impressive. Today Cornwall has the largest number of designated heritage assets of any county, and as sole Planning

Authority since 2009, Cornwall Council has the largest number of heritage designations to monitor of any council, and itself owns, and has responsibility for, more designated heritage assets than any other local authority.

When examining the last 25 years one can be forgiven for assuming that the position that we find ourselves in now is the result of purposeful strategic planning from the start. Reality is not that straightforward. Much of what has been achieved in Cornwall is as much the result of unexpected threat, as of the changing political fortunes of the heritage sector, and the personal academic interests of individuals and the availability of different grant streams.

The growth of developer-related archaeology – from 'rescue' to 'research'

The threats to archaeology by development, and how to deal with them, were the reason why the Cornwall Committee for Rescue Archaeology (CCRA) was created in 1975. In 1976 the Sites and Monuments Record (now Historic Environment Record) was established to incorporate all known archaeological sites, monuments and find spots, and this was to be the information bedrock upon which all advice was built. The HER now includes sites from remote prehistory up to the end of the Cold War (Hartgroves, this volume). The scope has expanded markedly to include industrial and military sites, marine archaeology, historic buildings and settlements and now include sites found through geophysics and aerial photography. These are held together and geo-referenced through GIS, and given historical context and time depth through Historic Landscape Characterisation (Herring, this volume). This comprehensive dataset, increasingly capable of complex interrogation, is used to demonstrate archaeological significance and to predict archaeological potential. Archaeologists have moved away from an instinctive 'preservation-at-all-costs' approach that was common 25 years ago, because today we are much more aware that the archaeological resource is significantly larger than was previously thought, and that threats to archaeology can yield predictable research gains in addition to unexpected discovery.

The threats to archaeology have changed over the intervening years, as have the means and scale of intervention. The introduction of the Planning Policy Guidelines (PPG16 in 1990 and PPG15

Table 1 Project work carried out in Cornwall, 1985-2010

Year	1. CAU/HES projects per year. (developer paid in brackets)	2. Non CAU/HES project reports	3. Total projects in Cornwall	4. Total industrial projects. (Mining related in brackets)	5. Total Geophysical surveys - (developer paid in brackets)	6. Total Maritime projects. (developer paid in brackets)
1985	26(3)	1	27	5(4)	1(0)	0
1986	13(3)	0	13	8(8)	0	0
1987	12(2)	2	15	4(4)	1(0)	0
1988	15(3)	1	16	6(6)	3(2)	0
1989	22(6)	5	27	13(12)	2(1)	0
1990	29(9)	6	35	5(4)	4(2)	0
1991	44(12)	6	50	11(8)	3(2)	0
1992	47(29)	14	61	9(9)	1(0)	0
1993	79(42)	10	89	22(21)	4(1)	0
1994	64(30)	18	82	13(13)	14(6)	0
1995	73(44)	16	89	19(18)	7(6)	1(0)
1996	70(46)	12	82	18(16)	10(9)	0
1997	77(52)	19	96	27(25)	9(4)	1(1)
1998	106(55)	31	137	33(27)	18(15)	3(1)
1999	116(73)	29	145	30(25)	9(7)	1(0)
2000	96(73)	19	88	41(32)	4(2)	2(2)
2001	96(70)	38	134	25(24)	17(14)	0
2002	76(47)	28	104	14(10)	7(6)	0
2003	83(63)	37	120	18(12)	8(7)	2(0)
2004	92(64)	53	145	37(35)	17(9)	3(1)
2005	83(71)	33	116	13(8)	3(2)	3(0)
2006	101(70)	28	129	25(23)	8(6)	3(1)
2007	115(64)	36	151	21(18)	7(5)	4(2)
2008	125(103)	45	170	25(20)	19(18)	4(1)
2009	120(79)	33	153	15(14)	14(12)	6(2)
2010	126(94)	40	166	16(13)	19(19)	3(0)

in 1994), for archaeology and historic buildings respectively, led to a steep increase in development related assessment and excavation work in the 1990s (see Table 1). Since 1985 there have been over 2,800 archaeological projects (assessment, excavation, survey, buildings recording), geotechnical projects, historical research projects, conservation management plans and urban surveys carried out in Cornwall. Over 2000 of these were carried out by the Cornwall Archaeological Unit/Historic Environment Service (CAU/HES; 1900 projects) and District Council Conservation staff (100). The remaining 800 were by more than 50 contractors, largely based outside Cornwall, of which 25 are archaeological contractors. Exeter archaeology (82 projects), Wessex Archaeology (40), Katherine Sawyer (16), AC Archaeology (12), and South West Archaeology (10), have carried out the most projects. Wessex Archaeology, Kevin Cammidge and HES have carried out most of the maritime projects, and Eric Berry, Keystone and HES have been responsible for much of the recording of historic buildings and structures.

'Grey literature'– and the information explosion

Whilst the Society's journal remains the principal means of publication for major excavations, field work projects and research, there are now other formats for publication and other means of dissemination. The 2,800 projects mentioned above have produced nearly 3,000 reports. Whilst some have found their way into journals and monographs, or have been published by the HES, the vast majority remain unpublished in the traditional sense, and are thus termed 'grey literature'. Many of the references in the articles in this volume are to 'grey literature'. Until recently this has implied that such reports are part of a vast, hidden, and largely unreachable resource that represents an unacceptable aspect of modern archaeology. This situation is now beginning to be resolved. Nationally, such schemes as OASIS are providing a searchable library for such reports, and in Cornwall most of the 1,942 HES reports (1975-2010) are available in pdf format on the www. historic-cornwall.org.uk website. These reports need to be treated with caution, however, since they have not been peer reviewed in the same way as journal articles, and it must be understood that initial interpretations in a preliminary 'archive' report on an excavation will be superceded by the conclusions of the published report – which, ironically, may be less readily available.

Traditional publications, including journals, now have to compete with the increasing amount of information being published on the internet. In addition, most of the well known, but expensive, antiquarian publications of the past are now available as print-on-demand scanned publications. In this fast changing information world the Society will need to consider whether it would like to follow the example of the National Library of Wales, and consider posting scanned versions of its own journals, and those of other Cornish archaeological journals, on the web. Cornwall has an extraordinary legacy of archaeological research and fieldwork and the full publication on the internet of its 'grey literature', and the making available online of its rich heritage of journal publications, would be a worthy outcome of this anniversary celebration.

Developments in archaeological detection

CCRA was an early convert to geophysical survey. The Ancient Monuments Laboratory (Inspectorate of Ancient Monuments) demonstrated, over three seasons (1978, 1980, 1982), that magnetometry worked very effectively in Cornwall (Rose, this volume). In 1991, at Penhale Round (Indian Queens), geophysics, combined with air photographs, was used for the first time on a major development site to guide where excavation trenches were to be located. However it was not until 1994, on the Probus bypass, that a systematic programme of magnetometry was paid for by the developer.

The results were good, and thereafter geophysics became an integral part of evaluation and mitigation in the Planning process.

There have been over 200 geophysical surveys between1978 and 2010 (see column 5, Table 1) covering a total of 16.59 km2 (1,659ha), and three significant marine surveys (e.g. side scanning sonar) in Mounts Bay (2552ha), Scilly (2009ha) and in advance of the Wave Hub off Hayle (2364ha). Over 20 specialist contractors have been involved in Cornwall, with the majority of the 159 developer paid surveys having been carried out by GSB Prospecting (88), and Stratascan (14) whilst the English Heritage Ancient Monuments Laboratory (41) and the Tamarside Archaeological Survey and several Universities have undertaken 67 research surveys between them.

New subjects for study and recording

The dramatic increase of surveys of historic mine sites in the early 1990s was in response to the availability to local authorities of 100% Derelict Land Grants in order to facilitate the 'clean up' of contaminated and unstable mine sites. Throughout the 1990s mine sites were under the constant threat of being 'tidied up' and 'suburbanised'. In order to record what was being lost and to try to assess which mining areas are of particular importance, CAU carried out surveys of threatened mine sites (see column 4, Table 1), and developed a number of large-scale mining landscape projects (Sharpe, this volume). In the period 1986-91 there was a burst of large-scale surveys to look at the potential of mining landscapes. This started with Bodmin Moor and was followed by detailed surveys at Minions, Luxulyan Valley, and Kit Hill, St Just Mining

District, and the St Austell China Clay district.

Whilst surveys in advance of grant aided 'remediation' to historic mine sites continued apace throughout the 1990s, these were gradually combined into large projects that have managed to incorporate the conservation of historic mine buildings and structures, with public access and interpretation in addition to the remedial work need for public safety (Sharpe, this volume). These included the Mineral Tramways Project 1989-2009, St Just Regeneration Project 2003-2008, Tamar Valley Mining Heritage Project (from 2003), Caradon Hill Area Heritage Project (from 2005), and East Cornwall Regeneration Project (2006-2008) with particularly significant conservation projects at Geevor (1993- 2009), and the Heartlands Project, South Crofty (2006-11). The fact that so much conservation work was going on was a major factor in the success of the World Heritage Site Bid in 2006.

Continuing china clay production, and now its retreat, combined with the Renewal of Old Mineral Permissions process, has necessitated much survey and recording, particularly in the Hensbarrow and Bodmin Moor china clay districts. As with historic mining, the threats to historic china clay works has resulted in the loss of important structures (such as Goonvean), but also a range of well documented and protected sites.

The archaeological response to changes in the farming economy

CAU was actively involved in discussions with the Countryside Commission in 1985/6 concerning the designation of Environmentally Sensitive Areas (ESA). This was intended to encourage traditional farming practices for the positive conservation of important habitats and historic landscapes. West Penwith, Bodmin Moor and the Lizard were submitted as candidate areas in 1986/7. The significance of the archaeology, as demonstrated by the surveys of the previous four years was crucial in the decision to designate West Penwith in 1987, and CAU was involved in defining the original boundary and its subsequent enlargement in 1991/92. At the same time CAU had been examining, since 1987, all applications for Forestry Grants. It was natural therefore that CAU/HES should take an active interest in all agri-environment schemes thereafter (Reynolds, this volume).

Towards better stewardship of the historic environment

From the early 1980s the National Trust commissioned archaeological surveys of its properties to guide a more informed management of the historic environment. There have been several campaigns of work that reflected contemporary concerns and campaigns. Thus, the West Penwith properties were surveyed in response to the conservation crisis of the early 1980s. Land reclamation grants paid for the surveys of mine sites and a major programme of acquisition secured vulnerable mining remains in St Just. More recently, work has concentrated on the great houses (Cotehele, St Michael's Mount and Trerice) and their associated parks and gardens.

English Heritage have also commissioned surveys in advance of repairs and development as well as for research, and to record earlier programmes of repair and rebuilding. Important surveys have been carried out at the castles at Pendennis, St Mawes, Launceston, Restormel, Penhallam, and Tintagel, and the Garrison walls on Scilly. Of their prehistoric sites only Chysauster still awaits a modern survey. Since 1985, the Cornwall Heritage Trust has acquired historic sites, including Castle an Dinas hillfort (St Columb Major), and now manages, on behalf of English Heritage, all non-custodial national monuments including Carn Euny, Trethevy Quoit and Dupath Holy Well. In recent years, many sites owned by local authorities have also been recorded including, Trevelgue Cliff Castle, Kit Hill, Carn Brea, Luxulyan Valley, Geevor Mine, Robinson's Shaft and many other individual sites and buildings. Again, many of these are as part of grant programmes.

In addition to the above, arising from concern about the care of sites in the late 1990s, including the protection of prehistoric monuments at risk from damage during the gatherings to observe the total eclipse in 1999, local groups such as the Cornish Ancient Sites Protection Network and more recently the Lizard Ancient Sites Network have become actively involved in conserving and monitoring monuments. This carries forward the work of the Old Cornwall Societies that started in the 1930s.

Changing research themes

Programmes of innovative research have been of particular note. The surveys of West Penwith and

Bodmin Moor, as well as mining and china clay surveys are examples where threat has been the spur to action. The huge increase in the recording of military sites (see Johnson, below), which includes the Plymouth defences (1991-2) and English Heritage castles and fortifications, are the result of threat to the resource and the need to record change.

Many research programmes were designed to enhance the HER. Early examples were the Rapid Identification Surveys of Stratton Hundred (1993-4) and East Wivelshire Hundred (1994-5) (Herring, this volume, 'Later medieval rural landscape'). The mapping of thousands of sites visible on aerial photographs through the 12-year National Mapping Programme (1994-2006) and the 100 reconnaissance flights flown by Steve Hartgroves for HES (Hartgroves, below), has transformed the HER. Cornwall is fortunate to have an HER that is based on sites identified from below by geophysics, and from above through aerial photography, in addition to sites identified through documents and field evidence. Survey work on Scilly to enhance the HER has led on to current research into historic sea level change (the Lyonesse Project; Johns, this volume).

The underlying principles of the characterisation of historic landscapes were being explored in Cornwall from the mid 1980s to give historical context to the thousands of sites in the HER. The landscape we see today is a mixture of ancient relict landscapes, historic farming patterns, more modern intakes from former moorland, and wholly modern land uses. The simple concept of time depth within a landscape has been formalized in Historic Landscape Characterisation (1994). The methodology was extended, to encompass urban areas using Historic Urban Characterization through the Cornwall and Scilly Urban Survey (2002-5). This developed from experience gained through the Cornwall and Scilly Industrial Settlements Initiative (1998-2004) that recorded the character of 50 industrial towns and villages. Historic Seascape Characterization was developed to encompass the marine historic environment in 2007.

HLC marked a significant intellectual milestone on the journey from the early struggles to record sites and landscapes in advance of the bulldozer and plough. We now have a unifying methodology that moves one from a world consisting of dots on maps representing individual sites, to the means of exploring whole complex human habitats, century by century, and most importantly, being better able to predict what might be found between those dots. HLC provides the ideal tool to identify areas that have archaeological potential, especially where there are no sites indicated on the HER. Much of the new archaeology discussed here has been found as a result of using HLC to target areas of archaeological potential, using geophysics to identify targets, and finally using excavation and palaeoenvironmental sampling to reveal new sites and information. The absorption of geophysical techniques, as well as those of aerial mapping and the application of HLC into the archaeological tool kit in Cornwall has made a significant impact over the last 15 years. Many important excavations over the last 20 years are the result of the predictive power of HLC and the HER.

Public grant programmes and the public sector

Archaeological work in Cornwall has been greatly aided by substantial and sustained grant funding from English Heritage. Cornwall has also benefited from national agri-environment grants and land reclamation grants, the latter being responsible for tens of millions of pounds worth of conservation to historic mine sites. Cornwall's archaeology, historic buildings and settlements have benefited handsomely from Heritage Lottery grants since 1994, and the European Objective One Programme kick-started the World Heritage Site Bid for Cornish Mining.

In addition to this massive public investment in Cornwall and Scilly's historic environment, the county has maintained, and grown, a stable archaeological service that has managed to remain intellectually curious and enthusiastic amidst the ups and downs of local authority politics and budgets. Few staff have left Cornwall, and so very little of the extensive archaeological knowledge accrued over many years, has leaked across the Tamar. This has meant continuity in projects and programmes from inception to publication. This is very unusual, and unlike most areas, Cornwall has very few archaeological projects where completion and publication is thought to be a problem.

ARCHAEOLOGY IN CORNWALL

Cornish Archaeology 50, 2011, 35–39

From Checklists to Historic Environment Record: the archaeological encyclopaedia of Cornwall and Scilly

STEVE HARTGROVES

Most of the country's professional archaeological services were established in the mid 1970s, in response to the perceived loss of archaeological information as a result of an ambitious programme of motorway construction and road building, and accelerating rates of urban redevelopment and renewal. Their creation, encouraged by funding from the Department of the Environment meant that archaeological considerations could henceforth be incorporated into decision-making through the planning process.

One of the first tasks was to bring information together and organise it systematically in Sites and Monument Records. The 1970s and the early 80s were definitely 'BC' – before computers – and the first SMRs were strictly paper-based, with mapping at imperial scales – it really was a different world!

The establishment of a Sites and Monuments Record (SMR) for Cornwall and Scilly began with the Urban and Rural Surveys inaugurated by the newly established Cornwall Committee for Rescue Archaeology (CCRA), established in 1975. The 'original' SMR consisted of a set of 1:10,560 scale (6 inches to the mile!) Ordnance Survey maps annotated with site details and backed up by hand-written A4 record sheets and A4 'Information Files' holding illustrations, photographs, case notes from the planning process and photocopies of articles.

The information files took on a life of their own filling numerous filing cabinets lining the walls and corridors of the Cornwall Archaeological Unit's offices.

Initial data gathering for the SMR relied heavily on two sources - the archaeological records created by the Ordnance Survey (the OS cards, many of them compiled by past CAS Presidents Norman Quinnell and Martin Fletcher), and the Cornwall Archaeological Society's Parochial Check-lists of Antiquities which followed the model set by Vivien Russell in her West Penwith Survey (Russell 1971). The Checklists provided detailed and extensive information on the archaeological and historical wealth of the county, covering about half of the county by 1984 (Johnson and Rose 1984, fig 1). Since its inception, the SMR has continued to be augmented by information from site investigations and recording exercises (often related to developments), by information from fieldworkers and the public, and by detailed SMR enhancement surveys of historic landscapes - for example the famous West Penwith and Bodmin Moor Surveys - and by studies of particular sites such as the Luxulyan valley, Kit Hill, and Perran Foundry.

By the mid 1980s the SMR held in excess of 25,000 records and was still growing. With increasing difficulties in managing, searching and

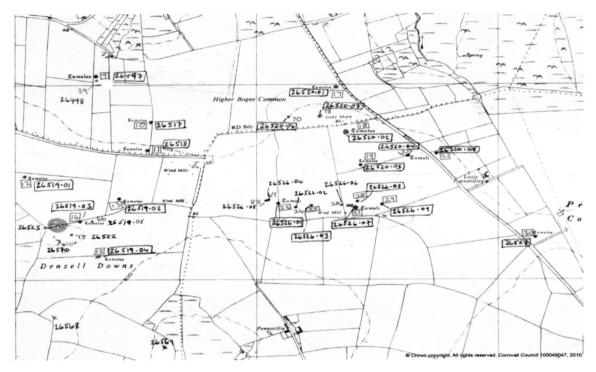

Fig 1. The old paper SMR maps had archaeological and historical information drawn on by hand. Conventions were adopted to increase the information content of the depictions - in this example, the barrow group on Denzell Downs - the SMR numbers of the Scheduled sites are drawn inside boxes. Sites were shown as points, when their exact locations were known, or crosses if they could be only approximately located. The actual extent of large sites could be indicated with an irregular polygon. When the paper SMR was migrated to database, a new number (the Primary Record Number or PRN) was allocated to each site and these had to be added to the paper SMR maps. A different colour was used to avoid confusion, but other conventions continued. The old SMR Number was red, the new PRN was Green. Sites with only a green number were new records added during the recasting of the record.

analysing the record it was clear that the SMR had outgrown its paper format and a computer-based system was essential. In 1983 a new post of SMR Officer was created with English Heritage and County Council support, and EH funding was secured for 'recasting' the content of the SMR into a computerised database. Recasting employed a staff of between 3 and 5 people for 10 years (1984-1994), and, with EH encouragement, 'Superfile' was the chosen database software.

Recasting provided the opportunity to enhance the SMR with information from the Institute of Cornish Studies' Place-names Index, compiled by Oliver Padel; this helped to identify all the settlements of medieval origin. Shortly thereafter, another ICS project was inaugurated

to create an SMR for the Isles of Scilly, and with CCRA guidance, information from this survey was added directly into the SMR database via an on-site PC.

On completion of the initial recasting project, the Royal Commission on the Historical Monuments of England (RCHME) provided support for the incorporation of another large and invaluable ICS-compiled dataset - the Industrial SMR - during the years 1994-8.

With these developments the SMR had grown to around 40,000 records and it was becoming clear that the Superfile software was finding it harder to cope with the sheer volume and complexity of the data, and would have to be replaced by a new and more sophisticated 'database engine'. The change would also provide the occasion for the system to take advantage of ongoing developments in software design - the emergence of standardised data formats meant that it had become feasible to transfer information directly between databases, word-processors and spreadsheets. Of even greater significance was the potential to link electronic databases to digital mapping in the form of Geographical Information Systems (GIS).

Consultations with English Heritage and with SMR Officers regionally and nationally confirmed that Microsoft's Access database had become the most commonly-used platform for SMR databases. Accordingly, an Access database was designed and implemented by Cornwall Archaeological Unit (CAU) staff, and the transfer of records from Superfile to Access (in a complicated process involving two intermediate steps via a flexible word processor (WordPerfect) and a database (Paradox)) was completed in 1998-2000. The design of the new database conformed more closely to the emerging 'national standard' data model for SMRs (MIDAS) developed through EH and ALGAO (the Association of Local Government Archaeological Officers), and terminology was also updated to accord with agreed national Thesauri for Site Types and Artefacts. The adoption of a single unified structure by individual SMRs across the country was seen as an essential precursor to the creation of a national network of linked local databases – a rather prescient concept for the time.

Forging the linkage between the SMR database and the CCC's corporate GIS (ArcView) was realised in a period of rapid development during the first few years of the new millennium. Additional data sets were acquired or in some cases created and various map layers were purchased, including the historic 1st and 2nd edition Ordnance Survey 25in: 1 mile maps of c 1880 and c 1907. Bespoke layers created for the GIS included the Events Record, detailing all the archaeological interventions (surveys, excavations, geophysics, etc) carried out in Cornwall and Scilly, and the NMP layer which depicted all the new features discovered from aerial photographs by the National Mapping Programme. A major dataset which proved ideal for digitisation was the Historic Landscape Characterisation. The HLC project had begun life as a paper-based mapping exercise and its transfer to GIS provided new ways to display the data, to interrogate the information and to explore and develop the insights which HLC had effected.

The 'old' SMR sites are now just one, albeit a crucial one, of many layers of information in the system; they can be plotted onto a range of historic and modern map bases, and viewed against a backdrop of aerial and satellite imagery, historic landscape character, and natural environment data such as geology and soil types, or contour and hydrographic data.

Recently we have seen moves to better integrate archaeological and historic building conservation in the planning system; this has meant measures

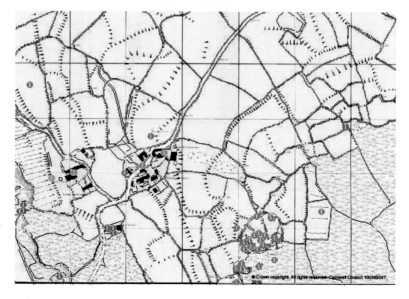

Fig 2. Surveys carried out by CAU over several decades have been digitised and can be displayed on the GIS. This extract of part of a survey of the area around the courtyard house settlement at Porthmeor in Penwith demonstrates the level of additional detail these sources can provide. Dots on the map indicate an entry in the SMR – the dots have been generated automatically from the National Grid Reference in the SMR. The points are colour-coded to indicate broad periods – the red dots represent prehistoric sites.

RECORDING THE PAST

to upgrade and improve the information held on the built environment, and on planning constraints and site and area designations. The GIS now allows users to select from a wide range of additional datasets and to display Scheduled Monuments, Listed Buildings, Conservation Areas and the World Heritage Site. It is also possible to display the locations of Designated Wrecks in the seas, and the extents of Historic Parks and Gardens and Historic Battlefields. All this has revolutionised the working practices of Historic Environment Service staff and transformed the archaeological record to such an extent that a new title is fully justified - the SMR is now just one element of this all-encompassing

collection of information known as the 'Historic Environment Record'.

This new extended environment was making demands on the database software that it was not designed to accommodate, and once again it was necessary to upgrade to a new system. Fortunately, a bespoke SMR database with integral links to GIS was available. It had been developed over several years by ExeGesIS SDM in partnership with English Heritage's National Monuments Record (NMR) and the Association of Local Government Archaeological Officers (ALGAO). Known as the HBSMR (Historic Buildings, Sites and Monuments Record), by 2010, this system had been adopted by

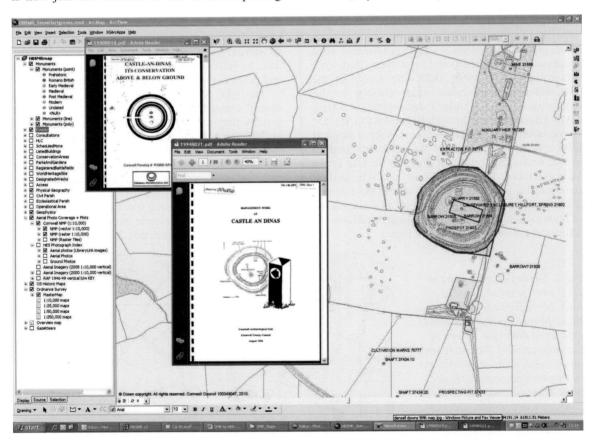

Fig 3. The GIS allows links to be made between different data sets via a common field. Clicking on any one of the coloured points on screen opens a window which displays the record from the HBSMR database. The GIS can forge links between a variety of datasets. One of the most useful is the Events theme, which shows where archaeological investigations have taken place – a couple of clicks with the mouse and you can be reading the project report (or reports) on screen. These can also be accessed online through the mapping pages on www.historic-cornwall.org.uk.

over half of the SMRs/HERs in England to manage their historic environment information and underpin their investigation and conservation activities. As our only realistic option, Cornwall Council made funding available for the acquisition of HBSMR, and our data was migrated to this new software platform early in 2009.

The move to HBSMR involved the reformatting of the old data and the adoption of the full 'national standard' for SMRs; this has had the beneficial effect of making it possible to add our data for Cornwall and Scilly to the national online archaeological database known as the Heritage Gateway. This means that for the first time the complete SMR can be consulted by anyone at any time in any part of the world from an internet-enabled computer.

The SMR today is a very different beast from the record founded in the mid 1970s. This is in large measure the result of the rapidly widening concept of what makes something historically significant. Thirty-five years ago the concept of what properly constitutes an 'archaeological site' was not the subject of a great deal of popular debate. In the intervening period however, we have become more aware of history as a process which should encompass everything up to and including the present (or at least, the recent past). The idea of the 'heritage asset' has evolved rapidly, and widened to include the sites and landscapes of the industrial revolution, the great houses amid their landscaped parks, the chapels and miners' institutes, the historic battlefields and vestiges in concrete from the two world wars of the twentieth century, that illustrate the 'big themes' in recent Cornish history; at the same time it has deepened its focus to incorporate the local and parochial, the humble terraces and marginal smallholdings, the milestones and finger posts, the stiles and drinking troughs, the allotments and hop gardens, the bee boles in the walls and the many small quays on the estuaries that altogether make the local environment so distinctive.

The history of the SMR is also the story of the race to stay abreast of developments in Information Technology - to fall behind would spell disaster. Each development ushers in a new and exciting range of possibilities, but each system has become outdated in a relatively short time. There is no indication that this process has arrived at any kind of conclusion.

To access the Heritage Gateway, go to: *www. heritagegateway.org.uk/gateway*. The Historic Cornwall website (*www.historic-cornwall.org. uk*) has further information from the Historic Environment Service, on the following topics:

- Archaeology and Historic Landscapes
- Aerial Archaeology
- Industrial Archaeology
- Townscapes and Urban Surveys

The mapping site on the Historic Cornwall website provides a map-based link to the HER and the Heritage Gateway. The mapping also shows the Events Record, with links to 'grey literature' reports.

References

Johnson, N, and Rose, P, 1984. Cornwall Committee for Rescue Archaeology 1983-4, *Cornish Archaeol*, **23,** 186-191

Russell, V, 1971. *West Penwith Survey*, Truro

RECORDING THE PAST

Cornish Archaeology 50, 2011, 41–44

The Cornwall (and Scilly) Aerial Survey Project

STEVE HARTGROVES

On 16 October 2010, the author carried out the 100th flight of the long-running Cornwall Aerial Survey Project. This milestone flight was made not to discover new sites but to record the impact of vegetation change and the growth of bracken on Bodmin Moor (Fig 2) as a result of newly introduced grazing regimes – a reflection of the maturity that this technique has attained over the past 25 years, and an indication of the way that it has become integrated with other archaeological activities.

The first flight by Cornwall Archaeological Unit staff was carried out in 1984. After a very hot dry summer, moorland fires in Penwith had burnt off the bracken and gorse which had masked archaeological features and restricted the activities of the West Penwith Survey Project. The one-off grant from the Royal Commission on the Historical Monuments of England (RCHME) for a rapid aerial assessment of the burnt areas became an annual grant to carry out a long-term programme of aerial survey of the county. The funding continued when the RCHME became absorbed by English Heritage, and a small grant has been received every year up to 2010.

The discovery of previously unrecorded sites through cropmark photography provided the initial impetus for the project, but from the very start the philosophy was to use this medium to create an archive of all aspects of the modern landscape. Our concepts of a 'suitable subject' for aerial recording have developed in tandem with

our ideas about the appropriate content of the SMR (see Hartgroves, this volume).

As with all other long-running projects, the technology has changed considerably since its inception. The original objective was to obtain high quality black and white prints which would provide the basis for the accurate transcription of archaeological features, by hand, onto paper maps. To this end a good quality medium format camera was obtained - a Mamiya 645 with a 70mm lens loaded with B/W 220 roll film inserts. A 35mm Pentax or Olympus SLR was used to provide colour images for slide shows, and the slides were rephotographed to provide colour prints for presentations, illustrations and exhibitions.

By 2004 however, the Historic Environment Service's project reports were being produced 'electronically', project staff were beginning to adopt digital cameras for illustrative images, and the Aerial Survey Project was no exception. Flight F64 in June 2004 was the first to use a digital camera to record colour images, and the technology proved itself over two flights; the slide camera was retired, to be replaced by a newly purchased Nikon D70 digital SLR with 28-55mm zoom lens from Flight F66 in August of that year.

A similar process of technological evolution was occurring with the transcriptions – and digital technology was rapidly taking over from pens and paper. Paper prints had become redundant, and from Flight 75 the B/W film camera was retired

Fig 1. A good example of a cropmark enclosure demonstrating why Iron Age enclosed settlements are colloquially known as Rounds. This site, at Roskymer overlooking the Helford near Gweek, is visible as a series of roughly concentric dark rings representing the courses of buried ditches. It can be assumed that a rampart would have been constructed on the internal lip of each ditch. The innermost ring is the thickest and darkest and represents the widest, deepest ditch, the second is much fainter, representing a slighter feature, and there are faint indications of a third ditch. The pattern of parallel pairs of lines running from side to side is created by the farmer's tractor in applying fertiliser to the growing crop.
(Photograph: Historic Environment, Cornwall Council, ACS 3273)

Fig 2. The impact of changing management regimes on Bodmin Moor is clearly illustrated in this image of bracken and gorse swamping an extensive and nationally important Bronze Age landscape of round houses, field systems and enclosures at Clitters on East Moor. Repeated photography over several years can chart the changes in the patterns of vegetation and illustrate the impact that this is having on archaeological features.
(Photograph: Historic Environment, Cornwall Council, F100/74)

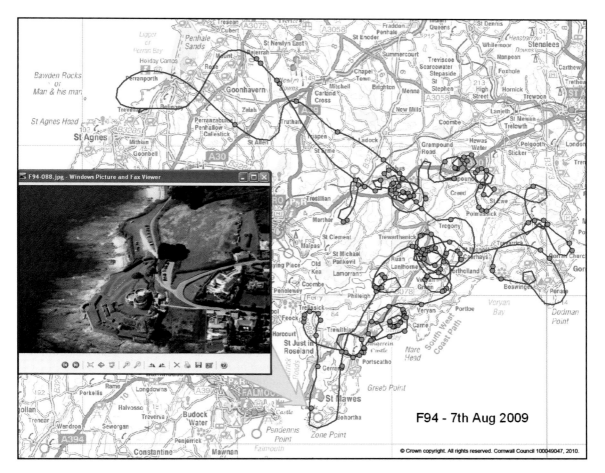

Fig 3. The continuous line overlaid on the GIS map shows the path of the aircraft and the dots along the line represent the location of the camera when a photo was taken; 'clicking' on the dot opens a window on screen to reveal the image. This image, representing the dot to the south of St Mawes town, shows St Mawes Castle and the early twentieth-century gun battery along the slope to the north.

Photograph: Historic Environment, Cornwall Council, F94/88. This map is based upon Ordnance Survey material with the permission of the Controller of Her Majesty's Stationery Office. © Crown Copyright. Unauthorised reproduction infringes Crown Copyright and may lead to prosecution or civil proceedings. Cornwall Council licence No. 100049047 2010.

and the air survey project relied exclusively on digital imagery.

Of course, technology refuses to stand still. In 2008 the camera was upgraded to a Nikon D300 with 28-70mm zoom lens. This camera has a socket on the body for a GPS. This enables us to record both the track of the flight (in the GPS) and the location of each photo; back on the ground, this information can be imported to the GIS to produce a very useful plot of the flight. Clicking on the photo symbol on screen opens

the appropriate image in a window (Fig 3). This gives us the useful feature that the flight track shows those areas which were overflown, but where no pictures were taken. This is very useful information when programmes of reconnaissance are being developed.

In the years from 1984 to 2010, the project has created an archive comprising 7,348 B/W prints and negatives, 5,711 colour slides and 5,995 digital images – a grand total of almost 20,000 aerial images of Cornwall and Scilly.

Fig 4. The Royal Naval Air Station Mullion was commissioned in 1916 as an airship station built to combat German submarines in the South-Western Approaches and the Channel. The site consisted of airship hangers, gas producing equipment and other technical buildings. Aircraft were also stationed here, mainly for aerial photography, and during World War II an experimental balloon station was set up and some areas of the site were used to house WAAF personnel working at the nearby wireless station. The concrete bases of the hangars and the remains of a number of buildings and other features associated with the station are visible on this air photo taken in April 2007. The area is currently the site of Bonython Wind Farm - representations by CAU to Kerrier District Council in connection with the proposed windfarm development secured the protection of these features from unnecessary disturbance during construction works. (Photograph: Historic Environment, Cornwall Council, F76/39)

This irreplaceable archive of aerial views of the county covers sites and landscape of every type and period. Of particular note are the images of 'upstanding remains' of prehistoric settlements and field systems, and ceremonial sites and landscapes in areas of moorland, the Iron Age/ Romano-British rounds and the ring ditches of Bronze Age barrows showing as cropmarks in the arable zone, the medieval landscape of settlements and churches, farmsteads and fieldsystems, the traces of 'modern' industries such as tin streaming, mining, quarrying and china clay extraction, and the 'concrete' remains of military sites from the seventeenth century onwards, including the remarkable site of a WW1 airship station on the Lizard (Fig 4).

Cornish Archaeology 50, 2011, 45–47

NMP - The National Mapping Programme in Cornwall

ANDREW YOUNG

The great value of aerial photographs for developing the Cornwall Sites and Monuments Record was identified at an early stage, and in the late 1970s and early 1980s copies from the National Monuments Record (NMR) collection were purchased systematically. Use was also made of Cornwall County Council's collections of vertical air photographs, many in overlapping stereo, including the RAF's post-war coverage from 1946, and several other partial sets, but mostly for *ad hoc* sketch plotting in particular areas rather than for systematic mapping of all sites.

In 1994 the Royal Commission on the Historical Monuments of England (RCHME) initiated the National Mapping Programme (NMP) - an ambitious programme of archaeological mapping from aerial photographs to address this very issue. Following the merger of the RCHME and English Heritage (EH) in 1999 the NMP has been administered and funded by EH. The aim of NMP is to enhance our understanding about past human settlement, by providing information and syntheses for all archaeological sites and landscapes visible on aerial photographs from the Neolithic to the twentieth century. Cornwall was one of a small number of NMP projects set up in the mid 1990s and mapping of the county was completed in 2006. In addition to the in-house AP archive, more than 50,000 aerial photos were consulted, most of them loaned to the project team from English Heritage's archive in Swindon.

NMP mapping of the whole of Cornwall was a huge task: some 30,000 archaeological features were mapped by the team (Andrew Young, Carolyn Royall, Emma Trevarthen), of which 75% were previously not listed in the HER. The project has transformed not only the amount of information known about Cornwall's archaeology, but also the ways in which it can be accessed. Whole historic and prehistoric landscapes have been mapped and, in conjunction with GIS, can be viewed in their entirety.

NMP has added significantly to our understanding of Cornish archaeology in a number of areas (Young 2006 and forthcoming). Of particular importance is the identification of more than 1,000 new enclosures dating from the later prehistoric or Romano-British periods; as a result a reappraisal of the settlement pattern in later Iron Age and Roman Cornwall is a priority for future research. In addition a range of prehistoric site types which are rare or were previously unknown in Cornwall were identified: these include several unenclosed roundhouse settlements, three possible henges, a Neolithic long barrow or mortuary enclosure and a possible cursus monument.

In upland areas the project resulted in the mapping of previously unsurveyed monument-rich landscapes, such as parts of the Lizard Peninsula and Hensbarrow Downs. Large numbers of new features were recorded, from Bronze Age barrows

RECORDING THE PAST

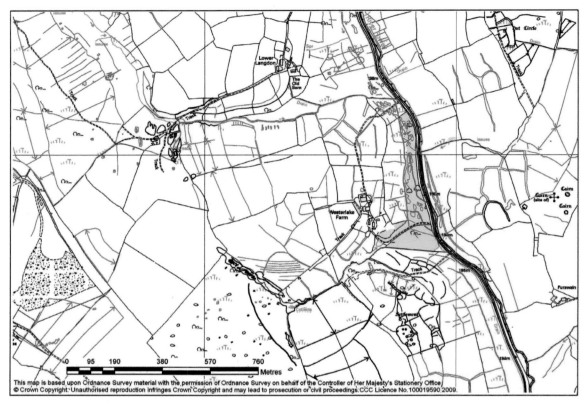

Fig 1. An extract of NMP mapping from the Siblyback area of Bodmin Moor, showing new sites transcribed from RAF vertical photography. For the most part these comprise medieval field boundaries and ridge and furrow (the direction of the ridges is shown by arrows). (© Cornwall Council 2011)

to post-medieval peat drying platforms. Many thousands of individual features associated with Cornwall's mining industries were mapped and NMP proved a key source of information for the Cornwall and West Devon Mining Landscape World Heritage Site bid. We also identified and plotted many early mining sites, including almost 300 previously unsurveyed tin streamworks. Another key outcome was the systematic recording of Second World War military and defensive features, which are nowadays seen as a valuable component of our heritage. At the outset very few features of this type were listed in the HER and the NMP mapped and recorded more than 500.

Perhaps the most significant value of the project data, made up as it is of a wide range of sites from all periods, is that it provides an overview of the archaeological landscape: while it can be argued that certain aspects of the mapping are of particular interest, the whole is greater than the parts. For this reason the publication of the project results took the form of a popular website which contains online access to the NMP mapping of the whole county, illustrated with lots of stunning images, information about the project and about aerial photography, an interactive time–line and a series of thematic summaries of those aspects of Cornish archaeology which feature in the mapping. The website is called 'Flying Past' and can be accessed easily by entering 'flyingpast' into Google, where it appears as the first entry.

References

Young, A, 2006. The National Mapping Programme in Cornwall, *Cornish Archaeol*, **45**, 109-116

Young, A, forthcoming. Prehistoric and Romano-British enclosures around the Camel estuary, *Cornish Archaeol*

Fig 2. On this wartime RAF photograph taken in 1942, attempts to camouflage the military airfield at Portreath by 'painting' the line of former field boundaries (using rubber chippings) can be clearly seen. The chance to consult contemporary photographs allowed NMP to record a number of short-lived, ephemeral features such as these. (Photograph: RAF/FNO/27 frame 6080 27 June 1942 © English Heritage [NMR] RAF Photography)

RECORDING THE PAST

Cornish Archaeology 50, 2011, 49–63

Field archaeology

PETER HERRING, ERIC BERRY, TONY BLACKMAN, ADAM SHARPE,
CHERYL STRAFFON and NIGEL THOMAS

Several non-invasive and repeatable ways of studying past people through examining above-ground remains have been effectively employed in the last quarter century. Most are within Society members' capacity and indeed the last 25 issues of *Cornish Archaeology* contain numerous member contributions based on field walking and survey, landscape study and buildings archaeology (Cave and Irwin 1990; Goodwin 1993; Langdon 1987; 1988; 1992; 1995; 1998/1999; 2006; Skellington 1998/1999; Steele 1987; 1988; 1991; Tangye 1991; 1994; 1995; 1997; Walford 1987; 1993; 1994; 1998/1999; 2000/2001). Major programmes of discovery have been undertaken by individuals working in a voluntary capacity, for example Alwyn Harvey's work on the Defence of Britain project (Johnson, this volume – post-medieval Cornwall).

Field surveys

Peter Herring

Analytical field survey involves making representations and critical observations of complexes of earthworks and structures to establish chronology, function and meaning. Such survey may help predict what lies beneath, but the main intention is usually to develop detailed narratives specific to particular places that also have more general relevance, informing understanding of Cornwall's prehistory, history and present-day landscape. Research, land management, planning, and appreciation of a community's sense of place all benefit from such work.

The period from 1986 saw continuations of major field survey programmes on Bodmin Moor and in West Penwith. On Bodmin Moor emphasis shifted from recording, analysing and interpreting predominantly prehistoric and medieval complexes (Johnson and Rose 1994) towards dealing similarly with the industrial (Fig 1) and post-medieval (Herring *et al* 2008).

As well as improving understanding and presentation, the Bodmin Moor Industrial Survey (largely funded by English Heritage) also provided an evidence base to support extension of statutory protection (Rose and Herring 1990) and enhancement of the Sites and Monuments Record (SMR) and National Monuments Record (NMR), providing planning archaeologists with the material to prepare adequate responses to proposed developments.

Similar considerations supported continuation of the West Penwith Survey (Fig 2), which had been rescue-recording prehistoric, medieval and industrial remains in advance of agricultural improvement (Johnson 1985). Establishment in 1987 of an Environmentally Sensitive Area in northern West Penwith saw a shift to survey in support of presentation and positive management, especially by land owning bodies like the National Trust, Cornwall Heritage Trust and Cornwall Wildlife Trust. Other surveys supported positive management delivered via agri-environment schemes.

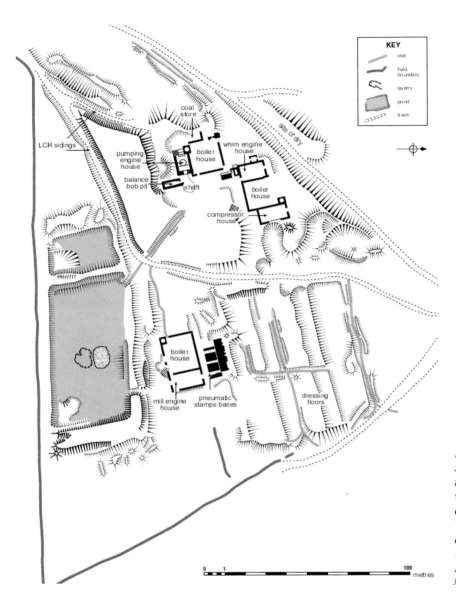

KEY

leat

field boundary

quarry

pond

track

Fig 1. Measured survey (using plane-table) of the unusually well-planned complex centred on the Prince of Wales Shaft on the site of the former Phoenix United mine near Minions. (From Sharpe 2008, fig 56; © English Heritage)

Elsewhere analytical field surveys provided material to support management of blocks of upland and marginal Cornwall either in public ownership or managed by public bodies. In these, and in surveys on Scilly (Ratcliffe 1988; 1993; Ratcliffe and Parkes 1990; Parkes 1990) and at Trerice (Parkes 2005) and Lanhydrock (Thomas 1994; 1998), measured surveys at a range of scales (usually between 1:100 and 1:1000 for intricate complexes and to 1:2500 for larger areas) informed understanding, interpretation and management. Recording also increasingly included sketch-plotting within accurate frameworks derived from OS mapping (contemporary or historical), aerial photographs (as at Godolphin; Herring 1997b), or within networks of accurately surveyed fixed points (as at Kit Hill; Herring and Thomas 1990).

Several surveys explored woodland archaeology and history, investigating both earlier remains preserved by woodlands' low intensity land use, and

Fig 2. Measured survey, using plane-table within the fixed framework of Ordnance Survey mapping, of the multi-period palimpsest at Bosigran, Zennor, undertaken by the Cornwall Committee for Rescue Archaeology and the National Trust in 1981-3. Field boundaries (from late prehistory and the medieval and post-medieval periods) survive either as standing structures (whose variety of form is recorded through conventions) or as lynchets and low banks and shallow ditches, all picked out with hachures.

remains of woodland working, like charcoal burning platforms, wood banks and woodsmen's trackways (Parkes 1997; 1998; 2006; Herring *et al* 1998).

In all these surveys, a 'total archaeology' approach also drew on extensive research on historic maps, documents, place-names and oral testimony to generate studies 'thick' with evidence (Herring 1986). Most also recorded and interpreted remains from many or all periods, not just that ostensibly under consideration, recognising that activity is usually affected by earlier features and memories or interpretations of them, while survival is affected by later activity. Most interpretation

in analytical field survey is based on empirical observation and analysis of patterns (using relative chronology principles when assessing relationships between discrete features) informed by continually deepening knowledge of Cornish landscape history. The value of integrating many approaches was displayed by a multi-disciplinary study of medieval industry and agriculture in St Neot (Austin *et al* 1989).

Survey methods used have been catholic, from total station EDM and sophisticated GPS to those most basic techniques, plane-tables and offsets from straight lines.

The Royal Commission on the Historical Monuments of England (RCHME), now within English Heritage, undertook fewer surveys in Cornwall and Scilly than in other parts of England because the Cornwall Archaeological Unit (CAU) / Historic Environment Service (HES) had developed its own survey capacity. Nevertheless RCHME/EH surveyed individual monuments (like Trencrom and De Lank tor enclosures: Oswald 1996; Wilson-North 1992) and complexes like the early gardens at Stowe and Godolphin (Wilson-North 1993; Fletcher 1995).

Historic landscape studies
Peter Herring

Total archaeology also informs less intensive historic landscape studies, working with smaller-scale mapping and often covering much larger areas. Again initial understanding of an area or theme is drawn from consideration of historic maps, documents, place-names, secondary histories and aerial photography, helping target subsequent rapid field surveys where recording is usually limited to annotation of existing mapping coupled with noting key features' form, dimensions, chronological relationships and then making functional and social interpretations.

Some such studies have aimed to improve the archaeological record in parts of Cornwall not subject to much previous work, like two RCHME-supported 'Rapid Identification Surveys' of parts of Stratton and East Wivelshire Hundreds (Herring and Thomas 1993; Thomas and Buck 1994) and 'audits' of the Fal, Fowey and Helford estuaries and Roseland Heritage Coast (Ratcliffe 1997; Parkes 2000; Reynolds 2000; Cole and Herring 2000). Others fed into more carefully designed land management, on Cornwall Wildlife Trust's nature reserves (Herring 2001), or when reinstating north Cornish habitats attractive to the Large Blue butterfly (Val Baker 2003; Craze *et al* 2006), or assessing areas subject to agri-environment scheme agreements (Johns and Herring 1996; Cole 1997a; 1997b).

A similar approach was adopted for assessing groups of National Trust properties (Thomas 1995; 2001; Ratcliffe 1998; Cole 2000; Gossip 2001; Taylor 2002a; 2002b; Parkes 2008). A Conservation Management Plan of the Trust's Ethy property integrated woodland and parkland archaeology with ecological surveys. Fungi, lichens and invertebrates supported by veteran trees of former wood pasture indicated essential continuity in tree life. This informed understanding of Ethy's landscape development while, conversely, archaeological analysis of earthworks and structures provided relative and absolute chronologies for those natural communities' host woods and trees, improving ecologists' appreciation that their subjects are historical as well as biological (Herring *et al* 1998).

Most post-1994 historic landscape studies made use of historic landscape characterisation (HLC), often deepening aspects of it, as in closer examination of west Cornwall's rough ground in the HEATH project (Dudley 2011; Kirkham 2011) and division of Anciently Enclosed Land into subtypes better representing medieval and post-medieval developments in the Roseland Heritage Coast study (Cole and Herring 2000). At Cotehele a finer grained HLC (Herring and Tapper 2006) formed the framework for recording in the field perceptual aspects of landscape, like activity levels, variety, open-ness, noisiness, harmony, degree of management. The form and conspicuousness of key components like trees, buildings and boundaries were also recorded (Herring and Val Baker 2004).

Such integrative work contributed to critical appraisal of the scientific and process-driven ways of working and thinking that archaeology had developed in the 1960s and 70s. A study of Cornwall's caves could now consider not only their utilisation, but also how they were perceived and feared (Rose 2000/2001).

Experiential archaeology
Peter Herring

In 1994 Chris Tilley reviewed the Bodmin Moor archaeological survey (Johnson and Rose 1994) and turned objectively recorded and described places into subjectively experienced landscape to make himself and his readers think imaginatively and critically about the social, economic, political and personal meanings that can be drawn from material remains. He drew 'natural' topography, including hills, tors, boulders and marshes into the prehistoric world (Fig 3), regarding them as 'symbolic resources of essential significance in the formation of personal biographies and the creation and reproduction of structures of power', especially when dramatic effects were revealed to others by those who knew (Tilley 1995, 5). For example he

Fig 3. People following the short stone row to the south east of Tolborough Tor are still drawn to the tor cairn (foreground). From here the traveller from the south gets their first view of the great tor-topped hills of north-western Bodmin Moor. Those who knew this world could point out Roughtor's topmost tors, poking over the long back of Brown Willy whose own orientation appears to have been deliberately echoed by the builders of a Neolithic long cairn (ringed) on shadowy Catshole.

noted that the Trippet Stones circle and Stripple Stones henge were carefully positioned so that the Moor's most distinctive tor-topped hill, Roughtor, could be shown disappearing from view on quitting the circle when headed towards the henge and then reappearing as that henge was entered through its north-west entrance (Tilley 1995).

Tilley thus extended a phenomenological approach to landscape (Tilley 1994) and for a while Bodmin Moor was central to development of an influential strand of archaeological method as University College London's Leskernick Project probed ever more imaginatively into Neolithic, Bronze Age and modern experience of a single hill and its surroundings. Its team included archaeologists, sociologists and artists and mixed orthodox excavation and survey techniques with more subjective and multi-disciplinary survey, enhanced and magnified through art installations (Bender *et al* 1995; 2007).

Such experiential archaeology is vulnerable to criticism, notably because of its inevitable subjectivity, layering of assumptions, and its sometimes uncertain relationship with verifiable evidence (Fleming 1999; 2005). Nevertheless a number of archaeologists have adopted elements of experiential archaeology, including in three doctoral theses (Altenburg 2003; Jones 2005; Robinson 2007), and it is likely to continue to develop in parallel and intertwined with more traditional or objective archaeology as

it recognises that past people would not have been driven by purely economic needs (Herring 2008a; 2008b; Farnworth *et al* forthcoming).

Earth Mysteries
Cheryl Straffon

'Earth Mysteries' is a generic term, first used in the 1970s to describe approaches to study of ancient sites which were not (at least at that time) normally used by 'orthodox archaeology'. Sometimes called 'alternative archaeology' or 'neo-antiquarianism', it encompassed alignments of sites ('ley lines'), earth 'energies', and anomalous phenomena experienced in a contemporary context at sites (including ultrasound, infrasound, and strange light phenomena). It also borrowed from other disciplines, such as folkloric studies, anthropological studies of contemporary stone-age cultures (in particular shamanic peoples), and archaeo-astronomy, as espoused in particular by researcher and mathematician Alexander Thom (Ruggles 1999). This potpourri approach allowed for some original thinking and research by so-called 'earth mystics', but did not generally find much favour with conventional archaeologists (e.g. Devereux 1999).

Times have changed, however, and in the last 20 or so years, many Earth Mysteries approaches and hypotheses are now routinely incorporated

RECORDING THE PAST

Fig 4. Chun Quoit appears to have been carefully positioned so that when standing beside it (capstone to the right) the sun sets at Midwinter solstice in a distinct notch on the striking silhouette of Carn Kenidjack.
(Photograph: Cheryl Straffon)

into the work of archaeologists. These include an interpretation of the belief systems of prehistoric peoples that focuses on their relationship to natural landscape features (tors, hills, cairns, etc) that were viewed as abodes of spirits, gods or ancestors, and their construction of monuments deliberately sited in relationship to these features, and which became the repository of ancestral legends and stories (e.g. Tilley 1994; Bender *et al* 2007). 'Orthodox' archaeology and 'earth mysteries' have converged a great deal, and especially so in Cornwall, where there have been good relationships between the two disciplines.

Highlights of Earth Mysteries research in Cornwall over this time include a number of discoveries of solar and lunar alignments from and to prehistoric sites. These include midwinter solstice sunset from Chûn Quoit to Carn Kenidjack notch (Fig 4); lunar standstill at and over Chapel Carn Brea from Ballowall Barrow when the 18.6 year cycle of the moon was observed, as it also was at Aberdeenshire recumbent stone circles (Burl 1980); lunar standstill through the Mên-an-Tol holed stone (Straffon 2004); and solar, lunar and stellar alignments at Nine Maidens (Boskednan) (Straffon 2004) and the Hurlers stone circles (Farnworth 2007; Tagney 2008). In addition, consideration of the nineteenth-century folklore studies by Robert Hunt and William Bottrell has produced new

theories of Cornish 'songlines', legends encrypted into the ceremonial landscape (Norfolk 2007); and interpretations of the use of stone circles for the worship or celebration of a Goddess or Earth Mother as the spiritual focus of the Neolithic and Early Bronze Age indigenous peoples (Straffon 1993). There are many other examples, but this brief overview does at least illustrate the fruitful nature of the on-going research and co-operation between the two approaches. More information can be found in *Meyn Mamvro* magazine (Straffon 1986 on) and in other publications (e.g. Straffon 2004).

Buildings
Nigel Thomas and Eric Berry

Standing buildings and structures, and complexes of them, are usually substantial, eye-catching elements of the historic environment. Their recording (combining measured plans and elevations, analytical description and scaled photography), analysis and interpretation throws valuable light on the buildings themselves and on their contexts, often providing a place's most closely dateable evidence for change and usually yielding evidence of the reasons for that change. Building function reveals much about the economy of an individual, their household or a locality and building design is revealing of status, motivation

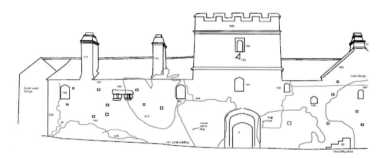

Fig 5. A photographic survey of Cotehele by Eric Berry and Cornwall County Council's Historic Environment Service (Berry et al 2004) was used as the basis for interpretative drawings showing architectural features and major changes in build.

RECORDING THE PAST

and ambition as well as architectural development and fashion. In short, buildings are among the archaeologist's most important subjects and it is therefore surprising that relatively little work had been done on Cornwall's standing structures (as opposed to ruined and buried ones) before the last quarter-century.

CAU/HES has been increasingly involved in recording buildings, partly on its own initiative, to enhance the Historic Environment Record and improve understanding of Cornwall's past, and partly as a result of external developments and initiatives that are summarised here (and see Table 1). In addition a number of other bodies, including other archaeological field units, historic buildings specialists and enthusiastic individuals have undertaken buildings archaeology in Cornwall over this period.

Much building recording has been undertaken as part of the planning process when PPGs 15 and 16 (and their successor PPS 5) have been used to support placing of conditions to record during either assessment (to better understand a structure's significance and the likely affects of the proposed change on that) or implementation

stages (taking opportunities that arise on revealing previously covered masonry and associated features). Recording conditions are normally applied to special buildings, either those that are Listed or are within their curtilage, those in the Cornwall and West Devon Mining Landscape World Heritage Site, or pre-1880 vernacular buildings (especially if these are to be demolished). These conditions take into account rarity and significance of building type and likely threats to fabric of the proposed change, such as the effects of modern engineering solutions on historic structures, like bridges.

Table 1 Numbers of building-related projects undertaken by CCRA, CAU and CC HES by five year period since 1975

Year Range	Projects
1975-1980	1
1981-1985	7
1986-1990	15
1991-1995	34
1996-2000	55
2001-2005	81
2006-2010	110

Fig 6. Samples being taken (by Robert Howard, University of Nottingham tree-ring dating laboratory) from the roof timbers at St Veep church for dendrochronological dating, part of an ad hoc *but purposeful programme of dating in Cornwall (see Arnold et al 2005).* (Photo by Eric Berry, for HE, Cornwall Council).

Buildings archaeology is also undertaken as part of management-oriented surveys aimed at improving understanding of functions, chronology, sequences of changes and circulation patterns (Fig 5). These help determine areas of relative significance, improve conservation management and enhance interpretation and are usually undertaken for major landowners like the National Trust (who commissioned extensive Vernacular Building Surveys of their Cornish properties in the 1980s and 1990s) and the Duchy of Cornwall, but also for English Heritage (especially buildings within their Guardianship Sites, but also when they desire more detailed information on Grade I and II* Listed Buildings for which they have special responsibility).

The trend towards proactive and targeted management of historic assets, including buildings, has stimulated a number of thematic surveys that include characterisations: mine buildings (Sharpe *et al* 1991), nonconformist chapels (Lake *et al* 2001), military structures (see Johnson this volume) and as strands of more holistic area studies, such as the St Austell China-Clay Area survey, which included rapid appraisal of farm buildings (Herring and Smith 1991) and the RCHME farmsteads survey in east Cornwall (Barnwell and Giles 1997; Herring and Giles 2008).

Table 2　Buildings that have been subjected to dendrochronological analysis

Pendennis Castle (Tyers 2004a)
St Michael's Mount, Chevy Chase Room (Berry and Thomas 2008; Arnold and Howard 2007d)
Duchy Palace, Lostwithiel (Tyers 2010)
St Mabyn church (Tyers 2008)
Lansallos church (Arnold and Howard 2006)
St Veep church (Arnold *et al* 2005)
St Martin by Looe church (Arnold *et al* 2006)
St Teath church (Arnold *et al* 2008)
Fowey church (Arnold and Howard 2010)
Poundstock Gildhouse (Arnold and Howard 2007a)
Cotehele House (Berry *et al* 2004)
Trerice House (Hurford *et al* 2009)
Godolphin House (Tyers and Tyers forthcoming)
Boconnoc House (Arnold *et al* 2008)
Cullacott, Werrington (Miles 1995)
Roscarrock, St Endellion (Tyers 2004b)
Welltown Manor, Trevalga (Tyers 2004c)
Molenick, St Germans (Miles 1994)
Treludick, Egloskerry (Arnold *et al* 2008)
Trerithick, Altarnun (Arnold and Howard 2007b)
Restormel Manor (Arnold and Howard 2007c)
Keigwin Place, Mousehole (Arnold *et al* 2009)

An informal programme of dendrochronology (Fig 6), mainly funded by English Heritage in response to proposed work on Scheduled Monuments and Grade I and II* Listed Buildings, is gradually establishing a Cornish tree-ring baseline (Table 2). This will increasingly effectively confirm dates of particular structures and tighten understanding of the historical context of key building forms and types.

Surveying Cornwall's industrial remains

Adam Sharpe

In 1986, little of Cornwall's industrial landscape had been recorded. The Trevithick Society – Cornwall's society for industrial archaeology – had concentrated on researching histories of its industry, but had done little recording of its sites. CCRA had, in 1983 at Cheesewring Quarry, proven that its survey techniques could be readily applied to industrial sites. From 1984, and building on the work undertaken by the National Trust West Penwith survey team (e.g. Herring 1987), site surveys were undertaken in West Penwith including industrial areas such as Ding Dong. On Bodmin Moor, key sites in the Caradon Mining District were recorded (Sharpe 1989); all industrial components in the Luxulyan Valley were either plane tabled or sketch surveyed (Smith 1988). Surveys of Kit Hill and Carn Brea produced detail plans of complex landscapes of mining, tin streaming and quarrying (Herring and Thomas 1990). Smaller but no less detailed mapping exercises were carried out at sites like Wheal Coates and Trevellas (Sharpe and Smith 1985b; Sharpe 1986) in St Agnes. At Lanivet stamps, Wheal Prosper, site survey was combined with photographic recording and detailed recording of components of stamps and waterwheel

(Gerrard and Sharpe 1985), while at Chapel Mill, St Stephen in Brannel, Cornwall's last-surviving intact china-stone mill was recorded in detail (Sharpe and Smith 1985a).

However, plane tabling, whilst capable of producing highly detailed and informative surveys, is inherently time consuming and expensive. The advent in the early 1990s of Derelict Land Funded 'reclamation' of industrial sites, initially within Kerrier District, required more rapid forms of survey for industrial sites threatened with sanitisation. Combining historic mapping with sketch survey allowed site plans to be quickly drawn up, key elements of sites identified, and management recommendations for site conservation made. Many sites were surveyed in this way, including East Basset Stamps (Sharpe 1992a), South Crofty and Cook's Kitchen (Sharpe 1993b), Wheal Uny (Herring 1992) and the Marriott's Shaft complex (Smith 1992a), Harvey's Foundry at Hayle (Smith 1999) together with Perran Foundry (Smith 1986) and the Kennall Vale gunpowder works (Smith 1985). Piecemeal surveys of breweries, industrial warehouses, clayworks, mines, brickworks, tramways, fishing coves, engine houses, quays and engineering works continued through the following decades.

Even so, most work continued to be reactive, and it was recognised that wider-ranging surveys of areas of Cornwall, or of particular industries was essential if

RECORDING THE PAST

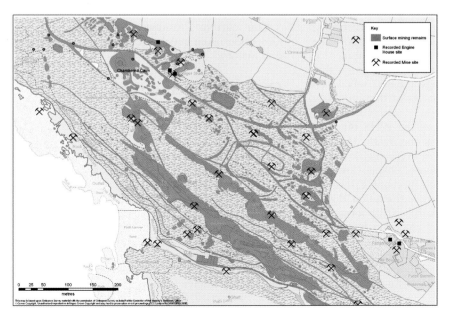

Fig 7. The mining landscape at Ballowal, near Cape Cornwall, part of the GIS mapping carried out to provide documentation for the Cornwall and West Devon Mining Landscape bid. (From Dudley 2011, fig 26)

Cornwall's archaeologists were to provide informed advice to planners or national agencies involved in grant-provision, designation and protection. Surveys of this type included the Bodmin Moor Survey (Herring *et al* 2008; see above, Field Surveys). The various Mineral Tramways projects, including the Engine House Survey, provided an overview and basic record of all surviving engine houses in this core mining district (Sharpe and Smith 1990; Sharpe *et al* 1991). Identification surveys reviewed industrial sites in the Tamar Valley (Buck 1998), and this was followed by more detailed assessments where conservation works were proposed (see Sharpe, this volume, below). Other work examined the St Austell china-clay area (Herring and Smith 1991; Smith 1992), coastal slate quarries near Tintagel (Sharpe 1990), Hayle's port and town (Buck and Smith 1995), Cornwall's granite quarries (Stanier 1999; Herring 2008c), the St Just Mining District (Sharpe *et al* 1992) and, following its closure, Geevor Mine (Sharpe 1993a).

Availability of digital mapping (GIS) has allowed Cornwall Council's Historic Environment service to draw together and combine a wide range of digitised information sources with digital aerial photographs, previous surveys and other material, to create new digital mapping information (Fig 7). Much of the work required between 2001 and 2005 to prepare a bid for World Heritage Site status for the Cornwall and West Devon Mining Landscape was based on this tool. Representations of extents of mine sites, miners' smallholdings and industrial settlements, the sites of over 2000 engine houses, 11,500 mine shafts and 872 Methodist chapels, the routes of all mine tramways and the industrial railways that succeeded them being amongst the data sets which allowed the complex boundaries of the ultimately successful bid to be defined.

A survey commissioned by the WHS office of all significant components of the World Heritage Site involved recording almost every engine house, chimney, wheelpit, count house, chapel, foundry, arsenic works, mining school, mechanics' institute and miners' terrace using high resolution digital photography. The survey (Sharpe 2010), forming a baseline condition survey to support a five-yearly monitoring programme, also provides, for the first time, a snapshot of the complex and diverse industrial landscape of Cornwall and West Devon linked, via GIS mapping, to existing site reports, surveys and site histories.

Oral evidence
Peter Herring

Thoughtful discussions with members of wider communities has helped archaeologists in a number of ways: guiding them to locally-known structures or earthworks not previously investigated; providing more locally grounded stories of explanation, including alternative interpretations (such as the possibility that Zennor clearance heaps may be stones annoyingly encountered during recent turf cutting rather than during prehistoric or medieval cultivation; the late Henry Symons, pers comm); and detailed memories of processes.

Most archaeological oral history takes the form of opportunistic conversations with owners and farmers, but there have also been more carefully designed programmes. In the 1970s Rosemary Robertson of the Institute of Cornish Studies recorded numerous interviews in the farming community (Robertson 1979) and the earlier University of Leeds dialect surveys have direct relevance to landscape history (Orton and Wakelin 1967; Wakelin 1975; North and Sharpe 1980). The Minions Area survey (Sharpe 1989) and the Tamar Valley AONB's market gardens survey (Lewis 2003; Herring 2008e) both included systematic oral history campaigns and the UCL Leskernick survey included several forms of interaction with individuals and local communities (Bender *et al* 2007). Other initiatives could be mentioned.

Our current President, Tony Blackman, has also undertaken much archaeologically oriented oral history.

Oral history and the Young Archaeologists Club
Tony Blackman

In 1994 a questioning of the then current identification of simple, common, circular and rectangular ditched platforms on Bodmin Moor led me into the houses of many elderly farmers where I soon realised that I was researching much more than these 'turf steads'. Firstly, their previous identification as peat drying platforms was demonstrably wrong (see Herring 2008d), but, more importantly, their investigation led to the closely-known and highly particular world of a distinctive part of Cornwall. Researching

Fig 8. Jack Parkyn, of Wimalford, St Cleer, using a turf iron to cut marsh turf for use in the household hearth. He and several other members of the community around Bolventor and the Drawnes Valley on Bodmin Moor, shared many details of moorland life and ways with Tony Blackman. (Photograph: Tony Blackman)

turf opened doors to many hospitable moorland households who tolerated a constant desire for conversation about the past and kindly allowed me to take photographic copies of family albums.

Here I met Jack Parkyn, who became a dear friend and who allowed me to participate in cutting, turning, saving, ricking and using turf and in the annual moorland farming cycle (Fig 8). Jack could find 365 reasons a year for not leaving the 123½ acres which had been his birth home and to which he was welded by process and intimacy; he generously shared the most common emotions felt about the Moor.

As well as helping interpret various modern archaeological remains, these discussions led to consideration of the degree to which an

understanding of modern moorland life could help interpret a more distant past. This helped inspire the careful construction, based on excavated evidence, of two replica upland Bronze Age roundhouses at Trewortha residential centre that have now seen many thousands of Cornish schoolchildren performing and experiencing ancient crafts, stimulating many discussions about the similarities and differences of recent moorland life and that of 3,500 years ago.

The Trewortha work showed that young people, with their open, active and unprejudiced minds, their keen eyes and their compulsive interest in stories and history, have a particular contribution to make to archaeology. So, in 1994 I started the Cornwall Branch of the Young Archaeologists Club and involved its members in research into various historical processes as we investigated diverse aspects of Cornish archaeology including, from prehistory, the propped stones like the Leskernick 'Quoit' found while leading a walk with Peter Herring (Herring 1997a) and other aspects of prehistoric landscape design. From more recent times, YAC has sought and recorded evidence of the splitting and dressing of granite moorstones.

Oral history and the YAC work have reaffirmed the value of a discipline like archaeology that links people with place and the past.

References

Altenberg, K, 2003. *Experiencing landscapes; a study of space and identity in three marginal areas of medieval Britain and Scandinavia*, Stockholm

Arnold, A, and Howard, R, 2006. *Church of St Ildierna, Lansallos, Cornwall: tree-ring analysis of timbers from the roofs and pews, Research Department Report Series*, **2006.49**, Nottingham (English Heritage)

Arnold, A, and Howard, R, 2007a. *The Gildhouse, Poundstock, near Bude, Cornwall: tree-ring analysis of timbers, Research Department Report Series*, **2007.9**, Nottingham (English Heritage)

Arnold, A, and Howard, R, 2007b. *Trerithick House, Polyphant, Cornwall: tree-ring analysis of timbers, Research Department Report Series*, **2007.94**, Nottingham (English Heritage)

Arnold, A, and Howard, R, 2007c. *Restormel Manor, Lostwithiel, Cornwall: tree-ring analysis of timbers, Research Department Report Series*, **2007.65**, Nottingham (English Heritage)

Arnold, A, and Howard, R, 2007d. *St Michael's Mount, Marazion, near Penzance, Cornwall: tree-ring analysis of timbers from the Chevy Chase Room, Research Department Report Series*, **2007.67**, Nottingham (English Heritage)

RECORDING THE PAST

Arnold, A, and Howard, R, 2010. *St Fimbarrus Church, Fowey, Cornwall: tree-ring analysis of timbers, Research Department Report Series*, **2010.46,** Nottingham (English Heritage)

Arnold, A, Howard, R, and Litton, C, 2005. *Tree-ring analysis of roof timbers at the church of Saint Ciricus and Saint Julitta, St Veep, near Lostwithiel, Cornwall. Research Department Report Series*, **2005.47,** Nottingham (English Heritage)

Arnold, A, Howard, R, and Litton, C, 2006. *Church of St Martin, East Looe, Cornwall: tree-ring analysis of roof timbers, Research Department Report Series*, **2006.46,** Nottingham (English Heritage)

Arnold, A, Howard, R, and Litton, C, 2008. List 197. Dendrochronology dates from Nottingham Tree-ring Dating Laboratory, *Vernacular Architecture*, **39,** 119-121

Arnold, A, Howard, R, and Litton, C, 2009. List 210. Dendrochronology dates from Nottingham Tree-ring Dating Laboratory, *Vernacular Architecture*, **40,** 111-112

Austin, D, Gerrard, G A M, and Greeves, T A P, 1989. Tin and agriculture in the Middle Ages and beyond: landscape archaeology in St Neot Parish, Cornwall, *Cornish Archaeol*, **28,** 7–251

Barnwell, PS, and Giles, C, 1997. *English farmsteads 1750–1914*, London (RCHME)

Bender, B, Hamilton, S, and Tilley, C. 1995. Leskernick: the biography of an excavation, *Cornish Archaeol*, **34,** 58-73

Bender, B, Hamilton, S, and Tilley, C, 2007. *Stone worlds, narrative and reflexivity in landscape archaeology*, Walnut Creek, California

Berry, E, Gossip, J, Mattingly, J, and Thomas, N, 2004. *Cotehele House, Calstock, Cornwall - historic building analysis*, Truro (Historic Environment Service, Cornwall County Council)

Berry, E, and Thomas, N, 2008. *St Michael's Mount, Cornwall - historic buildings analysis and watching brief of the summit buildings*, Truro (Historic Environment Service, Cornwall County Council)

Buck, C, 1998. *Preliminary assessment of the industrial sites of archaeological importance in the Tamar Valley*, Truro (Cornwall County Council)

Buck, C, and Smith, J R, 1995. *Hayle town survey and historic audit*, Truro (Cornwall County Council)

Burl, A, 1980. Science or symbolism: problems of archae-astronomy, *Antiquity*, **54,** 191-200

Cave, D, and Irwin, M, 1990. Another flint site on Trevose Head, *Cornish Archaeol*, **29,** 43-48

Cole, R, 1997a. I*vey and Hawkstor Farms, an archaeological assessment*, Truro (Cornwall Archaeological Unit)

Cole, R, 1997b. *Gear Sands, Perranzabuloe, an archaeological assessment*, Truro (Cornwall Archaeological Unit)

Cole, R, 2000. *St Just in Roseland, Cornwall - Rapid Archaeological and Historic Assessment*, Truro (Cornwall Archaeological Unit)

Cole, R, and Herring, P, 2000. *Roseland Heritage Coast Historic Audit*, Truro (Cornwall Archaeological Unit)

Craze, N, Herring, P, and Kirkham, G, 2006. *Atlantic Coast and Valleys Project - historic environment assessments of farms*, Truro (Historic Environment Service, Cornwall County Council)

Devereux, P, 1999. *Earth Mysteries*, London

Dudley, P, 2011. *Goon, hal, cliff and croft, west Cornwall's rough ground*, Truro (Cornwall Council)

Farnworth, R, 2007. Sightlines to the tors and stars, *Meyn Mamvro*, **63,** 10-11

Farnworth, R, Herring, P, and Tapper, B, forthcoming. The focus on Rough Tor and Stowe's Pound in the Neolithic and Early Bronze Age, *Cornish Archaeol*

Fleming, A, 1999. Phenomenology and the megaliths of Wales: a dreaming too far? *Oxford Journal of Archaeology*, **18 (2),** 119-125

Fleming, A, 2005. Megaliths and post-modernism: the case of Wales, *Antiquity*, **79,** 921-932

Fletcher, M, 1995. *Godolphin and its gardens*, Exeter (RCHME)

Gamble, B, and the World Heritage Site Bid Team, 2005. *Nomination of the Cornwall and West Devon Mining Landscape for inclusion on the World Heritage Site List*, Truro (Historic Environment Service, Cornwall County Council)

Gerrard, S, and Sharpe, A, 1985. Archaeological survey and excavations at Wheal Prosper tin stamps, Lanivet, *Cornish Archaeol*, **24,** 196-211

Goodwin, J, 1993. Granite towers on St Mary's, Isles of Scilly, *Cornish Archaeol*, **32,** 128-139

Gossip, J, 2001. *The Gannel Estuary, Cornwall - archaeological and historical assessment*, Truro (Historic Environment Service, Cornwall County Council)

Herring, P, 1986. *An exercise in landscape history. Pre-Norman and medieval Brown Willy and Bodmin Moor*, unpublished MPhil thesis, University of Sheffield

Herring, P, 1987. *Bosigran, Zennor. Archaeological assessment*, Truro (Cornwall Archaeological Unit)

Herring, P, 1992. *Wheal Uny, Redruth*, Truro (Cornwall Archaeological Unit)

Herring, P, 1997a. Early prehistoric sites at Leskernick, Altarnun, *Cornish Archaeol*, **36,** 176-185

Herring, P, 1997b. *Godolphin, Breage, an archaeological and historical assessment*, Truro (Cornwall Archaeological Unit)

Herring, P, 2001. *Wild Cornwall - archaeological assessments of Cornwall Wildlife Trust nature reserves*, Truro (Historic Environment Service, Cornwall County Council)

Herring, P, 2008a. Stepping onto the commons: south-western stone rows, in P Rainbird, ed, *Monuments in the landscape*, Stroud, 79-88

Herring, P, 2008b. Commons, fields and communities in prehistoric Cornwall, in A Chadwick, ed, *Recent approaches to the archaeology of land allotment*, Brit Arch Repts, Int Ser, **1875,** Oxford, 70-95

Herring, P, 2008c. Quarrying, in Herring *et al* 2008, 83-100

Herring, P, 2008d. Turf, in Herring *et al* 2008, 117-126

Herring, P, 2008e. Tamar Valley Orchards, in I Rotheram, ed, *Orchards and groves: their history, ecology, culture and archaeology*, Sheffield, Wildtrack Publishing, 86-95

Herring, P, and Giles, C, 2008. Agriculture, in Herring *et al* 2008, 139-162

Herring, P, Parkes, C, Pring, S, Green, E, Spalding, A, 1998. *Ethy Park, St Winnow - historic landscape survey*, Truro (Cornwall Archaeological Unit)

Herring, P, Sharpe, A, Smith, J R, and Giles, C, 2008. *Bodmin Moor: an archaeological survey. Volume 2: the post-medieval and industrial landscapes*, Swindon (English Heritage)

Herring, P, and Smith, J R, 1991. *The archaeology of the St Austell china clay area, an archaeological and historical assessment*, Truro (Cornwall County Council)

Herring, P, and Tapper, B, 2006. *Cotehele historic landscape characterisation and scoping survey for historic landscape survey*, Truro (Historic Environment Service, Cornwall County Council)

Herring, P, and Thomas, N, 1990. *The Archaeology of Kit Hill*, Truro (Cornwall County Council)

Herring, P, and Thomas, N, 1993. *Stratton Hundred - Rapid Identification Survey*, Truro (Cornwall Archaeological Unit)

Herring, P, and Val Baker, M, 2004. *The intangibles at Cotehele*, unpublished PowerPoint presentation, Truro (Historic Environment Service, Cornwall County Council)

Hurford, M, Arnold, A, Howard, R, and Tyers, C, 2009. *Trerice, Kestle Mill, Cornwall: tree-ring analysis of timbers, Research Department Report Series*, **2009.38,** Nottingham (English Heritage)

Johns, C, and Herring, P, 1996. *St. Keverne Historic Landscape Assessment*, Truro (Cornwall County Council)

Johnson, N, 1985. Archaeological field survey, a Cornish perspective, in S Macready and F H Thompson, eds, *Archaeological field survey in Britain and abroad*, Occasional Paper (New Series) VI, The Society of Antiquaries, 51-66

Johnson, N, and Rose, P, 1994. *Bodmin Moor, an archaeological survey Volume 1: the human landscape to c 1800*, London

Jones, A M, 2005. *Cornish Bronze Age ceremonial landscapes c 2500-1500BC*, Brit Arch Repts, Brit Ser, **394,** Oxford

Kirkham, G, 2011. *Managing the historic environment on west Cornwall's rough ground*, Truro (Cornwall Council)

Lake, J, Cox, J, and Berry, E, 2001. *Diversity and vitality - the Methodist and Non-Conformist chapels of Cornwall*, Truro (Cornwall County Council

Langdon, A, 1987. Ancient cross head discovered, *Cornish Archaeol*, **26,** 161-2

Langdon, A, 1988. More ancient crosses, *Cornish Archaeol*, **27,** 204-210

Langdon, A, 1992. Cornish crosses: recent news, *Cornish Archaeol*, **31,** 154-165

Langdon, A, 1995. Discovery of two medieval wayside crosses, *Cornish Archaeol*, **34,** 182-190

Langdon, A, 1998/99. The restoration of some North Cornwall crosses, *Cornish Archaeol*, **37-8,** 170-7

Langdon, A, 2006. Old Tom: the discovery of an unfinished cross on Catshole Tor, Bodmin Moor, *Cornish Archaeol*, **45,** 117-122

Lewis, J, 2003. *Sovereigns, Madams, and Double Whites, fruit and flower pioneers of the Tamar Valley*, Saltash, Tamar Valley AONB Service

Miles, D W H, 1994. *The tree-ring dating of Molenick Farmhouse, St Germans, Cornwall, Ancient Monument Laboratory Report*, Portsmouth (English Heritage)

Miles, D W H, 1995. *Tree-ring dating of the Old Farmhouse*

at Cullacott, Werrington, Cornwall, Ancient Monument Laboratory Report*, Portsmouth (English Heritage)

Norfolk, A, 2007. Songlines – legends in the landscape, *Meyn Mamvro*, **62,** 14-18; 63, 14-18

North, D J, and Sharpe, A, 1980. *A word-geography of Cornwall*, Redruth (Institute of Cornish Studies)

Orton, H, and Wakelin, M F, 1967. *Survey of English Dialects, vol IV (Southern)*, Leeds

Oswald, A, 1996. *Trencrom Castle, Ludgvan, Cornwall*, York (RCHME)

Parkes, C, 1990. *Fieldwork in Scilly March 1990 - early batteries on the Garrison, St Mary's*, Truro (Cornwall Archaeological Unit)

Parkes, C, 1997. *An archaeological and historical assessment of Cabilla and Redrice Woods*, Truro (Cornwall Archaeological Unit)

Parkes, C, 1998. *Home Farm, Minster - an archaeological and historical assessment*, Truro (Cornwall Archaeological Unit)

Parkes, C, 2000. *Fowey Estuary historic audit*, Truro (Cornwall County Council)

Parkes, C, 2005. *Trerice, Newlyn East, Cornwall - archaeological assessment*, Truro (Historic Environment Service, Cornwall County Council)

Parkes, C, 2006. *Turnaware Point, St Just in Roseland - an archaeological assessment*, Truro (Historic Environment Service, Cornwall County Council)

Parkes, C, 2008. *The Dodman and St Austell Bay archaeological survey of The Dodman and Penare, Lambsowden, Lamledra and Bodrugan*, Truro (Historic Environment Service, Cornwall County Council)

Ratcliffe, J, 1988. *Isles of Scilly archaeological management plan*, Truro (Cornwall County Council)

Ratcliffe, J, 1993. *Fieldwork in Scilly 1991 and 1992*, Truro (Cornwall Archaeological Unit)

Ratcliffe, J, 1997. *Fal Estuary historic audit*, Truro (Cornwall County Council)

Ratcliffe, J, 1998. *Treen and Rospletha Cliffs, Penberth Valley and Cove - an archaeological assessment*, Truro (Cornwall Archaeological Unit)

Ratcliffe, J and Parkes, C, 1990. *Fieldwork in Scilly September 1989*, Truro (Cornwall Archaeological Unit)

Reynolds, A, 2000. *Helford Estuary Historic Audit*, Truro (Cornwall County Council)

Robertson, R, 1979. The Institute's Oral History Project: Family Farming in West Penwith, 1919-39, *Cornish Studies*, **7,** 66-8

Robinson, G, 2007. *The prehistoric island landscape of Scilly*, Brit Arch Repts, British Ser, **447,** Oxford

Rose, P, 2000/2001. Shadows in the imagination: encounters with caves in Cornwall, *Cornish Archaeol*, **39-40,** 95-128

Rose, P, and Herring, P C, 1990. *Bodmin Moor, Cornwall: an evaluation for the Monuments Protection Programme*, Truro (Cornwall Archaeological Unit)

Ruggles, C, 1999. *Astronomy in prehistoric Britain and Ireland*, New Haven and London

Sharpe, A, 1986, *Trevellas, St. Agnes, Cornwall – an archaeological survey*, Truro (Cornwall Archaeological Unit)

Sharpe, A, 1989. *Minions: an archaeological survey of the Caradon Mining District*, Truro (Cornwall County Council)

Sharpe, A, 1990, *Coastal slate quarries - Tintagel to Trebarwith*, Truro (Cornwall Archaeological Unit)

Sharpe, A, 1992. *East Basset Stamps - an archaeological assessment for Kerrier Land Reclamation Scheme*, Truro (Cornwall Archaeological Unit)

Sharpe, A, 1993a. *Geevor and Levant - an assessment of their surface archaeology*, Truro (Cornwall Archaeological Unit)

Sharpe, A, 1993b. *South Crofty and Cooks Kitchen - an archaeological assessment*, Truro (Cornwall Archaeological Unit)

Sharpe, A, 2008. Mining, in Herring *et al* 2008, 29-82

Sharpe, A, 2010. *Cornish Mining World Heritage Site, Cornwall and West Devon: photo-monitoring project 2010*, Truro (Historic Environment Projects, Cornwall Council)

Sharpe, A, Edwards, T, and Sparrow, C, 1992. *St Just: an archaeological survey of the mining district*, Truro (Cornwall County Council)

Sharpe, A, Lewis, R, Massie, C and Partners, with Johnson, N, 1991. *The engine house assessment: Mineral Tramways Project*, Truro (Cornwall County Council)

Sharpe A, and Smith, J, 1985. *Chapel Mill, a survey*, Truro (Cornwall Committee for Rescue Archaeology)

Sharpe, A, and Smith, J R, 1985. *Wheal Coates, St Agnes - an archaeological survey*, Truro (Cornwall Committee for Rescue Archaeology)

Sharpe, A, and Smith, J R, 1990. *An archaeological assessment of the industrial landscape between Devoran, Portreath and Troon, with an evaluation of the potential of the disused mineral railways and mines*, Truro (Cornwall Archaeological Unit)

Skellington, W, 1998/99. White vein quartz tools in West Cornwall and the Isles of Scilly, *Cornish Archaeol*, **37-38**, 121-5

Smith, J R, 1985. *The Kennall Vale gunpowder works*, Truro (Cornwall Committee for Rescue Archaeology)

Smith, J R, 1986. *Perran Foundry - a new interpretation centre*, Truro (Cornwall Archaeological Unit))

Smith J R, 1988. *Luxulyan Valley Project - an archaeological and historical survey*, Truro (Cornwall County Council)

Smith, J R, 1992a. *South Wheal Frances - an archaeological assessment for Kerrier Land Reclamation Scheme*, Truro (Cornwall Archaeological Unit)

Smith, J R, 1992. *Cornwall's china-clay heritage*, Truro, Twelveheads Press

Smith, J R, 1999. *Harvey's Foundry, Hayle, Cornwall - an archaeological assessment*, Truro (Cornwall Archaeological Unit)

Stanier, P, 1999. *South West granite, a history of the granite industry in Cornwall and Devon*, St Austell (Cornish Hillside Publications)

Steele, P, 1987. Five flint implements from south-east Cornwall, *Cornish Archaeol*, **26**, 99-101

Steele, P, 1988. Backed blades from Bodwannick, Lanivet, *Cornish Archaeol*, **27**, 200

Steele, P, 1991. Flint scatters at Penatillie, St Columb Major, *Cornish Archaeol*, **30**, 253-259

Straffon, C, 1986-present. *Meyn Mamvro* magazine

Straffon, C, 1993. *Pagan Cornwall: land of the Goddess*, St Just

Straffon, C, 2004. *Megalithic mysteries of Cornwall*, St Just

Tagney, J, 2008. The Hurlers – sightlines to the sun, in *Meyn Mamvro*, **66**, 8-11

Tangye, M, 1991. A 17th-century fish cellar at Porth Godrevy, Gwithian, *Cornish Archaeol*, **30**, 243-252

Tangye, M, 1994. A huer's hut, Cribba Head, Penberth, St Levan, *Cornish Archaeol*, **33**, 183-186

Tangye, M, 1995. Lestowder, St Keverne: a previously unidentified stronghold, *Cornish Archaeol*, **34**, 176-181

Tangye, M, 1997. Rock-cut baths in Cornwall, *Cornish Archaeol*, **36**, 186-200

Taylor, S, 2002a. *Tintagel East, North Cornwall - a rapid archaeological and historic landscape assessment*, Truro (Historic Environment Service, Cornwall County Council)

Taylor, S, 2002b. *Dizzard, Tremorn and St Gennys - a rapid archaeological and historic landscape assessment*, Truro (Historic Environment Service, Cornwall County Council)

Thomas, N, 1994. *An archaeological assessment of the National Trust estate at Lanhydrock, Cornwall*, Truro (Cornwall Archaeological Unit)

Thomas, N, 1995. *An archaeological assessment of the coastal property of the National Trust between Godrevy and Portreath, Cornwall*, Truro (Cornwall Archaeological Unit)

Thomas, N, 1998. *Lanhydrock Park - a survey of an historic landscape*, Truro (Cornwall Archaeological Unit)

Thomas, N, 2001. *Gribbin Head to Lansallos, Cornwall - an archaeological assessment*, Truro (Historic Environment Service, Cornwall County Council)

Thomas, N, and Buck, C, 1994. *The Tamar Valley Rapid Identification Survey*, Truro (Cornwall Archaeological Unit)

Tilley, C, 1994. *A phenomenology of landscape. Places, paths and monuments*, Oxford

Tilley, C, 1995. Rocks as resources: landscapes and power, *Cornish Archaeol*, **34**, 5-57

Tyers, I, 2004a. *Tree-ring analysis of oak timbers from Pendennis Castle, Research Department Report Series*, **2004.38**, Portsmouth (English Heritage)

Tyers, I, 2004b. *Tree-ring analysis of oak timbers from Roscarrock near Port Isaac, Cornwall, Research Department Report Series*, **2004.30**, Portsmouth (English Heritage)

Tyers, I, 2004c. *Tree-ring analysis of oak timbers from Welltown Manor, near Boscastle, Cornwall, Research Department Report Series*, **2004.29**, Portsmouth (English Heritage)

Tyers, I, 2008. *Church of St Mabena, St Mabyn, dendrochronological analysis of oak timbers, Research Department Report Series*, **2008.74**, Portsmouth (English Heritage)

Tyers, I, 2010. *Old Duchy Palace, Lostwithiel, dendrochronological analysis of oak timbers, Research Department Report Series*, **2010.1**, Portsmouth (English Heritage)

Tyers, C, and Tyers, I, forthcoming. *Godolphin House, dendrochronological analysis of oak timbers, Research Department Report Series*, Portsmouth (English Heritage)

Val Baker, M, 2003. *Atlantic Coast and Valleys Project, Cornwall - historic landscape characterisation, habitat, species and landscape assessments*, Truro (Historic Environment Service, Cornwall County Council)

Wakelin, M F, 1975. *Language and history in Cornwall*, Leicester

Walford, G F, 1987. Possible Neolithic long barrow on Kit Hill, *Cornish Archaeol*, **26,** 102

Walford, G F, 1993. An underground passage rediscovered, *Cornish Archaeol*, **32,** 164-6

Walford, G F, 1994. Prehistoric stone implements found near Callington, *Cornish Archaeol*, **33,** 5-13

Walford, G F, 1998/99. Some thoughts on early enclosures in southeast Cornwall, *Cornish Archaeol*, **37-38,** 130-1

Walford, G F, 2000/01. Flint finds from Clicker Tor, Menheniot, *Cornish Archaeol*, **39-40,** 167-171

Wilson-North, R, 1992, *De Lank: an enclosure of possible Neolithic origin*, Exeter (RCHME)

Wilson-North, W R, 1993. Stowe: the country house and garden of the Grenville family, *Cornish Archaeol*, **32,** 112-127

Cornish Archaeology 50, 2011, 65–70

A short history of geophysical survey in Cornwall

PETER ROSE

History

In 1978 a team from the Department of the Environment's Ancient Monuments Laboratory (Alister Bartlett and Gerry McDonnell) was persuaded by Nicholas Johnson of the Cornwall Committee for Rescue Archaeology to survey eight sites in Cornwall. Although a few surveys had previously been attempted, this marks the effective start of geophysical survey in Cornwall. Encouraged by promising results from these first surveys the AM Lab team returned a further 12 times over the next 19 years, investigating some 43 sites by 1997, with more occasional visits subsequent to that. The most effective technique for Cornwall was found to be magnetometry (typically with the fluxgate gradiometer), with the highly magnetic topsoils producing an excellent magnetic response. Resistivity can produce useful results to complement the magnetic data but is overshadowed by the effectiveness of the magnetic data and the efficiency with which it can be collected. The more sensitive caesium magnetometer has been little used in Cornwall (e.g. at Crasken Round; Linford and Linford 2002), but may prove useful where there are more weakly magnetic soils or over igneous geologies (Neil Linford, pers comm). Work by the AM Lab has been focused on sites which were already known, driven variously by research aims, or to guide site management or in response to threats, addressing

specific issues such as confirming the existence of sites, investigating their character to clarify their type and potential, testing a range of site types and

Fig 1. Magnetometer survey in the olden days, Merthen fort, 1980. Andrew David of the Ancient Monuments Lab with a field chart recorder, plotting results directly onto paper.

techniques, and providing a context for significant finds and excavations.

By the '90s, a series of commercial companies had become well established, such as Geophysical Surveys of Bradford (GSB Prospection), Stratascan and Oxford Archaeotechnics. From around 1994 commercial surveys became a new and increasingly important component of the geophysical surveys in Cornwall. A few surveys were commissioned to guide site management (e.g. English Heritage: Restormel Castle and Pendennis; the National Trust: The Dodman promontory fort; and local authorities: Lescudjack Castle, Penzance) (Geophysical Surveys of Bradford 1994a; 1994b; GSB Prospection 2004; 2005a; 2005b), but most - about 120 of the 210 or so surveys - have been in response to development, particularly road schemes and pipelines. These surveys have been much less site-focused than the work by English Heritage. They have provided more random samples of a range of locations, and as they sometimes give transects through different historic landscape types they have been of value in comparing the historical processes behind them.

Fig 2. CAS carried out a magnetometer survey at Carwynnen Quoit, Camborne, in March 2009, working with the site's new owners, the Sustainable Trust. Centre is Les Dodd, with Peter Nicholas (right).

For example, coinciding with the development of historic landscape characterisation for the whole of Cornwall, two of the early surveys, in 1994, on the A390 Probus bypass and at Viverdon Down on the A388 allowed a comparison of archaeological potential in two historic landscape character types, respectively 'Anciently Enclosed Land' (medieval or earlier farmland) and 'Recently Enclosed Land' (former rough ground) (Geophysical Surveys of Bradford 1994c; 1994d). The earlier surveys tended to be limited to samples of the development corridor, sometimes concentrating on locations near to known archaeological sites, but it has become more usual to survey the full length of a road line or pipeline corridor.

As the value of geophysical survey as a research tool has become increasingly recognised it has also been taken up by academic researchers and by voluntary groups. A series of surveys undertaken by Laura Cripps of Durham University in 2004 concentrated on Iron Age enclosures and settlements as part of doctoral research. A survey by Exeter University (Dr Smart and Dr Claughton) in 2007 at Calstock, to investigate medieval industry, resulted in the unexpected discovery of a Roman fort (Smart in preparation). In 2005 Saltash Heritage secured a grant for the Tamarside Archaeological Survey, a three-year project supported by the Heritage Lottery Fund. Survey equipment was purchased and under the leadership of Peter Nicholas the team of volunteers surveyed a series of sites predominantly in south east Cornwall, including the spectacular Roman forts at Restormel. In partnership with Saltash Heritage, Cornwall Archaeological Society now also carries out geophysical surveys, led by Les Dodd and Peter Nicholas.

Results and discoveries

Magnetometer surveys in Cornwall have predominantly been carried out using the fluxgate gradiometer, with 20m grids, 1m traverse separation and reading intervals mostly 0.5m but sometimes 0.25m. Most surveys have been smaller than 2ha, some are in the region of 4-5ha, and surveys larger than that have until recently been uncommon. A number of extensive surveys, 10ha to 15ha or larger (mostly undertaken by ArchaeoPhysica and GSB Prospection), have taken place in late 2010 and the first part of 2011 as part of the assessment process required by

Planning archaeologists in response to proposals for solar farms and housing developments.

Magnetometry has proved best at locating ditches and large pits, and is therefore good at discovering sites which are well represented by these features – ditched settlements, ring-ditches, ditched field systems. It generally works well in the slate-derived soils and subsoils of lowland Cornwall but is more unpredictable on the granite and the metamorphosed rocks; sometimes this may be due to sub-surface boulders which confuse the picture (e.g. Crift, Lanlivery). Surveys that have been attempted in coastal or upland rough ground have generally been disappointing (e.g. Tintagel Island, Trevelgue Head, Rough Tor, and hillfort interiors at Castle-an-Dinas (Ludgvan) and Castle-an-Dinas (St Columb).

Although it has to be remembered that the technique only ever recovers part of the story, results can be spectacular, and it has proved effective at locating and plotting sites of most periods. From the Early Bronze Age, barrows have been identified as ring ditches at Trelowthas (Probus) and on the Dodman (Gorran) (Geophysical Surveys of Bradford 1994d; Nowakowski 1995; GSB Prospection 2004; 2005a). A feature at Trenoweth near Portreath proved on excavation to be a substantial pit, probably for a large timber post (Reynolds 2006). One important outcome has been in establishing that magnetometry can locate Middle Bronze Age houses. Where these take the form of discs that are slightly hollowed into the ground, they can appear on the surveys as circular blobs as at Callestick (Perranzabuloe), Penhale and Penhale Moor (St Enoder) and Boden (St Anthony-in-Meneage) (Jones 1998-9; Nowakowski 1994; Linford 1994). Unfortunately, there are also similar blobs which have turned out to be geological features, or mining-related, or, at Scarcewater, a Middle Bronze Age mound rather than a house (Jones and Taylor 2010), and so without excavation the results are inconclusive.

As Iron Age and Romano-British rounds are usually defined by fairly substantial ditches, geophysical survey has proved very effective at discovering new sites and confirming possible ones, for example new sites at Boden (St Anthony–in–Meneage), Tretherras (Newquay), Race Farm (Camborne), Little Quoit Farm (St Columb), Killigrew Round (St Erme), and St Tudy (Linford 1998; Gossip in preparation; Stratascan

1994; Geophysical Surveys of Bradford 1998a; 1998b; GSB Prospection 2008). A smaller and slighter enclosure at Tremough proved to be a single farmstead (Gossip and Jones 2007), and geophysical surveys have in a number of cases now identified ring-ditches which are likely to be Iron Age roundhouses in unenclosed settlements; such sites are likely to be common, but are not easily discovered through other means. A major complex of ring-ditches was recorded by the Ancient Monuments Lab team at Lellizzick, and subsequently investigated by Time Team (Nowakowski, this volume, fig 9), following discoveries of artefacts by Jonathan Clemes (Payne 1998; Thompson 2008). Other ring ditches surveyed at Penmayn near Rock and at Higher Besore near Truro have proved to be Iron Age houses; sites at Camelford School appear to be a mix of secular and ceremonial sites (GSB Prospection 2009; 2002; Gossip forthcoming; GSB Prospection 2007). Some work has been done on hillforts and other large enclosures. Two sites have been particularly interesting. Survey of the large enclosure at Gear (St Martin-in-Meneage) by GSB Prospection for Time Team, recorded numerous house sites (as ring-ditches), as well as enclosures and fields which may predate the enclosure (GSB Prospection 2001; Edwards and Kirkham 2008). A survey by the Ancient Monuments Lab outside the large enclosure at Carvossa (Probus) identified part of a complex of small ditched enclosures and probable hearths, presumably an extra-mural settlement (Bartlett 1980a).

Many of the surveys have recorded traces of field systems which appear to pre-date the current (medieval-based) fields, though few if any of the surveys have been extensive enough to give a clear idea of their character and pattern. Although small rectangular fields were surveyed at Penhale (St Enoder) (Nowakowski 1994), most appear to be fairly large and irregular or rectilinear, for example Boden, Stencoose (St Agnes), Tolgroggan (St Allen), and Race Farm (Camborne) (Linford 1998; Jones 2000-1; Bartlett 1980b; Geophysical Surveys of Bradford 1998a), but certainly quite different from the networks of small rectangular fields, thought to be of later prehistoric origin, that are characteristic of West Penwith.

So far no medieval settlements have been discovered through geophysical survey in Cornwall, perhaps because most have continued

RECORDING THE PAST

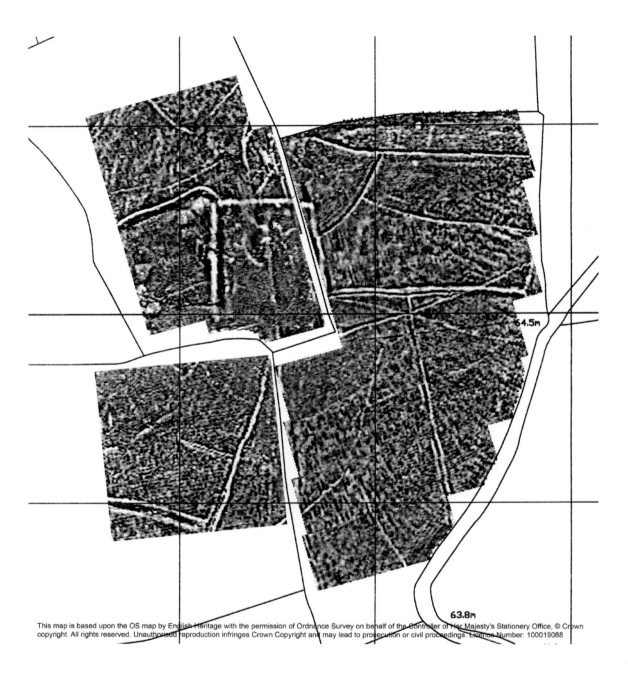

64.5m

63.8m

Fig 3. English Heritage's Ancient Monuments Lab undertook extensive magnetometer survey at Boden in 1993, following the discovery of a fogou by landowner Chris Hosken. This was followed by excavations by the Historic Environment Service in 2003 and by CAS in 2008. Most obvious are the rectangular Iron Age enclosure, field systems clearly of more than one phase, and further traces of settlement north of the enclosure. Scale: grids are 100m. (From survey detail provided by Neil Linford, English Heritage Centre for Archaeology)

in use and new roads and pipelines tend to avoid them. Surveys by English Heritage of the deserted settlements at Tybesta (Grampound) and Greys Farm, North Tamerton (file at Historic Environment Service, SW94NW; Cole 1994), recorded complexes of enclosures, and enclosures were also recorded adjoining Porthcollum, St Erth; these were excavated by Jim Navin and found to be early medieval (Linford 1992; Navin 1992). At Poundstock, a small motte or ringwork discovered during a Rapid Identification Survey in 1993 was surveyed; the mound and ditch were identified, and part of a possible bailey (AM Lab 1994c). However, at Restormel Castle as well as showing a lot of activity in the bailey, survey identified a probable additional enclosure to the south, perhaps another bailey (Geophysical Surveys of Bradford 1994a).

Magnetometry has huge potential for future investigation and research. It will continue to be a useful tool for looking at individual sites, to establish the context of important discoveries, to investigate the character of unusual sites and different types of site and for targeted research (for example, surveys around medieval settlements to identify evidence for prehistoric origins and explore the change from Romano-British to early medieval settlements). Geophysical survey could help to identify sites at risk from coastal erosion, in the context of Shoreline Management Plans, and Ground Penetrating Radar, as yet little used in Cornwall (e.g. at Boden, Linford 2004), could be tried in sandy coastal areas. The most important contribution will be from extensive surveys that can provide a clear view, at a landscape scale, of the changing patterns of settlements and field systems which at present we only see in fragments.

Acknowledgements

This paper is based on study of documentation at the offices of Historic Environment, Cornwall Council, including correspondence files, the Events Record and copies of surveys in the external reports library. The web-based English Heritage Geophysical Survey Database gives information on surveys up to 2004. I am grateful to Vanessa Straker and Neil Linford for their comments on a draft of this paper.

References

Ancient Monuments Laboratory, 1994. *Poundstock, Cornwall,* (mapping only, copy at Cornwall HER, ref ER 397)

Bartlett, A, 1980a. *Carvossa, Probus,* Cornwall, Ancient Monuments Laboratory Report, geophysics 4/80, London

Bartlett, A, 1980b. *St Allen, Cornwall,* Ancient Monuments Laboratory Report, geophysics 5/80, London

Cole, M A, 1994. *Greys Farm, Wilsworthy, North Tamerton, Cornwall,* Ancient Monuments Laboratory Report 25/94, London

Edwards, K, and Kirkham, G, 2008. Gear and Caervallack, St Martin-in-Meneage: excavations by Time Team, 2001, *Cornish Archaeol,* **47,** 49-100

Geophysical Surveys of Bradford, 1994a. *Restormel Castle, report no 94/31,* Bradford

Geophysical Surveys of Bradford, 1994b. *Pendennis Castle, report no 94/32,* Bradford

Geophysical Surveys of Bradford, 1994c. *A388 Viverdon Down, report no 94/112,* Bradford

Geophysical Surveys of Bradford, 1994d. *A390 Probus bypass, report no 94/113,* Bradford

Geophysical Surveys of Bradford, 1996. *A3076 Trispen bypass, report no 96/77,* Bradford

Geophysical Surveys of Bradford, 1998a. *Camborne to Portreath Sewage Treatment Works, report no 98/55,* Bradford

Geophysical Surveys of Bradford, 1998b. *Ruthvoes to Bears Downs, SWW Pipeline, St Columb Major, geophysical survey report 98/60,* Bradford

Gossip, J, forthcoming. Life outside the round - Bronze Age and Iron Age settlement at Higher Besore and Truro College, Threemilestone, Truro, *Cornish Archaeol*

Gossip, J, in preparation. The evaluation of a multi-period prehistoric site at Boden Vean, St Anthony in Meneage, Cornwall 2003, *Cornish Archaeol*

Gossip, J, and Jones, A M, 2007. *Archaeological investigations of a later prehistoric and Romano-British landscape at Tremough, Penryn,* Cornwall, Brit Arch Repts, Brit Ser, **443,** Oxford

GSB Prospection, 2001. *Caer Vallack & Gear Farm, report 2001/77,* Bradford

GSB Prospection, 2002. *Higher Besore Farm, Cornwall, geophysical survey report 2002/44,* Bradford

GSB Prospection, 2004. *Dodman Point, Cornwall, geophysical survey report 2004/41,* Bradford

GSB Prospection, 2005a. *Dodman Point II, Cornwall, geophysical survey report 2005/24,* Bradford

GSB Prospection, 2005b. *Lescudjack Hillfort, Cornwall, geophysical survey report 2005/77,* Bradford

GSB Prospection, 2007. *Camelford School, Cornwall, geophysical survey report 2007/72,* Bradford

GSB Prospection, 2008. *St. Tudy School, Cornwall, geophysical survey report 2008/51,* Bradford

GSB Prospection, 2009. *Land at Penmayne, Rock Cornwall, geophysical survey report 2009/50,* Bradford

Jones, A M, 1998-9. The excavation of a Later Bronze Age structure at Callestick, *Cornish Archaeol,* **37-8,** 5-55

RECORDING THE PAST

Jones, A M, 2000-1. The excavation of a multi-period site at Stencoose, Cornwall, *Cornish Archaeol*, **39-40,** 45-94

Jones, A M, and Taylor, S R, 2010. *Scarcewater, Pennance, Cornwall, archaeological excavation of a Bronze Age and Roman landscape,* Brit Arch Repts, Brit Ser, **516,** Oxford

Linford, N T, 1992. *Porthcollum, St Erth, Cornwall*, Ancient Monuments Laboratory Report 37/92, London

Linford, N T, 1994. *Geophysical survey at Penhale Moor, Penhale, Cornwall*, Ancient Monuments Laboratory report 34/94, London

Linford, N T, 1998. Geophysical survey at Boden Vean, Cornwall, including an assessment of the microgravity technique for the location of suspected archaeological void features, *Archaeometry*, **40, 1,** 187-216

Linford, N, 2004. *Boden Vean, St Anthony in Meneage, Cornwall, report on geophysical survey, October 2003*, English Heritage Centre for Archaeology Report Series, 11/2004

Linford, N, and Linford, P, 2002. *Crasken Farm, Helston, Cornwall: report on geophysical survey, February 2002*, English Heritage Centre for Archaeology Report Series, 26/2002

Navin, J, 1992. The Porthcollum project; interim statement, *Cornish Archaeol*, **31,** 129-30

Nowakowski, J, 1994. *Bypassing Indian Queens*, Truro (Cornwall Archaeological Unit)

Nowakowski, J, 1995. The excavation of a complex barrow at Trelowthas, Manor Farm, Probus, *Cornish Archaeol*, **34,** 206-11

Payne, A, 1998. *Report on geophysical survey July 1997 at Lelissick, Cornwall*, Ancient Monuments Laboratory report 58/98, London

Reynolds, A, 2006. An Early Bronze Age pit at Trenoweth, Portreath, and other results from the Reskadinnick to Portreath transfer pipeline, *Cornish Archaeol*, **45,** 71-95

Smart, C, in preparation. A Roman fort and medieval settlement at Calstock, Cornwall: excavation and survey 2008-2010, to be submitted to *Archaeological Journal*

Stratascan, 1994. *Tretherras School, Newquay*, Upton-upon-Severn

Thompson, S, 2008. *Lellizzick, near Padstow, Cornwall. Archaeological evaluation and assessment of results*, Salisbury (Wessex Archaeology; report reference: 65312.01)

Cornish Archaeology 50, 2011, 71–76

The work of the Portable Antiquities Scheme in Cornwall

ANNA TYACKE

The Portable Antiquities Scheme (PAS) was originally set up by the Department for Culture Media and Sport in 1997 to record the increased amount of material that had to be reported as Treasure under the new Treasure Act 1996. The Scheme was initially trialled in five counties and run by a central team based at the British Museum, and was then enlarged to cover all counties in England and Wales in 2002, with a grant from the Heritage Lottery Fund, paid by the Museums, Libraries and Archives Council. The post of Finds Liaison Officer (FLO) was set up in Cornwall in 2003 and the Scheme has this year come under the auspices of the British Museum and is guaranteed by the Government for a further four years. There are now about 2,500 objects from Cornwall on the PAS database (www.finds.org.uk), the great majority recorded to six figure grid-references or better by the Cornwall FLO, and finds come from across the county. Figure 1 shows the distribution of finds in Cornwall with clusters of finds represented by the black dots, and areas between these clusters partly indicative of where access to land is prohibited, private or protected.

Objects reported are not only metal artefacts discovered by detectorists. Reporting of finds from fieldwalking has also led to the discovery of important new sites. For example in Paul parish this has included Late Neolithic Grooved Ware (PAS reference number CORN-A55EA6), flint

manufacturing sites and a rock outcrop which may be a possible source for Group I greenstone axes, a Beaker bracer (CORN-B38773) and flint arrowheads, Bronze Age houses with Trevisker ware (CORN-F0E2C2), and concentrated material including metalwork, pottery, and querns from a ploughed out Romano-British round. This has led to staff at Cornwall Council's Historic Environment service (HE) and the PAS FLO applying for English Heritage funding, and the support of the Cornwall Archaeological Society, to record the 5000 finds and investigate the sites further with geophysical survey and test pits.

Bronze Age

Some major Bronze Age hoards have been reported through the Treasure process, notably those at Marazion (CORN-A8B9A0; Treasure reference number 2009 T557), St Erth (CORN-F4FC91; DCMS 2004, 20-22), Breage (2004 T71 and T262, DCMS 2007, 35-36) and Mylor (2005 T323, DCMS 2008, 50-52; Jones and Quinnell, this volume, fig 15). Metallurgical analyses have proven theories regarding trade from the Continent, particularly identifying imports in the Late Bronze Age (Northover 2005, 2). The Mylor Late Bronze Age socketed axe hoard findspot and fields around have been surveyed and test pits have been excavated to try to identify evidence of local manufacture. The

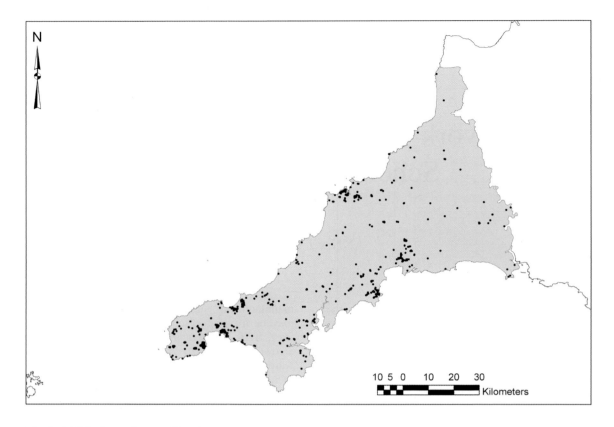

Fig 1. PAS finds in Cornwall (Copyright PAS)

33 axes were wrapped in bracken and placed in a pot that originally contained mutton. The axes are rich in lead and unfinished suggesting that they were not meant to be used as tools, but instead perhaps for exchange. The axes are about to be further analysed using the ICPMS (inductively coupled plasma mass spectrometer) at Camborne School of Mines which can identify the individual isotopes in the plasma gas and source the metal ore precisely.

Bronze Age gold, reported as Treasure, has also added to the Royal Institution of Cornwall's important Bronze Age collections, such as two twisted torc fragments of arm or neck ornaments, one from Gwithian (CORN-A99B98) and the other from Paul parish (CORN-B6B241) (Fig 2), which have both been sheared off at one end and folded in on themselves, ready to be placed in a crucible and melted down to be re-used.

Iron Age and Roman

Iron Age metal finds were exceptionally rare in the county before the Scheme was introduced (Tyacke 2002-3). Linch pins (to hold the wheel hub onto the axle; CORN-32D017), a horse cheek piece (CORN-B50AA7), a scabbard mount (CORN-AC1453) and a bucket escutcheon (CORN-DC8D13) are among the finds, and those inlaid with enamel and glass have also been analysed to show that they were locally made, such as the baldrick ring (Fig 3) (CORN-B177A3) from Constantine which has tin-rich solder under the copper-coloured glass. Iron Age coin finds have shown that although Cornwall was not minting its own coins at this time, it had connections with areas that did, ranging from Jersey to Gloucestershire.

Further metallurgical analyses have been carried out on a unique type of Roman Aesica-variant brooch, mainly found and perhaps produced in Cornwall, now called Cornish Type 31, with eight new brooches recorded on to the PAS database (e.g. CORN-DE55F7; Bayley and Tyacke forthcoming; illustrated in Nowakowski, this volume). High status individual Roman finds are also rare in Cornwall, but each year more are found and reported to the Scheme, like a gold bracelet fragment or necklace link from St Buryan (CORN-929E07; 2007 T140, DCMS 2009, 72-3), a gold finger ring from Bodmin (2006 T463; DCMS 2008, 60), and a gold amuletic pestle pendant (CORN-955DE8; 2008 T782) from Maker with Rame (Fig 4).

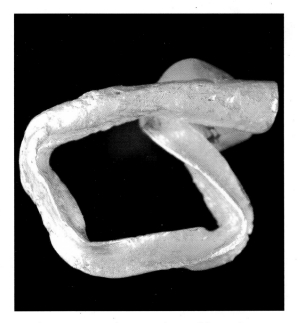

Fig 2. Fragment of Bronze Age gold torc from Paul parish, CORN-B6B241 (Copyright RIC)

The nature of the Roman occupation of Cornwall remains elusive, largely due to the scarcity of sites and finds. However, the PAS has played a significant role in the discovery of several new sites, including the fort at Restormel (Thorpe 2007). This Roman bivallate fort is still visible in the landscape but it was metal detecting activity and a Treasure find of Republican denarii (CORN-7E8363 and 7E10F8; 2005 T53, DCMS 2008, 188) as well as finds from fieldwalking around the fort that led to a project design by HE for further work. A geophysical survey carried out by the Saltash Heritage Group

Fig 3. Iron Age baldrick ring, which would have held a sword belt hanger, from Constantine, CORN- B177A3 (Copyright RIC)

under Peter Nicholas, revealed a second camp and external buildings, perhaps even including a bath house. The finds date from over 400 years of occupation, which is unusual for Cornwall as other Roman forts and camps were not long-lived.

Further down the Fowey estuary the Ethy hoard, St Winnow (Royal Institution of Cornwall accession number TRURI 2003.2) was found on a track that was known to have been used in medieval times,

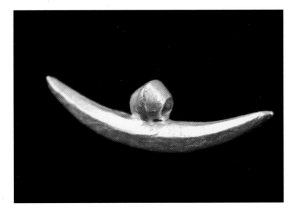

Fig 4. A Roman period gold pestle pendant (length 35mm) worn as an amulet but imitating bronze cosmetic pestles; from Maker with Rame, CORN-955DE8; 2008 T782 (Copyright RIC)

RECORDING THE PAST

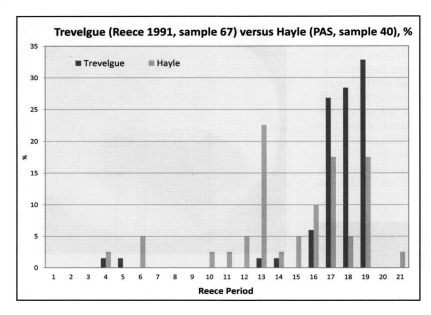

Fig 5. A comparison of the Roman coins found at Trevelgue (Reece 1991) with those recorded with the PAS from Hayle
(Copyright PAS)

but is likely earlier, leading from the Fowey river straight up to Restormel castle and fort. This hoard of over 1000 radiates was contained in a pot and was probably being traded for its metal content as the coinage was no longer legal tender. Other estuaries, on both the south and north coasts, appear to have been the focus for Roman activity. Major enclosures are known on the Fal, for example, though only Carvossa, Probus, has produced significant Roman-period finds (Carlyon 1987). The intriguing rectangular enclosures at Merthen, Constantine, on the Helford, remain undated.

Although very different in character, the rare gold aureus of Nero (CORN-DE6541) recently published by Bland and Loriot (2010, 128, No 75), and the most recent Antonine hoard of 'grots'

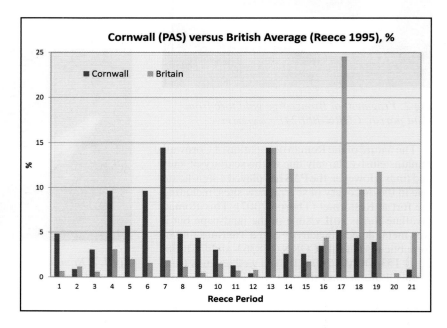

Fig 6. Roman coin finds for Cornwall (PAS) and Britain (Reece 1995) compared (Copyright PAS)

(CORN-A94205; 2009 T558) contribute equally in showing general trends and patterns. The bias of recovery and access to land must be taken into consideration but nonetheless, the steadily growing number of site-finds of Roman coins is a highly important dataset, adding considerably to the known coin finds recorded in Roger Penhallurick's corpus (Penhallurick 2009). Amongst these coins is a large assemblage from the Hayle area which, returning to the theme of estuaries, highlights the importance of this region in the late Roman period. The graph in Figure 5 shows the chronological distribution of coins from before AD 41 (Period 1) to AD 388-402 (Period 21). Hayle is shown against the only other comparable site from the whole of Cornwall, Trevelgue (Newquay). Both have coin finds from throughout the Roman period, but with a significant concentration of late Roman coins. This is different from the situation seen in Cornwall as a whole (as shown in Fig 6).

The Padstow area might also have been a Roman port with Roman finds on either side of the estuary and a late Roman coin hoard (2007 T576, DCMS 2009, 185) and early post-Roman site excavated by Time Team to the north of the town (Wessex Archaeology 2008, 11). And to the south a Treasure find of a hoard of silver denarii (2006 T3, DCMS 2008, 193), with the same goddess on the reverse of many of the coins, is suggestive of a religious site in the vicinity, or even a temple to a particular goddess. A square cropmark enclosure nearby, close to a spring, might tentatively be associated (HER: PRN 50446).

But as we move in from the coasts, the pattern of third to fourth-century coinage changes, probably linked to the tin trade which increased at this time as Spain's tin was running out (Penhallurick 1986, 100, 187-8, 205). Inland we find predominantly first to second-century coins, which might link with centralised military control. The PAS coins overall provide a higher proportion of late Roman coins than is shown by past coin hoards though these are still low relative to the national picture: the graph in Figure 6 shows how the coin profile over time for Cornwall is very different from the national average for Britain. The time periods range from pre-AD 41 (Period 1) to AD 388- 402 (Period 21) (Reece, 1995).

Cornwall has produced a number of Late Roman and Byzantine coins (e.g. CORN-72D1D7) from the Eastern Mediterranean, echoing the finds of imported post-Roman pottery best known in the large collection from Tintagel. This does suggest sea trade coming out of the Straits of Gibraltar and across the Bay of Biscay to Cornwall. Similar coins are also being found on the Isle of Wight and in fact, the PAS is showing that Cornwall and the Isle of Wight share much more in common than we had previously thought (pers comm, Sam Moorhead).

Medieval and later finds

Early medieval finds are extremely rare, especially Anglo-Saxon or Viking artefacts. But the far west of the county is providing new evidence of influence from these cultures, perhaps from the sea and the Scillies, rather than from the expanding kingdom of Wessex. So far two ninth to eleventh-century Hiberno-Norse buckles, three eleventh-century Anglo-Saxon stirrup strap mounts, and three eleventh-century coins have been found in Penwith. The two buckles, from Sennen and Phillack (CORN-902CE5 and CORN-EC5F13; Fig 7), have snake-like heads with circular eye sockets for stone settings at each apex of the D-shaped frame, commonly found on tenth-century strap ends in Hiberno-Norse Dublin (Tyacke 2004-5). The Sennen stirrup mount (CORN-C57246) has decorative silver wire and niello inlay of Anglo-Scandinavian style. The Paul stirrup mount (CORN-

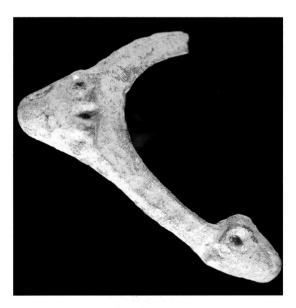

Fig 7. Hiberno-Norse buckle from Phillack,
CORN-EC5F13 (Copyright RIC)

9CABC7) has enamelled zoomorphic decoration, and the Ludgvan strap mount (CORN-CD2446) has a saltire cross dividing four lozenges. At the same time, silver cut halfpennies of Edward the Confessor (1042-1066) (CORN-F06E11 and CORN-635F45) and William I (1066-1087) (CORN-642B57) were being used in Phillack near Hayle.

Medieval and post-medieval finds are by far the most numerous on the database, and there are too many to discuss here, but it is worth mentioning a recent rare find that has been loaned to Penlee House Gallery and Museum, Penzance. This fifteenth-century silver iconographic ring from Paul (CORN-57E815) has two facets on the bezel depicting the Virgin Mary and a saint, not only images of devotion but also semi-magical protectors. The twists are engraved with five-petalled flowers, a reference to the five wounds of Christ, three on one side and four on the other, an allusion to the seven sorrows of the Virgin Mary. Another unusual trend for Cornwall has been identified by Geoff Egan (former PAS Finds Adviser) in looking at all of the medieval buckles (e.g. CORN-E53CD1); he recorded that their local manufacture is unique and differs from the mass-produced types outside of Cornwall and across Europe at the time (Geoff Egan, pers comm).

Modern finds are also recorded, such as buttons, seals, medallions and jewellery, especially when linked to Cornish families, industries and historical events, to enrich our knowledge of Cornwall's local history and encourage the public to learn more about it.

Acknowledgements

I would like to thank Sam Moorhead, National Finds Adviser for the Portable Antiquities Scheme, for allowing me to use his graphs and data for the section on Roman coins.

References

Bayley, J, and Tyacke, A, forthcoming. Romano-British brooches – of Cornish origin? in S Pearce, ed, *The archaeology of south western Britain: recent research. Papers in honour of Henrietta Quinnell*, Brit Arch Repts, Brit Ser, Oxford

Bland, R, and Loriot, X, 2010, *Roman and early Byzantine gold coins found in Britain and Ireland*, Royal Numismatic Society Special Publication, **46**, London

Carlyon, P M, 1987. Finds from the earthwork at Carvossa, Probus, *Cornish Archaeol*, **26**, 103-44

Department of Culture, Media and Sport, 2004. *Treasure Annual Report 2002*, London

Department of Culture, Media and Sport, 2007. *Treasure Annual Report 2004*, London

Department of Culture, Media and Sport, 2008. *Treasure Annual Report 2005/6*, London

Department of Culture, Media and Sport, 2009. *Treasure Annual Report 2007*, London

Northover, P, 2005. *Analysis of the St Erth hoards*, Oxford (Oxford Materials Characterisation Service, Oxford University)

Penhallurick, R D, 1986. *Tin in Antiquity*, Institute of Metals, London

Penhallurick, R D, 2009. *Ancient and medieval coins from Cornwall and Scilly*, Royal Numismatic Society Special Publication **45**, London

Reece, R, 1991. *Roman coins from 140 sites in Britain*, Cotswold Studies, Vol IV, Cirencester

Reece, R, 1995. *Site-finds in Roman Britain*, Britannia, **XXVI**, 180-206

Thorpe, C, 2007, *The earthwork at Restormel Farm, Lostwithiel, Cornwall: archaeological site and finds evaluation*, Truro (Historic Environment Service, Cornwall County Council)

Tyacke, A, 2002-3. Chariots of fire: symbols and motifs on recent Iron Age metalwork finds in Cornwall, *Cornish Archaeol*, **41-42**, 144-148

Tyacke, A, 2004-5. An early medieval buckle from Phillack, *Cornish Archaeol*, **43-44**, 169-170

Wessex Archaeology, 2008, *Lellizzick, near Padstow, Cornwall: archaeological evaluation and assessment of results*, Salisbury

Cornish Archaeology 50, 2011, 77–81

A top 10 of excavations, 1986 to 2011

PETER ROSE

For all the value of remote sensing there comes a point where the aerial photo and the magnetometer have to be set aside for the mattock and the trowel. Only then is it possible to investigate dates, structures, environmental evidence and artefacts. We should also expect the unexpected.

Over the past 25 years three trends in particular have made a difference to the nature of archaeological excavation in Cornwall. First, there is the expectation that developers should take responsibility for the recording of significant archaeological remains affected by their developments. This has been driven by the government's Planning Policy Guidance 16, issued in 1990 (and in 2010 replaced with Planning Policy Statement 5). In 1987, without setting any conditions for archaeological recording, Penwith District Council gave permission for a housing development on the known 'round' at Reawla, Gwinear, leaving English Heritage to step in to fund an excavation, and depending on the good will of the developers to allow access (Appleton-Fox 1992). It is hard to imagine this happening now – more probably a development would be steered away from a major, complex and potentially expensive site such as a round, as has indeed happened on more than one occasion. At the same time, agencies such as South West Water have adopted codes of conduct to ensure that their developments give due consideration to their impact on archaeology. Since the 1990s they have routinely arranged for assessments, geophysical surveys and archaeological monitoring and recording along their pipelines, resulting in the discovery and recording of many significant sites as well as a better understanding of the historic landscapes through which the pipelines cut (for example the Bronze Age roundhouse at Callestick, Perranzabuloe, Romano-British fields at Stencoose, St Agnes, a Bronze Age house and other sites at Newlyn East, and Beaker structures at Sennen; Jones 1998-9; Jones 2000-1; Jones and Taylor 2004; Jones *et al* forthcoming).

These factors, including the more rigorous process of assessment in advance, often with extensive areas checked out by magnetometer surveys, also led to the second major development in the last two decades – a dramatic change in the scale of investigations and excavations – 1.3ha on the St Austell North East Distributor in 1997 (Johns 2008), 3ha at Tremough, Penryn in 2002 (Gossip and Jones 2007), 17ha at Richard Lander School and Truro College, Truro (2004-5; Gossip forthcoming) and 30ha at Scarcewater, St Stephen in Brannel (Jones and Taylor 2010). Examination can be directed towards understanding samples of different types of historic landscape as much as recording known individual sites.

The third factor is regular and consistent sampling for environmental data, and for material for scientific dating (see Straker, this volume).

The key excavations below have made a real difference to our knowledge and understanding, or broken new ground in the exploration of particular types of site. From these examples it is interesting that research excavations, and excavations for training and 'outreach', have continued to play a major role alongside those driven by the need to make a record in advance of destruction.

RECORDING THE PAST

Fig 1. One of the largest excavations in Cornwall, the Richard Lander School site, Truro, in 2004 included a later Iron Age settlement. The ring gully of House 9, one of 12 structures, can be seen in the foreground.

Higher Besore (Richard Lander School and Truro College) (Gossip forthcoming)

These excavations in 2004 and 2005 led to the discovery and recording of a complete, unenclosed late Iron Age settlement for the first time in Cornwall. The excavation was large enough to see how the settlement was organised into a series of individual farmsteads. Remarkably, a settlement of Late Bronze Age houses was also recorded, contributing to understanding of the Late Bronze Age pottery sequence as well as house types.

Trethellan, Newquay (Nowakowski 1991)

This 1987 excavation of a complete Middle Bronze Age settlement (*c* 1500-1100 BC) established the site type for sunken-floored houses, and also explored the role of ritual within the settlement, in particular in the formalised closure of the house sites but also with at least two remarkable ritual structures.

Helman Tor (Mercer 1997)

Along with several other sites in Cornwall, Helman Tor had been suggested as a possible Early Neolithic

tor enclosure, comparable to the previously excavated example at Carn Brea. Roger Mercer's research excavation in 1986 confirmed that Helman Tor is indeed another example, and so we can be more confident that a series of other major sites in Cornwall (such as Trencrom, St Stephen's Beacon, Rough Tor and Stowe's Pound) are also important early centres.

A30 Fraddon to Indian Queens bypass (Nowakowski 1994 and in prep)

This programme of archaeological recording in response to the construction of a new stretch of the A30 in 1993-4 was designed to investigate the archaeological character and historical development of the two types of landscape through which it cut, namely areas of former open downland which had been enclosed in the eighteenth and nineteenth centuries (Recently Enclosed Land) and areas thought to have originated as farmland in the medieval period or before (Anciently Enclosed Land). Prehistoric settlement sites were found to be concentrated in the Anciently Enclosed Land, including two Middle Bronze Age settlements and a Romano-British round. Arguably the most

Fig 2. CAS members helped in the early stages of the excavations at Trethellan, Newquay, on the discovery of the Middle Bronze Age settlement. (Left, Geoff Walford, centre, Peter Brierley)

important site in its own right was an Early Neolithic rectangular building, so far unique in Cornwall.

Enclosure at Hay Close, St Newlyn East (Jones forthcoming)

The Society's research excavation in 2007 helped to lead to the recognition of a new range of Iron Age ceremonial sites. Interpreted from cropmark evidence as a henge, the enclosure was selected for excavation because of its potential to investigate the late Neolithic, a period little studied in Cornwall. Excavation confirmed that the enclosure had a bank outside the ditch, like a henge, but established that the site actually had its origins in the Iron Age. Other Iron Age ceremonial enclosures of various sizes and types have now been identified at Tremough (Penryn), Camelford, and Scarcewater (St Stephen in Brannel) (Jones 2010).

Tintagel Island (Barrowman *et al* 2007)

Research and survey in the 1980s had raised many questions about the nature of post-Roman Tintagel. Excavations by Glasgow University in the 1990s investigated some of the large number of slightly built rectangular buildings and demonstrated, through stratigraphic evidence and radiocarbon dating, a date range from the early fifth century AD to the late sixth or seventh century. The excavations

Fig 3. Roger Mercer's excavations at Helman Tor in October 1986 confirmed it as a Neolithic tor enclosure. Note the substantial stone rampart to the rear of terrace.

RECORDING THE PAST

reinforced earlier interpretations of Tintagel as a post-Roman stronghold of Dumnonian royalty, with extensive occupation of the fifth to seventh centuries right across it and demonstrably of high status, with contacts with the Mediterranean, south-west France and southern Spain, trade in wine, olive oil and exotic glass and with evidence for literacy (the 'Artognou' stone), implying a system of education and the use of Latin.

Tintagel Churchyard (Nowakowski 1992)

Research excavations in 1990 and 1991 provided a rare opportunity to explore the origins and development of a churchyard and demonstrated the survival of varied and complex remains, including many phases of burial in both cist graves and unlined graves, from post-Roman to post-medieval. Quantities of imported Mediterranean pottery of the sixth century AD suggested an association with Tintagel Island, and fires and areas of burning suggested graveside rituals. A rectangular building was interpreted as a pre-Norman church or chapel.

The sword and mirror burial from Bryher, Scilly (Johns 2006)

Following the discovery of an Iron Age sword and scabbard by farmer Paul Jenkins a painstaking excavation in 1999 showed that it was part of a remarkable and spectacular burial placed in a well-constructed stone-lined and stone-capped grave. The grave goods included the sword, a decorated bronze mirror, a brooch and a finger ring – an assemblage unique in the south west (Johns, this volume, fig 4).

Duckpool, Morwenstow (Ratcliffe 1995)

First discovered by CAS member RM Heard, this Romano-British and early medieval site stands out amongst contemporary settlements because of its coastal location, on the valley floor at the head of a beach, and its specialised industrial activity, including metalworking. The 1992 excavation, though small in scale, illustrates the complex settlement hierarchies to be expected at this time. It also suggests what we might expect to find at other 'porths'.

Glasney, Penryn (Cole 2005)

This evaluation exercise in 2003 was very successful in establishing the layout of the thirteenth and fourteenth-century collegiate church. John Allan's analysis of the artefacts also revealed much about the quality of stonework and its relation to medieval work elsewhere in the south west.

Fig 4. Glasney College, Penryn, 2003. A series of evaluation trenches recorded the layout of the collegiate church; here the buttressed south-east corner of the church is exposed. The excavation was run by Cornwall County Council's Historic Environment Service for the Friends of Glasney, funded by the HLF. Community involvement was a major objective; 64 volunteers participated and 500 visitors were given guided tours by Joanna Mattingly.

Of course other writers would come up with a different selection! Other highlights include a rare Beaker structure found on a pipeline at Sennen (Jones *et al* forthcoming); large scale excavations at Scarcewater, St Stephen-in-Brannel, which included Romano-British burials at the edge of a settlement (Jones and Taylor 2010); and fogous at Boden (St Anthony in Meneage) and, unexpectedly, at Penhale Round (St Enoder) (Gossip in prep; Hood 2007).

Whilst some of these excavations are still going through the process of analysis and final publication it is worth noting that the last 20 years have seen the publication of important 'backlog' excavations and major excavation campaigns of the 1960s and 1970s, including major sites that are representative of their type: Carn Euny courtyard house settlement, Halangy Porth and Launceston Castle; Mawgan Porth early medieval settlement; Trethurgy Round; West Lanyon deserted medieval settlement; and the excavations of C K Croft Andrew in the 1930s and 1940s, including Trevelgue cliff castle, Lamanna Chapel, and barrows on Davidstow Moor and the north coast.

Are there still themes which are poorly explored by excavation? Towards the top of a long list, in my opinion, should be early medieval settlements, medieval settlements in lowland Cornwall, and excavation in towns – all subjects on which excavation has done little to shed light in the past 25 years. We should also expect that research will be taken forward through completely unexpected discoveries.

References

Appleton-Fox, N, 1992. Excavations at a Romano-British round; Reawla, Gwinear, Cornwall, *Cornish Archaeol*, **31**, 69-123

Barrowman, R C, Batey, C E, and Morris, C D, 2007. *Excavations at Tintagel Castle, Cornwall, 1990-1999*, Reports of the Research Committee of the Society of Antiquaries of London, No. 74

Cole, D, 2005. *Glasney College, Penryn, Cornwall - archaeological assessment and evaluation trenching*, Truro (Historic Environment Service, Cornwall County Council)

Gossip, J, and Jones, A M, 2007. *Archaeological investigations of a later prehistoric and a Romano British landscape at Tremough, Penryn, Cornwall*, Brit Arch Repts, Brit Ser, **443**, Oxford

Gossip, J, forthcoming. Life outside the round - Bronze Age and Iron Age settlement at Higher Besore and Truro College, Threemilestone, Truro, *Cornish Archaeol*

Gossip, J, in preparation. The evaluation of a multi-period prehistoric site at Boden Vean, St Anthony in Meneage, Cornwall 2003, *Cornish Archaeol*

Harry, R, and Morris, C D, 1997. Excavations on the Lower Terrace, Site C, Tintagel Island 1990-4, *Antiq J*, **77**, 1-143

Hood, A, 2007. *Penhale Round, Fraddon, Cornwall; NGR SW9080 5725; archaeological excavation post excavation assessment*, Swindon (Foundations Archaeology, report no 541)

Johns, C, 2006. An Iron Age sword and mirror cist burial from Bryher, Isles of Scilly, *Cornish Archaeol*, **41-42**, 2002-3, 1-79

Johns, C, 2008. Excavations at Trenowah, St Austell North-East Distributor Road, *Cornish Archaeol*, **47**, 1-48

Jones, A M, 1998-9. The excavation of a Later Bronze Age structure at Callestick, *Cornish Archaeol*, **37-8**, 5-55

Jones, A M, 2000-1. The excavation of a multi-period site at Stencoose, Cornwall, *Cornish Archaeol*, **39-40**, 45-94

Jones, A M, 2010. Misplaced monuments?: a review of ceremony and monumentality in first millennium cal BC Cornwall, *Oxford Archaeological Journal*, **29**, 203-28

Jones, A M, forthcoming. Hay Close, St Newlyn East: excavations by the Cornwall Archaeological Society, 2007, *Cornish Archaeol*

Jones, A M and Taylor, S R, 2004. *What lies beneath . . . St Newlyn East and Mitchell, archaeological investigations 2001*, Truro (Cornwall County Council)

Jones, A M and Taylor, S R, 2010. *Scarcewater, Pennance, Cornwall, archaeological excavation of a Bronze Age and Roman landscape*, Brit Arch Repts, Brit Ser, **516**, Oxford

Jones, A M, Taylor, S R, and Sturgess, J, forthcoming. A Beaker associated structure and other discoveries along the Sennen to Porthcurno SWW pipeline, *Cornish Archaeol*

Mercer, R, 1997. The excavation of a Neolithic enclosure complex at Helman Tor, Lostwithiel, Cornwall, *Cornish Archaeol*, **36**, 5-63

Nowakowski, J A, 1991. Trethellan Farm, Newquay: the excavation of a lowland Bronze Age settlement and Iron Age cemetery, *Cornish Archaeol*, **30**, 5-242

Nowakowski, J, 1994. *Bypassing Indian Queens*, Truro (Cornwall Archaeological Unit)

Nowakowski, J A, and Thomas, C, 1992. *Grave news from Tintagel. An account of a second season of archaeological excavation at Tintagel Churchyard, Cornwall, 1991*, Truro (Cornwall County Council)

Ratcliffe, J, 1995. Duckpool, Morwenstow: a Romano-British and early medieval industrial site and harbour, *Cornish Archaeol*, **34**, 81-171

RECORDING THE PAST

Chysauster at dawn. Photograph by Paul Chrome, CAS member.

Cornish Archaeology 50, 2011, 83–87

Archaeological protection - legislation, designation and planning policy

NICHOLAS JOHNSON

In the 'rescue archaeology' decades of the 1970s and 1980s, the legal protection of archaeological monuments (Ancient Monuments), historic buildings (Listed Buildings) and historic settlements (Conservation Areas) was considerably enhanced. The last two decades have seen equally momentous changes in legislation and planning policy guidance. Cornwall now has a World Heritage Site, and archaeology and the built heritage are material considerations in the planning system. Also accepted is the principle that the 'polluter pays'. Developers now meet the cost of assessment and evaluation, and in the event of loss, mitigation through 'preservation by record'. Archaeology has become a profession (Institute for Archaeologists, founded 1982) and, since the early 1990s, a commercial profession. In January 2011, 3189 of the 5827 people in archaeological employment in the UK, were working in commercial and applied archaeology (Institute for Archaeology statistics). Changes in legislation, designation and planning policy have completely transformed the profile of archaeology within the national and local authority planning systems, the position of professionals in the wider heritage establishment, and the amount of archaeological work being carried out. The route showing how this came about is mapped out below.

The protection of archaeology has been the responsibility of the **Ministry of Works** (1943-1962), the **Ministry of Public Buildings and Works** (1962-1970), the **Department of the Environment** (DoE) (1970-1992), the **Department of National Heritage** (1992-1997), and now from 1997, the **Department of Culture Media and Sport**. The **Historic Buildings and Monuments Commission for England (English Heritage (EH))** was established under the **Heritage Act 1983** and the staff transferred from the DoE. In 1999 the **Royal Commission on Historical Monuments of England**, responsible for the National Monuments Record and survey, was absorbed into EH. EH is the archaeological advisor to Government, and with the **Heritage Lottery Fund** (since 1994), provides grants for archaeological research, recording and management. Along with the **National Trust**, EH is also a significant owner of national heritage sites. This triumvirate provides, between them, the national framework for protection, for grant aid and national best practice management of archaeology and the wider historic environment.

When the **Cornwall Committee for Rescue Archaeology** (CCRA) was formed in 1975 it reflected the 'rescue' ethos of the early 1970s. It was always intended by the sponsoring authority, the Department of the Environment, that such Units should become the responsibility of local authorities. It was to be 13 years (in 1988) before this happened in Cornwall. Titles give a good indication of the changing character of an organization. CCRA became the **Cornwall Archaeological Unit** (CAU)

Date	1. Advice staff	2. Number of Information staff	3. World Heritage Site staff	4. Project staff	5. Total CAU/HES staff	6. Hedgerow application consultations	7. Forestry consultations	8. Agri-environment schemes	9. ESA consultations	10 Development related projects undertaken
1985	1	1	-	6	8	-	-	-	-	3
1986	1	1	-	6	8	-	-	-	-	3
1987	1	1	-	11	13	-	-	-	-	2
1988	1	1	-	12	14	-	N/A	-	-	3
1989	1	1	-	9	11	-	N/A	-	N/A	6
1990	1	1	-	9	11	-	N/A	-	N/A	9
1991	1	1	-	10	12	-	N/A	-	N/A	12
1992	1	1	-	12	14	-	N/A	42	N/A	29
1993	1	1	-	13	15	-	N/A	41	N/A	42
1994	1	2	-	17	20	-	80	58	N/A	30
1995	1	2	-	16	19	-	103	50	N/A	44
1996	1	2	-	16	19	-	76	c.3	N/A	46
1997	1	2	-	17	20	-	64	46	N/A	52
1998	1	2	-	17	20	32	65	44	N/A	55
1999	1	2	-	19	22	33	70	88	N/A	73
2000	2	2	-	22	24	33	68	88	N/A	73
2001	5	4	4	20	33	24	60	214	N/A	70
2002	5	4	4	21	33	52	57	125	112	47
2003	5	5	3	25	38	13	50	92	96	63
2004	5	5	3	26	39	52	61	124	51	64
2005	5	5	3	27	40	44	25	36	24	71
2006	5	5	3	24	37	42	41	31	3	70
2007	5	5	3	23	36	38	37	50	3	64
2008	5	5	3	22	35	40	33	19	-	103
2009	5	6	3	20	34	19	33	33	-	79
2010	5	6	5	20	36	18	28	83	-	94

Table 1 CAU/HES capacity statistics 1985-2010

This table gives a broad impression of the increasing capacity and workload of the CAU/HES since 1985, with staff numbers in columns 1-5, agri-environment advice in columns 6-9, and the number of projects in column 10 that were paid for by developers as a result of the Spatial Planning process.

Note: Whilst advice was certainly given, no figures for consultations are available between1988-1993 for Forestry consultations (Column 7), and between 1989-2001 for ESA consultations (Column 9).

in 1985/6 and was much more pro-active within the planning system both as a 'curator' giving advice, and as a 'contractor', bidding for, and undertaking, projects. Table 1 demonstrates that advice and recording work has steadily increased over the last 25 years. CAU became the **Historic Environment Service** in 2000, and the **Sites and Monuments Record** (SMR) became the **Historic Environment Record** (HER) reflecting the indivisibility of archaeology and conservation. From the late 1980s CAU had been recording and giving advice on historic buildings, historic landscapes as well as archaeological sites. The trend of integration of historic environment advice, information and projects culminated in 2009 with the bringing together of the County Council archaeological service and the District Council conservation services in the new Cornwall Council's **Historic Environment** service. In 2010 Cornwall had one of the largest and most integrated local authority historic environment services in the country. It is 129 years since the ***Ancient Monuments Protection Act***

(1882) enshrined the division between monuments and buildings. Cornwall has often been ahead of the heritage curve and the new comprehensive service exactly reflects the new heritage zeitgeist. The *draft Heritage Protection Bill (2008)* intends the integration of all heritage designations into one with the hope that national, regional and local historic environment services should bring together archaeological and historic buildings services. Whilst the Heritage Bill is still awaited, the end of the heritage schism in Cornwall should bode well for the protection of our archaeological heritage.

Designation and Protection

The *Ancient Monuments and Archaeological Areas Act (1979)* replaced the *Ancient Monuments Consolidation and Amendment Act (1913)*, which replaced the *Ancient Monuments Protection Act (1882)*, and underpins archaeological protection to this day. The 1979 Act had originally intended that 'Archaeological Areas' could include important archaeological landscapes. This raised hopes that great archaeological relict landscapes on Bodmin Moor and in West Penwith could be protected as a sort of 'Archaeological Conservation Area'. In the event only the centre of historic cities, such as Exeter, were designated. Today Cornwall has 1581 Scheduled Monuments (some 2660 individual items).

Before 1986, sites were selected largely as a result of threat, personal interest, and unexpected discovery. A rapid assessment of all county Sites and Monuments Records in 1984 showed that only 2% of recorded sites were scheduled, and even these were unrepresentative of the national resource. In response, the **Monuments Protection Programme** (MPP) was established in 1986 to identify monuments for scheduling on the grounds of importance and conservation need (Darvill *et al* 1987; Startin 1991; 1995; English Heritage 1996; 1997). It was to provide a comprehensive reassessment and a better understanding of the archaeological resource, using a new classification system, in order to improve conservation, management and public appreciation. Approximately 225 classes of site were eventually identified and described, and many were evaluated. EH were also to consider forms of management or designation other than scheduling. This was to

prove of particular significance to Cornwall since the surveys of Bodmin Moor and West Penwith in the early 1980s and the surveys of historic mining sites in the late 1980s and 1990s identified hundreds of sites of national importance that proved beyond EH's resources to schedule. There are still a large number of sites awaiting designation. In Cornwall, programmes of scheduling from 1988 to 2003, as part of the MPP, were both area based and thematic, with coverage of EH properties, readily accessible monuments such as roadside crosses, parts of Bodmin Moor, some of the nationally important industrial sites and sites in Carrick District and part of Restormel Borough. The plug was pulled on the programme in the run up to the proposed review of the designation system that began in 2003 and culminated in the draft Heritage Protection Bill 2008. This has meant that the designation in Cornwall remains incomplete, with many nationally important monuments unprotected. This includes many sites and areas in West Penwith and on Bodmin Moor and many important industrial sites.

Although curtailed, the MPP provided the clear thinking required to reform the whole protection system and it provided, for the first time, systematic descriptions of the country's archaeological resource.

The **Register of Parks and Gardens**, established in 1983, built on the work of the Garden History Society, and locally the Cornwall Gardens Trust. They provided the surveys (almost 80 to date) for most of the 38 gardens (3720 ha) on the Register. The **Battlefields Register**, now advised by the Battlefields Trust, was established in 1995. Two of the 42 on the Register are in Cornwall (Braddock Down and Stratton, both 1643).

The United Kingdom ratified the *World Heritage Convention (1972)* in 1984 and The Cornwall and West Devon Mining Landscape (Cornish Mining - 18,222 ha, 5.5% of Cornwall) was inscribed in 2006 following a decision in 1998 to promote the role that the UK played in the Industrial Revolution. World Heritage Sites are not statutory designations but nonetheless have a measure of protection through planning legislation and guidance.

Historic buildings have been protected through the *Town and Country Planning Acts 1932, 1944 and 1971*, and most recently *The Planning (Listed Buildings and Conservation Areas) Act 1990*. Listed Building Consent was the responsibility of the

District Councils in Cornwall until 2009, and as with Scheduled Monuments there have been programmes of upgrading the Lists. In Cornwall the last major List review was in the early 1980s, followed by the recent review of nonconformist chapels. Cornwall has 12,660 Listed Buildings (about 15,000 individual buildings and structures). There are still many areas inadequately covered despite surveys over the last 15 years of towns and villages through the Cornwall Industrial Settlements Initiative, the Cornwall and Scilly Urban Survey programme and many Conservation Area Assessments and Management Plans. It is to be hoped that EH's **National Heritage Protection Plan (2010)**, developed in response to heritage protection reform, will result in the resumption of List Reviews.

Conservation Areas were introduced by the *Civic Amenities Act 1967*. Of the 145 (4070ha) Conservation Areas in Cornwall, most were designated in the 1980s and early 1990s, with a few recent industrial settlements added. There are two other categories of designation, which have quasi-legal protection. They are particularly important in Cornwall. **National Trust Inalienable Land** (10,026 hectares including 78 scheduled monuments) cannot be sold without an act of parliament. **National Heritage Properties** (7 properties- mostly large houses with their parks and gardens) have conditional exemption from Inheritance Tax, subject to a Conservation Management Plan, and breaking the agreement results in the withdrawal of the exemption. Finally, offshore there are 12 **Designated Wrecks** and 2 **Designated War Graves** (naval wrecks).

There are therefore a significant number of archaeological sites, historic buildings, historic maritime assets, and historic areas that are legally protected in Cornwall and Scilly. Beneficial management of change to this precious resource can only happen through the goodwill of owners, and or, through the strictures of the spatial planning process and or grant aid. The annual national **Heritage at Risk Register**, that includes monuments, buildings and conservation areas, is proving to be a useful indicator of how successful we are proving.

Spatial Planning legislation and guidance

The protection of archaeology from harmful development has been made possible through successive legislation: the *Town and Country*

Planning General Development (Amendment No 2) order 1985; the *Town and Country Planning Act 1990; the Planning (Listed Buildings and Conservation Areas) Act 1990*; the *Environment Act 1995;* the *Town and Country Planning (General Permitted Development) Order 1995*; the *Hedgerow Regulations 1997*; the *Town and Country Planning (Environmental Impact assessment) Regulations 1999*; the *Planning and Compulsory Purchase Act 2004*; and the *Environment Information Regulations 2004*. These seek to ensure that designated sites, and undesignated archaeology, historic buildings and historic areas are given proper consideration through the planning system and *Circular 07/09* ensures that World Heritage Sites are also brought within Planning regulations.

Planning Policy Guidance notes give advice on how legislation should be used within the planning system. *Planning Policy Guidance 16. Archaeology and Planning 1990* was critical in establishing the principle of 'preservation *in situ*' of nationally important archaeological remains, and the application of the principle of 'polluter pays' where archaeological remains will be damaged or destroyed by development. It gave advice on the handling of archaeological remains and discoveries under the development plan and development control systems including the use of planning conditions, the requirement for developers to provide adequate information on the impact of proposals on archaeological remains, and to arrange for recording and publication in mitigation. PPG 16 had an immediate effect on the level of archaeological work being carried out in Cornwall. The number of archaeological projects undertaken has increased from 98 in the 5 years before the introduction of PPG16 to an astonishing 769 projects carried out in the five years to 2010. Developer paid projects have risen from approximately 20% of all projects undertaken in 1985, to over 75% in 2010. During the same period, the number of planning advice staff has increased from 1 to 5 and project staff from 9 to over 20 (Table 1).

Planning Policy Guidance 15. Planning and the Historic Environment 1994 provided policies for the identifying and protection of historic buildings, conservation areas, and other elements of the historic environment, and explains the role played by the planning system in their protection and treatment as a material consideration in development proposals. Local planning authorities should have appropriately qualified specialist advice available, and were encouraged to ensure that comprehensive management plans are in place for World Heritage Sites. This guidance has resulted in an increasing number of building recording projects and these now routinely involve historic farm buildings in advance of conversion as well as many historic bridges in advance of the strengthening programme. Recording buildings and archaeology as part of the evaluation process, and as mitigation through 'preservation by record', is now routine and these guidance notes are responsible. Both PPGs have now been superseded by *Planning Policy Statement 5. Planning for the Historic Environment 2010* which defined two important new concepts- 'heritage asset' and 'significance':

1. A **heritage asset** is 'a building, monument, site, place, area or landscape positively identified as having a degree of significance meriting consideration in planning decisions. Heritage assets are the valued components of the historic environment. They include designated heritage assets as defined in this PPS (i.e. World Heritage Site, Scheduled Monument, Listed Building, Protected Wreck Site, Registered Park and Garden, Registered Battlefield or Conservation Area) and assets identified by the local planning authority during the process of decision-making or through the plan-making process (including local listing)'.
2. **Significance** is 'the value of a heritage asset to this and future generations because of its heritage interest. That interest may be archaeological, architectural, artistic or historic'.

The stated objectives of PPS 5 neatly encapsulate the *raison d'etre* for having a strong local authority Historic Environment service:

1. 'to deliver sustainable development in the historic environment by recognizing that heritage assets are a non-renewable resource, by taking account of the wider benefits of heritage conservation, and by recognizing that intelligently-managed change may sometimes be necessary to maintain assets long term'

2. 'to conserve assets in a manner appropriate to their significance by ensuring that decisions are based on that significance as investigated to a proportionate degree, by putting the assets where possible to an appropriate and viable use consistent with their conservation, recognizing and valuing their contribution to local character and sense of place; and integrating the historic environment into planning policies'
3. 'to contribute to our knowledge and understanding of our past by ensuring that evidence is captured and made publicly available'

Regional and Local Strategies and Plans

Planning legislation and guidance is translated into policy and practice through the **Draft Regional Spatial Strategy for the South West 2008**, and **Our Environment our Future - the Regional Strategy for the South West Environment 2004-14**. In Cornwall the **County Structure Plan 2004** and the six District **Local Plans** are superseded by the **Draft Cornwall Local Development Framework 2010**. These documents, and the legislation and planning guidance outlined above provide a substantial and coherent framework that can protect our heritage for future generations to value and interpret. The rest is up to owners, developers, and elected councillors, guided by public opinion and expert advice- and this must surely include the Cornwall Archaeological Society.

References

Darvill, T, Saunders, A, and Startin, B, 1987. A question of national importance: approaches to the evaluation of ancient monuments for the Monuments Protection Programme in England, *Antiquity*, **61**, 393-408

English Heritage, 1996. *The Monuments Protection Programme, 1986-96 in retrospect*, English Heritage leaflet

English Heritage, 1997. *The Monuments Protection Programme, an introduction*, English Heritage leaflet

Startin, B, 1991. Assessment of field remains, in J Hunter, and I Ralston, eds, *Archaeological Resource management in the UK: an introduction*, London

Startin, B, 1995. The Monuments Protection Programme: protecting what, how and for whom? in M A Cooper, A Firth, J Carman, and D Wheatley, eds, *Managing Archaeology*, London

CONSERVING THE PAST

Cornish Archaeology 50, 2011, 89–94

Curating the past: Cornish museums and galleries

JANE MARLEY

The Royal Institution of Cornwall (RIC) was regarded as the main archaeological repository for Cornwall as early as 1825. The distinctive archaeology collections contain material from the prehistoric period onwards: '...*the Council have much pleasure in stating that your Museum appears to be increasingly regarded as a proper depository for objects connected with the Antiquities of the County.*' (RIC AGM August 27th 1825).

The Royal Cornwall Museum (RCM) holds the majority of the archaeological finds and archives of Cornwall on behalf of the RIC, a charitable trust. Other local authority funded museums also keep local archaeological collections and some voluntary run community museums curate small numbers of local finds. The Isles of Scilly Museum, St Mary's, currently collects for the Isles of Scilly. English Heritage manages properties in Cornwall and some of the archives are held in a store in the Midlands while others are curated at the RCM.

In considering the preservation and conservation of finds in Cornwall over the last 25 years, the RCM, as the main county repository, reflects the progress and changes in museum archaeology within the

Fig 1. Box of packaging from Acc. No. 1959.38 Nanjulian before reorganisation in 2004. Archaeologists used to use anything that came to hand to store finds and did not repack them before deposition in the museum. Containers consisted of grocery boxes, paper bags, match boxes, tins and bottles and could contaminate finds for contemporary scientific analysis needs. Over time, as the boxes collapsed and the bags tore finds could be mixed up and/or crushed. Pencil or biro marking on notes and packaging could disintegrate or fade.

*Fig 2. Matthew Freeman, volunteer, repackaging
the collection in the Basement Store in 2008.
Finds after reorganization are stored in inert
storage materials such as plastic bags and
plastazote to prevent contamination. Finds
are placed in different stores or plastic sealed
boxes which provide microclimates to ensure the
appropriate temperature and humidity prevents
decay. Notes and markings on old packaging are
kept and new marking is with permanent ink pens
on finds and on bags and packaging.*

country. The museum is not typical of a regional
museum, however, as although the collections are
substantial and significant, it is a charitable trust
with fluctuating public funding.

Usually archaeological archives from Cornwall
are placed with the RCM which is a Museums,
Libraries and Archives (MLA) 'accredited'
museum and the designated English Heritage store
for Cornwall eligible for storage box grants (MLA
2004). The RCM also provides care for a proportion
of the collections of the Isles of Scilly and others
on loan from the Duchy, English Heritage and the
National Trust. Since 2004, where there are no finds
from an investigation, the documentary records are

placed with the Cornwall Record Office and a copy
of the final report is placed in the Courtney Library
on behalf of the RIC which administers it.

Over the last 25 years, the changing pattern
of the care of the archaeology collections reflects
the fortunes of the museum itself, the talents of its
staff, the wider heritage environment of the times
and the development of the museum profession
and related specialists. 1987 saw the retirement of
Leslie Douch, Curator of the RIC since 1951. Leslie
Douch was a highly capable and hardworking
curator who inspired and amused many; his
personality and some of his achievements are
outlined in tributes (JRIC 2003). His wide ranging
interests included archaeology, and he began
the task of arranging and compiling a variety of
descriptive lists and catalogues of the collections
as finding-aids, all beautifully hand written. Roger
Penhallurick, assistant to Leslie Douch, published
Tin in Antiquity (Penhallurick 1986). Roger
Penhallurick was also arranging the museum
collection of coins and tokens; his corpus of coins
found in Cornwall was posthumously published
in 2009 (Penhallurick 2009). These remarkable
works by Roger Penhallurick and the contribution
of Leslie Douch to the Cornwall Archaeological
Society Journal and Newsletter attest to much care,
study, analysis and scholarship with regard to the
archaeology collection at the RCM during their
tenure (JRIC 2003).

The changing role of the Curator can be
charted by looking at past records and comparing
the tasks and projects carried out over the last 25
years. For example, the Annual Report for 1985
for the year 1984/5 shows how the development
of the museum was being scrutinised and the
collecting policy for the museum was being
examined (RIC Council 1985).

Later, annual reports show the RIC took
advantage of new funding streams such as the
Heritage Lottery Fund and match funding. A
new position, the Curator of Human History, was
filled by Anna Tyacke, from 1990 to July 2003
to care for the collection and to work on the new
displays (Marley this volume). The creation of the
new environmentally controlled stores in 1996/7
enabled the archaeology collection to be curated to
a higher standard. Both projects were substantial
achievements that prepared the museum for
operation in the twenty-first century.

The introduction of a part-time Finds Liaison

Officer from 2003 (a post taken by Anna Tyacke) hosted at the museum to run the successful Portable Antiquities Scheme in Cornwall, is covered elsewhere in this journal.

In 2003 the RCM became one of only 14 museums across the country to receive temporary financial support from the Department for Culture, Media and Sport (DCMS), through a programme called Renaissance in the Regions (RiR). The purpose of the funding was to build capacity in important regional museums, enabling them to become centres of excellence. In 2004, the overall staffing trebled and many new, short term renewable contract posts were created. One of these posts was the Curator of Archaeology and World Cultures. Recent work has concentrated on,

firstly, preserving the collection by reorganising it to current standards, secondly, making it accessible to the public through documentation using powerful databases, and thirdly providing exhibitions, learning and digital access for the widest possible variety of audiences. As before, the Curator has the opportunity to publish articles and give lectures about artefacts or curatorial projects but only if they correspond with the priorities of the organisation.

Since 2004 the museum's acquisition and disposal policy (RIC May 2005) and deposition of archaeological archives (RIC December 2005) have been revised; new policies and guidance have been created (RIC Dec 2005, May 2006; RCM RIC Oct 2006; RIC Oct 2007; a 10-year *Collections*

Fig 3. Laura Pooley, Curatorial Assistant, reorganizing the Basement Store. New low acid boxes with brass staples fit the shelves to make the most of space and avoid damage to boxes on removal. Boxes are placed in accession order from 1820s onwards.

CONSERVING THE PAST

Fig 4. Laura Ratcliffe conserving the outer coffin lid of Iset-tayef-nakht, the unwrapped mummy, at Royal Cornwall Museum.

Management Plan (RIC March 2005) has been produced to reorganise and raise the standard of the care of the collection to current national standards (Brown 2007; Elliott 2002 ; Grant 1994; HMC/mda 2002; Longworth and Wood 2000; McKenna and Patsatzi 2007; MGC 1992; MGC 1996; Owen1995; SMA 1993).

RiR funded Curatorial Assistants (2005 – 2009) to undertake the large task of auditing, reconciling the documentation and repackaging the results of around 200 years of archaeology collecting. Around 95% of the documentation of the collection has been reconciled over five years with the assistance of volunteers and work placements and around 60% of the repacking (Figs 1, 2 and 3).

The history of documentation at the RIC is covered in detail elsewhere (Morgan 2008). The story of the RIC's improvements to reach national standards for documentation (Grant 1994; McKenna and Patsatzi 2007) and the impact of computers and digitisation will broadly mirror that of other museums in Cornwall.

By the recording of the location of finds on a database, the ability and speed to answer enquiries has increased from up to two days to under an hour. Many enquiries continue to be answered and visiting researchers include not only local people but those involved with high status academic projects and partnerships in Britain and Europe and universities around the world (see list of researchers/ funding institutions/aims/methodology under 'Cornish Archaeology' on the RCM web site, *www. royalcornwallmuseum.org.uk*. These enquiries require research and assistance from the curator and conservator and, appropriate space to work and equipment such as microscopes and scales.

Renaissance funding allowed a post of Conservator (2006 – 2010, full time and 2010 to present, part time) and enabled the creation of a Conservation Laboratory. Investigative conservation of finds, such as the Mylor Hoard led to more information becoming available and the opportunity to use analytical technologies (Jones and Quinnell this volume, fig 15); (Fig. 4).

Issues of current and future archaeological archives and museums and libraries

The pressures on the archaeology curators at regional museums such as the RCM have increased for three reasons: the introduction of the Portable Antiquities Scheme and the reporting of 'Treasure'; the increase in building development in the county; and the rise in researchers due to the growing numbers of people studying archaeology at university. Associated with this are a far greater proportion of administration and curatorial care and greater research needs.

Few realise that the RCM and other county museums play an important role within the county planning process through PPG 16 and now PPS 5 as county wide archaeological repositories. This is now under threat as a result of government cuts and the anomalous position of the museum which is not owned by the Cornwall Council. This anomalous position may become the norm as Council funded museums move towards trust status (Heywood 2010). Adequate funding would recognise this essential function of the museum in the planning process and ensure the future permanent preservation of, and access to, the archaeological collections of Cornwall.

The RCM and other museums in Cornwall currently operate in changing political and funding scenarios but must strive to keep up their profile and inform the public, stakeholders and funders about what they do. New types of funding such as strategic commissioning will, one hopes, fund current practice already carried out by charitable trusts. In Cornwall, more collections storage is required for around 100 archaeological archives on a waiting list for deposition to RCM, and for the archives from the next 25 to 50 years of excavations. Better research facilities are required for the increase in researchers. An Assistant Curator and a Conservator, or a budget to 'buy in' conservation would be of help. The establishment of a system to deposit digital born archives and digital archives in a recognised, permanent, 'Accredited' Digital repository such as the Archaeology Data Service (ADS) or a local repository is required. Increased support for the

RCM is required to keep up with the twenty-first century responsibilities of preserving and making the archaeological archives accessible on behalf of the county and people of Cornwall. Ideally an Archaeological Resources Centre could be created, perhaps together with the Cornwall Record Office and Historic Environment, Cornwall Council.

Acknowledgements

My thanks to Hilary Bracegirdle and Margaret Morgan for reading and commenting on this article.

References

Brown, D, July 2007. *Archaeological archives: a guide to best practice in creation, compilation, transfer and curation*, Archaeological Archives Forum

Elliott, P, ed, 2002. *Standards in Action Book 4: managing archive collections in museums*, Museum Documentation Association

English Heritage, 1991. *Management of Archaeological Projects (MAP2)*, English Heritage

Grant, A, ed, 1994. *SPECTRUM: the UK museum documentation standard*, Museum Documentation Association

Heywood, F, November 2010. 'Leaving local authority control', *Museums Journal*, 15

JRIC, 2003. 'Of perfect mind and memory.' A tribute to H L Douch, *Jnl Roy Inst Cornwall*, 9-28

McKenna, G, and Patsatzi, E, eds, 2007. *SPECTRUM: The UK Museum Documentation Standard (version 3.1)*, Museum Documentation Association

HMC/mda, 2002. *Code of practice on archives for museums and galleries in the United Kingdom*

Longworth, C, and Wood, B, 2000. *Standards in Action Book 3: Working with Archaeology*, Society of Museum Archaeologists and Museum Documentation Association

Morgan, M, 2008. Keeping track: documenting the collections in the Royal Cornwall Museum, *Jnl Roy Inst Cornwall*, 21-31

Museums and Galleries Commission, 1992. *1: Standards in the museum care of archaeological collections*, London

Museums and Galleries Commission, 1996. *Code of practice on archives for museums in the United Kingdom*, revised edition, London

Museums, Libraries and Archives Council, 2004. *Accreditation standard: the accreditation scheme for museums in the UK*, London

Owen, J, ed, 1995. *Towards an accessible archaeological archive. The transfer of archaeological archives to museums: guidelines for use in England, Northern Ireland, Scotland and Wales*, Society of Museum Archaeologists, London

CONSERVING THE PAST

Penhallurick, R, 1986. *Tin in Antiquity*, London

Penhallurick, R, (Guest, P, and Wells, N, eds) 2009. *Ancient and early medieval coins from Cornwall and Scilly*, Royal Numismatic Special Publication, No. 45 London

RIC Council, 1985. The 166th annual report of the Council, *Jnl Roy Inst Cornwall*, New Series IX, Part 4, 309-11

Royal Institution of Cornwall, *Minute Book* AGM August 7th 1825

Royal Institution of Cornwall, March 2005. *Collections Management Plan: Archaeology and World Culture*, Truro (Royal Institution of Cornwall)

Royal Institution of Cornwall, May 2005. *Collections management policies: policy on acquisition and disposal*, Truro (Royal Institution of Cornwall)

Royal Institution of Cornwall, December 2005. *Conditions of acceptance of archaeological archives,* Truro (Royal Institution of Cornwall)

Royal Institution of Cornwall, May 2006. *General guidelines for display of archaeological materials*, Truro (Royal Institution of Cornwall)

Royal Institution of Cornwall, October 2006. *Policy on human remains*, Truro (Royal Institution of Cornwall)

Royal Institution of Cornwall, October 2007 *Policy for sampling museum objects for analysis*, Truro, (Royal Institution of Cornwall)

Society of Museum Archaeologists, 1993. *Selection, retention and dispersal of archaeological collection – guidelines for use in England, Wales and Northern Ireland*, SMA

Cornish Archaeology 50, 2011, 95–100

Scheduled Monument Management: conserving Cornwall's past

ANN PRESTON-JONES

'Scheduled Monument Management' is the rather unsexy name of a project that has been running in Cornwall for over 15 years. As the name suggests, its focus has been on the management, repair and conservation of Cornwall's remarkable resource of extant monuments and historic landscapes.

Despite the fame and diversity of Cornwall's archaeology, which is responsible for helping to create the modern image of Cornwall as a timeless and special place on the wild Atlantic fringe, sites are not all perfectly managed. Help is constantly needed to keep them in a state which conserves both their landscape value and archaeological significance. Problems and threats can include stock erosion, scrub growth, root damage, development, vandalism, accidental damage, and natural deterioration.

The repair and conservation of monuments in Cornwall is not a new concept. Lanyon Quoit, for example, was restored through public subscription after it fell down in 1814 (Borlase 1972, 17-18; Barnatt 1982, 121-4) and Boscawen Un stone circle was 'restored' in 1862 when a hedge which bisected the circle was removed (Blight 1861, 72; 1865, 122; Barnatt 1982, 159-62). From their foundation in the 1920s, the Old Cornwall Societies have been much involved in the preservation of historic sites. Trequite Cross in St Kew was restored by the cross sub-committee of Wadebridge Old Cornwall Society in 1947 and Towan holy well was repaired by St Austell Old Cornwall Society in 1937 (Langdon 1996, 39; Lane Davies 1970, 36; Evans and Prettyman 1994,

37). The repair work, which was specified and supervised by Cuthbert Atchley, the Old Cornwall Societies' Consulting Architect, cost £18. Mr Atchley stated that 'in restoring the building no concrete has been used, the only new material is Pentewan Stone, to make good the missing ridge which has been of that stone' (Preston-Jones 2006, 11, 20). In this, he was leading the way with the principles that guide stonework repair even today. After repair, the well was re-dedicated by the Bishop of Truro.

From the 1920s, legal protection was provided for the most special monuments in Cornwall through designation as Scheduled Monuments with suggestions for the first 100 sites to be protected being made by, amongst others, Charles Henderson and Henry Jenner. Scheduling has continued sporadically since then. While the earliest monuments to be scheduled tended to be the iconic sites for which Cornwall is most famous – the quoits, standing stones, stone circles and crosses, plus a number of bridges - more recent Scheduling has focussed on the remarkable prehistoric landscapes of Bodmin Moor, industrial heritage and many less conspicuous but equally significant cropmark sites.

As the range of protected monuments has increased, so too has the range of associated problems. And while scheduling is of evident value in helping to protect against deliberate damage, it is of less help with issues of gradual deterioration, especially since the bureaucracy, never mind the cost, involved in carrying out repairs can be a considerable deterrent.

It was against this background that the Scheduled Monument Management project began in 1994. English Heritage suggested to the Cornwall Archaeological Unit (later the Historic Environment Service, now Historic Environment, Cornwall Council) that we might like to pilot a scheme whose intention was to carry out small scale conservation or restoration works with a minimum of bureaucracy, and to help carry out work on behalf of owners who lacked the resources to undertake it.

The project started with a budget of £10,000. In the first year, English Heritage gave a grant of £5,000, which was matched by £2,000 from the Cornwall Heritage Trust and £3,000 from Cornwall County Council. Partnership working, involving 'in kind' contributions from other individuals and organisations who give their time voluntarily, has always been a feature of the project. From that small beginning in 1994, the project has run continuously and grown so that it is now one of the cornerstones of the Historic Environment team's project work.

The same three partners have supported the project throughout, although in latter years it has benefitted additionally from grants from the Heritage Lottery Fund. To date, well over 100 monuments have been conserved.

Work began in 1994 with repairs to two medieval stone crosses (Whitecross, Wadebridge and St Teath churchyard cross), St Clether holy well and the Brane entrance grave. Both crosses were suffering from the deterioration of nineteenth-century repairs and the entrance grave from cattle erosion. The holy well, a late nineteenth-century reconstruction by Sabine Baring-Gould, was in need of timely maintenance (Preston-Jones 1995a, 1995b; Preston-Jones and Attwell 1995). These projects encapsulate the type of work and monuments which have dominated work over the last 15 years, although there have been many surprises and challenges along the way.

The major themes which have emerged are:
- Standing monuments prehistoric and medieval: crosses, standing stones, stone circles

Fig 1. Restoring a fallen stone at the Nine Maidens or Boskednan Stone Circle, Madron, in 2004.

Fig 2. Repairing erosion around one of the stones at the Trippet Stones stone circle in 2006.

CONSERVING THE PAST

- Structures: small ruined buildings like holy wells
- Earthworks: barrows, hillforts, methodist preaching pits

Projects involving standing stones and stone circles have undoubtedly been the most spectacular. Three stand out: the Gunrith menhir, the Nine Maidens Stone Circle, and the Trippet Stones stone circle. In January 2003 the 3m high Gun Rith Menhir, near the Merry Maidens in St Buryan parish, fell over. The accident was not witnessed, but in retrospect was no surprise, for the stone was leaning and was known to be loose. After careful planning the stone was lifted back into place and for security, as well as to help retain the former height and lean of the stone, it was socketted into a large granite base-stone, set flush with the ground (Preston-Jones 2004a).

At the Nine Maidens Stone Circle in Madron (Fig 1) we worked in partnership with the Commoners and Natural England to clear scrub, improve drainage and access, and restore three stones which had been uprooted during the nineteenth century. The restoration of the stones followed excavation to locate their sockets and has had the effect of dramatically enhancing both the appearance of the circle and the views from it (Preston-Jones 2008). Now,

the circle's relationship with nearby Carn Galva is emphasised by the circle's two tallest stones, and the circle has been 'rediscovered' by the media as an image of Cornwall's antiquity.

The focus of work at the Trippet Stones on Bodmin Moor (Fig 2) has been the repair of stock erosion. At the base of each stone was a massive hole up to 5 metres across and 0.5 metres deep, worn by cattle and ponies rubbing against the stones. Huge quantities of sand, stone, rab, earth and turf have been used to repair the holes, and in 2006 a recently fallen stone was re-erected (Preston-Jones and Attwell 2000, 2003; Gossip 2007). Local children, Commoners, farmers, landowners, volunteers and the former North Cornwall District Council's Countryside Service were involved in this partnership project.

Crosses have been the most numerous of our projects. The work has generally related to stabilisation through the provision of a base, or to the replacement of deteriorating ironwork used for past repairs. Occasionally emergency repairs have been needed. The most graphic demonstration of the problem that rusty ironwork can cause came while undertaking repairs to the lantern cross in Callington Churchyard. It had been noted that the top of the shaft beneath the head of this massive granite cross was cracked. When scaffolding was erected to give access

Fig 3. Repair of the Tremethick Cross, Madron, in 2008, after it had been hit by a lorry.

and the cross-head removed it was discovered that the central pin holding the head to the shaft was so rusty that it had expanded to twice its original size, causing the surrounding granite to crack. The iron pin was replaced with stainless steel and the broken granite shaft drilled and repaired with smaller pins. At the same time, the sculptured faces of the lantern cross were cleaned and recorded (Preston-Jones and Langdon 1998).

One of the most dramatic cross projects involved the repair of the Tremethick Cross (Fig 3), after it was hit by a lorry in 2006. The cross was broken into three; the head being flung some distance by the lorry's impact. Interestingly a microchip, fitted to the cross in the previous year, was still functioning, even after the accident (Preston-Jones and Langdon 2008).

Small stone structures have featured prominently in the project. Holy wells have been the most frequent, but also other small buildings like Roger's Tower, a folly near Penzance, Halwyn Dovecote in St Issey and Kennall Vale gunpowder

works (Cole 2003, Preston-Jones 1997, 2004b). At Rogers Tower, work principally involved the replacement of cement pointing with lime – a more sympathetic mortar for old buildings. At Towan holy well, repointing in lime mortar was carried out by the local Old Cornwall Society (Fig 4); our role was to organise and record the work. The latter included a historic building analysis by Eric Berry, who concluded that although the well's roof may have been repaired in the nineteenth century, and was restored in the early twentieth, it remains an outstanding example of late medieval stonework (Preston-Jones 2005). This contrasts with the conclusion of recording at St Ruan's (Grade) Well on the Lizard, which contains pieces of medieval carved stonework, but was thought by Eric to be of seventeenth-century origin, with nineteenth-century repairs (Preston-Jones and Sturgess 2003).

Erosion repair work has normally involved the British Trust for Conservation Volunteers. One of the most outstanding examples was at Bury Down hillfort, badly eroded where sheep tracked

Fig 4. Volunteers from St Austell Old Cornwall Society repointing Towan holy well in 2004.

along the steep face of the rampart. Repair on the rampart's steep face involved the construction of wooden revetments to retain the earth-filled sand bags, earthing and then turfing (Preston-Jones *et al* 1996). Although this worked well it was not until the site entered a Countryside Stewardship agreement and stocking rates in the field were reduced, that the repair finally stabilised.

Local volunteers have been involved in many of our schemes. The outstanding example was St Piran's Church (Fig 5), where we worked successfully with the St Piran's Trust and other volunteers to excavate sand from the old church and improve its conservation and display (Cole 2007a, 2007b). Just as successful, though less well known, was a recent project to set up a group of volunteers on the Lizard, to help with the maintenance and monitoring of sites. LAN – the Lizard Ancient Sites Network – has an enthusiastic team of regulars who have worked successfully to clear scrub from a number of sites not seen for many generations (Preston-Jones 2010).

After 15 years it is probably true to say that the main priorities have now been dealt with, and that new projects are likely to be those that arise as a result of more dramatic incidents. Nonetheless there is still a good deal to be done in raising awareness of the need for management and in ensuring that this message is understood by the younger generations, who will be the future guardians of the sites. Hence one of the latest achievements – with the help of funding from the Heritage Lottery Fund – has been to commission from 'Sense of Place' a new work unit for Key Stage 1 children called 'Found in the Ground'.

CONSERVING THE PAST

Fig 5. Volunteers help with excavation within the graveyard associated with St Piran's Church in 2005: the excavation was part of a project to improve understanding and presentation of the church site.

ANN PRESTON-JONES

References

Barnatt, J, 1982. *Prehistoric Cornwall: the ceremonial monuments*, Northampton

Blight, J T, 1861. *A week at the Land's End*, London

Bight, J T, 1865. *Churches of west Cornwall, with notes of antiquities of the district*, London

Borlase, W C, 1872. *Naenia Cornubiae: a descriptive essay, illustrative of the sepulchres and funeral customs of the early inhabitants of the county of Cornwall*, London and Truro

Cole, R, 2003. *Kennall Vale Gunpowder Works, Cornwall - repair to leat*, Truro (Historic Environment Service, Cornwall County Council)

Cole, D, 2007a. *The excavation of St Piran's Church, Perranzabuloe*, Truro (Historic Environment Service, Cornwall County Council)

Cole, D, 2007b. *St Piran's Church, Perranzabuloe, Cornwall: archaeological excavation, conservation and management works*, Truro (Historic Environment Service, Cornwall County Council)

Evans, R, and Prettyman, G W, 1994. *Pictorial Pentewan*, Pentewan

Gossip, J, 2007. *The Trippet Stones, Blisland*, Truro (Historic Environment Service, Cornwall County Council)

Lane Davies, Rev A, 1970. *Holy Wells of Cornwall*, Federation of Old Cornwall Societies

Langdon, A G, 1996. *Stone Crosses in North Cornwall*, Federation of Old Cornwall Societies, 2nd edition

Preston-Jones, A, 1995a. *Repairs to St Clether holy well*, Truro (Cornwall Archaeological Unit)

Preston-Jones, A, 1995b. *Repairs to the entrance grave at Brane, Sancreed, Cornwall*, Truro (Cornwall Archaeological Unit)

Preston-Jones, A, Lawson-Jones, A, and Vulliamy, C, 1996. *Management work at Bury Down fort, Lanreath, Cornwall*, Truro (Cornwall Archaeological Unit)

Preston-Jones, A, 1997. *Halwyn Dovecote, St Issey: consolidation and repairs*, Truro (Cornwall Archaeological Unit)

Preston-Jones, A, 2004a. *The Gun Rith menhir, Cornwall: archaeological recording and restoration of a fallen menhir*, Truro (Historic Environment Service, Cornwall County Council)

Preston-Jones, A, 2004b. *Castle an Dinas, Ludgvan, Cornwall: conservation work to Rogers Tower and ruined 19th century farmhouse*, Truro (Historic Environment Service, Cornwall County Council)

Preston-Jones, A, 2005. *Towan holy well, St Austell, Cornwall: recording and repointing*, Truro (Historic Environment Service, Cornwall County Council)

Preston-Jones, A, 2008. *The Nine Maidens, Madron, Cornwall: restoration (scrub clearance, drainage, re-erection of three fallen stones)*, Truro (Historic Environment Service, Cornwall County Council)

Preston-Jones, A, 2010. *The Lizard, Cornwall: monitoring and management of archaeological sites by local volunteers*, Truro (Historic Environment Projects, Cornwall Council)

Preston-Jones, A, and Attwell, D, 1995. *Repairs to the Whitecross, Wadebridge*, Truro (Cornwall Archaeological Unit)

Preston-Jones, A, and Attwell, D, 2000. *The Trippet Stones, Blisland, Cornwall: erosion repair*, Truro (Cornwall Archaeological Unit)

Preston-Jones, A, and Attwell, D, 2003. *The Trippet Stones, Blisland, Cornwall: erosion repair*, Truro (Historic Environment Service, Cornwall County Council)

Preston-Jones, A, and Langdon, A, 1998. *Repair of the lantern cross in Callington Churchyard*, Truro (Cornwall Archaeological Unit)

Preston-Jones, A, and Langdon, A, 2008. *Cross south-east of Tremethick, Cross, Madron, Cornwall: restoration following vehicle collision*, Truro (Historic Environment Service, Cornwall County Council)

Preston-Jones, A, and Sturgess, J, 2003. *St Ruan's Well, Grade: conservation and landscaping*, Truro (Historic Environment Service, Cornwall County Council)

100

Cornish Archaeology 50, 2011, 101–105

Caring for the historic countryside – agri-environment schemes and the historic environment

ANN REYNOLDS

Over the past 20 years government-funded national agri-environment schemes have become one of the most important means of caring for archaeological sites and historic landscapes in the countryside. These schemes were primarily set up to enhance the natural environment through good agricultural practice.

At the same time, through these schemes, farmers and landowners are acknowledged as important custodians of some of our finest archaeological sites, and the management of the historic environment is seen as an integral part of the conservation of the countryside as a whole.

Fig 1. Wheal Tom, Deer Park Farm, Luckett. Part of a small mid-nineteenth-century tin and copper mine. All associated buildings were consolidated through Higher Level Stewardship and incorporated into educational access visits to the farm.

CONSERVING THE PAST

Fig 2. As part of the Environmentally Sensitive Area scheme this complex of barns (including a mid-nineteenth-century Grade II Listed stable block and loft) at Higher Trewey near Zennor were renovated using traditional materials. (Image reproduced with kind permission of Natural England).

One of the first of these was the Environmentally Sensitive Areas scheme (ESA). ESAs were the UK's response to a European Regulation requiring member states to take action to protect and enhance traditional agricultural landscapes at risk. Introduced in 1987 by the Ministry of Agriculture Forestry and Fisheries (MAFF), the scheme offered incentives to encourage farmers to adopt practices which would safeguard and enhance land considered to be of high landscape, wildlife or historic value (often National Parks or Areas of Outstanding Natural Beauty).

This came at a critical time for Penwith, which throughout the 1970s and 1980s went through a period of agricultural intensification, resulting in land improvement and the removal of a number of features including ancient hedges, one of the defining features of this important landscape, and the breaking in of archaeologically rich rough ground, for example an area of ancient fields above Chysauster (Smith 1996). This motivated an extensive programme of mapping the historic landscape, carried out by the Cornwall Committee for Rescue Archaeology (CCRA). It included detailed surveys of selected areas, the mapping of rough ground and heathland loss from 1840 to the 1980s, the mapping of surviving prehistoric and medieval landscapes and a study of potential sites for scheduling around Zennor.

The Zennor survey revealed that the majority of the parish contained significant archaeological features, based on a surviving prehistoric landscape, that was of sufficient importance and quality to merit Scheduled Monument status. This raised obvious problems. Scheduling on this scale would be impractical in a working landscape; for example Scheduled Monument Consent would be required for every slight hedge repair and most ground works.

This dilemma coincided with the proposal of ESA status for West Penwith, which was seen as an excellent way of resolving the problem of conserving this unique landscape whilst allowing normal farming practice to continue. Land entered into the scheme would then be farmed in such a way as to be beneficial to the archaeological and historic features present. This included simple measures to prevent overgrazing or undergrazing of sites, maintenance of boundaries and boundary restoration, reinstatement of Penwith style iron gates and granite gateposts, and restoration of traditional buildings, all made possible with financial support available through the UK government and EU funded ESA scheme. The ESA was an immediate success, with a very large take-up and a near complete halt on the loss of ancient hedges and rough ground.

Countryside Stewardship (CSS) was introduced as a pilot scheme in 1991 and operated outside the Environmentally Sensitive Areas. It was launched by the Countryside Commission and transferred to MAFF and the Farming and Rural Conservation Agency (FRCA) which in turn evolved into the Department of the Environment, Food and Rural Affairs (DEFRA) and the Rural Development Service (RDS) – now part of Natural England.

Countryside Stewardship was the Government's main scheme for the wider countryside, aiming to 'improve the natural beauty and diversity of the countryside, enhance, restore and re-create targeted landscapes, their wildlife habitats and historical features, and to improve opportunities for public access' (Natural England website, closed schemes, CSS). It achieved this in a similar way to the ESA scheme, rewarding positive management of archaeological features and paying for more complex conservation works on those sites which required an extra level of care.

By 2000, around 100 Scheduled Monuments in Cornwall fell within areas managed under CSS. These included six hillfort complexes (Caer Bran, Roundwood, Castle Canyke, Cadsonbury, Tregeare Rounds, Warbstow Bury), a similar number of promontory forts (including The Dodman, The Rumps, Kelsey Head), Helman Tor Neolithic tor enclosure, Boscawen-Un stone circle, numerous barrows and two medieval earthwork castles (Kilkhampton and Poundstock) (Rose 2000, 1).

In 1998, the Monuments at Risk Survey was published by English Heritage. It demonstrated that since 1945, agriculture has been the single biggest cause of unrecorded loss of archaeological sites (Darvill and Foulton 1998). This coincided with an upturn in the number of applications into Agri-environment schemes. English Heritage responded to this by developing a pilot project in the south west to help fund Historic Environment Countryside Advisor (HECAS) posts in local authorities. This was at a time when the benefits of Agri-environment schemes, such as Countryside Stewardship and the ESA scheme, were being vigorously promoted as an alternative to the direct grants linked to production that dominated the agricultural policy for the last half of the twentieth century (Coe 2002, 1).

Cornwall County Council's Historic Environment Service (HES) was one of the first to establish this role in Spring 2000. Initially this was with funding from English Heritage, and from April 2001 with part funding from Cornwall County Council and the National Trust. Previously many of its functions had been carried out by other parts of CAU: consultations on agri-environmental schemes were dealt with by the Projects staff; whereas Hedgerow Regulations, Woodland Grant Schemes and Forestry Plans were dealt with by Development Control Officers. Various members of staff had attended meetings with partners in countryside affairs and helped to

Fig 3. Godolphin Hill, Breage, was initially entered into the Countryside Stewardship Scheme and then into Higher Level Stewardship, along with the wider farmed estate. Conservation grazing and targeted scrub clearance has enhanced the features on this prominent landmark. (Historic Environment, Cornwall Council, F85-134)

CONSERVING THE PAST

develop strategies. Ultimately all these functions were transferred to the Countryside Advice team, enabling for the first time, direct named points of contact with specific knowledge of rural issues. HECAS originally comprised two members of staff, Peter Herring and Ann Reynolds, later joined by Peter Dudley. It is now covered by a single post holder, Ann Reynolds.

The service offers detailed advice on the management of sites in the countryside, involving records and survey data, management recommendations and on site inspection and advice. This enhanced service helps increase the number of sites entering into beneficial management. Good working relationships have been established between various partners such as English Heritage, Natural England, Forestry Commission, Cornwall Wildlife Trust, Cornwall Farming and Wildlife Advisory Group, the Environment Agency and The National Trust, as well as with individual farmers, landowners and the larger private estates in Cornwall.

The increase in the number of pre-application consultations on all schemes and for rural advice in general, from partner organisations, agents and private individuals alike, provides ample evidence of the support and demand for the service since its creation.

By having a dedicated officer, HECAS can provide constructive comments on both county and national strategic consultations regarding rural schemes and policies. This has enabled significant input into consultations for the national and regional targeting statements for the Environmental Stewardship Scheme which has now replaced ESAs and Countryside Stewardship. A number of recommendations made by HES were incorporated into the scheme targets, enabling greater opportunities suited to specific features of the Cornish landscape such as dew

Fig 4. East Leigh Berrys, Stratton - possibly an adulterine motte with two baileys. Through Higher Level Stewardship, the modern fence cutting across the eastern enclosure has been removed, a permissive footpath has been created and the land is being managed to protect the earthworks. (Historic Environment, Cornwall Council, F87-187)

ponds found in West Penwith and Lizard, the medieval farmsteads of the China Clay area and the miners' smallholdings associated with areas of concentrated hard rock mining.

The main source of currently available funding for archaeological and historic sites in the countryside is now through Higher Level Stewardship (HLS), introduced in 2005. HLS involves more complex environmental management, with payments of up to 100% of costs on the protection of qualifying archaeological features, including necessary assessment surveys, management plans and archaeological recording. Management payments are also given for reverting important cropmark sites out of arable cultivation, beneficial grazing of features under grass and removal of scrub and bracken from sites. Cornwall's HECAS provides advice on every single application into HLS, identifying all sites with management potential under the scheme, and then works very closely with the local Natural England office to apply these management options where appropriate. In recent years this has led to the pro-active targeting of a number of important sites for HES and the Cornwall and West Devon Mining Landscape World Heritage Site, including the Wheal Maid Valley and both Castle an Dinas hillforts (St Columb and Ludgvan).

The future of the conservation of the rural historic environment in Cornwall will throw up many challenges, not least through the ending of the West Penwith ESA scheme in 2012 and further reform of the Common Agricultural Policy in 2013 impacting on agri-environment funds currently available through the Rural Development Programme for England. However, thanks to the development of strong partnership working with our natural environment partner organisations and agencies, Cornwall and HECAS is in a strong position to meet these changes head on.

References

Coe, D, 2002. *Historic Environment Countryside Advisory Service – 1st Review January 2002*, English Heritage

Darvill, T, and Fulton, A, 1998, *MARS: The Monuments at Risk Survey of England, 1995: Main Report*, Bournemouth University and English Heritage

Rose, P, 2000. Unpublished report to English Heritage (Historic Environment Service, Cornwall County Council)

Smith, G, 1996. Archaeology and environment of a Bronze Age cairn and prehistoric and Romano-British field system at Chysauster, Gulval, near Penzance, Cornwall, *Proc Prehist Soc*, **62**, 167-220

CONSERVING THE PAST

Cornish Archaeology 50, 2011, 107–114

Historic landscape characterisation and urban characterisation

PETER HERRING

Introduction

In the 18 years since its first devising (in Cornwall), historic landscape characterisation (HLC), a 'neat modern technique' (Carver 2009, 76; see also Rippon 2004), has become an important archaeological tool, widely used throughout Britain and further afield. HLC describes and interprets the character of the present-day landscape through the historical processes that have made it the way it is (see Fig 1 for example).

By recognising that all parts of Cornwall are historic and can be carefully managed and planned for, it complements more traditional approaches to conservation and heritage planning based on selection, designation and protection (Herring 2009a). HLC was first developed on Bodmin Moor in 1993 (Herring 1998) although aspects of its method were prefigured in work undertaken in the previous decade, especially by Nicholas Johnson, Peter Rose and Ann Preston-Jones (Johnson 1980; Johnson and Rose 1982; Preston-Jones and Rose 1986). English Heritage also actively supported the Cornwall method when developing its characterisation approach to historic landscape in the early 1990s (Fairclough *et al* 1999).

HLC delineates blocks of land sharing predominant historic character (Fig 2), assesses and interprets the historic attributes that make them

Table 1 Broad Types (originally HLC Zones) and Types defined in the 1994 Cornwall HLC

Broad Types	Types
Enclosed Land	Anciently Enclosed Land (AEL; medieval or earlier origins)
	AEL substantially altered in 18C and 19C
	AEL substantially altered in 20C
	Recently Enclosed Land (18C - 20C intakes)
Rough Ground	Upland Rough Ground
	Coastal Rough Ground
	Dunes
Intertidal Zone	
Navigable Rivers and Creeks	
Steep-sided valleys	(The typical locations in Cornwall of ancient woodland)
Industrial	Active Industrial
	Relict Industrial
Settlement	Pre-1900 urban cores and larger villages
	20C urban extensions
Ornamental	
Recreation	
Military	
Airfields	
Plantations	
Water Bodies	Reservoirs
	Natural water bodies

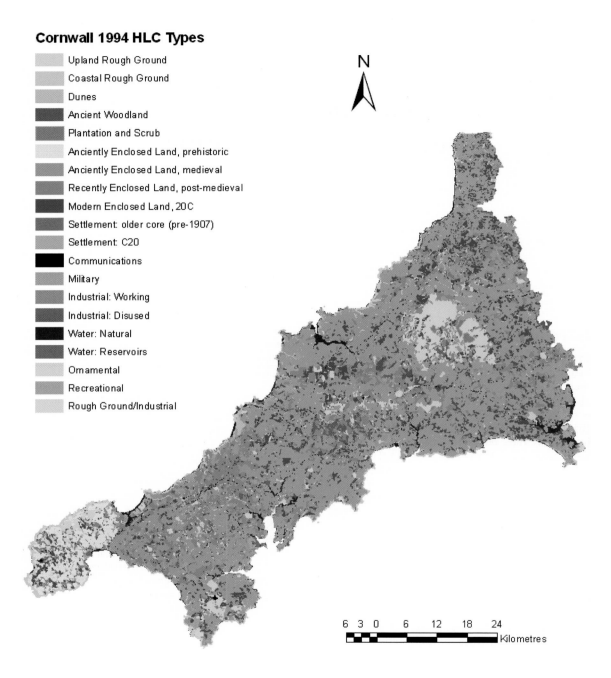

Cornwall 1994 HLC Types

- Upland Rough Ground
- Coastal Rough Ground
- Dunes
- Ancient Woodland
- Plantation and Scrub
- Anciently Enclosed Land, prehistoric
- Anciently Enclosed Land, medieval
- Recently Enclosed Land, post-medieval
- Modern Enclosed Land, 20C
- Settlement: older core (pre-1907)
- Settlement: C20
- Communications
- Military
- Industrial: Working
- Industrial: Disused
- Water: Natural
- Water: Reservoirs
- Ornamental
- Recreational
- Rough Ground/Industrial

Fig 1. The original 1994 Cornwall historic landscape characterisation, dominated by enclosed land (greens). Predominating is the green 'Anciently Enclosed Land'; the darker green 'Recently Enclosed Land' is mostly former rough ground, enclosed in the eighteenth and nineteenth centuries. Aside from the forms of rough ground (yellow) and woodland, all other Types, with brighter colours, have been imposed onto that fieldscape. (Copyright Cornwall Council)

distinguishable, and classifies them according to Broad Types (originally HLC Zones in Cornwall), subdivided where appropriate into Types and Subtypes (see Table 1). Initially designed to feed more comprehensive appreciation of historic landscape into Landscape Character Assessments of Bodmin Moor (LUC 1994) and Cornwall (LDA 1994; Countryside Commission 1996; Herring 1998; 2007; Herring and Johnson 1997), HLC was also designed to meet other predictable needs.

- Guiding holistic management of extensive areas (see Reynolds, this volume).
- Informing more sensitive planning, following Government policy that increasingly

Fig 2. *Distinctive, but repeating historic landscape character in Calstock on a 1947 RAF aerial photograph. Southern settlements (left) are dominated by large medieval hamlets (Harrowbarrow and Metherell) whose curving sided enclosures, with mature hedges with trees, are directly derived from their former open fields, divided into strips; the Anciently Enclosed Land. On Hingston Down (right) settlements are either cottages on the Callington to Gunnislake highway (the A390) or scattered isolated farmsteads, established in Recently Enclosed Land, the rigidly rectilinear enclosures, largely drystone-walled and lacking trees, created when the common grazing land enjoyed by the tenants of those medieval hamlets was subjected to nineteenth-century Parliamentary enclosure.* (CPE/UK 4134. Copyright Cornwall Council)

emphasises character and sense of place.

- Supporting partnerships with other environmentalists.
- Providing context for sites in the Historic Environment Record (HER).
- Framing archaeological research.
- Stimulating archaeological activity by predicting what remains are likely to survive beneath the ground surface.
- Helping individuals and communities appreciate the historic dimension of place.

Supporting its creation and application are several principles developed by the Cornwall Archaeological Unit (CAU) in association with Graham Fairclough of English Heritage; they have influenced all subsequent British HLCs (Herring 1998; Aldred and Fairclough 2003; Clark et al 2004; Alfrey 2007; Dixon 2007).

- HLC develops from recognition that a key quality of all landscape is time-depth, the legibility of our inheritance from the past.
- Nevertheless, HLC deals principally with today's landscape, the one we currently manage.
- HLC incorporates the semi-natural (land cover, woodland, rough land, etc) as all is affected to varying extents by human action.
- It deals with areas, not points; other record and interpretation systems (like HERs) accommodating those.
- Landscape being dependent on perception is always construed differently (Council of Europe 2000), so HLC's spatially organised historical interpretation serves as a framework in which all can recognise their place and engage with and contest other views.
- Such contested landscape therefore has no fixed values, so HLC does not build in fixed evaluations, but it does include in its associated text assessments of measures like rarity of itself and its components, typicality, condition, perceptions, contribution to landscape character, etc that will support evaluation when the need for that arises (see below).
- To give users confidence, all sources (usually map-based) and all decisions made in its creation, including interpretations, are clearly presented.

HLC is designed to use understanding of our landscape inheritance to guide form, location and scale of future change (English Heritage 1997; Herring 2007; HCA and EH 2009). As change is proposed or develops we assess a place's sensitivity to it, judging vulnerability and significance as issues arise. Once decisions about whether to proceed, or whether to redesign or relocate change have been made the HLC returns to being a value-neutral resource.

To help users, HLC mapping is accompanied by texts for each Type (CCC 1996; Herring 1998) setting out its distinctive attributes, current understanding of the historical processes that produced it and thus typical components either known or predicted to exist within it. Texts also consider how Types relate to each other. They consider the Type's rarity or whether it is distinctive or characteristic of Cornwall, or parts of Cornwall. Typical perceptions and current forces for change are summarised. Recent revisions (Herring 2009b) discuss how Types fit with the evidential, historical, aesthetic and communal ways that we tend to value the historic environment (see English Heritage 2008). General recommendations are then made for safeguarding the Type.

Further work

Scilly was characterised in 1996 (LUC 1996). In 2004 its HLC was extended to include aspects of the sea between and beyond the islands (Johns et al 2004), a forerunner of the now established Historic Seascape Characterisation (Hooley 2007). The Cornwall and Scilly HLCs are now part of the HER, having been digitised by Bryn Tapper and placed on Cornwall Council's GIS. Cornwall's HLC has been 'deepened' to satisfy a variety of users, either for selected areas, like the Lynher catchment, Cotehele estate or the north coast (e.g. Herring and Tapper 2002; 2006; Val Baker 2003) or for selected HLC Types, like west Cornwall's Rough Ground (Fig 3) (Dudley 2011). Such revisions, usually larger scale and more fine-grained, benefit from how HLC has developed elsewhere in Britain where characterisation is now more rigorously developed from first describing a block of land's main attributes (patterns, forms etc) and then at a second stage interpreting what they mean in terms of its history.

Using HLC to predict below ground remains has been especially valuable in previously poorly studied but extensive 'lowland' Cornwall. Much here is characterised from medieval field patterns and settlement origins as Anciently Enclosed Land (AEL). Accumulating evidence suggests this was also Cornwall's later prehistoric and Roman period agricultural heartland (Herring 1998). The Lowland Cornwall project critically assessed that evidence, fine-tuning Cornwall's HLC to increase its ability to serve as a predictive tool and more sensitively guide new

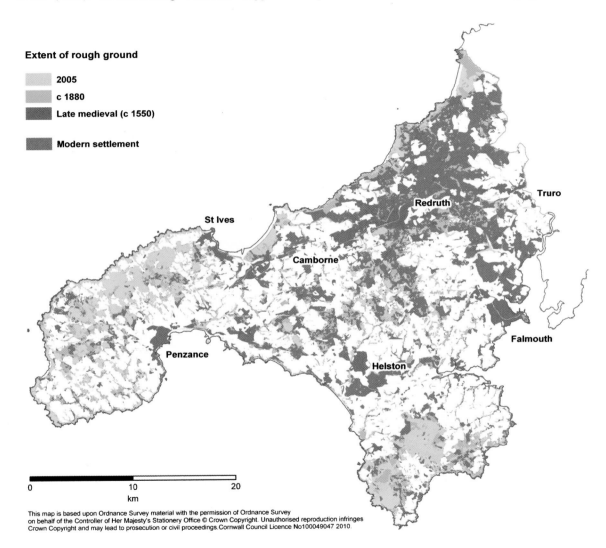

Extent of rough ground

- 2005
- c 1880
- Late medieval (c 1550)

- Modern settlement

Truro

Redruth

St Ives

Camborne

Penzance

Helston

Falmouth

0   10   20
km

This map is based upon Ordnance Survey material with the permission of Ordnance Survey on behalf of the Controller of Her Majesty's Stationery Office © Crown Copyright. Unauthorised reproduction infringes Crown Copyright and may lead to prosecution or civil proceedings. Cornwall Council Licence No100049047 2010.

Fig 3. More detailed historic landscape characterisation in west Cornwall used map regression analysis and landscape modelling to refine appreciation of the former area of rough ground to then inform future management. Modern extents in West Penwith and on the Lizard are much less reduced from medieval ones as in the large former open area around Redruth, mainly enclosed in the period to 1880. (From Dudley 2011, fig 24)

CONSERVING THE PAST

development while maximising potential to learn more about Cornwall's past (Young forthcoming). Consequently, HLC is now routinely used by Cornwall Council to guide the development management process, in particular with the expectation that AEL will have high potential for below-ground archaeology.

HLC is also used in more academic research. Representations of early medieval Cornwall created by simplifying and interpreting the HLC have stimulated discussions of landscape impacts of Christianity and transhumance (Turner 2006; Herring 2009c; forthcoming). HLC provides another dimension to all archaeological (and most historical) research. In a two-way process, HLC

gives spatial context to the research and the research feeds back into greater understanding of the HLC (Herring 1998).

Urban characterisation

Character-based approaches to the built environment have a long pedigree as Conservation Areas, in place since the late 1960s, are defined on the basis of valued character as well as historical and architectural importance (English Heritage 2006). In the 1970s and 1980s Policy Statements were prepared for some Cornish Conservation Areas, and since the 1990s detailed Character Appraisals of many more have been prepared

Fig 4. The Camborne part of the first use of fine-grained urban historic landscape characterisation in Cornwall, for an assessment of the Camborne-Pool-Redruth urban regeneration area. The mosaic of colours reflects the diversity of historical processes behind the town we see today; the types shown include Industrial workers' housing (orange), Middle-class housing, Large houses and grounds, nineteenth century commercial, twentieth century housing development (red), Urban open ground, Recreation and Sports Grounds, Education Facility and Grounds, Church/Chapel/Grounds. (From Herring et al 2005, fig 5.1a)

following national guidelines (English Heritage 2005), all with the aim of conserving the most significant elements and guiding tolerable change (e.g., Falmouth: Berry 1998; Truro: Herring *et al* 2005). The Cornwall Industrial Settlement Initiative (CISI), instigated in 1998, used descriptive, interpretative and characterisation methods developed from such appraisals to report on over 50 towns and villages that housed workers in Cornwall's great extractive industries – mining, granite and slate quarrying and china-clay working – or in associated ports (Cahill 2005).

More recently, following acceptance that all is historic and all can be appropriately managed, urban characterisation has moved into suburbs and modern housing estates in addition to historic town centres (Thomas 2006; Penrose 2007; Walsh and Partington 2010). However, English Heritage's Extensive Urban Survey programme was given a more traditional Conservation Area Appraisal twist when applied to Cornwall from 2002 as the Cornwall and Scilly Urban Survey (CSUS), which produced close studies of the historical topography, surviving historic fabric, modern use and consequent character of the pre-twentieth-century cores of 19

towns (Kirkham 2003). The main units of study were Character Areas, delineated through their shared history, morphology, condition, activity levels and management issues.

CISI and CSUS were prefigured by audits of the inherited fabric of three important Cornish settlements: Hayle, St Just in Penwith and Charlestown (Buck and Smith 1995; Buck and Berry 1996; Smith *et al* 1998). CSUS, however, also aimed to proactively guide regeneration (supported by Cornwall's European Union Objective One status). For each Character Area a series of recommendations (for management, conservation and heritage-led regeneration) were set out (e.g. Kirkham 2003).

A collation of HLC and the CISI and CSUS reports covering the Camborne-Pool-Redruth Urban Regeneration Company's area in 2005 (Herring *et al* 2005) stimulated the first systematic urban characterisation in Cornwall, following methods developed in midland and northern England (Thomas 2007). Here urban HLC Types (attribute-led subdivisions of residential, commercial, civic and industrial land) covered the twentieth-century parts of the CPR area as well as the earlier cores (see Fig 4 and Table 2).

Table 2 Additional urban HLC Types devised for the Camborne-Pool-Redruth characterisation (Herring *et al* 2005)

Recreation and sports grounds
Medieval planted town with burgage plots
Post-medieval urban development
Nineteenth-century commercial
Industrial workers housing
Middle-class housing
Large houses and ground
Twentieth-century housing development
Urban open ground
Allotment gardens
Education facilities and grounds
Church / chapel / cemetery
Caravan / chalet parks
Hospitals and grounds
Public and civic facilities
Urban ornamental parks
Twentieth-century industrial and commercial
Bus stations
Major road complexes
Car parks

References

Aldred, O, and Fairclough, G, 2003. *Historic Landscape Characterisation: taking stock of the method*, London (English Heritage and Somerset County Council)

Alfrey, J, 2007. Contexts for Historic Landscape Characterisation in Wales, *Landscapes*, **8.2,** 84-91

Berry, E, 1998. *Falmouth Conservation Area Appraisal*, Truro (Carrick District Council)

Buck, C, and Smith, J R, 1995. *Hayle town survey and historic audit*, Truro (Cornwall County Council)

Buck, C, and Berry, E, 1996. *St Just town survey and historic audit*, Truro (Cornwall County Council)

Carver, M, 2009. *Archaeological investigation*, Abingdon

Cahill, N, 2005. *Cornwall Industrial Settlements Initiative - methodology statement*, Truro (Historic Environment Service, Cornwall County Council)

Clark, J, Darlington, J, and Fairclough, G, 2004. *Using Historic Landscape Characterisation*, London (English Heritage and Lancashire County Council)

Cornwall County Council, 1996. *Cornwall Landscape Assessment 1994*, Truro (Cornwall County Council)

Council of Europe, 2000. *European Landscape Convention, European Treaty Series, no.176*, Florence (Council of Europe)

Countryside Commission, 1996. *Views from the past, CCWP 4*, Cheltenham (Countryside Commission)

Dixon P, 2007. Conservation not reconstruction: Historic

CONSERVING THE PAST

Land-Use Assessment (HLA), or characterising the historic landscape in Scotland, *Landscapes*, **8.2**, 72-83

Dudley, P, 2011. *Goon, hal, cliff and croft, west Cornwall's rough ground*, Truro (Cornwall Council)

English Heritage, 1997. *Sustaining the historic environment: new perspectives on the future*, London (English Heritage)

English Heritage, 2005. *Guidance on conservation area appraisals*, Swindon (English Heritage)

English Heritage, 2006. *Guidance on the management of conservation areas*, Swindon (English Heritage)

English Heritage, 2008. *Conservation principles*, Swindon (English Heritage)

Fairclough, G, Lambrick, G, and McNab, A, 1999. *Yesterday's world, tomorrow's landscape*, London (English Heritage)

Gillard, B, 2005. *Cornwall and Scilly Urban Survey. Historic characterisation for regeneration: Saltash*, Truro (Historic Environment Service, Cornwall County Council)

Herring, P, 1998. *Cornwall's historic landscape, presenting a method of historic landscape character assessment*, Truro (Cornwall County Council)

Herring, P, 2007. Historic landscape characterisation in an ever-changing Cornwall, *Landscapes*, **8.2**, 15-27

Herring, P, 2009a. Framing perceptions of the historic landscape: Historic Landscape Characterisation (HLC) and Historic Land-Use Assessment (HLA), *Scottish Geographical Journal*, **125.1**, 61–77

Herring, P, 2009b. *Cornwall HLC texts, reviewed*, Truro (Historic Environment Projects, Cornwall Council)

Herring, P, 2009c. *Early medieval transhumance in Cornwall, Great Britain, in J Klapste, ed, Medieval rural settlement in marginal landscapes, Ruralia VII*, Brepols, Turnhout (Belgium), 47-56

Herring, P, forthcoming. Shadows of ghosts: early medieval transhumants in Cornwall, in R Silvester, and S Turner, eds, *Papers in memory of Harold Fox*, Leicester (Medieval Settlement Research Group)

Herring, P, Newell, K, Tapper, B, and Val Baker, M, 2005. *Truro Conservation Area Appraisal*, Truro (Historic Environment Service, Cornwall County Council)

Herring, P, Newell, K, Tapper, B, Val Baker, M, and Powning, J, 2005. *Camborne, Pool and Redruth - historic characterisation for regeneration*, Truro (Historic Environment Service, Cornwall County Council)

Herring, P, and Johnson, N, 1997. Historic landscape character mapping in Cornwall, in K Barker and T Darvill, eds, *Making English landscapes*, Oxford, 46-54

Herring, P, and Tapper, B, 2002. *The Lynher Valley, Cornwall, historical and archaeological appraisal*, Truro (Historic Environment Service, Cornwall County Council)

Herring, P, and Tapper, B, 2006. *Cotehele historic landscape characterisation and scoping survey for historic landscape survey*, Truro (Historic Environment Service, Cornwall County Council)

Homes and Communities Agency and English Heritage, 2009. *Capitalising on the inherited landscape, an introduction to historic characterisation for masterplanning*, London (Homes and Communities Agency)

Hooley, D, 2007. England's Historic Seascapes – archaeologists look beneath the surface to meet the challenges of the ELC, *Landscape Character Network News*, **26**, 8-11

Johns, C, Larn, R, and Tapper, B, 2004. *Rapid Coastal Zone Assessment for the Isles of Scilly*, Truro (Historic Environment Service, Cornwall County Council)

Johnson, N, 1980. Later Bronze Age settlement in the south-west, in J Barrett and R Bradley, eds, *The British Later Bronze Age*, Brit Arch Repts, Brit Ser, **83**, Oxford, 141-180

Johnson, N, and Rose, P, 1982. Defended settlement in Cornwall, an illustrated discussion, in D Miles, ed, *The Romano-British countryside*, Brit Arch Repts, Brit Ser, **103**, Oxford,151-208

Kirkham, G, 2003. *Cornwall and Scilly Urban Survey, historic characterisation for regeneration*, Truro, Truro (Cornwall County Council)

Landscape Design Associates, 1994. *Historic Landscape Assessment, a methodological case study in Cornwall*, Bristol (Countryside Commission)

Land Use Consultants, 1994. *The landscape of Bodmin Moor*, Bristol (Countryside Commission)

Land Use Consultants, 1996. *Isles of Scilly: historic landscape assessment and management strategy*, London (Land Use Consultants)

Penrose, S, 2007. *Images of change, an archaeology of England's contemporary landscape*, Swindon (English Heritage)

Preston-Jones, A, and Rose, P, 1986. Medieval Cornwall, *Cornish Archaeol*, **25**, 135-185

Rippon, S, 2004. *Historic landscape analysis, deciphering the countryside, practical handbooks in archaeology, no. 16*, York (Council for British Archaeology)

Smith, J R, Berry, E, Johnson, N, and Thomas, N, 1998. *Charlestown, historical and archaeological assessment*, Truro (Cornwall Archaeological Unit)

Thomas, R M, 2006, Mapping the towns: English Heritage's Urban Survey and Characterisation programme, *Landscapes*, **7.1**, 68-92

Turner, S, 2006. *Making a Christian landscape, the countryside in early medieval Cornwall, Devon and Wessex*, Exeter

Val Baker, M, 2003. *Atlantic Coast and Valleys Project, Cornwall - historic landscape characterisation, habitat, species and landscape assessments*, Truro (Historic Environment Service, Cornwall County Council)

Walsh, D, and Partington, A, 2010. The Lincoln townscape assessment, valuing places, *Conservation Bulletin*, **63**, 39-40

Young, A, forthcoming. *Lowland Cornwall*, Truro (Historic Environment Projects, Cornwall Council)

Cornish Archaeology 50, 2011, 115–122

Conserving industrial remains 1985-2010

ADAM SHARPE

Public safety was, inevitably, a key driver behind the works undertaken on Cornwall's industrial sites over the past 25 years, and without doubt initially led to more fencing, shaft plugging, propping and buttressing than the archaeological community would have preferred. Given that much of the work undertaken during the early 1990s was driven and specified by non-archaeologists, there was a not unsurprising concentration of effort on shaft capping, and many industrial sites, valued more as nature conservation habitats or local amenities than sites of historic importance, were landscaped and made safe by local authority engineers. Some engine houses were stabilised, but the primary function of these decontextualised, monumentalised structures, set in sometimes over-sanitised rural parks, was to provide interesting stopping off points for those locals and visitors, riders, cyclists and walkers who wished to explore these trails. Archaeological assessments and watching briefs during these work programmes preserved some of the now-lost detail (as for example on the many shaft capping projects carried out by Kerrier District Council between 1989 and 1997), but it has to be admitted that much of the complexity of these sites was inevitably lost and, during the early years of this programme, the phrase 'watching brief' was a quite literal description of the role accorded to archaeologists. Fortunately, increasing input into conservation programmes by historic environment professionals over the years gradually began to tip the balance, and the sensitivity and importance of the sometimes less obvious components of the industrial landscape became better recognised and taken account of. Rather than observers and recorders, Cornwall's archaeologists increasingly became valued members of multi-disciplinary conservation teams, contributing to the development of project strategies, recording sites and structures in detail in advance of works, and providing advice on current best practice in conservation methodologies.

Prior to 1985, the only conserved industrial structures in Cornwall, apart from the two engine houses in the Danescombe Valley converted to holiday homes, were those at Wheal Coates where the National Trust had recognised the importance of its iconic Towanroath engine house, and at Botallack, where the restoration of the Crowns engine houses was very much a labour of love by the Carn Brea Mining Society, supported by a combination of a Manpower Services Commission programme and public subscription. None of this work was accompanied by either recording or advice from Cornwall's archaeological professionals. For years, these two sites remained the only ones to have been considered worth recognition and conservation. In contrast, by 2010, over 100 engine houses had been consolidated and large areas of the industrial landscape of the county have been safeguarded from inappropriate development, underpinning the successful 2005 bid for World Heritage Site status for the Cornwall and West Devon Mining Landscape (World Heritage Site Bid Team 2005a).

This change in attitudes was driven by a growing recognition that in taking forward the richness

Fig 1. Before and after - Wheal Edward stamps engine house near Botallack was one of the first industrial structures to be conserved by the National Trust on their St Just properties during the mid 1990s. Rather than the extensive rebuilding which had characterised their work at Wheal Coates in 1970 or that carried out by the Carn Brea Mining Society at Botallack Crowns in the early 1980s, the engine house at Wheal Edward and its neighbour at West Wheal Owles were conserved as ruins using a lime-based mortar, reconstruction being kept to an absolute minimum.

of Cornwall's landscape this had to include the physical evidence for those massive changes which had occurred during the industrial period from the late eighteenth century to the outbreak of the Great War. In some areas, particularly in mid-west Cornwall, the connections between a substantial expansion of mining activity, rapid population growth, the development of specialised miners' smallholdings in former downland, the appearance of towns such as Camborne, the need for specialised ports such as Hayle and the investment of newly-wealthy landowners in estates such as Scorrier and Carclew were relatively easy to articulate; this was particularly clear within the area between Camborne, Portreath and Devoran. The Mineral Tramways Project (1989-2009)

proved to be the unifying means which ensured not only recognition of the contribution made by industry in the evolution of the Cornish landscape, but also how it could contribute to the future economy of the county. The strategic approach taken through landscape surveys undertaken in the area surrounding Portreath, Camborne, Redruth, St Day and Devoran (Sharpe *et al* 1990), on south-east Bodmin Moor (Sharpe 1989), on Bodmin Moor (Rose and Herring 1990), Kit Hill (Herring and Thomas 1990), the Luxulyan Valley (Smith 1988) and in the St Just mining district (Sharpe 1992) provided much of the information required to make strong arguments for acquisition, informed management, designation and the prioritisation of resources.

The 1990s were notable for considerable levels of acquisition of former industrial sites by local authorities, most particularly by the former Kerrier District Council in the area surrounding Redruth-Camborne and eastwards towards Gwennap, and especially along the proposed long distance cycle and walking routes following the former mineral tramways and railways which had been constructed to link the copper mines around Scorrier, St Day, Chacewater and Redruth with the coast at Portreath and Devoran. Although the funds utilised to achieve this – initially the Derelict Land Grant and subsequently the Land Reclamation Fund – were originally devised to rehabilitate brownfield sites following the decline in UK manufacturing, it proved possible to make use of them not only to tackle safety issues but also to conserve the engine houses and other mine structures along these transport routes and to undertake the access works needed to create the path network. Over a 15 year period most of the surviving engine houses within this area were consolidated, the first being Wheal Uny near Redruth in 1993; during the remainder of the decade most of the engine houses along the Great Flat Lode to the south of Carn Brea received equivalent attention. The most recent programme of works (2003-8) included the prominent group at Wheal Peevor near Scorrier (Sharpe 2005) and those at Cusvey above Twelveheads (Sharpe 2008b).

In the far west of Cornwall, the final closure of Geevor Mine in 1991 seemed very likely to be followed by the disposal of its machinery, the demolition of its structures and the levelling of the site in advance of a new use as an industrial estate. Through the use of the National Heritage Memorial Fund it proved possible to safeguard the most important machinery, whilst in the following year Cornwall County Council took the bold step of purchasing the site with the intention of preserving this almost intact twentieth-century tin mine as Europe's largest industrial heritage site. Following initial archaeological and other surveys (Sharpe 1993) and several rounds of grant-aided safety works (Sharpe 1994, Sharpe 2010b) that focussed on the many early mine shafts scattered across the site, Geevor opened its doors to the public, who have continued to explore this unique site in ever-growing numbers. Further grant aided works on the site have included the very extensive rehabilitation of its building fabric and the construction of a brand new museum (Sharpe 2008a). A section of the eighteenth-century Wheal Mexico adit system had been identified, cleared and made safe for visitor access in the mid 1990s (Sharpe 2010b), and this has been doubled in length as a result of works undertaken as part of the World Heritage Site's *Discover the Extraordinary* project undertaken in 2010-11 (Sharpe 2011).

Elsewhere in West Penwith, guided by the St. Just Mining District Survey (Sharpe 1992), in 1995 the National Trust began a strategic 10 year programme of acquisition of coastal properties along the St Just coast, targeting in particular those sites with significant industrial remains, including the Kenidjack and Cot Valleys, Botallack, Wheal Cock and Wheal Owles, whilst also working with a dedicated group of volunteers to bring the Levant Whim back into steam. These acquisitions

CONSERVING THE PAST

Fig 2. Hedges around abandoned open shafts were the traditional method used to make them safe in Cornwall during the nineteenth century. This approach was adopted by the National Trust in West Penwith in the 1990s rather than the concrete plugs used elsewhere when tackling such hazards. This approach not only halved the costs of such work but ensured that the shafts remained as landscape features, as well as roost sites for threatened species such as Greater horseshoe bat.

Fig 3. The decontamination of the arsenic labyrinths at Botallack mine was an essential precursor to their conservation. Once the contaminated infill had been excavated and sent to a secure landfill site, the walls were pressure washed and the floors covered with a geotextile layer blinded with rab. Following some minor reconstruction to stabilise the structure and to enhance its interpretation, the masonry joints were repointed using a lime mortar.

were universally followed by the commissioning of archaeological management surveys and subsequently by any necessary shaft safety works. However, instead of the concrete plugs and slabs used almost universally in Kerrier District, traditional shaft hedges were almost always used in West Penwith (Sharpe 1996; 1997a; 1997b). A programme of conservation works for the engine houses and historic mine buildings on these new properties was also embarked upon, works being undertaken at Wheal Edward and West Wheal Owles, at Wheal Owles, West Wheal Owles and Wheal Drea (Sharpe 1999), at Levant (Sharpe 2010a), in the Kenidjack and Cot Valleys and at Botallack, where, in 1985, the Count House was purchased with its adjoining former carpenters' shop, the former carefully conserved to provide accommodation for a newly-appointed Area Warden, the latter being converted into a multi-purpose events space and office for the wardening staff. Close nearby, a bungalow constructed in the first decade of the twentieth century as a survey school for the Penzance School of Mines was purchased for conversion into NT volunteer accommodation and for workshops.

The National Trust had also, in the 1980s, undertaken the conservation of the clifftop mine buildings at Wheal Coates and at the nearby Great Charlotte and Charlotte United Mines near St. Agnes, as well as those at Carn Galva Mine at Rosemergy in West Penwith. In 1997, the National Trust had overseen the consolidation of Leed's Shaft engine house and chimney at Great Work following the acquisition of much of Godolphin Mine and park (Cole *et al* 2001), whilst the ruins of Wheal Pool engine house near Helston (Sturgess 2004) were also consolidated. Probably the most spectacular conservation project of its type to date was that undertaken at Trewavas Mine on the coast to the south of Tregonning Hill (Sharpe 2009a). The pair of engine houses at this mine were sited on remote cliffland in as difficult locations as it would be possible to find anywhere in Cornwall and their conservation was a spectacular tour de force.

For a variety of reasons, similar acquisitions and conservation works elsewhere in Cornwall were rather slower to take off. Although surveys of the surviving industrial heritage of the Minions area on south-east Bodmin Moor were originally undertaken in 1987, only relatively recently has work begun to secure the most important sites here. An initial phase of works in 1997-2001 by Caradon District Council, funded by the South West Regional Development Agency, concentrated on fencing shafts to make public access safe (Buck 1996; 2005), but included conservation of the Phoenix Stamps engine and boiler house in 2004 (Buck 2010). More extensive works on the engine houses in the area have been the focus of a successful bid to the Heritage Lottery Fund by Cornwall Council; the Caradon Hill Area Heritage Project started in 2010 with conservation work at West Phoenix, New Phoenix and Craddock Moor mines, and will continue at

West Caradon mine and South Caradon mine (Gossip 2003; Buck 2009a).

The importance of the industrial sites in the area eastwards from Kit Hill (Herring and Thomas 1990) to the Tamar Valley (Buck 1998) has long been recognised and over the last 15 years the necessary conservation, safety and access works have been under way, using a variety of grant funding. From 1996 to 1998 work focused on Kit Hill, Drakewalls and the Danescombe Valley (Buck 2000; 1999; 2003). A major programme in 2000-2002 organised by Cornwall County Council's Environmental Projects team included Okel Tor, Gunnislake Clitters, Holmbush and Coombe (e.g. Buck 2006a; 2006b; 2007b). The next phase, in 2006-2008, the East Cornwall Regeneration Project, run by CCC's Landscape and Urban Design Unit, included Hingston Down mine, Prince of Wales mine (Harrowbarrow) and further work at Holmbush and Drakewalls (e.g. Buck 2007a). Again, these works have been informed by detailed professional assessments of each individual site (for example, Buck 2006c).

Elsewhere in Cornwall, other local authorities had also carried out a small amount of industrial building conservation work. As examples, in the former North Cornwall district, the conservation and interpretation of the Prince of Wales quarry winding engine house in the late 1980s was an early exemplar of its type; Penwith District Council had secured the consolidation of Greenburrow engine house high on the moors at Ding Dong and of that at Giew Mine near Cripplesease, whilst Cornwall County Council had conserved an engine house at Cabilla Woods near Bodmin in 1998 and, in 1993, the early and unusual stamps engine house on the northern side of Carn Brea during the creation of a new Gypsy site at Tregajorran, whilst Carrick District Council had overseen the adaptive conversion for offices of the engine house at Wheal Kitty, St Agnes.

Running in parallel to these conservation works had been a sea change in the techniques used to achieve them. In the early days, the engineers in charge of the works had almost always specified the use of mortars based on Portland cement, the replacement of rotting timber lintels with those made of concrete or steel and the introduction of often intrusive props, straps and safety barriers. Moreover, the plaques attached to these conserved buildings tended to provide information about

Fig 4. Gunnislake Clitters riverside engine house – an award-winning conservation project in which a very ruinous engine house was reconstructed using a detailed building survey undertaken by CAU in the 1980s.

those who had undertaken or funded the works rather than provide useful interpretation for the visitor. Gradually, however, an approach initiated by the National Trust in West Penwith began to take hold. Where lintels had failed they were replaced in long-lasting oak, where pointing needed to be replaced, it was with mortars combining materials such as lime and locally-won aggregates which could breathe and flex in sympathy with any movements in the building brought about by heating and cooling. Despite initial scepticism, the superior performance of these traditional materials gradually began to be recognised, and they are now almost universally used. An important spin-off has been the rapid growth of skilled conservation masons within Cornwall, who can also turn their newly-won skills to work on other vernacular buildings in the county.

CONSERVING THE PAST

Fig 5. Geevor old ore bin before and after. This 1930s steel reinforced concrete structure adjacent to Victory Shaft had been thought beyond rescue given its condition, but was successfully rehabilitated using state of the art conservation techniques and products.

The increasingly crumbling poor quality concrete, corroding reinforcing steel and other ironwork used in the construction of many twentieth-century industrial structures had for many years, seemed destined to ensure that this period in Cornwall's industrial history would almost certainly soon be represented only in documentary form. However, pioneering work undertaken on the preservation of Geevor's 1930s ore bins and 1970s conveyors (Sharpe 2008a), as well as the other 'modern' buildings which make up the site has shown that this need not be the case, and that the materials and skills needed to conserve these 'difficult' materials are now readily available.

Much of what has taken place in the past 25 years has been reactive, yet the continuity provided by the relatively small group of archaeologists and other professionals involved in these conservation programmes has ensured that lessons are learned and past experience continues to be built on. The 2001-2005 Bid for World Heritage Site status drew widely on this collective experience, not only identifying and mapping those elements of Cornish history and the components it has contributed to its evolving landscape (WHS nomination document), but critically providing the overviews required for its appropriate management (WHS management plan). Recent work commissioned by the WHS team has included not only a complete photographic record of its component features (Sharpe 2010c), but also an attempt to identify those less tangible elements which provide its essential character (Sharpe 2009b) – its Universal Value. Taken together these studies allow not only the importance and character of the Site as a whole to be identified, but also its potential and its vulnerabilities to change.

But the picture has not all been positive. If, in the past, funding for the conservation of engine houses has been relatively easy to secure, that for other elements of its industrial heritage has not: iconic components of Hayle's town, foundry and harbour suffered repeated indignities as proposed regeneration schemes were announced, then failed to materialise; much of Charlestown Foundry has been demolished to make way for a housing estate; much of what remained of Perran Foundry – formerly one of Cornwall's premier ironworks – is on the verge of collapse; the Kennal Vale gunpowder works – one of the largest in Britain, is still in need of an extensive conservation programme; all of Cornwall's surviving tin smelting works are in less than sympathetic uses; Cornwall's largest surviving corn mill – Loggan's Mill at Hayle – has been shrouded in scaffolding for years, whilst many of Cornwall's maritime warehouses have been adapted for other uses, or have been demolished.

So what of the future? Cornwall Council's Historic Environment team and those with whom we regularly work have, by 2010, developed our understanding, not only of the resource as a whole, but of a wide range of appropriate techniques to deal with the conservation of timber, stone, concrete and metal (Sharpe 2008c). We have learned to negotiate with those primarily concerned with safety, with those whose concerns are primarily to do with bryophytes, badgers, bats or bridleways. However, we now face an uncertain future in which the availability of public funds to undertake further work is likely to be greatly restricted, and a significant degree of lateral thinking to achieve our conservation aims will inevitably be required. Natural England's Higher Level Stewardship scheme has the potential to be one source of funding for the conservation of industrial structures, as was demonstrated at Wheal Tom near Kit Hill in 2008 (Buck 2009b). But if adaptive reuse is to be the way in which the conservation of industrial structures is to be achieved in the foreseeable future, this must take place within the structure of a well-informed and sensitive strategic management plan, which must be adopted by those who fund and control such developments.

References

Buck, C, 1996. *Proposed shaft treatment at Minions, archaeological assessment*, Truro (Cornwall Archaeological Unit)

Buck, C, 1998. *Preliminary assessment of the industrial sites of archaeological importance in the Tamar Valley*, Truro (Cornwall County Council)

Buck, C, 1999. *Drakewalls Mine – an archaeological watching brief during Land Reclamation Fund works (Phases 2 and 3)*, Truro (Cornwall Archaeological Unit)

Buck, C, 2000. *Kit Hill, Cornwall – archaeological recording during structural consolidation and safety works*, Truro (Cornwall Archaeological Unit)

Buck, C, 2003. *Danescombe Valley – archaeological assessment and mitigation recording during Land Reclamation funded works*, Truro (Historic Environment Service, Cornwall County Council)

Buck, C, 2005. *Minions, Cornwall – mitigation recording during Phase I Land Reclamation funded works (1997-2005)*, Truro (Historic Environment Service, Cornwall County Council)

Buck, C, 2006a *Wheal Brothers, Harrowbarrow - watching brief*, Truro (Historic Environment Service, Cornwall County Council)

Buck, C, 2006b. *Coombe arsenic chimney, Harrowbarrow - watching Brief*, Truro (Historic Environment Service, Cornwall County Council)

Buck, C, 2006c. *Prince of Wales Mine, Harrowbarrow, Cornwall; archaeological assessment*, Truro (Historic Environment Service, Cornwall County Council)

Buck, C, 2007a. *Hingston Down Mine, Cornwall; mitigation recording during Land Reclamation funded works*, Truro (Historic Environment Service, Cornwall County Council)

Buck, C, 2007b. *Okel Tor Mine, Cornwall - recording during conservation and safety works, 2000/2001*, Truro (Historic Environment Service, Cornwall County Council)

Buck, C, 2009a. *Caradon Hill Area Heritage Project Mines, Cornwall – impact assessment report*, Truro (Historic Environment Projects, Cornwall Council)

Buck, C, 2009b. *Wheal Tom Mine, Luckett, Cornwall - report on building conservation works*, Truro (Historic Environment Projects, Cornwall Council)

Buck, C, 2010. *Phoenix United Stamps/boiler house, Minions - Report on building conservation works*, Truro (Historic Environment Projects, Cornwall Council)

Cole, R, Herring, P, Johns, C, and Reynolds, A, 2001. *Godolphin - archaeological research and recording*, Truro (Historic Environment Service, Cornwall County Council)

Gossip, J, 2003. *Minions LRF Phase II, Cornwall – archaeological assessment*, Truro (Historic Environment Service, Cornwall County Council)

Herring, P, and Thomas, N, 1990. *The archaeology of Kit Hill*, Truro (Cornwall County Council; reprint 1990 with minor amendments)

CONSERVING THE PAST

Rose P, and Herring, P C, 1990. *Bodmin Moor, Cornwall: an evaluation for the Monuments Protection Programme*, Truro (Cornwall Archaeological Unit)

Sharpe, A, 1989. *The Minions Project an archaeological survey of the Caradon mining district*, Truro (Cornwall County Council; 2 vols)

Sharpe, A, Edwards, T, and Sparrow, C, 1992. *St Just - an archaeological survey of the mining district*, Truro (Cornwall County Council; 2 vols)

Sharpe, A, 1993. *Geevor and Levant - an assessment of their surface archaeology*, Truro (Cornwall Archaeological Unit)

Sharpe, A, 1994. *Geevor DLG works, 1994*, Truro (Cornwall Archaeological Unit)

Sharpe, A, 1996. *Shaft safety works at Ballowall, St Just in Penwith*, Truro (Cornwall Archaeological Unit)

Sharpe, A, 1997a. *Shaft safety works at Ballowall, St Just in Penwith – the results of a watching brief during a second phase of engineering works*, Truro (Cornwall Archaeological Unit)

Sharpe A, 1997b. *Shaft safety and amenity works at Letcha, St Just in Penwith*, Truro (Cornwall Archaeological Unit)

Sharpe, A, 1999. *Wheal Owles, St Just United and Botallack – an archaeological watching brief during shaft safety and other remedial works undertaken for the National Trust at Wheal Owles and neighbouring mines, St Just in Penwith*, Truro (Cornwall Archaeological Unit)

Sharpe, A, 2005. *Wheal Peevor, Cornwall - results of an archaeological watching brief and additional assessment survey*, Truro (Historic Environment Service, Cornwall County Council)

Sharpe, A, 2008a. *Geevor Mine, Pendeen, Cornwall – historic environment consultancy and watching brief during conservation works*, Truro (Historic Environment Service, Cornwall County Council)

Sharpe, A, 2008b. *Cusvey, Twelveheads, Cornwall – historic environment consultancy during conservation works*, Truro (Historic Environment Service, Cornwall County Council)

Sharpe, A, 2009a. *Trewavas, Breage, Cornwall: historic environment consultancy and watching brief during conservation works*, Truro (Historic Environment Service, Cornwall County Council)

Sharpe, A, 2009b. *The Outstanding Universal Value of the Cornwall and West Devon Mining Landscape*, unpublished report to the Cornwall and West Devon World Heritage Site Office

Sharpe, A, 2010a. *Levant, Cornwall – recording and conservation works, 1999-2002*, Truro (Historic Environment Projects, Cornwall Council)

Sharpe, A, 2010b. *Geevor, Cornwall – archaeological consultancy during a second phase of land reclamation and structural works 1995-1998*, Truro (Historic Environment Projects, Cornwall Council)

Sharpe, A, 2010c. *Cornish Mining World Heritage Site, Cornwall and West Devon: photo-monitoring project 2010*, Truro (Historic Environment Projects, Cornwall Council)

Sharpe, A, 2011. *Wheal Mexico, Geevor: archaeological watching brief during works to the underground visitor tour*, Truro (Historic Environment Projects, Cornwall Council)

Sharpe, A, Smith, J, and Jenkins, L, 1990. *Mineral Tramways Project*, Truro (Cornwall County Council)

Smith J R, 1988. *Luxulyan Valley Project - an archaeological and historical survey*, Truro (Cornwall County Council)

Sturgess, J, 2004. *Wheal Pool engine house, Helston: archaeological building survey*, Truro (Historic Environment Service, Cornwall County Council)

World Heritage Site Bid Team, 2005a, *Nomination of the Cornwall and West Devon Mining Landscape: for inscription on the World Heritage Site List*, Truro (Cornwall County Council)

World Heritage Site Bid Team 2005b, *Cornwall and West Devon Mining Landscape: World Heritage Site Management Plan 2005-2010*, Truro (Cornwall County Council)

Cornish Archaeology 50, 2011, 123–126

Reconstruction archaeology

TONY BLACKMAN

Nearly 20 years ago the Wood family planned and built a lowland round house in a pleasant stream-valley situation at Saveock near Chacewater. Their aim was to be experimental and, indeed, that had to be the case as there was little, if any, experience outside of Butser. Shortly after, Graham Lawrence of Trewortha Farm and Tony Blackman built an upland, stone-walled roundhouse in the farm field on Bodmin Moor, not far from the remains of an original Bronze Age roundhouse – the house being built to the size and orientation of that building. Accompanying that project the Cornwall Branch Young Archaeologists built their own and children all under the age of 16 years transported their stones by human-pulled self-constructed sledge, cut their own timbers in the forest nearby, designed and constructed their porch and finally thatched with wheat straw. They planned that the major roof timbers should sit on granite pads placed around the outside of the wall as demonstrated at the excavation at Trethellan, Newquay (Nowakowski 1991).

The Wood family and Graham Lawrence were in the forefront of reconstruction archaeology: postgraduate research has shown that those first houses were in the first 10 reconstruction ventures nationally, whilst the third house at Trewortha became No. 54 – there had been an explosion in reconstruction.

But in both cases reconstruction became the environment for experimental archaeology. Adults tend to use it seriously whilst schools delighted in the opportunity to have a 'prehistoric day' for their children. Prehistoric has a loose

Fig 1. Chacewater Celtic Village, October 1994; (during Cornwall Archaeological Unit's Archaeology Alive week, involving a range of educational activities with schools).

PRESENTING THE PAST

*Fig 2. Trewortha,
September 1997*

translation and despite the fact that the Trewortha houses followed a Bronze Age theme all houses were soon labelled Celtic houses to help match National Curriculum requirements.

Later Fred and Penny Mustill built a single house at Bodrifty, in 1999-2001. Here too visiting school children are kept busy making pots, spinning, story-telling and other activities. It has to be said that several others have expressed an enthusiasm to do similar work but building this type of structure is time consuming and expensive where most of the money comes from the pockets of the originators.

The third and largest house at Trewortha built mainly by Nick Wright (flint knapper) and Graham Lawrence is perhaps unique by having no ties of any kind – all timbers are woven or pegged and it

Fig 3. Nick Wright and trainee knappers at Trewortha, July 2002

Fig 4. As well as demonstrating the skills needed in creating bronze tools, Neil Burridge's work gives a fresh insight into the bronze-work. For example, handling a replica such as this Late Bronze Age sword gives an appreciation of its weight, size and purpose.

PRESENTING THE PAST

is a remarkable achievement after the thousands of metres of bailer cord used in the earlier structures. Something we were to learn later was the need for maintenance and the disastrous weathering of wheat thatch which tends to be destroyed between exposed 'knuckles' and therefore can become 10 centimetres shorter each time the weather wins. The first two houses at Trewortha lasted no longer that 12 years before the savage upland conditions destroyed them. However, the structures themselves are immensely strong being immune to the worst the elements can deliver.

These houses became activity centres for children where querning, warp weighted loom weaving, thatching practice, ladder building and climbing and drop spindle spinning, with other activities, became regular educational activities. Indeed, as the Trewortha houses were centred on a Bronze Age moorland the children were able to walk relatively short distances to see Bronze Age landscapes and other archaeology. Children are always challenged to think about needs for survival from first principles and this questioning dictated the day's work. They were also encouraged to consider that they had ancestors alive through such times, no matter in which country those ancestors lived, and that they were at the roundhouses because their ancestors had through all their generations had the power of survival.

There is a certain atmosphere associated with roundhouses. Professor Tjeerd van Andel of Cambridge summed it up best when on a visit to Trewortha he kept walking in and out through the whole day and eventually burst out 'This is the most atmospheric structure I have ever been in!'

Experimental archaeology takes different interests. Trewortha Prehistoric Village has been associated with two highly skilled persons – Nick Wright and Neil Burridge. Nick Wright was already a practicing flint knapper when the Trewortha houses were built and centred himself for much of his demonstration work at Trewortha. We watched his constant improvement and I am proud to own a fine flint from a Young Archaeologist student of his which, when made at 16 years of age, was indistinguishable from a museum piece. Nick would talk about tiers of learning and on one occasion the CBA sponsored a visit abroad to a highly skilled expert when he needed help to reach the next tier.

Neil Burridge, similarly, was already along the trail of bronze casting expertise when he discovered the Trewortha houses. He has developed remarkably into one of the finest, if not the finest, prehistoric bronze casters in Britain and is much in demand nationally and internationally. However, these are rare people and their number can probably only be counted comfortably in tens in Britain.

Fig 5. Jane Stanley's painting, reconstructing the aftermath of a Civil War skirmish at Castle-an-Dinas, St Columb Major, is one of a series produced for the Cornwall Heritage Trust, and shows another approach to archaeological reconstructions. Jane's book, A Brush with the Past *(2009), interprets a broad range of sites, landscapes and scenes of many periods. Reconstructions also provide informative support to excavation reports, such as Rosemary Robertson's illustrations of Trethellan and Trethurgy; and for on-site information boards, as at Trevelgue Head, Kynance Gate settlement and Lescudjack hillfort. (By permission of Cornwall Heritage Trust and courtesy of Jane Stanley).*

Other things can be learned in a prehistoric learning environment. The author has spent most of his time on low level activities in his love of working with children but has a wide range of skills which sit alongside his love of landscape archaeology and running his young archaeological club.

Jacqui Wood developed her skills in prehistoric and historic cooking (Wood 2001; 2009) and fabric making for which she is internationally known.

Roundhouses fulfil other functions. They are magnets for interested people and some will travel miles just to stand in one and ask all the questions which become so familiar. The atmosphere in a roundhouse changes with the dark and a smoky fire such that children will sit for ages in silence just contemplating this unique and totally alien situation. It is a wonderful atmosphere for story telling.

References

Nowakowski, J, 1991. Trethellan Farm, Newquay: the excavation of a lowland Bronze Age settlement and Iron Age cemetery, *Cornish Archaeol*, **30**, 5-242

Stanley, J, 2009. *A brush with the past*, Truro (Jane Stanley and Cornwall Council)

Wood, J, 2001. *Prehistoric cooking*, Stroud

Wood, J, 2009. *Tasting the past*, Stroud

Cornish Archaeology 50, 2011, 127–132

The 'expert' amateur, professionalism and public engagement: the changing face of archaeology education in Cornwall from 1986 to 2011

HILARY ORANGE and CARADOC PETERS

Introduction

The last quarter century has seen challenges to the notion of who can practice and who can access archaeology. This notion depends on how archaeology itself is defined: whether it is a profession, an academic subject or a type of edutainment. This short paper reflects on a number of political and social trends, including the changing role of archaeology and its impact on education providers in Cornwall, including the Cornwall Archaeology Society (CAS), through the 1980s, 1990s and 2000s. A period which started with the decline of the 'expert' amateur, has largely been characterised by increasing professionalisation and has ended with a return towards community-centred provision but with diverse interests and approaches.

The 1980s through to the 1990s: the professional and the amateur

Just after the millennium, Charles Thomas reflected (in a similarly short paper) on the changing character of Cornish archaeology over the previous 30 years. He wrote that since the early 1970s there has been a 'complete national change in the way that archaeology is conducted' (2002, 83). This change was a growing distinction between research (including the kind of excavations that were traditionally run by many local historical and archaeological societies) and rescue archaeology. The emergence of rescue (or salvage archaeology, typically carried out in response to a threat to the archaeological record by development) led to the development of professional archaeological units, and consequently, an incremental professionalisation in terms of how archaeology was done. Many CAS members (including the second author of this article), and previously West Cornwall Field Club had gained many of their practical skills through joining CAS fieldwork projects such as fieldwalking, finds processing, surveying and excavation. This included excavations in the 1980s directed by 'amateur' archaeologists such as Daphne Harris (for example, at Shortlanesend and Poldowrian) and Pat Carlyon (for example, at Kilhallon), themselves the recipients of earlier CAS training.

However, certainly by the late 1980s, the technical requirements of modern excavation required the right expertise, the right equipment and considerable funding (Thomas 2002, 83). Indeed, presented with the possibility of excavation opportunities, the CAS projects sub-committee felt 'that Society members would not be welcome at' the site in question 'which was being dug by professionals as insurance policies would not cover amateurs' (CAS 1987). Rescue archaeology, then reinforced in the 1990s with the introduction of PPG16 (DoE 1990), and a ready supply of qualified graduates coming out of UK universities, fuelled the growth in contract archaeology (Speight 2002, 80-81). This trend towards professionalisation led to the marked decline in the number of projects run by the 'expert amateur' and far fewer opportunities, in the UK, for the public to participate in fieldwork. As Thomas noted:

'...amateur (i.e. unpaid, non-professional, not necessarily unqualified) participation in British archaeology has been steadily frozen out. Up to the 1970s the main focus of hundreds of archaeological societies, winter lectures apart, was some form of annual excavation' (2002, 83).

In 1992 Shanks and Tilley expressed a deep concern for the future of public engagement in archaeology, 'denying people their *active* participation in history, in the practice of making history and coming to an understanding of the present past' (1992, 25). This was echoed in CAS minutes of 1994, where the committee noted 'a strong feeling that excavation was desired by many people; it made them feel involved; it was a focus for activity in the Society', and that 'Many regretted the lack of this central activity' (CAS 1994). In reaction to the increasing dominance of 'official' approaches towards archaeological practice Neil Faulkner set up the Sedgeford Project in Norfolk, in 1996. Whilst one of its aims was to explore the origins and development of an English village, it was also an experiment in 'democratic archaeology' where '....fieldwork is rooted in the community, open to volunteer contributions, organised in a non-exclusive, non-hierarchical way...' (Faulkner 2000, 21). An approach which eventually led to local people taking on the formal positions as site bones specialists, fieldwork technicians and finds illustrators (Faulkner 2002, 19).

In terms of 'indirect' access the 1990s witnessed the Internet revolution and in 1994 the first episode of *Time Team* was broadcast on Channel 4, both examples of new media which highly popularised archaeology and led

to a plethora of web pages, archaeology-related TV programmes, books and computer games featuring archaeology related 'products' (Finn 2001; Hills 2003). Along with the increasing heritagisation of sites, archaeology was rapidly becoming a cultural resource (Holtorf 2005).

Active non-professional participation in fieldwork was, however, still tricky as the 1990s also brought in the health and safety culture which raised problems of insurance [Minute Book for 1985-2000] for archaeological societies, university departments and professional projects and further served to undermine the use of volunteers. Indeed, through the late 1980s and the 1990s, CAS focused less on developing its own fieldwork than previously and more on its walks and lecture series as they were seen to be an important way of getting people to engage with their historic landscape. On the other hand, interactive, independent fieldwork thrived in the Cornish branch of the Council for British Archaeology's Young Archaeologists Club (CBA YAC) which carried out practical fieldwalking and recording under the guidance of the current CAS president Tony Blackman (Denison 1997).

However, since 1970, the Truro office of the University of Exeter's Department of Continuing and Adult Education (DCAE) had provided adult education classes across Cornwall, organised by Henrietta Quinnell as Lecturer in Archaeology. For example, in 1986, weekly classes, for 10 or 20 weeks over the winter, were held in Bodmin, Bude, Camborne, Liskeard, Penzance and Truro, using a range of local experts such as Jacqueline Nowakowski and Peter Herring. A number of very successful day schools, on specialised themes, were also run in Bodmin. In 1986, to celebrate CAS's 25th anniversary the University organised a dayschool at Bodmin entitled *Carn Brea and Beyond* with Roger Mercer, Philip Dixon and Richard Bradley as invited speakers (Henrietta Quinnell, pers comm 2011).

In the early 1990s University policy began to decree higher charges and in addition the provision of suitable accommodation for classes in Cornwall became more difficult. Whereas previously there had been no requirement for students to provide written work, in 1994 the Department, in line with government policy, began to 'accredit' courses. In consequence syllabi became more fixed and students were required to write essays, increasing pressure on student time and staff workload. Accreditation could lead to a Certificate in Combined Studies, the equivalent to the first year of a university degree; however, the effect was a gradual decline in courses.

In the late 1990s Truro College began to play a role as a provider of formal archaeology education in Cornwall. The College has offered daytime 'A' Levels in Archaeology since 1998 for 16-19 year olds, many of whom have gone on to study archaeology in Higher Education. Since 2000 the Truro College 'A' Levels have been taught by Mike Dymond, and in addition, between 2000 and 2005 by the first author of this paper. A number of teachers have also taught evening classes to adults in at different venues in Cornwall. Whilst the University of Exeter's Institute of Cornish Studies (ICS) had an archaeological focus under the Directorship of Professor Charles Thomas, this changed in 1991, when Philip Payton took over as its director and turned the focus towards modern history (ICS 2010). However, from 1999 a university level Certificate of Archaeology was provided at Hayne Corfe, under the tutelage of Tina Tuohy, through the University of Exeter's 'Lifelong Learning Department' (rebranding of DCAE) (Henrietta Quinnell, pers comm 2011; Tina Tuohy, pers comm 2011).

Controversy in Cornwall

In terms of public engagement CAS, and Cornwall more broadly, has not avoided controversy and has figured within the debate surrounding 'who owns the past'. This question became a topical issue within academia following the first World Archaeology Congress held in Bournemouth in 1986 where delegates representing indigenous and minority groups challenged normative 'Western' standards regarding ownership of cultural resources (Ucko 1987).

At the end of the 1990s two initiatives, the Portable Antiquities Scheme (PAS) and the 1996 Treasure Act attempted to encourage responsible attitudes and codes of practice amongst members of the public (most commonly metal-detectorists) to report their finds. Initially the scheme drew some criticism from archaeologists who felt that PAS was 'effectively legitimising metal detecting' (Bland 2005a, 288). The Scheme's Director, Roger Bland, has argued that PAS has led not only to increased recording (and enhancement of archaeological knowledge) but also to improved communication between the public and professional organisations and an interest in archaeological education

within the detectorist community (Bland 2005b). 'Treasure' has now been acquired by the Royal Institute of Cornwall on a number of occasions and put on public display, including the group of Bronze Age axes and pottery vessel known as the Mylor Hoard (RIC 2009, 6; Jones and Quinnell this volume, fig 15).

Meanwhile, at Leskernick on Bodmin Moor in the late 1990s the local community resented the fact that archaeologists and anthropologists from University College London had not involved them from the beginning in the design of what was supposed to be a community project (Tony Blackman, pers comm 2011). However, the community still felt that the exercise had been a useful challenge. Chris Tilley, Barbara Bender and Sue Hamilton had regarded public involvement in their fieldwork at Leskernick on Bodmin Moor as a learning and research experience for the local community, their students and themselves and included a website containing a public forum (Basu and Locke 1995-1999). The whole venture has been published as *Stone Worlds* (Bender *et al* 2007), with some articles published earlier (Bender *et al* 1997; Tilley *et al* 1995).

Conversely, in 2005 the pages of *Current Archaeology* documented a debate sparked by a letter by Quinnell and Thomas (2005, 256) (President and Past-President of CAS at the time) who expressed a concern that as 'our archaeological heritage is a limited resource' Channel Four's *Time Team* 'Big Roman Dig' could legitimise 'excavation as an acceptable activity for amateurs' and, furthermore, could involve metal detectorists who would not have the expertise and funds to process the materials generated. Faulkner was one of the members of Time Team leading the Big Roman Dig and Features Editor of *Current Archaeology* (2005, 196), and this brought CAS into a major national debate. Quinnell and Thomas' position drew a very strong reaction from Carol Kirby, an amateur archaeologist and Guy de la Bédoyère, an academic historian and archaeologist with a keen interest in community archaeology. Kirby and de la Bédoyère accused Quinnell and Thomas of elitism, and de la Bédoyère even felt that public involvement was part of the academic debate and this could lead to a stifling of new ideas (2005, 308). In fact, Holtorf (2005) has developed the idea that the past (and therefore archaeology) is a renewable, rather than a 'finite' resource in that public involvement and debate enhances interpretation.

PRESENTING THE PAST

Archaeology and Education under New Labour

Where archaeology and heritage was concerned the New Labour agenda, since election in 1997, was firmly fixed on 'education, social inclusion and access' and a community-based ethos was reflected in the frameworks established by the Museums and the Renaissance project (MLA 2009, 5) and HLF funding, leading to the growth in a number of community related projects (including grants for the Royal Cornwall Museum, the Cornwall Heritage Trust and the West Cornwall and Isles of Scilly Maritime Archaeology Group according to the HLF website). However, vocational courses and heritage were 'in', extra-mural classes were 'out' and the withdrawal of funding led to the closure of adult education classes and centres of lifelong learning (BBC 2005). New Labour policies detached education from professional and elite groups of educationalists and transferred it to institutions so that it became 'knowledge-led rather than knower-led' (Leaton-Gray and Whitty 2010, 12). This meant community groups rather than traditional institutions were to achieve knowledge outreach.

Such educational tendencies had a direct impact on Cornwall. In 2004 there was a double-blow to archaeology education in Cornwall. Firstly, the University of Exeter axed the Certificate in Archaeology course at Hayne Corfe citing financial and student recruitment reasons (Lee 2009, 4). The University's Department of Continuing and Adult Education, by then renamed 'Life Long Learning', finally closed in 2005 (Henrietta Quinnell, pers comm 2011). Secondly, AQA (Assessment and Qualifications Alliance) axed the GCSE in Archaeology, which provided an introduction to the subject for both 14-19 year olds and adults, again citing low student numbers and administration costs (Wainwright 2004). CBA immediately campaigned against the decision but to little effect with Don Henson, CBA Education Officer, commenting on school history and its 'constant diet of Hitler and Stalin' whereas in his opinion the GCSE Archaeology course was 'an excellent introduction to archaeology as a whole. It provided a grounding in archaeological methods, along with a chronological approach to the whole sweep of human experience in Britain, including the medieval and post-medieval periods' (2005, 44). In Cornwall the course had been a popular choice for adults seeking an introduction to the subject and was taught at Truro College (led by Mike Dymond) and at other centres in Cornwall.

The withdrawal of Higher Education by the University of Exeter left a gap which Truro College and CAS tried to fill. At Truro College, Higher Education began as the HND validated by the University of Exeter from 1998 to 2003 and by the University of Plymouth from 2002 to 2005. From 2004, this became a Foundation Degree (FdSc) with a top-up third year making it a degree course from 2007 - the BSc (Hons) in Archaeology. The project began as a collaboration between the CAU and Truro College to create a more practical, vocational route for students in Higher Education. In fact the original HND was entitled the 'HND in Practical Archaeology'. The HND had followed on from the success of 'A' Level archaeology evening classes. From 1994 to 2000 Ann Reynolds and Dick Cole of the CAU ran such classes at Truro College and from 1995 to 2000 at St Austell College (Ann Reynolds, pers comm 2011). From 2000 to 2005, the first author of this paper ran the Truro College evening-class 'A' Level, so there was clearly a demand for archaeology in the county at a number of levels. The HND was therefore a logical next step. Subsequently, the concept of vocational has been broadened to reflect the nature of the cultural heritage sector. For example, as a result of input from the Royal Cornwall Museum more practical artefact and exhibition work has been added, and with input from the National Trust land and site management and conservation too.

At the same time that CAS was stoking the flames of controversy there was a recognition that Exeter's withdrawal left a gap in provision and the Society began to provide additional practical training and day-schools, including a 'sell-out' update series. In more recent years CAS re-established its own programme of training excavations, after a long hiatus, with successful excavations at St Newlyn East in 2007 (Jones and Taylor 2004; Jones 2008), Boden Vean in 2008 (Johns and Gossip 2009; Jones 2010) and Carn Galva and Bosporthennis in 2009 (Jones 2009), echoing the Society's origins as the West Cornwall Field Club. It is important to mention also the role of Cornwall's Historic Environment Service in these excavations. Aside from the CAS, a number of more localised or specialised societies – Lizard Ancient Sites Network (LAN), Cornwall Ancient Sites Protection Network (CASPN), Meneage Archaeology Group,

Cornwall Earth Mysteries Group – have sprung up with a range of fieldwork activities such as site clearance, excavation and field-walking. Indeed, such practical experiences have been a long term strength of the British archaeological education tradition (Collis 2001, 16).

In conclusion

Within the wider debate of 'who owns the past', education provides one avenue by which the public can access information, yet there exists the paradox that within many establishments opportunities for students to actively participate in fieldwork are comparatively limited compared to 50 years ago. Whilst some are concerned that more amateur involvement will threaten 'finite' resources through unscientific excavation or metal detecting, others see archaeology as a renewable resource. In this latter vein society at large has ownership of the past, requiring opportunities to be made to involve people directly and not just passively.

The changing face of archaeology education in Cornwall reflects both the shifting social and political debate. The long term approach in British politics is for more participatory government especially in the wake of the economic downturn and 'The Big Society' under the Conservative/Liberal Democrat Coalition is its latest incarnation. If archaeological education and training are not broadened, then support and understanding amongst the general public could evaporate. This in turn could lead to the public giving government the green light to cut archaeological budgets. Heritage is a key feature in promoting Cornwall as a tourist destination as well as an attractive location in which to do business. Therefore, archaeological education needs to be accessible to as wide an audience as possible to ensure continued support as well as helping to broaden the base of the community of archaeological ideas. There is a hint of optimism – there may not be much money for archaeology, but the trend appears to be moving firmly towards public engagement and hopefully therefore future political support.

Acknowledgements

The authors of this paper acknowledge the many other individuals who have contributed to archaeological education in Cornwall; the paper remains an abridged account of provision and teaching over the last 25 years. For providing details of course providers, dates and teachers the authors wish to thank Mike Dymond, Henrietta Quinnell, Ann Reynolds and Tina Tuohy for their recollections. We would also like to thank Tony Blackman, Roger Smith and Angela Broome for permission and assistance in accessing the CAS minutes.

References

Basu, P, and Locke, C, eds, 1995-1999. Leskernick project, London www.ucl.ac.uk/leskernick/home.htm (accessed 10/12/10)

Bender, B, Hamilton, S, and Tilley, C, 1997. Leskernick: stone worlds, nested landscapes, alternative narratives, *Proc Prehist Soc*, **63**, 147-78

Bender, B, Hamilton, C, and Tilley, C, 2007. *Stone worlds: narrative and reflexivity in landscape archaeology*, Walnut Creek, CA, USA

Bland, R, 2005a. The Treasure Act and the Portable Antiquities Scheme: a case study in developing public archaeology, in N Merriman, ed, *Public archaeology*, London, 272-291

Bland, R, 2005b. A pragmatic approach to the problem of portable antiquities: the experience of England and Wales, *Antiquity*, **79**, 440-7

CAS 1987. *Projects Sub-Committee Minutes from 20/06/1987.* Cornwall Archaeology Society

CAS 1994. *General Committee Minutes from 25/08/1994.* Cornwall Archaeology Society

Collis, J, 2001. Teaching archaeology in British universities: a personal polemic, in P Rainbird, and Y Hamilakis, eds, *Interrogating pedagogies: archaeology in higher education*, Lampeter Workshop in Archaeology 3, Brit Arch Repts, Int Ser, **948**, 15-20

De la Bédoyère, G, 2005, Letter: Cornish complaints, *Curr Archaeol*, **198**, 308

Denison, S, 1997. Youthful passions and real archaeology, *British Archaeology* **28**, www.britarch.ac.uk/ba/ba28/ba28int.html (accessed 11/01/2011)

DoE, 1990. *Planning Policy Guidance 16: archaeology and planning*, London

Faulkner, N, 2000. Archaeology from below, *Public Archaeology*, **1**, 21–33

Faulkner, N, 2002. The Sedgeford Project, Norfolk: an experiment in popular participation and dialectical method, in D Harris, ed., *Archaeology International* 2001/2002, Institute of Archaeology, UCL, 16-20

Faulkner, N, 2005. Roman Big Dig or National Archaeology Week: which do you prefer?, *Curr Archaeol*, **196**, 177

Finn C, 2001. Mixed messages: archaeology and the media, *Public Archaeology*, **1**, 261-268

Henson, D, 2005. Curriculum choice at 14+: who decides? *Historian*, **84**, 44-45

Hills C M, 2003. What is television doing for us?: reflections on some recent British programmes, *Antiquity*, **77 (295)**, 206–211

PRESENTING THE PAST

Holtorf, C, 2005. *Stonehenge to Las Vegas: archaeology as popular culture*, Oxford

ICS 2010. *About the Institute*, University of Exeter, www.exeter.ac.uk/cornwall/academic_departments/huss/ics/about_the_institute.shtml (accessed 27/07/2010)

Johns, C, and Gossip, J, 2009. The evaluation of a multi-period prehistoric site and fogou at Boden Vean, St Anthony-in-Meneage, Cornwall, Cornwall Council and English Heritage, ads.ahds.ac.uk/catalogue/archive/boden_eh_2009/index.cfm?CFID=4752422&CFTOKEN=62988771 (accessed 10/12/10)

Jones, A M, 2008. Excavations 2007; excavations at St Newlyn East, Cornwall Archaeological Society, www.cornisharchaeology.org.uk/excavations2007.htm (accessed 10/12/10)

Jones, A M, 2009. Excavations 2009; archaeological recording at Carn Galva and Bosporthennis, Cornwall Archaeological Society, www.cornisharchaeology.org.uk/excavations2009.htm (accessed 11/4/11)

Jones, A M, 2010. Excavations 2008; Boden excavation, Manaccan, Cornwall, Cornwall Archaeological Society, www.cornisharchaeology.org.uk/excavations2008.htm (accessed 10/12/10)

Jones, A M, and Taylor, S R, 2004. *What Lies Beneath - St Newlyn East and Mitchell: archaeological investigations 2001*. Truro (Cornwall County Council)

Kirby, C, 2005. Letter: Cornish complaints, *Curr Archaeol*, **198,** 308

Leaton-Gray, S, and Whitty, G, 2010. Social trajectories or disrupted identities? Changing and competing models of teacher professionalism under New Labour, *Cambridge Journal of Education*, **40,** 5-23

Lee, R, 2009. *Engaging with the historic environment: continuing education*, Final Version 1.0, CBA, www.britarch.ac.uk/sites/festival.britarch.ac.uk/files/node-files/EHE%20CE%20Report%202009_Draft%201.0.pdf (accessed 27/07/2010)

MLA 2009. *Renaissance in the Regions: Realising the Vision. Renaissance in the Regions, 2001-2008. Review of the Renaissance Review Advisory Group*, www.mla.gov.uk/what/programmes/renaissance/~/media/Files/pdf/2009/Renaissance_Review_Report (accessed 27/07/2010)

Newell, K, 2005. *Cornwall and Scilly urban survey: historic characterisation for regeneration. Penryn*, Truro (Cornwall County Council)

Quinnell, H, and Thomas, N, 2005. Letter: The Big Roman Dig, *Curr Archaeol*, **197,** 256

RIC, 2009. *Royal Institution of Cornwall Annual Review 2008/2009*, Truro

Shanks, M, and Tilley, C, 1992. *Re-constructing archaeology: theory and practice*, London (2nd edn)

Speight, S, 2002. Digging for history: archaeological fieldwork and the adult student 1943-1975, *Studies in the Education of Adults*, **34,** 68-85

Thomas, C, 2002. *Cornish Archaeology at the Millennium*, in P Payton, Cornish Studies, **10,** 80-89

Tilley, C, Bender, B, and Hamilton, S, 1995. The biography of an excavation, *Cornish Archaeol*, **34,** 58-73

Ucko, P J, 1987. *Academic freedom and apartheid: the story of the World Archaeological Congress*, London

Wainwright, M, 2004. Archaeology 'must not become history'. In the Guardian online 26/08/2004 www.guardian.co.uk/uk/2004/aug/26/schools.gcses20041 (accessed 19/05/2011)

Cornish Archaeology 50, 2011, 133–136

Presenting the past: the Cornish Mining World Heritage Site

AINSLEY COCKS

The landscapes of Cornwall and west Devon are well known for their metalliferous mining heritage and the inscription of World Heritage Site (WHS) status in 2006 reflected what many in Cornwall and Devon already appreciated, that these are indeed of global significance. The landscapes which comprise the WHS are both extensive and diverse; from mining along the dramatic coastline of West Penwith, through the concentration of sites along the Great Flat Lode near Camborne, to the high moors of Caradon, and the wooded seclusion of the Tamar Valley, the WHS is without doubt multi-faceted. It is also the largest WHS in mainland Britain, at just under 20,000 hectares, and its scale and diversity present significant management challenges.

Raising awareness and appreciation of the WHS and what makes it of exceptional international significance (its Outstanding Universal Value; UNESCO 2005, 14) is a principal aim set out in the policies of the WHS Management Plan (Thorpe *et al* 2005) which is addressed in a variety of ways. Public presentations are a well established feature of WHS

Fig 1. The Smokin' Chimneys event held on the Great Flat Lode near Camborne in June 2008; around 20 former mine chimneys were seen smoking during this event, the first time this had occurred since the late 1800s. (Ainsley Cocks © Cornwall Council)

Fig 2. The Portreath bicentenary event held in August 2009; Stephanos Mastoris, Head of the National Waterfront Museum, Swansea, is seen riding in a ceremonial coach (right) as part of the community's celebration of the historic links between Cornish copper and Welsh coal. (Ainsley Cocks © Cornwall Council)

outreach and since the commencement of the bid for WHS status in 2001 the WHS team, hosted within Historic Environment, Cornwall Council, have given around 200 presentations to local historical societies and other groups, and at professional conferences both at home, elsewhere in Britain and overseas. While presentations have been useful in expounding the Cornish mining story, particularly for local audiences, the number of people that can be reached by such means is limited.

The exponential growth of the worldwide web since the 1990s has led to the adoption of the internet as a primary means of information gathering and dissemination. In recognition of this the WHS team created a dedicated website for the bid in 2002 as an additional means to communicate the rather complex process of achieving World Heritage status. The content for this was drawn from the wealth of material then being prepared to inform

the nomination and later was to include the final bid Nomination Document and Management Plan. In recent years the website has been expanded to include the downloadable WHS newsletter *Cornish Mining* in addition to a range of information and links relating to mining heritage attractions and special events within the Site.

The WHS team are currently engaged in a significant tourism project to enhance visitor facilities and interpretation at mining heritage attractions across the Site. *Discover the Extraordinary* is a £2.5 million programme, with £1.94 million of this being funded by the South West RDA Rural Development Programme for England (RDPE). A new website is being created as part of this which will allow improved user navigation within the site, and provide ready access to tourism information that visitors to the WHS require. The forthcoming website, due to be online later in 2011, will also enable the creation of customised 'routes' within different areas of the WHS. A number of mobile interpretative tours will also be available as audio trails which can be downloaded and experienced on site via personal MP3 players, mobile phones and similar devices. This will provide an extra strand of interpretation which is informative, easy to use, environmentally sustainable and cost-effective. Cutting-edge technologies and specifically 'augmented realities' are to be explored as future additions to the website, with these giving an immersive experience with recorded interpretation delivered through personal devices dependent on the position and orientation of the user.

In order to engage audiences beyond those with an existing heritage interest, the WHS team has, in recent years, created a means by which the performing arts can be utilised to convey the World Heritage message to those who perhaps may be unfamiliar with the background to Cornish mining, but who are regular attendees of local plays and concerts. Since its inception in 2006 the WHS Cultural Events Programme has supported the staging of works and performances by a range of theatre groups, playwrights, songwriters and musicians, each producing or performing pieces which have a strong Cornish mining theme. Over 50 performances have been staged to date, engaging audiences across Cornwall and west Devon and generating much interest.

Support for community events has also been a key activity in promoting the Site. In 2008 the WHS was able to part fund the successful Smokin' Chimneys event, in partnership with the Mineral Tramways Project, along the Great Flat Lode near Camborne. An estimated 5,000 people gathered at the end of June to witness around 20 mine chimneys in smoke for the first time since the area's tin mining heyday in the late 1800s. In 2009 support

Fig 3. Morwellham Quay, west Devon; this excellently preserved copper shipping port was one of the launch venues for the WHS young person's activity guide Mine & Yours, published in 2008. (Kirstin Prisk © Cornwall Council)

was also given to the Portreath bicentenary event enabling the community to celebrate the laying of Cornwall's first tramroad, linking the prosperous copper mining area of Gwennap with this once important north Cornish mineral port. For younger people the WHS also commissioned its activity guide *Mine & Yours*, in 2008, which introduces the Site and highlights important places to visit in addition to interesting facts concerning the WHS and local mining history. *Mine & Yours* has also been made available to over 300 schools across Cornwall and west Devon to introduce young people to this important aspect of their heritage.

For further information on *Mine & Yours*, the World Heritage Site, and metalliferous mining in Cornwall please visit the website: *www. cornishmining.org.uk.*

References

Thorpe, S, and the World Heritage Site Bid Team, 2005. *Cornwall and West Devon Mining Landscape World Heritage Site Management Plan 2005 – 2010*, Truro (Cornwall County Council)

UNESCO 2005. *Operational guidelines for the implementation of the World Heritage Convention*, Paris

Cornish Archaeology 50, 2011, 137–139

'The end of a moving staircase': Industrial archaeology of the past, present and future

HILARY ORANGE

'Relics of 2,500 years of mining that litter the Cornish landscape were given World Heritage site status yesterday. The honour ranks the remains alongside the Taj Mahal, the Great Wall of China and the Pyramids at Giza' *(de Bruxelles 2006, 37).*

Fifty years ago, the idea that the remains of Cornwall's tin and copper mining industries would one day be considered as significant as the Taj Mahal or the Pyramids would likely have led to a mixture of confusion, derision and laughter. Nevertheless, as Nick Johnson has pointed out, archaeologists are positioned at the 'end of a moving staircase' (2006) and hence in time 'have to accept concrete buildings just as much as we accept brick buildings'. Indeed, the intervening years have led, not just to the World Heritage Site (WHS) but also to the iconisation of the Cornish engine house as a symbol of Cornish identity. This short paper considers changing perceptions of Cornish mining remains over the last 50 years and ends, by looking forward to the next 50 years, and with a forecast for the (industrial) archaeology of the future.

It has been suggested that in the post-war period mining sites, along with other relict industrial sites, held negative connotations. They were painful reminders of lost livelihoods (Cooper 2005) as well as being regarded as 'relics of sweated labour and unacceptable working practice' (Palmer and Neaverson 1998, 141). Interviews

within oral history archives in Cornwall (Cornish Audio Visual Archive; Geevor Mine Oral History Archive) to some extent concur with such a view with recollections of the frequent practice (before household waste and recycling centres were set up) of dumping rubbish at mine sites leading to the common descriptor of 'wasteland'. Johnson described the post-war St Just mining area as a 'beautiful but smashed and ruined landscape – a mirror to later deprivation – surrounded by areas traditionally reserved for fly-tipping, New Age Travellers and flat-roofed extensions' (1996, 150-151) but conceded that such areas were still 'home for local people' *(ibid)* and, undoubtedly, mining sites provided playgrounds for children and destinations for dog walkers and mineral collectors.

The demolition of the Doric Portico at Euston Station in 1962 is often cited as the key moment which kick-started British industrial archaeology and led to a groundswell of amateur groups and societies (Buchanan 1980, 25; Samuel 1994, 237, 276). In Cornwall, in the 1970s and 1980s, mining areas were targeted by a number of statutory reviews (Thorpe *et al* 2005, 18), moorland clearance subsidies and land reclamation schemes, the latter resulting in the capping of shafts for safety reasons (Palmer and Neaverson 1998, 129; Schwartz 2008, 120; Sharpe 2008, 21). During the 1980s and 1990s the Cornwall Archaeological Unit carried out a number of mining surveys (Johnson 2006; Sharpe 1989; 1992; Sharpe, this volume), members of local societies restored mine engines and buildings and the National Trust cleaned-up mining sites following acquisitions (a period covered in detail within Adam Sharpe's paper on conservation within this volume). Through such interventions the archaeological 'value' of industrial sites became more widely recognised. At the same time a UK-wide 'heritage boom' embraced mills, railways, foundries and mine buildings alongside long-established 'jewels in the crown' (Alfrey and Putnam 1992, 41). Whether the heritage industry resulted from top-down neo-Conservative policy or a bottom-up appropriation of cultural resources has been argued by Wright (1985) and Samuel (1994). Either way, by the 1990s industrial archaeology was firmly fixed on the heritage map.

The challenges of negotiating between different stakeholders who may hold potentially competing values is discussed in detail by Adam Sharpe (this volume) It is clear that advocates for 'bryophytes, badgers, bats or bridleways' (Sharpe, this volume) and advocates for the conservation of the historic record have been engaged in a call and response relationship for the last 20 to 30 years. For instance, while some considered the removal of mine dumps (eye-sores or sources of contamination) a 'good thing' others rued the loss of archaeological information and damage to wildlife habitats (Palmer 1993). In addition, for some local people, there was also a sense that local ownership was threatened; a feeling expressed by the Cornish writer Alan Kent in his 2005 poem *Identity Theft*.

> '*They've taken my landscape and put a tree museum in,*
> *Cleansed the earth and sanitized it*
> *Though I never asked them to;*
> *They've taken my time and told me*
> *How my history should be;*
> *Presented it in their cabinet,*
> *With their labels – not mine*'.

Despite such concerns in recent years the symbol of the engine house has become another marker of Cornish identity. Alongside Cornish tartan, Celtic crosses and the flag of St Piran's as shorthand for 'Made in Cornwall' it can be found on chocolate bars, car bumper stickers and bed and breakfast signs. Ainsley Cocks' discussion (this volume) illustrates how the value of the WHS now also extends into arts and tourism including WHS projects which focus on developing multiple ways of telling the stories of Cornish mining to different audiences.

But what of the (industrial) archaeology of the future? Trinder has argued that the process of heritage making includes a necessary, yet transitory 'stage of abandonment' through which the public come to terms with their 'disturbing' past and its connotations of socio-economic decline (2000, 39-41). Likewise, for Jackson 'an interval of neglect' provides ruination and 'the incentive for restoration' (1980, 102). The archaeology of the future is therefore that which is currently, or soon to be, abandoned and forgotten (Orange 2008). Returning to Johnson's metaphor of the 'moving staircase', the process of heritage making also depends on where the boundary is drawn between the past and the present. Whilst Symonds has argued that many people may perceive industrial remains as belonging in a period '*after* history, i.e., belonging to a slightly earlier version of *us*, just beyond living memory' (Symonds 2005, 36), when the BBC History Magazine asked its readership the question 'When does history begin?' the answers that came back ranged from 'one second ago' to 'before I was born' (2009). Whilst the passing of time is argued to be a necessity, the question remains – how much time?

In certain respects the answer may be 'no time at all'. Contemporary archaeologists are turning archaeological gaze and method towards the remains of the very recent past and considering Cold War bunkers, peace camps and prison complexes (Harrison and Schofield 2010). Meanwhile, the geographer Harvey has argued that

> 'If we try to be honest about the aspects of the present-day landscape that the people of the future will remember us for, then the A30 would be a very good example...In terms, of "our achievements" in the landscape, the road network (love it or hate it) is surely among the most enduring symbols of early twenty-first-century life...' (2006, 228).

At the end of June 2008 thousands of people gathered on Carn Brea to watch chimney stacks being re-lit (one last time?) as part of a week-long celebration of mining heritage. In 50 years time they might be back to better view the A30 or to watch the wind-turbines start to turn again.

References

Alfrey, J, and Putnam T, 1992. *The industrial heritage: managing resources and uses*, London

BBC Magazine, 2009. History? It started a second ago, www.bbchistorymagazine.com/feature/history-it-started-a-second-ago, accessed on 11 December 2010

Buchanan, R A, 1980. *Industrial archaeology in Britain*, London

Cooper, M A, 2005. Exploring Mrs Gaskell's legacy: competing constructions of the industrial environment in England's northwest, in E C Casella, and J Symonds, eds, *Industrial archaeology: future directions*, New York, 155-173

Cornwall Audio Visual Archive (CAVA), Institute of Cornish Studies, University of Exeter

de Bruxelles, S, 2006. Ruins of Cornwall's old mines become new world wonders, in *The Times*, July 14 2006, 37

Geevor Tin Mine Oral History Archive, Geevor Tin Mine, Pendeen, Cornwall

Harrison, R, and Schofield, J, 2010. *After modernity: archaeological approaches to the contemporary past*, Oxford

Harvey, D, 2006. Landscape as heritage and a recreational resource, in R Kain, ed, *England's Landscape: the South West*, London, 207-228

Jackson, J B, 1980. *The necessity for ruins and other topics*, Massachusetts

Johnson, N, 1996. Safe in our hands? in D M Evans, P Salway, and D Thackray, eds, *The remains of distant times: archaeology and the National Trust*, Woodbridge, 147-152

Johnson, N, 2006. Interview by Peter Fordham on behalf of the Cornwall Audio Visual Archive on the 23rd of November

Kent, A M, 2005. Identity theft, in *Assassin of grammar*, Penzance

Orange, H, 2008. Industrial archaeology: its place within the academic discipline, the public realm and the heritage industry, in D Gwyn, ed, *Industrial Archaeology Review*, Volume 30, 83-95

Palmer, M, 1993. Mining landscapes and the problems of contaminated land, in H Swain, ed, *Rescuing the historic environment: archaeology, the green movement and conservation strategies for the British landscape*, Warwick, 45-50

Palmer, M, and Neaverson, P, 1998. *Industrial archaeology: principles and practice*, London

Samuel, R, 1994. *Theatres of memory. Volume 1. Past and present in contemporary culture*, London

Schwartz, S P, 2008. *Voices of the Cornish mining landscape*, Truro (Cornwall County Council)

Sharpe, A, 1989. *The Minions survey: the Minions area archaeological survey and management*, Truro (Cornwall County Council and English Heritage)

Sharpe, A, 1992. *St Just: an archaeological survey of the mining district. Volume 1*, Truro (Cornwall County Council; 2 vols)

Sharpe, A, 2008. *Geevor and Levant, Cornwall: Historic Landscape Development*, Truro (Historic Environment Service, Cornwall County Council)

Symonds, J, 2005. Experiencing industry: beyond machines and the history of technology, in E C Casella, and J Symonds, eds, *Industrial archaeology: future directions*, New York, 33-57

Thorpe, S, Boden, D, and Gamble, B, 2005. *Cornwall and West Devon Mining Landscape: World Heritage Site Management Plan 2005-2010*, Truro (Cornwall County Council)

Trinder, B, 2000. Industrial archaeology: the twentieth-century context, in N Cossons, ed, *Perspectives on industrial archaeology*, London, 39-56

Wright, P, 1985. *On living in an old country: the national past in contemporary Britain*, London

PRESENTING THE PAST

Cornish Archaeology 50, 2011, 141–147

CAS excavations

JAMES GOSSIP, ANDY M JONES and PETER ROSE

Background

Peter Rose

In 2007 the Cornwall Archaeological Society ran its own training excavation for the first time in over 25 years. The Society had started with a strong tradition of set-piece excavations over its first 15 years.

    1962, Castilly Henge (and St Dennis); director Charles Thomas (Thomas 1964)

    1963, 1965, 1967, The Rumps; director R T Brooks (Brooks 1974)

    1964, Old Lanyon; director Mrs E Marie Minter (Beresford 1994)

    1968, Merther Euny; director Charles Thomas

    1968, Carvossa; director Les Douch

    1969, Crane Godrevy; director Charles Thomas (Thomas 1969)

    1970, 1971, 1972, 1973, Carn Brea; director Roger Mercer (Mercer 1981)

    1975, Killibury; director Henrietta Miles (Miles 1977)

These training excavations provided the special cultural experience that is unique to archaeological excavation, a social event mixed with the thrill of discovery and back ache. Following in the tradition of Charles Thomas's Gwithian campaigns

Fig 1. CAS Secretary Florence Nankivell leads a tour at the Society's excavations at The Rumps, 1965.
(Photograph: Charles Woolf Collection, reproduced with the kind permission of the Royal Institution of Cornwall, RIC).

Fig 2. The Rumps, 1967, Florence Nankivell and site director R T Brooks, with camp site to rear.
(Photograph: Charles Woolf Collection, reproduced with the kind permission of the Royal Institution of Cornwall, RIC).

(Nowakowski *et al* 2007, 20), the volunteer excavators could stay at a camp site (or in the case of Carn Brea, at Carnkie School) supported especially by the then Secretary, Mrs Florence Nankivell, and by a camp cook – Miss Jill Purser at the Rumps and Crane Godrevy, Mrs Muriel Edgington at Carn Brea.

The Society excavations catered for many volunteers – 51 at Old Lanyon, 157 at Carn Brea – but other long-running campaigns also gave opportunities, in particular on the Ministry of Public Buildings and Works and DoE excavations by Andrew Saunders at Launceston Castle

(1961-1983) and Paddy Christie at Carn Euny (1964-1972). Meanwhile in the early 1970s rescue excavations led by Henrietta Miles (later Quinnell) at Trethurgy and the St Austell barrows also drew in large numbers of volunteers, over 100 at Trethurgy (Quinnell 2004, ix; Miles 1975, 78), and skills were reinforced by Henrietta's classes with the University of Exeter Extra-mural Department so that from the mid 1970s, Society members themselves were leading and publishing rescue excavations, notably Daphne Harris, Peter Trudgian and Pat Carlyon at

Fig 3. Killibury hillfort, 1975. 'Rescue' excavations at Killibury were used by Henrietta Quinnell as a CAS and University of Exeter Extra-Mural Department training exercise.
(Photograph: Henrietta Quinnell)

Fig 4. Killibury, 1975; at the centre are Mary Irwin (left), then Secretary of CAS, and Daphne Harris (right), then Membership Secretary.
(Photograph: Henrietta Quinnell)

Fig 5. Stannon, St Breward, 'rescue' excavation by CAS in 1977; Charles Woolf, Daphne Harris and Peter Trudgian at the excavation of a cist. (Photograph: Charles Woolf Collection, reproduced with the kind permission of the Royal Institution of Cornwall, RIC).

Lesquite (1973), Bodmin bypass (1975), Stannon (1976-7), St Endellion (1978), Poldowrian (1978), Shortlanesend (1979) and Kilhallon (1985) (all reported in *Cornish Archaeology*). This was following in the tradition of Dorothy Dudley, who as an 'expert amateur' or second career archaeologist had led research and rescue excavations through the 1950s and up to 1967.

From 1978 to 1983 the Society again ran its own fieldwork programme – the Lizard Project, which involved a huge amount of fieldwalking as well as excavation – but this time as a joint exercise with

Fig 6. Shortlanesend, Truro; excavation of the 'round' in 1979 was funded by the Department of the Environment via the Cornwall Committee for Rescue Archaeology and was carried out by members of CAS directed by Daphne Harris. From the left: Nancy Reed(?), Pat Brierley (then Carlyon), Peter Brierley, Geoff Berridge (foreground), Pat Penhallurick (then Best), Archie Mercer and Daphne Harris. (Photograph: Peter Rose)

English Heritage's Central Excavation Unit (Smith 1986). During the 1970s an increasing awareness of the scale of resources and commitment, both for individuals and societies, required to see a programme of excavation through its complex stages of post-excavation analysis and publication, will have been a factor in encouraging CAS to look at other activities. Although CAS did not afterwards set up its own excavations until 2007, CAS members, as before, participated in many of the excavations that took place in Cornwall, and helped on excavations managed by the Cornwall Archaeological Unit and subsequently the Historic Environment Service (HES) of Cornwall County Council, including Bodmin Priory, Trethellan, Tintagel Churchyard, Trelowthas, Liskeard, Junior School and Stannon Down. The HES also set up excavations which had a strong element of community involvement, notably at Glasney College (2003), Boden, St Anthony-in-Meneage (2003), and St Piran's Church (2005). There were also training excavations established in the county: Jacqui Wood's excavations at Saveock Water, Chacewater, since 2001; and since 2003 the Slaughterbridge Training Excavation Project digging at Old Melorn near Camelford.

Hay Close, St Newlyn East, 2007

Andy Jones

The excavations partly arose because there was a desire by members of the Society to become directly engaged with fieldwork projects which involved the opportunity to learn archaeological techniques and partly because there was growing recognition that the Society could make a contribution to the archaeological knowledge of the county by targeted investigation of sites which fell outside the bounds of developer funded archaeology. However, it is also the case that the project was partially inspired by an impromptu excavation at the Eathorne Menhir (Hartgroves *et al* 2006), undertaken 12 months before, which had demonstrated how well volunteers and professional archaeologists could work together.

From the outset, therefore, the project had two major aims, to involve training for members of the Society, and to undertake a project which would make a significant contribution to the study of Cornwall's past. The site at St Newlyn East

Fig 7. St Newlyn East finds training session. Jane Marley and Laura Ratcliffe provided examples of finds from Royal Cornwall Museum to help volunteers recognise the sort of artefacts that they might recover. (Photograph: Andy Jones)

was chosen as an interesting crop-mark enclosure which had the potential to provide a suitable site for up to 30 volunteers from the Society to learn the techniques of archaeological excavation and recording over a two-week period.

Through the assistance of dedicated people we were able to provide instruction in fieldwalking, resistivity survey, planning and section drawing, and artefact recognition and processing, which were all enthusiastically taken up by volunteers. At the end of the fieldwork the finds from the excavation were catalogued at the Royal Cornwall Museum by volunteers from the Society.

We also wanted to provide outreach to the community that we had descended upon and at our open day we had somewhere in the region of 500 visitors. A follow-up exhibition at the village hall attracted around 100 people.

Fig 8. St Newlyn East: volunteers were encouraged to learn how to record the features they had excavated. This photograph shows the trench being prepared for section recording.
(*Photograph: Andy Jones*)

The project was hugely successful and the paper will shortly be published in *Cornish Archaeology* (Jones forthcoming).

CAS excavation at Boden Vean, St Anthony-in-Meneage, 2008

James Gossip

During September and October 2008 CAS carried out the excavation of a Bronze Age roundhouse in a field close to Boden Vean, just south of Manaccan on the Lizard peninsula. The site was chosen as a result of work carried out in 2003 when a team from the Historic Environment Service, Cornwall County Council undertook the evaluation of an Iron Age enclosure and fogou. This original work was funded by English Heritage and came about because of events that began in 1991, when pipe-laying by the landowner led to the rediscovery of a fogou (subterranean passage), documented in this area in the early nineteenth century but the whereabouts of which had since been forgotten.

The objectives of the excavation of 2008 were to recover missing parts of a very large Trevisker Ware vessel (Middle Bronze Age, *c* 1500 – 1200 BC) found during the original evaluation and to help understand the practices and extent of ritual deposition within the abandonment phases of Bronze Age domestic structures. The excavation was made possible by the kind assistance of the Meneage Archaeology Group and the landowner Chris Hosken.

Fig 9. CAS members uncover Trevisker Ware sherds on the floor of the Boden roundhouse, 2008.

The excavation of the 10m diameter, hollow-set roundhouse took place over five long weekends with the involvement of up to 15 CAS members on each day, giving everyone the opportunity to gain fieldwork experience. All participants were offered training in aspects of site recording such as surveying, planning, section drawing, context recording and environmental sampling. Some members took this up, whilst others were happy

Fig 10. CAS president Tony Blackman visiting the Boden excavation with the Young Archaeologists Club. (*Photograph: Andy Jones*)

PRESENTING THE PAST

Fig 11. Some of the CAS excavation team at the Boden roundhouse.

to hone their skills as excavators – this was a site rich in finds, and everyone was given the chance to discover a piece of the Bronze Age for themselves! An important task was the detailed recording of every artefact recovered, a task supervised by Laura Ratcliffe with the assistance of CAS members.

The excavation was very well publicised, with local press and television present on more than one occasion. Five local schools visited the site and were given a site tour and a talk on the history of the site as well as a chance to look at the finds with Anna Tyacke, Finds Liaison Officer with the Portable Antiquities Scheme. Despite horrendous weather a public open day was well attended giving people the chance to see the artefacts at close quarters and to watch the excavation taking place.

Once the excavations were complete CAS members were involved in the wet-sieving of eighty environmental samples and have carefully washed and marked over 600 artefacts retrieved from the excavation. Other post-excavation tasks have included inking-up plans in advance of digital scanning and the inputting of data into spreadsheets. Post-excavation analysis is being funded by Cornwall Archaeological Society and the Royal Cornwall Museum.

The excavation culminated with a party held by the Meneage Archaeology Group, celebrating the achievements of the dig. The outstanding

success of the excavation was in providing CAS members with first-hand experience of excavation whilst making a significant contribution to the study of Cornwall's past.

Carn Galva and Bosporthennis, Zennor, 2009

Andy Jones

The success of Hay Close in 2007 led to the development of a more ambitious excavation plan for 2009. The Society decided to develop

Fig 12. The trenches at Carn Galva and Bosporthennis were entirely hand dug. This photograph shows Laura Ratcliffe supervising volunteers uncovering the Carn Galva enclosure wall. (Photograph: Andy Jones)

Fig 13. At Bosporthennis, thanks to the enthusiasm of Les Dodd and Phil Hills, volunteers were given the opportunity to learn how to use a variety of field survey techniques, including geophysical survey, total station survey and levelling. In this photograph a student is being instructed in how to take readings using a dumpy level. (Photograph: Andy Jones)

a longer-term project to investigate sites in the Penwith. In the first year it was decided to split the excavations between two sites, the enclosure on Carn Galva and the chambered tomb at Bosporthennis. The excavations were smaller in scale but all the trenches were hand-dug by the volunteers, so we were again able to offer places for up to 30 people over a two week period.

We were also able to build upon the training that had been on offer in 2007. In addition to learning the techniques of excavation, volunteers were encouraged to become involved with geophysical

survey, total station surveying, planning and section drawing as well as finds processing. As at Hay Close, participation in these tasks was taken up with enthusiasm. Unfortunately the open days in 2009 were completely washed out by torrential rain. However, aside from this the project was a great success and a report is in preparation (Jones in preparation).

The excavations at Hay Close and Carn Galva demonstrate the potential for local societies to undertake training excavations and at the same time obtain valuable results. The success of the excavations have, however, been in no small part due to the people who gave up their 'day' jobs to help with the training. In no particular order, they include: Sean Taylor and Laura Ratcliffe, Paul Bonnington, Jane Marley, Les Dodd and Phil Hills, Peter Nicholas as well as Henrietta Quinnell and the members of the Excavation Committee, Tony Blackman and Sally Ealey, who worked behind the scenes.

References

Beresford, G, 1994. Old Lanyon, Madron: a deserted medieval settlement. The late E Marie Minter's excavations of 1964, *Cornish Archaeol*, **33**, 130-169

Brooks, R T, 1974. The excavation of the Rumps cliff castle, St Minver, Cornwall, *Cornish Archaeol*, **13**, 5-50

Hartgroves, S, Jones, A M, and Kirkham, G, 2006. The Eathorne menhir, *Cornish Archaeol*, **45**, 97-108

Jones, A M, forthcoming. Hay Close, St Newlyn East: excavations by the Cornwall Archaeological Society, 2007, *Cornish Archaeol*

Jones, A M, in preparation. CAS excavations at Carn Galva and Bosporthennis in 2009, *Cornish Archaeol*

Mercer, R, 1981. Excavations at Carn Brea, Illogan, Cornwall – a Neolithic fortified complex of the third millennium bc, *Cornish Archaeol*, **20**, 1-204

Miles 1975. Barrows on the St Austell granite, Cornwall, *Cornish Archaeol*, **14**, 5-81

Miles, H, 1977. Excavations at Killibury hillfort, Egloshayle 1975-6, *Cornish Archaeol*, **16**, 89-121

Nowakowski, J A, Quinnell, H, Sturgess, J, Thomas, C, and Thorpe, C, 2007. Return to Gwithian: shifting the sands of time, *Cornish Archaeol*, **46**, 13-76

Smith, G H, 1986. The Lizard Project: landscape survey 1978-1983, *Cornish Archaeol*, **26**, 13-68

Quinnell, H, 2004. *Trethurgy: excavations at Trethurgy round, St Austell: community and status in Roman and post-Roman Cornwall*, Truro (Cornwall County Council)

Thomas, C, 1964. The Society's 1962 excavation: the henge at Castilly, *Cornish Archaeol*, **3**, 3-14

Thomas, C, 1969. Excavations at Crane Godrevy, Gwithian, 1969, interim report, *Cornish Archaeol*, **8**, 84-88

Fig 14. Planning at Bosporthennis. The subtleties of making scaled drawings are being explained to two student volunteers. (Photograph: Andy Jones)

PRESENTING THE PAST

Cornish Archaeology 50, 2011, 149–152

The Time Team in Cornwall

CARL THORPE

Now entering its nineteenth season, Time Team has done more than any other television programme to raise the profile and popularity of archaeology in the public consciousness, not only within Britain but also world wide, inspiring a new generation of archaeologists. First broadcast in 1994 on Channel 4, the programmes marked a new approach to archaeology on British television, using the now familiar (but then revolutionary) formula of a three-day investigation to capture the excitement and immediacy of the process of discovery –

archaeology as it happened. At the same time the audience was introduced to the methods and language of the archaeological evaluation. Presented by Tony Robinson, the 'Team' currently consists of Mick Aston, Francis Pryor, Phil Harding, Stewart Ainsworth, John Gater, Henry Chapman, Helen Geake and Victor Ambrus, though early series also featured Carenza Lewis and the historian Robin Bush. Whilst its success and popularity is generally acknowledged, the series has not been without its critics, having been accused in the pages of *Cornish*

Fig 1. Roughtor, 2006. Phil Harding of Time Team and Ian Morrison of English Heritage discuss the Neolithic(?) bank cairn.

Fig 2. Lellizzick, 2007, excavating a roundhouse.

Archaeology of compromising archaeology as a serious subject, and of being 'superficial and misleading' (Gathercole *et al* 2002-3, 150, 152).

Cornish sites have now featured in six Time Team investigations, as well as occasional parts in Time Team Specials (on King Arthur in 2001 and on the wreck of the *Colossus* in 2002).

Their first outing to Cornwall was in 1995, to the well known fogou at Boleigh, near St Buryan (SW 4372 2519). They identified at least two ramparts forming an enclosure around the fogou. Pottery from the site suggested that the settlement was first occupied in the Early Iron Age and continued through the Late Iron Age, and perhaps into the fourth century AD (Young 2000). A geophysical survey was also carried out to locate the 'lost' fogou at Trevenegue, St Hilary which had been excavated in 1866, rediscovering it at SW 5477 3305.

In 1996 the Time Team came to St Leonards, Launceston, the site of a medieval leper hospital, following the chance discovery of human remains within a water pipe trench. This was a challenging programme as not much was actually found! However, the trenching established the limits of the cemetery, and suggested that the hospital buildings lay beneath the Launceston Sewage Works (SX 35069 84842). A single burial of a young woman was excavated; a radiocarbon date of cal AD 1040-1280 was broadly contemporary with the hospital which was founded in the thirteenth century (Harding *et al* 1997).

The sites investigated in 2001 were more immediately impressive - the two large enclosures at Gear (SW 721 248) and Caer Vallack (SW 7255 2455), near Helford. Evidence for activity prior to construction of both hill forts was found dating from the Neolithic and Bronze Age. The excellent geophysical survey of Gear was one of the largest to have been carried out in Cornwall and revealed dense activity of various phases, including several smaller enclosures and roundhouses, while the results from Caer Vallack showed the presence of indeterminate structures within the enclosures. It was suggested that Gear developed into a social and economic centre covering a large area while Caer Vallack could have been a site for the higher echelons of society (Edwards and Kirkham 2008).

Returning in 2006 the Time Team went to Bodmin Moor and the western flanks of Rough Tor (SX 14081 81735). The investigations focused on two sites. The first was a 500 metre long cairn (or bank cairn, a possible Neolithic ritual monument), running on an east-west alignment towards the tor (Fig 1). The other was a Bronze Age roundhouse settlement. Unfortunately no radiocarbon dating was achieved at either site though Trevisker pottery from the roundhouse trenches would be consistent with a Middle Bronze Age date (*c* 1500-1100 BC) (Thompson 2007).

At Lellizzick, on the Camel Estuary near Padstow, aerial photographs taken by archaeologist Steve Hartgroves, and two geophysical surveys by English Heritage's Ancient Monuments Lab, had shown dozens of circular and semi-circular shapes and lines running across the cliff top fields (Nowakowski, this volume, fig 9). Field walking and metal detecting by Jonathan Clemes had produced artefacts that dated from Neolithic through to early medieval. Time Team's excavations in 2007 confirmed that these were the outlines of roundhouses containing internal pits and hearths, dating from the Iron Age through to the Roman period (Fig 2). A bronze stylus, dated to about AD 200, is possibly the earliest evidence of writing yet discovered in Cornwall. The discovery of sherds of North African Red Slip ware and Bi amphora implied that trade with the Mediterranean had continued well into the fifth and sixth centuries AD connecting Cornwall with the Byzantine Empire (Thompson 2008).

In 2008 the Time Team came to Looe. Two sites were involved: the Lammana Chapel and nearby Monks House on the mainland (centred on SX 25113 52209), and St Michael's Chapel on Looe Island (centred on SX 25675 51437).

Trenches on the island discovered the ditches of an unexpected Romano-British enclosure on the summit and picked up the walling of the summit chapel belonging to a small priory documented from *c* AD 1200. An inhumation grave was uncovered which would have lain beneath the chancel arch. It was dated by a pottery find to the thirteenth century. A second inhumation burial, and a possible stone-lined cist grave, was found outside the southern wall of the chapel.

The mainland site (Fig 3) had been excavated by C K Croft Andrew in the 1930s and the results re-evaluated and published in 1994 (Olson 1994). The Time Team evaluation confirmed the ground plan of the chapel as a single phase construction with a southern porch and a secondary, northern entrance. There were indications of a rood screen. One disturbed inhumation burial was found beneath the chancel arch, and traces of two other possible graves, as well as a stone-lined possible reliquary. Bone from the disturbed inhumation provided a radiocarbon date of cal AD 1200-1280. The

Fig 3. Lammana Chapel, Looe, 2008. In the trench, centre, Tony Robinson and Jacqueline McKinley discuss bones.
(Photograph: Nigel Thomas)

Fig 4. Looe Island, 2008. Time Team founding members: Tony Robinson, Tim Taylor, Phil Harding, and Mick Aston.

evidence pointed to Lammana Chapel post-dating the island chapel in construction.

At Monks House, the south-western wall was exposed, and enabled a revision of Croft Andrew's stated dimensions of the building. No traces of associated buildings were found. Croft Andrew's finds indicated use of this building in the thirteenth to fourteenth centuries, and finds from the Time Team evaluation were of similar date (Thompson 2009).

The first three of Time Team's Cornish investigations have been published in *Cornish Archaeology*, and from the 2003 series onwards Wessex Archaeology have been commissioned to complete evaluation and assessment reports; these are available on the Wessex Archaeology web site. For the more recent Cornish investigations these reports have recommended that summaries are produced for *Cornish Archaeology*, though arguably the significance of the results would suggest that rather fuller accounts would be appropriate.

With well over 200 sites having been investigated, Time Team looks set to continue well into the future. Within Cornwall the wide variety of evaluations has provided information about monuments which would not otherwise have been investigated, and has also helped to raise the profile of archaeology within the county.

References

Edwards, K, and Kirkham, G, 2008. Gear and Caervallack, St Martin-in-Meneage: excavations by Time Team, 2001, *Cornish Archaeol*, **47,** 49-100

Gathercole, P, Stanley, J, and Thomas, N, 2002-3. Archaeology and the media: Cornwall Archaeological Society-Devon Archaeological Society joint symposium, *Cornish Archaeol*, **41-42,** 149-160

Harding, P A, Ainsworth, S, Gater, G, and Johns, C, 1997. The evaluation of a medieval leper hospital at St Leonards, Cornwall, *Cornish Archaeol*, **36,** 138-150

Olson, L, 1994. Lammana, West Looe; C K Croft Andrew's excavations of the chapel and Monks House, 1935-6, *Cornish Archaeol*, **33,** 96-129

Thompson, S, 2007. *Roughtor, Bodmin Moor, Cornwall. Archaeological evaluation and assessment of results*, Salisbury (Wessex Archaeology; report reference: 62500.01)

Thompson, S, 2008. *Lellizzick, near Padstow, Cornwall. Archaeological evaluation and assessment of results*, Salisbury (Wessex Archaeology; report reference: 65312.01)

Thompson, S, 2009. *Looe, Cornwall. Archaeological evaluation and assessment of results*, (Wessex Archaeology; report reference: 68734.01)

Young, A, 2000-1. Time team at Boleigh fogou, St Buryan, *Cornish Archaeol*, **39-40,** 129-145

Cornish Archaeology 50, 2011, 153–158

Presenting the past: Cornish museums and galleries

JANE MARLEY

Museums and galleries present the past and make it accessible to the public through displays, exhibitions, learning resources and educational activities which communicate effectively and provide access for the needs of different audiences (Fig 1). Due to lack of space, the focus of this article is on the presentation of archaeology collections in displays and exhibitions.

Museums and galleries proliferate in Cornwall and currently number around 41. Some evolved from mid-nineteenth-century learned institutions formed as a nucleus around which *Literati* of the county might concentrate for the diffusion of scientific information, the excitement of literary emulation and literary research based on antiquities, as proposed for the formation of the Cornwall Literary and Philosophical Institution in the year 1818.

The Royal Cornwall Museum holds collections for the Royal Institution of Cornwall (RIC), a charitable trust, which was founded in 1818, and the Penlee House Gallery and Museum collection was founded in 1839 by the Penzance Natural History and Antiquarian Society (Naylor 2010). Other museums were created more recently by small communities proud to promote their local history amongst themselves and to others; for example St Agnes Museum and Constantine Heritage Collection. Some collections, created by excavations, operate under private ownership such as Wayside Folk Museum, Zennor and Poldowrian

Museum in Poldowrian Gardens, near Coverack. The variety of each collection has roots in the time and nature of the foundation of the museum. The earliest museums tend to form collections of antiquarian interest concentrating on natural history, archaeology, ethnography, archives, photographs and art from Cornwall and beyond. During the twentieth century interest in social history resulted in the creation of many community museums. They have built up distinctive local collections relating to the land and the seafaring people of nineteenth and twentieth-century Cornwall, for example Helston Folk Museum and Charlestown Shipwreck and Heritage Centre.

The Royal Cornwall Museum holds the largest collection and display of archaeological finds and some of the finest artefacts in Cornwall. The collection was redisplayed in 1994 and on Maundy Thursday, 1994 the new exhibition was opened with a visit of the Queen and Prince Philip (RIC/RCM 1994). The displays were arranged in chronological and taxonomic order in traditional museum cases (Figs 2 and 3). In terms of physical and intellectual access, the walk-ways accommodated wheel chairs and the text was aimed at an adult audience with a strong interest in the subject. School parties could only be accommodated in groups of up to 15 maximum as most activities were designed purposefully to take place in the two education rooms and there was only one hands-on activity for family groups.

Fig 1. Children making Early Bronze Age
lunulae for the National Archaeology Day event
'Arteology' in 2006. Since the RIC was founded,
there has always been some provision for adult
and children's education but funding for this
has increased over the last 25 years. In 1988,
children's activities during school holidays were
introduced and 36 children and their parents
handled the museums prehistoric and Roman
pots and tried their hand at potting (Dudley 1989,
361). In 1995/6 funds were raised to set up a
schools service with a trial six-month programme
of workshops based on the museums collections
and linked directly to the National Curriculum.
This proved so successful that the post was
funded for another 3 years (Dudley 1996) and
the education service has continued to grow and
flourish up until the present day when education
activities, including archaeology, are available
for schools and families during the holidays
and are tailor-made for temporary exhibitions.
Loans boxes, including archaeology are available
for schools and higher education institutions
and Memory Boxes, including archaeology, are
planned for reminiscence sessions. In 2008 the
museum won the Sandford Award for Education.

In 2003, with Renaissance in the Regions (RiR)
funding, a series of improvements to the Royal
Cornwall Museum's local history and archaeology
gallery took place. The museum closed for six weeks
in 2007 for refurbishment of the older display cases.
Next, the background information was researched
with assistance from local specialists and new
information panels and graphics were added in
2009. In 2009/10 the main gallery was further
refurbished to raise the standard of the display

Fig 2. Pre-1991 main gallery at the Royal
Cornwall Museum. Archaeology and Social
History are displayed on the ground floor
alongside the outer coffin of Iset-Tayef-Nakht,
by the stairs. Natural History is displayed on the
Balcony.

(Fig 4). Four spaces were created to accommodate
corporate entertaining for fundraising and up to 30
school children for activities in each space relating
to chronological phases. Information panels, texts
and labelling were aimed at a general audience.
Large images of Cornish sites in the landscape were
added to the cases to link artefacts to landscapes and
encourage exploration outside the museum. Sadly,
no new interactives were introduced.

Another significant archaeology gallery in
Cornwall is at the Penlee House Gallery and
Museum. It was redisplayed in 2006, again
aimed at a general audience (Figs 5 and 6). The

Fig 3. Story of Cornwall Gallery at the Royal
Cornwall Museum, opened in 1994. The layout
enabled the visitor to choose a route through the
galleries.

Fig 4. Story of Cornwall Gallery at the Royal Cornwall Museum refurbishment, opened in 2010. The layout of the cases was reviewed to enable the architecture of the building and the stairs to be visible.

gallery, cases and artefacts, including loans from the RCM, are displayed to aesthetic effect. Vince Bevan, a photographer, won the commission to produce a series of black and white photographs of monuments in Penwith. Old prints and drawings are displayed alongside pertinent quotes.

Other museums in Cornwall, such as Helston Museum, Bodmin Town Museum, Lostwithiel Museum and Padstow Museum display local finds from their own collections alongside social history and natural history to illustrate the story of the town or area. At Lawrence House Museum, Launceston, the finds from the Augustinian Priory of St Thomas are displayed. Penryn Museum has material on display about the medieval Glasney College including loans from the RCM. The nature of the displays varies according to the funding,

Fig 5. Pre 2006 Prehistoric Penwith Gallery at The Penlee House Gallery and Museum, Penzance.

access to resources such as computers and whether the exhibition is made in-house or by a designer.

Callington Museum holds the collection of the Callington Local History Society which includes prehistoric stone implements collected by Cornwall Archaeological Society field walking over 10 years. Wayside Folk Museum, Zennor, founded in 1937 by Colonel Hirst, an archaeologist, exhibits finds from the locality. Poldowrian Museum houses artefacts from excavations carried out locally. The Cornwall Museums' web site currently lists 15 museums as having Industrial Heritage collections and these include Geevor Tin Mine, King Edward Mine, Wheal Martyn China Clay Country Park and the Redruth Old Cornwall Society Museum.

Fig 6. Archaeology gallery at The Penlee House Gallery and Museum, Penzance, after redisplay in 2006 now gives a sense of the archaeology of the area, both in terms of finds but also in the history of study and practice.

PRESENTING THE PAST

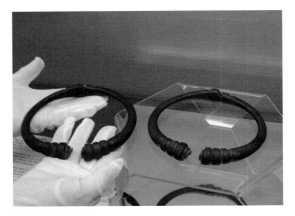

Fig 7. The Pentire neckring replica created for the Newquay Old Cornwall Society being held next to the original on display in the main gallery. Replicas can be useful for teaching. The RCM has supported adult education classes and 'A' Level courses through customised provision for the teacher and class. It has supported 1st & 2nd Year FdSc Archaeology Students from Truro College (University of Plymouth Partnerships), through a Working in Museums workshop and through providing annual 30 day work placements. The RCM applied as an employer partner for the one year stand-alone degree course for Archaeology at Truro College, Plymouth University in 2007 and has been involved with the course since then. The museum provides materials for adult PAST (Practical Archaeology Skills Training) for the Cornwall Archaeological Society.

St Agnes Museum and Geevor Tin Mine have recently obtained World Heritage Site funding for refurbishment of their exhibits.

In addition, Cornish collections may be found on display in other museums in Britain: Plymouth Museum and Art Gallery has Cornish collections obtained before museum collecting areas were created and has an Iron Age skeleton from Harlyn Bay on display; the British Museum holds finds of significance such as the Early Bronze Age Rillaton Cup and the ninth-century Trewhiddle Hoard; and the Ashmolean Museum has five Iron Age coins from the Carn Brea hoard.

Temporary exhibitions can be a successful way of presenting archaeology. Over the last 25 years at the RCM, notable amongst these are the Millennium Exhibition: *The History of Christianity in Cornwall AD 500-2000*, accompanied by a publication (Thomas and Mattingly 2000); *A Brush with the Past*, an exhibition of reconstructions of Cornish archaeology by local artist Jane Stanley, was an opportunity to support the launch of her book by the same name (Stanley 2009); an exhibition of *Masters of Mathematics: The Rhind Mathematical of Ancient Egypt* enabled the RCM to borrow the papyrus from the British Museum for an exhibition aimed at families and schools (RIC/RCM 2008); and *The Botallack Hoard* curated by artist, David Kemp, a 2010 exhibition about 'Relics, artefacts and god-dollies from the consumer cults that thrived on the South West Peninsula towards the end of the Second Millennium'. The new acquisition case was used to publicise finds acquired through the Portable Antiquities Scheme and the Treasure process as with the Late Bronze Age Mylor hoard (Jones and Quinnell this volume, fig 15). New archaeological archives such as the Tregony urns and the Pentire neckring (Fig 7) were exhibited, as were hidden treasures in store, such as the collection of cuneiform tablets. Each display provided an opportunity to create a press release to gain local press, radio and television interest for those involved and to raise the profile of archaeology in Cornwall.

Other community museums and organizations put on temporary displays of archaeological material, often on loan from the RCM: the Gerrans Heritage Centre for the open season and Newquay Old Cornwall Society for weekend long exhibitions for anniversaries. Callington Museum created a temporary exhibition including archaeological artefacts in 2010.

The future

The two main archaeology galleries of Cornwall have been redisplayed over the last 25 years. However, despite the Renaissance in the Regions funding, the current gallery at the Royal Cornwall Museum is a refurbishment created on a limited budget of £50,000 in a period of three months with a closure of three weeks. Overall, the refurbishment has been well received and the use of traditional style cases is generally popular with visitors and visiting specialists.

This century Somerset County Museum, Plymouth Museum and Art Gallery and Royal Albert Memorial Museum, Exeter have all tapped into substantial HLF and other funding to create new displays, including archaeology, costing millions and have closed for months and even years to achieve this. In future a new gallery on this scale would enable the RCM to redisplay the significant Cornish regional collection to current best practice standards (Lord and Dexter Lord 2001; Hooper-Greenhill 1994; Pearce 1994; Falk 1992; Renaissance East of England Hub 2008; Houtgraff *et al* 2008).

A new display would also satisfy a public now used to sophisticated contemporary exhibitions. These now place learning at the heart of the experience; have different levels of information aimed at different audiences; an emphasis on the 'stories' surrounding artefacts; learning through activities and handling materials in the gallery; and sensory learning. In future they will make information available on mobile phones and hand held devices. Due to the lack of future funding sources, more add-on refurbishments of these features are the most likely way ahead for the RCM in the immediate future.

Most small private or local museums present some archaeological material in their displays. Thanks to the enthusiasm and expertise of local volunteers with advice from Museum Development Officers and Curatorial Advisers and funding through the former these displays are being continuously renewed. World Heritage funding is currently a substantial source of funding to improve presentation of industrial archaeology museums and galleries in Cornwall. In future, it is likely there will

Fig 8. Staff mounting the Early Bronze Age Penwith lunula on loan from the British Museum into the Treasures from the Earth *at Penlee House Gallery and Museum in 2011.*

be more partnership working and more joined up approach to producing new displays.

The travelling exhibition *Treasures from the Earth*, created with HLF funding by the RiR, has been organised by South West Hub museum archaeological curators at Royal Cornwall Museum, Royal Albert Memorial Museum, Exeter and Plymouth Museum and Art Gallery. The exhibition will travel round community museums in Cornwall, Devon and Somerset to raise the profile of archaeology in the south west and enable more people to become involved. The exhibition will come to Cornwall in 2011/12. Containing loan artefacts from the main archaeological repositories, the exhibition is a chance to research and display new local finds and to organise activities, talks and walks. As part of the *Treasures from the Earth* exhibition, the RCM will be providing funding and staffing to produce educational materials for the four museums involved: Bude Museum; Lawrence House Museum, Launceston; the Penlee House Gallery and Museum; and the RCM (Fig 8). These generic materials will be available to all museums in Cornwall and the south west.

Future developments for the presentation of archaeology are likely to be the availability of archaeology museum collections on line and the use of social media such as Facebook and Twitter to communicate with audiences. A gallery guide and an illustrated publication summarising the archaeology of Cornwall that can be easily and regularly updated and aimed at the general public are much needed.

Most notably there has been a movement towards consulting the views of individuals, groups and organisations in the interpretation of museum collections. This trend can be seen at Penlee House Gallery and Museum where the Cornish Ancient Sites Protection Network (CASPN) was involved with the display of one case to emphasise sustainability issues of tourism and interest in archaeological monuments.

The opinions of archaeological experts have always been added to the records of artefacts. However, there is a move towards adding new or non-traditional knowledge held by individuals outside the organisation to museum collections databases with a view to developing audiences and finding new ways of engaging users with collections (*www.collectionstrust.org.uk/revcol*). The multi-vocal views of individuals and organisations may increasingly feature in the interpretation

PRESENTING THE PAST

of collections in public galleries and on online materials alongside the opinion of the curator and archaeological specialist.

Acknowledgements

My thanks to Hilary Bracegirdle and Margaret Morgan for reading and commenting on the article and to Lisa Mitchell for the latest references about museum displays.

References

Cornwall Museums Group, *Museums in Cornwall* web site, 15.9.2010, http://www.museumsincornwall.org.uk/

Dudley, C, 1989. Director's report, *Jnl Roy Inst Cornwall*, **X.3**, 360-1

Dudley, C, 1996. The Director's report, *Jnl Roy Inst Cornwall*, **2.3**, 9-10

Falk, J, 1992. *The museum experience*, Washington

Hooper-Greenhill, E, ed, 1994. *The Educational role of the museum*, London

Houtgraff, D, Vitali, V, and Gale, P, eds, 2008. *Mastering a museum plan: strategies for exhibit development*, Plymouth

Lord, B, and Dexter Lord, G, eds, 2001. *The manual of museum exhibitions*, Walnut Creek, California

Naylor, S, 2010. *Regionalizing science* no. 11, London

Pearce, S, ed, 1994. *Interpreting objects and collections*, London

Rennaisance East of England, Feb 2008. *Evaluation toolkit for museum practitioners*, East of England Museum Hub (http://www.collectionstrust.org.uk/revcol), 14.11.2010

Stanley, J, 2009. *A brush with the past*, Truro (Jane Stanley and Cornwall Council)

The Royal Institution of Cornwall Royal Cornwall Museum, October 1994, *Newsletter 16*

The Royal Institution of Cornwall, Royal Cornwall Museum and Courtney Library, October 2008. *Newsletter 44*

Thomas, C, and Mattingly, J, 2000. *The History of Christianity in Cornwall: AD 500 – 2000*, Truro (Royal Institution of Cornwall)

25 YEARS OF DISCOVERY AND RESEARCH

A review of our changing understanding of Cornwall's past

Hurlers at dawn. Photograph by Paul Chrome, CAS member.

Cornish Archaeology 50, 2011, 161–174

The Cornish landscape

PETER HERRING

Parts of Cornwall, like Bodmin Moor's commons, appear to have changed remarkably little since drastic alterations wrought by graziers around 4,000 years ago. Much seems ancient, while other parts appear repeatedly reworked. But all Cornwall's landscape is historic, and all is simultaneously thoroughly modern, of today: always changing, physically, in how it is used and in terms of our understanding of it (Fig 1).

Landscape is a tangled inheritance, its history more or less easily legible, with cognition and recognition playing important roles in forming it, making it 'a constantly emergent perceptual and material milieu' (Wylie 2007). Being ever-changing, transitory, with no original form, such a world is, of course, far from 'timeless', being full of the outcomes of discernible changes, each distinctively of their time, providing the evidence that allows landscape archaeologists to get to work (Fairclough 2006). And much landscape archaeology has been undertaken in Cornwall in the last quarter century, mixing

Fig 1. Cornwall's ever-changing landscape means different things to each person who perceives it. A farmer might be drawn to the invasion of Caradon by bracken, furze and trees as grazing levels are reduced, rather than to the stacks, engine houses and dumps of great Victorian copper mines. Survey and research continues to alter our understanding of all aspects of this part of Bodmin Moor, so that the perceptions of both farmer and industrial archaeologist are themselves always altering. *(Photograph: Peter Herring)*

DISCOVERY AND RESEARCH

Fig 2. A highly legible historic landscape: a medieval town, Boscastle, in one of several steep-sided and anciently wooded valleys running to one of north Cornwall's most sheltered harbours; the strips of Cornwall's last surviving open field on Forrabury Common echoed in the enclosed fields beyond the town and more quietly so in other field patterns in this anciently enclosed land. Here is the sea and there, far way, are Roughtor and Brown Willy high on Bodmin Moor. But somewhere is a place more important than any, at least for Thomas Hardy: a 'junction of lane and highway'. (Photograph: Peter Herring)

rigorous recording with deductive modelling (Herring forthcoming a). Some has been driven by academic querying, but most has originated in either a form of rescue landscape archaeology, recording in advance of threats, or as a means of informing positive land management (see Herring, Field Surveys, this volume).

A shift in the last 15 years away from Hoskins-inspired, narrative-based approaches, reflects developing appreciation that landscape is not just a separate place recorded and analysed, where two-dimensional representations of all that remains can be made to yield interesting stories. As well as that, we increasingly appreciate that we also live in landscape, creating it as we work

on it and think about it, so that Roughtor, Redruth and Roche exist within us as well as out there, and that they like us are plural, not singular.

Boscastle (Fig 2), while entirely historic, is more than a medieval town with castle, later medieval and modern houses, set in tractor-worked medieval fields, among ancient semi-natural woodlands, and linked by steep lanes to a rare north-coast harbour and by wider roads to moorland pastures (Kirkham 2005). It is a place entered, sensed (seen, smelt, heard), felt and responded to, remembered and pondered, a place like all the historic landscape that can make us smile or weep. Thomas Hardy evokes such a Boscastle, as Castle Boterel.

As I drive to the junction of lane and highway,
And drizzle bedrenches the waggonette,
I look behind at the fading byway,
And see on its slope, now glistening wet,
Distinctly yet

Myself and a girlish form benighted
In dry March weather. We climb the road
Beside a chaise. We had just alighted
To ease the sturdy pony's load
When he sighed and slowed…

…It filled but a minute. But was there ever
A time of such quality, since or before,
In that hill's story? To one mind never,
Though it has been climbed, foot swift, foot sore,
By thousands more.

We discover again what people seem to have once known easily, judging from how pre-enlightenment landscape design, prehistoric and medieval, appears to show how place was not objectivised and flattened through systematised observation, but fully rounded and filled with knowledge, memories, associations and individually and communally understood meaning, often made symbolic. The world as historic landscape is doubly cultural, culturally made over days, years, decades, centuries and millennia, and culturally perceived. A second modern definition of landscape, that has rapidly become influential, is that underpinning the European Landscape Convention. Again it marries the external and internal, the objective and subjective, with people as creators and perceivers. Landscape is 'an area, as perceived by people, whose character is the result of the action and interaction of natural and/or human factors' (CoE 2000, Article 1).

No two perceptions of place will exactly chime, so landscape will always be contested, encouraging constructive engagement with interpretation (and action). What follows is an outline landscape history of Cornwall as this author currently perceives it, drawing particularly on the last 25 years of landscape archaeology and recognising that its emphases and omissions are not simply the outcomes of a word limit. Framed as a narrative, it illustrates or suggests how people have changed and transformed place, functionally through industry, agriculture and other land use, socially through territory, property, tenure, and mentally through remembering, misremembering, and persuasion.

It does not treat landscape as a large archaeological site, and not as merely the context for archaeological sites, or assets, as that way of seeing Cornwall's historic environment is considered elsewhere in this volume. Instead it accepts those two recent definitions and regards landscape as an inherited place, full of meanings for communities and individuals, some signalled by those assets. It is our richest historical document (Hoskins 1955, 14), a form of literature, and even in places a work of art (Farnworth *et al* forthcoming).

Only in our present interglacial, from around 8000BC, did rising sea levels leave Cornwall's shape like something we might recognise. Mesolithic people used its newly re-vegetated terrain with patches of birch in sparse grasslands in ways we feel we understand – hunting, fishing and gathering (Berridge and Roberts 1986; Smith 1987; Herring and Lewis 1992). We stretch ourselves if we try to imagine how they might have felt about a place that just 2,000 years later, but still in the Mesolithic period, had so radically changed that the resources available to the small nomadic bands had become as spectacular as those in Eden (Gearey *et al* 2000a; 2000b; Tinsley 2004-5; Straker 2011). Untamed ungulates grazed within what may have been wood pastures (Fig 3) rather than dense forest (Vera 2000), reaching onto downs in which only the highest hilltops remained completely open. Following the seasons, our gatherers and hunters knew their world intimately, recognising and responding to landmarks everywhere, increasingly exerting control over flora (burning) and probably also fauna (herding), stepping towards domestication and their own large-scale landscape change, but not rushing towards agriculture (despite knowing it thrived a boat trip away across the Channel; Jones and Quinnell, this volume).

They may not have practiced much the magic of sowing, tending and harvesting crops, except perhaps on significant hills like Roughtor (Fig 4), Stowe's Hill and Carn Brea (Herring 2008a) and in significant places. Early Neolithic charred cereal grains have been found at Penhale on the slopes beneath Carliquoiter Rock, a tor at the NW corner of the Hensbarrow uplands (OS first-inch drawing), now submerged by china-clay tips, and at a possibly 'liminal' coastal site, celebrating land, sea and air, at Portscatho (Jones and Reed 2006, 14). They may not have settled, but from the permanent monuments they created, early Neolithic people do seem to have

Fig 3. A form of wood pasture on Pendrift Common, Blisland. Some distant clumps of oaks, but also many growing in the open, their lower branches browsed by ungulates (now mainly domesticated cattle and ponies, and some wild deer). (Photograph: Peter Herring)

devoted themselves to particular parts of what is now Cornwall. Their quoits, large slabs covering built chambers, still intriguing landmarks, were perhaps designed to mimic the inherited and perplexing natural tors and draw meaning and social power from them (Bradley 1998). The effort required to hoist such slabs suggests communal organisation, while the placing of quoits just where favoured hills, usually with greater tors, like Carn Galva, come into view when approached (Kirkham 2011), may have allowed rituals and ceremonies to acknowledge tor-building predecessors (ancestors even) and confirm commitment to early territories. Early Neolithic pits,

some containing carefully considered placements of valued or meaningful artefacts, also seem to be concentrated near distinctive natural outcrops (Jones and Reed 2006).

Those significant and favoured hills, and several others, have early enclosures that should be of the early fourth millennium BC on analogy with excavated Carn Brea and Helman Tor and more roughly examined Trencrom (Jones and Quinnell, this volume). From their scale and distribution, they appear to have been the gathering places for peoples of larger territories. They crossed the thresholds of several openings or gateways to enter spaces possibly regarded as liminal, linking the mundane and the supernatural or mystifying (*ibid*). We may imagine them playing different roles in various business: settling disputes (perhaps over resources), exchanging goods and gossip, performing various rites of passage ceremonies, being initiated into and reinforcing the community's cosmologies, finding life partners, feasting and cementing commitment to people and place through the enjoyment of shared pleasures (Herring *et al* 2000, 115-6; Herring 2011a). All tor enclosure hills are eyecatching, dramatic even; their significance perhaps having Mesolithic roots if their tors were notable nodes in a networking landscape. The quoits themselves may have predecessors in the still uncertainly dated propped stones; the Leskernick alignment of long mound to propped stone to early fourth millennium midsummer sunset post-dates the propped stone itself, which could even be Mesolithic (Herring 1997).

A form of landscape design that incorporated acculturated 'natural' features and respected inherited creations into arrangements of 'monuments' remained important in later Neolithic and Early Bronze Age complexes. In worlds that would have been closely explored, certain places were clearly especially significant; communities repeatedly returned to them, often over long periods (covering many generations). We become less surprised that there are few isolated early prehistoric monuments when we appreciate that place was a crucial component in ritual and ceremony, and that the meanings attached to that place would be enhanced or adjusted on each return. Elements within complexes were often separate from each other, but were linked by an intervisibility that was often carefully emphasised.

Each of three straight lengths of broad stony bank, the Roughtor bank cairn (Fig 4), was aligned

Fig 4. Time Team's Francis Pryor and Tony Robinson converse upon an apparently Neolithic bank cairn on Roughtor while Phil Harding, Megan Val Baker and two others excavate an exploratory trench through it, establishing how carefully the two stone faces were constructed. Survey had previously established how the cairn, up to 7m wide and nearly 400m long, is made up of three straight lengths each slightly differently constructed, those further uphill probably attached to those downhill, and each apparently deliberately aligned on a different one of Roughtor's skylined cheesewrings, further emphasising the importance of the great hill and its tors. It also nicely illustrates how few monuments were individual and single-phased; most were elements within complexes that often included 'natural' features like the tors, and most were added to and adjusted over time. (Photograph: Peter Herring)

on a different skylined cheesewring (tor) on Roughtor's long back (Herring 2008a, 74; Herring and Kirkham forthcoming).

Most Cornish stone circles were placed south of a dominant hill (Tilley 1995). An exception is the Altarnun Nine Stones, but here on a clear day Lundy neatly sits in the northern notch where two hills meet (Mary Pearce, pers comm). Roger Farnworth suggests that on a clear night the stars would appear to rotate around the Pole Star set above that northern hill (or Lundy) (2007; Farnworth *et al* forthcoming).

Treen, Pennance and Trewey entrance graves were placed precisely where Gurnard's Head's topmost carn is seen poking above Zennor's coastal plateau rim (Herring 2011b, 85).

Moving along stone rows, significant hills and features were displayed at key points, recalling local attachments when returning to summer grazings (Tilley 1995; Herring 2008b).

Some large hilltop cairns, like the Brown Gelly and Carburrow Tor groups, mimic or frame significant distant views (Herring 2008a). Others are positioned precisely where significant distant features come into view, and still others are added to earlier complexes, renewing relevance and reinforcing commitment (Tilley 1995; Jones 2005).

Intriguing, even startling, in themselves, *en masse* these and other instances of landscape design suggest that monuments were placed and people lived within a world filled with memory and meaning.

Clearance of forest (or wood pasture) continued apace, including in the lowland parts that were to become Cornwall's Anciently Enclosed Land (Herring 1998; Jones and Quinnell, this volume).

The balance between gathering/hunting and agriculture was shifting so that by the mid second millennium BC most people probably belonged to communities practicing recognisable farming regimes (*ibid*; Nowakowski 1991; Herring 2008a). On Craddock Moor (Jones and Quinnell, this volume, fig 13) round houses are in yards within organically accretive patterns of curvilinear fields. Lanes deliberately shaped to double as livestock processing pens, lead to open moorland, a form of common beyond what appear to be arable and meadow fields. Other settlements, such as those lacking enclosures, may have been the homes of either special pastoralists or transhumants (Johnson and Rose 1994; Herring 2008a). Round houses may have been carefully located and designed to relate to the wider landscape. Doorways at Leskernick appear positioned so that an emerging person had a direct view to a significant hill or to features inherited from earlier periods, like cairns and stone circles (Bender *et al* 2007). All 107 houses on the long west side of Roughtor were carefully positioned so that the much earlier bank cairn was skylined to their north (Herring 2008a, 74). People not only knew how to obtain food from the Moor, but they also knew its history; they created places that reflected both forms of understanding; we may liken them to landscape archaeologists and farmers.

Revisions of field patterns and extents of commons around the turn of the first millennium BC saw upland commons extended and emptied of permanent settlement, while parts of coastal and lowland Cornwall were farmed more systematically or intensively, forging the fundamental division between Upland Rough Ground and the core farmland, or Anciently Enclosed Land, that then persisted for nearly three millennia. The change appears to reflect awareness, perception, or observation that the Cornish environment was under pressure from levels or methods of agricultural exploitation (Herring 2008a). Those deciding to change ways, knowing how the world worked at local to regional scale, may be likened to landscape ecologists, and even landscape planners.

Fig 5. The great north Cornish Iron Age gathering place at Warbstow Bury is positioned not on its hill's summit, but on a north-eastern spur, tilting views towards the lands of Ottery, Tamar and Dartmoor, presumably deliberate design allowing the gathered crowd to view the country, or territory that was most meaningful to them. This view from the inner enclosure's western bank shows another aspect of the landscape design: the complex was drawn just far enough up the hill to allow those who knew it to point out a key feature of the wider north Cornish landscape, the topmost tors of Roughtor (marked here with a bar). Flowering furze marks the Bury's middle and outer banks, the slighter middle one possibly a remnant from an earlier enclosure. It may have been its builders who first found the view to Roughtor sufficiently significant. (Photograph: Peter Herring)

Fig 6. Ancient semi-natural grassland on Shallow-Water Common, Blisland, established and maintained by thousands of years of summer grazing, including through the transhumance that linked together separate parts of a secure and stable Cornwall in later prehistoric and early medieval times. (Photograph: Peter Herring)

Responses to such pressures on resources may also have been one cause, later in the first millennium BC and early in the first millennium AD, of the enclosure of many but not all settlements by substantial banks and external ditches, as rounds. Hillforts, 'central communal places' (Quinnell 2004, 211-5) gathering places and perhaps the occasional courts of those who organised local society, were also established in prominent and significant places (Fig 5). The numerous less archaeologically visible unenclosed settlements suggest that this was an essentially peaceful time with much the same area of Cornwall under productive agriculture as in the eighteenth century AD. Mixing of rounds and open settlements within the same areas (e.g. Gossip forthcoming) hints that differentiation of settlement form reflected some other variable than defensive need, the most likely being status. 'Defences' may have been analogous to medieval crenellation, with the right or licence to erect such a distinctive and understandable display being in the gift of a widely respected local authority. If so they seem now as they may have seemed then to represent a landscape that contained, amongst other things, power and position. An interpretation of the dominant settlement form (virtually all households being grouped into small hamlets) and associated regular brick-shaped field systems (in which households' holdings may have been intermixed to share potential and risk, to share the good and the bad, in a way familiar from medieval arrangements), suggests that the land was also seen as shared, a communal space where households cooperated (Herring 2008a).

Adding to the sense of a stable society working a fully organised land is appreciation that the uplands continued to be used for summer grazing (Fig 6), with households split for half of the year as some of their members accompanied flocks and herds to the hills, milking them and processing the proceeds (Herring forthcoming b). Even with the newly recognised Restormel and Calstock forts, the Romans made little impact on Cornwall, life for most apparently continuing much as before, perhaps with local leaders now acting as clients or revenue-collectors for the new power (Quinnell 2004, 235).

So the basic rural pattern of settled areas, fields and commons, and even the highways and by-ways that linked and gave access to them, with which we are familiar, may not have been forged in the early and later medieval periods as Hoskins and his followers presumed, but rather were inherited from later prehistory (Fox 2006; Herring 2006). That does not mean there were no major changes in forms and in ways of being within Cornwall in the early

DISCOVERY AND RESEARCH

medieval period. Rounds do not appear to have been occupied after the sixth or perhaps seventh century and also from around that time the later prehistoric and Roman period field systems of much of Cornwall were dismantled, hedges thrown down, ditches infilled, to be replaced by more open fields, still with intermixing, but now with the shares of land held in the much more easily measurable or assessable strips (Herring 1999; 2006; see Fig 2). Whether such a radical overhaul, which included loss of that licence to enclose rounds, can be directly associated with the arrival of a new ideology (Christianity) is of course intriguing, but uncertain, though Cornwall was increasingly filled with other structures and symbols of Christianity (Herring 1999; Turner 2006; Preston-Jones, this volume). The new field systems were still located at hamlet level, within small estates, not villages within manors. They were similar in scale and form to the Irish townlands, and are typified by those whose names have the *tre* prefix ('farming estate; Padel 1985); they may be seen as *tre*-lands (Herring forthcoming b).

Such *tre*-lands often contained areas of common shared only by the households of the hamlet (Dudley 2011), but there were also larger commons, shared by groups of *tre*-lands, equivalents of multiple estates, and to these members of the household, probably the young women, continued to transhume (Herring

Fig 7. Restormel castle within Cornwall's largest medieval deerpark (made clearly visible by the relatively large size of the post disparkment fields, including the three squarish ploughed ones). Early parks like this one (extant by 1250 and possibly part of a single creation with the twelfth-century castle) and Pinsla (Herring this volume, Later medieval, fig 5) were carefully designed to take aesthetic advantage of Cornwall's topography. They were also filled with social and economic meaning, being among the first examples of private enclosure in countryside that was otherwise largely open. It was part of a trend of enclosure, privatisation and exclusion that increasingly affected Cornwall (and much of Britain) in the next several hundred years. (Photograph: Peter Herring)

2009; forthcoming, b). Emotions associated with taking responsibility for the household's livestock, feeling the excitement of summer freedom, moving back to a wilder world with landmarks either remembered from previous years or pointed out by more experienced girls, and then in the autumn returning to the security and comfort of home, may have been similar to those experienced by early Bronze Age people following stone rows.

Estate centres, hamlets, strip fields and commons, with churches, crosses and other Christian structures, continued to dominate the Cornish landscape in the later medieval period (Turner 2006). Norman families established the French castle as symbol of power, especially in the east, and lords increasingly arranged deliberately designed landscape around these places which rapidly became castle-esque country houses. Medieval deer parks (Fig 7), once seen as venison larders, are now accepted as early examples of ornamental landscape design (Herring 2003; and this volume).

Much elsewhere was made to be familiar and understandable, reflecting various aspects of a shared culture; places were designed so that local visitors would know how things worked, and what to do. This extended all the way from the landscape of the interior of a typical longhouse, in which spaces, openings, movement schemes, and fittings were nearly always arranged the same way (Austin and Thomas 1990), to the townplaces, field systems and commons of farmland, to the interiors of churches (whose design was not driven by liturgical needs alone; Orme 2007, 98), and to the layouts of Cornwall's 'street towns' (Kirkham and Cahill, this volume).

As climate improved slightly in the later medieval period (Bell and Walker 1992), uplands were partly resettled (still with hamlets and strip fields). Resources (metals, slate, stone, wool, fish, etc) were also increasingly exploited and Cornwall developed an unusually diversified economy (Hatcher 1969; Fox 1999) and a semi-industrial society and landscape (Austin *et al* 1989). Tinning (streamworking and early lode working) meant substantial alteration to landforms and its waste silted up previously navigable rivers, causing shifts in transport networks and towns as it did so. People may have started to identify themselves with their local towns, adding that to an already complex personal and communal identity, which would have included their family (or household), their hamlet, their 'manor', tithing

(upholding law and order), parish, kin network, friendship network and workplace community (Herring forthcoming c). There was and is variety across Cornwall in the materials and forms used in domestic, urban, ecclesiastical and military architecture, in proportions of arable, pasture, woodland and rough ground within *tre*-lands, and in other local styles (including those of stiles). These allow locales (similar to the French *pays*) to be identified that reflected local ways of being and doing, and these too would have contributed much to a person's sense of identity, making them of Penwith, or the Roseland, or Fawymore, or the Culm.

With towns so close together (rarely more than 10 miles apart, or a couple of hours walk away) and with Cornish life so commercialised, this was already, 700 years ago, an unusually richly diverse place.

Some farming hamlets on Bodmin Moor were abandoned later in the medieval period, and their well-preserved remains (Johnson and Rose 1994)

Fig 8. The medieval hamlet at Garrow, St Breward shrank to a single seventeenth-century farmhouse, its kitchen fireplace fuelled by turf and furze. (Photograph: Peter Herring)

Fig 9. Cotehele Quay, with ferry slip and hand winch, on the tidal Tamar, part of the enhancement of Cornwall's transport infrastructure that oiled a range of industries which directly and indirectly transformed Cornwall's modern landscape. (Photograph: Peter Herring)

suggest original forms of the longhouse farmsteads and fields that preceded today's lowland farms, still often discernibly medieval, but so different now in the way they are firmly enclosed. Enclosure was a fairly universal force in later medieval and early post-medieval Cornwall. What was open, public and shared, or communal, became increasingly closed and private, and individual.

- Houses were divided into rooms, making space either public (where guests were entertained) or private (where they were less welcome, and where owned goods were stored) (Herring and Berry 1997)
- Fields were privatised when individual strips were either hedged in separately or exchanged so that bundles could be enclosed, creating the roughly rectangular fields we know today (Herring 2006)
- Commons were divided by stock-proof walls defining individual holdings of rough ground, or enclosed into smaller parcels as crofts (Dudley 2011)
- Hunting grounds, once ranging widely as open chases or forest, were enclosed as parks, keeping deer in and the public out (Herring 2003)
- Churches had screens inserted from the fourteenth century to separate the chancel (and priest) from the nave (and people) (Orme 2007, 98)
- Market places were partly rationalised, with many functions brought indoors into market houses (Kirkham and Cahill, this volume).

With separation of individuals from the formerly cooperative community, there was greater opportunity for some to grow and others to fail. From the fourteenth century onwards we see some Cornish yeomen farmers absorbing the lands of their former fellows and hamlets shrinking (Fig 8), often to the single farmsteads that are now so familiar they seem to some to be Cornwall's traditional settlement form (Herring 2006).

Post-medieval Cornwall developed from that already diverse medieval world. Its position in relation to the English nation, at the mouths of two great shipping channels, meant it became ever more commercialised (with coastal towns especially thriving) and increasingly heavily defended, fringed with breastworks and bristling with artillery forts and batteries representing and symbolising England more than Cornwall (Johnson, this volume).

A series of overlapping industrial surges swept over the granite-edge parts of post-medieval Cornwall: copper, lead, iron and arsenic being sought as well as tin (Sharpe, this volume); china clay and china stone (Smith 1992) as well as granite (Stanier 1999) and roofing slate; wool, fruit, flowers, potatoes, fish, dairy products as supplements to the traditional meat and grain. In a wage and tribute economy, working people were mobile, and numerous settlements developed to accommodate them, some being swollen older ones, some being wholly new (Kirkham and Cahill, this volume). New fields and smallholdings, with smaller simpler buildings and ruler-straight boundaries were cut out of the shrinking commons to intensify food production (and increase the lords' return from their land). This is the Recently Enclosed Land (Herring 1998; Turner 2007) that still contrasts so markedly with the irregular hamlets, mellow farmhouses, large buildings, sinuous-sided fields

Fig 10. Twenty-first-century rural landscape: large areas of ploughing (farmers no longer practice convertible husbandry), prefab farm buildings, campsites and in the distance a swollen hamlet and a modern brewery. The past still governs much of Cornwall; those features are attached to and reinforce the impact of earlier settlements and in this part of St Minver the local landmark is that seventeenth-century windmill tower; the early medieval boundary of Trevelver's tre-land curves round the hilltop on which it stands. Marshy land at the head of a stream on the right still supports willow; roads follow routes established for flocks and wagons; and tractor-drivers negotiate kinks and corners left when medieval fields were amalgamated. The brewery is at Pityme, an ironic name given by the post-medieval settlers who formed those distinctively straight-sided fields. (Photograph: Peter Herring)

DISCOVERY AND RESEARCH

*Fig 11. The Square, St Columb
Major, a once busier commercial
space, typical of the centres of
many Cornish market towns.*
(Photograph: Peter Herring)

with ancient trees and oft-repaired hedges of the Anciently Enclosed Land.

The frugality and thrift that uncertain futures fomented in these industrial and rural communities was made spiritual in the nonconformist Christianity that was itself made concrete in the hundreds of solid chapels (Lake *et al* 2001). Meanwhile industrialists grew rich, displaying their status and taste in great Georgian and Victorian country houses set within ornamental parklands, often some distance from the noisy, dusty and dangerous sources of their wealth (Petts 1999). More of our transport network was set up to meet the needs of industry (Fig 9) – the few canals were replaced and extended by railways that themselves stimulated further economic development, including that associated with those who could more easily come to enjoy the landscape that 6,000 years of change had created.

Competition from cheaper imports led to serious declines in Cornish copper and tin mining in the 1860s and 1880s respectively, and while quarrying and china-clay working continued through the twentieth century, these too have consolidated so that now only the St Austell china-clay area survives as an extensive industrialised landscape. Elsewhere active pits and quarries are as scattered as the edge of town industrial estates that grew through the last century.

Rural Cornwall is now widely seen as countryside, a place viewed and valued in relation to the urban places where most people work and an increasing proportion live (Figs 10 and 11). Parts of rural Cornwall have a declining permanent population

as many houses, especially near the coasts, are used for holidaying. Since the Second World War, the land itself has generally been used increasingly intensively, and in increasingly specialised ways. There were several later twentieth-century decades of major reorganisation of many farms with hedges removed to enlarge fields, marshes drained, scrub cleared. Many farms were indeed amalgamated with neighbours, their buildings becoming redundant. Many have been converted into dwellings.

At the same time, and partly in response to those trends there has been a significant development of sustainable land management, at first confined to the works of bodies like the National Trust, but increasingly, and partly through adjustments to agricultural support, but partly by the development of new markets, by the farming community at large. Much of this is led by natural environment initiatives, but thoughtful management of landscape and the historic environment have also become increasingly well established as drivers for such change.

References

Austin, D, Gerrard, G A M, and Greeves, T A P, 1989. Tin and agriculture in the Middle Ages and beyond: landscape archaeology in St Neot Parish, Cornwall, *Cornish Archaeol*, **28,** 7–251

Austin, D, and Thomas, J, 1990. The 'proper study' of medieval archaeology: a case study, in D Austin, and L Alcock, eds, *From the Baltic to the Black Sea: studies in medieval archaeology*, London, 43-78

Bell, M G, and Walker, M, 1992. *Late Quaternary environmental change: physical and human perspectives*, Harlow

Bender, B, Hamilton, S, and Tilley, C, 2007. *Stone worlds, narrative and reflexivity in landscape archaeology*, Walnut Creek, California

Berridge, P, and Roberts, A, 1986. The Mesolithic period in Cornwall, *Cornish Archaeol*, **25**, 7-34

Bradley, R, 1998. Ruined buildings, ruined stones: enclosures, tombs and natural places in the Neolithic of south-west England, *World Archaeol*, **30**, 13-22

Council of Europe, 2000. *European Landscape Convention, European Treaty Series, no.176*, Florence, Council of Europe

Dudley, P, 2011. *Goon, hal, cliff and croft, west Cornwall's rough ground*, Truro (Cornwall Council)

Fairclough, G, 2006. Our place in the landscape? An archaeologist's ideology of landscape perception and management, in T Meier, ed, *Landscape ideologies, Archaeolingua, Series Minor,* **22**, 177-197

Farnworth, R, 2007. Sightlines to the tors and stars, *Meyn Mamvro*, **63**, 10-13

Farnworth, R, Herring, P, and Tapper, B, forthcoming. The focus on Rough Tor and Stowe's Pound in the Neolithic and Early Bronze Age, *Cornish Archaeol*

Fox, H, 1999. Medieval urban development, in R Kain, and W Ravenhill, eds, *Historic atlas of South-West England*, Exeter, 400-7

Fox, H, 2006. Foreword, in S Turner, ed, *Medieval Devon and Cornwall*, Macclesfield, xi-xvi

Gearey, B R, Sharman, D J, and Kent, M, 2000a. Palaeoecological evidence for the prehistoric settlement of Bodmin Moor, Cornwall, south-west England: Part I – the status of woodland and early human impacts, *J Archaeol Sci*, **27**, 423-438

Gearey, B R, Sharman, D J, and Kent, M, 2000b. Palaeoecological evidence for the prehistoric settlement of Bodmin Moor, Cornwall, south-west England: Part II – land-use changes from the Neolithic to the present, *J Archaeol Sci*, **27**, 493-508

Gossip, J, forthcoming. Life outside the round: Bronze Age and Iron Age settlement at Higher Besore and Truro College, Threemilestone, Truro, *Cornish Archaeol*

Hatcher, J, 1969. A diversified economy: later medieval Cornwall, *Econ Hist Rev*, **22**, 208-227

Herring, P, 1997. Early prehistoric sites at Leskernick, Altarnun, *Cornish Archaeol* **36**, 176-185

Herring, P, 1998. *Cornwall's historic landscape, presenting a method of historic landscape character assessment*, Truro (Cornwall County Council)

Herring, P, 1999. Farming and transhumance in Cornwall at the turn of the first millennium AD, part 2, *Cornwall Assoc Local Historians*, Autumn 1999, 3-8

Herring, P, 2003. Cornish medieval deer parks, in R Wilson-North, ed, *The lie of the land, aspects of the archaeology and history of the designed landscape in the South West of England*, Exeter, 34-50

Herring, P, 2006. Cornish strip fields, in S Turner, ed, *Medieval Devon and Cornwall*, Macclesfield, 44-77

Herring, P, 2008a. Commons, fields and communities in prehistoric Cornwall, in A Chadwick, ed, *Recent approaches to the archaeology of land allotment*, Brit Arch Repts, Int Ser, **1875,** Oxford, 70-95

Herring, P, 2008b. Stepping onto the commons: south-western stone rows, in P Rainbird, ed, *Monuments in the landscape*, Stroud, 79-88

Herring, P, 2009. Early medieval transhumance in Cornwall, Great Britain, in J. Klapste, ed, *Medieval rural settlement in marginal landscapes, Ruralia VII,* Turnhout, Belgium, Brepols, 47-56

Herring, P, 2011a. Hilltop enclosures, in Dudley 2011, 84-86

Herring, P, 2011b. Chambered tombs, in Dudley 2011, 86-89

Herring, P, forthcoming a. The past informs the future; landscape archaeology and historic landscape characterisation, in S Kluiving, and E Guttmann, eds *Proceedings of Landscape Archaeology Conference 2010*, Amsterdam

Herring, P, forthcoming b. Shadows of ghosts: early medieval transhumants in Cornwall, in R Silvester, and S Turner, eds, *Papers in memory of Harold Fox*, Leicester, Medieval Settlement Research Group

Herring, P, forthcoming c. Multiple identities in Cornwall, in S Pearce, ed, *The archaeology of south western Britain: recent research*

Herring, P, and Berry, E, 1997. Stonaford, *Cornish Archaeol*, **36**, 151-175

Herring, P, and Kirkham, G, forthcoming. A bank cairn on Roughtor, *Cornish Archaeol*

Herring, P, and Lewis, B, 1992. Ploughing up gatherer-hunters: Mesolithic and later flints from Butterstor and elsewhere on Bodmin Moor, *Cornish Archaeol*, **31**, 1-14

Herring, P, Thorpe, C, Quinnell, H, Reynolds, A, and Allen, J, 2000. *St Michael's Mount archaeological Works 1995-98*, Truro (Cornwall County Council)

Hoskins, W G, 1955. *The making of the English landscape*, London

Johnson, N, and Rose, P, 1994. *Bodmin Moor, an archaeological survey Volume 1: the human landscape to c 1800*, London

Jones, A M, 2005. *Cornish Bronze Age ceremonial landscapes c 2500-1500BC*, Brit Arch Repts, Brit Ser, **394**, Oxford

Jones, A M, and Reed S J, 2006. By land, sea and air: an Early Neolithic pit group at Portscatho, Cornwall and consideration of coastal activity during the Neolithic, *Cornish Archaeol*, **45**, 1-30

Kirkham, G, 2005. *Boscastle, Cornwall - characterisation and recording in the aftermath of the August 2004 floods*, Truro (Historic Environment Service, Cornwall County Council)

Kirkham, G, 2011. Something different at the Land's End, in A M Jones, and G Kirkham, eds, *Beyond the core: reflections on regionality in prehistory*, Oxford

Lake, J, Cox, J, and Berry, E, 2001. *Diversity and vitality - the Methodist and Non-Conformist chapels of Cornwall*, Truro (Cornwall County Council)

Nowakowski, J, 1991. Trethellan Farm, Newquay: the excavation of a lowland Bronze Age settlement and Iron Age cemetery, *Cornish Archaeol*, **30**, 5-242

Orme, N, 2007. *Cornwall and the Cross: Christianity 500-1560*, Chichester

Padel, O J, 1985. *Cornish place-name elements,* Nottingham, English Place-Name Society, Vol LVI/LVII

DISCOVERY AND RESEARCH

Petts, D E, 1999. *Cornwall's parks and gardens*, Penzance

Quinnell, H, 2004. *Trethurgy, excavations at Trethurgy Round, St Austell: community and status in Roman and post-Roman Cornwall,* Truro (Cornwall County Council)

Smith, G, 1987. The Lizard project: landscape survey 1978-1983, *Cornish Archaeol*, **26,** 13-68

Smith, J R, 1992. *Cornwall's china-clay heritage*, Truro (Twelveheads Press)

Stanier, P, 1999. *South West granite, a history of the granite industry in Cornwall and Devon*, St Austell (Cornish Hillside Publications)

Straker, V, 2011. A review of the palaeo-environmental literature review, in Dudley 2011, 66-71

Tilley, C, 1995. Rocks as resources: landscapes and power, *Cornish Archaeol*, **34,** 5-57

Tinsley, H, 2004-5. Pollen analysis, in A M Jones, Settlement and ceremony: archaeological investigations at Stannon Down, St Breward, Cornwall, *Cornish Archaeol*, **43-44,** 48-70

Turner, S, 2006. *Making a Christian landscape, the countryside in early medieval Cornwall, Devon and Wessex*, Exeter

Turner, S, 2007. Fields, farms and agricultural innovation in late medieval and early modern south-west England, in J Finch, and K Giles, eds, *Estate landscapes: design improvement and power in the post-medieval landscape*, Woodbridge, 57-74

Vera, F, 2000. *Grazing ecology and forest history*, Hungerford

Wylie, J, 2007. *Landscape*, London

Cornish Archaeology 50, 2011, 175–186

Science and archaeology

VANESSA STRAKER

Introduction

The application of scientific techniques to address archaeological research questions has increased greatly in scope in the last 25 years. The principal techniques can be grouped into five subject areas:

- Geophysical survey
- Environmental archaeology
- Scientific dating
- Ancient technology
- Applied techniques

It would be misleading to give the impression that few scientific techniques were used prior to 1985. To take the largest subject area, Environmental Archaeology, Bell's 1984 review identified some 40 sites that had received some form of analysis and of these 20 were considered as major studies. Cornwall benefited from the early attentions of several leading scholars, including John Evans, who pioneered the study of molluscs on archaeological sites and Geoffrey Dimbleby, who did the same for soil pollen analysis and studied soils beneath barrows such as Wilsey Down and Otterham (Dimbleby 1964) and buried deposits at Carn Euny (Dimbleby 1978). Ian Cornwall, a leading early figure in archaeological soil science, worked with Dimbleby at Carn Euny. The value of pollen analysis on upland mires was also recognised early and the work of Connolly, Godwin and Megaw (1950) and Brown (1977) on Bodmin Moor resulted in a broad understanding of Holocene (the recent period since *c* 10,000 cal

BC) vegetation development and change. Brown's study at Hawk's Tor was supported by radiocarbon dates, and with a late glacial origin it is still one of the very few long pollen sequences in south-west England to cover the late glacial and Holocene periods. Miles' (1975) excavation of five barrows on the St Austell granite is still a seminal piece of work and was supported by the scientists of the Ancient Monuments Laboratory of the Department of the Environment, later to become English Heritage. The early clearance of oak-hazel woodland to be replaced by grass and heather heath was noted in pollen analysis of soils beneath the barrows and in ditch silting (Bayley 1975). Caseldine (1980) published a useful synthesis of the evidence for environmental change in Cornwall and Maltby and Caseldine (1984) drew on this and their work at Colliford to write on prehistoric soils and vegetation on Bodmin Moor.

The last 25 years
Geophysical survey

The application of geophysical survey techniques is, where soil conditions permit, a routine first stage in understanding archaeological potential. Geophysical survey is reviewed by Peter Rose (this volume, above) and is not considered further here.

Environmental Archaeology

Broadly defined as the study of past human economy and environment, Environmental Archaeology

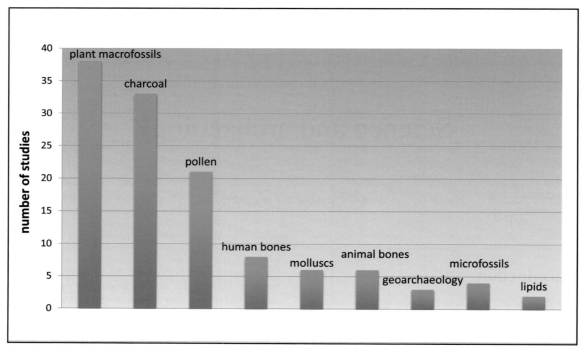

Fig 1. 1985-2010 Graph showing the number of studies using scientific techniques in the last 25 years.

uses earth and life sciences to study ecological, cultural, economic, and climate change. Figure 1 shows the range of techniques that have been used in Cornwall since *c* 1985. Most studies cover phases or sites of Neolithic – Iron Age date, with the majority being middle – late Bronze Age (Figure 2). Although a range of techniques has been used, most common were charred plant macrofossils (fruits, seeds), charcoal and pollen which reflects the soil preservations conditions and lack of settlement sites with waterlogged preservation.

This brief review summarises new information on the use of pollen and plant macrofossils to study vegetation history and change, the environmental setting of sites, the evidence for agriculture and the use of plant and animal resources.

Detailed summaries of the development of Cornwall's vegetation can be found in the period chapters (Palaeolithic and Mesolithic, Neolithic and early Bronze Age, Later Bronze Age and Iron Age, Romano-British, early medieval, post conquest medieval) within the South West Archaeological Research Framework (Webster 2008).

The early studies noted above established a basic vegetation sequence for upland Cornwall with oak-hazel dominated woodland established by the mid-Holocene. The lack of major peaks in pine pollen left open the question that the most exposed locations may have remained open moorland and that still remains a possibility. There was little detailed information on local conditions, setting of sites and dating resolution needed improvement. Furthermore, there was little or no information for much of central and west Cornwall.

Recent studies on Bodmin Moor have concentrated mainly on the Stannon-Rough Tor area (Figure 3) and Tresellern Marsh on east moor and the De Lank Valley. The results have added much detail to the general picture, describing well-dated vegetation changes and clearance episodes. For example, permanent grassland was established in the early Bronze Age after 2020-1760 cal BC (SUERC -3624) at Stannon (Tinsley 2004-5) and as at Rough Tor (Gearey, 1996; Gearey and Charman 1996; Gearey *et al* 2000b) grazing was intense in the middle Bronze Age with pasture in much of the

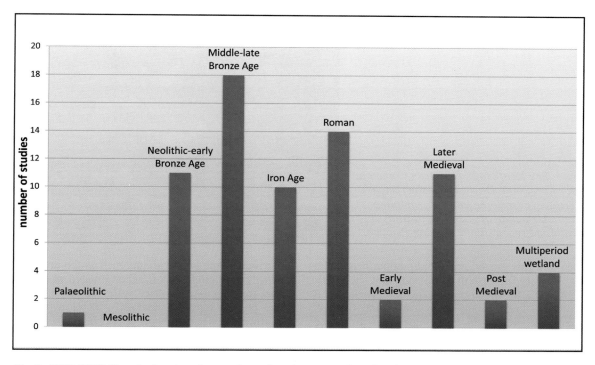

Fig 2. 1985-2010 Graph showing the number of environmental studies by period.

area and a little surviving woodland. Acid grassland and heath plants demonstrate soil deterioration and heath development from the early Bronze Age in places, but the main increase in heathers and woody heath plants such as gorse, evident from pollen and charcoal, is late prehistoric (especially Iron Age) and could result from all or a combination of increased soil acidification, reduced grazing and the

Fig 3. Stannon, 1998. Sampling with small monolith and Kubiena tins for pollen and soil analyses. (Photograph: Vanessa Straker)

use of fire to manage the balance of heather/grass moorland. Conclusive evidence for cereal cultivation in the mid-late second millennium BC is only clear from the more sheltered De Lank Valley (Jones and Tinsley 2000-1) and Tresellern Marsh (Gearey and Charman 1996; Gearey *et al* 2000a).

Heathland vegetation development in West Cornwall has been the focus of a recent study, the Heath Project (Robinson *et al* 2011; Straker 2011a; 2011b; Figures 4 and 5). Existing work was summarised and new studies undertaken to try to fill in gaps from Penwith and Carnmenellis with some interesting results including a late glacial sequence on Carnmenellis, a rare find for Cornwall. For the mid - late Holocene, in contrast to the Lizard where heath and heather heathland predated barrow construction, Penwith shows a very varied vegetation cover with oak-hazel woodland at Chysauster in the early Bronze Age. At Treen Common, some Neolithic arable farming is likely, followed by (possibly very local) renewed woodland growth (hazel, with birch, oak and willow) by the early Bronze Age. Further clearance is not recorded here until the early –middle Iron Age when from

DISCOVERY AND RESEARCH

Fig 4. The Heath project - Treen Common, February 2006. David Robinson (English Heritage) describing and sub-sampling a core for pollen assessment, to study heathland vegetation history on Penwith.
(Photograph: Vanessa Straker)

then onwards grazed grassland predominates with a temporary increase in woodland plants in *c* 900-1000 AD after which cereals and other agricultural indicators are present. Cross-leaved and Cornish heath are present in small quantities from the Neolithic. Both, but the Cornish heath in particular, expand in the early medieval period, probably when grazing pressure reduces. The pollen flora from a soil beneath a Romano-British boundary wall at Foage, Zennor, suggested largely herbaceous grassland with plants such as bedstraw, scabious, plantains, meadowsweet, tormentil and buttercups, with plants of the daisy, campion and cow parsley families among the grasses (Herring *et al* 1993).

Further evidence from other Penwith sites is now needed to better understand the chronology and variability of landuse change and vegetation development.

The other main area of new knowledge comes from coastal and intertidal sites. The west Cornwall studies are summarised briefly in Straker (2011a). Sites include Porthleven (Tinsley 1999a), Marazion Marsh (Healy 1993, 1995, 1996, 1999), Chyandour (James and Guttman 1992), Porthallow (Tinsley 1999b) and Church Cove, Gunwalloe (French 1996). Small coastal wetlands formed in valleys draining into the sea at many locations around the coast. The earliest date is on Mesolithic alder wood from Porthallow (early-mid sixth millennium BC) with the basal deposits at Marazion Marsh *c* 1000 years later. These developed directly or indirectly as a result of groundwater levels controlled by sea-level change. The wetland vegetation supported a rich tree and ground flora, principally of alder fen

carr with some local variants such as the inclusion of willow or birch. Oak-hazel dominated woodland was frequent on the drier valley slopes and hill and plateau tops. By analogy with elsewhere in Cornwall, this had probably developed by the eighth millennium BC.

On the Isles of Scilly a programme of recording and sampling intertidal and cliff sites was carried out from 1989 to 1993 (Ratcliffe and Straker 1996). Pollen and plant macrofossil evidence from earlier studies was summarised and new assessments demonstrated the potential for further analysis on intertidal deposits of late Mesolithic and later date on St Mary's, St Martin's and Tresco. The basic terrestrial vegetation sequence, showing development of oak-hazel woodland by the late Mesolithic with birch a major component of the Neolithic woodland, had been published by Scaife (1984) from Higher and Lower Moors. In this part of St Mary's the main phase of woodland clearance appeared to date to the latter half of the first millennium BC; elsewhere on Scilly a largely treeless environment is likely by the late Iron Age. The Lyonesse project, reported on by Johns (this volume) describes the new work that is taking place on both intertidal and sub tidal deposits and refining knowledge of sea level change and vegetation.

Vegetation in the historic period has been less well studied, but there have been some advances. With better dating resolution and a greater number of studies on Bodmin Moor and in central Cornwall, we are starting to appreciate that landuse and vegetation development was variable and locally distinctive. Ground clearance before extension of a

Fig 5. The Heath project - Treen Common, April 2006. David Robinson and Zoë Hazell (English Heritage) sampling peat for plant macrofossil analysis and radiocarbon dating. (Photograph: Vanessa Straker)

China Clay tip prompted analysis of soils beneath Cornish hedges. Although not independently dated, the hedges are thought to be medieval and the pre-enclosure landscape of open acid grass-heathland also included local hazel stands with alder on wetter soils and oak woodland with hornbeam and beech at some distance (Tinsley 1999c). Whether due to careful husbanding of a valuable resource or regeneration, local woodland stands are also evident on Bodmin, for example at Colliford (Maltby and Caseldine 1984), Stuffle (Walker 1989) and in the Rough Tor area (Gearey *et al* 1997; 2000b). At Rough Tor the mid-late prehistoric grass-heathland was replaced locally by species rich grassland similar to an old meadow flora. It may have lasted for up to 1000 years from the first to fourth centuries AD and been managed by light grazing with the possibility of a hay crop.

The killas and particularly the granite-derived soils in much of the county are acidic and bone (and shell) survival is poor or non-existent. They survive best on coastal sites where soils are enriched by blown shell-rich sand or in deeply stratified or urban sites. However, the only site in the latter category is the medieval castle at Launceston. As a result, as Figure 1 shows, there is now a reasonable body of information derived from charred remains of fruits, seeds and charcoal, whereas evidence of past animal husbandry and exploitation of wild animals is still slight. It is ironic that away from sand-enriched coastal soils, bones do not survive and thus

we have very little information on what must have been a major occupation for much of the population. Indirect evidence such as dairy fats in ceramics and landscape features interpreted as cattle pens are cited, but direct evidence is scarce.

Compared with the early 1980s, there is now a much better understanding of plant use and local environments based on studies of charred macrofossils, charcoal and pollen. For the recovery of the remains of crops, crop weeds and other wild plants, compared with some other counties, Cornwall has benefitted from comprehensive sampling strategies that have consistently used similar sample sizes and processing techniques on around 38 sites. This allows valid comparison between assemblages and periods. As well as many small projects, there have been several large-scale development-led projects in recent years, with assemblages recovered from features of many periods. These include Scarcewater (Jones and Taylor 2010), Tremough (Gossip and Jones 2007), Nancemere (Gossip forthcoming a) and Richard Lander School (Higher Besore) and Truro College (Gossip forthcoming b).

Prehistoric arable crops included emmer wheat and hulled barley in the Neolithic, with spelt wheat and celtic beans from the Middle Bronze Age and hulled and naked barley. These were supplemented by wild plants especially hazelnuts with fruits such as sloe (blackthorn) and crab apple. Oats (wild and domesticated species) tolerate poor soils and exposed conditions and wild oats are found occasionally from the Bronze Age. They become common from the Roman period onwards and are also thought to have been an important crop probably for both human and animal use. Nutritious tuberous roots of some plants (e.g. pignut) may also have been consumed though those that survive were probably components of turf (see below). The weeds include typical arable or disturbed ground species such as black bindweed, vetches, field madder, cleavers and others, but seeds of grassland and pasture such as buttercups, clover, plantains, self heal are always present too. Chaff remains are usually sparse and the grain, chaff and arable weeds are usually interpreted as crop cleaning waste from cultivation on a small scale or of crops brought in from elsewhere.

The plant food record for the Neolithic and early Bronze Age is improving with small assemblages from a growing number of features, some on multi-period sites. Examples include early Neolithic pits at Portscatho, containing charred emmer and barley grains with vetch, cleavers and hazelnuts (J Jones 2006), and Tremough. Here, Carruthers (2007) found hazelnut shells in both early and late Neolithic pits; however, in some of the later pits cereal grains were present. As well as arable, wild fruits and seeds suggested a damp fairly open grassland habitat, which had probably been disturbed or grazed.

On Scilly, the earliest direct evidence for arable comes from a cache of early Bronze Age naked barley at East Porth, Samson (Ratcliffe and Straker 1996).

Sites with good assemblages of arable crops and crop processing waste are rare, the most notable being the middle Bronze Age coastal settlement at Trethellan Farm, Newquay where the principal crop grown was naked barley (Straker 1991). Barley was also the main crop at Tremough (Carruthers 2007). There are few, if any, other assemblages from prehistoric or Romano-British settlements with clear evidence of arable farming on a reasonable scale. The growth or collection of plants in the cabbage family (*Brassica* or *Sinapis or Sisymbrium* sp.) for their oil content is a possibility at Trethellan, Tremough and Truro College (Carruthers forthcoming).

Very large numbers of samples were processed from the early and late Bronze Age and late Iron Age settlements at the Truro College (Carruthers forthcoming) and Higher Besore (J Jones forthcoming) sites. In both locations, macrofossil density was low but survival was better in the later prehistoric contexts on the Truro college sites giving further confirmation of the consumption of emmer and spelt wheats, with hulled barley that would have been useful as a human or animal foodstuff. As with earlier periods, wild plant foods such as tubers, nuts and fruits including elderberry supplemented crops in a system where rearing livestock was probably the main occupation. The few arable weeds such as brome and corn spurrey, typical of acid soils, were outnumbered by grasses and grassland weeds. Carruthers (forthcoming) speculates on a possible origin in burnt hay, or as a result of arable cultivation in fields not long ploughed from grassland. The well-sampled middle Bronze Age to Romano-British phases at Scarcewater produced broadly similar remains with the exception of a single stone-lined Romano-British cist. This contained several hundred grains of hulled wheat, oats and some barley, spelt chaff and many arable and grassland weeds (J Jones 2010). Their relationship with the cist is not clear.

In summary, the evidence suggests that husbandry of grazing animals predominated, with arable concentrated mainly on areas where soils were more favourable, such as the coastal fringes. This pattern is typical at least for much of later prehistoric and Roman Cornwall.

Our knowledge of crop history and plant use for the early and later medieval periods is also scarce, most coming from the late Roman to early medieval contexts at Tintagel Churchyard and Island (Straker 1992; 1997; 2007). Wheat, barley and especially oats were consumed, but details of their cultivation are few and they may well have been grown elsewhere and brought on to the island. Local vegetation was largely open with rough grassland and some scrub, identified from charcoal (Gale and Straker, 1997; Gale in Straker, 2007).

Charcoal has been studied, principally by Rowena Gale, from some 30 sites and complements the information gained from pollen and plant macrofossils. Typically oak and hazel predominate but there is also a wide range of other species, especially in later periods. An early example of woodland management comes from Lower Boscasawell early Bronze Age burnt mound and associated pits. The fast-grown roundwood typical of managed woodland is mainly oak, hazel and willow/poplar but there is also Pomoidae (includes hawthorn type), birch, ash, gorse/broom and blackthorn (Gale 2006).

Burning of turf for fuel is suggested by burnt tuberous roots of plants such as pignut and lesser celandine in rough ground and grassland assemblages. Examples include Stencoose (de Moulins 2000-1), Trenoweth and Tremough (Carruthers 2006; 2007).

As well as for food, fuel and construction, wild plants were used for many other purposes. Charred remains of, for example bracken, sedges, gorse and heathers have a likely origin as animal bedding, fodder and thatch. Many other plants would have been used for medicines and a wide range of raw materials. However, at present direct evidence is sparse with no studies of macrofossils from settlement and occupation sites with waterlogged or anoxic preservation. Charring tends to favour the preservation of cereal grains, crop processing waste (chaff and weed seeds), wood and other accidentally burnt domestic waste.

Unsurprisingly, most bone and shell assemblages have been recovered from Scilly from Bronze Age to medieval settlement sites at over 20 locations but the most substantial groups are from Halangy Down, Nornour and Tean. Much of the work was by the late Dr Frank Turk. The studies are summarised in Ratcliffe and Straker (1996). Early Scillonians were practising an integrated 'land-sea' economy raising crops and domestic mammals, hunting deer, catching birds and a wide range of inshore and offshore fish and collecting shellfish such as scallops, mussels, cockles and limpets. The limpets may have been eaten occasionally and used for bait. Cattle, sheep and pig are the main domestic mammals with occasional horse, goat, dog and cat. Marine mammals – whale, seal, dolphin and porpoise - were also exploited. The red and occasional roe deer are likely to have been transported to the island by boat, as were the domestic mammals. Several species of small mammal (Pallas's vole, the Lesser white-toothed (Scilly) shrew and the woodmouse) occur in deposits of Bronze Age and later date and discussion centred around whether they had been introduced or whether Pallas's vole and possibly the Scilly shrew survived as relicts of early postglacial populations. No firm conclusion has been reached. The bird bones are of residents, migrants and birds in passage; however a third are seabirds, emphasising their importance as a food resource. Of the impressive list of about 50 identified species, 12 are not found on the islands today. These include scaup, long-tailed duck, bean and brent geese, stone curlew, great auk, partridge,

barn owl, white stork, corn bunting, corncrake and a possible bittern. Rising sea levels and loss of freshwater, arable and woodland habitats will have been contributory factors.

On the Cornish mainland, recent publications include bone assemblages from old excavations, notably Gwithian, Trevelgue Head and Launceston Castle. Studies at Atlantic Road, Newquay and Duckpool, Morwenstow are the principal recent projects.

The main glimpse of Bronze Age animal husbandry comes from Gwithian where farming, fishing and hunting were part of life in the second millennium BC (Hammon, 2004, 2006, Nowakowski et al 2007). Bones of cattle, sheep/ goat, roe and red deer, dog, fish and a single whale bone survive. As well as arable and pasture, access to rougher and wooded or scrub vegetation is evident from wood charcoal of a range of species which would have provided forage and cover for pigs and red deer as well as fuel and building material. Crop remains themselves are sparse.

Trevelgue provides insight into Iron Age and Romano-British animal husbandry and exploitation of wild species (Hammon 2011). Further Roman data comes from Duckpool (Powell and Serjeantson 1995) and Atlantic Road (Ingrems forthcoming). At Trevelgue animals had many uses. Cattle were kept for meat, milk, traction and other by-products. The Iron Age cattle were a little smaller than their Romano-British counterparts, consistent with breed improvement by the Romans. Sheep (mainly) and goats were less numerous and provided meat, milk and wool. Horse may also have been eaten. Pigs and red deer imply that woodland was not far away and a single stingray suggests inshore fishing. The wild fauna from Atlantic Road included pine marten, badger and goose and fish (wrasse species).

In contrast, sheep were more important than cattle at Duckpool and in both the early and late Roman phases at Atlantic Road, though because of their large size, most meat consumption was probably beef. There was increasing demand for sheep's wool and milk in the later phase at both sites. The sheep at Trevelgue were larger than the contemporary Atlantic Road and Duckpool specimens. This poses the interesting possibility of the presence of two types or 'breeds'; a research question for future projects where bone survives.

The most comprehensive study of animal bones

DISCOVERY AND RESEARCH

is from Launceston Castle, covering the eleventh to twentieth, but principally the late thirteenth to mid nineteenth centuries (Albarella and Davis 1996). Cattle, sheep, pig and a wide variety of other mammals, birds and fish are represented. The authors comment that the assemblages from the late thirteenth and fifteenth centuries are similar to those from other castles while after a transitional phase, from the mid-seventeenth century onwards they resemble 'urban' assemblages in general. High status medieval feasting is attested by the wide range of species (e.g. red, roe and fallow deer, hare, a variety of fish, cetaceans, woodcock, plover, partridge, crane, gannet, swan, puffin, heron) in food debris with numerous hind limb bones of deer representing the remains of haunches. The decline of the castle's status in recent centuries is reflected in the range of the fauna. In common with elsewhere in England, the reduced importance of pig compared with cattle and sheep in the late medieval period is evident and thought to result from reduction of woodland providing pannage (Grant 1988). Increases in the size of pigs, sheep and cattle in the later phases are suggested to result from agricultural improvements started in Elizabethan times.

There are no studies of deeply stratified or anoxic medieval and later urban deposits from the county. Elsewhere these deposits preserve fish and mammal bone, insects and charred and waterlogged plant remains. This allows an insight into urban living conditions and the rural markets supplying the towns.

Marine and terrestrial snails from sands or sandy soils give detailed local information. On Constantine Island, open grassland established in the late Neolithic to early Bronze Age was grazed shortly before cairn construction (Walker 2008). Recent assessment of snails in 'layer 4' at Gwithian has shown that there were cultivated plots as well areas of scrub or woodland in the middle Bronze Age (Davies 2006). Stabilised dune grassland was evident in the Late Roman phase at Atlantic Road with further confirmation of the introduction of *Cernuella* sp. in the Roman period (Davies forthcoming).

Of particular note is the Roman to medieval industrial site at Duckpool. Here, shells of dog whelks had been carefully clipped to remove a gland from which a purple dye could be extracted (Light 1995).

Scientific dating

In the present context, this covers the application of Radiocarbon Dating, Dendrochronology and Optically Stimulated Luminescence (OSL) to understand the chronology of past events and environmental changes.

Prior to 1985, there were few radiocarbon dates from Cornwall, the sequence for Hawk's Tor (Brown 1977) and two dates from Watch Hill (Miles 1975) being early examples. The excavation in 1987 of the Bronze Age and later occupation at Trethellan Farm, Newquay (Nowakowski 1991) provided the opportunity for the first larger-scale dating programme. Fifteen dates were obtained to investigate the scale of duration and contemporaneity of domestic and ritual features in the Bronze Age settlement. It is now routine on excavations to make provision for an appropriate suite of dates where stratigraphy and suitable materials for dating permit.

Radiocarbon dating has developed in the last 20 years, most notably with the advent of Accelerator Mass Spectrometry (AMS) dating which enables very small samples, in the order of milligrams for some materials, to be dated. At the same time, this has emphasised the need for better understanding of the taphonomy of samples and their relationships with each other and the event to be dated. Dating of charred residues adhering to the inside of ceramics is proving a valuable approach; examples include Bronze Age features at Scarcewater (Jones and Taylor 2010) and Gwithian (Hamilton *et al* 2007) and on Iron Age pottery from Camelford (Jones and Taylor 2008).

Strategies for radiocarbon dating are carefully thought out and in future on appropriate sites the application of Bayesian modelling may be applied to better refine interpretation of chronology and duration of events.

Radiocarbon dating relies on the existence of organic remains and our limited ability to date mineral sediments with no organic content restricts understanding of chronology. OSL dating is now the principal method available and is based on the emission of light by quartz or similar minerals. The event dated is the last exposure of the mineral grains to daylight (Duller 2008). OSL dating at Gwithian was carried out on windblown sands above and below two Bronze Age occupation layers from which burnt residues on ceramics were radiocarbon dated. This pilot scientific dating programme combining two techniques gave a broad framework for the interpretation of human activity in the Bronze Age and demonstrated scope for an expanded programme to give a more precise chronology (Hamilton *et al* 2007). A combination of OSL and radiocarbon dating is also being used in the Lyonesse project (see Johns, this volume).

The application of dendrochronology (tree-ring dating) has so far been confined to some studies on buildings, often chosen to inform Listed building casework (Thomas and Berry, this volume, Field archaeology, Buildings, table 2). The chronology for Cornwall is poor compared with many other counties, at least partly because good quality locally sourced timber (principally oak) was in short supply. The survival of medieval timbers is rare and dendrochronology results achieved so far mainly post-date AD 1500. As more work is done, the chances of obtaining successful matches with reference chronologies will improve.

Ancient Technology

This encompasses the study of the early use of natural raw materials to produce and work metals, create glass etc.

Cornwall's rich mining heritage is recognised by its World Heritage Site status, but surprisingly little is known of its early history. Much of the evidence is indirect and rests on the discovery of objects made during eighteenth and nineteenth-century tin streaming, with an assumption that this has destroyed much of the evidence for earlier mining and metal working. No doubt some early sites have been lost, but these more recent activities have also buried earlier sites. Remediation of post-medieval sites provides a great opportunity to look for evidence of medieval and earlier activities.

The site most well-known for prehistoric metal working is Trevelgue Head, first excavated in 1939 by C K Croft Andrew. These excavations provided abundant evidence and although, as Dungworth (2011) notes, the results were not published promptly, Trevelgue swiftly became known as a nationally significant metalworking site. Extravagant claims were made for the scale of Iron Age iron production and the influence of the south west in introducing iron-smelting

into Britain. The detailed study of the Trevelgue assemblage has challenged these assumptions (Dungworth 2011). The assemblage comprises 183kg of bloomery iron smelting debris from middle to late Iron Age contexts. The site dating shows that iron manufacture at Trevelgue began several centuries after the technology was introduced to the British Isles. The quantity of slag recovered would probably derive from around 24 smelts and may have yielded approximately 100kg of iron. These figures suggest iron production of local and possibly regional importance, rather than on the scale envisaged by earlier writers.

Lawson-Jones (forthcoming a) summarises the sources of information for Romano-British tin and iron working, noting findings of iron slag and / or hammer scale at Little Quoit farm (Lawson-Jones forthcoming b), Killigrew (Cole and Nowakowski forthcoming) and Duckpool (Ratcliffe 1995), for example. Tin slag is very rare with most finds made before the mid twentieth century. Dungworth (forthcoming) used scanning electron microscope and energy dispersive spectrometer analysis on thin sections to confirm the presence of third to fourth-century smelting slag (rather than slag from a secondary melting process). This was found in a deliberately backfilled ditch near Botallack.

Applied techniques

The last 25 years has seen the development of a range of applied techniques including biomolecular studies such as the analysis of lipids (e.g. plant oils and waxes and animal fats), proteins (e.g. milk) absorbed into the fabric of objects such as cooking and storage vessels and DNA. Protein studies have yet to be carried out in Cornwall; however, lipid analysis on Bronze Age ceramics from Trethellan Farm found that 36% of the sherds analysed contained dairy ruminant (cow, sheep or goat) fats and ruminant and pig carcass fats (Copley *et al* 2005). This confirms the use of milk products and demonstrated the potential of the technique. As noted above, on most inland sites direct evidence for animal husbandry is poor or absent. The approach can also be used on non-settlement sites; work is in progress on lipids in pottery from a Bronze Age burial at Harlyn Bay (Andy Jones, pers comm).

Successful studies of ancient DNA have yet to be achieved. An attempt to determine gender using DNA was made on the fragmentary remains of a human skull from the Iron Age sword and mirror burial at Hillside Farm, Bryher, Scilly (Mays *et al* 2006).

There has been further development of the use of isotopes such as analysis of stable isotopes in the study of past human diets and movements of populations. These include carbon and nitrogen, and to a lesser extent oxygen, strontium, lead, suphur and hydrogen. The analysis is usually done on bone collagen, dentine and tooth enamel. As noted above, the geology and soils of most of Cornwall are not conducive to bone preservation and only modest populations have been recovered from shell-enriched coastal sediments. The only example for Cornwall and Scilly is from the Bryher sword and mirror burial. Analysis of carbon and nitrogen stable isotopes indicated that despite the coastal location, the individual derived only a small proportion of dietary protein from marine seafood sources (Mays *et al* 2006).

Priorities for the future

Environmental studies on sites or sequences with waterlogged / anoxic preservation (pollen, plant macrofossils, insects, microfossils such as diatoms, ostracods, foraminifera, testate amoebae etc as appropriate to the research questions asked)

- Further research into animal husbandry and breeding; exploitation of wild animals, fish and birds
- A better understanding of the mechanics of arable production and trade especially in the Iron Age and Roman periods
- Environmental studies on early medieval and later sites
- Comprehensive dating strategies with the inclusion of Bayesian modelling where possible
- Studies of environmental history (climate and vegetation) seen as long term ecology and better integrated with current land management practice in areas of historic landscape
- Lipids and isotope studies to investigate indirect use of animal and plant products
- Coastal change: long term research projects to ensure that funds are directed to research questions on sites and landscapes that are vulnerable, particularly to loss through flooding or erosion

Acknowledgements

I am very grateful to David Dungworth for information on Trevelgue and comments on early technology, Wendy Carruthers and Julie Jones for discussing unpublished work with me and Francis Kelly for comments on buildings and tree ring dating. I would also like to thank staff at Cornwall Historic Environment Service, particularly Bryn Tapper, Jane Powning, Charlie Johns, James Gossip, Andy Jones, Jacky Nowakowski and Ann Reynolds for kindly supplying information to me. Many thanks also to Peter Rose for his helpful comments.

References

Albarella, U, and Davis, S J M, 1996 for 1994. Mammals and birds from Launceston Castle, Cornwall: decline in status and the rise of agriculture, *Circaea, The Journal of the Association for Environmental Archaeology* **12 (1),** 1-156 www.envarch.net/publications/circaea/circaea-12-1.html

Barrowman, R C, Batey, C E, and Morris, C D, 2007. *Excavations at Tintagel Castle, Cornwall, 1990- 1999,* Reports of the Research Committee of the Society of Antiquaries of London, **74**

Bayley, J, 1975. Pollen, in H Miles, Barrows on the St. Austell granite, *Cornish Archaeol,* **14,** 60-66

Bell, M, 1984. Environmental archaeology in South West England, in H C M Keeley, ed, *Environmental archaeology. A regional review,* DOE Occasional Paper, **6,** 43-133

Brown, A P, 1977. Late Devensian and Flandrian vegetation history of Bodmin Moor, Cornwall, *Phil Trans Royal Soc London,* **B, 276,** 251-320

Carruthers, W, 2006. Charred plant remains, in A Reynolds, An early Bronze Age pit at Trenoweth, Portreath, and other results from the Reskadinnick to Portreath transfer pipeline, *Cornish Archaeol,* **45,** 87-90

Carruthers, W, 2007. Plant remains, in Gossip and Jones, 2007, 100-6

Carruthers, W, forthcoming. The charred plant remains (Truro College), in Gossip forthcoming b

Caseldine, C J, 1980. Environmental change in Cornwall during the last 13,000 years, *Cornish Archaeol,* **19,** 3-16

Cole, R, and Nowakowski, J, forthcoming. Excavations at Killigrew – an Iron Age and Romano-British industrial site on the Trispen Bypass, Cornwall, 1996, *Cornish Archaeol*

Connolly, A P, Godwin, H, and Megaw, E M, 1950. Studies in the post glacial history of British vegetation XI: late-glacial deposits in Cornwall, *Phil Trans Royal Soc London,* **B. 234,** 397-469

Copley, M S, Berstam, R, Dudd, S N, Aillaud, S, Mukherjee, A J, Straker, V, Payne, S, and Evershed, R P, 2005. Processing of milk products in pottery vessels through British prehistory, *Antiquity,* **79,** 895-908

Davies, P, 2006, Land snail assessment, in Nowakowski *et al* 2006, 21-23

Davies, P, forthcoming. Land molluscs, in Reynolds forthcoming

de Moulins, D, 2000-2001. Roots and Tubers, in A M Jones, 2000-1, 79

Dimbleby, G W, 1964. Pollen analysis of two Cornish barrows, *Jnl Roy Inst Cornwall (new series),* **IV (3),** 364-365

Dimbleby, G W, 1978. Pollen analysis, in P M Christie, The excavation of an Iron Age souterrain and settlement at Carn Euny, Sancreed, Cornwall, *Proc Prehist Soc*, **44,** 424-9

Dudley, P, 2011. *Goon, hal, cliff and croft: the archaeology and landscape history of west Cornwall's rough ground,* Truro (Cornwall Council)

Duller, G A T, 2008. *Luminescence dating: guidelines on using luminescence dating in archaeology,* Swindon (English Heritage)

Dungworth, D, 2011. Examination of metalworking debris from the 1939 excavations at Trevelgue Head, in Nowakowski and Quinnell 2011, 220-244

Dungworth, D, forthcoming. Examination of samples of tin slag from St Just, in Lawson-Jones forthcoming a

French, C N, 1996. Preliminary results of the pollen analysis of sediments from Church Cove, Gunwalloe, in M G Healy, ed, *Late Quaternary coastal change in west Cornwall, UK. Field Guide,* Durham (Environmental Research Centre, Department of Geography, University of Durham; International Geological Correlation Programme Project 367), 20-25

Gale, R, and Straker, V, 1997. Charcoal from heaths, layers, floors and stakeholes, in Straker *et al* 1997, 101-6

Gale, R, 2006. Charcoal, in Jones and Quinnell 2006, 49-50

Gale, R, 2007. Charred plant macrofossils and charcoal, in Straker 2007, 291-294

Gearey, B R, 1996. *Human-environment relations on Bodmin Moor during the Holocene,* unpublished PhD thesis, University of Plymouth

Gearey, B R, and Charman, D, 1996. Rough Tor, Bodmin: testing some archaeological hypotheses with landscape palaeoecology, in D J Charman, and R M Newnham, and D G Croot, eds, *The Quaternary of East Devon and Cornwall: Field Guide,* London: Quaternary Research Association

Gearey, B R, West, S, and Charman, D, 1997. The landscape context of medieval settlement on the south western moors of England. Recent palaeoenvironmental evidence from Bodmin Moor and Dartmoor, *Med Arch*, **41,** 195-208

Gearey, B R, Charman, D, and Kent, M, 2000a. Palaeoecological evidence for the prehistoric settlement of Bodmin Moor, Cornwall, Southwest England. Part I: The status of woodland and early human impacts, *J Archaeol Sci, 27,* 423-438

Gearey, B R, Charman, D, and Kent, M 2000b. Palaeoecological evidence for the prehistoric settlement of Bodmin Moor, Cornwall, Southwest England. Part II: Land Use Changes from the Neolithic to the Present, *J Archaeol Sci,* **27,** 493-508

Gossip, J, forthcoming a. Archaeological investigations at Nancemere, Truro, Cornwall 2002: a prehistoric and Romano-British landscape, *Cornish Archaeol*

Gossip, J, forthcoming b. Life outside the round - Bronze Age and Iron Age settlement at Higher Besore and Truro College, Threemilestone, Truro, *Cornish Archaeol*

Gossip, J, and Jones, A M, 2007. *Archaeological investigations of a later prehistoric and a Romano-British landscape at Tremough, Penryn, Cornwall,* Brit Arch Repts, Brit Ser, **443,** Oxford

Grant, A, 1988. Animal resources, in G Astill, and A Grant, eds, *The countryside of medieval England,* Oxford, 149-261

Hamilton, D, Marshall, P, Roberts, H M, Bronk Ramsay, C, and Cook, G, 2007. Appendix 1, in Gwithian: scientific dating, in Nowakowski *et al* 2007, 61-70

Hammon, A, 2004. Gwithian: assessment of the vertebrate remains, in Nowakowski 2007, 145-156

Hammon, A, 2006. Gwithian, Cornwall 2005 fieldwork (GMXVII). Assessment of the vertebrate assemblage, in Nowakowski *et al* 2006, 27-28

Hammon, A, 2011. Iron Age mammal and fish remains. Animal bone from late early IA, Middle IA and RB periods, in Nowakowski and Quinnell 2011, 294-305

Harry, R, and Morris, C D, 1997. Excavations on the Lower Terrace, Site C, Tintagel Island 1990-4, *Antiq Jnl,* **77,** 1-143

Healy, M G, 1993. *Holocene coastal evolution and relative sea-level change in west Cornwall, UK,* unpublished PhD thesis, National University of Ireland

Healy, M G, 1995. The lithostratigraphy and biostratigraphy of a Holocene coastal sequence in Marazion Marsh, west Cornwall, UK, with reference to sea-level movements, *Marine Geology*, **34,** 237-252

Healy, M G, 1996. *Late Quaternary coastal change in west Cornwall, UK, Field Guide,* IGCP Project **367,** Environmental Research Centre, University of Durham, 46-59

Healy, M G, 1999. Marazion Marsh, in J D Sourse, and M F A Furze, eds, *The Quaternary of west Cornwall, Field Guide,* Quaternary Research Association, London, 74-80

Herring, P, Crabtree, K, Straker, V, and West, S, 1993. Examining a Romano-British boundary at Foage, Zennor, *Cornish Archaeol,* **32,** 17-27

Ingrems, C, forthcoming. The animal bones and human mandible, in Reynolds forthcoming

James, H C L, and Guttman, E B, 1992. Late Holocene vegetational development at Chyandour near Penzance, west Cornwall, *Proc Ussher Soc*, **8,** 60-3

Jones, A M, 2000-2001. The excavation of a multi-period site at Stencoose , Cornwall, *Cornish Archaeol,* **39-40,** 45-94

Jones, A M, 2004-5. Settlement and ceremony: archaeological investigations at Stannon Down, St Breward, Cornwall, *Cornish Archaeol*, **43-44,** 1-140

Jones, A M, 2008. Excavation of a barrow on Constantine Island, St Merryn, Cornwall, *Cornish Archaeol,* **47,** 101-130

Jones, A M, and Quinnell, H, 2006. Cornish Beakers: new discoveries and perspectives, *Cornish Archaeol,* **45,** 31-69

Jones, A M, and Reed, S J, 2006. By land, sea and air: an early Neolithic pit group at Portscatho, Cornwall and consideration of coastal activity during the Neolithic, *Cornish Archaeol*, **45,** 1-30

DISCOVERY AND RESEARCH

Jones, A M, and Taylor, S, 2008. Camelford school excavations, summer 2008, Iron Age activity revealed, *CBA Southwest Journal*, **22,** 29-32

Jones, A M, and Taylor, S R, 2010. *Scarcewater, Pennance, Cornwall, archaeological excavation of a Bronze Age and Roman landscape*, Brit Arch Repts, Brit Ser, **516,** Oxford

Jones, A M, and Tinsley, H M, 2000-1. Recording ancient environments at De Lank, St Breward, Cornwall, *Cornish Archaeol*, **39-40,** 146-60

Jones, J, 2006. Charred plant remains, in Jones and Reed 2006, 14-15

Jones, J, 2010. Plant remains, in Jones and Taylor 2010, 142-9

Jones, J, forthcoming. The charred plant remains (Lower Besore), in Gossip forthcoming b

Lawson-Jones, A, 1999. *Porthleven Stream flood alleviation scheme: archaeological watching brief and peat sampling*, Truro (Cornwall Archaeological Unit)

Lawson-Jones, A, forthcoming a. Discoveries along the North Land's End pipeline, *Cornish Archaeol*

Lawson-Jones, A, forthcoming b. Little Quoit Farm, *Cornish Archaeol*

Light, J, 1995. Marine molluscs, in Ratcliffe 1995, 142-152

Light, J, forthcoming. Marine molluscs and crustaceans, in Reynolds forthcoming

Maltby, E, and Caseldine, C J, 1984. Prehistoric soils and vegetation development on Bodmin Moor, *Nature,* **297,** 397-400

Mays, S, Turner-Walker, G, and Brown, K, 2006. Human bone, in C Johns, An Iron Age sword and mirror cist burial, from Bryher, Isles of Scilly, *Cornish Archaeol,* **41–42,** 2002–3, 20-23

Miles, H, 1975. Barrows on the St Austell Granite, *Cornish Archaeol*, **14,** 5-82

Nowakowski, J A, 1991. Trethellan Farm, Newquay: excavation of a lowland Bronze Age settlement and Iron Age cemetery, *Cornish Archaeol*, **30,** 5-242

Nowakowski, J A, 2007. Excavation of a Bronze Age landscape and post Roman industrial settlement 1953-1961, Gwithian, Cornwall. Assessments of key datasets (2005-2006), Truro (Historic Environment Service, Cornwall County Council; 2 vols)

Nowakowski, J A, Quinnell, H, Sturgess, J, Thomas, C, and Thorpe C, 2007. Return to Gwithian: shifting the sands of time, *Cornish Archaeol*, **46,** 13-76

Nowakowski, J A, and Quinnell, H, 2011. *Trevelgue Head, Cornwall – an Iron Age cliff-castle: the story of the 1939 excavations by the late C K Croft Andrew*, Truro (Cornwall Council)

Nowakowski, J A, Sturgess, J, and Lawson-Jones, A, 2006. *Gwithian, Cornwall, report on palaeoenvironmental sampling fieldwork, Scheduled Monument Cornwall 771,* Truro (Historic Environment Service, Cornwall County Council)

Powell, A, and Serjeantson, D, 1995. Animal bones, in Ratcliffe 1995, 136-142

Ratcliffe, J, and Straker, V, 1996. *The early environment of Scilly: palaeoenvironmental assessment of cliff-face and intertidal deposits, 1989-1993*, Truro (Cornwall County Council and English Heritage)

Ratcliffe, J, 1995. Duckpool, Morwenstow: a Romano-British and early medieval industrial site and harbour, *Cornish Archaeol,* **34,** 80-171

Reynolds, A, forthcoming. Atlantic Road, Newquay: excavations on a Late Iron Age and Romano-British coastal site, *Cornish Archaeol*

Robinson, D E, Forster, E, Hazell, Z, and Straker, V, 2011. Recent studies of vegetation history in west Cornwall, in Dudley 2011, 72-74

Scaife, R G, 1984. A history of Flandrian vegetation in the Isles of Scilly: palynological investigation of Higher Moors and Lower Moors peat mires, St Mary's, *Cornish Studies,* **11,** 33-47

Straker, V, 1991. Charred plant macrofossils; Appendix 1, in Nowakowski 1991, 161-179; 234-5

Straker, V, 1992. *Charred plant macrofossils from Tintagel Churchyard*, unpublished report for Cornwall Archaeological Unit

Straker, V, with Gale, R, Payne, S, and Mays, S, 1997. The ecofactual assemblage, in Harry and Morris 1997, 82-108

Straker, V, 2007. The ecofactual assemblages (V Straker with contributions from P Baker, A Bayliss, C Bronk Ramsay, R Gale, J Heathcote, J Jones, M Robinson and H Tinsley), in Barrowman *et al* 2007, 280 – 301

Straker, V, 2011a. Past environments in west Cornwall: a review of the palaeoenvironmental literature, in Dudley 2011, 66-72 and Appendix 1

Straker, V, 2011 b. The rough ground historic environment. Palaeoenvironmental Research, in G Kirkham, *Managing the historic environment on west Cornwall's rough ground,* Truro (Cornwall Council and English Heritage), 14-16

Tinsley, H M, 1999a. Pollen analysis, in Lawson-Jones 1999, 23-8

Tinsley, H M, 1999b. *Pollen assessment of samples from buried peat at Porthallow, Cornwall*, unpublished report for Cornwall Archaeological Unit

Tinsley, H M, 1999c. Palynological analysis of three buried soils from Gaverigan, Cornwall, in R Cole, ed, *Wheal Remfry, Gaverigan Tip Extension. A programme of archaeological recording*, Truro (Cornwall Archaeological Unit)

Tinsley 2004-5. Pollen analysis, in Jones 2004-5, 48-72

Walker, M, 1989. Pollen analysis and radiocarbon dates, in D Austin, G A M Gerrard, and T A P Greeves, Tin and agriculture in the Middle Ages and beyond: landscape archaeology in St Neot parish, Cornwall, *Cornish Archaeol,* **28,** 179-189

Walker, T, 2008. Molluscs, in Jones 2008

Webster, C J, ed, 2008. *The archaeology of South West England. South West Archaeological Research Framework Resource Assessment and Research Agenda*, Somerset County Council

Cornish Archaeology 50, 2011, 187–196

Ancient Scilly: the last 25 years

CHARLES JOHNS

Introduction

1985, the year preceding Paul Ashbee's characteristically elegant reprise of Scillonian archaeology in the 25th anniversary edition of *Cornish Archaeology*, saw the publication of Charles Thomas' *Exploration of a Drowned Landscape*, a remarkable collection of essays which has influenced thought on aspects of Scillonian archaeology and history ever since. In particular, Thomas' model of sea level rise; based on 'Minimal Occupation Level' and place-name evidence and suggesting that during the Neolithic

the shallow lagoon between the northern islands was an area of ancient woodland subsequently cleared for settlement and agriculture which only became inundated in the late eleventh century AD, has gained a foothold in popular imagination.

Also noted with enthusiasm by Ashbee was the archaeological watching brief during the off islands electrification project, organised by Charles Thomas and the Institute of Cornish Studies and supervised by Jeanette Ratcliffe. Trenching in advance of cable laying was observed and recorded on St Martin's, Tresco, Bryher and St Agnes during the summer and autumn of 1985; the results of the

Fig 1. Air photo of North Hill Samson showing some of the stone walls in the intertidal zone, top.
(Photograph: Cornwall Council)

DISCOVERY AND RESEARCH

project were presented in *Lighting up the past in Scilly* (Ratcliffe 1991).

Jeanette subsequently became a field officer with the Cornwall Archaeological Unit (CAU) with special responsibility for projects in the Isles of Scilly. In 1988, with a team including Cathy Parkes, Carl Thorpe, and Andy Waters, she carried out a benchmark project for English Heritage to assess the archaeological resource of the islands resulting in an archaeological management plan for Scilly (Ratcliffe 1989).

Emerging from the plan's recommendations was the Coastal Erosion Project, a five year rolling programme of coastal monitoring and of intertidal peat sampling, culminating in *The Early Environment of Scilly* (Ratcliffe and Straker 1996) and 'The changing landscape and coastline of the Isles of Scilly recent research' (Ratcliffe and Straker 1997), which presented an alternative model for sea level rise suggesting that the disparity between sea level change in Scilly and Cornwall might be less than proposed by Thomas. The present author first visited Scilly in September 1991 to work on this project, which during its course involved many CAU and English Heritage staff. Michael Tangye has continued to record and monitor coastal sites independently.

In 1995 Gill Arbery was appointed as Field Monument Warden and Conservation Officer for Scilly, a post jointly funded by English Heritage and the Council of the Isles of Scilly. Gill did much valuable work in Scheduled Monument management and planning advice before she left in 2004. In 2007 Eleanor Breen was appointed as her successor, the post now renamed as Historic Environment Adviser.

The Scilly Sites and Monuments Register (SMR), set up by the Institute of Cornish Studies in 1983 and recognised as an important new development by Ashbee, is now maintained by Historic Environment Cornwall Council as part of the Cornwall and Scilly Historic Environment Record (HER).

In 1996 Historic Landscape Characterisation was applied to Scilly in the *Historic Landscape Assessment and Management Plan for Scilly* (Land Use Consultants and Cornwall Archaeological Unit 1996), which highlights the antiquity and archaeological potential of Scilly's landscape. A current landscape initiative is the recording project to inform conservation and sustainable management of field boundaries funded by the

Isles of Scilly AONB Unit (Johns 2010).

Following Murley MacLaran's death in 1988, Steve Ottery became Honorary Secretary of the Isles of Scilly Museum and later Honorary Curator. On his retirement Amanda Martin became Acting Honorary Curator. She was appointed as the first paid part-time Curator/Manager in September 2002. Under her stewardship the Museum has gained Full Accreditation status, improved and enlarged its archive storage capacity, and continues to be a valuable research resource.

Much of the development-led archaeological fieldwork undertaken in Scilly during the 1990s was associated with coast protection schemes, notably recording cliff-exposed Bronze Age remains at Porth Killier on St Agnes in 1996 (Johns *et al* forthcoming) and sampling peat deposits at Old Town Bay on St Mary's (Ratcliffe and Straker 1998), or cable laying such as the British Telecom trenching on St Martin's in 1992 when an Early Christian grave and medieval midden were discovered at Lower Town (Ratcliffe 1997).

Much more development-led work has been undertaken during the last decade, but these have mostly been small scale interventions. A watching brief during the construction of the new playing field at Dolphin Town, Tresco in 2003 revealed remains of a Middle Bronze Age settlement (Taylor and Johns forthcoming a) and a Late Bronze Age settlement was investigated in 2009/10 at a new affordable housing development at Annet Farm on St Agnes (Taylor and Johns forthcoming b). Rather surprisingly, considering its location near Ennor Castle, detailed evaluation on the site of the new Five Islands School Base at Carn Gwaval St Mary's did not reveal any archaeological remains other than removed post-medieval field boundaries (Johns *et al* 2010). Similarly watching briefs during the refurbishments of the off islands quays in 2007 were largely unproductive except for the discovery of two nested Bronze Age vessels on the site of the contactor's compound near Porth Conger, St Agnes (Johns and Sawyer 2008; Wessex Archaeology 2008; Johns and Quinnell forthcoming).

In 1992 the first edition of the popular booklet *Scilly's Archaeological Heritage* was published by Twelveheads Press (Ratcliffe 1992) and a second edition followed in 1995. The booklet provides a succinct chronological overview of the islands' archaeology and history with a gazetteer of sites to visit. A fully revised edition with colour illustrations was published in 2003 (Ratcliffe and Johns 2003).

Notable publications have included Paul Ashbee's report on the excavations of the prehistoric and Roman-period settlement Halangy Down, St Mary's between 1964 and 1977 (Ashbee 1996), Sarnia Butcher's reconsideration of Roman Nornour (Butcher 2000-1), Rosemary Parslow's new study of Scillonian flora (Parslow 2007), and English Heritage's new book on the military defences of Scilly (Bowden and Brodie 2011).

There has been continuing interest in Scilly by academic researchers. Fieldwork has been undertaken and interesting papers have been written by Trevor Kirk, formerly of Carmarthen College (Kirk 2004), Mary Ann Owoc of Mercyhurst College Pennsylvania (Owoc et al 2003), and Eleanor Breen (Breen 2006 and 2008). Gary Robinson drew together and reconsidered existing archaeological knowledge of Scilly for his PhD thesis, providing a valuable source of reference, although some of his claims must remain contentious (Robinson 2007). Since 2005, three seasons of fieldwork have been carried out by the ongoing 'Islands in a Common Sea' project directed by the present author and Jacqui Mulville of Cardiff University, including recording the cliff-exposed Bronze Age cairn at Pendrathen, St Mary's (Johns and Mulville 2011), an evaluation of Knackyboy Cairn (Mulville et al 2007) and archaeological investigation and building recording conservation work on the post-medieval buildings on Samson and Tean (Johns et al 2007; Johns et al forthcoming a and b).

The National Heritage Act of 2002, which extended English Heritage's remit into the marine zone, and the discovery of the stern carving from HMS Colossus brought maritime archaeology to the fore. The Time Team visited the islands to record its lifting in 2002. In 2003-4 HE Projects carried out the Rapid Coastal Zone Assessment Survey of the Islands (phase 1 desk-based assessment) for English Heritage which included entering all 771 recorded wreck sites into the Cornwall and Scilly Historic Environment Record (Johns et al 2004).

There are now two local maritime archaeology groups, the Cornwall and Isles of Scilly Maritime Archaeology Society (CISMAS) and the Islands Maritime Group (IMAG). Maritime projects have included ongoing work on HMS Colossus (e.g. Camidge 2005 and 2009), work on the Firebrand by Bristol University and the discovery of the Wheel Wreck by IMAG which has been designated under the Protection of Wrecks Act 2003. CISMAS have also spent two seasons of fieldwork surveying and recording the intertidal field walls on Samson Flats (Camidge et al 2011). Wessex Archaeology have carried out designated and undesignated site assessments of a number of wrecks for English Heritage. The Little Gannick wreck, discovered by IMAG, is protected under the Protection of Wrecks Act. It comprises a discrete mound of post 1850 Cornish mining equipment. The cargo is considered to be of national significance given its rarity and potential for informing use about the international trade in Cornish mining equipment and technology.

Aspects of Scillonian archaeology
Topography, submergence and the evolving environment

In 2009 English Heritage commissioned the Lyonesse Project, a two year study of the evolution of the coastal and marine environment of Scilly managed by HE Projects and including specialists from English Heritage and Aberystwyth, Cardiff, Exeter, and Plymouth Universities as well as the local maritime archaeological groups CISMAS and IMAG.

The initial impetus for the project was the discovery by Todd Stevens in 2005 of a submerged forest at a depth of 8m off Pendrathen in St Mary's Roads. A sample was recovered in that year, and further samples taken by divers in 2009 and 2010, including a large segment of tree trunk (willow). Radiocarbon determinations ranging from 5990 to 4350 cal BC date the submerged forest to the later part of the Mesolithic period. At this time sea level must have been below the points at which these samples were taken.

The project has involved an audit and verification of all recorded peat exposures in Scilly during two seasons of fieldwork. Marine geophysics has been used to map the submerged forest and to prospect for peat on the seabed. Reports of peat by local divers have been investigated and samples taken from St Mary's Roads and the seabed off Nornour. In the intertidal zone auger surveys, tied in with GPS, were then used to map the extent of peat deposits which are often buried by sand on Tresco, St Mary's, St Martin's and St Agnes.

The pollen spectra from the sub-marine samples show a sequence of vegetation change through

DISCOVERY AND RESEARCH

Fig 2. CISMAS divers Innes McCartney and Luke Randall taking a column sample of the submerged peat in St Mary's Sound. (Photograph: CISMAS)

the Mesolithic period from a herb-rich grassland, gradually colonised by oak, birch and hazel woodland. A large peak in charcoal at the transition to the overlying peat is associated with a peak in birch and a decline in oak, suggesting possible disturbance or clearance by fire, followed by a phase which sees recovery of oak dominated woodland, with an increasingly wet surface as shown by the presence of willow. The final phase sees a change to an open marsh dominated by sedges changing to grass dominance with increasing levels of salinity possibly from rising sea-levels.

Radiocarbon determinations and OSL ages from samples from Crab's Ledge and Bathinghouse Porth indicate a saltmarsh environment on the southern edge of Tresco by about 1200 cal BC and suggest that the realistic model for sea level rise is closer to that suggested by the 1989-93 work rather than Thomas' 1985 theory.

Palaeoenvironmental analysis and scientific dating of the samples is currently ongoing and the final results of the project will be disseminated in March 2012.

Mesolithic (*c* 7000 BC – *c* 4000 BC)

Ashbee (1986, 185) suggested that although there was meagre positive evidence of Mesolithic occupation in Scilly, rising sea levels may have obliterated much evidence for occupation during this period. Artefactual evidence has not greatly increased in the last 25 years, the main discovery being the 20 or so pieces collected from the cliff face at Old Town Quay, St Martin's indicating the only identified Mesolithic flintworking site on the Islands (Ratcliffe 1989, 33 and 1994, 13). However it has long been considered that although the evidence is sparse, Scilly was visited on a seasonal basis by groups of Mesolithic hunter-gatherers travelling by boat from the mainland (e.g. Ratcliffe 1989, 33 and 1992, 3).

Important new evidence for occupation during the Mesolithic is in the form of a charcoal peak in a core sample from the submerged forest in St Mary's Roads, indicating an episode of burning. As Ashbee stated, of vertebrate fauna the question of deer in Scilly is by far the most important, with bones of large and small red deer having been found at Halangy Porth, on St Agnes and on Nornour (Ashbee 1986, 145-6) and it is possible that red deer had been introduced in the Mesolithic period and the woodland burning was intended to encourage the growth of new willow shoots that would attract red deer to feed (J Mulville, pers comm) thus indicating an early controlled, insular deer economy as suggested by Ashbee.

Neolithic (*c* 4000 BC – *c* 2500 BC)

Evidence for occupation in Scilly during the Neolithic also remains sparse with a few small assemblages and some single finds of south western or Hembury style pottery and some flint artefacts. The pottery fabric is local granite-derived material with a single sherd of Lizard gabbroic clay from Old Quay, St Martin's probably representing the only ceramic import to the islands in this period (Quinnell forthcoming).

The calf's tooth recovered from the lower peat on Par Beach, St Martin's may represent the earliest evidence for animal husbandry in Scilly, if not the British Isles. A piece of oak in the surface of the peat was dated to 4460-4040 cal BC (GU-5222) and a sample from the base of the peat was dated to 4230-3820 cal BC (GU-6061) (Ratcliffe and Straker 1996, 19, 34). It is hoped that English Heritage will fund a new radiocarbon date on the tooth itself.

Although it has long been mooted that Scillonian entrance graves may have had their origins during the Later Neolithic period, current research by Katharine Sawyer for her PhD suggests that they date unequivocally to the Early Bronze Age (pers comm), as they do in Penwith (Jones and Quinnell, this volume). As part of the Islands in a Common Sea Project Katharine Sawyer and Jacqui Mulville have recently made a successful application to Oxford Radiocarbon Accelerator Dating Service for funding to date human bone from Knackyboy Cairn, Obadiah's Barrow and the Old Town cist burial, the results of which should clarify the date of these monuments.

Bronze Age (*c* 2500 BC – *c* 700 BC)

Current evidence suggests that Scilly was not permanently settled until the Bronze Age and that the Mesolithic and Neolithic artefacts found on the islands are the result of seasonal visits from Penwith (Thomas 1985, 101; Ratcliffe

Fig 3. Bronze Age structure on the St Agnes affordable housing site during excavation in October 2009.
(*Photograph: Cornwall Council*)

DISCOVERY AND RESEARCH

1989, 34; Ratcliffe and Johns 2003, 5; Robinson 2007, 64).

New discoveries relating to the Bronze Age include the settlement revealed during construction of the new playing field at Dolphin Town, Tresco in 2003 (Taylor and Johns forthcoming a), the settlement remains uncovered on the new affordable housing site at Annet Farm, St Agnes (Fig 3; Taylor and Johns forthcoming b), and the two nested vessels in pits unearthed in a field on St Agnes during the off island quays refurbishment in 2007 (Johns and Quinnell forthcoming). The first is important because of the range of pottery which suggests activity from a range of dates within the Bronze Age; an interesting feature of the second site was a group of shallow, sub-circular pits which seemed to have been dug to extract the soft natural clay in the valley bottom. The clay may have been used for making pots or possibly for coating pots to make them waterproof before insertion into pits in the ground, an almost complete clay-lined pot was found in one of the excavated structures. Another potentially significant discovery was the identification of a possible boat graffito on a potsherd from the site.

The two nested vessels, two large bases containing sherds of smaller pots and buried in pits clearly had a ritual purpose, although there were no associated features and the soil filling the vessels did not contain any cremated bone or charcoal.

Iron Age (*c* 700 BC – AD 43) and Roman (AD 43 – 410)

The discovery and excavation of the Bryher sword and mirror cist burial in 1999 was arguably the most important archaeological event in the Islands during the last 25 years. Within the cist were the fragmentary remains of a crouched human skeleton. In addition to a sword, which survived within a bronze scabbard, the grave goods included a mirror, shield fittings, a sword belt ring, a brooch and a spiral ring (all of copper alloy), together with a shattered tin object. There was also evidence for the grave having contained a sheepskin or fleece and woven textile incorporating goat and other animal hairs. This is the only known Iron Age grave to contain both a sword and mirror, raising interesting questions as to the gender significance of both these grave goods. The unique combination of metal objects will continue to be central to future discussions concerning the development of British Iron Age metalwork. A long bone fragment from the burial was radiocarbon dated, to 200-45 cal BC; the metalwork typology narrows this range to the first half of the first century BC. The dates indicate that the Bryher mirror is the earliest known British decorated bronze mirror and has important national implications for the study of the development of insular Celtic Art in Britain (Johns 2002-3).

An Iron Age fogou was found in a field on Peninnis Head in 2000, the only one so far identified on the

Fig 4. The Bryher swordand mirror.
(Photograph: English Heritage)

islands. The full extent of the fogou is undetermined and there is a possibility of associated features in the vicinity that are as yet unidentified.

In 2003 two cist graves were uncovered by ground disturbance at Lunnon Farm, St Mary's (Butcher 2003). Further investigation in 2005 showed that these were part of a more extensive cist grave cemetery which included an infant burial (Johns and Mulville 2011).

Two small pits on the St Agnes Affordable Housing site, in the same area as the pits described above, contained the rim of a pot and an Iron or Romano-British brooch, evidently the result of ritual deposition and suggesting that clay extraction on the site continued into this period. Two adjacent postholes indicate that the position of the pits may have been marked by posts (Taylor and Johns forthcoming).

Medieval (AD 410 – 1547)

The simple rectangular chapels possibly of the eighth to tenth centuries, such as St Helen's, Tean

and Chapel Brow, St Martin's were traditionally thought of as insular hermitages but were reinterpreted in the late 1980s as the earliest parish churches for Scilly, sited near to contemporary settlements (Ratcliffe 1989).

Large quantities of finds were recovered during the 1985 off islands electrification project and the possible location of the medieval settlements of *Sturtom* and *Bantom* identified on Bryher (Ratcliffe 1991).

The main focus of settlement on St Mary's during the medieval period was Ennor Castle at Old Town; however, detailed evaluation on the nearby site of the new Five Islands School Base at Carn Gwaval St Mary's did not reveal any evidence for medieval occupation other than a few fragments of pottery (Johns *et al* 2010).

Post-medieval and modern (1547 – 2010)

Ashbee pointed out that 'Scilly's Garrison, as progressively modified and developed down the years, is probably the most impressive work of its

Fig 5. Cardiff University students Cat Richards and Jesse Collins recording House P on South Hill Samson prior to consolidation works. (Photograph: Cornwall Council)

DISCOVERY AND RESEARCH

kind extant in England. Like the remarkable Civil War earth- and other works, it has never been planned nor described in detail, almost 40 years after the Ministry of Works began to consolidate the walls' (1986, 210). The collapse of the north-east corner of Lower Benham Battery in a storm in October 2004 provided an impetus for the development of a long awaited Conservation Plan for St Mary's Garrison, which was eventually completed in 2010 (Johns and Fletcher 2010). In May 2006 English Heritage carried out an evaluation of the seventeenth-century breastwork and a gun platform at Doctors Keys to inform the Conservation Plan (Fellows 2007). English Heritage's current 'Defending the Isles of Scilly' project has resulted in the publication of a volume within the Informed Conservation series of books and a major Research Department report on the Garrison Walls (Bowden and Brodie 2011; Brodie 2011).

The systematic scrutiny of Scilly's historic buildings, advocated by Ashbee (1986, 212) still remains to be carried out. However the booklet *Scilly's Building Heritage* by Peter Madden published in the Twelveheads Press heritage series provides a useful addition to Peter Laws' 1980 booklet. The Cornwall and Scilly Urban Survey of Hugh Town, a guide to heritage-led regeneration, was completed in 2003 (Kirkham 2003) and in 2010 Rachel Leung carried out an archaeological and historical assessment of the buildings affected by the Porthcressa regeneration scheme (Leung forthcoming).

Since 2006 a programme of conservation work has been carried out on the post-medieval buildings on Samson by the Isles of Scilly wildlife Trust (Fig 5). Investigation and recording prior to consolidation was carried out by the School of History and Archaeology Cardiff University and HE Projects, and consolidation work was undertaken by Western Maintenance under the supervision of historic buildings consultant Eric Berry (Johns *et al* 2007). The first year's work was funded through the Scheduled Monument Management Programme and the Isles of Scilly Area of Natural Beauty (AONB) Sustainable Development Fund (SDF). Inspired by the success of the 2006 work a similar project was undertaken on the post-medieval farmhouse on Tean in addition to the continuing work on Samson, both sponsored by the AONB SDF (Johns *et al* forthcoming a and b). Since 2008 the work on the Samson buildings

has continued with grant from English Heritage's Historic Buildings, Monuments and Designed Landscape Fund.

The future

In October 2010 English Heritage commissioned the preparation of a Research Framework for the historic environment of the Isles of Scilly, which will guide future management and research in the Islands (Johns and Breen, eds, forthcoming). The research framework will be achieved in three stages: Resource Assessment, Research Agenda and Research Strategy. The Resource Assessment will assess the historic environment resource on Scilly and identify significant gaps in current knowledge. The Research Agenda will quantify the main risks to the resource and identify sites and landscapes that are at risk; and identify key research themes that are either unique to the Islands or situate Scilly within a broader regional or national context. The Research Strategy will produce a five-year plan detailing research priorities and suggesting possible directions for future research and be reviewed after five years.

References

Ashbee, P, 1986. Ancient Scilly: retrospect, aspect and prospect, *Cornish Archaeol,* **25,** 186-219

Ashbee, P, 1996. Halangy Down, St Mary's, Isles of Scilly, excavations 1964-1977, *Cornish Archaeol,* **35**

Bowden, M and Brodie, A, 2011. *Defending Scilly,* London (English Heritage)

Breen, E, 2006. Constructing meanings from the architecture of landscape on the Isles of Scilly, in V O Jorge, with the assistance of J M Cardoso, A M Vale, G L Velho, L S Periera, eds, Approaching "prehistoric and protohistoric architectures" of Europe from a "dwelling perspective", *Journal of Iberian Archaeology,* **8,** 265 – 280

Breen, E, 2006. Constructing meanings from the architecture of landscape on the isles of Scilly, in Approaching "prehistoric and protohistoric architectures" of Europe from a "dwelling perspective": proceedings of the TAG session, Sheffield 2005 , V O Jorge, with the assistance of J M Cardoso *et al*, eds, *Journal of Iberian Archaeology,* **8**

Breen, E 2008. Encounters with place in prehistory: writing a case study for Shipman Head Down, Isles of Scilly, in A Chadwick, ed, *Recent Approaches to the Archaeology of Land Allotment*, Brit Arch Repts, Brit Ser, **1875,** Oxford, 97-109

Brodie, A, 2011. *The Garrison, St Mary's, Isles of Scilly: the defences of the Garrison 1500-1545, Survey Report,* English Heritage Research Department Rept Ser no **29-2011**

Butcher, S, 2000-1. Roman Nornour, Isles of Scilly: a reconsideration, *Cornish Archaeol*, **39-40,** 5-44

Butcher, S, 2003. Cist graves at Lunnon Farm, St Mary's, Isles of Scilly, unpublished typescript

Camidge, K, 2005. *HMS Colossus stabilisation trial*, unpublished report for English Heritage, Penzance (CISMAS)

Camidge, K, 2009. HMS Colossus, an experimental site stabilization *Conservation and Management of Archaeological Sites*, **11 (2),** 161-88

Camidge, K, Charman. D, Rees, P, and Randall, L, 2011. *Samson Flats inter-tidal field survey project report 2010*, Penzance (CISMAS)

Fellows, D, 2007. *The Garrison, St Mary's, Isles of Scilly: archaeological evaluation report project 4792*, English Heritage Research Department, Report Series no 69/2007

Johns, C, 2002-3. An Iron Age sword and mirror burial from Bryher, Isles of Scilly, *Cornish Archaeol*, **41-42,** 1-79

Johns, C, 2010. *Field boundaries on the Isles of Scilly: feasibility study to inform conservation management*, Truro (Historic Environment Projects, Cornwall Council)

Johns, C, Berry, E, and Edwards B, 2007. *The Samson buildings project 2006-7, Samson, Isles of Scilly: lichen assessment, archaeological recording and building consolidation*, Truro (Historic Environment Service, Cornwall County Council)

Johns, C, Berry, E, and Mulville, J, forthcoming a. *The Samson buildings project 2007-8, Samson, Isles of Scilly: archaeological recording and building consolidation*, Truro (Historic Environment Service, Cornwall County Council)

Johns, C, Berry, E, and Mulville, J, forthcoming b. *Tean farmhouses project 2007-8, Tean, Isles of Scilly: archaeological recording and building consolidation*, Truro (Historic Environment Service, Cornwall County Council)

Johns, C, and Breen, E, eds, forthcoming. *Research framework for the historic environment of the Isles of Scilly: resource assessment,* Truro (Cornwall Council and English Heritage)

Johns, C, and Fletcher, M, 2010. The Garrison, St Mary's, Isles of Scilly: Conservation Plan, Truro (Historic Environment Projects, Cornwall Council)

Johns, C, Larn, R, and Tapper, B P, 2004. *Rapid Coastal Zone Assessment for the Isles of Scilly,* Truro (Historic Environment Service, Cornwall County Council)

Johns, C, and Mulville, J, 2011. *Islands in a Common Sea: archaeological fieldwork in the Isles of Scilly September 2005*, Truro (Historic Environment Projects, Cornwall Council)

Johns, C, and Quinnell, H, forthcoming. Two nested Bronze Age vessels from St Agnes, Isles of Scilly, *Cornish Archaeol*

Johns, C, Ratcliffe, J, and Young, A, forthcoming. St Agnes Coast Protection Scheme: results of archaeological recording 1996, *Cornish Archaeol*

Johns, C, and Sawyer, K, 2008. *Off islands quays refurbishments Isles of Scilly 2007: archaeological recording*, Truro (Historic Environment Service, Cornwall County Council)

Johns, C, Sturgess, J, and Shepherd, F, 2010. *The new Five Islands School Base proposed site, Carn Gwaval, St Mary's Isles of Scilly: archaeological assessment, evaluation and building recording*, Truro (Historic Environment Projects, Cornwall Council)

Kirk, T, 2004. Memory and materiality: the Isles of Scilly in context, in V Cummings, and C Fowler, eds, *The Neolithic of the Irish Sea: materiality and traditions of practice*, Oxford, 233-44

Kirkham, G, 2003. *Cornwall and Scilly Urban Survey: Hugh Town, St Mary's, Isles of Scilly*, Truro (Cornwall County Council)

Land Use Consultants and Cornwall Archaeological Unit, 1996. *Isles of Scilly historic landscape assessment and management strategy*, Truro (Cornwall County Council)

Laws, P, 1980. *The buildings of Scilly,* Isles of Scilly Museum Publication, **12,** Scilly and Redruth

Leung, R, forthcoming. The changing landscape of Porthcressa, *Cornish Archaeol*

Madden, P, 1996. *Scilly's building heritage*, Chacewater

Mulville, J A, Dennis, I, Johns, C, Mills, S, Pannett, A, and Young, T, 2007. *Islands in a Common Sea: archaeological fieldwork in the Isles of Scilly 2006 (St Mary's and St Martin's),* Cardiff Studies in Archaeology Specialist Rep No **27**

Owoc, M A, Adovasio, J M, Illingsworth, J, Greek, M, and Manske, K, 2003. *Perishables and pots in later prehistory: unravelling a distinctive Scillonian cultural tradition*, paper presented at the 68th Annual Meeting of the Society for American Archaeology, Milwaukee

Parslow, R, 2007. *The Isles of Scilly,* London

Quinnell, forthcoming. Assessment of prehistoric and Romans ceramics, in Johns and Breen, eds, forthcoming

Ratcliffe, J, 1989. *The archaeology of Scilly: an assessment of the resource and recommendations for its future*, Truro (Cornwall Archaeological Unit)

Ratcliffe, J, 1991. *Lighting up the past in Scilly: archaeological results from the 1985 electrification project*, Camborne and Truro (Institute of Cornish Studies and Cornwall Archaeological Unit)

Ratcliffe, J, 1992. *Scilly's archaeological heritage*, Chacewater (Twelveheads Press)

Ratcliffe, J, 1994. *Fieldwork in Scilly, July 1994,* Truro (Cornwall Archaeological Unit)

Ratcliffe, J, 1997. *British Telecom Trenching on St Martin's, Isles of Scilly, Summer 1992: the results of the archaeological watching brief,* Truro (Cornwall Archaeological Unit)

Ratcliffe, J, and Johns, C, 2003. *Scilly's archaeological heritage*, Chacewater (Twelveheads Press)

Ratcliffe, J, and Straker, V, 1996. *The early environment of Scilly*, Truro (Cornwall County Council)

Ratcliffe, J, and Straker, V, 1997. The changing landscape and coastline of the Isles of Scilly: recent research, *Cornish Archaeol*, **36,** 64-76

Ratcliffe, J, and Straker, V, 1998. *Old Town Bay coast protection scheme, St Mary's, Isles of Scilly: results of the archaeological recording*, Truro (Cornwall Archaeological Unit)

DISCOVERY AND RESEARCH

Ratcliffe, J, and Straker, V, 1998. *Old Town Bay Coast Protection Scheme, St Mary's, Isles of Scilly: Results of Archaeological Recording*, Truro (Cornwall Archaeological Unit)

Robinson, C, 2007. *The prehistoric island landscape of Scilly*, Brit Arch Repts, Brit Ser, **447,** Oxford

Taylor, S R, and Johns, C, forthcoming a. Archaeological recording on the site of the new sports field at Dolphin Town, Tresco, Isles of Scilly, *Cornish Archaeol*

Taylor, S R, and Johns, C, forthcoming b. St Agnes Affordable Housing, Higher Town, St Agnes, Isles of Scilly: archaeological recording, *Cornish Archaeol*

Thomas, C, 1985. *Exploration of a Drowned Landscape*: *archaeology and history of the Isles of Scilly*, London

Webster, C J, ed, 2009. *The Archaeology of south west England: South West Archaeological Research Framework resource assessment and research agenda*, Taunton (Somerset County Council)

Wessex Archaeology 2008. *Tresco quays watching briefs*, Salisbury (Wessex Archaeology)

Cornish Archaeology 50, 2011, 197–229

The Neolithic and Bronze Age in Cornwall, *c* 4000 cal BC to *c* 1000 cal BC: an overview of recent developments

ANDY M JONES and HENRIETTA QUINNELL

In 1986 Roger Mercer and Patricia Christie wrote the chapters on the Neolithic and Bronze Age of Cornwall for the 25th-anniversary volume of *Cornish Archaeology*. These pieces magisterially summarised the then current state of knowledge. For students of Cornish prehistory their contribution was invaluable and they continue to be useful and much sought after introductions. They remain the last thorough synthesis of the Neolithic and Bronze Age periods in Cornwall.

In many ways these two papers constituted the culmination of a particular tradition of archaeological research and presentation. They were written in the period immediately before the advent of large-scale developer-led archaeology (for example, Nowakowski 1991; Gossip and Jones 2007), and before the publication of large-scale surveys in the Penwith uplands and on Bodmin Moor (for example, Johnson and Rose 1983; 1994). The chapters were therefore biased towards the discussion of particular site types found in upland areas, where preservation was good. By contrast, the lowland 'Anciently Enclosed Land' (Cornwall County Council 1996), where we now know much of Cornwall's archaeology lies buried, was under represented. In 1986 radiocarbon determinations from Cornwall were still few in number and it was several years before high-precision AMS

dating was to become available. For example, just three radiocarbon determinations were considered adequate for the Neolithic enclosure at Carn Brea (Mercer 1981), as opposed to the six dates which have recently been obtained from a small group of pits at Tregarrick Farm, Roche, (Cole and Jones 2002-3). As a result, the period interpretations put forward in 1986 were biased towards excavations of upstanding sites, and most dating was based on artefactual typology and affinities with, often, quite distant sites. Conversely, unrecognised limitations in the data also gave aspects of monument and artefact sequences a certainty which now is now known to be fallacious.

The volume of new data collected in the last 25 years on all aspects of the Neolithic and Bronze Age is too great for this paper to attempt to match the scope of the 1986 chapters. Instead it will focus upon key findings from recent archaeological investigation.

The Early Neolithic (*c* 4000 cal BC to 3400 cal BC)

In 1986 Mercer argued that the start of the Neolithic was contemporary with the first agriculture, stone axe production, ceramics, tor enclosures and chambered tombs. He considered that these

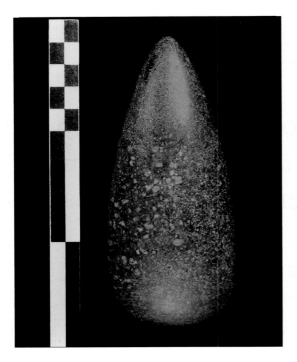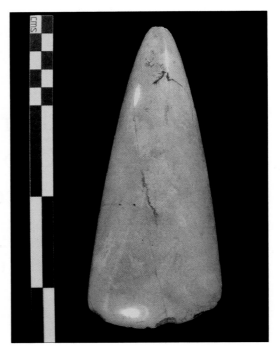

Fig 1. Neolithic polished axe-heads. Left, a highly polished greenstone axe-head from House Field, Moorgate Farm, Fletchersbridge (Accession No. 1992.25) and right a jadeite axe found in Falmouth (Accession No. 1831.16.4). The jadeite axe originated in the Alps where they were quarried in the Early Neolithic. By the time it reached Cornwall it would have been a treasured heirloom. The greenstone axe was probably made from rocks which outcrop in the west of the county. It too would have been a prized possession and its green colour, like that of the jadeite axe may have been significant.
(Reproduced with permission of the Royal Institution of Cornwall).

changes resulted from acculturation of Cornish hunter-gather communities through contacts with Neolithic farmers in western France. More recently large-scale dating projects of enclosures and long barrows (Bayliss *et al* 2008; Whittle *et al* 2007) have revealed that the first cultivated plants and pottery appear around *c* 4000 cal BC and that the construction of tombs and then enclosures follows on a little later from *c* 3800 cal BC to 3600 cal BC. These new dates can be used to support a rapid colonisation from Europe or acculturation, with scope for regional variation. The interpretation of the Neolithic has become more fragmented. There is currently a division between those who see the Neolithic introduced by the arrival of immigrants from Europe, who developed stable sedentary societies with defined territories (Sheridan 2000; 2004; Sheridan and Schulting 2008), and those who

argue that the change was more ideological, a matter of mind-set, and that Early Neolithic communities essentially developed from a Mesolithic life-style and combined small-scale agriculture with seasonal movements (Thomas 1991; 1999; Whittle 1997).

Along the Atlantic facade, there is some evidence for an exchange of material culture with Continental Europe during the Neolithic (Sheridan 2000; Cunliffe 2010) and in Devon a passage tomb at Broadsands has been argued to be of a similar type to those in Brittany and Normandy (Schulting and Sheridan 2008). Where preservation of human bone has allowed stable isotope analysis which provides evidence for protein sources, there also appears to have been a rapid switch from a marine to a terrestrial meat-based diet (Schulting 2004). Recently, radiocarbon modelling has been used to suggest both a case for an increase in

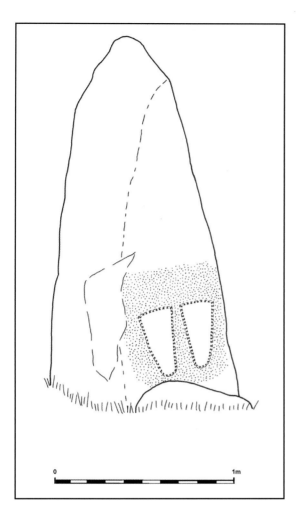

Fig 2. Standing stone in the centre of the Boscawen-un with axe carvings near to the foot of the stone. (After Herring 2000a)

evidence for the movement of Group I axes from Cornwall across the Irish Sea.

Monuments also provide evidence for the circulation of ideas. Chambered tombs are likely to represent knowledge of widespread monument forms rather than indigenous development. Other undated monuments may indicate continental links. The 'D'-shaped enclosure of small orthostatic stones on East Moor, Bodmin Moor (Johnson and Rose 1994, 29) has certain similarities with the non-circular settings or cromlechs found in Brittany (Burl 2000, 340-2). Similarly, the 'axe-shaped' standing stone in the centre of the Boscawen-un stone circle (Fig 2) has two apparent axes in relief close to its base (Herring 2000a; forthcoming). The 'axe'-shape of the stone is a feature of some Breton standing stones and axes are sometimes found carved upon them (Tilley and Thomas 1993, 231; Patton 1993, 58 60). In Brittany many of these decorated menhirs ended up reused in chambered tombs (Bradley 1990, 53) The Boscawen-un standing stone may represent an Early Neolithic site currently without parallel in south west Britain and it is of note that it became the focal point for a stone circle. However, the axes on Breton standing stones are generally of more Alpine shape and often depicted as being hafted (Alison Sheridan, pers comm) and what appear to be broad cutting edges on the Boscawen-un stone may be more similar to Early Bronze Age axes, such as those depicted on a stone from a cairn Nether Largie, in Argyll, south west Scotland (RCHMS 1999, 33).

Early Neolithic evidence is still very scanty. There are no Neolithic animal bone assemblages from the south west, and the earliest dated sites have rarely been found to contain much in the way of cereals or grain processing tools (Cole and Jones 2002-3; Jones and Reed 2006). Furthermore, there is not enough human bone from either the Mesolithic or Early Neolithic periods in the south west to provide information on dietary strategies or the possible effect of the adoption of a diet based on domesticated animals on Mesolithic-type lifestyles.

Arguably, the evidence from flint scatters might suggest a degree of continuity, as Early Neolithic assemblages are frequently intermixed with earlier, Mesolithic scatters (Lawson-Jones forthcoming), and at Poldowrian (Smith and Harris 1982) late Mesolithic and Neolithic radiocarbon determinations were obtained from adjacent layers

population linked with appearance of cereals and also that agriculture may have been introduced by migrants from France into southern England, with a broadly defined south west region being one of the first to be colonised (Collard *et al* 2010). In Cornwall there is quite limited evidence for early contacts with Europe. The three jadeite axes known, including one from Falmouth (Campbell-Smith 1963; Pétrequin *et al* 2008) (Fig 1), came from the Continent and are likely to date to the early centuries of the fourth millennium cal BC. Likewise, recent petrological study of greenstone axes found in Ireland (Mandal 1997) provides

Fig 3. Carn Brea from the north west showing low stone ramparts of the tor enclosure. (Steve Hartgroves
© HE, Cornwall Council)

and features. Unfortunately Mesolithic studies in Cornwall have not moved on significantly beyond Berridge and Roberts's 1986 paper and secure dating of Late Mesolithic sites in Cornwall remains poor. Sites with mixed Mesolithic and Neolithic lithics are most likely to result from patterns of landscape use first developed as Mesolithic clearings. Such usage indicated by flint scatters continued on into the Later Neolithic and most of the Bronze Age but much of the material can be difficult to date closely if diagnostic types are not present. As with the Mesolithic, there has been little useful work on Neolithic and later assemblages, apart from those from excavated sites, in the last 25 years.

The limited evidence for the movement of artefacts and the construction of widely distributed monument forms during the Early Neolithic shows that communities around the British Isles had contact with those on the Continent. However, it is possible that this contact was of a localised and variable nature (Cummings 2009; Garrow and Sturt 2011). The origins of the Neolithic inhabitants of Cornwall are uncertain and the nature of their diet is currently unresolved.

More positively the last 25 years have witnessed a substantial growth in the known number of Early Neolithic sites and in the availability of radiocarbon dates (Jones and Reed 2006). From these it is now

possible to begin to establish the character of the earliest Neolithic period in Cornwall. Mercer's excavations at Carn Brea (Fig 3) and Helman Tor demonstrated that significant hill-tops (Figs 4 and 5) had been enclosed by stone ramparts early in the fourth millennium cal BC, from *c* 3900-3600 cal BC, and that these places were both the focal points for the exchange of greenstone axes and for the deposition of early ceramics (Mercer 1981; 1997). The enclosures were interpreted by the excavator as permanent agricultural settlements (see below). Since 1986 a further nine enclosure sites have been recorded (Oswald *el al* 2001, 158-9). Several tor enclosures have been surveyed, such as Trencrom (Fig 4; Oswald 1996) where a flint assemblage has been recovered (Herring 1999). However, excavation has been confined to a small number of trenches on Carn Galva which confirmed the presence of walling but did not lead to the recovery of anything datable (Jones in preparation a).

New unenclosed Neolithic sites have also been identified. With the exception of a rectangular structure and a lightly built circular structure at Penhale, which have been dated to the Early Neolithic (Griffith *et al* 2008, 82), these take two forms, flint scatters and pit groups. Flint scatters of Early Neolithic date are being increasingly identified in the west half of the county, where they can be large and widespread (Gossip and Jones 2007; Lawson-Jones forthcoming). Small bowl-shaped pits containing pottery, flint and charcoal are an increasingly recognised feature of the British Neolithic in general and the Early Neolithic period in particular. In the last 10 years several sites have been excavated across Cornwall with radiocarbon dates which indicate

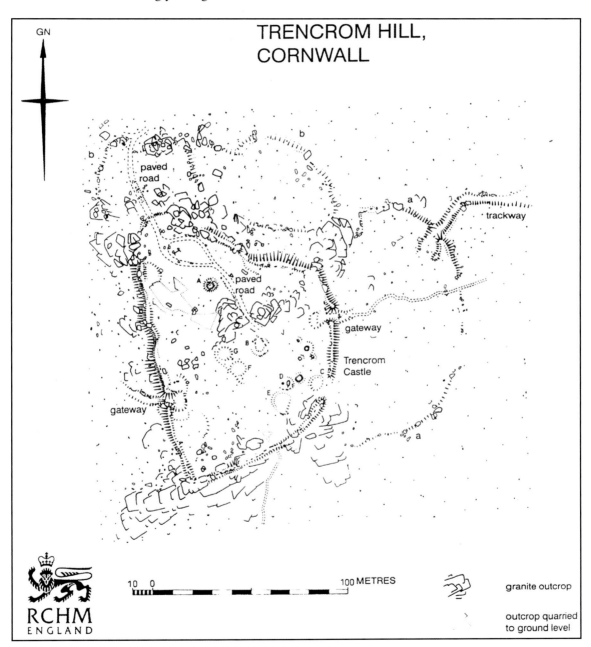

Fig 4. Plan of Trencrom showing the tor enclosure. (©Crown copyright. NMR)

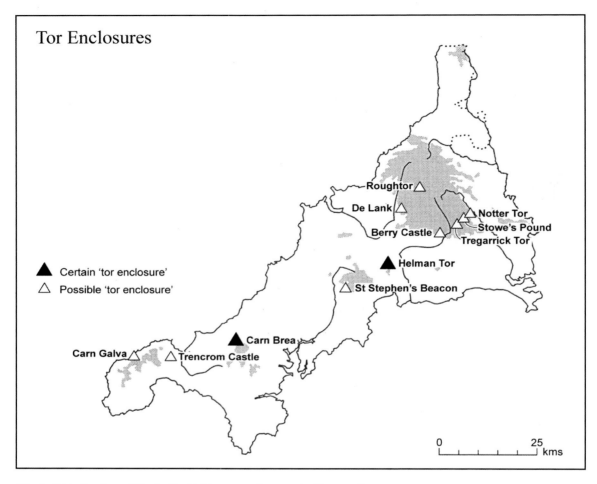

Fig 5. Distribution of Early Neolithic tor enclosures in Cornwall.

contemporaneity with the tor enclosures (Cole and Jones 2002-3; Jones and Reed 2006). Although these pits contain charcoal, most do not seem to have been used for cooking and may instead have been dug to hold special deposits which included curated sherds of pottery and other heirlooms. Interestingly, stone axe-heads are rare finds in pits. These pits may have been a ritualised way of clearing up when a site was left (Cole and Jones 2002-3), linked with a life-style that still involved considerable mobility. Radiocarbon determinations indicate that not all the pits within a group were contemporary, and this implies that certain locales may have been special and periodically revisited. Chris Tilley (1995; 1996) in a pair of particularly important papers has argued that rocky outcrops,

such as those on Bodmin Moor, may have been especially significant places in the landscape and it is relevant here that several pits have been found near to rocky outcrops (Smith and Harris 1982; Cole and Jones 2002-3).

Current evidence suggests that the Cornish landscape was well-used during the earlier part of the Neolithic but that tor enclosures were not permanently occupied settlements. Excavations at Carn Brea and Helman tor revealed little in the way of evidence for substantial structures and the worked stone assemblages lack the querns and rubbers which are commonly found on settlement sites. Instead, their locations on dramatically-sited hills may have made them liminal places; that is to say, they were places

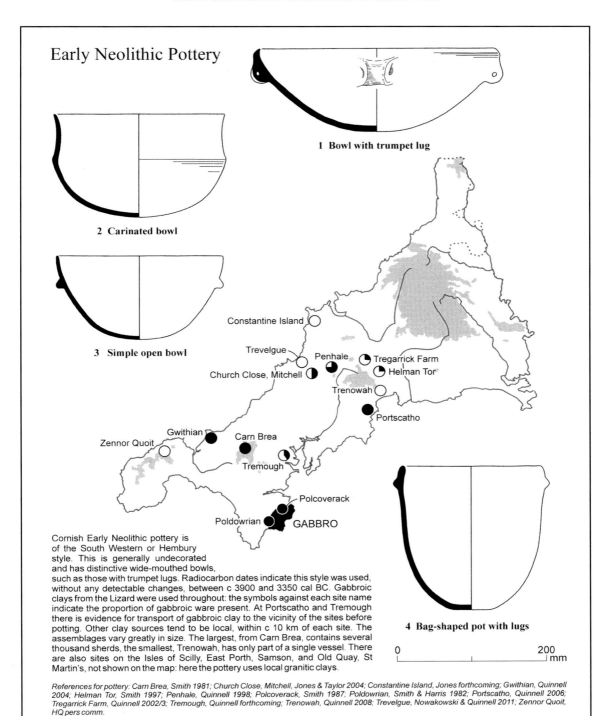

Early Neolithic Pottery

1 Bowl with trumpet lug

2 Carinated bowl

3 Simple open bowl

Constantine Island
Trevelgue
Penhale Tregarrick Farm
Church Close, Mitchell Helman Tor
Trenowah
Portscatho
Gwithian
Zennor Quoit Carn Brea
Tremough
Polcoverack
Poldowrian GABBRO

Cornish Early Neolithic pottery is
of the South Western or Hembury
style. This is generally undecorated
and has distinctive wide-mouthed bowls,
such as those with trumpet lugs. Radiocarbon dates indicate this style was used,
without any detectable changes, between c 3900 and 3350 cal BC. Gabbroic
clays from the Lizard were used throughout: the symbols against each site name
indicate the proportion of gabbroic ware present. At Portscatho and Tremough
there is evidence for transport of gabbroic clay to the vicinity of the sites before
potting. Other clay sources tend to be local, within c 10 km of each site. The
assemblages vary greatly in size. The largest, from Carn Brea, contains several
thousand sherds, the smallest, Trenowah, has only part of a single vessel. There
are also sites on the Isles of Scilly, East Porth, Samson, and Old Quay, St
Martin's, not shown on the map: here the pottery uses local granitic clays.

4 Bag-shaped pot with lugs

0   200
└─────────┴─────────┘ mm

References for pottery: Carn Brea, Smith 1981; Church Close, Mitchell, Jones & Taylor 2004; Constantine Island, Jones forthcoming; Gwithian, Quinnell 2004; Helman Tor, Smith 1997; Penhale, Quinnell 1998; Polcoverack, Smith 1987; Poldowrian, Smith & Harris 1982; Portscatho, Quinnell 2006; Tregarrick Farm, Quinnell 2002/3; Tremough, Quinnell forthcoming; Trenowah, Quinnell 2008; Trevelgue, Nowakowski & Quinnell 2011; Zennor Quoit, HQ pers comm.

DISCOVERY AND RESEARCH

Panel 1 Early Neolithic pottery

Fig 6. Cornish chambered tombs. Left, the portal dolman Zennor Quoit, and right, the simple Chun Quoit.
(Photographs: Andy Jones).

which were thought to occupy thresholds between the everyday and the supernatural. As such they may have been considered as places which held magical powers. This in turn may have made them suitable for periodic gatherings and for the exchange of greenstone axes and other objects by dispersed communities who spent most of their time in the lower lands around them. A case has been made for links between the artefactual assemblages deposited in pits and those made within tor enclosures; the two forms of deposition represented part of the same system of ordering objects and depositing them at particular places in the landscape (Jones 2005, 136).

It is also clear that greenstone axes appear in the earliest Neolithic contexts in Cornwall. Greenstone axes have been found in large numbers at tor enclosure sites and also frequently occur as unstratified stray finds (Fig 1). Identification of potential greenstone sources (Keiller *et al* 1941; Clough and Cummins 1988) suggested the existence of axe 'factories' (see Mercer 1986, fig 2). In the 1990s, the absence of the identification of any actual axe making sites led to the existence of axe 'factories' being questioned by Berridge (1993, 47). However, recent petrological study of greenstone outcrops undertaken by Markham (2000) has confirmed that Group I axes were derived from a source or sources in Penwith. Although it is likely that some axes were manufactured from beach pebbles, it is possible that detailed investigation of *in situ* greenstone outcrops with close petrological matches to finished axes could lead to the identification of production sites. There

have been substantial advances in our knowledge of Early Neolithic pottery, and especially the use of gabbroic clays (Panel 1).

The last strand of the Early Neolithic relates to the ceremonial and funerary monuments. As elsewhere in western Britain, chambered tombs and a small number of simple long mounds are found. The chambered tombs include simple tombs such as Chun (Fig 6), as well as portal dolmens and unclassifiable tombs such as Sperris Quoit (Thomas and Wailes 1967). Very limited new excavation has taken place within any of the Cornish chambered tombs (Jones in preparation a); however, new radiocarbon dates of *c* 3600-3500 cal BC from Sperris and *c* 3350-3000 cal BC from Zennor Quoit (Fig 6) on cremated human bone confirms that these sites were in use during the fourth millennium cal BC, and that cremation was an early mode of burial (Kytmannow 2008, 105-6). However, their initial date of construction remains to be established. Simple long mounds, such as the Catshole long barrow on Bodmin Moor (Johnson and Rose 1994, 24) are mostly found in the eastern part of the county. They are entirely undated but are presumed to belong to the Early Neolithic period on broad analogy with those from other parts of Britain.

Entrance graves, small chambered tombs found in Scilly and Penwith, were also included within Mercer's Neolithic chapter. The dating of these sites has been open to question and some writers have suggested an Early Neolithic origin (Ashbee 1982). However, recent study of these sites strongly suggests that they are of Early Bronze Age date (Jones and Thomas 2010; Robinson 2007, 144).

The Middle to Late Neolithic period (*c* 3400 cal BC to 2400 cal BC)

Few Middle Neolithic (*c* 3400-3000 cal BC) sites have been identified in Cornwall. A handful of pits, at Trenowah and Metha (Johns 2008; Jones and Taylor 2004) have radiocarbon determinations which fall within this period, as does the cremation from Zennor Quoit (*c* 3350-3000 cal BC). However, currently only one site has produced Peterborough Ware, a pit at Helston (information Foundations Archaeology), and, unlike other parts of the country (Gibson 2007), none of the investigated large round barrows have been found to be of later Neolithic date. A couple of possible crop-mark cursus-type sites have been identified by the National Mapping Programme at Trifle in East Cornwall (see Young 2006, fig 2) and near Portscatho on the Roseland. The embanked avenue on Craddock Moor (Johnson and Rose 1994, 26-8) could also be allied to cursus monuments. These are undated and unexplored; however, if they are cursus-type sites, they are likely to be Middle Neolithic, dating to *c* 3600-2900 cal BC (Barclay and Bayliss 1999, 25). Likewise, the bank cairn on the slopes of Rough Tor (Herring and Kirkham forthcoming) could, if related to the wider class of bank barrows found in southern England and Scotland, date to the middle to later part of the fourth millennium BC (Brophy 1998, 103; Sharples 1991, 103). However, the recent excavation of a trench across the bank cairn did not lead to the recovery of any secure dating material (Thompson and Birbeck forthcoming).

It could be argued (for example, Whittle 1978; Collard *et al* 2010), that the apparent decline in the number of Middle Neolithic sites and radiocarbon dates may equate with a population fall. However, given that until recently many radiocarbon determinations have been obtained from monuments, the apparent 'decline' may be little more than a pause in monument construction. In a Cornish context, the potential biases in data can be demonstrated by the recent developments in the Late Neolithic.

In 1986 evidence for the Cornish Late Neolithic was limited to a few class I henge monuments, such as Castilly, and a small number of Grooved Ware sherds (Mercer 1986; Christie 1988; Cleal and McSween 1999; Jones 2005, chapter 3). Excavation of Castilly henge and the Stripple Stones did not lead to the recovery of any diagnostic artefacts (Thomas 1964; Grey 1908). This meant that their assignment to the Late Neolithic is dependant upon henges which have been dated elsewhere (for example, Harding 2003). No henges have been excavated in the county since 1986. Until recently, the only ceremonial monument associated with a Later Neolithic radiocarbon date or Grooved Ware was the post-circle beneath barrow Davidstow 25 on Bodmin Moor (Christie 1988).

However, since the mid 1990s, several Grooved Ware sites have been excavated (Nowakowski forthcoming; Gent 1997; Gossip and Jones 2007, 8). All of these sites are associated with clusters of small pits, which were found to contain structured deposits of selected sherds of Grooved Ware pottery and of flint. The pits are very similar in content to those of the earlier Neolithic, and probably represent a continuing tradition of ritualised deposition. In common with the earlier pits, cereal remains are uncommon and it is likely that the pit groups were the work of small-scale communities. Current knowledge of Grooved Ware in Cornwall, and again the use of gabbroic clays, is presented in Panel 2.

A few ceremonial monuments have been securely dated to the later Neolithic period. A pit circle / timber circle recently excavated at Royalton on Goss Moor has been dated to *c* 2900-2600 cal BC (Clark and Foreman forthcoming). The site was devoid of artefacts, which highlights the especial importance of radiocarbon determinations for sites without dateable artefacts. The chronology of many monument forms poses a problem. In 1986 Mercer placed stone circles in the Neolithic period, on a few analogies from elsewhere in Britain, whereas post-rings, single standing stones and stone rows were briefly discussed in Christie's Early Bronze Age chapter. Although it is possible that some Cornish stone circles are contemporary with henges and date to the later Neolithic period (for example, Burl 2000, 174), currently, the only radiocarbon determination from a stone circle is from Leskernick, which was 1750-1550 cal BC (Bender *et al* 2007). Standing stones are also difficult to date. As discussed above, the Boscawen-un stone (Fig 2) may date from either the Early Neolithic or the Early Bronze Age, whereas the possible post- or stone-socket associated with the pit at Trenoweth was dated to the late third millennium cal BC (Reynolds 2006), and cremated bone from the cist beside the Try menhir (Jones and Quinnell 2006a) was dated to the second millennium cal BC. Indeed, the only secure determination from a

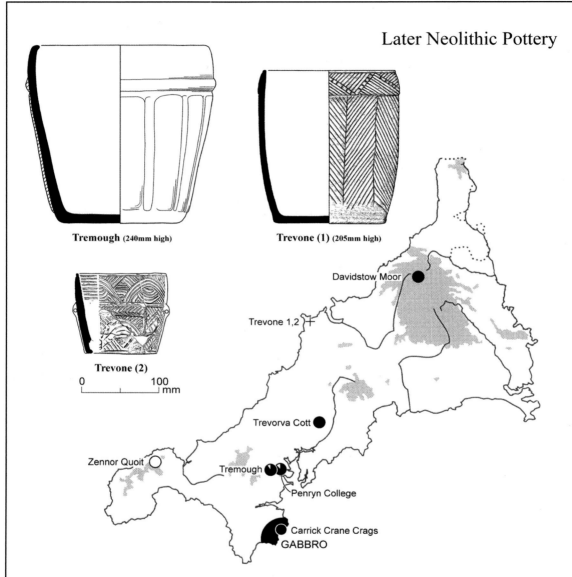

Later Neolithic Pottery

Tremough (240mm high)

Trevone (1) (205mm high)

Trevone (2)

0   100 mm

Davidstow Moor

Trevone 1,2

Trevorva Cott

Zennor Quoit

Tremough

Penryn College

Carrick Crane Crags

GABBRO

Middle Neolithic pottery, Peterborough Ware, c 3400-2900 cal BC, is only known from an unpublished find at Helston. Grooved Ware in Cornwall currently has radiocarbon dates ranging from 2900 to 2200 cal BC. This is the first flat-bottomed pottery in Britain. It has a variety of broadly tub-shaped forms and is usually decorated extensively, often by close-set incisions or patterns of applied clay strips. Gabbro clays were extensively used: the proportion of gabbro clay present is indicated by the map symbols, + indicating that the fabric is not known. At Tremough there was evidence for transport of some gabbroic clays for potting near the site. The largest assemblage comes from Tremough with at least 21 vessels present; the other sites have far less material. No Later Neolithic pottery is known from the Isles of Scilly.

References for pottery: Carrick Crane Crags, Longworth & Cleal 1999 No 44; Davidstow Moor, Longworth & Cleal 1999 No 42; Penryn College, Quinnell in prep. a; Tremough, Gossip & Jones 2007; Trevorva Cott, Nowakowski forthcoming; Trevone (1) Buckley 1972; Zennor Quoit, HQ pers comm.

Panel 2 Later Neolithic pottery

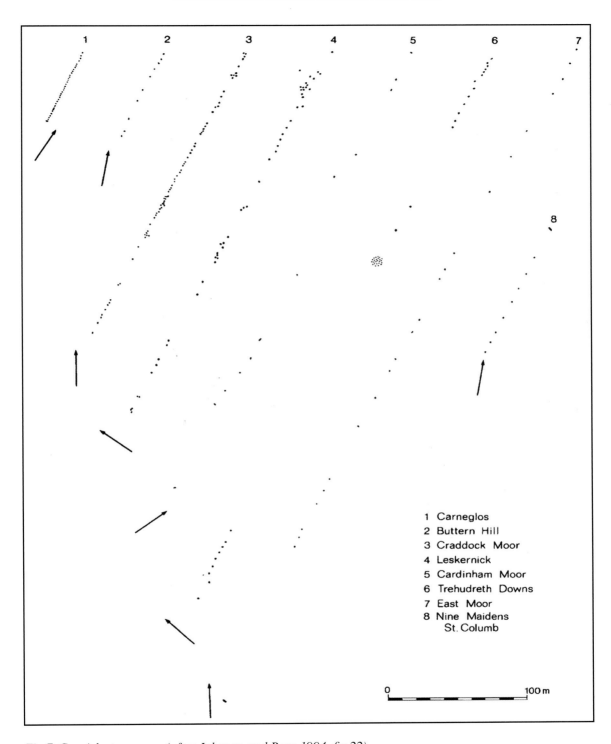

1 Carneglos
2 Buttern Hill
3 Craddock Moor
4 Leskernick
5 Cardinham Moor
6 Trehudreth Downs
7 East Moor
8 Nine Maidens
  St. Columb

DISCOVERY AND RESEARCH

Fig 7. Cornish stone rows (after Johnson and Rose 1994, fig 22).

standing stone came from the socket of the Eathorne menhir and this fell in the first to second centuries AD (Hartgroves *et al* 2006).

Stone rows present similar difficulties (Fig 7). Around 9 rows have been identified in Cornwall, the majority of which have been found on Bodmin Moor (Johnson and Rose 1994, 33-4; Herring 2008). Dating for these sites is as problematic as that for standing stones and stone circles. No radiocarbon determinations are available from the Cornish sites, but recently dating from a stone row on Dartmoor at Cut Hill falls in the first half of the fourth millennium cal BC (Fyfe and Greeves 2010) – or the earlier part of the Neolithic. By contrast, other Dartmoor sites such as Merrivale (Butler 1997, 220) seem to be very closely associated with Bronze Age cairns and the implication is that they are broadly contemporary. This means that stone rows are likely to have had an extended chronology, although, as with standing stones, it is likely that the meanings associated with them altered over time.

The final monuments of possible third millennium cal BC date are propped stones, which are found on the tops of tors (Blackman in preparation). They comprise a large stone which, as at Carn Galva in Penwith, has been raised or 'chocked' up by one or more smaller stones. Secure dating will be difficult to obtain given that most sites were constructed on bare rock. Support for a fourth or early third millennium cal BC date has been suggested (Herring 1997) for the propped stone on top of the hill at Leskernick on Bodmin Moor, as this was arranged so that the midsummer sun would been seen setting behind the propped stone when viewed from a nearby long mound. This alignment would have been accurate during the fourth to third millennium cal BC. One recently excavated site with similarities to the propped stones has associated radiocarbon dating. A stone setting near Sennen comprised a cluster of pits and posts erected around an arrangement of large granite boulders (Jones *et al* forthcoming). Although the stone setting could not be dated, the postholes have a series of radiocarbon determinations of *c* 2140-1510 cal BC, which suggests that the site had been an important focal point over several centuries. This should imply that the veneration of natural places first identified for the Early Neolithic (Tilley 1995) continued into the Early Bronze Age.

It would therefore seem likely that monument forms such as standing stones, stone rows and stone circles are extremely long-lived and potentially span the fourth to first millennium cal BC. This lengthy chronology is certainly borne out by the better dated free-standing post-rings (Panel 6) which can date to the Neolithic or the Bronze Age (Gossip and Jones 2007, 116; Clark and Foreman forthcoming).

The Beaker using period (*c* 2400 cal to 1700 cal BC)

For Christie in 1986, Beaker sites in Cornwall were restricted to a small group of largely incomplete vessels mostly derived from barrow-related contexts (for example, Clarke 1970, 477), and only one site, a burnt mound at Poldowrian on the Lizard, was associated with a radiocarbon determination (Harris 1979; Jones 2005, 21; Jones and Quinnell 2006a). However, in the last 10 years the number of sites and radiocarbon dates has greatly increased (Jones and Quinnell 2006a; Jones and Taylor 2010, 158-60; Jones *et al* forthcoming). The emerging picture from the new evidence is that the earliest Beakers in Cornwall (*c* 2400-2100 cal BC) are not found at barrows and cists but are instead on sites which may have been associated with the preparation of food such as the cooking mound and pit at Boscaswell (Jones and Quinnell 2006a) and with small pits, as at Scarcewater and Treyarnon (Jones and Taylor 2010, 5; forthcoming) where sherds are often found with flints and charcoal. Again, these pits have much in common with those of the Neolithic, although evidence for cereals is more commonly found, as well as hazelnut shells. Current interpretation of these sites suggests that Beakers were associated with the consumption and sharing of food as part of ritualised social events.

Recently, Beakers have also been found in association with the earliest Early Bronze Age structure to be identified in the county. This was found at Sennen, in Penwith (Jones *et al* forthcoming). The site comprised a small sub-oval structure, measuring approximately 4m long by 3m wide with small postholes and stakeholes around the edge of a hollow. Posts outside the structure indicated that it was set within a slight enclosure and other external features included a stone-lined hearth, which contained charred cereal grains. Four radiocarbon determinations from the site indicate that occupation probably occurred *c* 2400-2100 cal BC, making this the oldest securely dated Beaker associated activity in the county and the oldest post Neolithic structure

Beaker Pottery

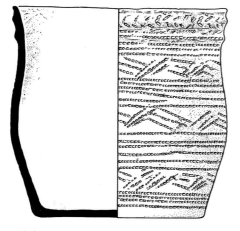

1 Sennen. S-profile Beaker, reconstructed

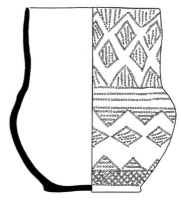

2 Long-necked Beaker, based on Boscaswell

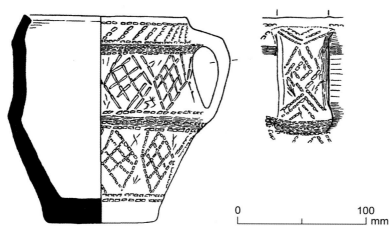

3 Try, Gulval. Late Beaker

0   100
|_____|_____| mm

Beaker pottery c 2400-1700 cal BC. This has been given a variety of complex classifications in the literature. The earliest, carinated, forms have not yet been found in Cornwall. S-profiled forms, as at Sennen, are the earliest to appear. Next are long-necked forms, as at Boscaswell, from at least 2100 cal BC. The Try Beaker is one illustration of a range of late unclassifiable forms, sometimes found in barrows. Eleven sites, with 13 + vessels represented, are barrows or burial-related. Fourteen sites, with parts of 80 + vessels, represent various forms of domestic rubbish disposal. Only one vessel from a barrow/burial is gabbroic. Five other sites have gabbroic vessels only, another five both gabbroic and other clays, and four sites non-gabbroic vessels. At the domestic sites at Sennen, Treyarnon and Nancemere gabbroic clays have been transported and mixed with local materials. No Beakers have yet been identified in the Isles of Scilly.

References for Beakers: general, Needham 2005, Jones & Quinnell 2006a with catalogue; Sennen, Jones et al forthcoming: Treyarnon, Jones & Taylor forthcoming; Boscaswell, Jones & Quinnell 2006a; Try, Russell & Pool 1964.

Panel 3 Beaker Pottery

DISCOVERY AND RESEARCH

in the south west. The small size of the structure together with the slenderness of its supporting posts suggests that it was a flimsy building, associated with a short-term occupation, although the presence of a large assemblage of grain processing stones and charred grains indicates cultivation in the vicinity, which might imply repeated visits to the area. The stonework assemblage from the Sennen structure is unusually good for Britain as a whole.

Radiocarbon dating for Beaker-associated burials is limited to one site (Jones and Quinnell 2006a), but the associations of Beakers with other ceramic forms, including Trevisker Ware, and Food Vessels suggests that it is only after *c* 2000 cal BC that Beakers were deposited into barrow-associated contexts.

Interestingly, unlike Ireland (O'Brien 2004), none of the Beaker assemblages can currently be shown to be linked with early metalworking or with the extraction of tin or copper. The lack of human remains means that it is impossible to be certain

whether the long-distance population mobility which has been identified elsewhere (for example, Price *et al* 1998; Fitzpatrick 2009) occurred in Cornwall. However, the localised, non-burial contexts for Beakers in Cornwall and their deposition alongside regional ceramic forms suggests that any Beaker-using people from outside Cornwall were rapidly assimilated into local communities.

In summary, the available evidence would suggest that the earliest Cornish Beaker-associated sites, such as the Sennen structure (Jones *et al* forthcoming) fall within the first period of Beaker use *c* 2400-2250 cal BC (Needham 2005). However, most, including those from the burnt mound at Boscaswell occurred during the period *c* 2250-1950 cal BC. It is also possible that there was a gradual shift over time from Beakers use on sites associated with ritualised cooking and social activity to use within ceremonial monuments *c* 2000-1700 cal BC. A summary presentation of Cornish Beaker pottery is given in Panel 3.

Fig 8. Bosiliack entrance grave from the south east during excavation in 1984. (*Photograph: Charles Thomas*)

The Early Bronze Age (*c* 2050 to 1500 cal BC)

The chronology of the periods of the British Bronze Age has been enhanced by the application of radiocarbon dating to metal-associated contexts over the last decade. As a result the dates now used are generally a little earlier than those presented in 1986 (Needham 1996).

From *c* 2000 cal BC barrows and cairns were constructed in large numbers. Around 3,500 have been recorded and they form a wide variety of site types, ranging from mounded barrows to open enclosure barrows, such as ring cairns (Johnson and Rose 1994, 34-42; Miles 1975). Radiocarbon determinations from newly excavated sites and material held in museum archives (Jones and Thomas 2010; Jones *et al* in preparation) have demonstrated that the period *c* 2000-1500 cal BC is marked by monument construction on a scale not been seen since the earlier Neolithic. Currently the evidence for

barrow building after *c* 1500 cal BC is limited to a few small-scale monuments.

A number of barrows and cairn groups have been investigated over the last 25 years, including individual sites at Harlyn Bay, Littlejohhns Barrow, Gaverigan and Trelowthas (Rose and Preston-Jones 1987; Jones *et al* in preparation; Johns 1994; Nowakowski 1995; 2007), and the cairn complex on Stannon Down (Jones 2004-5). The re-examination of older sites and new excavations has demonstrated the longevity of both individual barrows and cairns, and the complexes in which they are found. Radiocarbon dating has revealed that the use of monuments could extend over more than a century (Jones and Quinnell 2006b).

It has long been clear that there was a good deal diversity in their use, much of which was not burial-related (for example, Miles 1975). The excavation of five cairns at Stannon revealed that only one site had probably been used for burial and at Littlejohns Barrow and Gaverigan there was none at all (Jones

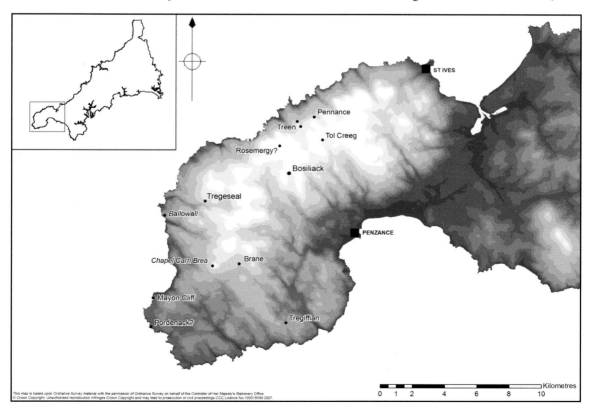

Fig 9. Distribution of Penwith entrance graves.

DISCOVERY AND RESEARCH

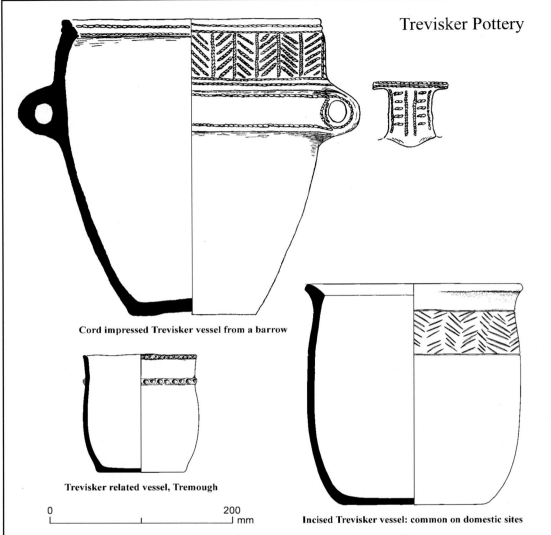

Trevisker Pottery

Cord impressed Trevisker vessel from a barrow

Trevisker related vessel, Tremough

0   200
|_____| mm

Incised Trevisker vessel: common on domestic sites

Trevisker ceramics originate in Cornwall and form the principal ceramics of the 2nd millennium cal BC. Some has decoration made by impressed cord, some by incisions; other techniques such as comb-stamping also occur. Early attempts to show chronological variation in decoration have been proved wrong. However, most vessels from the Early Bronze Age are cord-impressed as this was the preferred style for barrow deposition. Even so, incised vessels do occur, notably at Harlyn Bay. In the Middle Bronze Age, domestic settlements have a mixture of incised and cord-impressed decorations. Some vessels, such as that from Tremough with finger-nail impressions on cordons are best described as Trevisker-related. Fabrics are usually tempered with rock fragments and are described as 'admixtures'. In the Early Bronze Age gabbroic, granitic and other clays are used with rock admixtures. In Middle Bronze Age settlements, about 90% of vessels are of gabbroic admixture. Several sites of this date now have evidence for the transport of gabbroic clay and its mixing with local material. These are Gwithian, Tremough, Carnon Gate, Nancemere, Scarcewater and Stannon. Trevisker ceramics are not found on the Isles of Scilly, where a slightly different range of cord-impressed and incised vessels occur.

References for Trevisker pottery: general, Parker-Pearson 1990, Woodward & Cane 1991; Harlyn Bay, Jones et al in prep; Tremough, Gossip & Jones, 2007; Gwithian, Quinnell 2004; Carnon Gate, Gossip & Jones forthcoming; Nancemere, Quinnell in prep. b; Scarcewater, Jones & Taylor 2010; Stannon, Jones 2004/5.

Panel 4 Trevisker Pottery

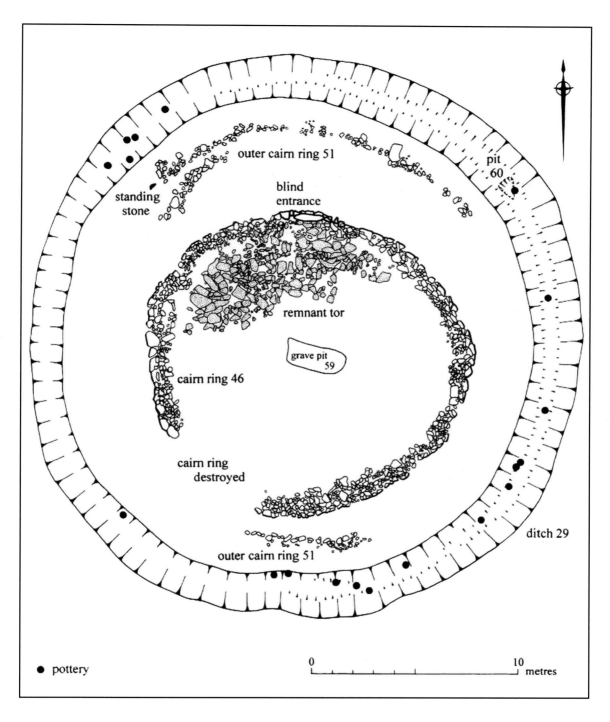

Fig 10. Plan of the Watch Hill barrow showing the remnant tor, the primary cairn ring and central burial feature (after Jones and Quinnell 2006b).

Watch Croft: blending the cultural and the natural in the Early Bronze Age

1 'Cairn' group viewed from the east

2 Cairn in group

3 Cairn and outcrop

4 Natural rocky outcrop

A recurring feature of Cornish prehistory is the association of ceremonial sites with distinctive natural places, such as tor and smaller rocky outcrops. Many upland Early Bronze Age cairns have been found to be associated with distinctive natural places. This relationship is clearly shown at Watch Croft in Penwith. In profile, the summit of Watch Croft appears to have been crowned by a linear cairn group (1). Closer inspection reveals that this is not entirely the case. One of the sites in the group is a cairn (2); however, other cairns clearly include natural outcrops within them (3), and two of the 'cairns' are wholly formed by natural 'cairn-like' outcrops (4). It is possible that the 'cairn-like' outcrops on Watch Croft were perceived as being 'ancestral' cairns or the work of supernatural beings. The Early Bronze Age cairns referenced and manipulated the outcrops by being aligned onto or physically incorporating them into their fabric. In doing so, bonds were forged between sacred locales, monuments and their builders.

Photographs: A M Jones 2009.

Panel 5 Watch Croft, West Penwith, blending the cultural and the natural in the Early Bronze Age

2004-5; Johns 1994; Nowakowski 1994). Analyses have revealed a wide variety in the manner that human remains were treated, and there is no evidence that inhumations occurred before cremation burials (Jones in preparation b). Radiocarbon dating suggests that token and multiple and single cremations occurred throughout Needham's (1996) Periods 3 and 4 (2050-1700 cal BC and 1750-1500 cal BC). Many barrows have been found to contain very tiny, token, amounts of human bone (for example,

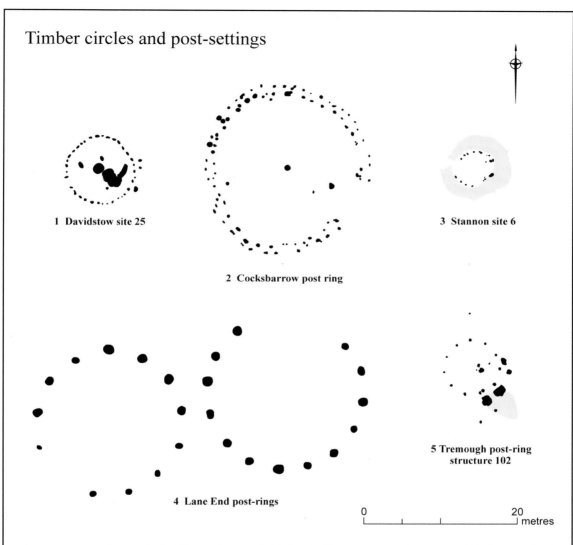

Timber circles and post-settings

1 Davidstow site 25

2 Cocksbarrow post ring

3 Stannon site 6

4 Lane End post-rings

5 Tremough post-ring
structure 102

0   20
|____|____|____| metres

DISCOVERY AND RESEARCH

Large-scale excavation over the last 20 years has revealed that post-settings were a recurring element within the repertoire of ceremonial monuments during the latter part of the third and second millennium cal BC. The publication of the Davidstow barrow complex demonstrated the presence of a later Neolithic post-ring beneath Davidstow site 25 (1). During the first half of the second millennium cal BC, post-rings and timber settings are found in association both with Early Bronze Age barrows and ring-cairns (2 and 3) and as free-standing structures (4). In the second half of the second millennium cal BC, post-rings were erected, near to settled areas, as at Tremough (5) where a linear complex of timber rings was constructed. It is probable that these sites were associated with shifting sets of meanings and it has been suggested that the later Bronze Age post-rings may have shared a symbolic link with the structural post-rings which were contained inside the centre of domestic roundhouses.

References for timber rings: Davidstow site 25, Christie 1988; Cocksbarrow, Miles and Miles 1971; Stannon site 6, Jones 2004-5; Lane End post-rings, Clark and Foreman forthcoming; Structure 102, Tremough, Gossip and Jones 2007.

Panel 6 Timber circles and post-settings

Christie 1985; 1988), whereas, at the other end of the scale, others have been found to contain multiple cremation deposits (Harris *et al* 1984; Smith 1996). The cist in the barrow at Trelowthas contained the cremated remains of several individuals (Nowakowski 1995). The recently analysed urned cremation deposit from Harlyn Bay has shown that an apparently homogenous burial was actually a multiple cremation which comprised parts of the ashes of several young people and animal bone (Jones *et al* in preparation). By contrast, the analyses of an, apparently primary, cremation from the entrance grave at Bosiliack dated to 1690-1500 cal BC was associated with the remains of a single individual (Jones and Thomas 2010) (Figs 8 and 9). As discussed above, entrance graves are probably best seen as being part of the diverse range of monuments, ritual and burial practices found in Cornwall during this time.

Where artefacts are recovered from barrows, they are frequently not directly associated with the burial. Aside from pottery, artefacts are not particularly common, and metalwork and other high status objects are especially scarce prior to *c* 1750 cal BC (Jones in preparation c). Gold is exceptionally rare, although there are a small number of lunulae dating to *c* 2000 cal BC, which demonstrate early contacts with Ireland. Two of these came from a barrow at Harlyn Bay although no burial was identified (Mattingly *et al* 2009). The only other barrow-associated gold object is the Rillaton Cup, which is much later, dating to *c* 1750 cal BC (Needham *et al* 2006). It may have been obtained through contacts with a wider European tradition of precious cup use which linked communities either side of the English Channel (Needham 2009). It is tempting to associate cross-channel contacts with the circulation of Cornish tin and copper, but evidence for securely dated Early Bronze Age metallurgy in the south west remains scarce. Little evidence remains for prehistoric mining, most of it probably having been destroyed by later activity. Hammerstones have been found in west Cornwall, which could date to the Bronze Age (Craddock and Craddock 1997) and tin slag was found within the Caerloggas I barrow, which probably dates toward the latter part of the Early Bronze Age (Miles 1975). Although later in date, Middle Bronze Age finds from stream-works are indicative of second millennium cal BC tin mining. Over 40 prehistoric artefacts, including antler picks, oak shovels, and metal tools, have

been recorded as being discovered in reworked tin stream-works (Penhallurick 1986, 173; 1997); however, the contexts for most of these finds are not well-documented. It is not until the Late Bronze Age when ingots and bronze moulds (Herring 2000b, 46; Gossip forthcoming) are found that there is more substantive evidence for metalworking.

Pottery is often found, especially Trevisker Ware (Panel 4). Recent radiocarbon dating of barrows and cairns has confirmed the establishment of this regionally distinctive ceramic tradition from around *c* 2000 cal BC, which continued to be made throughout the second millennium cal BC. Other barrow associated ceramic finds such as the Accessory Vessel from Colliford CRIVC (Griffith 1984) or the Collared Urn and Food Vessel from Cataclews (Christie 1985) provide evidence for the occasional inclusion of ceramic styles widely found in other parts of Britain.

Many Cornish barrows were associated with small-scale ritualised offerings in pits and ditches (Jones and Quinnell 2006b; Jones in preparation b). It has also been found that many sites were aligned on, adjacent to, encircled by or sometimes even covered prominent, if small, rock outcrops (Fig 10). Watch Croft in West Penwith (Panel 5) demonstrates a complex linkage between natural and manmade features. Tors such as Rough Tor on Bodmin Moor and Carn Galva in Penwith seem to have been particularly important focal points for barrows and other ceremonial monuments (Tilley 1995; Jones 2005 chapter 4; in preparation a). This link with landscape markers strengthens the interpretation of many of the region's barrows and cairns as focal points for ritual, rather than primarily as places of burial.

Other types of ceremonial monuments have been identified, such as the free-standing timber-rings (Panel 6) at Goss Moor (Clark and Foreman forthcoming), post-ring structure 66 at Tremough (Gossip and Jones 2007, 11) and the segmented enclosure at Highgate, near Indian Queens (Nowakowski 1994); the centre of which contained a Collared Urn holding a cremation burial and an awl. The stone-setting at Sennen, mentioned above, also had pits erected beside it during this period (Jones *et al* forthcoming). As Christie noted, several barrows are associated with cup-marks (for example, Christie 1985). Other cup-marks have been found on *in situ* boulders, as at Stithians reservoir (Hartgroves 1987) and Bodrifty.

However, in addition to incorporation within Bronze Age monuments, they have also been found on the capstones of megaliths such as Mulfa (Rose 2009, 19). This means that, like the standing stones and stone circles, their dating remains uncertain and their context needs to be better understood.

Although evidence for formal ceremonial activity is common, settlement evidence for the period prior to *c* 1500 cal BC remains extremely scarce and, with the exception of structure 1642 (formerly described as the Beaker structure) at Gwithian which has been dated to 1890-1610 cal BC (Nowakowski *et al* 2007), no 'domestic' structures are known from this period. Small pits, containing flint, charcoal and often hazelnut shells continue to occur from

during the first half of the second millennium cal BC, as at Trenoweth and at Tremough (for example, Reynolds 2006; Gossip and Jones 2007, 11). These sites are comparable to the small Neolithic and Beaker pits that have been discussed above and probably represent practices associated with the ritualised clearing, following on from the communal consumption of food.

The Middle Bronze Age (*c* 1500 cal BC to *c* 1100 cal BC)

In 1986, most of the known roundhouses dating to the Bronze Age were those in upland areas such as Bodmin Moor. However, in the last 25 years one of

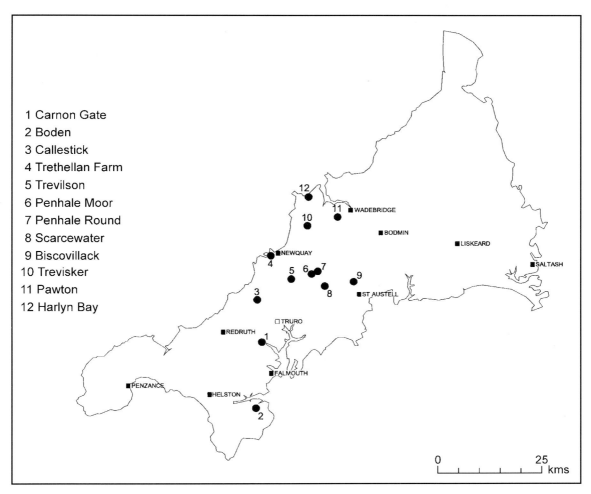

1 Carnon Gate
2 Boden
3 Callestick
4 Trethellan Farm
5 Trevilson
6 Penhale Moor
7 Penhale Round
8 Scarcewater
9 Biscovillack
10 Trevisker
11 Pawton
12 Harlyn Bay

Fig 11. Distribution of Middle Bronze Age lowland sunken floored roundhouses.

DISCOVERY AND RESEARCH

Fig 12. Middle Bronze Age roundhouse 1500 at Scarcewater, from the south, showing post ring in bottom of the house hollow. (© HE, Cornwall Council)

the major developments in the Cornish Bronze Age has been the identification of widespread settlement activity across the lowlands (Fig 11). Lowland house-building is associated with a regionally distinctive form of roundhouse architecture. This building tradition takes the form of sunken-floored roundhouses, which range from around 6m to 15m in diameter and are characterized by hollows that are lined with stone walling and contain a post-ring set within the interior of the hollow. As a result of the corpus of radiocarbon determinations, which currently stands at around 40 dates (Gossip and Jones 2008), it is evident that this architectural tradition dates to the period *c* 1500 cal BC-1100 cal BC.

Around 20 sunken-floored roundhouses have been recorded in Cornwall. They include sites at Trevisker and Trethellan, Callestick and Trevilson (ApSimon and Greenfield 1972; Nowakowski 1991;

Jones 1998-9a; Jones and Taylor 2004). They have been found across the lowlands from Boden on the Lizard (Gossip in preparation) to more marginal areas, such as the Carnon Gate roundhouse, situated near to the Carnon River (Gossip and Jones 2008) and Scarcewater, located on the edge of the St Austell Granite (Jones and Taylor 2010). A probable house has also been located at Staddon, Plymouth (Exeter Archaeology Projects 4648 and 4813) and has produced radiocarbon dates, calibrating to 3118 $\pm$ 37 BP, 1440 – 1250 BC (Wk-15104) and to 3122 $\pm$ 42 BP, 1450 – 1210 BC (Wk-15105).

The uncovering of complete lowland settlements is uncommon, and only two, Trethellan and Scarcewater, have been excavated in their entirety (Nowakowski 1991; Jones and Taylor 2010). However, despite having sunken interior floors, typically there are relatively few occupation-related layers and comparatively little is known about daily-life. At Scarcewater, a settlement comprising three roundhouses was excavated (Fig 12), yet most of the artefacts associated with the roundhouses were either recovered from ritualised deposits in pits or postholes, or were found in backfill layers, which had been placed into the houses when they were being abandoned. As a result, many of the discussions about roundhouses in Cornwall have been focussed upon the ritualised patterns of roundhouse abandonment, rather than on evidence for occupation (for example, Nowakowski 2001; Jones 1998-9a). From recent excavations it is apparent that many roundhouses underwent episodes of transformation at the end

of their occupation: they were monumentalised and would have ended up looking similar to Early Bronze Age cairns or barrows. This resemblance is likely to have been intentional and drawn from earlier Bronze Age ritual traditions associated with barrows and cairns (Jones 2008).

In Devon post-ring roundhouses were constructed instead (for example, Butler 1997; Fitzpatrick *et al* 1999). The most westerly is that recently excavated at Langage Farm, Plympton (Exeter Archaeology Project 5504). The uniqueness of Cornish lowland architecture is significant because it indicates regionalised identity in the lowlands, as well as localised responses to wider changes

Fig 13. The settlement on Craddock Moor, Bodmin Moor, from the south. (Aerial photograph: Steve Hartgroves © HE, Cornwall Council)

in settlement organisation which were occurring in the middle part of the second millennium cal BC. However, metalwork assemblages comprised widely found forms, such as the palstave hoard from Truro (Rowlands 1976, 228), and the discovery of Trevisker-style pottery in a Middle Bronze Age settlement in France indicate that long-distance contacts were maintained (Marcigney *et al* 2007).

Stone-walled houses were constructed in the uplands, especially on Bodmin Moor where large numbers have been recorded (Johnson and Rose 1994, 55-76) (Fig 13). Unfortunately, the only moorland settlements associated with radiocarbon determinations are those at Leskernick on Bodmin Moor (Bender *et al* 2007) and Bosiliack in Penwith (Jones and Quinnell in preparation). Both settlements have been dated to the middle centuries of the second millennium cal BC. However, the picture at Bosiliack is complex as the two investigated houses have been found to have been reoccupied in the first

Fig 14. *An exposed boundary of probable Middle Bronze Age date found near to Bossiney along the North Cornwall pipeline, 2009.* (© *HE, Cornwall Council*)

millennium cal BC – possibly by transhumant pasturalists (*ibid*).

The rapidly increasing number of sites indicates that both the lowlands and the uplands were quite densely occupied by the middle of the second millennium cal BC. The relationship between the uplands and the lowlands is incompletely understood, although it seems likely that there would have close links between the two zones and possible that some upland settlements may only have been occupied during the summer months.

The way in which communities from lowland and upland settlements used the land is problematic. Evidence for cereal cultivation increases during the second millennium cal BC, with charred cereals found on several settlements, especially Trethellan, where barley and wheat were identified (Nowakowski 1991). Elsewhere, the evidence for cultivation has been sparser, for example at Scarcewater, where, despite large-scale sampling, low quantities of charred cereals were recovered from the Middle Bronze Age roundhouses (Jones and Taylor 2010, 34). Environmental evidence indicates an expansion of farming from the middle centuries of the second millennium cal BC (Wilkinson and Straker 2008; Jones and Tinsley 2000-1). Pasture and rough grazing may have made up a large part of the landscape, and on Stannon Down pollen evidence indicated the spread of grassland after *c* 1500 cal BC (Jones 2004-5). Areas of woodland were still present although of unknown extent.

Field systems are well-documented in the uplands (Johnson and Rose 1994, 59-65; Yates 2007, 68-71) and are closely integrated with settlements, as at Bosiliack (Jones and Quinnell in preparation). It is not yet possible to demonstrate that the initial dates for fields and for roundhouses were contemporary in the county. Two unpublished radiocarbon dates from peat beneath field boundaries at Stannon Down, on Bodmin Moor, 1780-1520 cal BC (GU-5172) and 1700-1490 cal BC (GU-5170) indicate that some boundaries were being laid out in the middle centuries of the second millennium cal BC. Late Bronze Age metalwork finds from within field systems in west Cornwall demonstrate that boundaries had been established by *c* 1000 cal BC (Johnson 1980).

Because field boundaries rarely survive later ploughing, it has proved more difficult to identify field systems in the lowlands. On current evidence, many sunken-floored roundhouses seem to be unenclosed, but this picture is probably incorrect. Where post-settlement deposits have formed over houses, these have associated field walls and banks. At Trethellan the remains of a lynchetted boundary were found, and at Gwithian stone banks were uncovered (Nowakowski 1991; Nowakowski *et al* 2007). Recently, stone walling associated with Trevisker pottery has been found beneath hill-wash deposits near Bossiney on the north Cornish coast (information Andy Jones) (Fig 14). It seems probable, therefore, that large tracts of the lowlands were enclosed during the middle centuries of the second millennium cal BC.

Where large-scale excavation has occurred, evidence is emerging for the 'zonation' of space. A range of buildings are now known in addition to roundhouses, and some are non-domestic. Roundhouses, non-circular post-built structures, activity hollows and small ceremonial monuments were contemporary with one another and there was spatial separation of 'task-scapes', 'dwelling' and 'ritual' areas (Nowakowski *et al* 2007; Nowakowski 2001; Johns 2008; Jones 2008; Jones and Taylor 2010). At Scarcewater, three sunken-floored roundhouses were excavated, with several flimsy structures and pits located just beyond them. Various features in this area produced muller and quern fragments suggesting the grinding of cereals, and it was likely that many activities took place outside the roundhouses. An area down-slope of the settlement held a group of three ploughed-down mounds, probably small barrows. The evaluative excavation was too limited to determine whether they held burials, although trenching through one mound produced part of a vessel filled with pebbles arranged in circles (Jones and Taylor 2010, 34). A radiocarbon date from the vessel revealed that the mound was contemporary with the roundhouses.

Small-scale ceremonial sites are increasingly being recognised in areas adjacent to settlements. At Trethellan and Callestick non-domestic buildings were sited close to roundhouses (Nowakowski 1991; Jones 1998-9a). At Tremough, five timber post-rings were erected, and at Stannon a ring cairn of Early Bronze Age origin beside a roundhouse settlement was refurbished (Gossip and Jones 2007; Jones 2004-5, 25). In the middle centuries of the second millennium cal BC, ceremonial activity shifted away from distant barrows to sites which were close to settlements. However, a crouched inhumation burial inside a cist beneath

a cairn built over an earlier barrow on Constantine Island has been dated to 1320-1110 cal BC (Jones forthcoming). This suggests that some formal burials may have been situated within older sites during the latter half of the second millennium cal BC, although the practise of constructing large barrow mounds appears to have ceased.

As elsewhere in Britain (for example, Brück 1995; Bradley 2005, 52), ritual and burial activity seems to have moved into the areas of settlements in the middle of the second millennium cal BC. An inhumation burial was found beneath a hearth within one of the roundhouses at Trethellan (Nowakowski 1991) and cremations were found at Gwithian in residential structures and within pits along field boundaries (Nowakowski *et al* 2007). A token amount of probable human bone was also found within a vessel inside a pit outside the roundhouses at Scarcewater (Jones and Taylor 2010, 68). The variable, but generally small, amounts of human bone from the ritual foci on settlements demonstrates, as does the barrow-like appearance of abandoned roundhouses, continuity from Early Bronze Age barrow-associated practices. Continuity is also indicated by the Trevisker pottery, which occurs in settlements until the end of the second millennium cal BC (Quinnell 2004-5; 2007). The current evidence suggests that people, roundhouses and settlements had interrelated biographies.

The Late Bronze Age
(*c* 1100 cal BC to 800 cal BC)

In 1986, the Late Bronze Age was largely represented in Cornwall by metalwork finds, often recovered during later tin streaming, and a small number of pits (Pearce 1983; Penhallurick 1986; Miles *et al* 1977). The character of settlement and the post Trevisker pottery sequence was not well-understood. Today large-scale area excavation has led to the discovery of Late Bronze Age settlements (for example, Gossip forthcoming) and the arrangements for reporting artefacts has greatly increased the number of documented metalwork find-spots (Department of Culture Media and Sport 2004; 2008) (Fig 15). However, burials are still unknown from this period.

Environmental information from Bodmin Moor (Tinsley 2004-5) does not show a marked deterioration in conditions, which means that there was no environmental reason for the disuse of the

DISCOVERY AND RESEARCH

Fig 15. The Late Bronze Age Sompting axe hoard with pottery container found at Mylor (Royal Cornwall Museum Accession Number 2008.12). (© Bernie Pattinson)

uplands in the Late Bronze Age, which was widely suggested in the 1980s (for example, Burgess 1980). Indeed, upland areas, such as Bodmin Moor and Penwith have provided evidence for the continuing use or reoccupation of earlier, Middle Bronze Age, roundhouses. This is suggested by the radiocarbon dating of two roundhouses at Leskernick (Bender *et al* 2007, 88-9) and from a roundhouse at Bosiliack (Jones and Quinnell in preparation). It is possible that any reuse of structures may have been of a seasonal nature, perhaps associated with the movement of animals to upland pastures.

Evidence is also emerging for settlement in the lowlands after 1000 cal BC when radiocarbon dates indicate that the sunken-floored roundhouses disappeared. Two Late Bronze Age settlements have been excavated. At Truro College, a settlement comprised of four post-ring structures with diameters of up to 8m has been securely dated to the tenth and ninth centuries cal BC (Gossip forthcoming). At Scarcewater, a post-ring roundhouse approximately 8m in diameter with a porched entrance on the south east was partly enclosed by a palisade (Fig 16). The palisade was probably not defensive, as it was only wide enough to support split timbers or planks and was open on its western side. The porch and palisade together may have formed a grand façade for the roundhouse when approached from

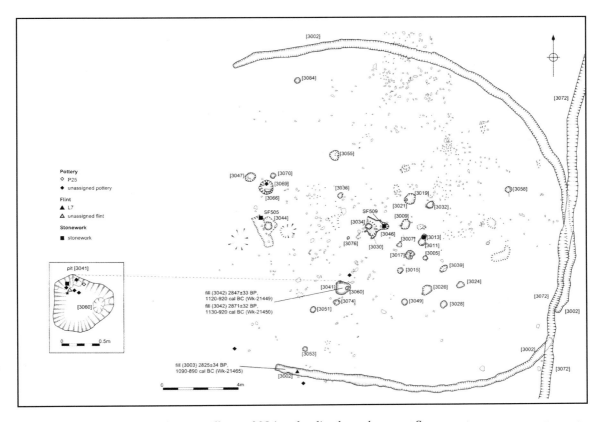

Fig 16. Plan of Late Bronze Age roundhouse 3084 and palisade enclosure at Scarcewater. (© HE, Cornwall Council)

lower ground (Jones and Taylor 2010, 83). The radiocarbon determinations from the site fell in the range 1130-890 cal BC. Another ditched enclosure, dating to 1396-840 cal BC, was excavated at Liskeard. However, the Liskeard enclosure ditch was much more substantial and the enclosure far larger than the Scarcewater palisade. Unfortunately truncation of the site made it uncertain whether it had encircled a settlement (Jones 1998-9b).

The Late Bronze Age post-ring roundhouses at Truro and Scarcewater are comparable with houses that are found across southern Britain (for example, Guilbert 1982; Ladle and Woodward 2009, 364-7), and it seems likely that this type of domestic architecture spread into Cornwall from Devon.

The aggrandisement of the entrance was a feature of the recently excavated roundhouse at Trevalga on the north Cornish coast (Fig 17). This had a dry-stone walled entrance and an internal wall lined with non-structural, vertical set slates.

The site has not been radiocarbon dated yet, but the presence of a stone mould for a triangular-shaped razor suggests a date at the end of the Late Bronze Age. The mould suggests contacts with France, where triangular razors are much more common (for example, Burgess 1968; Nallier and Le Goffic 2008) than in south west Britain (Pearce 1983) (Fig 18).

After nearly a millennium, the regional Trevisker Ware ceramics disappear from around 1000 cal BC and versions of styles common across much of Britain appear. Late Bronze Age Plain Ware pottery has been found within the settlements at Truro College and Scarcewater (Gossip forthcoming; Quinnell 2010), as well as residually at Trevelgue cliff castle and possibly from a roundhouse on St Michael's Mount (Nowakowski and Quinnell 2011; Quinnell 2000, 39-40).

Metalwork is also being recovered, for example, the St Erth hoard (Department of Culture Media

DISCOVERY AND RESEARCH

Fig 17. Trevalga roundhouse, near Tintagel, excavated in 2009 on the North Cornwall pipeline, showing dry-stone walling around the entrance. (© HE, Cornwall Council)

and Sport 2004), the Mylor Hoard (Ratcliffe and Marley 2009) and the St Michael's Mount find-spot (Herring 2000b; Jim Parry, pers comm). The growing body of metalwork, especially socketed axes (Henderson 2007, fig 3.2), enhances the data for contacts across a wide area of Britain. The hoard of Sompting-type axes found within a pot at Mylor shows that this contact continued until the very end of the Bronze Age. Late Bronze Age gold-work has long been known, for example the well-documented hoard of probable Irish goldwork, including torcs and bracelets from Towednack (Pearce 1983, 426), but there have been additional finds such as the bracelets from Rosemorran and a strip of gold found with the St Erth hoard (Department of Culture Media and Sport 2004). These new metalwork finds reinforce the indications of increasing contacts along the Atlantic façade (Henderson 2007, 57; Cunliffe 2010), and show that Cornwall was part of a network of long-distance connections. However, while metalwork, the form of post-ring roundhouses and the ceramics demonstrate widespread connections, some locally established traditions persisted.

The settlements at Scarcewater and Truro College were both adjacent to pits with structured deposits. At Scarcewater sherds of pottery were placed in a pit dating to 1000-830 cal BC (Jones and Taylor 2010, 83). At Truro College a pit dating to *c* 1150-1000 cal BC contained part of a Wilburton type clay sword mould (Gossip forthcoming) and pottery. This is the first Late Bronze Age sword mould found in Cornwall, and its burial may have been a formal, ritualised event. Likewise, metalwork hoards are often in contexts suggestive of structured deposition, and as in other parts of Britain it is possible that certain types of topographical locale were favoured for ritualised deposition (Yates and Bradley 2010). The Mylor axe hoard was buried in pot inside a pit and several Late Bronze Age metalwork hoards were buried close to distinctive rock outcrops, as at Carn Brea, Viaduct Farm and the recent St Michael's Mount hoard (Borlase 1769, 263; Thomas 2004; Jim Parry pers comm). This

Fig 18. The Late Bronze Age razor mould recovered during the excavation of the Trevalga roundhouse. (Photograph: Anna Tyacke)

manner of deposition is evident back in the Early Neolithic, and, while details of the beliefs involved are likely to have changed through the millennia, long-established traditions may have enhanced the importance of distinctive places in the landscape and influenced the sorts of deposits considered appropriate at them.

Conclusion

The last 25 years have witnessed a dramatic increase in knowledge of the Neolithic and Bronze Age periods, and has largely been brought about by developer-funded projects on lowland areas. It is now clear that well-preserved monuments represent only a small part of human activity and that the lowlands were at least as densely occupied as the moors. However, unsurprisingly, questions still remain. In particular, the transition from the Mesolithic to the Neolithic is poorly understood, and Middle Neolithic sites are still few and far between. Similarly, the nature of Early Bronze Age settlement remains to be established, our knowledge of the Late Bronze Age is still sparse and the context for hoards of all periods needs to be better understood. The evidence for Bronze Age mining and metallurgy remains elusive and

targeted archaeological investigation is badly needed to identify extraction and production sites. Perhaps most importantly, targeted research projects are needed in the next 25 years to investigate those types of sites, such as stone rows and stone circles, which have not been recently excavated because they have been considered 'safe' from development.

Acknowledgements

The authors would like to thank Jane Read for the maps and illustrations and Jane Marley Curator of Archaeology and World Cultures at the Royal Cornwall Museum for providing access to the collections and for giving us permission to reproduce Figures 1 and 15. Thanks are also due to Anna Tyacke PAS Finds Liaison Officer for Cornwall for photographing the axes in Figure 1 and the razor mould in Figure 18, and to English Heritage for giving us permission to reproduce the survey plan of Trencrom. We are grateful to Tim Gent of Exeter Archaeology for permission to use the illustration of Grooved Ware from Trevone in Panel 2.

References

ApSimon, A M, and Greenfield, E, 1972. The excavation of the Bronze Age and Iron Age settlement at Trevisker Round, St Eval, Cornwall, *Proc Prehist Soc*, **38**, 302-81

Ashbee, P, 1982. Mesolithic megaliths? The Scillonian entrance graves: a new view, *Cornish Archaeol*, **21**, 3-22

Barclay, A, and Bayliss, A, 1999. Cursus monuments and the radiocarbon dating problem, in A Barclay, and J Harding, eds, *Pathways and ceremonies*, Oxford, 11-29

Bayliss, A, Whittle, A, and Healy, F, 2008. Timing, tempo and temporalities in the Early Neolithic of southern England, in H Fokkens, B J Coles, A L Vian Gijn, J P Kleijne, H P Hedwig, and C G Slappendel, eds, *Between foraging and farming*, Leiden, 25-42

Bender, B, Hamilton, S, and Tilley, C, 2007. *Stone worlds: narrative and reflexivity in landscape archaeology*, Walnut Creek, California

Berridge, P, 1993. Cornish axe factories: fact or fiction, in N Ashton, and A David, *Stories in stone*, London, 45-56

Berridge, P, and Roberts, A, 1986. The Mesolithic period in Cornwall, *Cornish Archaeol*, **25**, 7-34

Blackman, T, in preparation. From pseudo-quoit to propped stones

Borlase, W, 1769. *Antiquities historical and monumental of the County of Cornwall*, Oxford

Bradley, R, 2005. *Ritual and domestic life in prehistoric Europe*, London

Brophy, K, 1998. Cursus monuments and bank barrows of

DISCOVERY AND RESEARCH

Tayside and Fife, in G J Barclay, and G S Maxwell, *The Cleaven Dyke and Littleour, monuments in the Neolithic of Tayside*, Edinburgh, 92-108

Brück, J, 1995. A place for the dead: the role of human remains in Late Bronze Age Britain, *Proc Prehist Soc*, **61**, 245-78

Buckley, D G, 1972. The excavation of two slate cairns at Trevone, Padstow, 1972, *Cornish Archaeol*, **11**, 9-18

Burgess, C, 1968. The later Bronze Age in the British Isles and north western France, *Arch Jnl*, **125**, 1-45

Burgess, C, 1980. *The Age of Stonehenge*, London

Burl, A, 2000. *Stone circles of Britain Ireland and Brittany*, Newhaven

Butler, J, 1997. *Dartmoor atlas of antiquities, volume 5*, Tiverton

Campbell-Smith, W, 1963. *Jade axes* from sites in the British Isles, *Proc Prehist Soc*, **29**, 133-72

Christie, P, 1985. Barrows on the north Cornish coast: wartime excavations by C K Croft Andrew, *Cornish Archaeol*, **24**, 23-122

Christie, P, 1986. Cornwall in the Bronze Age, *Cornish Archaeol*, **25**, 81-110

Christie, P, 1988. A barrow cemetery on Davidstow Moor, Cornwall: wartime excavations by C K Croft Andrew, *Cornish Archaeol*, **27**, 27-169

Clark, P, 2007. A30 to *Indian Queen to Indian Queens road improvement scheme: post-excavation assessment and updated project design*, Oxford (Oxford Archaeology)

Clark, P, and Foreman, S, forthcoming. The archaeology of the A30 Bodmin to Indian Queens road scheme, *Cornish Archaeol*

Clarke, D L, 1970. *Beaker pottery of Great Britain and Ireland*, Cambridge

Cleal, R, and MacSween, A, 1999. *Neolithic Grooved Ware in Britain and Ireland*, Oxford

Clough, T H McK, and Cummins, W A, 1988. *Stone axe studies, volume 2*, London

Cole, R, and Jones, A M, 2002-3. Journeys to the Rock; archaeological investigations at Tregarrick Farm, Roche, Cornwall, *Cornish Archaeol*, **41-42**, 107-43

Collard, M, Edinborough, K, Shennan, S, and Thomas, G, 2010. Radiocarbon dating evidence indicates migrants introduced farming to Britain, *J Archaeol Sci*, **37**, 866-70

Cornwall County Council, 1996. *Cornwall landscape assessment 1994*. Report prepared by CAU and Landscape Design Associates, Cornwall County Council, Truro

Craddock, P T, and Craddock, B R, 1997. The inception of metallurgy in south-west Britain, in P Budd and D Gale, eds, *Prehistoric extractive metallurgy in Cornwall*, Truro, 1-14

Cunliffe, B, 2010. Celtization from the West: the contribution of archaeology, in B Cunliffe, and J T Kock, eds, *Celtic from the West: alternative perspectives from archaeology, genetics, language and literature*, Oxford, 13-38

Cummings, V, 2009. An Irish Sea change: some implications for the Mesolithic-Neolithic transition, in K Brophy, and G J Barclay, eds, *Defining a regional Neolithic: the evidence from Britain and Ireland*, Oxford, 53-65

Department of Culture Media and Sport, 2004. *Treasure annual report 2002*, London

Department of Culture Media and Sport. 2008. *Treasure annual report 2005/6*, London

Fitzpatrick, A, 2009. In his hands and in his head: the Amesbury Archer as a metalworker, in P Clark, ed, *Bronze Age connections, cultural contact in prehistoric Europe*, Oxford, 176-88

Fitzpatrick, A, Butterworth, C A, and Grove, J, 1999. *Prehistoric and Roman sites in east Devon: the A30 Honiton to Exeter Improvement DBFO Scheme, 1996-9*, Salisbury

Fyfe, R, and Greeves, T, 2010. The date and context of a stone row: Cut Hill, Dartmoor, south-west England, *Antiquity*, **84**, 55-70

Garrow, D, and Sturt, F, 2011. Grey waters bright with Neolithic argonauts? maritime connections and the Mesolithic-Neolithic transition within the 'western seaways' of Britain, c. 5000-3500 BC, *Antiquity*, **85**, 59-72

Gent, T, 1997. *Padstow to Harlyn: a transect across the landscape*, Exeter (Exeter Archaeology)

Gibson, A, 2007. A Beaker veneer, in M Larsson, and M Parker Pearson, eds, *From Stonehenge to the Baltic, living with cultural diversity in the third millennium BC*, Brit Arch Repts, Int Ser, **1692**, Oxford, 47-64

Gossip, J, forthcoming. Life outside the round - Bronze Age and Iron Age settlement at Higher Besore and Truro College, Threemilestone, Truro, *Cornish Archaeol*

Gossip, J, in preparation. The evaluation of a multi-period prehistoric site at Boden Vean, St Anthony in Meneage, Cornwall 2003, *Cornish Archaeol*

Gossip, J, and Jones, A M, 2007. *Archaeological investigations of a later prehistoric and a Romano- British landscape at Tremough, Penryn, Cornwall*, Brit Arch Repts, Brit Ser, **443**, Oxford

Gossip, J, and Jones A M, 2008. A Bronze Age roundhouse at Carnon Gate, Feock, *Cornish Archaeol*, **47**, 101-115

Gray, H St G, 1908. On the stone circles of east Cornwall, *Archaeologia*, **61**, 1-60

Griffith, F M, 1984. Archaeological investigations at Colliford Reservoir, Bodmin Moor 1977-78, *Cornish Archaeol*, **23**, 47-140

Griffith, F, Healy, F, Jones, A M, Lawson, A, Lewis, J, Mercer, R, Mullin, M, Nowakowski, J, Pollard, J, Wickstead, H, and Woodward, P, 2008. Neolithic and Early Bronze Age, in C Webster, ed, *South West Archaeological Research Framework: the archaeology of south west England*, Taunton, 75-102

Guilbert, G, 1982. A Sussex style of post ring layout in Bronze Age roundhouses, *Sussex Archaeological Collections*, **120**, 209-13

Harding, J, 2003. *The henge monuments of the British Isles*, Stroud

Harris, D, 1979. Poldowrian, St Keverne: a Beaker mound on the gabbro of the Lizard peninsula, *Cornish Archaeol*, **18**, 13-32

Harris, D, Hooper, S, and Trudgian, P, 1984. Excavation of three cairns on Stannon Down, St Breward, *Cornish Archaeol*, **23**, 141-55

Hartgroves, S, 1987. The cup-marked stones of Stithians reservoir, *Cornish Archaeol*, **26**, 69-84

Hartgroves, S, Jones, A M, and Kirkham, G, 2006. The Eathorne menhir, *Cornish Archaeol*, **45,** 97-108

Henderson, J, 2007. *The Atlantic Iron Age: settlement and identity in the first millennium BC,* London

Herring, P, 1997. Early prehistoric sites at Leskernick Altarnun, *Cornish Archaeol*, **36,** 176-85

Herring, P, 1999. *Trencrom, Lelant, archaeological and historical assessment*, Truro (Cornwall Archaeological Unit)

Herring, P, 2000a. *Boscawen-un, St Buryan, Cornwall, archaeological assessment,* Truro (Cornwall Archaeological Unit)

Herring, P, 2000b. *St Michael's Mount, archaeological works, 1995-8,* Truro (Cornwall County Council)

Herring, P, 2008. Stepping onto the commons: south-western stone rows, in P Rainbird, ed, *Monuments in the landscape*, Stroud, 79-88

Herring, P, forthcoming. Boscawen-Un: stone circle and stone axes, *Cornish Archaeol*

Herring, P, and Kirkham, G, forthcoming. A bank cairn on Rough Tor, *Cornish Archaeol*

Johns, C, 1994. Littlejohns Barrow: the damage and reprofiling of the round barrow west of Hensbarrow, Roche, *Cornish Archaeol, 33,* 22-35

Johns, C, 2008. The excavation of a multi-period archaeoloical landscape at Trenowah, St Austell, Cornwall, 1997, *Cornish Archaeol, 47,* 1-48

Johnson, N, 1980. Later Bronze Age settlement in the South-West, in J Barrett, and R Bradley, R, eds, *Settlement and society in the British later Bronze Age*, Brit Arch Repts, Brit Ser, **83,** Oxford, 141-180

Johnson, N, and Rose, P, 1983. *Archaeological survey and conservation in west Penwith*, Truro (Cornwall Committee for Rescue Archaeology)

Johnson, N, and Rose, P, 1994. *Bodmin Moor: an archaeological survey, volume 1,* London

Jones, A M, 1998-9a. The excavation of a Later Bronze Age structure at Callestick, *Cornish Archaeol*, **37-8,** 5-55

Jones, A M, 1998-9b. The excavation of a Bronze Age enclosure at Liskeard Junior and Infant School, *Cornish Archaeol*, **37-8,** 56-71

Jones, A M, 2004-5. Settlement and ceremony; archaeological investigations at Stannon Down, St Breward, Cornwall, *Cornish Archaeol*, **43-44,** 1-141

Jones, A M, 2005. *Cornish Bronze Age ceremonial landscapes c. 2500-1500 BC*, Brit Arch Repts, Brit Ser, **394,** Oxford

Jones, A M, 2008. Houses for the dead and cairns for the living: a reconsideration of the Early to Middle Bronze Age transition in south-west England, *Oxford J Archaeol*, **27,** 153–74

Jones, A M, forthcoming. Excavation of a barrow on Constantine Island, St Merryn, Cornwall, *Cornish Archaeol*

Jones, A M, in preparation a. CAS excavations at Carn Galva and Bosporthennis in 2009

Jones, A M, in preparation b. Without Wessex; the local character of the Early Bronze Age in the south west peninsula

Jones, A M, in preparation c. *Going west: ceremony, barrows and cairns in the south west peninsula*

Jones, A M, Marley, J, Quinnell, H, and Hartgroves, S, in preparation. On the beach: new discoveries at Harlyn Bay, *Proc Prehist Soc*

Jones, A M, and Quinnell, H, 2006a. Cornish Beakers: new discoveries and perspectives, *Cornish Archaeol*, **45,** 31-70

Jones, A M, and Quinnell, H, 2006b. Redating the Watch Hill Barrow, *Arch Jnl, 163,* 42-66

Jones, A M, and Quinnell, H, in preparation. Bosiliack a later prehistoric settlement in Penwith, Cornwall, *Arch Jnl*

Jones, A M, and Reed, S J, 2006. By land, sea and air: an Early Neolithic pit group at Portscatho, Cornwall and consideration of coastal activity during the Neolithic, *Cornish Archaeol*, **45,** 1-30

Jones, A M, and Taylor, S R, 2004. *What lies beneath . . . St Newlyn East and Mitchell, archaeological investigations 2001*, Truro (Cornwall County Council)

Jones, A M, and Taylor, S R, 2010. *Scarcewater, Pennance, Cornwall, archaeological excavation of a Bronze Age and Roman landscape*, Brit Arch Repts, Brit Ser, **516,** Oxford

Jones, A M, and Taylor, S R, forthcoming. Discoveries along the Treyarnon SWW pipeline, *Cornish Archaeol*

Jones, A M, Taylor, S R, and Sturgess, J, forthcoming. A Beaker associated structure and other discoveries along the Sennen to Porthcurno SWW pipeline, *Cornish Archaeol*

Jones, A M, and Thomas, A C, 2010. Bosiliack and a reconsideration of entrance graves, *Proc Prehist Soc,* **76,** 271-96

Jones, A M, and Tinsley, H M, 2000-1. Recording ancient environments at De Lank, St Breward, Cornwall, *Cornish Archaeol*, **39-40,** 145-60

Keiller, A, Piggott, S, and Wallis, F S, 1941. First report of the subcommittee of the South-western federation of museums and art galleries on the petrological identification of stone axes, *Proc Prehist Soc*, **7,** 50-72

Kytmannow, T, 2008. *Portal tombs in the landscape, the chronology, morphology and landscape setting of the portal tombs of Ireland, Wales and Cornwall,* Brit Arch Repts, Brit Ser, **455,** Oxford

Ladle, L, and Woodward, A, 2009. *Excavations at Bestwall Quarry, Wareham, 1992-2005, volume 1: the prehistoric landscape*, Dorchester

Lawson-Jones, A, forthcoming. Discoveries along the North Lands End pipeline, *Cornish Archaeol*

Longworth, I, and Cleal, R, 1999. Grooved Ware gazetteer, in R Cleal, and A MacSween, 1999, 177-206

Mandal, S, 1997. Striking the balance: the roles of petrography and geochemistry in stone axe studies in Ireland, *Archaeometry*, **39,** 289-308

Markham, M, 2000. Provenance studies of British prehistoric greenstone implements using non-destructive analytical methods, unpublished PhD thesis, Open University

Marcigny, C, Ghesquiere, E and Kinnes, I, 2007. Bronze Age cross-channel relations. The Lower-Normandy (France) example: ceramic chronology and first reflections, in C Burgess, P Topping, and F Lynch, eds, *Beyond Stonehenge, essays on the Bronze Age in honour of Colin Burgess*, Oxford, 255-67

DISCOVERY AND RESEARCH

Mattingly, J, Marley, J, and Jones, A M, 2009. Five gold rings? Early Bronze Age gold lunulae from Cornwall, *Jnl Roy Inst Cornwall*, 95-114

Mercer, R, 1981. Excavations at Carn Brea, Illogan Cornwall: a Neolithic fortified complex of the third millennium bc, *Cornish Archaeol*, **20**, 1-204

Mercer, R, 1986. The Neolithic in Cornwall, *Cornish Archaeol*, **25**, 35-80

Mercer, R, 1997. The excavation of a Neolithic enclosure complex at Helman Tor, Lostwithiel, Cornwall, *Cornish Archaeol*, **36**, 5-63

Miles, H, 1975. Barrows on the St Austell Granite, *Cornish Archaeol,* **14,** 5-81

Miles, H, and Miles, T, 1971. Excavations on Longstone Downs, St Austell, St Stephen-in-Brannel and St Mewan, *Cornish Archaeol*, **10**, 5-28

Miles, H, Davey, U, Harris, D, Hooper, S, Moreton, P, Padel, O, and Staines, S, 1977. Excavations at Killibury hillfort, Egloshayle 1975-6, *Cornish Archaeol*, **16**, 89-121

Nallier, R, and Le Goffic, M, 2008. Rosnoen 60 ans apres. Complements et revision concernant le depot de l'Age du bronze final de Penavern (Finistere), *Bulleten de la Societe prehistorique francaise*, **105**, 1-27

Needham, S. 1996. Chronology and periodisation in the British Bronze Age, *Acta Archaeologia*, **67**, 121-40

Needham, S, 2005. Transforming the Beaker culture in north-west Europe: processes of fusion and fission, *Proc Prehist Soc*, **71**, 171-218

Needham, S, 2009. Encompassing the sea: 'maritories' and Bronze Age interactions, in P Clark, ed, *Bronze Age connections, cultural contact in prehistoric Europe*, Oxford, 12-37

Needham, S, Parfitt, K, and Vardell, G, 2006. *The Ringlemere cup, precious cups and the beginning of the Channel Bronze Age,* London

Nowakowski, J, 1991. Trethellan Farm, Newquay: the excavation of a lowland Bronze Age settlement and Iron Age cemetery, *Cornish Archaeol*, **30**, 5-242

Nowakowski, J, 1994. *Bypassing Indian Queens*, Truro (Cornwall Archaeological Unit)

Nowakowski, J, 1995. The excavation of a complex barrow at Trelowthas, Manor Farm, Probus, *Cornish Archaeol*, **34**, 206-11

Nowakowski, J, 2001. Leaving home in the Cornish Bronze Age: insights into the planned abandonment process, in J Brück, ed, *Bronze Age landscapes tradition and transformation*, Oxford, 139-48

Nowakowski, J. 2007. Digging deeper into barrow ditches: investigating the making of early Bronze Age memories in Cornwall, in J Last, ed, *Beyond the grave; new perspectives on barrows*, Oxford, 91-112

Nowakowski, J A, forthcoming. Trevorva Cott, Probus. A Late Neolithic site in lowland Cornwall, *Cornish Archaeol*

Nowakowski, J, Quinnell, H, Sturgess, H, Thomas, C, and Thorpe, C, 2007. Return to Gwithian: shifting the sands of time, *Cornish Archaeol*, **46**, 13-76

Nowakowski, J, and Quinnell, H, 2011. *Trevelgue Head cliff castle: the 1939 excavations by CK Croft Andrew*, Truro (Cornwall Council)

O'Brien, W, 2004. *Ross Island: mining, metal and society in early Ireland*, Galway

Oswald, A, 1996. *Trencrom Castle, Ludgvan, Cornwall*, Cambridge (Royal Commission Historic Monuments England)

Oswald, A, Dyer, C, and Barber, M, 2001. *The creation of monuments*, Swindon

Parker-Pearson, M, 1990. The production and distribution of Bronze Age pottery in south-west Britain, *Cornish Archaeol*, **29**, 5-32

Patton, M, 1993. *Statements in stone, monuments and society in Neolithic Brittany*, London

Pearce, S, 1983. *The Bronze Age metalwork of south western Britain*, Brit Arch Repts, Brit Ser, **120**, Oxford

Penhallurick, R, 1986. *Tin in antiquity*, London

Penhallurick, R, 1997. The evidence for prehistoric mining in Cornwall, in P Budd, and D Gale, eds, *Prehistoric extractive metallurgy in Cornwall*, Truro, 23-34

Pétrequin, P, Sheridan, A, Cassen, S, Errera, M, Gauthier, E, Klassen, L, Le Maux, N, and Paillier, Y, 2008. Neolithic Alpine axeheads from the Continent to Great Britain the Isle of Man and Ireland, in H Fokkens, B J Coles, A L Vian Gijn, J P Kleijne, H P Hedwig, and C G Slappendel, eds, *Between foraging and farming*, Leiden, 261-79

Price, T D, Grupe, G A, and Shröter, P, 1998. Migration in the Bell Beaker period of Central Europe, *Antiquity*, **72**, 405-12

Quinnell, H, 2000. First millennium BC and Roman period ceramics, in Herring 2000b, 39-45

Quinnell, H, 1998. Neolithic ceramics, in J A Nowakowski, *A30 Project, Cornwall – Archaeological Investigations along the route of the Indian Queens Bypass 1992-1994*, **2**, 136-7, Cornwall Archaeological Unit Report to English Heritage

Quinnell, H, 2003-3. Early Neolithic pottery, in Cole and Jones 2002-3, 113-121

Quinnell, H, 2004. Appendix 2: assessment of the prehistoric and Roman period pottery, in J A Nowakowski, *Archaeology Beneath the Towans: Excavations at Gwithian, Cornwall 1949-1969: Update Project Design. Cornwall County Council*

Quinnell, H, 2004-5. The pottery, in Jones 2004-5

Quinnell, H, 2006. Neolithic pottery, in Jones and Reed 2006, 5-9

Quinnell, H, 2007. Prehistoric, Roman and early medieval pottery, in Gossip and Jones 2007, 51-78

Quinnell, H, 2008. The prehistoric pottery, in Johns 2008

Quinnell, H, 2010. Prehistoric, Roman, and early medieval pottery, in Jones and Taylor, 2010, 93-139

Quinnell, H, forthcoming. Early Neolithic pottery, in J Gossip forthcoming, Neolithic pits and tree throws at Tremough, Penryn

Quinnell, H, in prep. a. The pottery, in J Gossip in prep, Archaeological excavations at Penryn College, Cornwall, *Cornish Archaeol*

Quinnell, H, in prep. b. The pottery, in J Gossip in prep, Archaeological investigations at Nancemere, Truro, Cornwall 2002: a prehistoric and Romano-British landscape

Ratcliffe, L, and Marley, J, 2009. The Mylor axe hoard, *CBA Archaeology South-West Journal*, **23,** 13-14

RCHMS, 1999. *Kilmartin, prehistoric and early historic monuments*, Edinburgh

Reynolds, A, 2006. An Early Bronze Age pit at Trenoweth, Portreath and other results from the Reskadinnick to Portreath transfer pipeline, *Cornish Archaeol*, **45,** 71-96

Robinson, G, 2007. *The prehistoric island landscape of Scilly*, Brit Arch Repts, Brit Ser, **447,** Oxford

Rose, P, 2009. *Mulfra Hill, Madron, Cornwall, archaeological survey 1988-9*, Truro (Historic Environment Service, Cornwall County Council)

Rose, P, and Preston-Jones, A, 1987. Mrs Hurn's Urn, *Cornish Archaeol*, **26,** 85-96

Rowlands, M J, 1976. *The organisation of Middle Bronze Age metalworking*, Brit Arch Repts, Brit Ser, **31,** Oxford

Russell, V, and Pool, P A S, 1964. Excavation of a Menhir at Try, Gulval, *Cornish Archaeol*, **3,** 15-26

Schulting, R, 2004. An Irish Sea change: some implications for the Mesolithic-Neolithic transition, in V Cummings, and C Fowler, eds, *The Neolithic of the Irish Sea, materiality and traditions of practice*, Oxford, 22-8

Sharples, N, 1991. *Maiden Castle: excavations and field survey, 1985-6*, London

Sheridan, A, 2000. Achnacreebag and its French Connection: *vive* the 'Auld Alliance', in J Henderson, ed, *The prehistory and early history of Atlantic Europe*, Brit Arch Repts, International Series **861,** Oxford, 1-16

Sheridan, A, 2004. Neolithic connections along and across the Irish Sea, in V Cummings and C Fowler, eds, *The Neolithic of the Irish Sea, materiality and traditions of practice*, Oxford, 9-21

Sheridan, A, and Schulting, R, 2008. Re-visiting a small passage tomb at Broadsands, Devon, *Proc Devon Archaeol Soc*, **66,** 1-26

Smith, G H, 1987. The Lizard Project: landscape survey 1978-1983, *Cornish Archaeol*, **26,** 13-68

Smith, G, 1996. Archaeology and environment of a Bronze Age cairn and prehistoric and Romano-British field system at Chysauster, Gulval, near Penzance, Cornwall, *Proc Prehist Soc*, **62,** 167-220

Smith, G, and Harris D, 1982. The excavation of Mesolithic, Neolithic and Bronze Age settlements at Poldowrian, St. Keverne, 1980, *Cornish Archaeol*, **21,** 23-62

Smith, I F, 1981. The Neolithic pottery, in Mercer 1981, 161-85

Smith, I F, 1997. The Neolithic pottery, in Mercer 1997, 29-37

Thomas, A C, 1964. The Society's 1962 excavations: the henge of Castilly at Lanivet, *Cornish Archaeol*, **3,** 1-14

Thomas, A C, 2004. *The Neolithic in the Gwithian area*, privately published

Thomas, A C, and Wailes, B, 1967. Sperris Quoit; the excavation of a new Penwith chamber tomb, *Cornish Archaeol*, **6,** 9-22

Thomas, J, 1991. *Rethinking the Neolithic*, Cambridge

Thomas, J, 1999. *Understanding the Neolithic*, London

Thompson, S, and Birbeck, V, forthcoming. A Time team evaluation at Roughtor, Bodmin Moor, Cornwall, *Cornish Archaeol*

Tilley, C, 1995. Rocks as resources: landscapes and power, *Cornish Archaeol*, **34,** 5-57

Tilley, C, 1996. The powers of rocks: topography and monument construction on Bodmin Moor, *World Archaeology*, **28,** 161-76

Tilley, C, and Thomas, J, 1993. The axe and the torso; symbolic structures in the Neolithic of Brittany, in C Tilley, ed, *Interpretative archaeology*, Oxford

Tinsley, H, 2004-5. Pollen analyses, in Jones 2004-5, 48-72

Whittle, A, 1978. Resources and population in the British Neolithic, *Antiquity*, **52,** 34-42

Whittle, A, 1997. Moving on and moving around: Neolithic settlement mobility, in P Topping, *Neolithic landscapes*, Oxford, 15-42

Whittle, A, Barclay, A, Bayliss, A, McFayden, L, Schulting, R, and Wysocki, M. 2007. Building for the dead, process and changing worldviews from the thirty-eighth to thirty fourth centuries cal BC in southern England, *Cambridge Archaeol J*, **17,** 123-47

Wilkinson, K, and Straker, V, 2008. Neolithic and Early Bronze Age environmental background, in C J Webster, ed, *The archaeology of South West England, South West archaeological research framework, resource assessment and research agenda*, Taunton

Woodward, A and Cane, C, 1991. The Bronze Age pottery, in Nowakowski 1991, 103- 131

Yates, D, 2007. *Land, power and prestige: Bronze Age field systems in southern England*, Oxford

Yates, D, and Bradley, R, 2010. The siting of metalwork hoards in the Bronze Age of south-east England, *Antiq Jnl*, **90,** 41-72

Young, A, 2006. The National Mapping Programme in Cornwall, *Cornish Archaeol*, **45,** 109-17

DISCOVERY AND RESEARCH

Cornish Archaeology 50, 2011, 231–240

A summary of Cornish ceramics in the first millennium BC

A brief illustrated guide to the sequence of Cornish ceramics in the first millennium BC derived from analysis of excavated sites undertaken since 1986.

HENRIETTA QUINNELL

During the last 25 years a number of projects, mostly undertaken by the staff of Historic Environment, Cornwall Council, have provided information on the chronology and sequence of ceramic styles in Cornwall during the first millennium cal BC. The understanding of the ceramic sequence has been greatly assisted by the now regular practise of obtaining multiple radiocarbon dates from excavated sites, a practise that was only just beginning 25 years ago. New information has been especially important for the Late Bronze Age, which has only been recognised in the last decade, and for the Middle and the Late Iron Ages. Data are still scanty for the Earliest and Early Ages. This summary is intended as a guide to current knowledge and as the basis for refinement as new data becomes available. Much background discussion is presented in the publication on Trevelgue Head cliff castle, Newquay (Quinnell 2011).

Late Bronze Age Plain Ware (Fig 1)

Trevisker ware, in which vessels have a geometric pattern beneath the rim (Jones and Quinnell current volume), was used through much of the second millennium BC. It was probably current in the early part of the Late Bronze Age, defined by metalwork

as starting *c* 1150 cal BC (Needham 1996). Radiocarbon dates from the settlement at Gwithian indicate that Trevisker pottery was still in use in the tenth century cal BC (Nowakowski *et al* 2007, 30), dates corroborated by recent determinations for the eleventh and tenth centuries cal BC from a pit group at Porthleven (information Bryn Morris). There was almost certainly some overlap with the subsequent ceramic style, Late Bronze Age Plain Ware.

The term Late Bronze Age Plain Ware was first used by John Barrett (1980) when he realised that, with frequent radiocarbon dating, much of the pottery previously considered Iron Age in Wessex and South East England in fact was contemporary with the typical bronze artefacts of the Late Bronze Age. The term 'Plain Ware' was contrasted with 'Decorated Ware' as, in those parts of England, there was a clear sequence between plain and decorated versions of the same styles. These consisted broadly of simple jars with straight or slightly curved walls, jars with marked shoulders and bowls with carinated (sharply angled) profiles. The 'Decorated' version of Late Bronze Age Ware has not been identified in Cornwall or Devon and it is probable that Plain Ware forms were current here for longer than further east.

Excavations at Higher Besore/Truro College in 2004 (Gossip forthcoming) provided the first

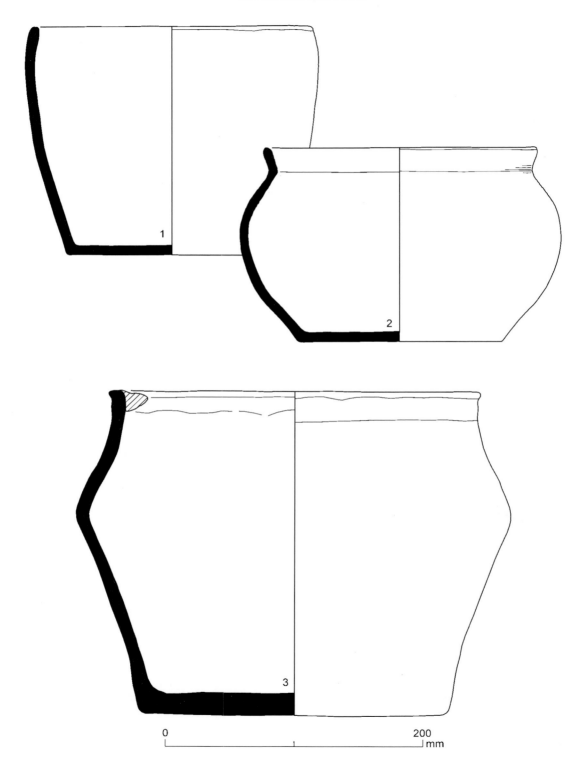

0   200
                                    └── mm

Fig 1. (Previous Page) Late Bronze Age Plain Ware vessels, c 1050 – 800 cal BC. No 1 straight-walled vessel, No 2 necked bowl, No 3 jar with internal flange. (Drawing: Jane Read)

good data on Late Bronze Age Plain Ware. Simple straight-walled jars were found in a pit with the clay mould for a sword hilt (see Fig 1 No 1). The latter is of distinctive form and should date *c* 1150-1000 cal BC: there is no radiocarbon date for its context. Other features have radiocarbon dates calibrating to the tenth and ninth centuries BC and straight-walled vessels are accompanied by necked vessels with rounded and angular bodies (see Fig 1, Nos 2, 3). A second site excavated in 2004 at Scarcewater, on the south west corner of the St Austell granite, produced a straight-walled vessel and a carinated jar with a radiocarbon date again calibrating to the tenth and ninth centuries BC (Quinnell 2010, 107, fig 53).

At both Higher Besore/Truro College and Scarcewater gabbroic clays from the Lizard were used. At both sites some gabbroic clay was imported to the vicinity of the sites where it was mixed with local materials before potting.

Two other settlements, Bodrifty, Mulfra (Dudley 1956) and Nornour in the Isles of Scilly (Butcher 1978), have well-established sequences of, probably, continuous activity from the Middle Bronze Age until the Late Iron Age and Roman period respectively. Both have straight-walled Plain Ware vessels (Dudley 1956, fig 9, 17-18; Butcher 1978, fig 26) and a range of other forms. The straight-walled jar form can also be recognised at the Bronze Age building at Callestick, Perranzabuloe (Quinnell 1998/9, fig 9, No 4).

A date range from the late eleventh century cal BC through to *c* 800 cal BC is the 'best fit' that the chronology for Late Bronze Age Plain Ware currently allows.

Earliest Iron Age (Fig 2)

This term is used for the period *c* 800 – 600 cal BC. The Iron Age, with the regular use of iron, can now be seen to start *c* 800 cal BC (Needham 2007). Barry Cunliffe (2005, fig 2.2) has distinguished a break around 600 cal BC in ceramic styles further east in England and refers to the periods before and after this date as 'Earliest' and 'Early'. This usage can be adopted for Cornwall where there appears to be a similar break in ceramics.

The only site with Earliest Iron Age pottery supported by radiocarbon dating is the cliff castle at Trevelgue Head, Newquay (Nowakowski and Quinnell 2011, 7.7). There, a large shouldered vessel and a smaller carinated jar (Fig 2, Nos 1, 2) are associated with a date which calibrates to the eighth century BC (Quinnell 2011, fig 7.3). These are made of gabbroic clay. A very similar large shouldered vessel was found containing a hoard of Sompting bronze axes at Mylor (Treasure Annual Report 2005/6, Department of Culture Media and Sport 2008; author, pers comm; Jones and Quinnell this volume, fig 15). The axes belong to the last phase of the Bronze Age, Late Bronze Age 3 or Halstatt C, and underline a very confusing fact, that artefacts of both the latest Bronze Age and the Earliest Iron Age can be correctly assigned to the eighth century cal BC.

Some of the ceramics from both Bodrifty and Nornour should belong to the Earliest Iron Age. (It is not possible to separate Late Bronze Age Plain Ware and Earliest Iron Age forms stratigraphically as both sites had rebuilds and many artefacts appear to be redeposited). The vessels with finger-tip decoration at Bodrifty may well be Earliest Iron Age (Dudley 1956, fig 9, Nos 11-12) as may the carinated bowls in a group at Nornour (Fig 2, No 3; Butcher 1978, fig 24). St Michael's Mount probably has pottery of this period (Quinnell 2000, fig 12, No 4); this site shows us that granitic, as well as gabbroic, clays were used at this time. The similarities between the shapes illustrated in Figs 1 and 2 show that on current knowledge Late Bronze Age and Earliest Iron Age ceramics are very similar.

The Earliest Iron Age is the period of the first millennium BC about which we know least, and this scarcity of information is also true for Devon (Gent and Quinnell 1999, 68). Sites of this date are not being recognised and possibly one reason for this is that there was little use of ceramics across the peninsula at this time. (The cliff castle at Maen, Sennen, has been judged 'Early Iron Age', but re-examination of the assemblage (author) shows that some vessels (Crofts 1954/5, fig 24) are in fact Trevisker and others (ibid , fig 23) belong to the subsequent Early Iron Age after 600 cal BC. Any sites referred to as 'Earlier Iron Age' in our previous anniversary publication (Quinnell 1986, 112) and not mentioned here can only be regarded, with more recent knowledge, as occupied at some date during

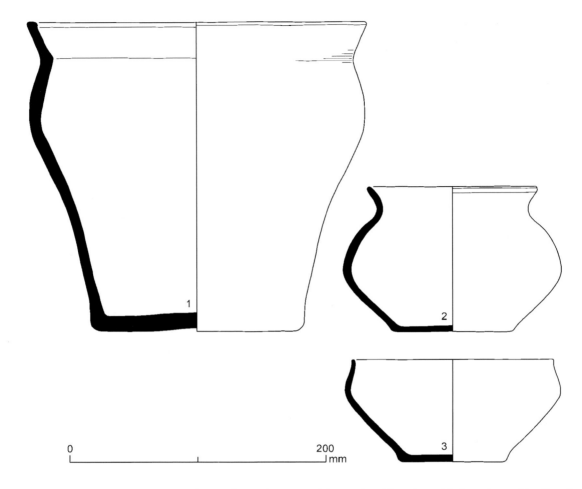

Fig 2. Earliest Iron Age vessels, c 800 – 600 cal BC. No 1 large shouldered jar, No 2 carinated jar/bowl, No 3 open carinated bowl. (Drawing: Jane Read)

the use of Late Bronze Age Plain Ware, Earliest Iron Age and Early Iron Age Plain Jar Group pottery.

Early Iron Age Plain Jar Group (PJG) (Fig 3)

Several sites, notably Carn Euny, Sancreed (Christie 1978) and Halligye (Elsdon and Quinnell forthcoming) with Middle Iron Age activity have Early Iron Age pottery in their earlier levels and every indication of continuous occupation. This pottery consists of a range of jars without decoration, and has now been termed 'Plain Jar Group' (Quinnell 2011, 7.8). The most distinctive form (Fig 3, No 1)

has a concave neck with a slight carination at the top of a gentle shoulder: other forms have a shorter neck which may be either vertical or out-turned (Fig 3, Nos 2, 3). Vessels are generally smaller than the shouldered vessels of the Earliest Iron Age. This pottery was the only style found in levels associated with the enclosure and related fogou at Boden, St Anthony-in-Meneage (Quinnell forthcoming) which radiocarbon dating placed securely in the fourth century cal BC. A wide-ranging review of Iron Age ceramics incorporated in the report on Trevelgue Head cliff castle (Quinnell 2011) concluded that the Plain Jar Group was probably current from the sixth to fourth centuries cal BC. One well known

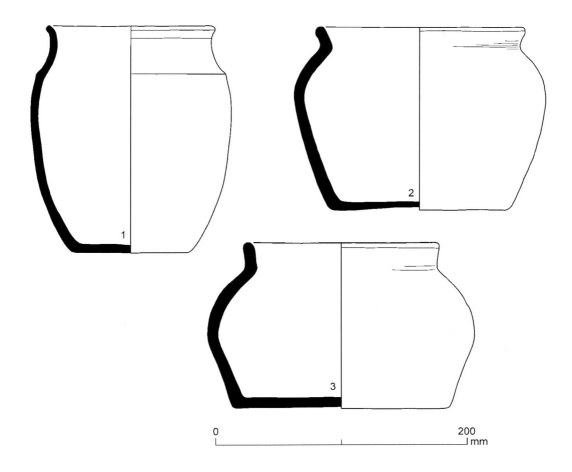

Fig 3. Early Iron Age Plain Jar Group (PJG) vessels, c 600 – 300 cal BC. No 1 jar with carination at base of neck, No 2 jar with everted rim, No 3 jar with upright rim. (Drawing: Jane Read)

previously published site, Gurnard's Head cliff castle, Zennor, has clear examples of Plain Jar Group material (Gordon 1941, fig 7, P8-9, fig 8, P2) as does Maen cliff castle (author pers comm). Occasional stamped decoration occurs on vessels from Gurnard's Head (Gordon 1941, P9) and Carn Euny (Christie 1978, fig 53, Nos 4-5). The use of stamped decoration, which continued on Middle Iron Age vessels, may indicate some North French contact (Schwappach 1969) by communities using late Plain Jar Group pottery.

While gabbroic clays were used for the majority of vessels, a variety of different granitic fabrics were also current. This is true in the West Penwith area

and at Trevelgue Head (Quinnell 2011) some 30% of Plain Jar Group vessels were granitic, sourcing to the St Austell Granite. During the Early Iron Age more use was made of granitic fabrics than at any other period in the first millennium BC. Use of pottery generally appears to have gradually become more frequent than in the preceding Earliest Iron Age.

Middle Iron Age South Western Decorated ware (SWD) (Fig 4)

South Western Decorated ware, and its Somerset equivalent Glastonbury ware, is distinguished by the presence of geometric, sometimes curvilinear,

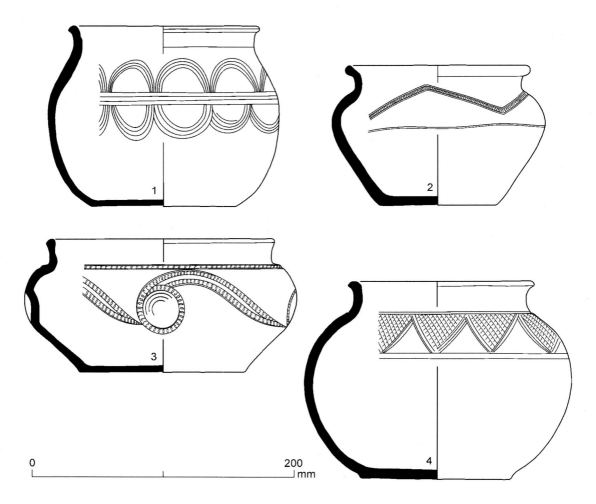

Fig 4. Middle Iron Age South Western Decorated ware, c 300 cal BC until late first century cal BC; the Outline Style probably starts in the late fourth century BC. No 1 BD6.1 form with Outline decoration, No 2 BD6.2 form with Standard, rouletted, decoration, No 3 BD6.1 form with Accomplished (curvilinear) decoration, No 4 BD6.2 form with Standard (angular geometric) decoration. (Drawing: Jane Read)

decoration which appears to echo that found on metalwork. In Cornwall, and Devon, only one basic vessel form was used, with a few minor variations (Fig 4). This form may well derive from the basic forms in the preceding Plain Jar Group. Study of the ware at Trevelgue Head, where a range of stratified groups have good radiocarbon dates, has provided a new framework for its dating.

The basic form of vessel is described, following the Danebury/Trevelgue system, as **BD6**, a smallish bowl or jar with an upright rim and good burnished finish. This has been divided at Trevelgue as follows:

BD6.1 Variety with gently rounded shoulder (Fig 4, Nos 1, 3-4). Occurs throughout currency of South Western Decorated vessels.

BD6.2 Variety with sharply rounded shoulder (Fig 4, No 2). Introduced in the third or second centuries BC, with a tendency to occur in contexts at the end of South Western Decorated currency.

BD6.3 Variety with a very short slightly everted rims and variously rounded shoulders (see

Quinnell 2011, fig 7.8, No 122). Not common.

BD6.4 Variety with gently rounded shoulder and slightly everted rim (*ibid,* fig 7.8, No 121). The distinctive feature is the addition of an internal lip inside the neck to restrict width and provide a definite lid seating. The few examples known are all large. This belongs at the end of South Western Decorated currency.

All vessel variants were generally fired in reduced conditions, conditions in which oxygen was restricted, so that a grey to black colour was hopefully obtained.

The ware has previously (Quinnell 1986, 113) been considered to have become current around 400 cal BC. The work at Trevelgue, together with total absence from fourth century contexts at Boden (Quinnell forthcoming), suggests a date for the general adoption of this style around 300 cal BC. The Trevelgue sequence shows that a simply decorated form of this ware occurs around the end of the fourth century. This has simple, often untidy, geometric designs, and with no areas of infill, and uses BD6.1 vessels. Handles sometimes occur. This version of the ware has been termed *Outline* (Fig 4, No 1), using only BD6.1 vessels (see below). At Trevelgue Outline style vessels only are found stratified in a series of middens which accumulated against the innermost rampart between the late fourth and the late first centuries BC; there are obviously factors involved here in vessel choice which are now impossible to understand. Outline style vessels continued to be made throughout the use of the ware until the late first century BC. The only other site at which an Outline vessel has a radiocarbon date before 300 BC is Scarcewater (Quinnell 2010, 108).

The main currency of South Western Decorated ware has two variants, *Standard* and *Accomplished,* which occur from around 300 cal BC until the late first century BC. *Accomplished* (Fig 4, No 3) has curvilinear patterns sometimes so regular that use of a compass may have been involved; infill of areas with additional tooling/incision is frequent. *Standard* style (Fig 4, No 4) has regular angular geometric designs, again often with areas infilled. Stamps occur occasionally throughout. The use of rouletting, decoration incised by use of a small wheel, is generally, but not always, a late feature, and was often used for vessels which appear, from their findspots, to have been regarded as special: good examples are the sherds found buried beneath the rampart at Castle Dore (Radford 1951, 81) and those placed in a posthole at Trevelgue (Quinnell 2011 fig 7.8 No 80). The detail of decoration in all the styles varies a great deal, so much so that currently no one decorative pattern has been found to have been replicated.

While some granitic fabrics were used for SWD, the proportions of pottery made from these decreased very markedly from those in the preceding Early Iron Age PJG. The amount of gabbroic fabrics, usually well-made, correspondingly increased. By the end of the Middle Iron Age assemblages are almost entirely gabbroic and the first gabbroic vessels are found in the Isles of Scilly. The quantity of ceramics used in the Middle Iron Age continues to increase, following the trend in the Early Iron Age.

Previous studies (Quinnell 1986, 114) have indicated a link between South Western Decorated ware and the first rounds or small enclosures. This link has now been shown to have been broken by the occurrence of Early Iron Age Plain Jar Group material in the enclosures at Boden and Halligye. There still seems to be a link between SWD and the development of multiple enclosure hillforts such as Killibury (Miles 1977) but, with cliff castles at Trevelgue Head, Maen Castle and Gurnard's Head producing Earliest and Early Iron Age material, linkage between enclosure and pottery groups can be seen to be complex.

Late Iron Age Cordoned ware (Fig 5)

Cordoned ware is the latest Iron Age style, its introduction usually dated to the first century BC and its origins related to French styles which are found as imports in Dorset and in Devon (Quinnell 1986, 119). The style lacks decoration but many forms have added horizontal clay strips or 'cordons'. An alphanumeric type series was established by Threipland (1956) in the publication of her excavations at a small hillfort at Carloggas, St Mawgan-in-Pydar which still works well (see Fig 5). Cordoned ware is generally very well made and finished, with a good burnish; it is possible that limited use of the potter's wheel was introduced. The use of gabbroic fabrics became even more widespread than in the Middle Iron Age and were almost universal by the start of the Roman period. Cordoned ware has frequently been found in association with South Western Decorated ware but only recently have

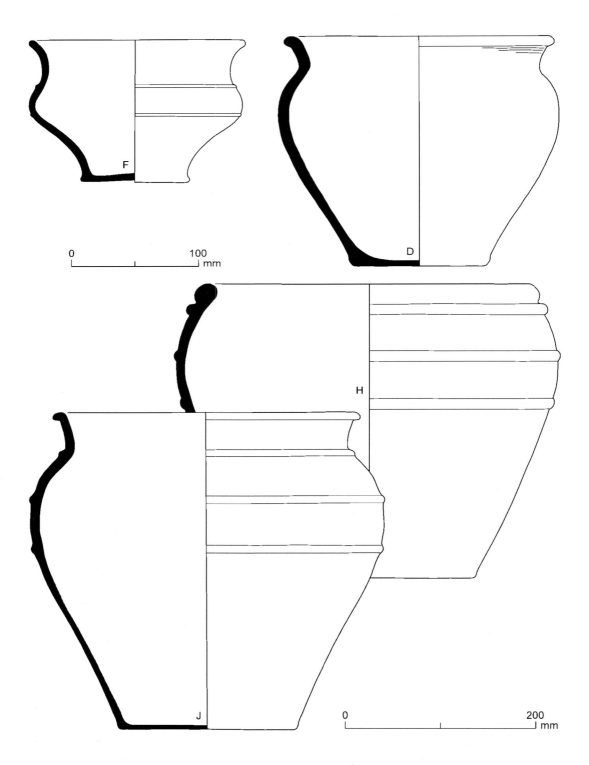

0   100
mm

F

D

H

J

0   200
mm

Fig 5. (Previous Page) Late Iron Age Cordoned ware. Late second century BC until, and after, the Roman Conquest. Type F and Type D scale 1:3, Type H and Type J scale 1:4. (Drawing: Jane Read)

excavations revealed the complicated relationship between these Cornish styles.

Recent work on the settlement at Higher Besore/ Truro College (Quinnell in Gossip forthcoming) has greatly increased our knowledge of Cordoned ware. Here a group of houses with multiple radiocarbon dates produced both Cordoned and South Western Decorated ware. Cordoned ware storage jars, Types H and J (Fig 5, H, J), and serving/drinking vessels, Types F/G (Fig 5, F) were introduced here in the late second century cal BC. Neither storage vessels nor specialised serving/drinking vessels were present in South Western Decorated ware, in which the universal form BD6 was multipurpose. SWD ware was present throughout the use of the Higher Besore/ Truro College settlement, which lasted until a date in the first century cal BC. It seems highly probably that the new Cordoned ware forms were introduced to meet changing needs and social practises, more storage of grain and more elaborate service in meals and drinking. The new forms show an awareness of ceramic trends in Northern France.

At Higher Besore/Truro College SWD vessels appear to have been used for general purpose culinary purposes. At the adjacent round of Threemilestone (Schwieso 1976) undecorated versions of basic cooking vessels, Cordoned ware Types D/E (Fig 5, D) appear; these tend to be taller and less bowl-like than SWD form BD6 and had no decoration. The amount of SWD present at Threemilestone is small and, although there are no radiocarbon dates from this site, it appears to belong to the end of the settlement sequence in the immediate area. By this time the presence of incised decoration on vessels must have lost its significance. Two further Iron Age Cordoned ware types occur at the Rumps cliff castle (Brooks 1974) but not at Higher Besore/Truro College. These are Type O, a small jar with an everted rim, and Type C, a large roll-rimmed jar with rim-set handles (Threipland 1956, figs 26 and 17).

The Cordoned ware used during the late Iron Age may be described as First Phase Cordoned ware. Second phase Cordoned ware was in use after the arrival of Rome until around the middle of the second century AD. Subsequently vessels with cordons are found throughout the remainder of the Roman period and may be described as Third Phase. Gabbroic clays continued to be used almost universally throughout the Roman period. The continuance of cordoned ware features on Roman period pottery has caused great misunderstandings of chronology in the past, in particular causing courtyard houses to be incorrectly dated to the Late Iron Age (Quinnell 1986, 120). The First, Second and Third Phases of Cordoned ware, and the distinctive sequence of Roman period gabbroic ceramics, are fully addressed in the publication of the Trethurgy Round settlement (Quinnell 2004, 110).

Acknowledgments

I am grateful to J A Nowakowski, J Gossip and C Thorpe for use of drawings awaiting publication in the preparation of the illustrations which have been drawn by Jane Read.

The drawings have been funded by payment received by the author for the obituary of the late Paul Ashbee, a former President of the Society and a great proponent of the appropriate use of graphics in archaeological publications.

References

Barrett, J, 1980. The pottery of the later Bronze Age in lowland England, *Proc Prehist Soc,* **46,** 297-321

Brooks, R, 1974. The excavation of the Rumps cliff castle, St Minver, Cornwall, *Cornish Archaeol,* **13,** 5-50

Butcher, S A, 1978. Excavations at Nornour, Isles of Scilly, 1969-73: the pre-Roman settlement, *Cornish Archaeol,* **17,** 29-112

Christie, P M, 1978. The excavation of an Iron Age souterrain and settlement at Carn Euny, Sancreed, Cornwall, *Proc Prehist Soc,* **44,** 309-434

Crofts, C B, 1954-5. Maen Castle, Sennen: the excavation of an Early Iron Age promontory fort, *Proc West Cornwall Field Club,* **1.3,** 98-115

Cunliffe, B, 2005. *Iron Age Communities in Britain,* London (4th edition)

Department of Culture Media and Sport 2008. *Treasure annual report 2005/6,* London

Dudley, D, 1956. An excavation at Bodrifty, Mulfra, near Penzance, *Arch Jnl,* **113,** 1-32

Elsdon, S, and Quinnell, H, forthcoming. The pottery, in W Startin, Excavations at Halligye Fogou, *Cornish Archaeol*

Gent, T H, and Quinnell, H, 1999. Excavations of a causewayed enclosure and hillfort on Raddon Hill, Stockleigh Pomeroy, *Proc Devon Archaeol Soc,* **57,** 1-76

DISCOVERY AND RESEARCH

Gordon, A S R, 1941. The excavation of Gurnard's Head, an Iron Age cliff castle in western Cornwall, *Arch Jnl,* **97,** 96-111

Gossip, J, forthcoming. Life outside the round - Bronze Age and Iron Age settlement at Higher Besore and Truro College, Threemilestone, Truro, *Cornish Archaeol*

Miles, H, 1975. Excavations at Woodbury Castle, East Devon, 1971, *Proc Devon Archaeol Soc,* **33,** 183-208.

Needham, S. 1996. Chronology and periodisation in the British Bronze Age, *Acta Archaeologia,* **67,** 121-40

Needham, S, 2007. The Great Divide, in C Haselgrove, and R Pope, eds, *The Earlier Iron Age in Britain and the near Continent* ,Oxbow, Oxford, 39-63

Nowakowski, J A, and Quinnell, H, 2011. *Trevelgue Head, Cornwall: the importance of C K C Andrew's 1939 excavations for prehistoric and Roman Cornwall,* Truro (Cornwall Council)

Nowakowski, J A, Quinnell, H, Sturgess, J, Thomas, C, and Thorpe, C, 2007. Shifting the sands of time, *Cornish Archaeol,* **46,** 13-76

Quinnell, H, 1986. The Iron Age and the Roman period in Cornwall, *Cornish Archaeol,* **25,** 111-34

Quinnell, H, 1998/9. Bronze Age pottery, in A M Jones, The excavation of a Later Bronze Age structure at Callestick, *Cornish Archaeol,* **37-8,** 19-26

Quinnell, H, 2000. First millennium BC and Roman period ceramics, in P C Herring, *St Michael's Mount, Cornwall. archaeological works, 1995-8,* Truro (Cornwall County Council), 39-46

Quinnell, H, 2004. *Trethurgy. Excavations at Trethurgy Round, St Austell: community and status in Roman and post-Roman Cornwall,* Truro (Cornwall County Council)

Quinnell, H, 2010. Prehistoric and Roman pottery, in A M Jones, and S R Taylor, *Scarcewater, Pennance, Cornwall. Archaeological excavation of a Bronze Age and Roman landscape,* Brit Arch Repts, Brit Ser, **516,** Oxford, 93-113

Quinnell, H, 2011.The pottery, in Nowakowski and Quinnell 2011

Quinnell, H, forthcoming. The pottery, in J Gossip, The evaluation of a multi-period prehistoric site at Boden, St Anthony-in-Meneage, Cornwall, 2003, *Cornish Archaeol*

Radford, C A R, 1951. Report on the excavations at Castle Dore, *Jnl Roy Instit Cornwall,* **I,** Appendix

Schwappach, F, 1969. Stempelverzierte Keramik von Armorica, *Marburger eiträgezur Archäologie der Keltern (Festschrift Wolfgang Dehn)*

Schwieso, J, 1976. Excavations at Threemilestone, Kenwyn, near Truro, *Cornish Archaeol,* **15,** 51-67

Threipland, L M, 1956. An excavation at St Mawgan-in-Pydar, North Cornwall, *Archaeol J,* **113,** 33-81

Cornish Archaeology 50, 2011, 241–261

Appraising the bigger picture – Cornish Iron Age and Romano-British lives and settlements 25 years on

JACQUELINE A NOWAKOWSKI

Principal advances

Discoveries of new sites through aerial photography, the results of the National Mapping Programme (NMP), geophysical surveys, and opportunities from developer-funded evaluations and larger open-area excavations have all made significant contributions to our understanding of Iron Age and Romano-British settlement over the past 25 years. Metal objects recorded through the Portable Antiquities Scheme have added new knowledge as has routine scientific dating with the growing application of Bayesian modelling. Important themes are apparent in the emergent picture of the complexities of the social and cultural landscapes for these periods: the specialised characters of settlements, the importance of control over agricultural land and metal resources, the maintenance of a distinctive regional identity and Cornwall's place in a changing wider world.

Publication of two backlog excavations has set benchmarks: for the Iron Age, the pre-war excavations at the complex Iron Age cliff castle of Trevelgue Head, Newquay (Nowakowski and Quinnell 2011) and for the Romano-British period, the 1970s excavation of Trethurgy Round, St Austell (Quinnell 2004).

An emergent chronological framework

The chronological framework for these periods has, until recently, relied heavily on diagnostic finds but these can provide no more than spot dates. Routine scientific dating (AMS radiocarbon dates with a focus on pot residues and event dating) has begun to lay the foundations of a regional chronological framework (P Marshall, in Nowakowski and Quinnell 2011, appendix to chapter 6, CD). Our developing knowledge of the ceramic sequence is discussed by Quinnell (this volume).

Dates from the partially excavated hilltop enclosure at Liskeard School, east Cornwall, (Jones 1998-9), could suggest that some large enclosures have Late Bronze Age origins although the wide-ranging scientific dates mean that identification of active sites dating to the earliest Iron Age (*c* 800–600 BC) remains a future priority (*cf* Quinnell 1986). The start of the elaborate sequence at Trevelgue cliff castle, Porth, may be early (Nowakowski and Quinnell 2011, chapter 17). A modelled sequence of dates from Boden, St Anthony-in-Meneage, shows activities from the earliest Iron Age; here, a fogou and the enclosure in which it sits have an active though discontinuous history into the Romano-British period (with a notable gap in the Middle Iron Age; Gossip forthcoming a). The open middle

Fig 1. Bird's eye view of Bosigran Farm, Zennor, where detailed archaeological survey has demonstrated that upstanding field patterns perpetuate prehistoric landscapes of international importance. Here clusters of courtyard houses have been shown to be tied into blocks of fields. (See also Hartgroves, this volume, Checklists to HER, fig 2; and Herring, this volume, Field surveys, fig 2). (Photograph: © Historic Environment, Cornwall Council)

Iron Age site at Atlantic Road, Newquay (see below and Reynolds forthcoming), the field systems at Bar Point, Isles of Scilly (Evans 1983), the uninvallate hillfort at Gear, Helford (Edwards and Kirkham 2008), open settlements at Halangy Porth, St Mary's, Scilly (Ashbee 1996) and West Porth Samson, Scilly (Ratcliffe and Straker 1996) have all produced middle to late first millennium BC radiocarbon dates in association with South West Decorated wares. There are also a number of spot dates for a range of enclosures for the Romano-British period such as Reawla, Gwinear (Appleton-Fox 1992), Penhale Round, Fraddon (Johnston 1998/9; P Marshall in Nowakowski and Johns forthcoming), Trethurgy, St Austell (Quinnell 2004), Killigrew, St Erme (Cole and Nowakowski forthcoming), Little Quoit Farm, St Columb (Lawson-Jones forthcoming), Tremough, Penryn (Gossip and Jones 2007) and Pollamounter, Newlyn East (Jones and Taylor 2004). Although we have more scientific dates than 25 years ago, there are still *few dated sequences* and as settlement variety becomes more apparent, opportunities to secure series of dates from different site types continues to be a major priority. Here the application of Bayesian modelling, applying statistical methods to dates from a stratigraphic sequence, will have a crucial role to play with its potential to refine chronology to events and decades.

Scoping the resource – fieldscapes and settlements

Detailed field surveys over the last 30 years in West Penwith have captured a great deal of information on the varied characters of settlement for the Iron Age and Romano-British periods. On the coastal plateau within Zennor parish the present day fields were laid out in later prehistory: here the patterns of ancient terraced fields have survived as upstanding stone hedges, built upon the earlier enclosures (Figs 1 and 2). In places ruinous Romano-British courtyard

houses are shown tied into blocks of fields (e.g. Bosigran Farm and Bosporthennis Farm; Herring 1987 and Nowakowski 1987 respectively). Detailed surveys of courtyard houses reveal considerable variety: solitary houses such as Carnaquidden, Gulval or clustered houses such as at Nanjulian, Sennen (Nowakowski and Sharpe 1986a; 1986b). The fields were used for both arable cultivation and stock farming. Limited investigations through early boundaries identified at Foage, Zennor (Herring 1993b) and Chysauster, Gulval (Smith 1996) have provided useful background environmental data. At Foage, pollen analysis of a buried soil beneath a lynchet assumed of Roman date, suggested open herbaceous grassland (Crabtree, Straker and West in Herring 1993b). Pollen analysis of a localised peat-filled channel found within the catchment area

Fig 2. A 'modern' stone hedge sits upon an earlier lynchetted boundary at Bosigran Farm, Zennor, August 2010. Heavily overgrown ancient terraces can be seen across the valley on the upper slopes of neighbouring Porthmeor Farm. (Photograph: © J Nowakowski)

DISCOVERY AND RESEARCH

of the 1984 investigations of the Romano-British landscape at Chysauster showed a rise in grassland in the first millennium BC, confirming a dominant pastoral and stock farming economy (R Scaife in Smith 1996). While the concept of field enclosure was well established by the second millennium BC (e.g. Gwithian, Nowakowski *et al* 2007), expansion of enclosure and inroads into blank zones is evident. In Sennen early fields appear to lie under the Iron Age cliff castle at Maen (Herring 1986a; 1994a), while a terraced field system, undated but with a possible Later Bronze Age origin, has been recorded at Trevelgue Head, Porth (Nowakowski and Quinnell 2011, chapter 2). Elsewhere in Cornwall, blocks of 'hidden' fields (hidden because their patterns have not survived through into modern fieldscapes) have been found in large open area excavations. An Iron Age ditched field system was found at Trenowah, St Austell (Johns 2008), and blocks of 'brick-shaped' fields, thought to be characteristic of the first millennium BC (Herring 2008), have been examined as ditched systems at Tremough, Penryn (Gossip and Jones 2007) and at Pennance, Scarcewater (Jones and Taylor 2010, fig 32). There is clearly variety in field enclosure as large irregular rectilinear fields rather than 'brick-shaped' systems have more commonly been identified by the NMP and geophysical surveys across lowland Cornwall (Andrew Young, pers comm) and managed landscapes with blocks of fields and lanes are also apparent (e.g. Camelford School, Sean Taylor, pers comm).

Across the county a major advance in identifying the settlement resource has been boosted by Historic Landscape Characterisation (HLC). Zones of 'Anciently Enclosed Land', as fieldwork opportunities have shown, reveal considerable time-depth: these are the areas where traces of later prehistoric and Romano-British settlement may be predicted. The predictive value of HLC can be very effective when combined with other sources of data. Drawing on the results of NMP with HLC and Historic Environment Record data, Andrew Young has, for example, been able to analyse settlement patterns and land use in the Camel Estuary in north Cornwall (Young forthcoming). Enclosures interpreted as later prehistoric and Romano-British settlements are highly visible on aerial photographs and geophysical surveys. Young has shown that the density of enclosed settlement around the Camel estuary has increased fivefold: 20 years ago, only 19 enclosures were recorded and now at least 103 have been mapped (Young forthcoming). In the wider Camel estuary area, enclosed 'settlements' are almost exclusively confined to Anciently Enclosed Land with the higher Rough Ground seemingly peripheral. There is, by contrast, a higher concentration of Early Bronze Age barrow cemeteries within Rough Ground and, to a large degree, these zones appear substantially unaltered in later prehistory. These are the likely key areas of upland pasture: access to these, and the resources they offered, may well have been tightly controlled in later prehistory as communities developed and pressure on land grew. Some of the settlements of stone-walled roundhouses can be seen in this context. Seven individual roundhouses examined on rough ground at Wicca Round, Zennor (Dudley 1957) may be the rare survivals of early transhumance. Field survey in 1986 demonstrated that the Wicca buildings were located in an earlier (co-axial) system of enclosure where it is apparent that control over common areas of grazing was an increasingly important factor in daily life (Herring 1986b; Herring 2008). On Bodmin Moor an Iron Age building re-using a Bronze Age ring cairn at Stannon, St Breward, is thought to represent temporary occupation as part of the management of upland grazing (Jones 2004-5).

The present overriding impression is of densely populated areas across the entire lowlands, current estimates suggesting two enclosures (rounds) per km² (Quinnell 2004, 211), whilst the uplands and coastal belts were key areas for pasture.

Appraising settlement variety in the Cornish Iron Age

Cornish Iron Age settlement research had, in the past, been largely characterised by studies of stone-walled roundhouses either located within coastal settings (e.g. Gurnard's Head, Zennor, Gordon 1941) or as groups on the moors (e.g. Garrow, Bodmin Moor, Dudley 1957-8; Bodrifty, Dudley 1956). On form, stone-walled roundhouses (on Bodmin Moor and West Penwith) are assumed to mostly date from the late second millennium BC (Johnson and Rose 1994). The visible lack of distinction however between upland Bronze Age and later roundhouses and the potential for Iron Age reuse (e.g. Kynance Gate, Thomas 1960; Bodrifty, Dudley 1956; Stannon Down, Bodmin Moor, Jones 2004-5; and Nowakowski in press) sets future challenges for accurate dating.

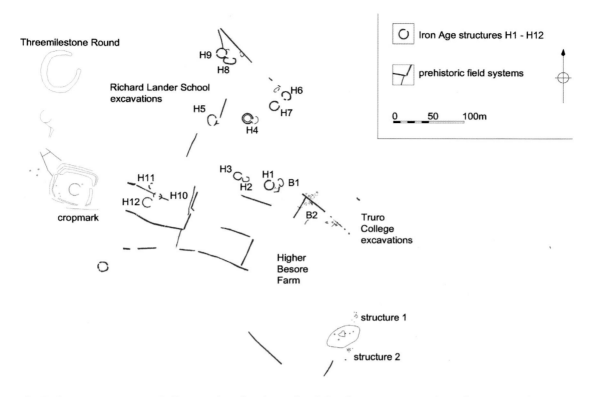

Fig 3. Higher Besore, Truro College and Richard Lander School excavations - plan of open Iron Age settlement excavated in 2004-5. Up to 10 roofed structures (including 5 roundhouses, 3 oval, 1 sub-rectangular and 1 round building) were found, some paired with unroofed stock-enclosures. Structures H1, H5 and H6 may have been industrial buildings (Gossip forthcoming b). These separate households shared the surrounding open spaces and a set-aside block of five rectangular (ditched) fields. Close by is Threemilestone Round where excavations in the 1960s and 1970s found the remains of contemporary settlement. Also close by lies an intriguing sub-rectangular ditched enclosure, unexcavated but interpreted as a possible contemporary shrine. (Plan: © Historic Environment, Cornwall Council; Gossip forthcoming b)

A variety of shapes and sizes of enclosures, (Johnson and Rose 1982; Quinnell 2004; Young forthcoming) are classed as rounds. Generally these small (often univallate) enclosures served as settlements for small autonomous farming communities throughout the Romano-British period (Quinnell 2004), though where field investigations have taken place it is clear that not all enclosures served as settlements involved in full scale agricultural production (see below). Rounds are regarded as the main settlement type but few have clear Iron Age origins (see below).

Until recently, open settlements of the first millennium BC have been less easy to identify with confidence, although increasingly field

investigations, most notably at Higher Besore, are pointing up the importance of looking at areas beyond the enclosure.

Higher Besore - excavations at Richard Lander School and Truro College

A key excavation has been at Higher Besore, Truro College, Threemilestone, to the west of Truro in 2004 and 2005 (Gossip forthcoming b). Extensive open area excavations (11.5ha) in advance of development discovered a remarkable series of gullied buildings and enclosures (Figs 3 and 4). Radiocarbon dates span the third to first centuries cal BC. The buildings with their associated

245

Fig 4. Higher Besore Iron Age roundhouse 3 during excavation. At Higher Besore five roundhouses defined by shallow gullies were found. Each building had the sockets for single post-rings but only slight evidence for domestic hearths and, interestingly, limited evidence for occupation surfaces or floors.
(Photograph: © Historic Environment, Cornwall Council)

small unroofed enclosures have the appearance of a planned but open settlement. They represent separate, individually distinct but related households with shared access to surrounding open spaces and nearby fields (a block of five fields set apart lay to the south and west). Discoveries of scarce Dressel 1 amphorae sherds hint at participation in a wider exchange network (the amphorae are continental imports usually containing wine; Peacock and Williams 1986). The overall picture for the Higher Besore settlement is a small kinship stock-farming community. Despite the absence of animal bone, the discovery of a collection of unusual notched slates suggests the importance of processed animal products. There is limited evidence for cereals. Iron ores, smelting slag, a hammerstone, fragments of

crucibles and tuyères reveal the routine importance of small-scale iron production although this may only have been an occasional activity. The status of the Higher Besore community is unknown although it is likely that households were part of a larger community which included the nearby Threemilestone Round, probably constructed towards the end of the Higher Besore sequence (Quinnell, this volume). Partial excavations of this multiple ditched site (during the 1960s and 1970s: Dudley 1960; Schwieso 1976) showed an Iron Age origin and a confusing pattern of overlapping circular and oval buildings, suggesting a dynamic settlement history. A little South West Decorated pottery but mainly Cordoned Wares were found at Threemilestone but there was no evidence for continued use into the Romano-British period (Quinnell this volume; Schwieso 1976).

Excavations at Higher Besore provide an intriguing picture of associated open and enclosed settlement during the latter part of the first millennium BC which has yet to be matched by other excavated examples, though potentially similar sites are known from aerial photography and geophysics.

Updating cliff castles, hillforts and coastal settlement

The multivallate cliff castle at Trevelgue Head, one of at least 60 sites along the Cornish coastline, is outwardly the most complex Iron Age coastal site in south-western Britain. The small-scale pre-war excavations revealed that the complex rampart arrangement is the outcome of a long history (with good evidence for Later Bronze Age activity). Rampart 7, one of the largest on the headland, was built upon an earlier boundary. Industrial scale iron production at Trevelgue, for which there is unequivocal evidence, ensured the emergence of a significant place in the middle Iron Age, a place where the active community who occupied the headland worked out rich local iron seams which they owned and tightly controlled. David Dungworth's analysis of the considerable quantities of metallurgical debris found during the 1939 excavations suggests production of a high quality product which had a value well beyond the region (Nowakowski and Quinnell 2011, chapter 9). On present evidence Trevelgue's influence seems to have waned by the later Iron Age (Nowakowski and Quinnell 2011).

During the first millennium BC the communities at Trevelgue are likely to have made extensive use of the seaways for inter-regional contact as well as participation in distant exchange. Non-local goods such as glass beads (from Somerset) show how widely connected it was with southern Britain and the cobalt nickel-rich iron ore from Cornwall

Fig 5. The remarkable roundhouse, House 1, found during the 1939 excavations at the complex cliff castle at Trevelgue Head, Porth, Newquay, has been interpreted as a communal building - it is very large (at 14m diameter), with an architecturally impressive stone build. (Source: © Trevelgue Head Croft Andrew Archive)

DISCOVERY AND RESEARCH

(the Great Perran Lode which lies to the south of Trevelgue) was traded into Wessex during the earlier Iron Age (Ehrenreich 1994; Morris 1996; Hingley 1997). For Cornwall, Trevelgue was clearly significant and while there is no definitive evidence to show that Trevelgue participated in continental cross-channel exchange, despite the increasing evidence for a rich metalwork trade throughout this millennium, the site, in its heyday, may well have been connected to major foci for trade such as the coastal promontory of Hengistbury Head, near Christchurch harbour, Dorset (Cunliffe 1987; D Dungworth in Nowakowski and Quinnell 2011). Whether other key sites such as St Michael's Mount (Herring 1993a) and Mount Batten, Plymouth (Cunliffe 1988) reached such regional prominence can only be verified with future research.

In Diodorus Siculus' description of *Belerion* (the name ascribed to the Land's End area) around the fourth century BC, he names a place where tin was traded – *Ictis* (Cunliffe 2001). The isle of *Ictis* was also know to the remarkable Greek adventurer Pytheas of Massilia, who on recalling his journey to Britain *c* 300 BC noted that *Ictis* was a 'collecting point where ingots of tin are brought to be traded to the merchants who carried it over to Gaul' (Cunliffe 2002). Some have suggested that **St Michael's Mount** in Mount's Bay is the most appropriate candidate for *Ictis* as it matches his description of a place cut off at high tide, close to the most prolific sources of tin in the south west (Herring 1993a). To date no Iron Age structures have conclusively been identified on the Mount although in recent years roundhouse platforms have been surveyed and later prehistoric pottery and bits of copper ingots have been found indicating some level of activity during the first millennium BC (Herring *et al* 2000; Jones and Quinnell, this volume).

It is clear that coastal sites emerge as key contact places during this period and another interesting site is **St George's Island**, Looe, in south east Cornwall, also suggested by some as a possible candidate for *Ictis* (C Thorpe, pers comm). Looe Island is connected by a causeway to the mainland and is larger than St Michael's Mount. A copper 'ox-hide' ingot (Beagrie 1985) and the complete rim, neck and handle of Dressel 2-4 amphora (first century BC to first century AD) were recovered from the seabed close to the island. In 2008 Channel Four's Time Team located an enclosure ditch on the island and this produced Roman pottery and

coins dating from the third to fourth centuries AD (Thompson 2009).

Key socio-economic links between enclosed settlement and significant metal resources can be proposed for some similar coastal sites (such as the cliff castles at **Tubby's Head**, St Agnes; **Gurnard's Head**, Zennor or **Kendijack**, St Just in Penwith) as well as inland settlements such as **Castle Dore**, Fowey (Radford 1951) and **Carloggas**, St Mawgan-in-Pydar (Threipland 1956). All lie within or close to metal rich areas. The earliest phase of very limited metal production at Castle Dore is, for example, third to first centuries BC, broadly contemporary with Trevelgue and Higher Besore. What Trevelgue lacks however, unlike Higher Besore, is clear evidence of definitive iron production in the later Iron Age and early Roman period at a time when Dressel 1 amphorae were occasionally introduced into the region (Cunliffe 1987).

Trevelgue emerged as a major regional site which operated within a wider hinterland drawing upon the resources of other contemporary settlements (e.g., Porth Veor, White 1955-56; Tretherras, Craze *et al* 2002; Glendorgal, Dudley 1962; see Nowakowski 2009). Trevelgue's position at the head of an important deep harbour at Porth provided major access inland to sites up-valley such as the impressive hillfort at **Castle-An-Dinas,** 12km to the east, which overlooks Goss Moor. There has been only limited work at Castle-an-Dinas (by Bernard Wailes in the 1960s) and the full results are unpublished; a small quantity of South Western Decorated pottery was found. South-western hillforts require some serious research to look at their complex site histories and the variety of social roles they played.

Some hints of a greater social pressure on land and on the importance of participating in wider exchange networks in the late first millennium BC are clear and this may partly explain the appearance of settlement on estuaries (e.g. **Lellizzick, Padstow,** Fig 9) and the coastal belt. Well-preserved land surfaces which date to the later Iron Age (*c* 100 BC) and the Romano-British periods (second to fourth centuries AD) were found sealed beneath layers of wind-blown sand at **Atlantic Road** on the edge of Fistral Bay, Newquay. Here in 1998 keyhole excavations sliced through the tantalising remains of a very rich site. Footings for small circular stone buildings, stone-lined hearths, middens containing many artefacts, animal bone and cereals reveal

Fig 6. Boden Vean fogou during HES excavations in 2003. (Photograph: © Historic Environment, Cornwall Council)

stock farming and arable cultivation. Linear Romano-British ploughmarks were also found (Reynolds forthcoming). Continued use of the site, despite the hazards of sand blows, shows the pressure on land at this time.

Enigmatic fogous

The enigmatic subterranean structure known as the fogou, a site type associated with the Cornish Iron Age, has been investigated in modern excavations from the 1960s to 1990s at Carn Euny, Sancreed (Christie 1978), Halligye, Mawgan-in-Meneage (Startin forthcoming) and Boleigh, St Buryan (Young 2000-1); and more recently at Boden, St Anthony-in-Meneage, and Penhale, Fraddon (Gossip forthcoming a; Hood 2007). Function and interpretation of fogous has been the subject of much debate from the prosaic such as below ground storage chambers for food produce, to places of refuge and sacred places and cult centres associated with pre-Roman

religious practices (MacLean 1992; Cooke 1993; Herring 1994b).

The **Boden Vean** fogou (Fig 6) was rediscovered by farmer Chris Hosken in 1991 and its context established firstly by geophysical survey (Rose, this volume, Geophysical survey, fig 3) and then in 2003 by evaluation trenching. Excavations revealed

Fig 7. Inscribed coinage is an indication of social distinction. Two rare staters of late Iron Age date have been recorded from west Cornwall by the PAS in recent years, this silver Armorican stater from Gwithian (CORN-0FCF32; RIC newsletter 42 October 2007) and a Dobunnic gold stater from Ludgvan (CORN-DE0E02; RIC Acc. No. 2005.10). This is evidence for trade and political networks between local tribal groupings across Britain and beyond in the later Iron Age (Tyacke 2002-3). The Dumnonii (the principal tribal grouping identified in south-western Britain) were not politically centralised and lacked locally minted coins. These staters, minted upcountry and in continental Europe, reveal contact with the wider world but do not represent a fully developed monetary economy. Continental trade which existed via Britanny and the Atlantic seaways to south-west France (with Hengistbury Head, Dorset, serving as a major port of trade) was later disrupted with the Roman invasion of Gaul in first century AD (Cunliffe 2001). (Photograph: Portable Antiquities Scheme © A Tyacke, Royal Institution of Cornwall)

DISCOVERY AND RESEARCH

the fogou as a reasonably well-preserved site: a well-built stone-lined and capped corbelled linear passage (at least 9m long) appended to which was an unlined approach, and an earth-cut creep which gave access beyond the enclosure. Boden fogou was built during one construction phase which has been dated by statistically consistent radiocarbon dates to before the Later Early Iron Age *c* 420-350 cal BC (Hamilton *et al* in Gossip forthcoming a). The fogou was in use at the same time as the rectangular enclosure in which it was situated but it was also deliberately infilled and concealed in one major closure episode while 'settlement' activities within the enclosure continued well into the early Romano-British period (Gossip forthcoming a). The early date, fourth century BC or earlier, for a rectangular Iron Age enclosure with a fogou, is significant and highlights the varied character of enclosures for this period.

Until recently fogous have only been identified with certainty in the western part of the county, but their wider currency is suggested by the discovery of an exceptionally well-preserved stone-built fogou during a watching brief at **Penhale Round**, Fraddon, in 2006. This is the most easterly example and is well beyond the previously known range. Limited time permitted only a rapid exploration but the Penhale fogou was a subterranean structure accessed by a series of steps and lay within the centre of a long-lived round (Johnston *et al* 1998-9; Nowakowski 1998; Hood 2007; Nowakowski and Johns forthcoming). Like Boden, the fogou at Penhale Round had a clear dependant association with an enclosure and was concealed beneath the houses of the community who lived within its boundaries (Hood 2007).

Iron Age burial traditions

A late Iron Age cemetery found at **Trethellan Farm**, Newquay in 1987 where at least 21 deep unlined grave pits were discovered (Nowakowski 1991) adds to a recognised regional tradition of inhumation in formal graves (*cf* Whimster 1981). The skeletons at Trethellan were poorly preserved but the dead had been buried clothed with some wearing jewellery. Bronze brooches were found in each grave, and date the cemetery to the later Iron Age, *c* 200 BC to *c* AD 100. One bronze brooch had coral inlay. This non-local material would have been highly valued although materially there

is otherwise little social distinction between the individual graves which included men, women and children and probably represents a cross section of a typical Iron Age community. The context of the unique leaded bronze late Iron Age **Pentire neck-ring**, which was found close by some years later is unknown (Nowakowski *et al* 2009). The object had probably been placed within a grave and by wearing such an item social distinctions were marked.

This is highlighted by a stone-lined cist grave found on **Bryher, the Isles of Scilly** where a crouched body accompanied by a sword, shield and decorated mirror was found. The find is of international importance and unique in Western Europe: the sword and the mirror are rare finds for Cornwall. The mirror, if contemporary with the sword (on stylistic grounds dated to between *c* 250 and 125 BC), is one of the earliest to be found in the UK (Johns 2002-3; Johns, this volume, fig 4). The Bryher grave goods and the Pentire neck-ring are examples of high craftsmanship and if made locally their discoveries point up the possibility of a flourishing independent south-western school of metalworking (Johns 2002-3; Nowakowski *et al* 2009). Some of the recent metal objects recorded by the Portable Antiquities Scheme (PAS) would appear to confirm this (Tyacke, this volume). Examples are parts of horse gear such as a rare copper alloy cheekpiece (PAS data base reference CORN-B50AA7; RIC Acc No 2005.8), a decorated scabbard mount (CORN-AC1453; RIC Acc No 2005.1) (Tyacke 2002-3, 146) and a silver enamelled baldrick ring (CORN-B177A3; report RIC newsletter 42, October 2007). Finds of copper-alloy linch pins indicative of wheeled vehicles/chariots are also on the increase in the county (Tyacke 2002-3 and CAS newsletter June 2010).

Emergent Iron Age cultural and ceremonial practices

Compared to the rich artefact-dense domestic settlements of the Middle and Later Bronze Age (e.g. Trethellan Farm, Newquay, Nowakowski 1991; 2001; Gwithian, Nowakowski *et al* 2007; Pennance, Scarcewater, Jones and Taylor 2010), buildings of later Iron Age settlement and settlement-related sites are, to date, by comparison, artefact-poor. Where the interiors of Iron Age roundhouses have been excavated, floors are generally thin or absent and hearths insubstantial (e.g. Penhale Point, Smith 1988; Higher Besore, Gossip forthcoming b). Evidence for the removal of floors has been recorded at roundhouses excavated at Penhale Point (Smith 1988), the Rumps (Brooks 1974) and at Trevelgue (e.g. House 1, Nowakowski and Quinnell 2011). Whether this is evidence of widespread cultural and social practice can only be substantiated in future excavations.

The large middens identified as key later prehistoric sites in southern Britain (e.g. Potterne and East Chisenbury, Wiltshire: Lawson 2002 and McOmish 1996; Whitchurch, Warwickshire: Waddington and Sharples 2007) have not yet been identified in Cornwall. These are notable for their size and unusual composition of quantities of artefacts and settlement debris but are without buildings. Artefact-rich Iron Age sites in Cornwall have to date been middens found for example at **The Rumps**, St Minver and **Trevelgue Head**, St Columb Minor (Brooks 1974; Nowakowski and Quinnell 2011). At Trevelgue, three middens were thrown up against Rampart 7 and these contained large quantities of settlement waste with evidence for deposition of special deposits (Nowakowski and Quinnell 2011). Parts a human skull found in the midden at The Rumps is so far anomalous (Brooks 1974, 48). These trends do however replicate wider social practice (recorded elsewhere in southern Britain) where special treatment of settlement boundaries has been interpreted as the need to communicate distinction as well as confirm group affiliation, kinship and identity (Hill 1996, 102; Hingley 1990).

Investigation of a number of enclosures, of varying sizes, points to the classification of a new range of Iron Age ceremonial sites in Cornwall (Jones 2010). One such is **Hay Close, St Newlyn East**, investigated as a research project by the Cornwall Archaeological Society in 2007. Discovered as a cropmark, this single-ditched enclosure, 60m in diameter overall, has an external bank and was therefore initially classified as a potential henge of likely third millennium BC date. Small-scale excavations revealed a substantial rock-cut ditch but no traces of early prehistoric ritual or even later domestic activities were found within. Instead the ditch produced two distinct groups of pottery: a collection of plain wares, typical of early to mid first millennium BC and late post-Roman wares including Mediterranean imports. These two principal phases of activity were supported by

scientific dates (C Thorpe, pers comm; Jones 2010, 206). It is suggested that Hay Close, which occupies a high position on the edge of a spur, emerged as a central place attracting Iron Age communities to gather, meet, forge alliances and perhaps participate in ritual feasting. Such gatherings may have been cyclical and fostered inter-community networks where shared interests were played out perhaps through story telling, ritual games, exchange and even communal feasting. A similar ceremonial scenario, albeit on a more local level, has been suggested for a smaller (20m diameter) ditched enclosure with external bank which was investigated at **Sir James Smith's School, Camelford** in 2008 (Jones 2010). Here the sparse artefacts found were confined to a ditch terminal but included some later Iron Age pottery, confirmed by a radiocarbon date. A solitary slate-capped pit was the only feature within.

Romano-British settlements: living within and beyond the round

Enclosures termed 'rounds' dominate settlement research for the Romano-British period and some have shown long histories illustrating continuity of stable lifestyles during this period. Across the lowlands a far greater density than previously recorded is now apparent but few still have been excavated and recent excavations have shown that not all were settlements (see below). Generally however enclosures or 'rounds' do belong predominantly to the Roman period, with few definitely dated to the Iron Age (e.g. Boden Vean, Gossip forthcoming a) and provide the impression of an increasingly utilised landscape with expanding populations.

Trethurgy Round, St Austell, provides us with the most comprehensive study of settlement life for the Romano-British period to date. This is an enclosed agricultural village with distinctive oval stone-walled houses which variously served as dwelling houses and ancillary buildings (a granary, a byre, stores, workshops and a possible family shrine) and which were built around a central cobbled shared space. The impressive stone-flagged entrance into the village was closed by a substantial double-leaved wooden gate. The evidence for small-scale metalworking (smithing), distinctive gabbroic coarse wares and the Trethurgy type stone bowls and mortars which served the needs of 'the middle social tier' of a wider society, revealed a longevity and stability which prevailed from the mid second to

DISCOVERY AND RESEARCH

sixth centuries AD and which we might expect to be typical across the general scene during the Romano-British period (Quinnell 2004). Roman material culture and ideas were only selectively absorbed, revealing a confident independent community with a keen sense of identity and status. Beyond west Cornwall and the Isles of Scilly, areas dominated by courtyard houses, the oval houses revealed at Trethurgy are now regarded as the common Roman period house form in Cornwall.

A similar picture has recently emerged from

Fig 8. Stone weights from Killigrew Round, St Erme. Left, cylindrical stone mensuration weight of greisen with surviving part of metal suspension hook, designed to be used with a steel yard; weight 406g. This is a rare example for Cornwall. Right, trapedzoidal mensuration weight of fine grained granite worked to a smooth finish; weight 806g (H Quinnell and R Taylor in Cole and Nowakowski forthcoming). Stone weights, bowls, moulds and mortars have been found on a variety of Romano-British sites (e.g. Trethurgy, Quinnell 2004, 139-142; Nancemere, Gossip 2005; Higgins 2009; Tremough, Gossip and Jones 2007; Killigrew, Cole and Nowakowski forthcoming). Roman lead weights have also been found at the cliff castle at Maen Castle, Sennen (Herring 1994) and the settlement at Atlantic Road, Newquay (Reynolds forthcoming). Stone weights are a sign of the routine practice of accuracy in recording commodities for exchange and show understanding of market value in local exchange networks where coinage was not widespread. (Photograph C Thorpe, © Historic Environment, Cornwall Council)

excavations at **Penhale Round, Fraddon** in 1993, 1995-6 and 2006 (Nowakowski and Johns forthcoming; Johnston *et al* 1998-9; Hood 2007). With a late Iron Age origin, major structural changes at Penhale reveal how the appearance of a place could be dramatically transformed: initially a single ditch enclosure, Penhale acquired another when the impressive stone-lined entrance was remodelled. Inside lay a well-made fogou: the first conclusive association to be found outside west Cornwall of a fogou (which probably offered below-ground storage for surplus) and a round (Hood 2007); the date of the establishment of this fogou is not yet apparent. Round gullied wooden buildings as well as oval stone-walled buildings found within Penhale reveal variety. A network of ditched boundaries, the remains of former surrounding fieldbanks and enclosures, was found alongside evidence of a solitary contemporary gullied oval building lying on the outskirts (Nowakowski and Johns forthcoming). Settlement-related activities were thus not solely confined within the round. Throughout the Romano-British period, Penhale became well nested into its local setting, indicative of stability. Following its abandonment in the later Roman period it became neglected, was not reoccupied, and the pattern of later medieval fields ignored earlier enclosure (Nowakowski and Johns forthcoming).

Within this landscape of villages and hamlets other sites appear. Some may indicate increasing social pressure to colonise and claim new ground where access and control of good pasture was essential. At **Tremough, Penryn** a solitary timber-built oval building was found centrally located in a small, shallow-ditched enclosure (Gossip and Jones 2007, 23). The radiocarbon dates span the Romano-British period but rather than representing a single farmstead as has been suggested, the building may have operated as an occasional workshop (for blacksmithing and/or salting/food processing) or even as an occasional shelter for a stockperson. Its principal inhabitant may well have routinely lived in a settlement located on the lower slope. This unusual building within its equally unusual open-ended enclosure (Gossip and Jones 2007, fig 19), presumably designed to control stock, was probably only in occasional use.

A small stone U-shaped single-cell building dating to the Romano-British period was found at **Stencoose, St Agnes** built into the corner of

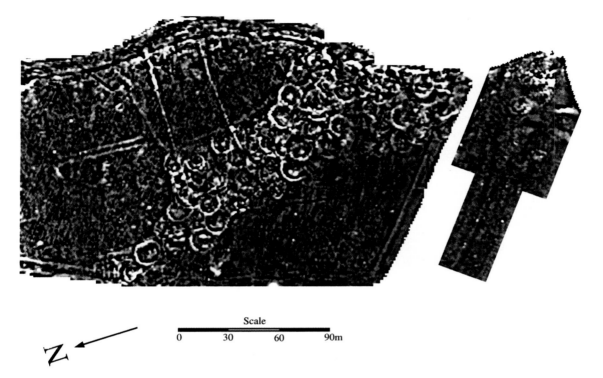

Scale

0   30   60   90m

Z

Fig 9. Lellizzick geophysical survey (source: AM Lab report, Payne 1998; © English Heritage). Aerial photography, geophysical surveys (1990, 1997 and 2007), metal-detected surface finds and small-scale excavations by Channel 4's The Time Team in 2007 confirmed the existence of a remarkable open long-lived roundhouse settlement on the low sea cliffs overlooking Padstow Bay and the Camel Estuary, which lie to the top of the picture. A number of roundhouses with stone foundations set in hollows with flagged floors were discovered alongside trackways and enclosures. The dense pattern of at least 70 individual and overlapping buildings shows successive phases of settlement. From form of settlement – roundhouses defined by ring-gullies – one would expect an Iron Age date, but finds from the excavations indicate activities from at least the first into the fifth and sixth centuries AD and some imported post-Roman pottery (African Red slip ware and B Ware) indicates a major coastal trading settlement. A late Roman coin hoard (27 coins spanning the second to fourth centuries AD) was found (Wessex Archaeology 2008).

a field. It has been suggested that this was used seasonally to keep watch over grazing cattle and sheep (Jones 2000-1).

Specialist sites and the rise of craft industries

Not all Romano-British enclosures were solely residential: some served particular functions.

Excavations at **Nancemere, Truro,** in 2004-2005, examined the larger part of a substantial ditched enclosure with a long history of use dated to the second to fourth centuries AD (Gossip

forthcoming c; Higgins 2009). A fine stone-built entrance was found alongside stone and wooden open-ended workshops, a variety of open hearths and one possible furnace (Higgins 2009). Artefacts suggested iron smelting, textile and leatherworking alongside stone working as principal activities, as well as food processing, with some possible evidence for brewing (samples of germinated grains, Stevens in Higgins 2009). Pottery comprised standard Trethurgy Type 4 cooking pots (H Quinnell, pers comm) as well as large storage vessels made of local clays with only a small percentage of imported Dorset black burnished

Fig 10. Iron carding comb from Atlantic Road, Newquay. Spindle whorls for spinning fleece are common finds on many Cornish Iron Age sites and show the importance of livestock farming but this rare find emphasises the importance of wool production. With pressures on land, enclosure for pasture, access to commons and control of grazing areas is paramount, since livestock farming requires far more land than arable production, and some areas would have been managed through transhumance with its seasonal control over land and commons for grazing (Herring 2008). (Photograph: C Thorpe, © Historic Environment, Cornwall Council)

wares. Stone weights were also discovered. No residential houses were found and Nancemere has been interpreted as a specialised place, the focus for craft workshops and a place for the exchange of goods serving nearby settlements (Higgins 2009).

Other industries are apparent within the coastal zone. An unusual late Roman site (radiocarbon dated to the third to fourth centuries AD) was excavated in 1992 at **Duckpool, Morwenstow**, in the base of a deep-sided valley in a small cove north of Bude. Here well-preserved small industrial hearths with good evidence for secondary metal-working (lead, pewter and copper alloy) alongside the manufacture of dyes from marine molluscs were found on the shoreline (Ratcliffe 1995). Marked by rich middens, this place was not enclosed, showed no conclusive evidence for permanent settlement and so was probably seasonally frequented and activities here served the needs of nearby farms. Other specialised coastal sites reveal another key industry: salt-making. Manufacture of this important commodity for preserving animal meats and fish has been found at **Trebarveth, St Keverne** (Peacock 1969), **Carngoon Bank, Lizard** (McAvoy 1980) and **Porth Godrevy, Gwithian** (Nowakowski *et al* 2007). The ability to make salt is fundamental to a society desiring to store surplus produce and to capitalise on their principal wealth: animal stock.

Inland other specialised sites are apparent at **Killigrew, St Erme** (Cole and Nowakowski forthcoming) and **Little Quoit Farm, St Columb Major** (Lawson-Jones forthcoming) which show that some enclosures met differing needs and requirements. These enclosures, a multiple ditched one at Killigrew and the single-ditched one at Little Quoit Farm were industrial centres. Investigations at Little Quoit Farm were keyhole, but several large hollows interpreted as working areas were found with clear evidence for secondary metalworking (blacksmithing iron). An anvil base was found *in situ*. An intact metalworking furnace was found at Killigrew where, like Little Quoit Farm, no residential buildings were found. A unique broken tin plate of Roman date was found at Killigrew (see below). At Killigrew iron-smelting in a purpose-built furnace started in the later Iron Age and the site may have become enclosed through time. It is possible, given the overall small quantities of iron slag recovered, that the smelted ore at Killigrew was reworked into ingots or bars elsewhere. Food was brought to the site for consumption by the specialist metalworkers and the repaired tin dish is probable evidence for the working of other metals. Long sequences of activities at Little Quoit Farm and Killigrew were dated by pottery to at least 200 or 300 years (second to fourth centuries AD) and their proximity to local sources of iron/ manganese bearing rock must have influenced their development and local standing. They probably served surrounding farms and villages. At least 19 enclosures lay within a 1.5km radius of Killigrew: a number of these probably small farming hamlets which used the services it provided. Multiple banks and ditches which developed could be read as a sign of their specialised local standing and status as well as marking ownership of the resources and/or services they operated.

At **Reawla, Gwinear** evidence for secondary industrial metalworking operated on a farmstead level and here is perhaps a more typical reflection of the scale of craft industry which would have been played out in village life across the general farming scene – that is blacksmithing for the repair and maintenance of iron agricultural tools (Appleton-

Fox 1992, 77). Scales of industrial production clearly varied but the rise of the specialist craft place within the wider landscape reveals complex social and economic networks between communities at a local level. Just as we have seen in the Iron Age, some places may have emerged as specialist centres where production and exchange were the key activities supported by the local economy.

Evidence for other craft industries such as the possible working of shale (shale spindle whorls from Reawla, H Quinnell in Appleton-Fox 1992, 109 and Nancemere, Higgins 2009, and fragments of shale bracelets found at Trethurgy, Quinnell 2004, 144-145) points up a continuing craft tradition which appears in the later Iron

Fig 11. Calstock Roman Fort, outer ditch. The multiple-ditched square enclosure was discovered by geophysical survey and has been examined with slot trenching in 2008 and 2009 (Rippon 2008; Claughton and Smart 2008; Smart 2010 and Smart in prep). Measuring 150m by at least 120m, it is considerably larger than the Restormel fort. Deep ditches and structural evidence for wooden towers set into the major rampart were found. Within, the imprints of timber buildings, pits and settlement rubbish and a roadway have been found, together with iron chain mail, hobnails for boots and studs for plate armour. Outside an iron smithing furnace dating to the first century AD was found. Pottery and coins suggest principal activity in the first century AD. (Photograph: © C Thorpe)

Age in Cornwall (e.g. Castle Dore, Radford 1951) and continues into the later Roman period (e.g. Gwithian, Nowakowski *et al* 2007). This non-local resource (from Kimmeridge, Dorset) again emphasises the importance of coastal trade and contact with communities in southern Britain. Alongside this grew a distinctive worked stone industry whose bowls, mortars and weights promoted a confident regional identity (Quinnell 1993 and see Fig 8). These artefacts copying imported Roman forms were very much a Cornish production although occasionally found elsewhere as far afield as London and Richborough (H Quinnell, pers comm).

Roman burial traditions

To date we know very little about Roman burial practice, which makes the discovery of a Roman cremation at **Tregony** in 2005 highly significant. Here a single female cremation was found in two complete pots. The burial lay within a small square enclosure (Taylor forthcoming). Both vessels date to the second century AD, and although locally made, copied Dorset black burnished styles. Two inhumation burials of Roman date were found at **Scarcewater, St Stephen in Brannel** (Jones and Taylor 2010). Although poorly preserved, one individual was buried face down and wore hob-nailed boots. Clearly clothed, the body wore a brooch dating to the first and second centuries AD. The Tregony cremation shows potential for enclosed Roman burial grounds – a tradition more in keeping with areas beyond the Tamar (*cf* White 2007) - while the Scarcewater burials appeared to be interred on the edge of a network of fields, revealing future potential variety and likely accidental discovery (Jones and Taylor 2010).

Roman forts – new evidence for military presence

The discovery of two new Roman forts, at Restormel, Lostwithiel (Thorpe 2007; Hartgroves and Smith 2007; 2008) and at Calstock, south-east Cornwall (Fig 11; Rippon 2008; Claughton and Smart 2008, Smart in prep), to add to the one previously known site at Nanstallon near Bodmin, suggests a far greater Roman military presence in Cornwall than previously realised although the implications are still far from clear. Fieldwalking on the Restormel site, a square earthwork sited on a spur which overlooks the River Fowey, has produced pottery including native and large numbers of imported wares (including Samian), Roman coins, quern fragments, alongside glass, gaming counters and significant quantities of iron slag (Thorpe 2007). Activities date from the first to fourth centuries AD which must indicate activity continuing subsequent to the phase of military occupation. Large-scale geophysical surveys carried out at Restormel by the Tamarside Archaeological Survey have detected a well-preserved multiple bank-and-ditched square enclosure with opposing entrances on all four sides. Interestingly this has been shown to sit upon a potentially earlier 'camp' with traces of a roadway adding to the site's clear complexity and interpreted by some as a possible marching camp (C Thorpe, pers comm). Steve Hartgroves and John Smith have suggested that Restormel's location on a prominent spur, alongside quantities of iron slag found in the vicinity, are key to understanding its significance (Hartgroves and Smith 2008). The site dominates the highest navigable position of the River Fowey and may well have controlled a major river highway. A major iron lode lies less than 300m from the site. The clear importance of iron for Roman military needs (tools, nails, hobnails, horse shoes etc) could mean that Roman military presence here prospected for workable metal mineral deposits. The site clearly merits excavation and its relationship to surrounding native farming settlements requires detailed research.

Along with being located on navigable routes, the sites at Restormel and Calstock are located close to rich metal mineral resources (tin, iron and silver) and this is likely to be significant with implications for control of metal resources. The socio-economic relationships between a Roman military presence and local communities will be key in future research. Aside from creating opportunities for market exchange, opportunities for social interaction will have offered new contexts for the introduction of new technology, ideas and even changes in fashion.

Cornish Romano-British lifestyles and material culture

The most up to date commentary on life in Cornwall during the Romano-British period by Henrietta Quinnell has emphasised the dominance of a distinctive social structure of autonomous

Fig 12. Copper alloy Roman Aesica variant hinged brooch, with cruciform bow and fantail foot (PAS CORN-DEC722). This first to second century AD example from St Hilary is one of a number of this type recorded by the Portable Antiquities Scheme in Cornwall (Tyacke, this volume). These elaborate enamelled objects with spherical bosses and knobs are evidence for the fusion of late La Tène decoration with a Roman-style object and as Cornish Variants, likely made in the county, show a pick-and-mix attitude to new styles and fashion. (Photograph: © A Tyacke, Royal Institution of Cornwall)

communities living in rounds, as reflected in the material culture found at Trethurgy (see above and Quinnell 2004). Here it seems that community and status were bound up with a continuance of strong late Iron Age cultural traditions and a pragmatic approach towards Roman influence and trends prevailed (e.g. the Trethurgy stone bowls which may copy Roman metal bowls, or local native wares copying Roman styles found in Samian from Carvossa: Carl Thorpe, pers comm; Quinnell 2004, 110). In stylistic terms the Pentire neck-ring (see above) captures a spirit of experimentation and

'showiness' which denotes increasing contact with Romanizing influence (Nowakowski *et al* 2009). Such influences are likely to have arisen through regular contact with representatives of the Roman regional administration based at Exeter (*Isca Dumnoniorum*) although Quinnell has raised the question to what degree the areas west of Bodmin Moor were wholly integrated into the *Civitas Dumnoniorum* (Quinnell 2004). The relationship between the military and local settlements is wholly unexplored and an area ripe for future research (see above).

Finds of Roman coins, in particular through the PAS, are pointing towards areas of particular potential, for example around Hayle, and are providing data, in terms of date range, that can be compared with national patterns (Tyacke, this volume). In recent years other types of typical Roman finds have been found and they give some insights into aspects of personal and public life for some people. Their discoveries show that some people acquired Roman things, but they are likely to have been regarded as exotic, and are related to matters of eating, dress and the body and reveal something about different levels of interaction, contact and openness to new trends.

The head of a small copper alloy spoon found at the courtyard house settlement at Chysauster, Gulval in 2003 is a *cochlear* type (Thorpe 2004) and is a common find in Roman Britain (first and second centuries AD, De la Bédoyère 1989). Another example was found at Atlantic Road, Newquay (Reynolds forthcoming). Both have small delicate bowls with fragments of a long prong-like handle and these may have been used for eating shellfish; the pointed ends used for winkling snails or other delicacies out of their shells (Allason-Jones 1989). These discoveries suggest fine dining. A Roman manicure set or *chatelaine* was found at Penryn College in 2007 (Crummy forthcoming) and these distinctive hygiene or toilet kits (comprising tweezers, ear-pick and nail cleaner all hung on a single link) were common across urban Roman Britain (De la Bédoyère 1989) and reveal increasing importance of personal grooming (Allason-Jones 1989, 131-132). Initially associated only with high status Roman burials, personal toilet sets became more widespread in use by the larger society in towns and small settlements across southern Britain after the Conquest. The Penryn example is extremely interesting for its rarity, being the only one to have

DISCOVERY AND RESEARCH

been found in the county to date, and for its pair of nail-cleaners (two are rare, Crummy *ibid*). The use of nail-cleaners was a particularly Romano-British trait and Nina Crummy has suggested that the Penryn example must have been an important object with a perceived value that expressed social distinction. A rare gold pendant amulet from Maker with Rame recently recorded by PAS is interpreted as a symbolic version of the more common copper alloy cosmetic grinders, used for the application of make-up (CORN-955 DE8; 2008T782; Tyacke, this volume, fig 4). Several finger rings have also been recorded by PAS in Cornwall. Roman finger rings were decorative items and took all forms but they could also be practical as a convenient way of carrying seals and were therefore very personal to the wearer (Allason-Jones 1989, 125). All of these types of personal objects betray an increasing preoccupation about appearance and the importance of marking social distinction.

Occasionally tin objects of Roman date have been recorded and the recent discovery of a flat tin plate at Killigrew Round is of interest (see above). Although found buried in a pit in a fragmented poor condition, X-ray fluorescence analysis showed it was almost entirely made of tin (95%) with small traces of lead, copper and iron (Starley forthcoming). A second century AD date has been suggested, making it one of the earliest tin objects found in the county. It may have been made at Killigrew (H Quinnell in Cole and Nowakowski forthcoming). With the discovery of a lead ingot found at Reawla, Gwinear (Appleton-Fox 1992, 118), this may suggest that by the Romano-British period experimentation with metal alloys, perhaps a mixture of traditional techniques with Roman influence, was in some quarters being gradually absorbed. Pewter plate manufacture almost certainly happened in Cornwall and a number of stone moulds have been found (e.g. Halangy Down, Ashbee 1970, plate VIIb; 1996; St Just in Penwith, Brown 1970; and Penhale Round, C Thorpe in Nowakowski and Johns forthcoming). Further evidence of a Romanizing influence may be seen in the recent discoveries of a handful of Roman Aesica hinged brooches recorded by PAS (Fig 12), variants which appear to be a Cornish phenomenon and show to a degree how some native objects encapsulated a cherry-picking approach to absorbing new influences (A Tyacke, pers comm, and this volume).

Two other aspects of Roman period material culture brought out with Trethurgy's publication deserve comment. It is apparent that later Roman ceramics, in the gabbroic fabrics which are almost universal in Cornwall, continued without change in the fifth and probably the sixth centuries AD. The 'end of Roman Cornwall' is not apparent in the archaeological record. This is related to the other significant aspect, the general scarcity of coins and the likelihood that the economy operated at a local level without coinage, with bartering clearly an enduring and successful strategy.

Endnote

Trevelgue cliff castle appears to have regained some regional significance in the later Roman period. House 1, formally abandoned at the end of the Middle Iron Age but left as a ruin with its walls intact, was revisited during the third century AD. At the beginning of the fifth century the building was concealed from view by settlement rubbish which contained the largest collection of late Roman coins found to date in the county (R Reece in Nowakowski and Quinnell 2011). The function served by the site and House 1 at this period is not clear but it is a reminder of the complexities of activities played out at a local level alongside wider social changes. Clearly food for thought and future research.

Acknowledgements

Many thanks are extended to James Gossip, Joanna Higgins, Andrew Hood, Charles Johns, Ann Reynolds, Sean Taylor, Anna Tyacke, Chris Smart and Andrew Young for sharing information on unpublished data in advance of full publication. Many thanks to Carl Thorpe and James Gossip for supplying plans and photographs and to Anna Tyacke for photographs of the Iron Age stater and the Romano-British Aesica brooch. Many thanks are also given to Carl Thorpe, Henrietta Quinnell and Peter Rose for their very helpful comments.

References

Allason-Jones, L, 1989. *Women in Roman Britain*, London
Appleton-Fox, N, 1992. Excavations at a Romano-British round: Reawla, Gwinear, *Cornish Archaeol*, **31**, 69-123
Ashbee, P, 1970. Excavations at Halangy Down, St Mary's, Isles of Scilly, 1969-70, *Cornish Archaeol*, **9**, 69-76

Ashbee, P, 1996. Halangy Down, St Mary's, Isles of Scilly, excavations 1964-1977, *Cornish Archaeol*, **35**, 9-201

Beagrie, N, 1985. A bronze 'ox-hide' ingot from Cornwall, *Cornish Archaeol*, **24**, 160-162

Brooks, R T, 1974. The excavation of The Rumps Cliff Castle, St Minver, Cornwall, *Cornish Archaeol*, **13**, 26-34

Brown, P D C, 1970. A Roman pewter mould from St Just in Penwith, *Cornish Archaeol*, **9**, 107-110

Champion, T C, and Collis, J R, 1996. *The Iron Age in Britain and Ireland: recent trends*, Sheffield (J R Collis publications)

Christie, P M, 1978. The excavation of an Iron Age souterrain and settlement at Carn Euny, Sancreed, Cornwall, *Proc Prehist Soc*, **44**, 309-434

Claughton, P, and Smart, C, 2008. The Bere Ferrers Project and discovery of a Roman fort at Calstock, *Journal of the Friends of Morwellham*, **30**, 4-15

Cole, R, and Nowakowski, J A, forthcoming. Excavations at Killigrew - an Iron Age and Romano-British industrial site on the Trispen bypass, Cornwall, 1996, *Cornish Archaeol*

Cooke, I M, 1993. *Mother and Sun, the Cornish fogou*, Penzance

Craze, N, Gossip, J, and Johns, C, 2002. Tretherras School, Newquay, Cornwall; archaeological evaluation, Truro (Historic Environment Service, Cornwall County Council)

Crummy, N, forthcoming. The toilet set, in Gossip forthcoming d

Cunliffe, B, 1987. *Hengistbury Head, Dorset Volume 1: the prehistoric and Roman settlement, 3500 BC-AD 500*, Oxford University Committee for Archaeology Monograph **13**

Cunliffe, B, 1988. *Mount Batten, Plymouth. A prehistoric and Roman port*, Oxford University Committee for Archaeology Monograph **26**

Cunliffe, B, 2001. *Facing the Ocean, the Atlantic and its peoples*, Oxford

Cunliffe, B, 2002. *The extraordinary voyage of Pytheas the Greek: the man who discovered Britain*, London (rev edn)

De la Bédoyère, G, 1989. *The finds of Roman Britain*, London

Dudley, D, 1956. An excavation at Bodrifty, Mulfra, near Penzance, *Arch Jnl*, **113**, 1-32

Dudley, D, 1957. Late Bronze Age and Early Iron Age settlements in Sperris Croft and Wicca Round, Zennor, Cornwall, *Jnl Roy Inst Cornwall*, ns, **3.1**, 66-82

Dudley, D, 1957-8. The early Iron Age in Cornwall, *Proc West Cornwall Field Club*, **2.2**, 47-54

Dudley, D, 1960. Pendeen Earthwork, Threemilestone, Truro, Cornwall, *Jnl Roy Inst Cornwall*, Supplement, 2-13

Dudley, D, 1962. The excavation of a barrow at Glendorgal, Newquay 1957, *Cornish Archaeol*, **1**, 9-17

Edwards, K, and Kirkham, G, 2008. Gear and Caervallack, St Martin-in-Meneage: excavation by Time Team, 2001, *Cornish Archaeol*, **47**, 49-100

Ehrenreich, R M, 1994. Ironworking in Iron Age Wessex, in A P Fitzpatrick, and E L Morris, eds, *The Iron Age in Wessex: recent work*, Salisbury (Wessex Archaeology), 16-18

Evans, J, 1983. Excavations at Bar Point, St Mary's, Isles of Scilly, 1979-1980, *Cornish Studies*, **11**, 7-33

Gordon, A S R, 1941. The excavation of Gurnard's Head, an Iron Age cliff castle in western Cornwall, *Arch Jnl*, **97**, 96-111

Gossip, J, forthcoming a. Excavations at Boden, St Anthony-in-Meneage, *Cornish Archaeol*

Gossip, J, forthcoming b. Life outside the round – Bronze Age and Iron Age settlements at Higher Besore and Truro College, Threemilestone, Truro, *Cornish Archaeol*

Gossip, J, forthcoming c. Excavations at Nancemere Fields 2003, *Cornish Archaeol*

Gossip, J, forthcoming d. Prehistoric activity and Romano-British settlements at Penryn College 2007, *Cornish Archaeol*

Gossip, J, and Jones, A M, 2007. *Archaeological investigations of a later prehistoric and a Romano-British landscape at Tremough, Penryn, Cornwall*, Brit Arch Repts, Brit Ser, **443**, Oxford

Gwilt, A, and Haselgrove, C, eds, 1997. *Reconstructing Iron Age societies*, Oxbow Monograph, **71**, Oxford

Hamilton, D, forthcoming. Radiocarbon dating, in Gossip forthcoming a

Hartgroves, S, and Smith, J R, 2007. *A second Roman Fort is confirmed in Cornwall*, Truro (Historic Environment Service, Cornwall County Council)

Hartgroves, S, and Smith, J R, 2008. A second Roman Fort is confirmed in Cornwall, *Britannia*, **39**, 237-239

Herring, P C, 1986a. *National Trust archaeological survey Mayon and Trevescan Cliffs*, Truro (Cornwall Archaeological Unit), 2 vols

Herring, P C, 1986b. *National Trust survey of Wicca Farm, Zennor*, Truro (Cornwall Archaeological Unit)

Herring, P C, 1987. *National Trust archaeological survey of Bosigran, Cornwall*, Truro (Cornwall Archaeological Unit), 4 vols

Herring, P C, 1993a. *St Michael's Mount*, Truro (Cornwall County Council)

Herring, P C, 1993b. Examining a Romano-British boundary at Foage, Zennor, *Cornish Archaeol*, **32**, 17-28

Herring, P C, 1994a. The cliff castles and hillforts of West Penwith in the light of recent work at Maen Castle and Treryn Dinas, *Cornish Archaeol*, **33**, 40-56

Herring, P, 1994b. Review: 'Mother and Sun, the Cornish fogou', by Ian M Cooke, *Cornish Archaeol*, **33**, 245-7

Herring, P C, 2008. Commons, fields and communities in prehistoric Cornwall, in A M Chadwick, ed, *Recent approaches to the archaeology of land allotment*, Brit Arch Repts, Int Ser, **1875**, Oxford, 70-95

Herring, P, Thorpe, C, Quinnell, H, Reynolds, A, and Allan, J, 2000. *St Michael's Mount: archaeological works 1995-8*, Truro (Cornwall County Council)

Higgins, J, 2009. *Archaeological excavations at Nancemere Fields, Truro, Cornwall*, Perranporth, (South West Archaeology)

Hill, J D, 1996. Hill-forts and the Iron Age of Wessex, in Champion and Collis 1996, 95-116

Hingley, R, 1990. Boundaries surrounding Iron Age and Romano-British settlements, *Scottish Archaeol Rev*, **7**, 96-103

Hingley, R, 1997. Iron, ironworking and regeneration: a study of the symbolic meaning of metalworking in Iron Age Britain, in Gwilt and Haselgrove, 9-18

DISCOVERY AND RESEARCH

Hood, A, 2007. *Penhale Round, Fraddon, Cornwall – archaeological excavation, post excavation assessment*, Wiltshire (Foundations Archaeology, rep 541)

Johns, C, 2002-3. An Iron Age sword and mirror cist burial from Bryher, Isles of Scilly, *Cornish Archaeol*, **41-42**, 1-79

Johns, C, 2008. The excavation of a multi-period archaeological landscape at Trenowah, St Austell, Cornwall, *Cornish Archaeol, 47*, 1-48

Johnson, N D, and Rose, P G, 1982. Defended settlement in Cornwall – an illustrated discussion, in D Miles, ed, *The Romano-British countryside: studies in rural settlement and economy*, Brit Arch Repts, Brit Ser, **103,** Oxford, 151-207

Johnson, N D, and Rose, P G, 1994. *Bodmin Moor. An archaeological survey volume 1: the human landscape to c 1800*, London (English Heritage and RCHM England Supplementary Series 11)

Johnston, D A, Moore, C, and Fasham, P, 1998-9. Excavations at Penhale Round, Fraddon, Cornwall, 1995-9, *Cornish Archaeol*, **37-38**, 72-120

Jones, A M, 1998-9. The excavation of a Bronze Age enclosure at Liskeard Junior and Infant School, *Cornish Archaeol*, **37-38**, 56-71

Jones, A M, 2000-1. The excavation of a multi-period site at Stencoose, Cornwall, *Cornish Archaeol, 39-40*, 45-94

Jones, A M, 2004-5. Settlement and ceremony; archaeological investigations at Stannon Down, St Breward, Cornwall, *Cornish Archaeol*, **43-44**, 1-141

Jones, A M, 2010. Misplaced monuments? A review of ceremony and monumentality in first millennium cal BC Cornwall, *Oxford J Archaeol*, **29 (2)**, 203-228

Jones, A M, and Taylor, S, 2004. *What lies beneath …St Newlyn East and Mitchell: archaeological investigations summer 2001*, Truro (Cornwall County Council)

Jones, A M, and Taylor, S, 2010. *Scarcewater, Pennance, Cornwall. Archaeological excavation of a Bronze Age and Roman landscape*, Brit Arch Repts, Brit Ser, **516**, Oxford

Lawson, A, 2002. Potterne 1982-85: animal husbandry in later prehistoric Wiltshire, *Wessex Archaeol*, **17**

Lawson-Jones, A, forthcoming. Smithing in the round: pipeline excavations at Little Quoit Farm, St Columb Major, Cornwall, *Cornish Archaeol*

MacLean, R, 1992. The fogou: an investigation of function, *Cornish Archaeol, 31*, 41-64

McAvoy, F, 1980. The excavations of a multi-period site at Carngoon Bank, Lizard, *Cornish Archaeol*, **19**, 17-62

McOmish, D, 1996. East Chisenbury: ritual and rubbish in the British Bronze Age Iron Age transition, *Antiquity*, **70**, 68-76

Morris, E, 1996. Artefact production and exchange in the British Iron Age, in Champion and Collis, 41-65

Nowakowski, J A, 1987. *National Trust archaeological survey of Bosporthennis Farm, Zennor*, Truro (Cornwall Archaeological Unit)

Nowakowski, J A, 1991. Trethellan Farm, Newquay: the excavation of a lowland Bronze Age settlement and Iron Age cemetery, *Cornish Archaeol*, **30**, 5-242

Nowakowski, J A, 1998. *A30 Project, Cornwall – archaeological investigations along the route of the Indian Queens bypass 1992-1994. Assessment and updated project design*, Truro (Cornwall Archaeological Unit)

Nowakowski, J A, 2001. Leaving home in the Cornish Bronze Age: insights into planned abandonment processes, in J Brück, ed, *Bronze Age landscapes tradition and transformation*, Oxford, 139-148

Nowakowski, J A, 2009. Introduction to prehistoric Newquay, *Old Cornwall*, Autumn Vol **XIV, No 1**, 27-38

Nowakowski, J A, in press. Telling tales from the roundhouse. Researching Bronze Age buildings in Cornwall, in S Pearce, ed, *Recent archaeological work in south western Britain. Papers in honour of Henrietta Quinnell*, Brit Arch Repts, Brit Ser, Oxford

Nowakowski, J A, and Johns, C, forthcoming. *Bypassing Indian Queens, Cornwall – archaeological excavations 1992-1994. Prehistoric and Romano-British landscapes and settlements*, Truro (The Highways Agency and Cornwall Council)

Nowakowski, J A, Gwilt, A, Megaw, J V S, and La Niece, S, 2009. A Late Iron Age neck-ring from Pentire, Newquay, Cornwall, with a note on the find from Boverton, Vale of Glamorgan, *Antiq Jnl*, **89**, 35-52

Nowakowski, J A, and Quinnell, H, 2011. *Trevelgue Head, Cornwall: the importance of C K Croft Andrew's 1939 excavations for prehistoric and Roman Cornwall*, Truro (Cornwall Council and English Heritage)

Nowakowski, J A, Quinnell, H, Sturgess, J, Thomas, C, and Thorpe, C, 2007. Return to Gwithian: shifting the sands of time, *Cornish Archaeol*, **46**, 13-76

Nowakowski, J A, and Sharpe, A, 1986a. *Carnaquidden/ Chysauster – survey, protection and management*, Truro (Cornwall Archaeological Unit)

Nowakowski, J A, and Sharpe, A, 1986b. *Nanjulian courtyard house settlement*, Truro (Cornwall Archaeological Unit)

Payne, A, 1998. *Report on Geophysical Survey, July 1997 at Lellizzick, Cornwall*, Ancient Monuments Laboratory Report no 58/98.

Peacock, D P S, 1969. A Romano-British salt-working site at Trebarveth, St Keverne, *Cornish Archaeol*, **8**, 47-65

Peacock, D P S, and Williams, D F, 1986. *Amphorae and the Roman economy*, London

Quinnell, H, 1986. The Iron Age and Roman period in Cornwall, *Cornish Archaeol*, **25**, 111-134

Quinnell, H, 1993. A sense of identity: distinctive Cornish stone artefacts in the Roman and post-Roman periods, *Cornish Archaeol*, **32**, 29-46

Quinnell, H, 2004. *Trethurgy. Excavations at Trethurgy Round, St Austell: community and status in Roman and post-Roman Cornwall*, Truro (Cornwall County Council and English Heritage)

Radford, C A, 1951. Report on the excavations at Castle Dore, *Jnl Roy Inst Cornwall*, **1,** Appendix

Ratcliffe, J R, 1995. Duckpool, Morwenstow: a Romano-British and early medieval industrial site and harbour, Cornwall, *Cornish Archaeol*, **34**, 81-171

Ratcliffe, J R, and Straker, V, 1996. *The early environment of Scilly*, Truro (Cornwall County Council)

Reece, R, 2011. The coins, in Nowakowski and Quinnell 2011, 245-256

Reynolds, A, forthcoming. Atlantic Road, Newquay: Late Iron Age and Romano-British site, *Cornish Archaeol*

Rippon, S, 2008. Third Roman fort discovered in Cornwall, *Curr Archaeol*, **271**, 5

Schwieso, J, 1976. Excavations at Threemilestone, Kenwyn, near Truro, *Cornish Archaeol*, **15**, 51-67

Smart, C, 2010. Unearthing Roman and medieval Calstock: discovery and investigation 2008-9, *CAS newsletter*, **122**, February 2010

Smart, C, in prep. A Roman fort and medieval settlement at Calstock, Cornwall: Excavation and Survey 2008-2010, *Archaeol Jnl*

Smith, G, 1988. Excavation of the Iron Age cliff promontory fort and of Mesolithic and Neolithic flint-working areas at Penhale Point, Holywell Bay, near Newquay, 1983, *Cornish Archaeol*, **27**, 177-199

Smith, G, 1996. Archaeology and environment of a Bronze Age cairn and prehistoric and Romano-British field system at Chysauster, Gulval, near Penzance, *Proc Prehist Soc*, **62**, 203-239

Starley, D, forthcoming. Metalworking debris, in Cole and Nowakowski, *Cornish Archaeol*

Startin, B, forthcoming. Halligye fogou: excavations 1980-1982, *Cornish Archaeol*

Taylor, S, forthcoming. Excavations of a Roman and post-Roman site in Penlee House, Tregony: a cremation burial and other burning issues, *Cornish Archaeol*

Thomas, I, 1960. The excavations at Kynance Gate 1953-1960, *The Lizard*, **1**, 2nd series, 5-16

Thompson, S, 2009. *Looe Island, Cornwall. Archaeological evaluation and assessment of results*, Salisbury (Wessex Archaeology, report 68734.01)

Thorpe, C, 2004. *Chysauster disabled access improvements, Cornwall: archaeological watching brief*, Truro (Historic Environment Service, Cornwall County Council)

Thorpe, C, 2007. *The earthwork at Restormel Farm, Lostwithiel, Cornwall, archaeological site and finds evaluation*, Truro (Historic Environment Service, Cornwall County Council)

Threipland, L M, 1956. An excavation at St Mawgan-in-Pydar, north Cornwall, *Arch Jnl*, **113**, 33-81

Tyacke, A, 2002-2003. Chariots of fire, symbols and motifs on recent Iron Age metalwork finds in Cornwall, *Cornish Archaeol*, **41-42**, 144-148

Young, A, 2000-1. Time Team at Boleigh fogou, St Buryan, *Cornish Archaeol*, **39-40**, 129-145

Young, A, forthcoming. Prehistoric and Romano-British enclosures in the Camel Estuary, *Cornish Archaeol*

Waddington, K E, and Sharples, N M, 2007. Pins, pixies and thick dark earth, *British Archaeol*, **94**, 28-33

Wessex Archaeology, 2008. *Lellizzick, nr Padstow, Cornwall. Archaeological evaluation and assessment of results*, Salisbury (Ref 65312 September 2008)

Whimster, R, 1981. *Burial practices in Iron Age Britain. A discussion and gazetteer of the evidence c 700 BC – AD 43*, Brit Arch Repts, Brit Ser, **90**, Oxford

White, G, 1955-1956. *Private notebooks with field notes on sites around Newquay*, no 3370, Newquay Old Cornwall Society

White, R, 2007. *Britannia Prima – Britain's last Roman province*, Stroud

DISCOVERY AND RESEARCH

Cornish Archaeology 50, 2011, 263–286

Early medieval Cornwall

PETER HERRING, ANN PRESTON-JONES, CARL THORPE
and IMOGEN WOOD

Introduction

Peter Herring

Ann Preston-Jones and Peter Rose's admirable 1986 survey of then current understanding of the medieval period has supported and stimulated most of what has happened since. By selecting highlights from the body of subsequent work, these two updates (early and later medieval Cornwall) leave the CA 25 chapter as an enduringly valuable quarry of material and ideas. For the early medieval, three areas of study have seen particularly great changes in our understanding: rural landscape; Christianity and its ramifications; regional and local identity as reflected in pottery and the sourcing of potting clay. Underpinning each, and much other work on this period, is a greater certainty that rather than being the period when Britain's fabric and society was moulded, as Hoskins and others proposed, most early medieval arrangements and perhaps also ideologies and identities, developed from and were to varying degrees inherited from later prehistoric and Romano-British ones. Of course, the enhanced awareness of the scale, stability and complexity of early medieval Cornish society then has implications for our appreciation of later prehistory.

NB Unless otherwise stated, all dates in this section are AD.

Early medieval rural landscape

Peter Herring

Historic Landscape Characterisation (HLC) enables Cornwall's early medieval landscape to be modelled (Fig 1): anciently enclosed land, largely inherited from later prehistory, in the better drained lowlands and more sheltered upland valleys, upland and coastal rough ground (including towans), again perpetuating prehistory's proto-commons, and woodland (largely in steep-sided valleys) (Herring 2007; Dudley and Young forthcoming). Tidal creeks, less silted than now, were longer, piercing our undulating peninsula more deeply, dissecting it more thoroughly (e.g. Nowakowski and Thomas 2007, 58).

Transhumance (where part of the household accompanied summering livestock), probably originating in the second millennium BC (Herring 2008) appears to have ceased in Cornwall some time in the first millennium AD. The early medieval evidence provides the clearest view of a practice of great importance to mixed farming revealing much about levels of social and economic security over that long period. Most prosaically it increased production by exploiting seasonally available resources while reducing risk by removing livestock from growing hay and ripening crops. That it did so by linking separated property, holdings and rights in uplands and lowlands and by dividing households for half the year immediately reveals a complex and stable rural society (Fox 1996; Herring 1996; forthcoming).

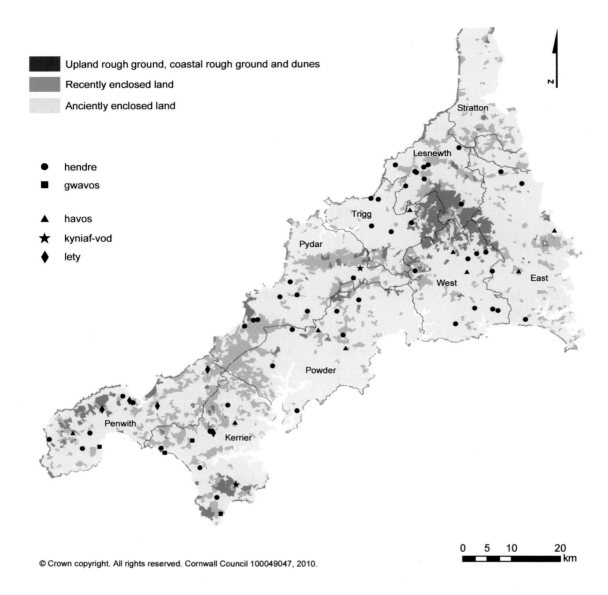

Fig 1. Transhumance place-names plotted against a simplified Cornwall historic landscape characterisation. Rough ground and recently enclosed land indicate the likely extent of early medieval open grazing land. **Havos** *(summer dwelling) and* **kyniaf-vod** *(autumn dwelling) names are associated with seasonal movement of herds and livestock away from* **hendre** *(old farming estate) and* **gwavos** *(winter dwelling) settlements, largely in lowland anciently enclosed land. Later* **lety** *(milk-house) names on the edges of west Cornwall's rough ground may represent a gradual shift away from the old practice of transhumance. The nine Hundreds equitably divided Cornwall's rough ground and access to its coastline (from Herring forthcoming).*

Pre-Norman Cornish place-name forms, notably *havos* ('summer dwelling') and *hendre* ('old or winter farming estate'), shared with the Welsh, confirm seasonal settlement was both widespread and early (Padel 1985; Herring 1996; 2009; forthcoming). Archaeological remains on Bodmin Moor include clusters of small sub-rectangular huts (good examples on Brockabarrow Common, Brown Willy, and Leskernick and Stowe's Hills), associated pens, and pounds for distraining trespassing livestock (Johnson and Rose 1994; Herring 1986; 1996; 2009). A small sub-rectangular structure of the fifth to seventh centuries excavated at Stencoose, St Agnes, may also be a transhumance hut (Jones 2000-2001).

The HLC supports modelling of transhumance's scale and shows how it affected not just upland and coastal rough ground, but also the lowland farmland from whence came herds and flocks that we can predict amounted to the equivalent of about 90,000 modern cows in Cornwall (Herring forthcoming). Such numbers would have achieved continued suppression of upland shrub and tree growth by grazing pressure (Fig 2) (Gearey *et al* 1997; 2000) and fit with early medieval lowland agricultural practice and settlement density (Herring forthcoming).

The lowland's individual households are now most visible in transhumance settlements where single-person huts are spaced out to leave room for tethering around them their owned animals. So too is the communal hamlet of which the household was part, represented by the loose groupings of transhumance huts. Pens were shared, as no doubt were risk, danger, company and pleasure, and again this probably reflects similar communalism in the lowland hamlet (Herring 1996; 2009; forthcoming). Numbers of households sending members to the hills suggests the need for labour there to routinely process the animals, presumably milking and then making butters, cheeses, etc, maximising outputs from the uplands. The nine large hundreds, Cornwall's administrative subdivisions, some or all of which were possibly established in late prehistory (Padel 2010c), probably policed rights and limits of transhumance, preventing trespass and ensuring rights were not exceeded (Herring 1996; see Fig 1).

Fig 2. Around a third of early medieval Cornwall would have been open rough ground, probably mainly commons supporting ancient semi-natural grasslands. Among those never subsequently enclosed is West Moor in Altarnun where transhumants made their huts within ruined Bronze Age round houses on Leskernick Hill (right) and would have encountered Bronze Age cairns, as skylined on distant Bray Down. (Photograph: Peter Herring)

DISCOVERY AND RESEARCH

Fig 3. Trebarwith (left) and Trecarne, two farming hamlets in Tintagel parish, each set within the clearly defined 'townland' (perimeters following streams, etc) that was the tre, or 'farming estate'. Fields have slightly sinuous boundaries but form roughly rectangular shapes, derived from later medieval enclosure of open fields probably established in the early medieval period. (Photograph: Peter Herring)

Recent British ethnographic evidence and reflection on household roles suggest that the member tending, milking and churning was probably a young woman. Transhumance brought them vivid experiences: the two great annual journeys (probably around May Day and October's end); partings and reunions; pleasures experienced, trust shared and responsibilities shouldered (Herring 2009; forthcoming).

Many *hendre* settlements are 4-5 kilometres from rough grazing (Herring 2009), similar to more recent transhuming distances elsewhere in Britain (Ó Danachair 1983-4; Bil 1990; Davies 1984-5). But they are also found throughout lowland Cornwall, some being over 10 kilometres from extensive rough ground (in Gerrans, Morval and St Germans). It seems each early medieval settlement in Cornwall's anciently enclosed land was effectively a *hendre*, as expected when considering the importance of clearing livestock from summer fields. The name *hendre* contains the Cornish element *tre*, 'farming estate' (Padel 1985, 223-232). Almost all 1300 or so surviving *trefs* are in anciently enclosed land, and their spacing, typically half a kilometre apart when in clusters (maps in Preston-Jones and Rose 1986; Turner 2006a), suggests that 'estates' typically contained around 50 hectares (*c* 125 acres) (Fig 3). HLC shows that each contained a mix of land, some rough (Fig 4). Such areas probably supported groups of four or

five households rather than single farmsteads if early medieval households could manage the 30 acres (12 hectares) of a typical post-medieval Cornish mixed farm. The limited archaeological evidence also suggests that later first millennium households were grouped into hamlets (e.g. Bruce-Mitford 1997). The *tre* was therefore close in concept and form to the ancient Irish townland (Glassie 1982; Aalen 1997; Herring 1999) and closer still if it followed the Welsh *hendra* and had close kinship links between its households (Davies 1984-5, 76).

Hamlet, constituent household and individual may have been fairly autonomous, despite being within larger landholding units, equivalents of multiple estates, represented unevenly in Cornwall as Domesday Book 'manors'. Individual households were more or less free (reflected in Domesday Book's statuses; Thorn and Thorn 1979), but it seems unlikely that those hamlet dwellers with privately held property, including livestock, as in Mawgan Porth's proto-longhouses (Bruce-Mitford 1997), were slaves owned and directed by higher levels of society (Fox 2006; but see Padel 2009). They did, however, live, farm and practice transhumance within the confines of broader proprietorial, customary and cultural structures. Examination of transhumance demonstrates freedom and the various legal, social or customary constraints upon it (Pearce 2004, 210; Herring 2009; forthcoming).

Development of convertible husbandry, perhaps in the 'long' eighth century if recent work in Devon can guide understanding of Cornish practices (Fyfe 2006; Rippon *et al* 2006), may explain the decline of transhumance. While much emphasis is placed on convertible husbandry's arable element with its 3-4 years cropping, it may be that the 6-10 years of grass reveals the driver as a desire (or need) to draw the household in during the summer, to milk in fields or cowhouses (Herring forthcoming). Summer grazing on rough ground persisted for another 1200 years, but fewer people were needed to accompany and check livestock no longer milked on the moors (Herring 2004). Origins of Cornwall's small-scale, hamlet or *tre*-level strip fields are also sought around the eighth century and most surviving strip systems do have the 10 or so cropping units that fit best the convertible husbandry regime (Herring 1999; 2006). The establishment of strip field systems and the apparently open hamlets that farmed them

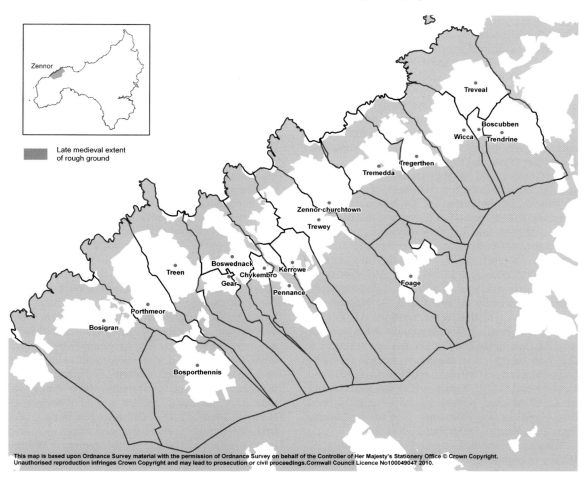

Fig 4. Zennor's ribbon-shaped 'townlands' as mapped from the 1840s parish Tithe Map and plotted against later medieval rough ground to show how each shared land of varying potential and many also had direct access to coastal resources. Their origins may be sought at least as early as the early medieval period when many had tre 'farming estate' place-names. Dots mark locations of the hamlets, placed within patches of anciently enclosed land inherited from later prehistory, perhaps like the townlands themselves. Such equity suggests that a higher level of rural organisation facilitated this allotment, presumably the prehistoric precursor of the parish itself. (From Dudley 2011, fig 43)

DISCOVERY AND RESEARCH

over most of Cornwall's anciently enclosed land appears to have been preceded by the wholesale dismantlement of later prehistoric and Roman period fields whose lines can be detected as crop marks on aerial photographs or through geophysical survey, a revision that was so radical that an ideological basis for it has been suggested, perhaps associated with the arrival of Christianity (Herring 2008, 91-3; see Preston-Jones, below). Here it is suggested that a deeper continuity from prehistory can also be detected in the dispositions of land use types and within their framework the townlands (which were normally delineated by topographical features like streams) and draped over them the administrative structure represented by the hundreds. On the more local level of individual farming settlements, Peter Rose and Ann Preston-Jones noted how distributions of surviving courtyard house hamlets in West Penwith tended to mach the spacing and patterning of early medieval ones (identified through place-names), again suggesting that the latter perpetuated the former (Rose and Preston-Jones 1995).

Full publication of the Trethurgy excavations sets out the evidence for continuity of occupation of this round (and that at Grambla, Wendron) from the Roman period and through the fifth and sixth centuries, and suggests why this might be a model for continuity of settlement, house form and economy for much of the western half of Cornwall (Quinnell 2004, 238-244). We are also starting to recover early medieval material and patterns from heartland anciently enclosed land. At Nancemere, east of Truro, a sixth-seventh centuries AD E-ware sherd found eroding from a round's inner rampart suggests continuing activity. Ditches in a field system that later incorporated the round yielded sherds of Grass-Marked pottery and a radiocarbon date of the eleventh and twelfth centuries (Gossip, forthcoming b). Grass-Marked pottery has also recently been discovered for the first time at a *tre* settlement: Trelissick, Feock (Taylor and Thorpe 2008).

Charcoal from an elongated clay-lined pit at St Blazey Gate produced late Roman or early medieval radiocarbon dates. Its excavator considered it a cooking pit, but upright stones in its fill suggest a 'floor' may have been laid across and the pit used in either malting or corn drying (Lawson-Jones forthcoming; Graeme Kirkham, pers comm). Other possible corn drying kilns may also be identified (Graeme Kirkham, pers comm). A long, narrow pit at Ruthvoes, St Columb Major had evidence of

burning (fifth and sixth centuries AD radiocarbon date) and a fill containing roasted, partially hulled barley grains with some wheat and oats, while another long pit, partly stone lined, at Black Cross, St Enoder, produced charcoal and oat grains and fifth to seventh-centuries AD radiocarbon dates (Nowakowski 1998, 87-91). None of these pits, all found during investigations of linear developments (pipelines etc), was associated with contemporary occupation, but it should be noted that because of the fire risk, kilns were normally located away from settlements (Evans 1957, 123; Jones 1985, 155; Herring 1986, vol 2, 103).

Late Roman and early post-Roman coastal agriculture at Atlantic Road, Newquay, involved a particular response to the local environment, creating a soil by adding to wind-blown sand massive quantities of domestic midden material, apparently deliberately drawn from earlier dumps nearby. Plough-marks were cut through this soil into the underlying sand (Reynolds forthcoming).

The forms of early medieval dwellings and buildings remains uncertain, though it seems likely that they were varied. Those small sub-rectangular transhumance huts, probably with simple ridges supporting thatched roofs, may echo the shapes, if not the sizes of lowland structures (Herring 1996), and may have developed from the oval houses (exemplified by those in the rounds at Trethurgy and Grambla) that seem to have been the norm in Roman period Cornwall and continued to be built as late as the sixth century (Quinnell 2004). The Stencoose building had a splayed quadrilateral plan, open on one side, and some of the structures excavated at Gwithian were equally irregular (Nowakowski 2007, fig 11). Ring-ditches on a south-facing slope, by a stream, at Lanhainsworth, St Columb Major, produced early medieval radiocarbon dates and may have been drip gullies around roundhouses (Lawson-Jones 2001, 47-51). Mawgan Porth's later first millennium rectangular structures, including proto-longhouses, were neatly arranged around courtyards (Bruce-Mitford 1997).

While agriculture may have driven Cornwall's early medieval economy, excavated archaeological sites usually illuminate other activities. As with transhumance, the most revealing material is generally found at the margins. Tintagel, St Michael's Mount and Lammana are dealt with below (Preston-Jones). Review of the material recorded north of the Red River in Camborne parish as part of the 1950s

Gwithian project suggests that small stone-built fifth to eighth-century structures perched above the then tidal river were not domestic settlements, but workshops. Crafts and industries included working of iron, bronze, bone and leather and 'the recycling of imported ceramics' (Sturgess 2007, 44). Duckpool, a beach-head Romano-British metalworking site in the far north of Cornwall was re-occupied from the seventh to the eleventh centuries and again used for industry, perhaps, like Gwithian's workshops in association with coastal trade (Ratcliffe 1995). Pottery consistent with seventh to ninth-century Grass-Marked wares and a ninth to tenth century AMS determination date a large settlement (up to 750m by 150m in extent) comprising stone-walled structures cut into Gunwalloe's dunes. Here soil micro-morphology and molluscs, coupled with middened cattle, sheep, pig, bird, crab, fish (wrasse and hake), shellfish, hare and amphibians provide evidence of a rich diet and a mixed landscape. Links to the adjacent early church site and to the great estate centre of Winnianton, caput of Kerrier in 1086, indicate that ongoing excavations are revealing an important settlement (Wood 2010).

The early medieval church
Ann Preston-Jones

The last 25 years have seen considerable progress in early medieval Cornish church archaeology. Scholarly surveys placed Cornwall in its British context while local studies increased knowledge of individual facets of the church. Excavations, often development-related, have provided remarkable insights, although there have been no research excavations of the sort undertaken by Charles Thomas in 1950s and 1960s.

Nothing, however, has altered the long-held perception that in Cornwall the period falls into roughly three parts. The first couple of centuries, termed variously 'sub-Roman' 'post-Roman', 'Early Christian', and 'Late Antique', represent continuation of ways and styles of Roman-period Dumnonia, with a strong Roman period legacy evident in the Christian sites and monuments. Little new information has illuminated the following true 'Dark Age': yet this was when Devonian Dumnonia came under English control and Cornwall was first named as an entity, for around a century being independent and self-governing. From the ninth-century Cornwall

too came under English control and in the tenth was fully integrated administratively. From the late ninth century a flowering of material culture suggests a re-awakening as Cornwall emerged as an English county with a distinctive character (Padel 2009, 4-5; 2010b).

Cornwall's position in relation to the British Isles and Europe is seen in John Blair's masterly study of all aspects of the church, especially the minster-monasteries which dominate first millennium English Christianity's structure (Blair 2005). Nicholas Orme has summarised the local historical background, emphasising the relationship of the church in Cornwall with the Anglo-Saxons (Orme 2007; 2010), while in the same VCH volume Oliver Padel identifies the Celtic aspects which survived Cornwall's incorporation (Padel 2010a). In numerous articles and works, Padel's contribution to our understanding of the period has been great. From his 1976-77 work on place-names of ecclesiastical sites to his 2010 VCH study, he has done much to push forward boundaries of knowledge and understanding. Meanwhile, Nancy Edwards has reiterated the many similarities between pre-Norman Cornwall and Wales: the result of a shared culture (Edwards and Lane 1992; Edwards 2009).

No evidence has yet emerged to show whether Cornwall was Christian, or even partly so, in the Roman period. But as more evidence of Roman military activity in the county emerges (Claughton and Smart 2008; Penhallurick 2009; Nowakowski this volume; Smart forthcoming) so too does the possibility grow that at least pockets of Christianity existed; as also does the possibility that Cornwall was more attuned to Roman culture than previously acknowledged and therefore likely to be receptive to an essentially Mediterranean-derived religion. On Tintagel Island, newly discovered evidence of Roman activity (Morris and Harry 1997; Barrowman *et al* 2007, 309-13) surely forms the backdrop to the remarkable post-Roman activity. At Calstock we now have the first definite Cornish instance of a church established at an important Roman site, a feature common elsewhere in the country (Blair 2005, 54), and although the relationship between the Calstock fort, the church and an even larger enclosure about both (established by geophysics) is not yet understood, the discovery of Grass-Marked pottery (Carl Thorpe, pers comm) suggests some sort of continuity. Forms and locations of St Hilary and Lelant churchyards, intervisible across

Fig 5. Excavations at Tintagel churchyard in progress in 1991. In the foreground can be seen a cist grave and a stone-built grave and beyond Ursula Davey and Archie Mercer is a possible pre-Norman church (with director Jacky Nowakowski to the right). (Photograph: HES Archive)

the Penwith isthmus, suggest these churches may be set within small Roman forts or signal stations (Pete Herring, pers comm and Preston-Jones 1994, 83, fig 6). Locations and distribution of Roman period 'milestones' also hint at continuity: four of the five are at or near church or chapel sites. The idea that they simply mark Roman roads requires reconsideration (Preston-Jones 2011, appendix 2).

Origins of Christianity in the west have been debated, with the influences of Roman-period Christianity, the Mediterranean, Gaul, Wales and Ireland and the rise of monasticism, all seen to contribute to the character which emerged (Blair 2005, 15-22). The contribution of the pre-existing landscape and ritual practice cannot be ignored. Carver (2009) emphasises its influence in monasticism in northern and western Britain and in Cornwall where the legacy of earlier cultures is so evident, incorporation of some sites and aspects of earlier practice seems inevitable.

The earliest evidence for Christianity in Cornwall is now from Tintagel church (Fig 5), on the mainland opposite the Island. Tintagel's status as a post-Roman citadel involved in and perhaps controlling trade with the Mediterranean was affirmed during the 1990s (Barrowman *et al* 2007), but excavations at the church have been of equal importance (Nowakowski and Thomas 1990; 1992). Here, in a surface radiocarbon dated to the very early fifth century, were revealed long-cists, dug graves and evidence of graveside ritual and feasting compared by the excavators with Mediterranean funerary customs. Associated with the graves were small white pebbles, incised slates (one with a cross) and imported pottery linking the site to the Island.

Investigations on St Michael's Mount, potentially the famed 'Ictis', or one of several such ports of trade, have raised the possibility that this too was a post-Roman citadel with Roman-period antecedents, of perhaps equal importance to Tintagel (Fig 6). There are now several post-Roman imported sherds from the Mount and an early medieval grave (though of broadly ninth century date) suggests a burial ground (Herring 1993; Herring *et al* 2000, 22-3, 33, 121-124; Sturgess 2010, 20-23). Sadly, Time Team's (admittedly limited) excavations on Looe Island failed to shed light on this other potential post-Roman citadel and early Christian site, although Roman activity was located and a sherd of early medieval pottery has previously been found (Olson 1989, 42, 103; Wessex Archaeology 2009, 22).

Despite these early signs of Christianity at coastal emporia, the process of conversion probably proceeded more slowly inland. At Trethurgy Round possible evidence of Christianity's impact on Cornish communities was found with the sixth-century abandonment of a feature interpreted as a shrine (Quinnell 2004, 237). Equally notable evidence for pagan activity continuing into the sixth century was found in an enclosure close to Newlyn East church (Jones forthcoming), while at Tremough excavation

in 2010 revealed structural deposition reminiscent of prehistoric ritual in a possibly sixth-century timber building (James Gossip, pers comm). So the portrayal of sixth-century Cornwall in the *Life of St Samson* as 'nominally Christian but still engaged in some pagan practices' may, as Orme (2010, 8) has suggested, be not far from the truth. A cist cemetery at Forrabury, discovered in 2009, has revealed a remarkable mix of pagan and Christian practice (Carl Thorpe, pers comm).

Alongside this exciting new information, the more conspicuous and well-known aspects of the fifth to seventh centuries continue to attract attention. The early inscribed stones – the period's most tangible Christian relics – have been the subject of two major volumes and discussion aired in *Cornish Archaeology*. The two works are complementary. One, by an experienced epigrapher (Okasha 1993) comprehensively catalogues and provides extensive bibliographies, while the other, by a distinguished Cornish archaeologist, presents a model of early medieval immigration from Wales and Ireland and the associated development of Christianity in Cornwall (Thomas 1994). Okasha highlights the Cornish stones' distinctive character (1993, 41-2) and in comparing the inscriptions with some from Pictland concludes that literacy there was more widespread and of a higher standard than in the south west (Okasha 1996). Further study by Thomas finds hidden meanings behind certain texts (Thomas 1997; 1998; 1999) in theories which do

Fig 6. On the basis of its distinctive character and limited finds of post-Roman imported wares made in the last 20 years, St Michael's Mount has been suggested as a possible south coast equivalent of the 'citadel' of Tintagel.

DISCOVERY AND RESEARCH

Fig 7. The curving line of roads around the churchyard at Lanivet is believed to represent the boundary of an early Christian lann. The name of Lanivet, Lannived in 1268, means 'church-site (or lann) at the place called Neved'; Neved, meaning 'pagan sacred place' must have been a pre-existing place-name in the area (Padel 1976-7, 19; 1988, 106). (Historic Environment Service, Cornwall Council, F86, 131)

not receive universal approval (McKee and McKee 2002; Blair 2005, 16), though such models stimulate discussion that can help move scholarship on to greater understanding. Meanwhile, inscribed stones continue to be discovered, for example at Kerris (Okasha 1998-9; Thomas 2000-1) and Lanivet, the latter by CAS member Carole Vivian. An unexpected date for charcoal from the socket of Eathorne menhir hints at an early medieval origin for this apparently un-inscribed stone (Hartgroves *et al* 2006, 105-6) and a rock-cut socket in Tintagel Churchyard's earliest levels may have accommodated a roughly cylindrical but also uninscribed granite pillar now re-erected in the churchyard (Nowakowski and Thomas 1992, 4, 7). Taken together, they may suggest a new monument type for this period.

Whether Cornish churchyard shapes signify very early Christian sites or *lanns*, has received full appraisal (Fig 7). Seen 25 years ago as 'enclosed developed cemeteries', likely *lanns* were discussed

and compared to suggest that status and chronology may be discernible in their physical attributes (Preston-Jones 1994). Although the early enclosure and use of *lanns* as cemeteries has been usefully questioned (Petts 2002, 30, 39-42; Turner 2005, 173; 2006a, 6, 9-10), the way the enclosure form mimics that of rounds suggests they may have originated as a specialised form, their Christian function established at a date when rounds were still a common settlement type – at least for certain members of society, the bank and ditch perhaps demonstrating the status of the occupants (Herring 2008, 91). As rounds generally went out of use by the sixth or seventh centuries, the tradition of the enclosure of *lanns* is likely to have been established by that date. Linguistic evidence supports this, the word being well established from as early a period as documentary references (including place-names) exist capable of showing it, including Somerset, Dorset and Devon, where the names can hardly have been created later than *c* 700 (Oliver

Padel, pers comm). Discoveries of Mediterranean wares at Mullion churchyard, a *lann* on a site which may be a reused round or hillfort, is strong evidence for use of the site at this period, although whether at that date the pottery represents use of the site as a round, a *lann*, or both is of course difficult to establish (Thorpe 2003, 26-31). Absence of early graves in the admittedly small area excavated at least shows that activity in this area did not involve burial (Carl Thorpe, pers comm). St Buryan may be another reused prehistoric site (Preston-Jones 1987). From another perspective, Padel concludes that in the early period *lanns* were specialised settlements, distinguished from most contemporary settlements by presence of a religious focus, perhaps graves and other features which might not show archaeologically (Padel 2002, 308-313; 2010a, 116-9; forthcoming). With time, and especially as churchyard burial became the norm, they may have acted as a base for local evangelism, leading to development as a parochial centre.

So, while accepting their early origin, we have over the last 25 years developed a rather different interpretation of *lanns*. Petts (2002, 42-44) considers that until the eighth century, lay cemeteries were more likely to be located on reused barrows, along major trackways, or in conspicuous landscape locations. For the select few, burial sites may have been represented by inscribed stones; for the majority burial may have been within extensive unenclosed cemeteries. Tintagel may have begun as one such: its early origin mentioned above. Further apparently unenclosed long-cist cemeteries have been discovered at Forrabury, Trevenen, Treharrock (a children's cemetery, perhaps associated with a Bronze Age barrow) and a single cist at St Issey (Carl Thorpe, pers comm; Johns and Preston-Jones 1996; St Issey cist: HER PRN 26510). Most remain undated except through landscape relationships (Trudgian 1987, 147-50). Such sites, apparently distinct and different from *lanns,* have no known Cornish name, perhaps because they became redundant fairly early (Oliver Padel, pers comm). Some, like St Endellion, developed into church sites, others did not. So the concept of the 'enclosed developed cemetery' certainly still exists, but not in relation to *lanns*. Blair (following Driscoll 1988, 184) suggests that the decline in the use of lay cemeteries and inscribed stones is linked to the point at which the power and importance of the church was outstripping that of the ancestors (Blair 2005, 63-4).

Sam Turner uses HLC to weave these well-known elements together and show Christianity's impact across the whole Cornish landscape (Turner 2003; 2005; 2006a). Religious sites are seen in the context of an already well-developed landscape, its settled core represented by the hundreds of places with *tre-* names which gradually replaced rounds as the major settlement type (Herring, above). Like both rounds and *trefs*, *lanns* were settlements surrounded by an associated estate of land for the community's support. Herring argues that the new Christian ideology may have influenced the change from rounds to unenclosed settlements and led to development of strip field systems (2006, 73; 2008, 91-3; and pers comm). Close relationships between early Christian and secular centres at Tintagel, Bodmin (with *Dinuurin*: Olson 1989, 51-6; Oliver Padel, pers comm) and possibly St Michael's Mount, suggest a link with the secular administrative framework and a means by which such ideology/influence could be disseminated. However, we still know little of secular power structure and despite discussion by Turner (2005, 56-61), identification and understanding of secular centres remains speculative.

So within a couple of centuries there may have been established a multitude of religious settlements, memorials and cemeteries, many of which are still in use. From amongst these, we discern a handful of larger, more complex sites of greater status that appear at the end of the period in sources including Domesday Book as land-owning churches with communities of clerics (Olson 1989; Orme 2010, 126-135; Turner 2006a, 156-7). There may have been more sites than the bald documentary record implies and archaeologically they are represented as sites with evidence of larger enclosures (Preston-Jones 1994, 86). Associated with their later decline in status are 'shrinking churchyards', already identified at Crantock (Olson 1982), but now also at Padstow (below) and possibly Fowey (Exeter Archaeology 1998-99, 222), whose monastery was postulated by Thomas (1994, 231-2). This diversity is different from the way the church is thought to have developed in Anglo-Saxon England. There, the minsters – powerful churches served by communities of priests, linked to secular power centres and associated with provision of pastoral care – developed in the seventh century to form the pillars of England's ecclesiastical system (Blair 2005). Only gradually was their network expanded and infilled with large numbers of lesser sites. As Padel points out, certain Cornish churches with minster-like properties only appear towards the end of the period, flourishing under English benevolence (Padel 2010a, 119).

The English minsters peaked in the eighth century and although their power declined in the ninth they nonetheless remained embedded in the landscape as economic and cultural centres and bases for pastoral care. This contrasts strongly with Cornwall, apparently already thick with small religious sites by the eighth century. The next two centuries are archaeologically quiet and we must suppose that many early *lanns* continued to develop a local role, becoming in time parochial centres. By the early tenth century, the Cornish 'List' of saints' names suggests elements of a parochial system were already emerging (Olson and Padel 1986, 68-9; but see Turner 2006a, 155).

An important excavation at Padstow uncovered long-cists of this middle period just outside the modern churchyard, but apparently related to the church site. As at Crantock and Fowey, Padstow's religious enclosure had contracted. A sherd of rare 'Hamwih ware' discovered here is a small but significant indicator of wide trading contacts of a site that in the late tenth century was of sufficient importance to attract Viking raiders (Manning and Stead 2002-3; Padel 2010a, 119; Olson 1989, 69-72).

In the late ninth century, two special things break the silence: a famous cross shaft near St Cleer and the Trewhiddle Hoard. The Doniert Stone may be an early example of the sculpture that characterises tenth and eleventh-century Cornwall: its significance lies also in its possible commemoration of *Dungart*, the last recorded Cornish king, though this is not universally accepted (Okasha 1993, 215). Hidden in the late ninth century and found in the late eighteenth, the Trewhiddle Hoard remains one of the important hoards of this period nationally and still defines an English art style (Wilson and Blunt 1961, 100). It is thought to have been buried in an active tin streamwork in times of Viking threat, 'as likely by the Danish "host" as by the Saxons' (Penhallurick 1986, 181-4; 2009, 228). Described by Wilson in 1961 as 'the moveable treasure of a church' (Wilson and Blunt 1961, 117) and defined by him entirely in relation to Saxon English art, it now needs reassessment, especially since a horn mount similar to that at Trewhiddle has been interpreted as belonging to a hunting-, rather than a drinking-horn (Graham Campbell 1976, 51).

Fig 8. A pre-Norman cross shaft recently identified in the north wall of Paul Church by Jill Hogben and Aidan Hicks. Decorated in multi-strand interlace, this is a typical West Penwith-style shaft, which may originally have been associated with the cross-head on the churchyard wall (Fig 9). (Photograph: Andrew Langdon)

Fig 9. Lighting is used to display and record decoration on pre-Norman crosses for the proposed corpus of early Cornish sculpture. In this illustration Andrew Langdon is photographing the cross-head on Paul churchyard wall; like most Penwith-style crosses, the head features an image of the Crucifixion on the main face. (Photograph: Anne Preston-Jones)

The later part of the period sees Cornwall coming increasingly under English authority. Despite this some Cornish sites were respected so that in the tenth century, St Germans cathedral was established in a *lann* (Padel 1978; Orme 2010, 129-30), while St Petroc's became Cornwall's most powerful monastery. Other land-owning religious houses become more apparent, identified by documentation, enclosures, names in *lann*, dedications to patron saints whose relics may have been preserved in shrines in the churches, occasionally extended sanctuaries, and perhaps multiple chapels (Padel forthcoming; Olson 1989; Petts and Turner 2009). These attributes differ from the more extensive range of features expected of early monasteries elsewhere (Carver 2009, 335-6). Place-names and the churchyard survey mentioned above show most Cornish parish churches to be based on early sites, while other lesser sites increasingly filled the landscape (Preston-Jones

1994, 79-81, 92; Turner 2006a, 161). Excavations at St Mawgan, St Minver, and others have revealed the depth of deposits and great potential of these anciently-established sites, but also the difficulties of excavating on sites in constant use for burial for over a thousand years (Thorpe 1998; 2001; 2003). From South Hill and Tintagel churches comes evidence that use of long-cists continued beyond the Norman Conquest (Nowakowski and Thomas 1992, 17-25; Gossip 2002; forthcoming) while Mawgan Porth shows that some unenclosed cemeteries continued in use into the tenth and eleventh centuries (Bruce-Mitford 1997, 63-70).

Crosses remain the most tangible evidence for the later period (Figs 8 and 9). Work by Preston-Jones, Okasha *et al* is well advanced on a comprehensive catalogue, in the same series as the *Corpus of Anglo-Saxon Stone Sculpture for the South-West* (Cramp *et al* 2006) and related to two *corpora* for South Wales (Redknap and Lewis 2007; Edwards 2007).

DISCOVERY AND RESEARCH

Though the appearance of crosses coincides with arrival of English rule and their form and motifs can be paralleled all over the British Isles, careful appraisal is establishing their distinctively Cornish identity. Charters confirm the importance of crosses as boundary markers (Hooke 1994; Turner 2006a, 161-5; 2006b, 31-40); they also show that boundaries both parochial and secular might be marked by earthworks, ancient burial mounds, prehistoric standing stones and natural features, while a name like *Carn Peran* 'the tor of St Peran' on the bounds of Tywarnhayle manor, shows that by the tenth and eleventh centuries Christianity had permeated the entire landscape (Hooke 1994, 28-30; Herring and Hooke 1993).

Church buildings, however, remain elusive. Although documentation, for example in the Bodmin Manumissions, indicates their existence in pre-Norman times (Bodmin, Padstow, Liskeard: Hooke 1994, 70-82; Padel 2009, 6-7) there has been a failure, other than at St Germans Cathedral (Olson and Preston-Jones 1998-9) to positively identify any church buildings of the period: the date of an east-west building located to the north of Tintagel Church, with pieces of a possible font built into its wall, remains to be confirmed (Fig 5; Nowakowski and Thomas 1992, 14-16; Thomas 1993, 108-9) while early stonework proposed for Minster and St Piran's churches has now been rejected (Allan 2004-5, 150; Allan and Blaylock 2007; 27, 31). However, a proposed future project at St Piran's Oratory may help in establishing some truth about this building, still popularly claimed to be the earliest Christian building in the country (see Carter 2001, 10-11 for a more pragmatic view).

Early medieval pottery
Carl Thorpe and Imogen Wood

Cornwall is one of few places in the British Isles where pottery production and use have been almost continuous from the Neolithic to the present day. Work here has played a prominent role in early medieval ceramics studies, especially in identification and understanding of French and Mediterranean imported wares. Cornwall is also one of few regions where manufacture of early medieval 'native' wares can be demonstrated. Professor Charles Thomas was first to identify and classify both native and imported wares (Thomas 1957; 1959; 1960; 1968; 1981). Knowledge of these

has progressed significantly in the past 25 years with publication and study of important sites like Trethurgy (Quinnell 2004), Boden Fogou (Gossip forthcoming), Gwithian (Nowakowski *et al* 2007), Mawgan Porth (Bruce-Mitford 1997), Launceston Castle (Saunders 2006), Hay Close, Newlyn East (Jones forthcoming) and Tintagel (Barrowman *et al* 2007).

In the late Roman period (fourth and fifth centuries AD) a well developed Cornish pottery industry flourished (Fig 10). Manufactured mostly from gabbroic clays (see Wood, below), principal forms were slack-profiled jars (Trethurgy Type, TT 4), flanged bowls (TT 22), flat grooved-rim bowls and large storage jars with cordons (TTs 21 and 13) and large cooking pots (TT 16). The Trethurgy material showed that basic Roman period patterns of cooking and eating endured until the fifth and possibly sixth centuries (Quinnell 2004).

Unlike large parts of Britain where production or use of ceramics either declined or ceased completely in the late fifth and sixth centuries, in Cornwall native pottery was experimental and innovative, developing rapidly in many directions (Thorpe forthcoming). Material first identified during the Gwithian excavations and consequently termed 'Gwithian Style' wares (Thomas 1956; 1960) was seen as continuing late Roman potting traditions. Its fabric (usually gabbroic, but locally granitic or slate) was even finer and harder fired, its bases often sanded and its surfaces better finished than before (wiped, burnished or patterned; Thorpe forthcoming). Forms include jars and bowls (sometimes flanged) with curved and everted rims, often with concave internal rim bevels. A completely new form, unrelated to the Romano-Cornish gabbroic repertoire, is the low walled (sometimes un-walled) platter, its introduction perhaps connected to changes in preparing and serving food. Sites where Gwithian Style wares have been recognised include Gwithian, Goldherring, Carngoon Bank, Boden, East Porth, Samson, and Tintagel, but it does not occur at Trethurgy (Thorpe forthcoming, a publication that will include example illustrations of the range of forms).

Gwithian Style ware is dated to the sixth to late seventh centuries through association at Gwithian and Hay Close with imported Mediterranean wares: Late Roman 1 (Bii), and Late Roman 2 (Bi) amphorae, African and Phocean Red Slipped Wares.

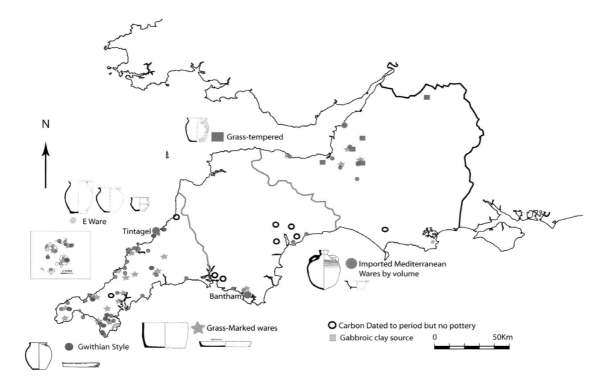

Fig 10. Distributions of principal post-Roman sites in Cornwall, Devon and the combined counties of Somerset, Dorset and Wiltshire (Wood 2011, fig 4.1). Tintagel and Bantham have the greatest volume of imported pottery, Devon lacks the perceived availability seen in Cornwall, and in Somerset it is generally restricted to hillforts, suggesting differing social hierarchies within the south west. E-ware is predominantly coastal in Scilly and Cornwall and has now been found elsewhere in the south west, often associated with Mediterranean imports. Similarly, Gwithian style is no longer restricted to western Cornwall having also been found in the north east. The concentration of Grass-tempered pottery in Somerset may be linked to similar Anglo-Saxon traditions in the Thames Basin, suggesting communication.

Supporting this are radiocarbon determinations of cal AD 550-650 from internal residue on a sanded platter sherd from Gwithian (Nowakowski *et al* 2007); cal AD 590-670 from residue within a platter at Boden (Gossip forthcoming); and cal AD 390–540 from bone in a sealed pit fill containing Gwithian Style ware and imported Mediterranean ware at Hay Close (Jones forthcoming). Gwithian Style ware is thus contemporary with imported western French E ware that may have influenced adoption of stylistic features such as concave internal rim bevels (Thorpe forthcoming). Two possible complete Gwithian Style jars have recently been excavated at Forrabury and Tremough Campus (Thorpe, pers comm) and the

ware has also been identified at East Porth, Samson (Neal et al forthcoming). Platters without grass-marking were also found at Goldherring (Guthrie 1969) and Carngoon Bank (McAvoy 1980).

Wide ranging international trading contacts are a feature of early medieval Cornwall, evidenced by numerous **imported wares** within ceramic assemblages. Since Charles Thomas published his influential corpus (Thomas 1981), several new sites have added to our understanding of these wares, whose characteristics are summarised here.

The first group is of Mediterranean wheel-made wares including tableware, amphorae and coarsewares. The fine red slip tableware comprises **Phocean**

Red Slip Ware (PRSW) from western Turkey and **African Red Slipped Ware** (ARSW) from near Carthage, Tunisia (Hayes 1972; 1980). Produced from the fourth to seventh centuries, their forms changed rapidly, making them useful for dating; those found in Cornwall are from around 450-550.

Amphorae are **Class Bi** (also known as Late Roman 2 amphora; Peacock and Williams Form 43; PW43) from Greece (for wine and olive oil); **Class Bii** (Late Roman 1; PW44) from Cilicia, south-east Turkey (wine and olive oil); **Class Biv** (Late Roman 3; PW45) from Sardis, western Turkey (wine or fine oil); and **Class Bv** (PW33/34) from Byzacena, northern Tunisia (olive oil). In use from the fifth to seventh centuries, their importation and distribution in Britain appears to have been largely from the late fifth to mid sixth centuries (Thomas 1981; Fulford and Peacock 1984; Peacock and Williams 1986; Tyers 1996; Dark 2001).

Most of the imported **coarsewares** found at Tintagel have not been closely provenanced, but appear to be eastern Mediterranean. Forms include jugs, bowls, casseroles and amphorae (Thomas and Thorpe 1988; forthcoming).

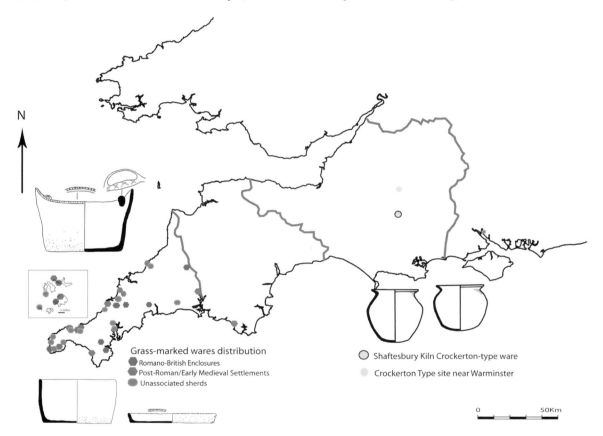

Fig 11. Distributions of principal early medieval sites yielding ceramic finds in Cornwall, Devon and the combined counties of Somerset, Dorset and Wiltshire (Wood 2011, fig 4.14). Cornwall continued its strong tradition of native pottery production and an emerging industry is seen in Dorset and Wiltshire. Devon appears to have been an aceramic buffer zone within the south west possibly hindering ceramic influences overland from the rest of the south west which began to adopt forms typical of southern Britain in this period. The presence of Grass-marked platters in Romano-British settlements marks the last phases of their occupation before this ware's distribution shifts to the coastal areas in a wider range of forms.

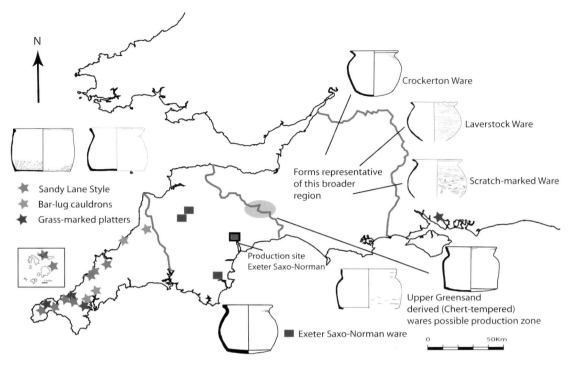

Fig 12. Distributions of principal post-Norman Conquest sites in Cornwall, Devon and the combined counties of Somerset, Dorset and Wiltshire (Wood 2011, fig 4.18). The production of Exeter Saxo-Norman and possibly Upper Greensand derived (Chert-tempered) wares ended a five century aceramic period in Devon after which pottery styles in Cornwall begin to imitate common forms seen in Somerset, Dorset and Wiltshire and southern England as a whole. It is clear ceramic influences progressed overland once more. Norman settlements utilised Grass-marked wares briefly, before importing the majority of pottery from elsewhere, signalling the decline of Cornwall's native potting tradition, partly through its absorption into first Anglo-Saxon and then Norman England.

Apart from Tintagel (Thomas 1993; Barrowman *et al* 2007) and Gwithian (Nowakowski *et al* 2007), several other sites have recently yielded Mediterranean material: East Porth, Samson (Neal *et al* forthcoming), St Michael's Mount (Herring *et al* 2000; Sturgess 2010), Mullion Church (Thorpe 2003), Lelissick, near Padstow (Thompson 2008) and Hay Close (Jones forthcoming).

The second group is **E ware**, wheel-made, hard-fired 'kitchen' wares from France (Gaul) (Thomas 1990), most recently discussed by Campbell (2007). Deduced dating of late sixth to early eighth centuries, perhaps around 575-700 (Campbell 1991; 1996; 2007; Hill 1998), is supported by radiocarbon dates of cal AD 605-660 of internal residue from an excavated sherd from Loch Glashan crannog (Crone and

Campbell 2005) and cal AD 390-540 at Hay Close (Jones forthcoming). E ware has also been identified on Bryher, Scilly (Johns 2002-3), Mays Hill, St Martins (Carl Thorpe, pers comm), Nancemere (Gossip forthcoming b) and Hay Close (Jones forthcoming).

Sometime before the seventh century a major cultural change included introduction into Cornwall of a pottery production technique involving use of chopped grass to protect surfaces prior to firing (Fig 11). The resultant impressions on vessel bases and sides led to identification as Grass-Marked ware, again first identified and described by Charles Thomas at Gwithian (Thomas 1956; 1966; 1968). Hand made, softer, thicker and less well finished than Gwithian Style, and variably fired, Grass-Marked ware is often of gabbroic clay, but can be granitic, as on Scilly (Thorpe forthcoming).

Grass-Marked ware was introduced when pottery production re-emerged in Somerset, Dorset and Wiltshire, but not in Devon, an aceramic buffer zone, presumably reflecting cultural differences that may have hindered eastern influences entering Cornwall, encouraging native innovation rather than Frisian/Irish influences as previously suggested (Bruce-Mitford 1956; Dunning et al 1959; Thomas 1957-8; cf Wood 2011). Pottery production and use in Cornwall were far greater than elsewhere in Britain. At the very least this indicates that Cornish ceramic traditions were strong and that demand continued, but the limited range of forms in platters, dog dish bowls, cooking pots and bar-lug cauldrons also marks a dramatic change in eating habits, turning away from the individual dining and serving sets common in the Roman period and to a range of vessels that seem to reflect more communal eating. This change is seen elsewhere in England at this time falling into the 'stew pot' tradition (Hagen 2006).

The two earliest radiocarbon dates for Grass-Marked ware are both cal AD 540-660, from residue on a platter at Penhale Round (Nowakowski forthcoming) and from Gwithian (Nowakowski et al. 2007). The latest date at Gwithian is cal AD 650-780, indicating that adoption of bar-lugs was before the end of the eighth century (ibid). Sixth and seventh-century dates, based on associations with imported wares, from Carngoon Bank (McAvoy 1980), Mullion (Thorpe 2003), East Porth, Samson (Neal et al forthcoming) and Tean (Ratcliffe and Straker 1996) suggest that Grass-Marked platters were used prior to the significant settlement shift represented by abandonment of rounds. A further radiocarbon date of cal AD 856-996 was obtained from Gunwalloe where a possible new fifth vessel form has been identified (Wood 2010).

Another radiocarbon date, from Nancemere, of cal AD 1010-1160, the latest so far recorded (Gossip forthcoming b), corresponds nicely with dendrochronology dates of AD 1080 and AD 1155 obtained from Waterford, Ireland (Gahan and McCutcheon 1997). There, Grass-Marked ware was unique to one house in the Hiberno-Norse coastal longphort, providing the first evidence of a link between Cornwall and Ireland and exportation of this style outside Cornwall and

Scilly. The Waterford examples have decoration on the outer lug, also identified at Trelissick in Cornwall (Taylor and Thorpe 2008) where an incised cross suggests a later style. Towards the end of this ware's life (in the eleventh century) 'grass-marking' as a technique appears to have declined: very little was observed at Mawgan Porth (about 11% of the entire assemblage) and even less at Launceston Castle (Bruce-Mitford 1997; Saunders 2006). Other eleventh and twelfth-century examples of Grass-Marked wares were found at Truro (Allan and Langman, 1998-9) and Old Lanyon (O'Mahoney 1994), confirming that this ceramic tradition remained virtually unchanged for around 500 years.

Discovery of late forms of Grass-Marked ware at early Norman centres might suggest it was being purchased (Fig 12). Such a market would help explain its subsequent replacement on some sites with **Upper Greensand-tempered ware** (UGTW) produced in the Blackdown Hills (Devon-Somerset border) and an indicator of early Norman occupation throughout the south west. UGTW is found at Launceston Castle, Tintagel and Lammana Chapel in Cornwall (Bruce-Mitford 1997; Saunders 2006; Olson 1994; Wood 2011).

Grass-Marked ware was replaced in most of Cornwall during the twelfth and early thriteenth centuries by Cornish medieval coarsewares manufactured in granitic fabrics (such as Bunnings Park / Stuffle ware) that replicate vessel forms and functions found elsewhere in the south west. However, there is some evidence for continuation of the early medieval ceramic tradition in west Cornwall. Thomas recognised a developing sequence of wares continuing the 'grass-marked' tradition and utilising gabbroic fabrics that persisted until the late twelfth or early thirteenth centuries. The type site is Sandy Lane in Gwithian (Thomas 1964; 1968; 1991). Three styles of Sandy Lane ware were described, evolving in shape and mode of manufacture through time, the Sandy Lane styles thus representing absorption into a native potting tradition of the medieval cooking pot with everted rim and sagging base, and use of a wheel. There are unfortunately no absolute dates and the furthest east this material has been identified is Penhale Round, Fraddon (Cole and Thorpe 1996). Sandy Lane wares appear not to have been produced on the same scale as Grass-Marked wares.

Changing the fabric of life in early medieval Cornwall

Imogen Wood

Society's fabric has many threads woven in specific and unique ways and expressed in the attributes of every object made within it. By helping define the region's heritage, Cornish gabbroic pottery offers an opportunity to unravel aspects of the society that produced it. Pottery's physical attributes are suited to empirical analysis such as David Peacock's petrographic identification of the gabbroic clay source (Peacock 1969a; 1969b), but pottery's social attributes have thus far received less attention. My theory-led study (for a PhD) utilises the social implications of petrographic analyses to address meanings in gabbroic clay.

Preferential selection of gabbroic clay, from the St Keverne area, for pottery production for over 4000 years since the Neolithic period has been attributed to its technological superiority (Peacock 1969b; Quinnell 1987), but research has demonstrated that its performance can be equalled by many other regional clays (Harrad 2003, 41). This suggests that an unexplored social importance of gabbroic clay may have motivated its procurement. Fabric analysis has already suggested gabbroic clay use fluctuated over time (Quinnell 1987, 2004; Parker-Pearson 1990; Harrad 2003). Ratios of gabbroic and non-gabbroic clay use might therefore reflect social and economic change (Fig 13).

Petrographic analyses of Lizard peninsula assemblages from Trebarveth (second to sixth centuries AD), Carngoon Bank (fourth to seventh) and Gunwalloe (seventh to tenth) demonstrate that the proportions of gabbroic clays in fabrics declined and that locally sourced clay was increasingly used. This trend supports a social rather than a technical motivation behind preference for gabbroic clay. The interplay of gabbroic and local clays appears to represent two diagnostic facets of society, that of the region, in gabbro, and that of the individual settlement or local social group, in local clays.

Use of gabbroic clays might have represented regional social cohesion and continuity maintained through distribution via kinship networks which reinforced regional identity, traditions and a shared social reality. Transportation of gabbroic clay between settlements maintained networks uniting people not only through family but also through shared practice. Its fairly continuous use through prehistory suggests it became a tradition, perhaps with a totemic significance reinforcing maintenance of social norms and customs. Local clays, however, probably represented everyday life and requirements of individual settlements, which when mixed with gabbro reaffirmed adherence to a wider regional identity. Ratios of gabbro and other clays in each pot may thus have represented levels of adherence to regional traditions and identity.

Gabbro's totemic significance is perhaps best appreciated in its period of gradual decline from sixth-century Carngoon Bank to its abandonment at ninth to tenth-century Gunwalloe where it is only found heavily diluted by local clays (Fig 13). As in prehistory, periods of fabric change coincide with other change in Cornwall; firstly, the abandonment of rounds and arrival of Christianity and secondly, new systems of land ownership, ecclesiastical markets and acceptance of the English Church. Such correlation suggests erosion of ancient traditions as new social beliefs

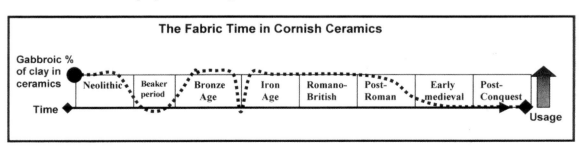

Fig 13. Schematic representation of the fluctuating use of gabbroic clay (as a proportion of all Cornish ceramics) from the Neolithic period to its post-Norman Conquest period demise (Imogen Wood).

and ways of being, possibly associated with Christianity, unsettled long-established values represented by use of gabbroic clay. Turning to local clays might also suggest people became isolated from ancient networks and instead began to form new non-regional identities.

Locating St Keverne's ninth or tenth-century monastery (Olson 1989) in gabbro country may not have been coincidental. In a region without urban centres a crucial clay source may have been a central place in Cornwall's socialised landscape, frequently visited and offering a captive audience for spreading God's word. This Christian practice may have been used at other Cornish locations with similar congregational attributes, like trade centres and routeways. Appropriation and absorption of pagan traditions was common in this conversion era and the use of gabbroic clay may have been initially drawn into the new Christian ideology, only to be later suppressed as representing the old order. Christianity and introduction of ecclesiastical markets could have destabilised and fragmented regional identity, networks and society maintained through gabbroic usage. This need not, however, have been a uniform process; some settlements appear to have maintained old traditions longer. Piecemeal selection of gabbroic rather than local clays in Grass-Marked bar-lug cauldrons at Launceston Castle (Brown *et al* 2006), contrasting with granitic-derived examples at Mawgan-Porth (Bruce-Mitford 1997), suggests curation of old traditions by some, but not all.

Plantation of Norman towns and markets created new social and economic networks and Cornish pottery forms, such as Sandy Lane ware, were united once again with those of the rest of the south west for the first time since their post-Roman diversion into Grass-Marked wares. Cornish pottery production appears to have declined in volume, suggesting the ancient local pottery production was displaced by centralised urban control or new lifestyles associated with freedom from past traditions. Gabbroic clay's decline echoed that of a regional identity and tradition that had spanned several millennia. In terms of important aspects of Cornish life, the impacts first of Christianity and then of Norman towns broke a peculiarly long-lived and apparently deeply meaningful practice. In a very literal sense the fabric of life in Cornwall changed forever, but life continued in a different form.

Suggestions for further work

- Excavation of a typical *lann* to confirm its early medieval (and earlier?) origins, subsequent development, and any cultural impact of English ecclesiastical administration
- Photographic record of inscribed stones
- Full publication of Tintagel Churchyard excavation, perhaps following further targeted excavation
- Research to illuminate that middle period of transition between late Roman and pre-Norman parts of the period
- Padstow and Bodmin have great potential when considering major ecclesiastical sites: origins, development, impacts of English take-over and Viking attacks, development of pre-Norman church building, sculpture workshops and metamorphosis at Bodmin into Augustinian priory
- Further research and excavation on high status early medieval sites, including later lys sites – Liskeard, Helston, Lesnewth, etc
- As models of early medieval economy and society develop, the need to examine early medieval levels of a well-preserved *tre* site and a Bodmin Moor transhumance hut group becomes more urgent
- Continue work to establish early medieval 'core' settlement areas
- Analytical study of routeways to draw out primary communication lines, early medieval or earlier
- Draw Cornwall into wider discussions of West Saxon Kingdom in the south west
- More closely date Grass-Marked pottery sequence to establish how continuous was post-Roman and early medieval Cornish pottery production
- Target petrographic analysis on non-gabbroic early medieval pottery production.
- Put effort into locating any Cornish pottery kiln sites (either early or later medieval).
- Undertake petrological analysis and ICP (inductively coupled plasma-atomic emission analysis) to enable Cornish wares to be identified beyond Cornwall.
- Correlate late seventh-century changes, including from Gwithian Style to Grass-Marked ware, with political and ideological

change
- Explain why Grass-Marked ware lasted for over 500 years
- Explain why no E ware was found at Tintagel, knowing it was occupied into the seventh century

References

Aalen, F H A, 1997. The Irish rural landscape: synthesis of habitat and history, in F H A Aalen, K Whelan, and M Stout, eds, *Atlas of the Irish Rural Landscape,* Cork, 4-30

Allan, J, 2004-5. After the flood: building recording at Minster church, Boscastle, in 2005, *Cornish Archaeol,* **43-44,** 145-58

Allan, J, and Blaylock, S, 2007. Notes towards a structural history of the church, in D Cole, *St Piran's Church, Perranzabuloe, Cornwall: archaeological excavation, conservation and management works,* Truro (Historic Environment Service, Cornwall County Council)

Allan, J P, and Langman, G, 1998-9. The pottery: investigations at nos 4-6 Pydar Street, Truro, *Cornish Archaeol,* **37-38,** 180-189

Barrowman, R C, Batey, C E, and Morris, C D, 2007. *Excavations at Tintagel Castle, Cornwall, 1990-1999,* London

Bil, A, 1990. *The shieling 1600-1840, the case of the Central Scottish Highlands,* Edinburgh

Blair, J, 2005. *The Church in Anglo-Saxon Society,* Oxford

Brown, D H, Thomson, R, and Vince, A, 2006. The pottery, in A D Saunders, ed, *Excavations at Launceston Castle, Cornwall,* Society of Medieval Archaeology Monograph, **24,** 269-281

Bruce-Mitford, R L S, 1956. *A Dark Age settlement at Mawgan Porth, Cornwall,* in R L S Bruce-Mitford, ed, *Recent archaeological excavations in Britain,* London, 167-196

Bruce-Mitford, R L S, 1997. *Mawgan Porth: a settlement of the late Saxon period on the north Cornish coast, excavations 1949-52, 1954 and 1974,* English Heritage Archaeology Rep, **13,** London

Campbell, E, 1991. *Imported goods in the early medieval Celtic West with special reference to Dinas Powis,* unpublished PhD thesis, Univ Wales, College of Cardiff

Campbell, E, 1996. The archaeological evidence for contacts: imports, trade and economy in Celtic Britain AD 400-800, in Dark 1996, 83-96

Campbell, E, 2007. *Continental and Mediterranean imports to Atlantic Britain and Ireland, AD 400 – 800,* CBA Res Rep, **157,** London

Carter, E, 2001. *In the shadow of St Piran,* Padstow

Carver, M, 2009. Early Scottish monasteries and prehistory: a preliminary dialogue, *Scottish Historical Review,* **88 (2),** 332-351

Claughton, P, and Smart, C, 2008. *The Bere Ferrers Project and discovery of a Roman Fort at Calstock,* Exeter (Exeter University)

Cramp, R, and Higgitt, J, and Worssam, B, and Bristow, R, 2006. *Corpus of Anglo-Saxon stone sculpture Vol VII, South West England,* Oxford

Cole, R, and Thorpe, C, 1996. *Penhale Round/SWEB 5 - an archaeological watching brief,* Truro (Cornwall Archaeological Unit).

Dark, K R, ed, 1996. *External contacts and the economy of Late Roman and post-Roman Britain,* Woodbridge, Boydell

Davies, E, 1984-5. Hafod and Lluest, the summering of cattle and upland settlement in Wales, *Folk Life,* **23,** 76-96

Driscoll, S, 1988. The relationship between history and archaeology: artefacts, documents and power, in S Driscoll, and M Nieke, eds, *Power and politics in early medieval Britain and Ireland,* Edinburgh, 162-187

Dudley, P, 2011. *Goon, hal, cliff and croft, west Cornwall's rough ground,* Truro (Cornwall Council)

Dudley, P, and Young, A, forthcoming. *Lowland Cornwall,* Truro (Historic Environment Projects, Cornwall Council)

Dunning, G C, 1959. Anglo-Saxon pottery: a symposium, IV. Pottery of the late Anglo-Saxon period in England, *Med Arch,* **3,** 31-78

Edwards, N, 2007. *A corpus of early medieval inscribed stones and stone sculpture in Wales, Vol II, South-West Wales,* Cardiff

Edwards, N, ed, 2009. *The archaeology of the early medieval Celtic Churches: proceedings of a conference on the archaeology of the early medieval Celtic Churches, September 2004,* Society for Medieval Archaeology Monograph, **29,** Society for Church Archaeology Monograph, **1**

Edwards, N, and Lane, A, eds, 1992. *The early church in Wales and the West: recent work in Early Christian archaeology, history and place-names,* Oxbow Monograph, **16**

Evans, E E, 1957. *Irish folk ways,* London, Routledge and Kegan Paul

Exeter Archaeology, 1998-9. Exeter Archaeology Cornish projects 1996-1999, *Cornish Archaeol,* **37-38,** 220-223

Fox, H, 1996. Introduction: transhumance and seasonal settlement, in H S A Fox, ed, *Seasonal settlement,* Leicester, 1-23

Fox, H, 2006. Foreword, in S Turner, ed, *Medieval Devon and Cornwall: shaping an ancient landscape,* Macclesfield, xi-xvi

Fyfe, R, 2006. Palaeoenvironmental perspectives on medieval landscape development, in S Turner, ed, *Medieval Devon and Cornwall: shaping an ancient landscape,* Macclesfield, 10-23

Gahan, A, and McCutcheon, C, 1997. Medieval pottery, in M F Hurley, O M B Scully, and S W J McCutcheon, eds, *Late Viking Age and medieval Waterford: excavations 1986-1992,* Waterford (Waterford Corporation), 285-359

Gearey, B R, West, S, and Charman, D J, 1997. The landscape context of medieval settlement on the south-western moors of England. Recent palaeoenvironmental evidence from Bodmin Moor and Dartmoor, *Med Arch,* **41,** 195-208

Gearey, B R, Charman, D J, and Kent, M, 2000. Palaeoecological evidence for the prehistoric settlement of Bodmin Moor, Cornwall, south-west England: Part II – land-use changes from the Neolithic to the present, *J Archaeol Sci,* **27,** 493-508

DISCOVERY AND RESEARCH

Glassie, H, 1982. *Passing the time; folklore and history of an Ulster community*, Dublin

Gossip, J, 2002. *St Sampson's Church, South Hill, Cornwall, archaeological watching brief during drainage improvements*, Truro (Historic Environment Service, Cornwall County Council)

Gossip, J, 2010. *St Piran's Oratory evaluation*, Truro (Historic Environment Projects, Cornwall Council)

Gossip, J, forthcoming a. The evaluation of a multi-period prehistoric site and fogou at Boden Vean, St Anthony-in-Meneage, Cornwall, 2003, *Cornish Archaeol*

Gossip, J, forthcoming b. Archaeological investigations at Nancemere, Truro, Cornwall 2002: a prehistoric and Romano-British landscape, *Cornish Archaeol*

Graham Campbell, J, 1973. The ninth-century Anglo-Saxon horn-mount from Burghead, Morayshire, Scotland, *Med Arch*, **17,** 43-51

Guthrie, A, 1969. Excavation of a settlement at Goldherring, Sancreed, 1958-61, *Cornish Archaeol*, **8,** 5-39

Hagen, A, 2006. *Anglo-Saxon food and drink: production, processing, distribution and consumption*, Stroud

Harrad, L, 2003. *The production and trade of prehistoric ceramics in Cornwall*, unpublished PhD thesis, University of Oxford

Hartgroves, S, Jones, A M, and Kirkham, G, 2006. The Eathorne Menhir, *Cornish Archaeol*, **45,** 97-108

Hayes, J W, 1972. *Late Roman pottery*, London

Hayes, J W, 1980. *A supplement to Late Roman pottery*, London

Herring, P, 1986. *An exercise in landscape history: pre-Norman and medieval Brown Willy and Bodmin Moor*, unpublished MPhil thesis, University of Sheffield

Herring, P, 1993. *St Michael's Mount*, Truro (Cornwall County Council)

Herring, P, 1996. Transhumance in medieval Cornwall, in H S A Fox, ed, *Seasonal settlement*, Leicester, 35-44

Herring, P, 1999. Farming and transhumance in Cornwall at the turn of the first millennium AD, *Journal of the Cornwall Association of Local Historians,* **37,** 19-25 and **38,** 3-8

Herring, P, 2004. Cornish uplands: medieval, post-medieval and modern extents, in I D Whyte, and A J L Winchester, eds, *Society, landscape and environment in upland Britain,* Society for Landscape Studies, supplementary series 2, 37-52

Herring, P, 2006. Cornish strip fields, in S Turner, ed, *Medieval Devon and Cornwall: shaping an ancient landscape,* Macclesfield, 44-77

Herring P, 2007. Historic landscape characterisation in an ever-changing Cornwall, *Landscapes*, **8.2,** 15-27

Herring P, 2008. Commons, fields and communities in prehistoric Cornwall, in A Chadwick, ed, *Recent approaches to the archaeology of land allotment*, Brit Arch Repts, Int Ser, **1875,** Oxford, 70-95

Herring, P, 2009. Early medieval transhumance in Cornwall, Great Britain, in J Klapste, ed, *Medieval rural settlement in marginal landscapes, Ruralia VII,* Turnhout, Belgium, Brepols, 47-56

Herring, P, forthcoming. Shadows of ghosts: early medieval transhumants in Cornwall, in R Silvester, and S Turner, eds, *Papers in memory of Harold Fox*, Leicester (Medieval Settlement Research Group)

Herring, P, and Hooke, D, 1993. Interrogating Anglo-Saxons in St Dennis, *Cornish Archaeol*, **32,** 67-75

Herring, P, Thorpe, C, Quinnell, H, Reynolds, A, and Allan, J, 2000. *St Michael's Mount: archaeological works 1995-8 (including watching briefs on a foul sewer trench and a land drain, surveys at the summit and on the lower slopes, and archaeological trenching at the summit)*, Truro (Cornwall County Council)

Hooke, D, 1994. *Pre-Conquest charter bounds of Devon and Cornwall*, Woodbridge

Johns, C, 2002-3. An Iron Age sword and mirror cist burial from Bryher, Isles of Scilly, *Cornish Archaeol,* **41-42,** 1-79

Johns, C, and Preston-Jones, A, 1996. *Delabole to St Endellion: water main renewal archaeological watching brief*, Truro (Cornwall Archaeological Unit)

Johnson, N, and Rose, P, 1994. *Bodmin Moor, an archaeological survey Volume 1: the human landscape to c 1800*, London

Jones, A, 2000-2001. The excavation of a multi-period site at Stencoose, Cornwall, *Cornish Archaeol*, **39-40,** 45-94

Jones, A, forthcoming. Hay Close, St Newlyn East: excavations by Cornwall Archaeological Society, 2007, *Cornish Archaeol*

Jones, G R J, 1985. Forms and patterns of medieval settlement in Welsh Wales, in D Hooke, ed, *Medieval Villages O.U.C.A. Monograph No. 5*, Oxford, 155-169

Lawson-Jones, A, 2001. *Bear's Down to Ruthvoes SWW pipeline - an archaeological watching brief*, Truro (Historic Environment Service, Cornwall County Council)

Lawson-Jones, A, forthcoming. An early medieval pit at St Blazey Gate, Par, Cornwall, *Cornish Archaeol*

Manning, P, and Stead, P, 2002-3. Excavation of an Early Christian cemetery at Althea Library, Padstow, *Cornish Archaeol,* **41-42,** 80-106

McAvoy, F, 1980. The excavation of a multi-period site at Carngoon Bank, Lizard, *Cornish Archaeol*, **19,** 31-62

McKee, H, and McKee, J, 2002. Counter arguments and numerical patterns in early celtic inscriptions: a re-examination of *Christian Celts: Messages and Images*, *Med Arch*, **46,** 29-40

Morris, C D, and Harry, R, 1997. Excavations on the Lower Terrace, Site C, Tintagel Island 1990-94, *Antiq Jnl*, **77,** 1-144

Neal, D S, and Johns, C, forthcoming. Excavations at East Porth, Samson, Isles of Scilly, 1970-1, *Cornish Archaeol*

Nowakowski, J, 1998. *A30 Project, Cornwall. Archaeological investigations along the route of the Indian Queens bypass 1992-1994. Assessment and updated project design*, Truro (Cornwall Archaeological Unit)

Nowakowski, J, forthcoming. *Bypassing Indian Queens, Cornwall - archaeological excavations 1992-1994. Prehistoric and Romano-British settlements and landscapes*

Nowakowski, J A, and Thomas, C, 1990. *Excavations at Tintagel parish churchyard Cornwall, spring 1990: interim report,* Truro (Cornwall County Council)

Nowakowski, J A, and Thomas, C, 1992. *Grave news from*

Tintagel: an illustrated account of archaeological excavations at Tintagel Churchyard, Cornwall, 1991, Truro (Cornwall County Council)

Nowakowski, J A, Quinnell, H, Sturgess, J, Thomas, C, and Thorpe, C, 2007. Return to Gwithian: shifting the sands of time, *Cornish Archaeol,* **46,** 13-76

Nowakowski, J A, and Thomas, C, 2007. Gwithian – emerging themes and future potential, in Nowakowski *et al* 2007, 49-59

Ó Danachair, C, 1983-84. Summer pasture in Ireland, *Folk Life,* **22,** 36-41

Okasha, E, 1993. *Corpus of Early Christian inscribed stones of South-West Britain,* London

Okasha, E, 1996. The Early Christian carved and inscribed stones of South-West Britain, in Barbara E Crawford, ed, *Scotland in Dark Age Britain,* Aberdeen, 21-36

Okasha, E, 1998-9. A supplement to Corpus of Early Christian inscribed stones of South-West Britain, *Cornish Archaeol,* **37-8,** 137-52

Olson, B L, 1982. Crantock, Cornwall as an early monastic site, in S M Pearce, ed, *The Early Church in Western Britain and Ireland,* Brit Arch Repts, **102,** Oxford, 177-86

Olson, L, 1989. Early monasteries in Cornwall, Woodbridge

Olson, L, 1994. Lammana, West Looe; C K Croft Andrew's excavations of the chapel and Monks House, 1935-6, *Cornish Archaeol,* **33,** 96-129

Olson, B L, and Padel, O J, 1986. A tenth century list of Cornish parochial saints, *Cambridge Medieval Celtic Studies,* **12,** 33-71

Olson, B L, and Preston-Jones, A, 1998-9. An ancient cathedral of Cornwall? Excavated remains east of St Germans Church, *Cornish Archaeol,* **37-8,** 153-69

O'Mahoney, C, 1994. The pottery from Lammana: the mainland chapel and Monks House, in Olson 1994, 115-125

O'Neill, H E, 1965. Excavation of a Celtic hermitage on St Helens, Isles of Scilly, 1956-58, *Arch Jnl,* **121,** 40-69

Orme, N, 2007. *Cornwall and the Cross: Christianity 500-1560,* Chichester

Orme, N, 2010. *A history of the county of Cornwall II: religious history to 1560,* London

Padel, O J, 1976-77. Cornish names of parish churches, *Cornish Studies,* **4/5,** 15-27

Padel, O J, 1978. Two new pre-Conquest charters for Cornwall, *Cornish Stud,* **6,** 20-7

Padel, O J, 1985. *Cornish place-name elements,* Nottingham, English Place-Name Society, Vol LVI/LVII

Padel, O J, 2002. Locals saints and place-names in Cornwall, in A Thacker, and R Sharpe, eds, *Local saints and local churches in the early medieval west,* Oxford, 303-60

Padel, O J, 2009. Slavery in Cornwall: the Bodmin Manumissions, *Kathleen Hughes Memorial Lecture 7,* Hughes Hall and Department of Anglo-Saxon, Celtic and Norse, University of Cambridge

Padel, O J, 2010a. Christianity in Cornwall: Celtic aspects, in N Orme, *History of the County of Cornwall II: Religious History to 1560,* London, 110-125

Padel, O J, 2010b. *When did Cornwall become English?* Lecture at Royal Cornwall Museum 13.11.2010

Padel, O J, 2010c. Ancient and medieval administrative divisions of Cornwall, *Proc Dorset Nat Hist Archaeol Soc,* **131,** 211-214

Padel, O J, forthcoming. *Celtic aspects of the Church in medieval Cornwall,* Department of Anglo-Saxon, Celtic and Norse, University of Cambridge

Parker-Pearson, M, 1990. The production and distribution of Bronze Age pottery in South-West Britain, *Cornish Archaeol,* **29,** 5-33

Peacock, D P S, 1969a. A contribution to the study of Glastonbury Ware from South-Western Britain, *Antiq Jnl,* **49,** 41-61

Peacock, D P S, 1969b. Neolithic pottery production in Cornwall, *Antiquity,* **43,** 145-149

Peacock, D, and Williams, D, 1986. *Amphorae and the Roman economy, an introductory guide,* London and New York.

Pearce, S, 2004. *South-western England in the Early Middle Ages,* London

Penhallurick, R D, 1986. *Tin in Antiquity,* London

Penhallurick, R D, 2009. *Ancient and early medieval coins from Cornwall and Scilly,* London

Petts, D, 2002. Cemeteries and boundaries in Western Britain, in S Lucy, and A Reynolds, eds, *Burial in early medieval England and Wales,* Society for Medieval Archaeology Monograph, **17,** 24-46

Petts, D, and Turner, S, 2009. Early medieval chapel groups in Wales and western England, in N Edwards, ed, *The archaeology of the early medieval Celtic Churches: proceedings of a conference on the archaeology of the early medieval Celtic Churches, September 2004,* Society for Medieval Archaeology Monograph, **29,** Society for Church Archaeology Monograph **1,** 281-300

Preston-Jones, A, 1987. Road widening at St Buryan and Pelynt Churchyards, *Cornish Archaeol,* **26,** 153-60

Preston-Jones, A, 1994. Decoding Cornish churchyards, *Cornish Archaeol,* **33,** 71-95

Preston-Jones, A, 2011. *Trethevey, Tintagel: Roman inscribed stone repair and re-presentation,* Truro (Historic Environment Projects, Cornwall Council)

Preston-Jones, A, and Rose, P, 1986. Medieval Cornwall, *Cornish Archaeol,* **25,** 135-185.

Quinnell, H, 1987. Cornish gabbroic pottery: the development of a hypothesis, *Cornish Archaeol,* **26,** 7-12

Quinnell, H, 2004. *Excavations at Trethurgy Round, St Austell: community and status in Roman and post-Roman Cornwall,* Truro (Cornwall County Council)

Ratcliffe, J, 1991. *Lighting up the past in Scilly; archaeological results from the 1985 electrification project,* Truro (Cornwall County Council)

Ratcliffe, J, and Straker, V, 1996. *The early environment of Scilly. Palaeoenvironmental assessment of cliff-face and intertidal deposits 1989 – 1993,* Truro (Cornwall County Council)

Ratcliffe, J, 1995. Duckpool, Morwenstow: a Romano-British and early medieval industrial site and harbour, *Cornish Archaeol,* **34,** 81-171

Redknap, M, and Lewis, J M, 2007. *A corpus of early medieval inscribed stones and stone sculpture in Wales volume 1, Glamorgan, Breconshire, Monmouthshire, Radnorshire and geographically contiguous areas of Herefordshire and Shropshire,* Cardiff

Reynolds, A, forthcoming. Atlantic Road, Newquay: excavations on a Late Iron Age and Romano-British coastal site, *Cornish Archaeol*

Rippon, S J, Fyfe, R M, and Brown, A G, 2006. Beyond villages and open fields: the origins and development of a historic landscape characterised by dispersed settlement in South-West England, *Med Arch*, **50**, 31-70

Rose, P, and Preston-Jones, A, 1995. Changes in the Cornish countryside, in D Hooke, and S Burnell, eds, *Landscape and settlement in Britain AD 400-1066*, Exeter, 51-68

Saunders, A, 2006. *Excavations at Launceston Castle, Cornwall*. Society for Medieval Archaeology Monograph, **24**, Leeds

Smart, C, forthcoming. *Excavations at Calstock, Roman fort and late medieval settlement*, Swindon, English Heritage

Sturgess, J, 2007. Post-Roman Gwithian, in Nowakowski *et al* 2007, 38-44

Sturgess, J, 2010. *St Michael's Mount watch tower and gateway complex - archaeological building survey and evaluation, archive report*, Truro (Historic Environment Projects, Cornwall Council)

Taylor, S, and Thorpe, C, 2008. Grass-marked pottery found at Trelissick, Feock, *Cornish Archaeol*, **47**, 177-182

Thomas, A C, 1956. Excavations at Gwithian, Cornwall 1955, *Proc West Cornwall Field Club*, **1.3**, 122-3

Thomas, A C, 1957. Some imported post-Roman sherds in Cornwall and their origin, *Proc West Cornwall Field Club*, **2**, 15-22

Thomas, A C, 1957-58. Cornwall in the Dark Ages, *Proc West Cornwall Field Club*, **2.1**, 59-72

Thomas, A C, 1959. Imported pottery in Dark Age Western Britain, *Med Arch*, **3**, 89-111

Thomas, A C, 1960. People and pottery in Dark Age Cornwall, *Old Cornwall*, **5.11**, 452-60

Thomas, C, 1964. Minor sites in the Gwithian area, *Cornish Archaeol*, **3**, 37-62

Thomas, A C, 1968. Grass marked pottery in Cornwall, in J M Coles, and D D A Simpson, eds, *Studies in Ancient Europe*, Leicester, 311-332

Thomas, A C, 1981. A provisional list of imported pottery in post-Roman Western Britain and Ireland, Pool, Institute of Cornish Studies, Special report, no 7

Thomas, A C, 1990. *Gallici Nautae de Galliarum Provinciis* – A sixth/seventh century trade with Gaul reconsidered, *Med Arch*, **34**, 1-26

Thomas, A C, 1991. Early medieval pottery, in Ratcliffe 1991, 87-92

Thomas, A C, 1993. *Tintagel, Arthur and archaeology*, London

Thomas, C, 1994. *And shall these mute stones speak? Post Roman inscriptions in Western Britain*, Cardiff

Thomas, C, 1997. Christian latin inscriptions from Cornwall in Biblical Style, *Jnl Roy Inst Cornwall*, new series II, volume II, part 4, 42-66

Thomas, C, 1998. *Christian Celts: messages and images*, Stroud

Thomas, C, 1999. *Penzance Market Cross: a Cornish wonder re-wondered*, Penzance

Thomas, C, 2000-2001. A supplement to Corpus of Early Christian inscribed stones of South-West Britain, by Elisabeth Okasha: some comments, a correction and an addition, *Cornish Archaeol*, **39-40**, 218-227

Thomas, A C, and Thorpe, C, 1988. *Catalogue of finds from Tintagel Castle, Cornwall*, Institute of Cornish Studies: Tintagel 88 Projects No 2

Thomas, A C, and Thorpe, C, forthcoming. *The imported Mediterranean coarse wares from Tintagel*

Thompson, S, 2008. *Lellizzick, near Padstow, Cornwall. archaeological evaluation and assessment of results*, Salisbury (Wessex Archaeology, report reference: 65312.01)

Thorn, C, and Thorn, F, 1979. *Domesday Book: 10 Cornwall* (from a translation by O Padel), Chichester

Thorpe, C, 1998. *St Minver parish church: an archaeological watching brief, July 1997*, Truro (Cornwall Archaeological Unit)

Thorpe, C, 2001. *St Felicitas' Church, Phillack, Cornwall*, Truro (Historic Environment Service, Cornwall County Council)

Thorpe, C, 2003. *Mullion Church, Cornwall: archaeological watching brief*, Truro (Historic Environment Service, Cornwall County Council)

Thorpe, C, forthcoming. The early medieval native pottery of Cornwall (*c* 400-1066) in S Pearce, ed, *Recent archaeological work in south western Britain. Papers in honour of Henrietta Quinnell*, Brit Arch Repts, Brit Ser

Trudgian, T P F, 1987. Excavation of a burial ground at St Endellion, Cornwall, *Cornish Archaeol*, **26**, 145-52

Turner, S, 2003. Making a Christian landscape: early medieval Cornwall, in M Carver, ed, *The Cross goes North: processes of conversion in Northern Europe*, York

Turner, S, 2005. Converting the British landscape, *Brit Archaeol*, September-October 2005, 21-25

Turner, S, 2006a. *Making a Christian landscape*, Exeter

Turner, S, 2006b. The Cornish landscape: churches, chapels and crosses, in S Turner, ed, *Medieval Devon and Cornwall: shaping an ancient countryside*, Macclesfield, 24-43

Wessex Archaeology 2009. *Looe, Cornwall: archaeological evaluation and assessment of results*, Salisbury (Wessex Archaeology)

Wilson, D M, and Blunt, C E, 1961. The Trewhiddle Hoard, *Archaeologia*, **98**, 75-122

Wood, I E E, 2010. *A new light on Dark Age Gunwalloe: excavations summer 2010. Interim report for the National Trust*

Wood, I E E, 2011. *Changing the fabric of life in post-Roman and early medieval Cornwall: an investigation into social change through petrographic analysis*, unpublished PhD thesis, University of Exeter

Cornish Archaeology 50, 2011, 287–314

Later medieval Cornwall

PETER HERRING, GRAEME KIRKHAM, NICK CAHILL, NIGEL THOMAS,
ERIC BERRY, ANN PRESTON-JONES, ANDREW LANGDON,
ADAM SHARPE and CARL THORPE

Introduction

Peter Herring

This summary of recent work on the later medieval period (1066-1540) is again necessarily selective, concentrating on the several areas where changes in understanding in the last 25 years have been most substantial. Attention has shifted from the uplands to the lowlands when considering settlement, farming and the rural landscape. Here too we have seen the more substantial work on buildings: dwellings, castles, churches and crosses. Mining studies have emphasised how early the working of lodes was in Cornwall. Finally, systematic characterisation of towns shows that, as in many other aspects of its medieval life, particular places closely adhere to clear and strong Cornish patterns. In all areas of study we see increasingly rapid change in a place that was unusually diversified and distinctive in its economy, society and culture.

Rural landscape

Peter Herring

Work over the last 25 years has generally concentrated on identifying and understanding broad patterns rather than deepening knowledge of individual sites or site types. Minimal excavation has been offset by considerable progress on contextualising medieval settlements, establishing typical attributes, seeing patterns, and relating them to field, pasture and farming systems. Historic landscape characterisation has helped extend the relevance of work undertaken in particular parts of Cornwall to others with similar medieval historic character.

Medieval farming settlements in upland and lowland Cornwall were dispersed but nucleated, that is hamlets rather than isolated farmsteads (Beresford 1964; Padel 1985, 227; Herring 2006a). Their dense patterns help make sense of the network of routeways. Early medieval highways, ways and lanes (Herring and Hooke 1993), used for carrying information and orders as well as for travel and transport (Fleming 2009), became the various later medieval roads and lanes. These and the paths and the navigable creeks are all still poorly recorded and little analysed, despite their crucial role in making medieval Cornwall work, linking settlements and connecting them to downs, towns, churchtowns, services and the sea. It is easy to over-indulge early modern critics bringing new-fangled coaches down Cornwall's ancient steep and twisting roads that were quite adequate for the wagons and carts for which they were made; the Cornish would have made their communications systems work because their unusually commercialised economy depended on them. Surviving later medieval bridges, fords and ferry points (for which still see Henderson and Coates 1928) confirm how little the basic patterns of lowland Cornwall have changed in the last 600

DISCOVERY AND RESEARCH

years. Inherently solid rural fabric encouraged conservatism: buildings, at least from the early thirteenth century, were largely of stone or cob (Herring and Berry 1997), and stock-proof field perimeters were heavily constructed stone-faced banks (Herring 1986; Bull 1999). Hedged-in lanes and stone bridges were also difficult to shift, and as weirs and leats were easier to maintain than adjust,

watermills were also long-lived (Unwin 1977).

Even so the later medieval period saw substantial changes to rural life and thus to those patterns and the detail within them. Margins also moved, settlements and fields generally pushing onto uplands (and so reducing extents of commons) in the twelfth, thirteenth and early fourteenth centuries, retreating in the later fourteenth and early fifteenth

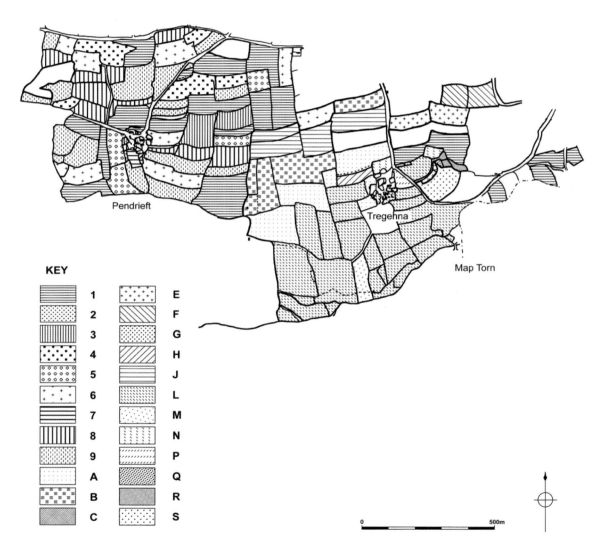

Fig 1. Intermixing of holdings in the enclosed but formerly open strip fields around the hamlets of Pendrieft (Pendrift) and Tregenna in Blisland. Each field system seems to have originally been organised into around a dozen cropping units, suitable for the application of convertible husbandry. (From Herring 2006a, fig 27)

centuries, and edging up again in the sixteenth (Johnson and Rose 1994). Despite these ebbings and flowings, at any one time roughly one-third of later medieval Cornwall was rough ground, with most of the remaining two-thirds subject to mixed farming (arable, pasture and meadow). Convertible husbandry, originating in the early medieval period (Herring, above), dominated Cornish farming and still influences modern practice (Dodgshon and Jewell 1970; Fox 1971; Herring 1986; 1999; 2006a; 2006b). The typical numbers of main fields, containing arable 'land', usually between 8 and 14, apparently depended on the number of years, usually between 5 and 11, that was the farm's length of 'ley' (i.e. years under grass) being added to the 3 or 4 that reflected the years of the cultivation round. The latter normally involved a first year of ground preparation that involved skimming off the matted turf, drying and burning it (and so destroying weeds and pests) and then spreading the consequent ashes with other dressings (dung, seasand and seaweed, middens and ditch cleanings) before ploughing or hand digging in advance of a first winter-sown crop, usually wheat. Spring-sown barley and oats followed, with grass undersown with the last to

ensure a strong crop of hay grass at the beginning of the ley (Herring 2006b)

As noted, and as in later prehistory and the early medieval period, most later medieval farming settlements were hamlets, their lands, still mainly within 'townlands' (see early medieval), worked cooperatively, with extensive resources like rough grazing and fuel grounds used by the several households in common. It seems increasingly likely that land was held as shares, expressed on the ground as the intermixing of narrow strips defined by low banks or balks scattered through the 8 to 14 fields, the sub-rectangular cropping units that were the smaller Cornish equivalents of Midland English furlongs (Fig 1; Herring 2006a). Those cropping units have generally survived best the reorganisations that followed the breakdown of the hamlets' communal systems, which sometimes occurred as early as the later thirteenth century (e.g. Brown Willy: Herring 2006b), was generally complete by the late fifteenth, but was occasionally delayed until the nineteenth (Herring 2006a). Forrabury Stitches are a nationally rare survival (Fig 2; Wood 1963; Dudley 2003). Scattered through Cornwall are patterns of enclosed strips (from Gooseham

Fig 2. Stitches on Forrabury Common, Cornwall's last surviving medieval open field. Low banks separate strips of land held individually, but grazed in common when not cultivated. (Photograph: Peter Herring)

DISCOVERY AND RESEARCH

to Escalls by Metherell, Trenilk, Treskilling, Trevarrian and many others), arrangements that reveal how difficult the negotiations to reallocate holdings upon enclosure could be, in turn revealing the strengths of relationships, and of tensions, between the interests of the several individual households and the small cooperating community, the hamlet, that they formed.

Nevertheless, by the end of the medieval period large numbers of farmsteads were isolated, either through shrinkage of hamlets to single farms or division of townlands into two or more parts, their new farmsteads having distinguishing names, like Higher, Lower, West, East, etc (Herring 2006a). Too few later medieval settlements that are still

occupied have been examined archaeologically, but a watching brief at Tregays, St Winnow hinted at their potential, producing Roman period sherds, having an early medieval name, yielding further sherds from the twelfth century through to modern (Thorpe 2001), and having architectural fragments from the sixteenth century onwards reused in later buildings. It also has a typical pattern of enclosures (yards, mowhays, gardens), arranged around the interstices of the several roads and lanes that enter the open townplace. In north Cornwall earthworks of numerous shrunken hamlets were recorded in farmstead enclosures of now isolated farms during the Stratton Hundred Rapid Identification Survey (Herring and Thomas 1993). To better appreciate

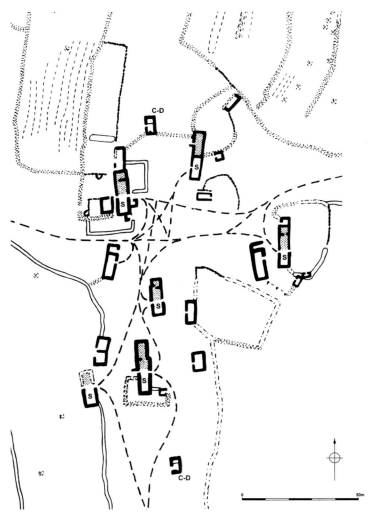

Fig 3. An abandoned later medieval hamlet within Brown Willy's extensive open field system (see Fig 4). Six farmsteads, five with longhouses, each have outhouses and small garden or mowhay enclosures that would have contained privately held property. They were arranged around a central communal space, the townplace, emphasised here by broken lines showing how cattle were moved from the six shippons (cowhouses) to the three main access lanes. Also common to all were two corn-drying barns (labelled C-D) set at each end of the hamlet so that whatever the wind direction one could safely be in use. (From Herring 2006b, fig 39)

what the archaeological potential might be, Peter Rose (pers comm) analysed the results from the southernmost seven parishes in the Hundred. Twenty-four of the 179 known medieval settlements are now deserted (13%); 45 (25%) have evidence for shrinkage and another 16 are deserted but unlocated. Extrapolated, this might suggest 730 deserted and 1,400 shrunken medieval settlements in Cornwall, although the heavy culm soils might have rendered the Stratton settlements a little more marginal than those in some other parts.

Detailed surveys, descriptions and interpretations have been produced of Bodmin Moor's numerous completely abandoned later medieval hamlets, with their longhouses, outhouses and farmstead and townplace enclosures (Fig 3; Herring 1986; Johnson and Rose 1994). Social meanings of repetition in plans and arrangements of internal fittings of excavated longhouses throw light on local identities (Austin and Thomas 1990; Herring forthcoming). A complex longhouse and part of a second, both tentatively dated to the later thirteenth and early fourteenth centuries, were excavated at Bunnings Park in 1979 and 1983 in advance of the Colliford Lake reservoir (Austin *et al* 1989, 54-62), while another partially explored at Crift, high on Lanlivery's hills, had been reused as a tin smelting house (McDonnell 1993; McDonnell *et al* 1995). A western longhouse at Old Lanyon excavated by the Cornwall

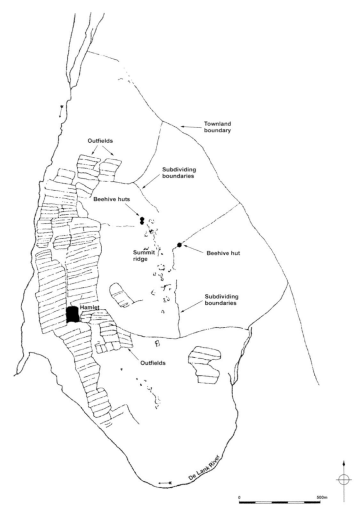

Fig 4. Brown Willy's medieval townland was largely enclosed by streams, but to the north east by a stock-proof boundary, a ring fence, separating it from West Moor's extensive commons. Within the ring fence the six households (see Fig 3) shared a 'hamlet common', initially undivided and apparently managed by herds who could shelter in early beehive huts, but by the later thirteenth century broken into six large pieces by subdividing boundaries. Here we see the shift from the open and common to the enclosed and individual.
(*From Herring 2006b, fig 43*)

DISCOVERY AND RESEARCH

Archaeological Society under the direction of E Marie Minter in 1964 was also published (Beresford 1994), the writer maintaining that the stone buildings had been preceded by stake and turf ones, despite growing evidence from Devon that the evidence for these is at best equivocal, and most likely absent (Austin 1985; Henderson and Weddell 1994). Nevertheless, we are still unsure what pre-thirteenth-century Cornish rural (and urban) dwellings comprised.

Most rough ground, coastal and upland, was used in common, principally for seasonal grazing, but also for fuel (turf and furze, or peat and gorse) and bedding (ferns, or bracken). There was variety in its extent. Much was within ring fences of townlands and so common only between the hamlet's households. Some contiguous hamlet commons were undivided and would have been grazed as one, though fuel, stone and other materials were retained for particular hamlets (e.g. Boswednack, Treen and Gear Commons in Zennor; Dudley 2011). Still more extensive commons were shared by several estates, as on Altarnun's West and East Moors (Johnson and Rose 1994). The late medieval privatisation of the formerly communal affected commons as well as fields; some were divided into separate holdings by long stockproof walls (as on Brown Willy, Fig 4; Herring 2006b), while in west Cornwall the earliest crofts, privately held and securely enclosed blocks of rough ground that contained valuable stands of furze, are later medieval (Dudley 2011).

A few commons were wholly or partially lost to deer parks, lordly enclosures of land previously enjoyed by their tenants (like Godolphin, Carn Brea and Hingston Down, the last partially enclosed as Carrybullock Park; Herring 1997; 2001; Schofield forthcoming; Tangye 1981; Pitman 1990). These were purified places where peasants and their domestic livestock were excluded and replaced by prettier, more sportive fallow deer. Recent work on Cornwall's medieval parks demonstrates that such marginal parks were not the norm; most were cut out of better land nearer or even surrounding the lord's home. These represented a still greater loss to tenants and indeed some hamlets and their fields appear to have been entirely lost to emparkment – several can be expected to have lain within the 550 acre Restormel park created by 1250 and perhaps a century earlier (Herring 2003, 39) by the Cardinans, the greatest Cornish family of the eleventh, twelfth and early thirteenth centuries (Soulsby 1976). As well as imposing the lord's status and flaunting their power, as those slightly later (probably later thirteenth century) parks high on hills at Godolphin and Carn Brea appear principally designed to do, many medieval Cornish deer parks displayed subtle landscape design (Fig 5). The Cardinan family parks at Pinsla, Restormel and Penhallam all had deep central valleys and their pales were run just beyond the crest of the valleysides so that from most places within the park there was no sight of the farmed world beyond, creating the fantastical

Fig 5. Pinsla Park was the home deer park of the Cardinham family whose castle stood a short distance north east. The wooded many-armed central valley lies at the heart of a great sack-shaped park whose pale ran, like at other Cardinham parks at Restormel and Penhallam, just beyond the crest of the valley sides. This left the park relatively secluded and the surrounding farmland out of sight when enjoying a hunt; a fine example of medieval landscape design. (Photograph: Peter Herring)

impression that their created world, cleaned of all mundaneity, ran on for ever (Herring 2003).

Deer parks represent an extreme form of a widespread process in later medieval Cornwall in which the open, common or communal became enclosed, divided, controlled, individual and private. This extended right down to creation of chambers and rooms within formerly open houses and castles (Johnson 2010), erection, largely from the fourteenth century, of the screen between chancel and nave in churches (Orme 2007, 98), and of course enclosure of formerly open fields and commons (above and Landscape, this volume). We may identify economic and social benefits for lords and peasants, but there seems to have also been an important element of ideology too (Hanawalt and Kobialka 2000). Ideas were being made real through changing ways of being and doing, and thus changing the medieval material world that survives to us as archaeologists.

This archaeology of ideas has been extended to a medieval equivalent of experiential archaeology at Bodmin Moor longhouse hamlets (Altenberg 2003), and to folkloric archaeology in neighbouring Devon (Franklin 2006). In doing so the medieval world is turned into medieval landscape, a place perceived as much as a place exploited or created, and a place whose form could be carefully calculated. As well as those designed deerparks, forerunners of early modern landscaped parks, we have inherited several highly important later medieval pleasure places, again enclosed and controlled. Peter Rose draws us into and around Earl Richard's walled, subdivided, pathed and lawned quadrangular 'intimate small world', a garden placed quite crazily, but perfectly properly for a fashionable mid-thirteenth-century fantasist, on Tintagel Island's windswept top (Rose 1994). Closer to homes, and more immediately available for contemporary enjoyment, were the more complex terraced gardens at Godolphin – possibly fourteenth century in origin and extensively reworked in the later fifteenth century – and Cotehele, apparently predating the mid-sixteenth-century tower (Herring 1997; Schofield forthcoming; Herring and Tapper 2006).

Standing rural buildings
Eric Berry and Nigel Thomas

As noted elsewhere (Thomas and Berry above), buildings archaeology developed rapidly in the last quarter century (there being just one short paragraph in Preston-Jones and Rose 1986). Nevertheless, surviving medieval building fabric is rarely found in existing houses as these have usually been extensively and repeatedly rebuilt, the main clues to their medieval origins being plan-forms and relationships with local topography. A former longhouse at Codda, Altarnun exemplifies this, its walls having been largely rebuilt in the post-medieval period, probably the seventeenth century, and its upper end further rebuilt in the nineteenth century to resemble a typical double-fronted house. Examination of the lower end's floor confirmed, however, that this had been a cowhouse reached via a through-passage from the uphill dwelling. Survey showed how the house related to probably medieval enclosures (yards, mowhays, domestic gardens etc) and the earthworks of another abandoned longhouse (Herring and Thomas 2000).

At Stonaford, North Hill, a central drain and remains of stalls indicated that the lower end housed cattle while bases of raised crucks confirmed that the longhouse was later medieval (Rosevear 1994; Herring and Berry 1997). Remains of the lowest room (probably a cowhouse) of another through-passage house were revealed in excavations in advance of works beyond the current lower end of Mennabroom, St Neot (Thomas 1996a). They added weight to the developing realisation that the 'end entry-passage' house form noted by Veronica and Frank Chesher (1968, 57) may be a misnomer, with supposed examples having evidence of the loss of one part, usually the lower end.

Surviving longhouses have also been identified in lowland east Cornwall. Halbathick, near Liskeard, was recognised during the 1992 list review and the lower end's cowhouse was recorded by Abigail Armstrong Evans and Vaughan Upson (Herring and Berry 1997). Dendrochronology at Cullacott, Werrington, suggests a late fifteenth-century origin for a dwelling that remained a longhouse until the 1650s, even though the parlour end had been subjected to high quality rebuilding and extension and both hall and chamber over the entrance had been plastered and decorated with wall paintings (*ibid*; Figs 6 and 7).

Indeed, many of Cornwall's greater houses developed from simpler through-passage layouts. Godolphin's porched hall (of *c* 1475) had high and low cross-wings closed off by an

DISCOVERY AND RESEARCH

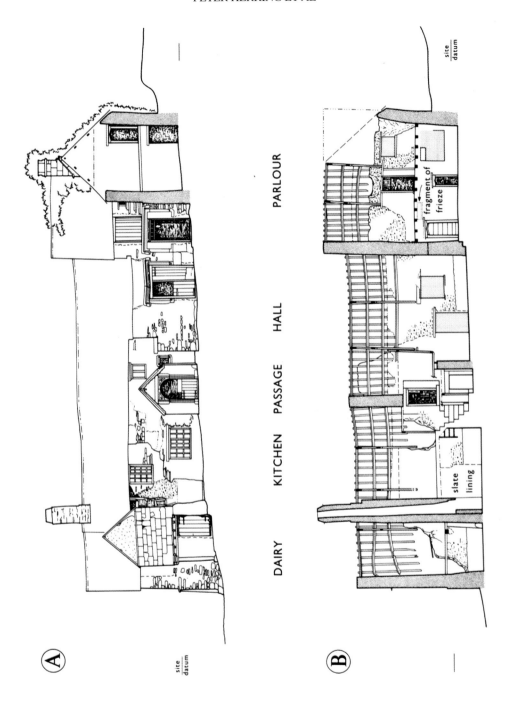

Fig 6. Long east elevation and cross section of the surviving later medieval through-passage plan house at Cullacott, Werrington. Examination of the kitchen's floor yielded evidence of the cowhouse, which confirmed that this was a longhouse. (© Keystone Historic Buildings Consultants)

Fig 7. Reconstruction of the hall at Cullacott with its higher end wall painting. The painting, centred on a figure in a mandorla, and here shown as The Virgin, was imaginatively reconstructed on the basis of recorded surviving fragments and researching contemporary manuscript and wall painting images. Reconstruction by Rhoops with advice from John R L Thorp, Jo Cox and following discussion with many others. (© Rhoops and Keystone Historic Buildings Consultants)

DISCOVERY AND RESEARCH

Fig 8. The west range of St Michael's Mount. Granite steps lead to the through-passage of a typical late medieval accommodation block with service rooms to the north (left) and hall to south. (Eric Berry for HE, Cornwall Council)

early sixteenth-century curtain wall to form a courtyard with square corner towers (Herring 1997; Schofield 1999; Cox 2009). Remnant quoin masonry beside the rear porch of Trerice, Newlyn East suggests the 1570s house occupies a similar footprint to that of a predecessor whose hall (by convention) probably lay north (up slope) of the through-passage, a layout reversed in the late sixteenth-century redevelopment. The house shares a common axis with the barn behind, suggesting a courtyard layout (Berry 1998; Berry and Sturgess forthcoming). St Michael's Mount's defended western range retains a through-passage (that provided controlled access to the Chapel), with hall to its south and service rooms to its north (Fig 8). The southern monastic buildings were joined to this western range by construction of the south-west link containing Sir John's Room when converted to later residential accommodation (Berry and Thomas 2008). Even Restormel Castle's domestic arrangements revolved around a passage separating hall and higher status rooms from a service end (Thomas 1996b). Although Cotehele has no through-passage, it has a higher end lit by a large window and heated by a fireplace

and a lower status part beyond the main doorway (Berry *et al* 2004).

Examination and research confirmed that Tintagel Old Post Office was not after all a former manor house. Before radical sixteenth-century reroofing and insertion of the hall fireplace with its lateral stack, it was a substantial later medieval town house (in Trevena borough), single-storeyed and again based on a through-passage plan (Berry *et al* 2003).

Castles and defended houses

Nigel Thomas, Eric Berry and Peter Herring

Cornwall's medieval castles have been contextualised through landscape study and documentary research and so shown to serve various social and symbolic functions, either as well as or instead of the orthodox military ones (Creighton 2002; 2009; Liddiard 2005; Creighton and Freeman 2006). Strategically placed fortresses, like Mortain's Launceston, the de Valletorts' Trematon and the Cardinans' Cardinham, had direct relationships with the early designed landscape of deer parks, while others appear to have been primarily hunting lodges or early country houses (Carn Brea, Restormel, Penhallam) (Herring 2003; Creighton 2009) and Tintagel's castle may have been primarily a symbolic creation.

Several individual castles have been subjected to close study. Full publication of the 1961 to 1983 excavations at Launceston Castle details structures, artefacts and arrangements dating from the eleventh century through all principal periods to the nineteenth century. As well as initial construction as a major fortification, these include Earl Richard's mid-thirteenth-century development of a palatial administrative centre in which the insertion of the high tower diminished the keep's defensive capacity (but created a remarkable position from which to view, among other things, the deer park). Richard also swept away the bailey's buildings to accommodate several fine new buildings, including as a centre-piece a 'large ceremonial great hall' (Saunders 2006). Also at Launceston detailed survey by the Cornwall Archaeological Unit (CAU) of the shell keep, high tower, and south gatehouse and barbican informed repairs and interpretation

of surviving features via paper reconstruction of original architectural forms and features. These included the former stepped passage ascending the motte, the shell keep's gateway, and a two-storey defensive position in the keep's north-west sector overlooking the approach to the bailey's north gate. Layout of the high tower's rooms and likely forms of the original roof, floor, fireplace and window of the upper floor room were established. Limits of the south gatehouse's gates, portcullis, barbican, ditch and removable road were also either determined or projected (Thomas and Berry 1994).

Since becoming a public monument in the 1920s, Restormel Castle has rarely been examined, so to inform repair and interpretation, English Heritage arranged a programme of documentary research, photogrammetry of standing walls, geophysical survey, core sampling of the ringwork's ditch, and topographical survey (Thomas and Buck 1993; Buck 1993; Thomas 1994 (with interpretational input from Eric Berry); 1996b; Thomas and Rosevear 1994; Travers 1995). This included examining the bailey's perimeter and establishing likely positions

Fig 9. Close analysis of the relationships of Restormel Castle's internal buildings and the thirteenth-century stone shell keep has indicated that all are of one build. Consideration of the defensive capabilities of its design and its immediate and wider contexts suggests that it was, at least in this late phase, less a castle and more a castle-esque country house, or even a very grand hunting lodge. (Nigel Thomas for HE, Cornwall Council)

DISCOVERY AND RESEARCH

of bailey buildings. The long-standing view that the interior buildings and the chapel post-date the shell keep was overturned and; architectural features strongly suggest a thirteenth-century origin for the surviving structure (Fig 9). A fragment of a large stone building, most likely part of the great hall, was also discovered during a watching brief in the bailey (Johns 2009).

Restormel is now regarded as a ringwork and bailey constructed by the great Cardinan family around the turn of the eleventh century as they encouraged the growth of Lostwithiel; its encompassing deer park, the largest in Cornwall, may even have been created contemporaneously, as part of a single design (Thomas 1996b; Herring 2003). After the Earls of Cornwall moved their administrative base to Lostwithiel on acquiring town and manor in the thirteenth century, it was probably Edmund, son of Richard, who built Restormel's shell keep as a castle-esque early country house. The house's large windows afford views over the park and to Lostwithiel further down the Fowey valley. The bailey defences were not strengthened and surviving sources suggest the castle was never directly involved in medieval conflict. While maintained in the fifteenth century, the castle was abandoned by 1540 to be briefly re-occupied when ruinous during the Civil War.

A rapid survey of St Michael's Mount in 1992, the first since Dr William Borlase's descriptions in 1731 and 1762 (Pool 1975), established that more of the medieval castle survives than commonly thought: the west range's square towers, a guardhouse, steps and vestigial curtain wall (Herring 1993). Watching briefs during service trenching fleshed out the curtain walls (Herring et al 2000) and detailed examination of the main summit pile separated out military, ecclesiastical and domestic uses and tightened chronologies (Berry and Thomas 2008). Examination of the so-called Watch Tower on the north slope revealed that the standing walls pre-date the Civil War, but were modified at that time to include the present Watch Tower and other defensive embrasures (Sturgess 2010).

Oliver Padel drew together the evidence for Tintagel Castle being a fanciful construction by Earl Richard around 1230 of Arthur's legendary residence (1988), while minor excavations improved dating and interpretation of surviving fabric (Hartgroves and Walker 1988; Appleton et al 1988; Batey et al 1990). Subsequent work

has concentrated on improving the record and analysis of surviving fabric (e.g. Reynolds 2006) and has occasionally involved hazardous working conditions, including drawing the Inner Ward's curtain wall when suspended from ropes (Grove 1994). Bossiney Castle meanwhile remained relatively overlooked, despite being the centre of the manor in which Tintagel stands and being a well-preserved ringwork (surveyed by our former President Martin Fletcher in 1976), with a western bailey located and surveyed in 1991 (Rose 1992).

Other north Cornish ringworks (or low mottes) at Week St Mary and Boscastle have now been placed in their urban contexts, in both cases being at the broader ends of triangular market places (Preston-Jones and Rose 1992; Kirkham 2005a). However, similar sized castles are also found in rural locations. That at Penhallam, fully recorded by Cathy Parkes in 1989, lying at the east end of a deer park, may have served the Cardinans as a grand hunting lodge (Herring 2003, 39). Kilkhampton Castle, probably of the twelfth century, and possibly built by the Grenvilles, was cleared of scrub and resurveyed by CAU in 1988 (Preston-Jones 1988), and placed within its landscape context by both Thomas (1992) and Reynolds (1999), the latter noting how the main hollow-way from the town to the castle cut through earlier strip fields. Eastleigh Berrys, the peculiar double-baileyed enclosure in Launcells (Reynolds, this volume, fig 4), has been subjected to geophysical survey that suggests a possible origin as a round, and indicates numerous extramural structures clustered close by the castle (Wright 2010). A previously unnoticed ringwork found west of Poundstock church (Herring and Thomas 1993) had internal buildings and a northern bailey identified through geophysical survey (AM Lab 1994).

At Godolphin the location of another lost castle (or defended house) mentioned as ruined by William Worcestre in 1475 and possibly constructed in the early fourteenth century, postulated through identification of its surrounding precinct (Herring 1997), was to a degree supported by ditches located nearby in service trenches (Johns 2008).

Other semi-fortified great houses include Cotehele where historic building analysis places the southern gatehouse in the period 1550-1560, roughly contemporary with its builder Piers Edgcumbe's much more modern Mount Edgcumbe, another castellated building (Berry et al 2004). Cotehele's inward-looking early character is illustrated by the few external openings in the south range. The tall north-west tower at Cotehele was shown to be comparable with Pengersick's and analysis of both has brought revisions in likely dating: Cotehele tower now of the 1560s (not 1630s) and Pengersick of the 1550s, not the fifteenth century (Berry *et al* 2004; Herring *et al* 1998). Both towers are also recognised as being primarily residential, being vertical stacks of chambers, though Pengersick's basement is clearly defensive, with original gun-loops.

Churches, priories and chapels

Eric Berry, Nigel Thomas and Ann Preston-Jones

Good progress has been made since 1986 with 'the basic ground-work' on the study of the later medieval church in Cornwall that was then considered required (Preston-Jones and Rose 1986, 162). Nicholas Orme has drawn together thinking on the post-Conquest fortunes and foundations of monasteries and friaries and described the effects of the Reformation in Cornwall, setting that alongside a vivid delineation of the extent to which Christianity impinged upon ordinary Cornish people as parishioners in the late medieval period (Orme 2007; 2010). Ongoing work by Peter Beacham on the third edition of Nikolaus Pevsner's Cornwall volume of the *Buildings of England* series will draw together much historical architectural material, while Joanna Mattingly has also produced a number of important papers, expertly mixing documentary research with buildings and features analysis on aspects of Cornish churches (2005a), such as guilds (1989; 2005b), bench ends (1991), stained glass (2000; Mattingly *et al* 2001), and saints' cults (2003).

Excavation linked to documentary and architectural analysis has transformed our understanding of Glasney College, Penryn (Berry *et al* 2003; Cole 2005). Evaluation work has established its layout (*ibid*) and close study of architectural fragments, tiles and pottery revealed a remarkably sophisticated early fourteenth-century design and high quality of execution. 'Its refinement and…close artistic links to the output of the Exeter Cathedral workshop place [Glasney] … in the mainstream of English Decorated art' (Allan and Blaylock, in Cole 2005, 40). The magnificent scale and rich decoration of Launceston Priory's stone-vaulted church (Fig 10) also suggests a status on a par with

Glasney College and Exeter Cathedral (Gossip 2002; 2011). Being within towns both College and Priory have been extensively robbed out, remaining loose stones being predominantly less usable pieces of window tracery. The fine tiled pavements laid in the thirteenth century within each of these is exemplified by that still surviving on the site of the demolished monks' choir at St Germans (Olson and Preston-Jones 1998-9, figs 4 and 8).

Historic buildings analysis on St Michael's Mount confirmed that the religious complex developed around the medieval chapel of St Michael, built on the highest granite outcrop. This chapel with its distinctive crossing tower was built in the fourteenth century, completely replacing an earlier, probably smaller building; rose windows were added to each end most likely in the fifteenth century. In the partially enclosed and more private space immediately to its south are the necessary buildings for a small monastic community: refectory, dormitory, kitchen, prior's quarters, and guest accommodation. The 'Lady Chapel', on a separate rock outcrop east of the summit, was entirely rebuilt later in the eighteenth century (Berry *et al*, this volume, Post-medieval, fig 22) and further modified by the addition of Roman cement exterior decoration in the early nineteenth century (Berry and Thomas 2008).

At the opposite end of the monastic scale, recent excavations by Time Team at Lammana, Looe, the site of a small cell of Glastonbury Abbey, have established relative twelfth and thirteenth-century dates for chapels on Looe Island and the mainland respectively and revealed the walls of the Monks' House: perhaps the reception place for pilgrims to this less popular alternative to St Michael's Mount (Wessex Archaeology 2009; Olson 1994). At St Leonard's, Launceston, Time Team located, but found few remains of, one of Cornwall's major leper hospitals (Harding *et al* 1997).

Individual studies have shed light on the development of churches at Lanlivery (Rodwell 1993), Minster (Allan 2004-5), and St Piran's Church, Perranzabuloe (Cole 2007), amongst others. At Tintagel removal of Victorian plaster enabled examination of the development of the best surviving example in Cornwall of a Norman cruciform church that retained its transepts and never developed aisles as was commonplace elsewhere (Gould 2000-2001).

Involvement during roof repairs has provided the opportunity to examine several churches, and

Fig 10. (Previous page) Reconstruction of St Thomas' Priory. Detailed analysis of stonework was undertaken by John Allan of Exeter Archaeology as part of a programme of conservation work on the ruins. This work suggested that the surviving remains constitute rebuilding of the Norman priory during the late thirteenth and early fourteenth centuries resulting in what was probably the grandest Decorated work in Cornwall. Artistic links can be found in Exeter Cathedral (the choir windows, high altar screen, and the earliest floor-tiles). (Drawn by Richard Parker, © Exeter Archaeology)

to take samples for dendrochronological analysis. This has revealed that some church aisles are not fifteenth century as previously supposed from stylistic dating, but were instead roofed after the Reformation (Berry 2007). Another Norman cruciform church at St Martin by Looe had its transepts rebuilt when aisles were added (Berry *et al* 2006) and at St Veep different stylistic designs in the three roofs, two of which are of very closely similar dates, suggest their variety reflected the different status of the aisles (Berry 2005).

Survey to inform conservation work established that the medieval chapel and former hermitage site on Rame Head, maintained as a post-medieval beacon and watch house, was built to withstand extreme weather and still retains its medieval barrel vault stone roof (Thomas 1993a). Reuse as a school until the later nineteenth century also explains the survival at Bodmin of St Thomas chantry chapel, with its charnel house beneath, that was probably associated with town guilds. Again surveyed in advance of conservation, it is a good and rare example of fourteenth-century construction and window design (Thomas 1993b).

Poundstock's stone and cob built Gildhouse, a meeting place for the parish guilds, venue for the parish Revel and for feasts to raise money for parish church and poor, was subject to detailed survey, dendrochronological analysis (indicating mid sixteenth-century roofing and flooring) and interpretation. Its ground floor contained kitchen, brewhouse, stores and meeting rooms, leaving the long first floor open to accommodate festivities (Keystone 2005; Arnold and Howard 2007).

Cornish Crosses

Andrew Langdon

A significant year in the study of Cornwall's stone crosses, 2011 marks the centenary of the deaths of two renowned Victorian artists and antiquarians. Both John Thomas Blight (1835-1911) and Arthur Gregory Langdon (1852-1911) brought awareness of stone crosses to the wider public and were the forerunners

Fig 11. An unusual cross, neither wheel-headed nor latin and dating from anywhere between the twelfth and fifteenth centuries, was buried in a back garden at Rock Farm, Roche. (Andrew Langdon)

Fig 12. One of the most surprising discoveries has been the fragment of a four-holed cross at Trelay, Pelynt. This is of an eleventh-century group found east of Padstow and St Columb that has trefoil shaped holes and triquetra knots on the arms.
(Andrew Langdon)

in promoting and encouraging their restoration and preservation (Blight 1856, 1858; Langdon 1896, 1906). Their work still forms the foundation of more recent work, including a series of guide books (Langdon, 1992 to 1999) and more detailed books on Penwith's crosses (Cooke 1999 to 2004).

Since Langdon's day there have been many new discoveries, the pace accelerating during the last 25 years, when 31 crosses and fragments have been discovered (Figs 11 and 12), while 63 have been either re-erected, repaired or restored and 32 re-sited or re-positioned. A further five crosses and four cross-bases are now either lost or missing (Langdon forthcoming).

A significant interpretative breakthrough came through recognition that simple wayside crosses, often previously assumed to be early medieval, are mostly post-Conquest, representing a tradition continuing and developing from cross-carving begun in the late ninth and tenth centuries with richly decorated crosses like Cardinham and Lanherne (Langdon 1896, 354-60). In west Cornwall, 43 wayside crosses display simple and crude Crucifixions, clearly copying the earlier and better executed Penwith group of sculpture (Preston-Jones and Langdon 1997, 118-19). Symbolism on some wayside crosses indicates a post-Conquest date; those at Egloshayle, St Mabyn and Lesnewth have in place of the cross

a *fleur de lys*, a characteristically thirteenth-century emblem more often seen on grave slabs and coffin lids (Allan and Langdon 2008). Crosses in Stithians and Wendron display chevron work of a type normally associated with Norman architecture.

Blight (1856; 1858) illustrated fifteenth and sixteenth-century lantern crosses that were only listed by Langdon (Langdon 1896 425-6); neither explained their significance. These monuments have recently received more attention (Langdon 2004) and restoration work has helped suggest they were originally painted, like everything else in the parish church at the time. With stained glass windows, wall paintings telling biblical stories, and painted woodwork, the church would have been a colourful place, and the lantern crosses were a continuation of this, but out in the churchyard. A lantern cross at St Michael's Mount, once cleaned, was found to have the outline of the patron's shields carved on each side in such low relief that they could not have been recognised unless originally painted (Preston-Jones and Langdon 2003, 12).

Cornish crosses were set up to mark Christian burial grounds, routes to the parish church, or boundaries of glebe or parish. Over the last two decades, however, these religious monuments have gained further significance as cultural symbols in Cornwall, with many modern and replica crosses being produced.

Artefacts

Carl Thorpe and Peter Herring

Since 1986 there have been several important publications of Cornish later medieval artefact assemblages, including some that describe, summarise and interpret collections made from earlier excavations, like Launceston Castle (Saunders 2006), Lammana (Olson 1994) and Old Lanyon (Beresford 1994). Launceston's enormous body of finds (requiring over 200 pages) includes a particularly rich collection related to Earl Richard's mid-thirteenth-century use of the castle as his regional power base. Dining was extravagant (in the range of food and the utensils used to create and serve it), dress was highly fashionable and equipment, including that of the military, sophisticated. A whole whale, the 'king's fish', was brought here, apparently sometime in the thirteenth century, a period when that mammal's meat was enjoyed (Mould and Vince 2006; Brown *et al* 2006; Mould 2006; Tyson 2006; Riddler 2006). This site and others including St Michael's Mount (Herring *et al* 2000), Scilly (Allan 1991), Bury Court, Penhallam (Beresford 1974), Lammana (Olson 1994), Pydar Street, Truro (Stead *et al* 1998-1999), Garrow (Dudley and Minter 1962-3), Treworld (Dudley and Minter 1966), Tresmorn (Beresford 1971), Davidstow Moor and Treligga (Christie and Rose 1987), Stonaford (Herring and Berry 1997), Colliford and Bunning's Park (Austin *et al* 1989), contain either much or some material imported into Cornwall, mainly from further east in southern Britain, but some from the continent. The time has come for detailed analysis of the contents of such assemblages, and a review of the material recorded within grey literature produced from watching briefs and minor excavations undertaken by CAU/Historic Environment Service and others to inform understanding of trade and other contacts, and of the social structures and ideologies that such artefacts can be made to reveal.

Key aspects of the study of native Cornish medieval pottery are also still poorly developed, largely because of continuing imprecise dating, due in part to paucity of stratified sequences. Much still depends on relating Cornish wares to broad regional traditions in which coarseware forms in particular were long-lived; some Exeter rim forms endured from the late tenth to the early fourteenth century (Allan 1984). Work on Old Lanyon, Lammana, Tintagel and Bunning's Park enabled Cathy O'Mahoney to work out the main Cornish coarseware types (O'Mahoney 1989a; 1989b; 1994a; 1994b). Continuing study by Carl Thorpe, as principal finds officer for numerous more recent projects, has refined understanding of ranges of forms (often limited) and chronologies.

- **Cornish Medieval Coarsewares** (late twelfth to late fourteenth centuries). Handmade, thin-walled vessels, sometimes wheel-finished, with hard-fired micaceous granitic fabric. Long-lived practical designs like jugs and cooking pots (Allan 1984; O'Mahoney 1989a; 1989b; 1994a; 1994b).
- **Bunnings Park Ware** (thirteenth to fifteenth centuries). Handmade, often wheel-finished, thin-walled, micaceous granitic fabric with many inclusions of rounded quartz grains, hard fired with pink-buff exterior and grey core. Probably made in or near Lostwithiel, though no kiln sites known possibly clamp-fired. Mainly cooking pots and jugs (O'Mahoney 1989b)
- **St Germans Ware** (thirteenth to fifteenth centuries). Hard-fired, wheel-thrown, thin-walled. Micaceous with quartz temper and black mica plate inclusions. Grey exterior and black core. White slip or incised geometric decoration. Cooking pots, jugs, bowls and cisterns. Kiln excavated at St Germans in 1957 (Guthrie 1957-8, 76), but might be other kilns; clay may derive from either Dartmoor or Bodmin Moor.
- **Lostwithiel Ware** (fifteenth century onwards). Wheel-thrown, hard-fired, pink to grey-brown exterior with a grey core. Similar to *Bunnings Park*, which it probably replaces and distinguished from it by being thicker walled and with large flakes of white mica and more angular white feldspar inclusions visible. Cooking pots, cisterns, lid-seated jugs with rod handles, two-handled jars and bowls/pancheons with complicated rims and shoulder carinations. Bases have more rounded, gently sloping angles. Decoration includes stabbed rod handles, horizontal painted bands of white slip, and lines of white slip forming simple geometric patterns. Incised lines, and applied thumb-pressed strips are also present, but rarer. Called Lostwithiel Ware despite no kilns having been found there, though large quantities of pottery wasters in this fabric have been

(Miles 1976; 1979; O'Mahoney 1989a; 1989b). There is documentary evidence for potting in Lostwithiel from the fifteenth to nineteenth centuries (Douch 1969).

Industry

Adam Sharpe and Peter Herring

In 1984, Sandy Gerrard joined the Cornwall Committee for Rescue Archaeology, bringing the results of his detailed investigation of several Bodmin Moor tin streamworks. Through comprehensive documentary research, survey and excavation at Colliford (as part of Austin *et al* 1989) and for doctoral research (Gerrard 1986), Sandy had established a method for characterising these early elements of our industrial landscape based on their morphologies, but incorporating understanding that these reflected sophisticated knowledge of hydrodynamics and exploitation of relative mineral densities to achieve optimal resource recovery –

something that continues to underpin most mineral dressing processes to this day.

Surveys of Bodmin Moor's industrial sites in 1988-9 (Rose and Herring 1990; Herring *et al* 2008), the Minions Area (Sharpe 1989) and Kit Hill (Herring and Thomas 1990) substantially confirmed Gerrard's streamwork typology. Cornwall's archaeologists have spent much of the past two and half decades charting the technological shift from working secondary tin deposits in streamworks (e.g. Fig 13) to the exploitation of lode deposits, the process that would eventually underpin Cornwall's transition into a major force in development of hard rock mining worldwide.

Surveys and watching briefs routinely confirm that what initially appear to be single-phase nineteenth-century mines had, in almost every case been preceded by exploitation of the lode outcrops, this work having been preceded by careful prospecting (for example, on Minions Moor; Sharpe 2008). Elsewhere such early remains have been

Fig 13. Walkers provide an idea of the scale of this apparently later medieval eluvial streamworks in the saddle between Leskernick and Buttern Hills on West Moor, Altarnun. The depth suggests that it has been re-cut several times and the patterns of dumps on either side of the central drainage channel, which reflect the arrangements of working tyes, are therefore of the last operation. (Peter Herring)

Fig 14. Gashes in Hermon cliff, St Just, mark the working of coastal outcrops from an early date. Radiocarbon dating of a timber pipe from Wheal Hermon gives evidence for sixteenth-century workings.
(Adam Sharpe)

plotted from aerial photographs by the National Mapping Programme (Young 2006). Far from being a vernacular industry, the emerging impression is of a systematised set of craft skills shared by a specialised workforce. Watching briefs showed that shaft and adit mining (characterised by self-draining workings) seems to have arrived on the scene more or less fully developed as early as the mid 1500s in parts of Cornwall (Sharpe 2008, 59-61).

In some areas like coastal West Penwith and St Agnes we now see that exploitation of cliffside lode outcrops clearly occurred earlier than previously thought. Discovery and subsequent radiocarbon dating of a timber pipe column from Wheal Hermon (Fig 14; National Trust 2002) showed that by the mid-sixteenth-century pumping technology was already sufficiently advanced for miners to be attempting to work below natural drainage levels – in Wheal Hermon's case below sea level. Another recently-discovered submarine shaft complete with similar pumps found on the shore at St Agnes suggests this was not the only early mine to be operating in this fashion (Wayne Ridgeway, pers comm). Survey on Godolphin Hill has provided additional archaeological evidence for early lode mining, fourteenth century or earlier (Herring 1997), as has research into a well documented phase of thirteenth-century silver mining in the Tamar Valley (Mayer 1990; Rippon *et al* 2009).

Investigations at Crift, Lanlivery uncovered evidence of later medieval or early post-medieval tin smelting within a ruined medieval longhouse (Buckley and Earl 1990; McDonnell 1993; McDonnell *et al* 1995; Malham *et al* 2002; Dudley 2005). The relationship between tinning and farming in the moulding of the medieval Cornish upland landscape was more thoroughly explored in the parish of St Neot, and especially in those parts to be flooded by the Colliford Reservoir. Extensive survey was coupled with excavation of leats, stamping mills

DISCOVERY AND RESEARCH

and tinners' shelters and palaeo-environmental analysis and interpretation to generate a model of the development of miner-farmer communities (Austin *et al* 1989).

Medieval towns

Graeme Kirkham and Nick Cahill

In 1986 Ann Preston-Jones and Peter Rose noted that, despite the variety and interest of Cornish towns, there had been little analysis of urban topography and limited recovery of material from excavations (1986; also Preston-Jones and Rose 1992). A quarter of a century later there has been progress, but Cornwall's medieval urban history is still poorly understood and below-ground urban archaeology remains almost completely obscure.

Harold Fox (1999) thought Cornwall having the third largest proportion of boroughs in relation to

land area in England was due to its diverse economy (exporting tin and fish, trading in stone, slate and cloth and importing wine and salt, all through urban markets), to the multiplicity of landowners with relatively small landholdings, and to geographical difficulties of communication. By about 1350 'few people would have been without easy access to a town of moderate size' (*ibid*, 406).

Fourteen towns with medieval origins – Bodmin, Callington, Camelford, Helston, Launceston, Liskeard, East and West Looe, Penryn, Penzance, Redruth, St Ives, Saltash and Truro (see bibliography) – were studied by the Cornwall and Scilly Urban Survey and the Cornwall Industrial Settlements Initiative. Boscastle, Lostwithiel and Trevena (Tintagel) have also been characterised (Kirkham 2005a; Berry *et al* 2008; Berry *et al* 2003) and topographical interpretations published for Tregony and East and West Looe (Slater 1999),

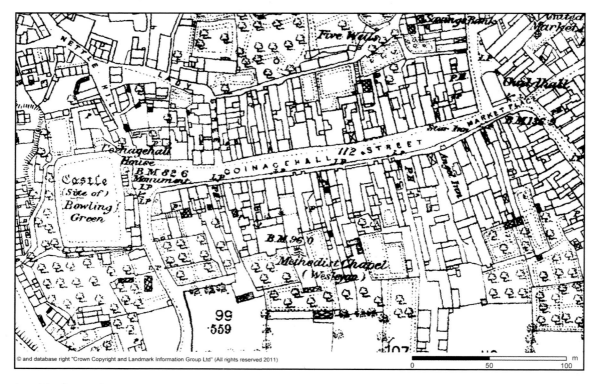

Fig 15. The medieval core of the planned 'street town' of Helston, shown on the 1st edition Ordnance Survey 25in: 1 mile map of 1879. The long, wide axial street extends east along a ridge top from the site of the castle, with the early triangular market space at its western end. Narrow, elongated burgage plots run back from the street frontage on both sides. A later market focus developed at the eastern end of Coinagehall Street.

Fig 16. The walled town of Launceston developed around the precinct of the early post-Conquest castle, with the medieval layout still distinct in the late nineteenth century (Ordnance Survey 1st edition 25in: 1 mile map, 1884). Although Launceston is more complex in its topography than many of Cornwall's medieval 'new towns', the 'street town' element represented by Northgate Street (north of the castle) is still relatively clear.

and for Week St Mary's 'failed' town (Preston-Jones and Rose 1992). New research on Mousehole emphasises its medieval urban character (Mattingly 2009). The potential of documentary sources for urban research has been noted by Fox and Padel (2000, xcvi-xcviii).

These studies, data on borough status (Beresford 1988; Fox 1999) and market and fair charters (Letters 2006), suggest most Cornish medieval towns were deliberate creations by major landowners. Proprietors 'planted' urban settlements on their estates to stimulate economic activity and create a local focus for civil authority. Most such new towns appear to be of the thirteenth and earlier fourteenth centuries, their locations dictated by potential for trade, most being ports. Tregony, Truro and Lostwithiel at the highest navigable points and lowest crossing places on major rivers served much larger hinterlands than towns established on the coast (like Penzance and Boscastle) or nearer river mouths (Padstow,

East and West Looe, Fowey, Penryn, St Mawes). 'Thoroughfare' towns like Camelford, Mitchell and Grampound took advantage of major routeway traffic (Fox 1999, 403).

All medieval Cornish settlements investigated were 'street towns', much the most frequent medieval urban form in southern Britain (Slater 2005, 19). Long axial main streets, sometimes following the spine of a ridge or spur, as at Truro, Tregony, Boscastle, Helston and Penryn, have burgage plots running back from narrow frontages on both sides (Figs 15-17). Most had a market space, often triangular, at one end of these principal streets, which were usually aligned on a focal point: castles at Helston, Truro, Tregony and Boscastle, quays or landing places at Saltash, Penryn, East and West Looe, Lostwithiel and Millbrook, a recently recognised early fourteenth-century 'new town' (Cornwall HER PRN 6201), and river crossings at Grampound, Wadebridge and

307

Camelford. Excepting Launceston and Tintagel (Fox 1999), castles had little prolonged influence in shaping development of adjacent towns, and apart from at Week St Mary (Preston-Jones and Rose 1992), churches and religious houses appear not to have provided such a focus, being typically set back from settlement cores. Religious foundations could, however, be key elements in the founding of towns and in their economic life, as at Bodmin and Penryn. Chapels were sometimes located adjacent to market sites, as at Tregony, Helston, St Ives, Truro, Boscastle, Camelford and Lostwithiel (Sheppard 1980; Russell 2002; Newell 2005a; Kirkham 2003; 2005a; Herring and Newell 2005; Berry *et al* 2008).

Lostwithiel has sometimes been suggested as having been laid out on a grid plan (e.g. Sheppard 1980), but here too the original twelfth-century form was a single street running north from a quay on the Fowey; the partly causewayed parallel street to the east was added when the new bridge was built before 1280 (Slater 1999, 409; Berry *et al* 2008). Launceston, created as a walled town alongside the castle enclosure in the first half of the thirteenth century, also apparently has a complex plan, but a 'street town' (Northgate Street) with burgage plots is again present within the walls, running steeply uphill from the North Gate to a large irregular market space (Herring and Gillard 2005). A 'street town' (Chapel Street) aligned on an early market space also formed one phase of the development of medieval Penzance (Cahill 2003). At Bodmin a new 'street town' (Fore Street) was almost certainly an initiative by the priory established there in the early twelfth century (Kirkham 2005b). Bodmin's new street appears to have been added to an earlier urban settlement, attested by a tenth-century reference to a municipal official (a portreeve) there and the 1086 Domesday record of 68 houses and a market. This earlier town may itself have derived from a late-Saxon *burh* (*ibid*). Similarly, at Helston and Liskeard, 'street towns' were added to earlier centres of economic activity (Russell 2002; Gillard 2005a).

At Mousehole, physical constraints, division between two manors and a larger-than-usual market space reflecting its role as both trading port and fishing centre produced a different plan: an axial street with buildings only to the west formed one side of the market area, with additional housing facing onto it from the north and south (Mattingly 2009, fig 3).

While simple 'street towns' underlie many Cornish medieval settlements, subsequent development was often topographically complex. Some market places were re-located and older ones infilled or encroached upon, as at Truro (Kirkham 2003), Tregony and West Looe (Slater 1999). Growth was achieved by adding linear extensions to street towns in Tregony (Slater 1999) and Bodmin (Bore Street) (Kirkham 2005b). In Penzance, Market Jew Street, itself a 'street town', was added perpendicularly to Chapel Street (Cahill 2003). Complexity also resulted where towns like Lostwithiel, Mousehole and St Mawes were divided between manorial proprietors (*cf* Slater 1999; Berry *et al* 2008; Mattingly 2009; Sheppard 1980).

Fig 17. Tregony from the north east, showing the town's unusually well-preserved medieval stripfield system. This was probably laid out to accompany the creation of the new town in the late twelfth century, providing the inhabitants with agricultural holdings in addition to the trade and craft activities which the town accommodated. Few other stripfield systems associated with towns survive. (Photograph: Historic Environment, Cornwall Council F69-108, 2005)

Fig 18. Part of the former Duchy of Cornwall administrative complex in Lostwithiel, one of the few surviving medieval urban structures in Cornwall, photographed in the 1860s. (The tramway to the left carried iron ore from Restormel Royal mine to Lostwithiel Quay.) (Photograph reproduced with the kind permission of the Royal Institution of Cornwall (RIC) LOStn005).

There is a need to measure burgage plots and other components to assess whether new Cornish towns were either carefully pre-planned or simply developed in accordance with a broad preference for the 'street

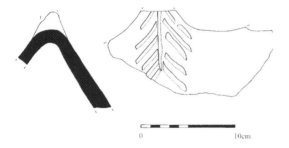

Fig 19. A crested medieval ridge tile, probably locally made, from excavations in Quay Street, Lostwithiel. Relatively little is known of Cornwall's medieval urban building forms and materials. (Drawing: Carl Thorpe)

town' form. Trenches possibly marking out burgage plots were uncovered at Week St Mary (Johns and Thorpe 1995). At Camelford and perhaps also Truro, Bodmin and Redruth, the size and alignment of burgage plots may have derived from the medieval open field strips over which they were laid out.

Excavation in Cornwall's medieval towns over the past 25 years has been generally disappointing in terms of specifically urban archaeology (leaving aside castle, priory and friary sites in urban contexts). Little or no evidence of the form of early buildings has been recovered; they may have been largely ephemeral timber or cob structures or sites may have been comprehensively cleared between building phases. Stratified artefactual assemblages are also rare and most medieval pottery recovered, for example, has been residual or re-deposited (e.g. Stead 1998-9). Cornish towns have yielded little to compare with the deep urban stratigraphies and rich harvest of finds and environmental evidence from features like wells and cess pits in medieval towns elsewhere in Britain. An exception was a portion of the town ditch (Dockey) in Launceston examined under rescue conditions in 1987, from which various well-preserved organic artefacts were recovered (Herring 1988). A series of probably fifteenth-century riverside revetment walls of the first reclamation episode were recorded in Quay Street, Lostwithiel, as were more substantial walls and floors associated with late medieval pottery that probably represent portions of late medieval buildings closer to the street frontage (Gossip forthcoming). The location of Lostwithiel's pottery industry, as with other medieval urban industries, remains obscure. There, as elsewhere, much remains to be done.

NB. Reports produced by the Cornwall and Scilly Urban Survey and Cornwall Industrial Settlements Initiative can be viewed online at www.historic-cornwall.org.uk

References

Allan, J P, 1984. *Medieval and post-medieval finds from Exeter 1971-1980,* Exeter Archaeological Reports, **3,** Exeter

Allan, J P, 1991. Medieval and post-medieval pottery, in J Ratcliffe, *Lighting up the Past in Scilly,* Truro (Institute of Cornish Studies and Cornwall County Council), 93-100

Allan, J, 2004-5. After the flood: building recording at Minster Church, Boscastle, in 2005, *Cornish Archaeol,* **43-4,** 145-58

Allan, J, and Langdon, A G, 2008. Medieval gravestones and architectural fragments from the churchyard of St Michael's, Lesnewth, *Cornish Archaeol,* **47,** 129-145

Allan, J and Blaylock, S, 2005. The architectural fragments, in Cole 2005, 32-40

Altenberg, K, 2003. *Experiencing landscapes; a study of space and identity in three marginal areas of medieval Britain and Scandinavia,* Stockholm

AM Lab, 1994. *Poundstock Castle resistivity survey,* Portsmouth (English Heritage)

Appleton, N, Fox, T, and Waters, A, 1988. *Tintagel Castle - survey and excavation at the Inner Ward, the Chapel and Site 4 and the Garden,* Truro (Cornwall Archaeological Unit)

Arnold, A, and Howard, R, 2007. *The Gildhouse, Poundstock, near Bude, Cornwall,* Research Department Report Series, **2007.9,** Nottingham (English Heritage)

Austin, D, 1985. Dartmoor and the upland village of the South-West of England, in D Hooke, ed, *Medieval Villages,* OUCA Monograph, **5,** Oxford, 71-79

Austin, D, Gerrard, G A M, and Greeves, T A P, 1989. Tin and agriculture in the Middle Ages and beyond: landscape archaeology in St Neot Parish, Cornwall, *Cornish Archaeol,* **28,** 7-251

Austin, D, and Thomas, J, 1990. The 'proper study' of medieval archaeology: a case study, in D Austin, and L Alcock, eds,

From the Baltic to the Black Sea: studies in medieval archaeology, London, 43-78

Batey, C E, Sharpe, A, and Thorpe, C M, 1990. Tintagel Castle: archaeological investigation of the Steps area 1989 and 1990, *Cornish Archaeol,* **32,** 47-66

Beresford, G, 1971. Tresmorn, St Gennys, *Cornish Archaeol,* **10,** 55-73

Beresford, G, 1974. The medieval manor of Penhallam, Jacobstow, Cornwall, *Med Arch,* **18,** 90-145

Beresford, G, 1994. Old Lanyon, Madron: a deserted medieval settlement. The late E Marie Minter's excavations of 1964, *Cornish Archaeol,* **33,** 130-169

Beresford, M W, 1964. Dispersed and grouped settlement in medieval Cornwall, *Ag Hist Rev,* **12,** 13-27

Beresford, M, 1988. *New towns of the Middle Ages: town plantation in England, Wales and Gascony,* Gloucester (rev edn)

Berry, E, 1997. *Trerice House: building analysis, report for the National Trust,* Truro (Eric Berry)

Berry, E, 2005. *St Veep Church Roof, Cornwall - archaeological survey,* Truro (Historic Environment Service, Cornwall County Council)

Berry, E, 2007. *Rapid assessment of a selection of eight Cornish churches for the Victoria County History,* Truro (Eric Berry)

Berry, E, Blackman, T, Buck, C, Cahill, N, Colwill, S, Mattingly, J, Powning, J, and Thomas, N, 2008. *Lostwithiel: 'the fairest of small cities'. Historic characterisation,* Truro (Cornwall County Council)

Berry, E, Cahill, N, Mattingly, J, and Thomas, N, 2003. *Tintagel, Cornwall: characterisation assessment,* Truro (Historic Environment Service, Cornwall County Council)

Berry, E, Gossip, J, Mattingly, J, and Thomas, N, 2004. *Cotehele House, Calstock, Cornwall - historic building analysis,* Truro (Historic Environment Service, Cornwall County Council)

Berry, E, Lawson-Jones, A, and Mattingly, J, 2003. *Glasney College, Penryn, Cornwall - archaeological assessment and evaluation,* Truro (Historic Environment Service, Cornwall County Council)

Berry, E, Mattingly, J, and Thomas, N, 2003. *The Old Post Office, Tintagel, Cornwall - historic building analysis,* Truro (Historic Environment Service, Cornwall County Council)

Berry, E, Newell, K, and Thomas, N, 2006. *St Martin by Looe, Cornwall - archaeological survey of the church roof,* Truro (Historic Environment Service, Cornwall County Council)

Berry, E, and Sturgess, J, forthcoming. *Trerice House, Newlyn East, Cornwall: historic building analysis,* Truro Historic Environment Projects, Cornwall Council)

Berry, E, and Thomas, N, 2008. *St Michael's Mount, Cornwall - historic buildings analysis and watching brief of the summit buildings,* Truro (Historic Environment Service, Cornwall County Council)

Blight, J T, 1856. *The ancient crosses and other antiquities of west Cornwall,* London and Penzance

Blight, J T, 1858. *The ancient crosses and other antiquities of east Cornwall,* London and Penzance

Brown, D, Thomson, R, Vince, A, and Williams, D, 2006. The

pottery, in Saunders 2006, 269-296

Buck, C, 1993. *Restormel Castle - historical and documentary register,* Truro (Cornwall Archaeological Unit)

Buckley, A, and Earl, B, 1990. Preliminary report on the tin and iron working site at Crift farm, *Jnl Trevithick Soc*, **17,** 66-77

Bull, E, 1999. *Cornwall's field boundaries,* Truro (Cornwall Archaeological Unit)

Cahill, N, with Russell, S, 2003. *Cornwall and Scilly Urban Survey. Historic characterisation for regeneration: Penzance,* Truro (Cornwall County Council)

Cahill Partnership and Cornwall Archaeological Unit, 2002a. *Cornwall Industrial Settlements Initiative: Looe,* Truro (Cornwall County Council)

Cahill Partnership and Cornwall Archaeological Unit, 2002b. *Cornwall Industrial Settlements Initiative: Redruth and Plain an Gwarry,* Truro, (Cornwall County Council)

Chesher, V M, and Chesher, F J, 1968. *The Cornishman's house,* Truro

Christie, P, and Rose, P, 1987. Davidstow Moor, Cornwall: the medieval and later sites, wartime excavations by C K Croft Andrew 1941-2, *Cornish Archaeol*, **26,** 163-194

Cole, D, 2005. *Glasney College, Penryn, Cornwall - archaeological assessment and evaluation trenching,* Truro (Historic Environment Service, Cornwall County Council)

Cole, D, 2007. *The excavation of St Piran's Church, Perranzabuloe, Cornwall - archaeological excavation, conservation and management works,* Truro (Historic Environment Service, Cornwall County Council)

Cooke, I M, 1999. *Crosses and churchway paths in the Land's End peninsula* I *St Just in Penwith,* Penzance (Men-an-Tol Studios)

Cooke, I M, 2000. *Crosses and churchway paths in the Land's End peninsula* II *Sennen and St Levan,* Penzance (Men-an-Tol Studios)

Cooke, I M, 2000. *Crosses and churchway paths in the Land's End peninsula* III *St Buryan,* Penzance (Men-an-Tol Studios)

Cooke, I M, 2001. *Crosses and churchway paths in the Land's End peninsula* IV *Paul and Sancreed,* Penzance (Men-an-Tol Studios)

Cooke, I M, 2002. *Crosses and churchway paths in the Land's End peninsula* V *Madron and Morvah,* Penzance (Men-an-Tol Studios)

Cooke, I M, 2002. *Crosses and churchway paths in the Land's End peninsula* VI *Gulval and Ludgvan,* Penzance (Men-an-Tol Studios)

Cooke, I M, 2003. *Crosses and churchway paths in the Land's End peninsula* VII *Lelant, St Ives and Towednack,* Penzance (Men-an-Tol Studios)

Cooke, I M, 2004. *Crosses and churchway paths in the Land's End peninsula* VIII *Zennor,* Penzance (Men-an-Tol Studios)

Cox, J, 2009. *Godolphin, Breage, Cornwall, Conservation Management Plan,* Exeter (Keystone)

Creighton, O H, 2002. *Castles and landscapes: power, community and fortification in medieval England,* London

Creighton, O H, 2009. *Designs upon the land: elite landscapes of the Middle Ages,* Woodbridge

Creighton, O, and Freeman, J, 2006. Castles and the medieval landscape, in S Turner, ed, *Medieval Devon and Cornwall,* Macclesfield, 104-122

Dodgshon, R A, and Jewell, C A, 1970. Paring and burning and related practices with particular reference to the south-western counties of England, in A Gailey, and A Fenton, eds, *The spade in Northern and Atlantic Europe,* Belfast (Ulster Folk Museum), 74-87

Douch, H L, 1969. Cornish earthenware potters, *Jnl Roy Inst Cornwall,* **6,** 33-64

Dudley, D, and Minter, E M, 1962-3. The medieval village at Garrow Tor, Bodmin Moor, Cornwall, *Med Arch,* **4-5,** 272-294

Dudley, D, and Minter, E M, 1966. The excavation of a medieval settlement at Treworld, Lesnewth, 1963, *Cornish Archaeol,* **5,** 34-58

Dudley, P, 2003. *Forrabury Strips, Forrabury and Minster, Cornwall - archaeological assessment,* Truro (Historic Environment Service, Cornwall County Council)

Dudley, P, 2005. *Helman Tor CWT properties, Cornwall - archaeological assessments,* Truro (Historic Environment Service, Cornwall County Council)

Dudley, P, 2011. *Goon, hal, cliff and croft, west Cornwall's rough ground,* Truro (Cornwall Council)

Fleming, A, 2009. The making of a medieval road: the Monk's Trod Routeway, mid Wales, *Landscapes,* **10 (1),** 77-100

Fox, H, 1971. *A geographical study of the field systems of Devon and Cornwall,* PhD thesis, University of Cambridge

Fox, H, 1999. Medieval urban development, in R Kain, and W Ravenhill, eds, *Historic atlas of south-west England,* Exeter, 400-7

Fox, H S A, and Padel, O J, eds, 2000. *The Cornish lands of the Arundells of Lanherne, fourteenth to sixteenth centuries,* Exeter Devon and Cornwall Record Soc, **ns 41**

Franklin, L, 2006. Imagined landscapes: archaeology, perception and folklore in the study of medieval Devon, in S Turner, ed, *Medieval Devon and Cornwall,* Macclesfield, 144-161

Gerrard, G A M, 1986. *The early Cornish tin industry: an archaeological and historical survey,* unpublished PhD thesis, Saint David's University College, University of Wales

Gillard, B, 2005a. *Cornwall and Scilly Urban Survey. Historic characterisation for regeneration: Liskeard,* Truro (Cornwall County Council)

Gillard, B, 2005b. *Cornwall and Scilly Urban Survey. Historic characterisation for regeneration: Saltash,* Truro (Cornwall County Council)

Gillard, B, Cornwall Archaeological Unit, and The Cahill Partnership, 2002. *Cornwall Industrial Settlements Initiative: Callington.* Truro (Cornwall County Council)

Gossip, J, 2002. *St Thomas' Priory Launceston, Cornwall, archaeological survey,* Truro (Historic Environment Service, Cornwall County Council)

Gossip, J, 2011. *St Thomas' Priory Launceston, Cornwall,* Truro (Historic Environment Projects, Cornwall Council)

Gossip, J, forthcoming. On the waterfront: excavations at Quay Street, Lostwithiel, Cornwall, 2002, *Cornish Archaeol*

Gould, J, 2000-2001. Recording churches and churchyards, *Cornish Archaeol*, **39-40,** 215-7

Grove, J, 1994. *Tintagel Castle - archaeological recording of the Great Hall cliff section*, Truro (Cornwall Archaeological Unit)

Guthrie, A, 1957-8. The medieval period in Cornwall, *Proc West Cornwall Field Club*, **2.2,** 73-7

Hanawalt, B A, and Kobialka, M, eds, 2000. *Medieval practices of space*, Minneapolis

Harding, P, Ainsworth, S, Gater, J, Johns, C, Burgess, G J, and Thorpe, C, 1997. The evaluation of a medieval leper hospital at St Leonards, Launceston, *Cornish Archaeol*, **36,** 138-50

Hartgroves, S, and Walker, R, 1988. Excavations in the Lower Ward, Tintagel Castle, 1986, in A C Thomas, ed, *Tintagel Papers, Cornish Studies*, **16,** 9-30

Henderson, C, and Coates, H, 1928. *Old Cornish bridges and streams,* Exeter

Henderson, C G, and Weddell, P J, 1994. Medieval settlements on Dartmoor and in west Devon: the evidence from excavations, *The archaeology of Dartmoor, perspectives from the 1990s, Devon Archaeological Society Proceedings*, **52,** 119-40

Herring, P, 1986. *An exercise in landscape history. pre-Norman and medieval Brown Willy and Bodmin Moor,* unpublished MPhil thesis, University of Sheffield

Herring, P, 1988. Launceston town wall, the Dockey, *Cornish Archaeol*, **27,** 170

Herring, P, 1993. *St Michael's Mount, an archaeological evaluation*, Truro (Cornwall County Council)

Herring, P, 1997. *Godolphin, Breage, an archaeological and historical assessment*, Truro (Cornwall Archaeological Unit)

Herring, P, 1998. *Cornwall's historic landscape, presenting a method of historic landscape character assessment*, Truro (Cornwall County Council)

Herring, P, 1999. Farming and transhumance in Cornwall at the turn of the first millennium AD, *Journal of the Cornwall Association of Local Historians* **37,** 19-25 and **38,** 3-8

Herring, P, 2001. The deer park, in R Cole, P Herring, C Johns, and A Reynolds, *Godolphin - archaeological research and recording*, Truro (Historic Environment Service, Cornwall County Council), 17-23

Herring, P, 2003. Cornish medieval deer parks, in R Wilson-North, ed, *The lie of the land, aspects of the archaeology and history of the designed landscape in the South West of England*, Exeter, 34-50

Herring, P, 2006a. Cornish strip fields, in S Turner, ed, *Medieval Devon and Cornwall*, Macclesfield, 44-77

Herring, P, 2006b. Medieval fields at Brown Willy, Bodmin Moor, in S Turner, ed, *Medieval Devon and Cornwall*, Macclesfield, 78-103

Herring, P, forthcoming. Multiple identities in Cornwall, in S Pearce, ed, *The archaeology of South Western Britain: recent research*

Herring, P, and Berry, E, 1997. Stonaford, *Cornish Archaeol*, **36,** 151-175

Herring, P, and Hooke, D, 1993. Interrogating Anglo-Saxons in St Dennis, *Cornish Archaeol*, **32,** 67-75

Herring, P, Thorpe, C, Quinnell, H, Reynolds, A, and Allan, J, 2000. *St Michael's Mount archaeological works 1995-98*, Truro (Cornwall County Council)

Herring, P, and Gillard, B, 2005. *Cornwall and Scilly Urban Survey. Historic characterisation for regeneration: Launceston*, Truro (Cornwall County Council)

Herring, P, and Newell, K, 2005. *Cornwall and Scilly Urban Survey. Historic characterisation for regeneration: Camelford*, Truro (Cornwall County Council)

Herring, P, Sharpe, A, and Smith, J R, 2008. *Bodmin Moor: an archaeological survey. Volume 2: the post-medieval and industrial landscapes*, Swindon (English Heritage)

Herring, P, and Tapper, B, 2006. *Cotehele historicl landscape characterisation and scoping survey for historic landscape survey*, Truro (Historic Environment Service, Cornwall County Council)

Herring, P, and Thomas, N, 1990. *The archaeology of Kit Hill*, Truro (Cornwall County Council)

Herring, P, and Thomas, N, 1993. *Stratton Hundred Rapid Identification Survey*, Truro (Cornwall Archaeological Unit)

Herring, P, and Thomas, N, 2000. *Codda, Altarnun, Cornwall, historic building and farmstead survey*, Truro (Cornwall Archaeological Unit)

Herring, P, Thorpe, C, and Morley, B, 1998. *Pengersick Castle, Breage - an archaeological and historical assessment*, Truro (Cornwall Archaeological Unit)

Johns, C, 2008. *Godolphin House, Breage - archaeological watching briefs, 1999-2004*, Truro (Historic Environment Service, Cornwall County Council)

Johns, C, 2009. *Restormel Castle, admissions building and power supply - archaeological investigations 2006-2008*, Truro (Historic Environment Service, Cornwall County Council)

Johns, C, and Thorpe, C, 1995. *An archaeological evaluation of land at the rear of Malaga Cottage, The Square, Week St Mary, Cornwall*, Truro (Cornwall Archaeological Unit)

Johnson, M, 2010. *English houses 1300-1800: vernacular architecture, social life*, London

Johnson, N, and Rose, P, 1994. *Bodmin Moor: an archaeological survey. Volume I: the human landscape to c 1800*, London (English Heritage)

Keystone Historic Buildings Consultants, 2005. A *Conservation Plan for the Gildhouse, Poundstock, Cornwall*, Exeter (Keystone)

Kirkham, G, 2003. *Cornwall and Scilly Urban Survey. Historic characterisation for regeneration: Truro,* Truro (Cornwall County Council)

Kirkham, G, 2005a. *Boscastle, Cornwall. characterisation and recording in the aftermath of the August 2004 floods*, Truro (Historic Environment Service, Cornwall County Council)

Kirkham, G, 2005b. *Cornwall and Scilly Urban Survey. Historic characterisation for regeneration: Bodmin*, Truro (Cornwall County Council)

Langdon, Arthur G, 1896. *Old Cornish crosses*, Truro

Langdon, Arthur G, 1906. Early Christian monuments, *Victoria County History of Cornwall*, London vol **I**, 407-445

Langdon, Andrew G, 1992. *Stone crosses in north Cornwall,* Federation of Old Cornwall Societies (2nd edn 1996)

Langdon, Andrew G, 1994. *Stone crosses in mid Cornwall,* Federation of Old Cornwall Societies (2nd edn 2002)

Langdon, Andrew G, 1996. *Stone crosses in east Cornwall,* Federation of Old Cornwall Societies (2nd edn 2005)

Langdon, Andrew G, 1997. *Stone crosses in West Penwith,* Federation of Old Cornwall Societies

Langdon, Andrew G, 1999. *Stone crosses in west Cornwall,* Federation of Old Cornwall Societies

Langdon, Andrew G, 2004. *Illuminating our lantern crosses: Cornish distinctiveness during the fifteenth century,* unpublished MA dissertation, University of Exeter

Langdon, Andrew G, forthcoming. Works on Cornish crosses 1986-2011, *Cornish Archaeol*

Letters, S, 2006. *Online gazetteer of markets and fairs in England and Wales to 1516* <http://www.history.ac.uk/cmh/gaz/gazweb2.html>: [Cornwall: last updated 17 November 2006]

Liddiard, R, 2005. Macclesfield

Malham A, McDonnell, J G, Aylett J, and Higgs, E, 2002. Tin smelting slags from Crift Farm, Cornwall and the effect of changing technology on slag composition, *Historical Metallurgy*, **36,** 84-94

Mattingly, J, 1989. The medieval parish guilds of Cornwall, *Jnl Roy Inst Cornwall*, **X.3,** 290-329

Mattingly, J, 1991. The dating of bench-ends in Cornish churches, *Jnl Roy Inst Cornwall*, **NS II, I.1,** 58-72

Mattingly, J, 2000. Stories in the glass – reconstructing the St Neot pre-Reformation glazing scheme, *Jnl Roy Inst Cornwall*, **NS II, III. 3 and 4,** 9–55

Mattingly, J, Buckley, A, and Hall, J, 2001. A tin miner and a bal maiden – further research on the St Neot windows, *Jnl Roy Inst Cornwall*, **2001,** 96–100

Mattingly, J, 2003. Pre-Reformation saints' cults in Cornwall – with particular reference to the St Neot windows, in J Cartwright, ed, *Celtic hagiography and Saints' Lives*, Cardiff, 249-70

Mattingly, J, 2005a. *Looking at Cornish churches*, Redruth (Tor Mark Press)

Mattingly, J, 2005b. Going a-riding; Cornwall's late-medieval guilds revisited, *Jnl Roy Inst Cornwall*, **2005,** 78-103

Mattingly, J, 2009. *Cornwall and the coast: Mousehole and Newlyn,* Chichester

Mayer, P, 1990. Calstock and Bere Alston silver-lead mines in the first quarter of the fourteenth century, *Cornish Archaeol*, **29,** 79-95

McDonnell, J G, 1993. Further work at Crift Farm, *Jnl Trevithick Soc*, **20,** 48-50

McDonnell J G, Hoaen, A, and Loney, H, 1995. The Crift Farm project - second interim Report, *Jnl Trevithick Soc,* **22,** 50-57

Miles, T J, 1976. Late medieval potters' waste from Lostwithiel, *Cornish Archaeol*, **15,** 115-7

Miles, T J, 1979. Late medieval potters' waste from Lostwithiel, *Cornish Archaeol*, **18,** 103-4

Mould, Q, 2006. The metal finds, in Saunders 2006, 301-340

Mould, Q, and Vince, A, 2006. Introduction to the finds, in Saunders 2006, 261-268

National Trust, 2002. *Wheal Hermon timber pipe column,* Bodmin (The National Trust)

Newell, K, 2004. *Cornwall and Scilly Urban Survey. Historic characterisation for regeneration: Redruth,* Truro (Cornwall County Council)

Newell, K, 2005a. *Cornwall and Scilly Urban Survey. Historic characterisation for regeneration: St Ives,* Truro (Cornwall County Council)

Newell, K, 2005b. *Cornwall and Scilly Urban Survey. Historic characterisation for regeneration: Penryn,* Truro (Cornwall County Council)

Olson, L, 1994. Lammana, West Looe; C K Croft Andrew's 1935 and 1936 excavations of the chapel and Monk's House, *Cornish Archaeol*, **33,** 96-129

Olson, L, and Preston-Jones, A, 1998-9. An ancient cathedral of Cornwall? Excavated remains east of St Germans Church, *Cornish Archaeol*, **37-8,** 153-69

O'Mahoney, C, 1989a. The medieval pottery from Tintagel Castle, *Inst Cornish Studies Spec Rep*, **8,** 67-68

O'Mahoney, C, 1989b. The pottery: Bunnings Park, in Austin *et al* 1989, 133-147

O'Mahoney, C, 1994a. The pottery from Lammana: the mainland chapel and Monks House, in Olson 1994, 115-125

O'Mahoney, C, 1994b. The pottery from Old Lanyon, in Beresford 1994, 152-166

Orme, N, 2007. *Cornwall and the Cross: Christianity 500-1560,* Chichester

Orme, N, 2010. *A history of the county of Cornwall Vol 2, religious history to 1560*, Woodbridge

Padel, OJ, 1985. *Cornish Place-Name Elements,* Nottingham, English Place-Name Society, Vol LVI/LVII

Padel, OJ, 1988. Tintagel in the twelfth and thirteenth centuries, *Cornish Studies*, **16,** 61-66

Pitman, S, 1990. *Kerrybullock. The evolution of the royal deer park in Stoke Climsland*, Stoke Climsland Parish Archive

Pool, P A S, 1975. 'The ancient and present state of St Michael's Mount, 1762' by William Borlase, *Cornish Studies*, **3,** 29-47

Preston-Jones, A, 1988. *Kilkhampton Castle – archaeology, history and management,* Truro (Cornwall Archaeological Unit)

Preston-Jones, A, and Langdon, A, 1997. St Buryan crosses, *Cornish Archaeol*, **36,** 107-28

Preston-Jones, A, and Langdon, A, 2003. *St Michael's Mount, Cornwall: conservation and recording of lantern crosses,* Truro (Historic Environment Service, Cornwall County Council)

Preston-Jones, A, and Rose, P, 1986. Medieval Cornwall, *Cornish Archaeol*, **25,** 135-85

Preston-Jones, A, and Rose, P, 1992. Week St Mary, town and castle, *Cornish Archaeol*, **31,** 143-53

Reynolds, A, 1999. *Kilkhampton Castle Farm - an archaeological and historical assessment*, Truro (Cornwall Archaeological Unit)

Reynolds, A, 2006. *Repairs to Tintagel Castle, Cornwall, 1998/9, archaeological recording,* Truro (Historic Environment Service, Cornwall County Council)

DISCOVERY AND RESEARCH

Riddler, I, 2006. Stone, bone, antler and ivory finds, in Saunders 2006, 357-380

Rippon, S, Claughton, P and Smart, C, 2009. *Mining in a medieval landscape: the royal silver mines of the Tamar Valley*, Exeter, University of Exeter Press

Rodwell, W, 1993. Lanlivery Curch, its archaeology and architectural history, *Cornish Archaeol*, **32**, 76-111

Rose, P, 1992. Bossiney Castle, *Cornish Archaeol*, **31**, 138-142

Rose, P, 1994. The medieval garden at Tintagel Castle, *Cornish Archaeol*, **33**, 170-182

Rose, P, and Herring, P, 1990. *Bodmin Moor, Cornwall: an evaluation for the Monuments Protection Programme*, Truro (Cornwall Archaeological Unit)

Rosevear, M, 1994. *The Stonaford rescue project - archive report of the rescue excavation and standing building recording conducted at Stonaford, North Hill*, Truro (Cornwall Archaeological Unit)

Russell, S, 2002. *Cornwall and Scilly Urban Survey. Historic characterisation for regeneration: Helston*, Truro (Cornwall County Council)

Saunders, A, 2006. *Excavations at Launceston Castle, Cornwall*, Society for Medieval Archaeology Monograph, **24**, Leeds

Schofield, J, 1999. *An architectural history of Godolphin House*, Godolphin (John Schofield)

Schofield, J, forthcoming. The appearances of Godolphin, in D Dawson, ed

Sharpe, A, 1989. *Minions: an archaeological survey of the Caradon mining district*, Truro (Cornwall County Council; 2 vols)

Sharpe, A, 2008. Mining, in Herring *et al* 2008, 29-82

Sheppard P, 1980. *The historic towns of Cornwall: an archaeological survey*, Truro (Cornwall Committee for Rescue Archaeology)

Slater, T R, 1999. Medieval town plans, in R Kain and W Ravenhill, eds, *Historic atlas of south-west England*, Exeter, 408-12

Slater, T R, 2005. Planning English medieval street towns: the Hertfordshire evidence, *Landscape History*, **26**, 19-36

Soulsby, I N, 1976. Richard Fitz Turold, Lord of Penhallam, Cornwall, *Med Arch*, **20**, 146–48

Stead, P, 1998-9. Investigations at Nos 4-6 Pydar Street, Truro, *Cornish Archaeol*, **37-8**, 178-85

Sturgess, J, 2010. *St Michael's Mount watch tower and gateway complex - archaeological building survey and evaluation*, Truro (Historic Environment Projects, Cornwall Council)

Tangye, M, 1981. *Carn Brea, a brief history and guide*, Redruth

Thomas, N, 1992. *An archaeological assessment of the Kilkhampton area*, Truro (Cornwall Archaeological Unit)

Thomas, N, 1993a. *A brief historical and archaeological survey of St Michael's Chapel, Rame Head*, Truro (Cornwall Archaeological Unit)

Thomas, N, 1993b. *The chapel of Thomas a Becket, Bodmin, Cornwall*, Truro (Cornwall Archaeological Unit)

Thomas, N, 1994. *Restormel Castle: auger tests on inner ditch*, Truro (Cornwall Archaeological Unit)

Thomas, N, 1996a. Mennabroom, St Neot - an archaeological investigation, Truro (Cornwall Archaeological Unit)

Thomas, N, 1996b. *Restormel Castle, an archaeological survey*, Truro (Cornwall Archaeological Unit)

Thomas, N, and Berry, E, 1994. *An archaeological investigation of the keep buildings at Launceston Castle, Cornwall*, Truro (Cornwall Archaeological Unit)

Thomas, N, and Buck, C, 1993. *An historical and archaeological investigation of Restormel Castle, Cornwall - an interim study*, Truro (Cornwall Archaeological Unit)

Thomas, N, and Rosevear, M, 1994. *Restormel Castle: interpretation of geophysical survey results*, Truro (Cornwall Archaeological Unit)

Thorpe, C, 2001. *Tregays Farm, near Lostwithiel, Cornwall - archaeological watching brief*, Truro (Historic Environment Service, Cornwall County Council)

Travers, A, 1995. *Restormel Castle, Cornwall - a report on primary sources*, Truro (Cornwall Archaeological Unit)

Tyson, C, 2006. The glass, in Saunders 2006, 341-356

Unwin, A, 1977. The water mills of St Keverne, *Jnl Roy Inst Cornwall*, **NS VII.4**, 292-301

Val Baker, M, 2003. *Atlantic Coast and Valleys Project, Cornwall - historic landscape characterisation, habitat, species and landscape assessments*, Truro (Historic Environment Service, Cornwall County Council)

Wessex Archaeology, 2009. *Looe, Cornwall: archaeological evaluation and assessment of results*, Salisbury (Wessex Archaeology)

Wood, P D, 1963. Open field strips, Forrabury Common, near Boscastle, *Cornish Archaeol*, **2**, 29-33

Wright, M, 2010. *A geophysical survey of East Leigh Berrys*, unpublished TS held at Cornwall Council Historic Environment

Young, A, 2006. The National Mapping Programme in Cornwall, *Cornish Archaeol*, **45**, 109-116

Cornish Archaeology 50, 2011, 315–350

Post-medieval Cornwall

PETER HERRING, GRAEME KIRKHAM, NICHOLAS JOHNSON,
ADAM SHARPE, NICK CAHILL, ERIC BERRY and NIGEL THOMAS

Introduction

Peter Herring

This period of often rapid change, involving radical revisions of Cornwall's already complex societies, economies, ideologies and landscape, has left highly varied and densely detailed remains: the material culture of us and of our unevenly documented recent ancestors, or predecessors. Archaeology, as the study of people through their physical remains, uses that wealth of material to better understand the post-medieval, modern and contemporary Cornish. As people have always responded to earlier arrangements, even in modern times, the present-day landscape contains the variably legible patterns, stories and meanings inherited from medieval and prehistoric times that have featured in earlier sections.

Given its wide interest and its contribution to understanding the rate, direction and effects of change, and its drivers or causes, it is perhaps surprising that more have not been actively involved with Cornwall's current and recent archaeology. We should expect and encourage greater engagement with post-medieval and modern archaeology in the next quarter century.

Post-medieval and modern archaeology do not just provide illustrative support for history prepared from the more traditionally relied upon documents, images and testimonies. It also provides material from which alternative and critical narratives can be composed; ones that may either challenge or qualify accounts derived from sources that are often more partial (especially so for buildings and industrial and agricultural history) and officially controlled (most obviously in military history). For example, interpretation of material remains, patterns and associations may critically inform discussions of local and Cornish identity (Herring forthcoming). The study of remains and patterns, such as those of gardens, fields and routeways, may also inspire historical research.

Again, this section is selective, drawing attention to areas where archaeological work has made the greatest impact on understanding recent Cornwall. All papers emphasise how its affairs (industrial, agricultural, commercial, administrative, military, social) were increasingly influenced by regional, national and international trends and pressures, politics, economies and ideologies. Most also show how the trend established in the later medieval period towards individualism (and enclosure, exclusion and separation) at the expense of the communal (the open and mutual) had also continued. It seems though that it was not until the mid nineteenth century that an essentially medieval mentality, supported by custom, folklore and various forms of popular culture was largely diminished. The nonconformist church played a crucial role in inculcating a modern world-view among those working within an already mature and heavily capitalised industrial economy and society (Lake *et al* 2001, 2-3; Deacon 2009).

Fig 1. Documentation for this nineteenth-century track separating two holdings on Tolborough Tor is minimal, restricted to OS mapping. However, its material remains reveal the variability of custom through the decisions of North Tolborough farm to use drystone walling to the east (left) and Tober Barton to prefer Cornish hedging to the west. Then twentieth-century maintenance provides evidence for unevenness of individual fortune in a marginal landscape transformed by the Rodd family's early Victorian flurry of determined improvement. (The lane makes for Bolventor, 'Bold Venture', the village planted around previously lonely Jamaica Inn.) Archaeologists inform recreation of the meanings crowding in on a person moving through the modern landscape, driving, riding or walking down that roughly cobbled way.

The selections are intended to encourage deepenings, critiques and the making of connections, and the study of other more neglected aspects of our world.

Mining
Adam Sharpe

Work in the last 25 years has confirmed that the transition between medieval and post-medieval industry in Cornwall was not gradual. The former was characterised by the vernacular, the small-scale, a part-time workforce, relatively low levels of capitalisation, and technologies based on wood, water and handcrafted machine components; the latter depended on a dedicated, full-time workforce with specialised roles living in new kinds of settlements, dependent for food and other goods on not only the local population but on national (and international) producers, and on complex technologies used on a daily basis, but manufactured perhaps hundreds of miles away. It encapsulated the birth of the modern age.

However, if at first this equipment, and the expertise to produce and improve it, had to be sourced from elsewhere in Britain, Cornish-based miners, engineers and entrepreneurs such as Davey, Trevithick, Hornblower and Murdoch soon became part of an indigenous industry, especially involved in designing steam pumping engines, which quickly made Cornwall a centre of innovation during Britain's industrial revolution. Specialised towns such as Camborne and Redruth (Cahill and CAU 2002b, 2002e, 2002i, 2002j) or Hayle/Copperhouse developed as centres of technological excellence, their emerging status on the world stage (Smith 1999, Cahill and CAU 2000) underpinned by the growing mercantile and banking power of towns like Penzance and Truro (Pool 1974; Kirkham 2003b).

Former dependence on water power had in many cases resulted in separation between the productive areas of mines, perforce located over the lodes, and their dressing floors, sited near watercourses (Gerrard 1985; Stanier 1987; Sharpe 2008a). As mines became larger and production rose, these inherent inefficiencies could become economically significant. Adoption of steam as the prime mover on mines during the later eighteenth century and especially in the nineteenth (Sharpe *et al* 1991) allowed mines to bring together all operations on a single site. However, reliance on an essential imported raw material – coal – demanded an entirely new and coordinated approach to exploitation of Cornwall's most valuable raw materials – copper and tin. Those whose fortunes were invested in Cornish mines increasingly diversified into construction of workers' housing and the industrial ports and railways needed to get their outputs to market and to import the vital coal and timber consumed in vast amounts during their operation. Rewards for supplying the capital needed to keep all at work (or indeed from simply receiving the mineral dues) could be substantial, even huge, as can be seen in those of Cornwall's great houses, parks and gardens built

Fig 2. Hayle was Cornwall's pre-eminent industrial port. From early beginnings during the eighteenth century as a small-scale coal-importing point on the north Cornwall coast, Hayle rapidly evolved into a specialised industrial town and port, siting a copper smelter at Ventonleague (Copperhouse). The establishment of John Harvey's iron works at Foundry (Penpol) and its rival operated by Sandys, Carne and Vivian at Copperhouse at the end of the eighteenth century spurred large scale urban development and substantial civil engineering works to create extensive wharves and quays along the shores of the estuary, together with the massive tidal holding ponds used to flush sand from the routes out to the harbour entrance. In 1837, Hayle became connected to the mines around Camborne-Redruth by the Hayle Railway allowing the transport of massive quantities of copper ore from the mines of the district to Hayle for export to the South Wales smelters, and for the dispersal of return cargoes of coal and timber. Harvey's iron works developed into Cornwall's principal constructor and exporter of beam engines, though also produced a wide range of mine equipment as well as diversifying into ship building. Industrial activity at Hayle continued long after the decline of Cornwall's mining industry, coal continuing to be imported here until 1977. (Historic Environment, Cornwall Council, F78/040)

Fig 3. This recent view looking west from Robinson's Shaft at the former South Wheal Crofty epitomises many of the changes which have taken place within the Cornish mining industry over the past century. When Robinson's Shaft was being developed in the early nineteenth century on a mine which had been worked for two centuries, beam engines were still the means by which the tens of thousands of kilometres of underground workings were kept dry and workable. This view shows the pumping engine house with its boiler houses clustered around it, together with those for the former steam winding engine and the compressor house. The twentieth-century mine seen in the background, focussed on New Cook's Shaft, relied on electric power for pumping, winding and ore dressing operations. Robinson's engine finally stopped work in 1955 as South Crofty expanded and modernised. However, the international tin crash of October 1985 made mining here increasingly uneconomic. When South Crofty closed in 1999 it had been the last working tin mine in Cornwall. The Robinson's Shaft site is now at the centre of the Heartlands development, whilst South Crofty, under new management, is proposed for a re-opening. (Photograph: Adam Sharpe, Historic Environment, Cornwall Council)

with mining wealth (Pett 1998; Gamble *et al* 2005). All these developments radically altered substantial parts of Cornwall – its ports and harbours, transport infrastructure, towns and villages (including new industrial settlements) and its downland, huge swathes of which were enclosed to provide miners' smallholdings or new farms to feed its burgeoning population (Sharpe 2008c).

However, this industrial revolution coincided with a significant expansion of the British Empire. As previously untouched mining areas were discovered in every continent, the particular skills of Cornish miners and engineers became increasingly in demand. Drawn abroad, these specialists soon established thriving new mining fields whose production quickly outstripped the home industry and inexorably drove down prices on the international market (Todd 1997; Payton 2005). By the 1860s it had become almost wholly uneconomic to mine copper in Cornwall and

within two decades local tin production was also under threat. The mining migrants were soon being followed by a second wave of men and their families who saw no future in Cornwall (Schwartz 2008); its technologies were increasingly seen as old fashioned and inefficient. Most foundries, engineering works, candle and boot factories and other undertakings that had relied on Cornish mining success folded, bereft of their former markets. By the century's end Cornish mining was virtually extinct and a third of the population had emigrated.

When efforts were made to revive Cornwall's mining industry early in the twentieth century it was to American or European technology to which new promoters turned to ensure success. When Geevor was reopened in 1907 by men returning from South Africa, new ways of working were put in place that diverged radically from how Cornish mining had operated for centuries. Shafts were vertical,

Fig 4. Geevor tin mill. Advances in mining technology developed and employed in Cornwall during the late eighteenth century and during much of the nineteenth century had placed the region at the forefront of the hard rock mining industry, but in the rapidly-globalising, highly competitive market at the beginning of the twentieth century, Cornish miners increasingly had to turn to new, increasingly sophisticated

technologies to retain their economic efficiency. As a result, the Cornish stamps and relatively simple buddles and frames which had been found on tin dressing floors for well over a century had to be replaced with vanners, classifiers, shaking tables and flotation cells, resulting in highly complex, scientifically-designed multi-stream dressing floors such as that at Geevor. (Photograph: Adam Sharpe, Historic Environment, Cornwall Council)

buildings concrete, and electrical rather than steam power was used for most purposes. Compressed air piped underground powered drills and other machines (Sharpe 1993).

Across Cornwall and west Devon are a number of key sites, the study of whose surface remains can still be used to chart the stages in this gradual process of technological breakthrough, world ascendency, decline, attempted adaptation and eventual final closure. These include The Gwennap Consolidated Mines (Sharpe 2009), Botallack (Sharpe 2008b), Levant (Sharpe 1993), the Caradon Mines (Sharpe 1989a), South Crofty (Sharpe 1999, 2003, 2007), Wheal Coates (Sharpe 1986), Devon Great Consols (Buck 2002), Geevor (Sharpe 1993), Perran Foundry (Smith 1991), Kennall Vale gunpowder works (Smith 1986) and the port of Hayle (Smith 1999, Cahill and CAU 2000, Gillard and Newell 2005).

Many of these sites, utilitarian, commonplace, and built for temporary use, are relatively poorly documented. Change was frequent and the sites' detail was of little interest to those documenting the period. The archaeological record almost always provides evidence for dynamic landscape and rapid change. These are sites only understood when considering the economic and social context in which they were created, evolved, and were eventually abandoned.

Its Industrial Revolution might have been short-lived and localised, but it radically changed the trajectory of Cornwall's history and contributed very substantially to the landscape of the Cornwall we now occupy or enjoy.

Other extractive industry
Peter Herring

As for metal mining, numerous detailed studies of the remains of other extractive industries – granite, slate, china clay and china-stone – show how all developed rapidly in the nineteenth and twentieth centuries from earlier small-scale, often part-time and generally superficial workings (e.g. Herring and Thomas 1990; Herring 2008a; Sharpe 1990c; Herring and Smith 1991; Smith 1992; 2008a, b). Again, capitalisation and exploitation of rapidly

DISCOVERY AND RESEARCH

Fig 5. The northern of Carbilly Tor's four well-preserved late nineteenth and twentieth-century granite dimension stone quarries. It sent building and monument stone to London and Birmingham until the 1960s. Most material was unsuitable and now forms the three long finger dumps; those to the left are from a neighbouring quarry. A hand crane's column still stands on its built stack, now an island in the flooded main pit. (Photograph: Peter Herring)

growing local, national and international markets spurred rapid technological innovation. Plug-and-feather splitting of granite, invented or introduced from around 1800, enabled development in all Cornwall's granite areas of an industry supplying precisely shaped dimension stone for architect-designed lighthouses, bridges, harbours and public buildings (Stanier 1985a; 1985b; 1985c; 1986a; 1986b; 1986c; 1992; 1999). The industry still survives in De Lank's twisting gorge (Herring 2008a).

Fig 6. Ramped dumps, mica lagoons, wide haul-roads, re-seeded slopes and turquoise flooded pits: the sublime industrial landscape at Dubbers, in the heart of the St Austell china-clay area. (Photograph: Peter Herring)

Delabole, the greatest roofing slate quarry, also continues (Lorigan 2007; Cahill Partnership and CAU 2002g), while all others, save a few of its nearest satellites, have closed, leaving gloriously dramatic abandoned sites, notably those cut into north Cornwall's sheer slate cliffs (Sharpe 1990c; Sturgess 2000; 2004a; Craze *et al* 2006). Outlying china-clay works, those on Bodmin Moor (Smith 2008b) or in the far west (Herring 1995; Taylor 2002), or those beyond the St Austell clay country's heart, are now all closed. Remarkable transformations continue to be wrought in the core area, maintaining a culture as peculiar as that of mining and a community as loyal to its place as any in Cornwall (Herring and Smith 1991; Smith 1992; 2008a; Turner 2000).

Transport and communications
Adam Sharpe

As long as the greater part of Cornwall's economy relied on small-scale, local production and on exchange and consumption of agricultural

goods, there was no reason why essentially local arrangements of lanes and tracks connected to a few major highways, of which the sea was one, should not continue unchanged. However, by the mid eighteenth century, development of large-scale copper mining in several parts of Cornwall put this network under increasing strain. We know from late eighteenth-century accounts that many thousands of mules were employed in transporting copper ore from the Gwennap and Camborne-Redruth mines to new north coast harbours for shipment to South Wales for smelting and then moving return cargoes of coal to pumping engines, and timber to support ever-deepening mine workings (Sharpe and Smith 1989).

A purpose-built engineered plateway (an early form of railway) linking the Scorrier, Chacewater and Gwennap mines to Portreath therefore added a new element to Cornwall's transport network in 1819 (*ibid*). All major early modern Cornish transport developments followed a similar pattern – ports and harbours funded by mining entrepreneurs

Fig 7. The Royal Albert Bridge, designed by Isambard Kingdom Brunel, was built between 1853 and 1859 to provide a link between the Cornwall Railway and the South Devon Railway. The bridge is 1100 feet long and was designed so that its central spans would be 100 feet above the Tamar to allow Royal Navy shipping to pass beneath the bridge. The opening of the bridge, finally connecting Cornwall to the British main line rail network, had significant impacts on the economy of the county, allowing the rapid movement of products and people in both directions. In Cornwall, the dairying and soft fruit industries were clear beneficiaries, farmers gaining access to national markets for their products, but there were also unexpected consequences, such as the development of tourism, the decline in local manufacturing of products such as shoes and clothing, the spread of new ideas and an erosion of Cornish cultural distinctiveness.
(*Photograph: Charles Winpenny www.cornwallcam.co.uk, copyright reserved*)

DISCOVERY AND RESEARCH

Fig 8. This milestone on a road junction outside St Just, like many others around the County, reflects the dramatic change in the mobility of people, products and raw materials which was driven by the growth of industrial activity in Cornwall. Before the early nineteenth century, the poorly-surfaced roads and tracks which made up the surface transport network in West Penwith constrained local mines' abilities to import the massive quantities of coal needed to fuel their pumping, winding and stamping engines or to export their tin and copper ore for smelting. Like the tramways and railways built elsewhere, these road improvements dramatically enhanced economic efficiency, allowing local mines to flourish. (Photograph: Adam Sharpe)

were linked by tramways or railways (and in a few cases, canals) to enable development of, and subsequently to service, inland mines and other industrial undertakings including engineering works, quarries and local manufactories, stimulating a population boom which transformed the rural

landscape. These initiatives included the Redruth and Chasewater Railway (1826), East Cornwall Mineral Railway (1872), Hayle Railway (1837), Bodmin and Wadebridge Railway (1834), Cornwall Minerals Railway (1873), Pentewan Railway (1829) and Liskeard and Caradon Railway (1840), supplementing the Liskeard-Looe Canal. Elements of these transport systems have been surveyed (Smith 1988; Sharpe 1989a; Sharpe and Smith 1989). These remained independent and unconnected undertakings for most of the nineteenth century, and it was not until 1859 when Brunel's Royal Albert Bridge across the Tamar linked the Cornwall Railway to the South Devon Railway that Cornwall finally became connected overland via a trunk line to the rest of Britain (Stengelhofen 1988).

The consequences for Cornwall were considerable, now that journey times between it and centres of population and manufacture were reduced to hours rather than days or weeks. Market gardens and orchards (on sheltered southern slopes and in the Tamar and Fowey Valleys) and dairies were now economically viable (Herring 2008b; Herring and Giles 2008). However, while Cornwall gained access to wider markets, its local industries were also subjected to greater competition. As railways increasingly carried passengers as well as goods, new ideas must also have become introduced to a relatively remote part of Britain.

While requirements of efficiency and effectiveness impelled improvement in industrial transportation, increased commerce throughout Cornwall also stimulated a rather slower-paced development of more rural networks. Surveys show how most fords were replaced or supplemented with bridges, even on byways, in the eighteenth and nineteenth centuries (Thomas 1995; 1998a; Oxford Archaeology 2003), while the King's or Western Road (now the A30) and most (but not all) the lesser highways were re-engineered, their lines smoothened, through the investments raised by turnpike trusts (Taylor 2001). At least 54 toll houses still stand sentinel and 331 milestones measure out for strangers distances to local market towns and for locals the distance to London (www.turnpikes.org.uk/TurnpikesinCornwall). Estuary surveys have confirmed how important the long tidal creeks were for rural traffic; most adjacent farms have early (probably later medieval) lanes hollowed by use leading to tiny stone-faced quays; beside some moulder the boats abandoned when tarmac and vans

Fig 9. Charlestown harbour. In 1790, the small fishing haven at West Polmear began to be developed by Charles Rasheigh into a port capable of exporting the copper produced by local mines for smelting in South Wales, the first wet dock gates being set up in 1799. As at other mineral ports developed in Cornwall about this time, a specialised new town developed, the original population of 9 rising to over 3000 by the end of the nineteenth century. With the demise of the local copper mines, Charlestown developed into a specialised china clay exporting port, though always overshadowed by the neighbouring port of Par, developed by Joseph Treffry between 1829 and 1840 and still in use today. (Photograph: Adam Sharpe)

made them redundant (Ratcliffe 1997; Parkes 2000; Reynolds 2000; Gossip 2001).

Management plans have been prepared for Cornwall's two main canals. Bude Canal, first proposed in the 1770s and built in stages from the late 1810s, reached as far south as Druxton, outside Launceston. It transported sea sand to inland farms and South Welsh coal to domestic fires (Dyer and Collings 2000; Atkins 2004). The Liskeard and Looe Union Canal opened in 1828, again initially to carry sea sand and lime for improving farmland, and ran the six miles inland to Moorswater (British Waterways 1999). Both canals declined in the late nineteenth century, largely as railways took their business.

Most medieval harbours were enhanced to accommodate larger vessels and increased

volumes of traffic: piers, quays and wharves were extended, heightened and resurfaced, as at St Michael's Mount and Penzance (Herring 1993; Cahill 2009), while some coves were provided with wholly new stone piers (e.g. Mullion; Ruddle and Thomas 2005) or docks (e.g. Charlestown; Smith *et al* 1998). Falmouth and Flushing benefited hugely as the base for the post office's Packet Service from 1688 to 1850, being the gateway for the country's overseas mail. Notorious tragedies provoked improvements in coastal safety in the form of coastguard lookouts, lighthouses, daymarks, rocket stations and the like.

Cornwall's ports were also increasingly serving another growing market as huge numbers of emigrants from failing mining districts took ship to search for better opportunities on every

DISCOVERY AND RESEARCH

continent across the World. Some returned wearing sombreros, talking of far-flung places, but many of those who used the new railways and ports to leave their parishes for the first time to travel to the carnage of the Great War did not.

By the late nineteenth century, newly-accessible Cornwall was increasingly promoted as a tourist destination (e.g. Mattingly 2009), initially via railway, but from the early twentieth century also by improved roads, which were of considerable local interest (Smith 2008c). People went to look when tarmac was first laid along the A30 across Goss Moor in the 1920s (Len Guest, pers comm to John Smith). Villages on new roads soon boasted garages and filling stations, cafes and shops to cater to passing trade. In places like Indian Queens, newly established businesses faced the highway, indicating the road's importance.

In the late nineteenth and twentieth centuries Cornwall played a prominent role in the history of world telecommunications. First, Porthcurno was used by the Cable and Wireless Company from 1870 as a communications centre receiving cable links with countries across the world. Then on 23 January 1901 Marconi received the first wireless transmission from beyond the horizon, at the Lizard Wireless Station. Amazingly his two wooden huts have survived and have been conserved by the National Trust (Johns 1998f).

Of a similar age to the Cornwall Archaeological Society is the first of the antennae at the Goonhilly Satellite Earth Station, built in 1960-1962, receiving the first live television transmission from the United States on 11 July 1962, and now a Grade II listed structure (Sturgess 2004b).

Change continues: Cornwall is now connected to the world by road, rail, sea, air and broadband, the last carried along the fibre-optic cables running up Porthcurno beach, replacing telegraph cables that formerly linked up the Empire. Laptops come from China; cut flowers from Kenya. Changes in transport and communications have played key roles in the evolution of Cornish identity and landscape. What is unclear is how both will change during the next 50 years.

Post-medieval towns
Graeme Kirkham and Nick Cahill

By 1986, other than Sheppard's (1980) review, a few local histories and isolated architectural studies (e.g. Truro Buildings Research Group 1981), relatively little archaeological work had been carried out on Cornish towns. That situation changed significantly in the last two decades as the Cornwall and Scilly Urban Survey, Cornwall Industrial Settlements Initiative and other characterisations investigated more than 30 towns and proto-towns (see references).

Fig 10. Two mid-sixteenth-century timber-framed merchant's houses at 11-13 High Street, Launceston, rare survivals of early post-medieval urban buildings. (Photograph: Graeme Kirkham)

Fig 11. Warmington House, in Camelford market place, has been closely tied to Camelford's history of parliamentary patronage: it was built in the late seventeenth century as Sir James Smith's town house, sold to George Warmington in 1704 and then to Lord Falmouth in 1722, before being bought by the Earl of Darlington in the early nineteenth century (Herring and Newell 2005). (Photograph: Historic Environment, Cornwall Council)

More local histories have been published and most Conservation Areas now have appraisals reviewing historic buildings and architectural styles. Some buildings have been closely recorded and analysed, and several post-medieval urban sites excavated (below). Two important Cornish architects, Trevail and Hicks, have been studied (Perry and Harradence 2008; Perry and Schwartz 2001).

The impression that Cornwall's post-medieval towns were more diverse than its medieval ones partly reflects our ignorance of the subtle distinctions which probably existed between medieval towns, but there certainly appears to have been a widening in towns' functional range and a tendency towards dominance by certain functions. While Camborne, Hayle and St Just were centres of industry, Redruth and Liskeard served adjacent industrial areas. Other towns were primarily administrative centres (Launceston, Bodmin, Truro), ports (Falmouth, Penryn), fishing harbours (Mevagissey, Newlyn, St Ives, Polperro) and resorts (Newquay, Bude), although most maintained several functions the relative importance of which shifted over time. Markets were key elements of almost all, but Penzance notably combined many roles: agricultural market, servicing industry; port, communications hub, genteel residential centre and resort (Cahill 2003).

Some specialisations affected surviving urban morphology and character. Bodmin rapidly gained various major institutional buildings – county asylum, enlarged county gaol, military barracks, Shire Hall and Judges' Lodgings – together with enhanced turnpike and then railway links after supplanting Launceston as *de facto* county town in the early nineteenth century (McLaren 1999; Kirkham 2005b). The later nineteenth-century shift of county administration (following the creation of Cornwall County Council) to Truro, coinciding with acquisition of diocesan and city status and establishment as Cornwall's primary commercial and retail centre, was similarly accompanied by new building there, including the cathedral and impressive new bank and shop premises (Kirkham 2003b). (These changes of county town, which in the medieval period had included Lostwithiel as well as Launceston, are distinctive elements of Cornwall's urban history.)

Prominently positioned clusters of substantial eighteenth and early nineteenth-century houses in towns like Camelford, Grampound and Lostwithiel can be linked to functions as pocket boroughs (Herring and Newell 2005; Berry *et al* 2008); similarly superior houses in Launceston reflect its eighteenth-century role as assize town (Herring and Gillard 2005). Penzance's 1843 promenade attests to its reputation for health and leisure well before railway tourism (Cahill 2003).

Diversity is particularly apparent in post-medieval new towns. Falmouth's sheltered position in Carrick Roads, adjacent to northern Europe's long-distance maritime trading routes, prompted its seventeenth-century rise from a landing place with inns and fishermen's cabins to the most important port, busiest commercial centre and largest town in Cornwall (Berry 1998a; Kirkham 2005c). Torpoint developed with deliberate planning from a mid eighteenth-century ferry landing with a few industrial facilities to an early

DISCOVERY AND RESEARCH

Fig 12. High-quality granite paving on the Terrace, Market Jew Street, Penzance, a distinctive example of the improvements in the urban public realm which many Cornish towns experienced from the later eighteenth century.
(Photograph: Graeme Kirkham)

Victorian genteel satellite to Dock (now Devonport) across the Hamoaze (Herring 2005). Hugh Town, the seventeenth-century garrison settlement on St Mary's, Scilly, grew in the nineteenth century to become the principal maritime trading centre and ship-building town on the archipelago (Kirkham 2003a). And Newquay, once a small fishing settlement, became a mineral port and from the mid nineteenth century a purpose-built and railway-based pleasure resort (Newell 2003).

The rapid sixteenth and seventeenth century rise of mining also stimulated new towns. Some rural churchtowns, probably containing just church and a few farmsteads in the mid sixteenth century, grew rapidly, acquired markets and became urban. St Austell, near Polgooth's rich mines, already had 'great trade in corn, fish and tin . . . [and] a fair market house' when petitioning for a market charter in 1638 (Hammond 1897, 30n). St Just's markets also probably began in the seventeenth century and St Agnes and Camborne had markets in the eighteenth century's first decade (Buck and Berry 1996; Cahill and CAU 2002h; 2002a; 2002i; Newell 2004b). Hayle and adjacent Copperhouse grew from the early eighteenth century through involvement in local mining, copper smelting, heavy engineering

and by servicing a substantial part of western Cornwall as a port (Buck and Smith 1995; Cahill and CAU 2000; Gillard and Newell 2005).

Population estimates further emphasise the diversity of post-medieval Cornish towns (Barry 1999, table 53.1). Older urban centres away from mining areas – like Tregony, Grampound, Lostwithiel, Bodmin, Penryn and Saltash – roughly doubled in size between *c* 1660 and 1805. Industrial towns experienced much greater rises over the same time: Camborne sevenfold to around 2,400, Redruth tenfold to 3200, while smaller industrial centres also saw major growth. St Agnes and Mevagissey (fishing), both rose tenfold to around 1,000. Commercial centres grew rapidly too, Penzance and Truro fivefold from 1660 to around 4,000 and 4,750 respectively by 1805 and Falmouth nearly sevenfold to over 5,500.

Until well into the nineteenth century most older towns saw little physical expansion as population increases were largely accommodated within existing urban footprints by multiple occupancy of buildings and development of back lots or burgage plots accessed via opes and entries (Brayshay

Fig 13. The impressive Italianate façade of St Austell market house, built 1844. Such market houses were clear expressions of civic prosperity and pride but also served to place market functions under more direct municipal control and remove from the streets what was often a dirty and chaotic element. (Photograph: Historic Environment, Cornwall Council)

326

Fig 14. Three early to mid nineteenth-century urban buildings in Fore Street, St Columb Major, all slate-hung over timber framing, with a spectacular later nineteenth-century 'Jacobethan'-styled bank in brick and granite. The architect for the latter is not known but was clearly influenced by the eclectic styles and use of materials typical of other Cornish architects at this period, most obviously Sylvanus Trevail and James Hicks.
(Photograph: Graeme Kirkham)

1999; Kirkham 2003b; 2005b). The resulting dense occupation often persisted until later nineteenth and twentieth-century slum clearances.

There were exceptions. Upper Fore Street, Redruth, and West Street in Penryn were both post-medieval axial extensions to medieval 'street towns' (Newell 2004a; 2005b). Seventeenth-century Cross Street, Helston, appears to be completely separate from the medieval town, and Penzance's Queen Street developed during the seventeenth or early eighteenth century along a new south-western route into the town (Cahill 2003). The rapid seventeenth-century increase in Falmouth's population prompted a sequence of planned extensions (Kirkham 2005c).

Within most older towns the medieval topography and hierarchy of spaces persisted largely unchanged. Again there were exceptions. Truro's original 'street', Pydar Street, was supplanted by Boscawen Street; the market house, coinage hall and homes of leading merchants were located there by the mid seventeenth century (TBRG nd). Helston's focal market moved from the lower end of Coinagehall Street to its upper end (Russell 2002) and Liskeard's commercial centre moved uphill from medieval Market Street to a new axis on what is now the Parade during the eighteenth century (Gillard 2005a).

From the mid eighteenth-century civic improvement is evident in features such as public water supplies and street paving and in Truro (from the 1770s) and Helston (early nineteenth century?)

elaborately engineered leat systems helped keep streets clean (Watson 1992; Johns 2006). Markets were progressively removed from open streets to nearby off-street spaces, clearing away dirty and disorganised elements and reshaping primary urban spaces. Gilbert (1820, 688) observed that Redruth had been 'greatly improved…. when the market house, which greatly interrupted the thoroughfare,

VIVIAN BROTHERS,
THE EMPORIUM, CAMBORNE.

Fig 15. The new retail premises of Vivian Bros, Camborne, illustrated in an advertisement in the Royal Cornwall Gazette (21 September 1899).

DISCOVERY AND RESEARCH

PETER HERRING ET AL

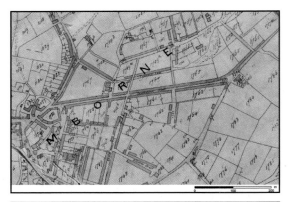

Fig 16. The rapid expansion of working-class housing in industrial settlements is demonstrated by comparison of part of the Camborne tithe map of 1840 with the same area shown on the 1st edition Ordnance Survey 25in: 1 mile map of 1879.

together with several other ancient buildings, were taken down, and the principal street, being laid open, is now very commodious'. In the same decade, the 1790s, Tregony and Truro market houses were similarly removed from positions in the middle of principal streets. Middle Row buildings, previously splitting Truro's Boscawen Street, were also demolished and new routes (New Bridge Street and Lemon Street) brought into the newly open central commercial area (Kirkham 2003b). In the early nineteenth century, Falmouth's market was moved from Market Strand to the Moor; a new space that soon became the town's primary civic focus (Kirkham 2005c).

Architecturally distinguished purpose-built market houses, highly visible symbols of civic pride, include those at Redruth (built 1826-

8), Penzance, Bodmin and Helston (all 1838), Launceston (*c* 1840), St Austell (1844) and Truro (1847). Universally, the primacy of core urban areas was reinforced by aggregating new prestige buildings, including churches (predominantly nonconformist), banks and public buildings. Retail provision also became increasingly ostentatious; in 1802 Robert Southey noted Truro's 'superb shops' windowed rather than shuttered (Chope 1967, 300-1) and Davies Gilbert (1838, III, 385) thought Redruth's 'main street is rendered splendid on both sides by continued lines of shops...'. Purpose-built late Victorian retail premises with large street-level and first-floor windows became highly visible urban elements: Redruth's included Trounson's grocery emporium (1870), West End Stores (1886) and the Tower House and Arcade (1885) (Cahill Partnership and CAU 2002b).

Fig 17. The proto-urban settlement of Pool shown on the 1st edition Ordnance Survey 25in: 1 mile map of 1880. During the nineteenth century the influence of mining prompted a number of small but fast-growing settlements to develop urban or proto-urban characteristics. These included high-density workers' housing and middle-class dwellings combined with a variety of services and institutions (shops, schools, chapels, inns, police stations, public open spaces) in relatively formal streetscapes. Early examples include Calstock, Chacewater and St Blazey and later Bugle, Gunnislake, Praze an Beeble, Portreath and Pool (Cahill Partnership and HES 2005; Gillard et al, 2004b Gillard et al, 2004c; Cahill Partnership and CAU 2002d; 2002e).

Fig 18. Morrab Terrace, Penzance, probably built in the 1840s. The stuccoed elegance of the 'Cornish Regency' style is a significant contributor to urban character in several other Cornish towns, including Truro, Falmouth and Liskeard, but parallels slightly earlier architectural developments in places such as Cheltenham and Brighton. (Photograph: Historic Environment, Cornwall Council)

Rapid population growth through the nineteenth century, particularly in mining towns and those servicing mining areas, stimulated substantial expansion and creation of the first predominantly residential areas. Much was working class housing, usually in grid-like patterns of rows and terraces. Camborne grew from about 2400 people in 1801 to a little under 4,400 by 1841 and more than doubled in size, with substantial areas of new housing (Newell 2004b) while St Just more than tripled in area during the 1830s (Cahill and CAU 2002h).

Planned middle-class suburban quarters are also distinctive elements of many Cornish towns. Most were speculative ventures by landowners of blocks of land adjacent to historic urban cores. Lemon Street in Truro, Dunstanville Terrace in Falmouth and Tregenna Place and Tregenna Hill in St Ives all date from around 1800 (Kirkham 2003b; 2005c; Newell 2005a) while the stuccoed Regency developments of Regent Square, Morrab Place and North Parade in Penzance and Ferris Town in Truro, date from the 1820-40s (Cahill 2003; TBRG 1985). Launceston's St Thomas Road was created in the 1830s: 'builders and others speculated in the erection of houses, and

the necessary conveniences sprang up numerously and with great rapidity' (Richard Robbins, 1856, quoted in Herring and Gillard 2005).

Cornwall's commercial and professional sector continued to prosper even after the 1860s mining decline and genteel suburban development, predominantly as detached or semi-detached villas and terraces of substantial houses, continued strongly in the second half of the century. The Clinton and Albany Road area of Redruth was created in the 1870s by landowner Lord Clinton and architect James Hicks (Perry and Schwartz 2001). Also later Victorian are Alexandra and Morrab Roads in Penzance, Dunheved Road in Launceston, the Narrowcliff area of Newquay and Hannafore, in West Looe, the latter created as a hotel and villa estate (Cahill 2003; Herring and Gillard 2005; Newell 2003; Cahill Partnership and CAU 2002f).

The themes and generalisations touched on above derive primarily from characterisation studies based on urban history, historic topography analysis and the evidence of surviving buildings and streetscapes. There have also been a few archaeological investigations on post-medieval sites, but most reveal frustratingly little information as later re-development was usually prefaced by razing previous structures, leaving little evidence of their form or artefacts associated with their use. In Truro the most significant finding concerns post-medieval reclamation along the Allen and Kenwyn rivers, mainly to create private quays for riverside properties (Kirkham 2003b; Exeter Archaeology 1997; Berry *et al* 1997; Gossip 2002; Jones and Reynolds 1997). Comparable evidence for river frontage reclamation has been excavated at Lostwithiel (Gossip forthcoming), inferred from historic maps in Penryn (Newell 2005b) and is evident from documentary sources in Falmouth (Tom Weller, pers comm).

Standing historic buildings may reveal considerable detail of Cornwall's post-medieval urban history, particularly in clarifying local architectural traditions and chronologies of development. Listed Building descriptions, now available online, offer a huge resource in this respect. Original form and subsequent changes to buildings are not always immediately evident, however, and analytical recording can produce surprises: at 20 Lower Bore Street, Bodmin, a superficially simple late eighteenth-century house was shown to have originated around 1600 as a 'town house of some importance', subsequently undergoing several rebuildings (Berry *et al* 2001). Programmes of building recording targeted on particular streets or quarters or on specific themes, successful elsewhere in Britain, could transform understanding of Cornish towns. One such theme could be the impressive surviving timber structures of Launceston and East Looe, probably mostly seventeenth century (Herring and Gillard 2005; Cahill Partnership and CAU 2002f). The survey in the late 1970s of many historic buildings in Penryn has yet to be fully published (Berry 1980).

Contributions of particular individuals to the distinctive characters of towns also merit attention. Truro's early nineteenth-century Cornish Regency was associated with architect Philip Sambell (TBRG 1985) and recent studies of Silvanus Trevail and James Hicks highlight their influence on several towns (Perry and Harradence 2008; Perry and Schwartz 2001). Others like Launceston's Otho Peter, Liskeard's Henry Rice and Penzance's John Mathews and William White of St Columb remain relatively obscure. Further documentary research modelled on that established in Truro by Veronica Chesher and June Palmer would aid these and all other urban studies considerably.

Finally, the studies cited here almost all treat individual towns in isolation; there is a need for a synthetic and comparative approach taking account of the range of urban histories in the county and region. Most themes touched on here are familiar in British and European post-medieval

Fig 20. The single-storeyed dwelling, at Higher Penquite, St Breward, probably of the eighteenth century, is a rare survival of a type that may be expected to have been much more common in early modern Cornwall (see Thomas 2008). (Photograph Nigel Thomas, for HE, Cornwall Council)

urban studies. The truly distinctive elements of Cornwall's historic towns can be better understood when reviewed in that broader perspective and with that understanding, they will be better valued, conserved, enhanced and celebrated.

Fig 19. Trerithick; a fine sixteenth to eighteenth-century manor house in Altarnun arranged around two courtyards, but whose principal element was still a typical, albeit very fine, cross-passage house (see Berry 2006b). (Photograph Eric Berry, for HE, Cornwall Council)

Fig 21. Entering the square forecourt garden reveals the full width of Godolphin's great north front, built around 1630 for Sir Francis Godolphin to a radically innovative design. The roof of the saloon above the pillared loggia was originally leaded and flat with the two central chimneys strong vertical lines behind the castellated parapet that effectively drew into the front's unity the two corner towers. These were inherited from sixteenth-century developments from the house's fifteenth-century core and were refaced with granite ashlar. (Photograph: Peter Herring)

Fig 22. Another remarkably advanced structure created in the west of Cornwall is the rebuilt Lady Chapel on St Michael's Mount, a 1740s neo-gothic confection for Sir John St Aubyn that was apparently built a few years before Horace Walpole's Strawberry Hill. (Photograph: Eric Berry, for HE, Cornwall Council)

Buildings

Eric Berry, Nigel Thomas and Peter Herring

There is great variety among post-medieval and modern Cornish buildings, ranging from Georgian hunts kennels (Thomas 1998b) and lighthouses (Nicholas 1996) to early modern terraced workers' housing (eg Cahill Partnership and CAU 2002b) and tanneries (Jones 2001) and later twentieth-century housing and telecommunications complexes (Johns 2000; Sturgess 2004b). Even where members of a class seem broadly similar, as in nonconformist chapels, we find historically significant subtypes and appreciate that each example usually has a particular and often complex history (Lake *et al* 2001). Consequently this brief section can only introduce broad patterns and inevitably omits major building types.

Cornish post-medieval farmhouses were mainly developed forms of the medieval through-passage dwellings although it seems longhouses were no longer constructed and surviving medieval longhouses no longer accommodated cattle, but had their lower rooms either converted to domestic use (Herring and Berry 1997) or removed (Thomas 1996a). New farmhouses normally had fully developed first floors and increased subdivision of space, to increase privacy and capacity, and the variety and definition of function. As the Cheshers demonstrated nearly half a century ago, this trend was followed by farmhouses of all sizes, from tiny Leaze (Chesher and Chesher 1968), through the yeomen homes like Treludick (Berry 2006a) and Cutmadoc (Sturgess 2004c) to substantial manor houses at Pendeen and Trerithick (Berry 2006b). Single-storeyed houses were probably also common until the mid nineteenth century (the late seventeenth-century Lanhydrock Atlas shows most houses thus; Holden *et al* 2010) and a few survive, often reused as outhouses. Most were the cottage homes of labouring families, like that at Higher Penquite in St Breward (Berry 2008), but some in Zennor were farmhouses. Reminiscent of Irish cabins, each had a single entrance, probably two ground floor rooms, only one of which, the kitchen,

Fig 23. Restormel Manor's small eighteenth-century country house, developed from a Tudor farmhouse, was partially Gothicised in the nineteenth century. (Photograph: Eric Berry, for HE, Cornwall Council)

was heated by a gable-end fireplace. Examples include those at Carne, Boswednack, and Bosigran Mill (Herring 1987b; Nowakowski 1987; Herring 1987a). Single-storey houses are also known on Scilly (Berry 1994).

For the great and middling families their relationship with developing ideas, as represented to us by architectural style, is especially interesting. Some surviving Cornish houses were amongst the most fashionable in Britain, including London, and indicate not just the wealth and ambition of their owners, but also how well connected they were with wider intellectual movements, and over the whole post-medieval period. By 1550 Sir Richard Edgcumbe crested the long rise from Cremyll with a house that looked both backwards to an ancient family's history (through its castellated form) and, unlike most other mid sixteenth-century gentry houses which turned inwards to secluded courtyards, forwards in its aspect to the great country house surveying its landscape (and seascape) (Gaskell Brown 1998).

At Trerice in the 1570s Sir John Arundell reversed his inherited inward-looking house to create an outward-looking one with a front made to appear more symmetrical than it was by the use of an eye-catching pattern of Dutch gables (Berry 1998b; Parkes 2005, 53; Berry and Sturgess forthcoming). In the 1630s Sir Francis Godolphin created Cornwall's most remarkable architectural statement, again intimately linked to its designed landscape. The north front at Godolphin still satisfies through repetitive use of classical proportions, emphasised by the remarkable double loggia whose pillars support palatial first-floor accommodation. Staged revelation was effected by several pinch-points along the northern approach (Herring 1997; Schofield forthcoming).

The rebuild of St Michael's Mount's Lady Chapel shortly before 1744 as two delicately gothic reception rooms, containing some of Cornwall's finest plaster, seems to have been completed a few years before Horace Walpole's internationally famous gothic creation at Strawberry Hill (Herring 1993, 72; Berry and Thomas 2008). The chapel's builder, Sir John St Aubyn, was an active correspondent with, amongst other intelligentsia, the antiquarian Dr William Borlase (Pool 1975), whose skill and influence as a gardener and polite architect may have been under-acknowledged. Caerhays Castle, another south coast gothic confection, conjured in 1807 by John Nash to satisfy the vanity and ultimately almost destroy the sanity of John Bettesworth Trevanion, is one of few survivors of his several romantic castles (Williams et al 2011).

Fig 24. A slate-clad nineteenth-century granary stands on staddle stones to one side of a fine seventeenth-century barn at Bokelly, St Kew while a single-storeyed stable completes the small open-sided rear courtyard. Such survivals are rare as most Cornish farm buildings were replaced in a form of Great Rebuild in the middle and late decades of the nineteenth century. (Photograph: Eric Berry, for HE, Cornwall Council)

Fig 25. The four-storey nineteenth and twentieth-century Town Mills at St Columb Major after recent restoration. (Photograph: Eric Berry, for HE, Cornwall Council)

Most other house-builders have followed fashion, using it to establish status and to signal their belonging to county or courtly circles. Golden Keep, despite being the earliest known brick building in Cornwall, is an example, being apparently 'constructed [by the Tregian family in the 1530s] to the order of people who had wealth and knowledge of current building trends' (Thomas 1997, 18). Examples of trend-followers are of course more numerous and among those recently studied are the small but imposing Restormel Manor, an eighteenth-century country house with some early nineteenth-century gothicisation, developed from a probably late sixteenth-century farmhouse (Berry *et al* 2010).

As one small corner of a once large mansion, Golden also reminds us that many important buildings have for a variety of reasons either been reduced, places like Trewarthenick (Parkes 2008a), Godolphin itself (Herring 1997; Schofield forthcoming), Pengersick (Herring, Thorpe and Morley 1998) and Tehidy (Parkes forthcoming), or have completely gone, like Pendarves, Trebartha, Whiteford (Dudley 2004) and Stowe (Wilson-North 1993), or apparently so – Nash's Caerhays Castle may stand upon the largely buried lower ground floor of its Tudor predecessor (Stephen Tyrrell, in Williams *et al* 2011). Many houses are multi-period, some spectacularly so; Godolphin's surviving courtyard displays fragments of great houses on each of its four sides, dating from the 1470s to the 1630s (Schofield forthcoming).

Studies of farmsteads and their buildings have included wide-ranging overviews of particular areas (the Hensbarrow uplands, east Cornwall, Bodmin Moor and Gerrans) intended to understand a variable and vulnerable resource (Herring and Smith 1991; Barnwell and Giles 1997; Herring and Giles 2008; Thompson 1993) and detailed studies of individual structures, usually in advance of conversion to secondary uses.

Unlike dwellings, few Cornish farm buildings survive from before the nineteenth century, other than a small number of seventeenth and eighteenth-century farm buildings and the great medieval and Tudor barns (like those at Cotehele, Trerice, Bodrugan and Cargoll; Herring and Tapper 2006; Parkes 2005; Cole 2003; Berry 2009) and stables (like Godolphin; Herring 1997). Some farms then erected buildings for the first time (having previously used pens, folds and ricks) and most others replaced small low structures with larger and more specialised ones.

Being functional structures, farm building forms, especially from the later eighteenth century onwards, closely reflect a farm's scale and regime and can vividly indicate changing practice and fortunes. Former dwellings were often reused as barns, stables and cowhouses on smaller farms that struggled to invest in wholly new structures. Whereas before the nineteenth century most farmsteads were relatively irregular in their layout, from the early Victorian period larger holdings, and especially barton farms (those working a lord's home land), began to establish planned arrangements of spaces (yards, mowhays, gardens etc) and buildings, the latter often set around rigidly rectangular courtyards, model farms when entirely newly created (Barnwell and Giles 1997), as for example at the Edwin Mucklow farms in Whitstone and Poundstock parishes (Herring and Thomas 1993, 17).

Decline in enforcement of multure freed up the millers' market, but the consequent competition obliged them to become more efficient, investing in better technology (Unwin and Thomas 2004, 12). Several corn mills have been surveyed or recorded, ranging from small structures like Bosigran mill in Zennor, reused as a tin calciner (Herring 1987) to the nineteenth-century industrial scale roller mill known as Loggans Mill near Hayle (Thomas 1998c).

Cornwall, Scilly and the military
Nicholas Johnson

The archaeology of defence has been transformed in Cornwall and Scilly over the last 20 years. Research has been proactive, being part of planned programmes, as well as reactive, the result of development pressures and unexpected discovery. Of particular note have been large-scale assessments of seaward and landward defence complexes surrounding Plymouth, at Falmouth and on Scilly (Plymouth: Thomas 1974; Pye *et al*, 1996; Woodward 1990; 1998; Falmouth: Heggie and Lane 1989; Linzey 2000a; 2000b; Ratcliffe 1997; Scilly: Keystone 1993; Johns and Fletcher 2010; Bowden and Brodie 2011). Surveys exist now for Padstow (Parr nd), Penzance (Cahill 2009), St Michael's Mount (Herring 1993; Herring *et al* 2000; Sturgess 2010), Hayle (CCHES HER records), the Submarine Telegraphy Station at Porthcurno (Foot 2009) and the Fowey and Helford estuaries (Parkes 2000; Reynolds 2000).

Coastal raiding in the late fifteenth century necessitated construction of artillery towers to protect the Hamoaze and Plymouth (Pye *et al* 1996), Fowey (Parkes 2000), and St Ives (Newell 2005a) and coastal batteries on St Michael's Mount (Herring 1993), and 50 years later blockhouses were built at St Mawes and Pendennis (Pasfield Oliver 1875; Kenyon 1982; 1983; Linzey 2000a; 2000b), at Fowey again (Thomas 1999), and at St Ives (Newell 2005a). In the 1540s and 1550s Tresco and St Marys on Scilly were protected with forts and blockhouses (Saunders 1962; Miles and Saunders 1970; Quinnell 1978; Brodie forthcoming a). This was followed in the 1590s by the construction of Pendennis Fortress (Linzey 2000a; 2000b; Johns 1997c), Star Castle and the first part of the Garrison Walls on St Marys (Adams 1984), and in the late 1620s with outworks to King Charles's Castle and the Blockhouse on Tresco and hornworks at Pendennis (Brodie forthcoming a; Linzey 2000a; 2000b).

The Armada, the Dutch Wars, the Wars of Spanish and Austrian Succession, also the Seven Years War, the American and Napoleonic wars (Ratcliffe and Sharpe 1990; Guy 1990; Goodwin 1993; Palmer 2000; Bowden and Brodie 2011: Brodie forthcoming, b), French re-armament of the 1860s (Woodward 1998) and the German naval arms race in the late nineteenth century, all resulted in upgraded and new coastal defences (Higham 1987; Saunders 1989), and reliable military signalling: signal stations in 1795 (Kitchens 1989; 1990a; 1990b; Ratcliffe and Sharpe 1990, 11-17; Goodwin 1993; Thomas and Herring 2001; Parkes 2008b); telegraphy in 1847; submarine telegraphy in 1852 (Foot 2009); wireless in 1903. These were to prevent invasion, and to protect harbours and anchorages against a naval *coup de main*.

Cornwall was one of the first counties mapped by the Ordnance Survey. Accurate mapping was essential for construction and maintenance of fortifications by the Board of Ordinance, and for the disposition of troops and construction of fieldworks by the Quartermaster General's Department. Cornwall was part of the Plymouth Division, and second only to Portsmouth in strategic importance. Scilly, Falmouth and Plymouth (Smith 1989) were the first and last ports of call for both the Navy's blue water squadrons and the merchant ships of the growing empire that was linked by trade routes and a reliable Packet Service (Sturgess 2001). It is not surprising therefore that mapping was completed for the county by 1816 (Margary 1977).

Fig 26. Dennis Fort, a very well preserved, but little known Civil War fort. The outer defence cuts off the headland and divides the two pasture fields, with a projecting hornwork close to the inlet at the bottom of the photo. The fort has semicircular bastions. A covered way is visible leading from the left side of the fort downhill, via two levelled platforms, to a battery platform on the cliff edge. Built by Sir Richard Vyvyan of Trelowarren in 1643 to cover the entrance to the Helford River, it was surrendered in March 1646 with 22 guns and 200 arms, along with the army at Tresillian Bridge and the strongholds of St Mawes

Castle and St Michael's Mount. Pendennis Castle and Scilly resisted for many months thereafter, and in the case of Scilly, it was re-captured and held for the crown until 1651. (Photograph: Historic Environment, Cornwall Council, ACS/1138)

There have been three other areas of significant advance in record and understanding: the English Civil Wars; late nineteenth-century rearmament, and twentieth-century defences.

Cornwall's part in the English Civil Wars has been known since Lord Clarendon's *History of the Great Rebellion* (Macray 1888), and Sir Ralph Hopton's *Bellum Civile* (Chadwyck-Healey 1902) became widely available. Coate's work (1963) and now Stoyle's extensive researches (Stoyle 1996; 1998; 1999; 2000a; 2000b; 2002; 2005; 2008) confirm Cornwall's important role. Its western coastal location, religious conservatism, the importance of tin revenues to the crown, and the sense of cultural difference, all influenced the war in Cornwall and the formation of the Cornish Army. Fieldwork has confirmed that there are considerable remains of contemporary fortifications (Barratt 2005), including on Scilly (Quinnell 1978; Thomas 1989; Ratcliffe 1993; Johns and Fletcher 2010; Bowden and Brodie 2011), and at St Michael's Mount (Herring 1993; Herring *et al* 2000, Sturgess 2009; 2010; Sturgess 2010), Dennis Fort on the Helford (Vyvyan 1910), Pendennis Castle (Carpenter

1984; Johns and Johnson 1994; Johns and Thomas 1995; Johns 2001b), and on the Cornish side of the Hamoaze (Pye *et al* 1996, 106-108). The battlefields of Stratton and Braddock Down are now defined and protected (English Heritage 1995). Research continues into the siege and battle of Lostwithiel 1644 (Foard 2008), the associated earthwork redoubts, the re-fortification of Restormel Castle (Radford 1980; Thomas and Buck 1993; Thomas 1996b), the related engagement at Tywardreath (CC HES HER records) and the evidence of destruction at the Duchy Palace and St Bartholomew's Church in Lostwithiel, and collateral damage elsewhere (Holmes 1989). In contrast, the square, bastioned enclosure on the summit of Kit Hill, Scheduled as a 'Civil War Redoubt', has now been confirmed as a late eighteenth-century gentleman's folly castle (Herring 1989; Herring and Thomas 1990).

Whilst the military are still present at RNAS Culdrose, Penhale Camp, HMS Raleigh, Tregantle Fort and the TA Depot in Truro, it is now rare to see service personnel in uniform about the streets. This is a far cry from earlier days when the military (especially the Navy) was a huge part of government

Fig 27. Grenville Battery (Redoubt No 4) and Maker Battery, Maker with Rame. The Plymouth Defences Survey Project, 1991-95 (Pye and Woodward 1996) identified, for the first time, the complexity and extraordinary survival of 216 individual defence works spanning 500 years. Redoubt No 4 (top of photo) is the southernmost of the line of 4 redoubts built (1779-1782) across Maker Heights during the War of American Independence to resist the capture of the high ground above Plymouth Sound. The guns were originally placed on the platform facing the camera to face inland. Converted (1887) to a sea facing battery (Grenville Battery) with two 12.5-inch RML guns. Together with Maker Battery (1886-7) in middle and lower half of photo, they formed part of the late nineteenth century and early twentieth-century coastal defences that covered Cawsand Bay and the approaches to the Plymouth naval base and anchorage. (Photograph: Historic Environment, Cornwall Council, ABW F4/50/1985)

expenditure. Between 1540 and 1956 Falmouth had a permanent garrison and Bodmin was base for the Duke of Cornwall's Light Infantry from 1881 to 1959 (White 2000). During the Jacobite Rebellion of 1745, but particularly in the Napoleonic Wars, many Volunteer and Militia Companies were

formed – Infantry Volunteers, Yeomanry/Cavalry, Artillery Volunteers and Sea-Fencibles (Thomas nd; 1957; 1958a; 1958b; 1959a; 1959b; 1959c; 1960a; 1960b). Again in the late 1850s and early 1860s, Rifle, Yeomanry and (coastal) Artillery Volunteer Companies were formed (Milne 1885). Most had rifle ranges and the Artillery Volunteers had Drill Sheds and practice Batteries. We now know that substantial remains survive at Charlestown (Smith *et al* 1998), Padstow (Parr nd), St Ives (Newell 2005a), St Just (Sharpe 1990a), Marazion, Penzance (Cahill 2009), and Pendennis (Linzey 2000a; 2000b) and many rifle ranges as well.

One of the revelations of the defences surveys of Falmouth (Harris 1985; Hartgroves *et al* 1989; Walker 1989; Sharpe 1989b; 1990b; Johns *et al* 1992; GSB 1994; Linzey 1995a; 1995b; 1995c; 1995d; 1999; Kiernat and Johnson1996; Heason nd; Johns 1997a; 1997b; 1997d; 1998b; 1998c; 1998e; 1999a; 1999b; 1999d; 1999e; 1999h; 1999k; 2001a; 2003; Gossip 2000a; 2000b; Johns and Sturgess 2005; Thomas 2006), Plymouth (Sheppard 1975; 1976; Hunt 1980; Payton 1987;

Fig 28. Penzance Battery. Recent work by Cahill (2009) has demonstrated that the stonework below the Penzance war memorial is the original hexagonal shaped stone walled platform of Penzance Battery completed in 1740 on Battery Rocks with an associated causeway and bulwark to defend Penzance harbour. The platform was walled and gated and mounted three 24 pdr guns manned by a Volunteer Company in the Napoleonic Wars. The battery is now Listed. A 1940 Emergency Battery (now removed) was built behind the battery adjacent to the Jubilee Pool. (Photograph: Nick Cahill)

*Fig 29. US field artillery position on Letter
Moor, St Neot. The typical entrenched position
dug for field artillery in the run up to D Day.
One of 10 positions here dug in two sets facing
north (this being one of a battery of 4 guns, with
another battery of 6 guns close by to the east).
Corresponding shell holes are found on the
eastern slopes of Brown Willy. Such ephemeral
remains have been recorded as part of the
Bodmin Moor Survey (Herring et al 2008).
Sites recorded include Davidstow Airfield, its
associated defences, anti landing obstructions,
and aircraft crash sites, as well as rifle and
grenade ranges, tented army training camps,
associated searchlights, infantry foxholes,
ammunition dumps, bomb craters and lookouts.*
(Photograph: Cornwall Council)

Pye *et al* 1996; Breslin 1998; Buck 1999; Kinross
1999; Young 2002; WA Heritage 2008a) and
Scilly (Ratcliffe 1989; Parkes 1990; CAU 1997;
Linzey 1994; Ratcliffe and Johns 2003; Johns and
Sawyer 2005; Fellows 2007; Johns 2010a; Johns
and Fletcher 2010) has been the survival of a wide
range of late nineteenth/early twentieth-century
sites. These (Hogg 1974; Dorman 1990; Linzey
2000a; 2000b, Pye *et al* 1996; WA Heritage
2008a; Bowden and Brodie 2011) illustrate the
development, of Rifled Breech Loading guns,
Range Finding Cells (Johns 1999i), Telegraphy,
Electric Defence Light installations with engine
rooms (Johns 2000; 2001b), and the Submarine
Minefield in Falmouth (Johns 1998d) with its
Volunteer Submarine Miners establishment
(Cavanagh-Mainwaring 1913) and associated
Quick Fire Batteries (Johns 1999c; 1999f).

English Heritage has, since 1994, commissioned
studies into the defence heritage, many forming
part of the *Twentieth-century Fortifications in
England* project (Lowry 1998; Schofield 2004).
Documentary sources helped identify what was
built and where. For Cornwall the following
studies are relevant: the identification of bombing
decoys (Dobinson 1996c), anti-aircraft artillery
1914-46 (Dobinson 1996a; 2000e), anti-invasion
defences (Dobinson 1996b; Foot 2006; Herring
et al 2008), Operation Overlord preparatory sites
(Dobinson 1996d), airfields and airfield defences
(Ashworth 1990; Andrew 1995; Dobinson 2000b;
2000c), aircraft crash sites (English Heritage
2002), acoustics and radar (Dobinson1996f), coast
artillery 1900-56 (Linzey 1992; Dobinson 1996e;
Corney 2008), civil defence, experimental and
training sites (Dobinson 2000a), barracks (Douet
1995), military camps (Evans and Foot 2006),
prisoner of war camps and drill halls (Thomas
2003), depots (Exeter Archaeology 2001) and Cold
War installations (Cole 1999; Dobinson 2000d).

This research has revealed the widespread
preparations for D Day from late 1942 (Anon 1994).
The US 29th Infantry Division was in Cornwall *en
route* for Omaha Beach and was accommodated
in tented camps (Young 2006) and large country
houses across the county. Eighty military camps are
known in Cornwall of which over 70 are connected
with D Day (Sharpe 2011b), whilst 3 others are anti-
aircraft training camps (Johns 1998a; Dudley 2007).
To these can be added camps associated with coastal
defence batteries, wireless and radar stations, and
airfields (Shapland 1989; Herring 1992; Johns
1999j; Young 2001; Herring *et al* 2008, 133-6). In
addition the more permanent accommodation at
Pendennis Castle (Johns 1999g; J Taylor 2002; Johns
2005), St Mawes Castle (Taylor 2006), St Anthony
Battery, Bodmin (White 2000), Scraesdon Fort,
Tregantle Fort (Sage 2003), Fort Picklecombe and
Maker Heights (Keystone 1999) was expanded with
temporary camps. Recent fieldwork has revealed
trench systems at St Anthony (Linzey 2000b, 223),
at Pendennis (Linzey 2000b, 223; Johns 1998d), and
at Scraesdon and Tregantle (WA Heritage 2008b)
that appear to be training works from World War
One. Airships also worked from Cornwall against
U-boats in the Great War (London 1999).

Site survival has been verified by checking historic
photographs, and through field visits. This task has
been greatly helped by the *Defence of Britain Project*

DISCOVERY AND RESEARCH

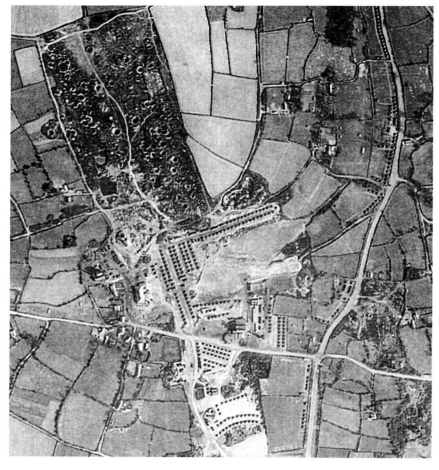

Fig 30. Defence of Britain Project. 29th US Division camp at Wheal Busy, Chacewater in March 1944. Ten-man tents and nissen huts are laid out across the old mine site, and also along the Chacewater road to the right of the photo. There were many tented camps ('Sausage camps') around Truro (Devoran, Perranwell, Shortlanesend, Treliske, Lower Penair, Pencalenick, Boscawen Park, Carvedras, Threemilestone, Penstraze, Chiverton Cross, United Downs) spread out along the approach roads to the 'embarkation hards', at Turnaware, Polgerran Wood (Tolverne), and Falmouth on the Fal, and Trebah on the Helford. Work began on the hards in late 1942 and the troops began arriving in camps in autumn 1943. The majority of camps in this area were empty again by the 12th June, the troops having landed on Omaha Beach.

The extraordinary range of sites identified by the Defence of Britain project include 24 drill halls, 32 rifle ranges, 8 RNAS airfields, 5 RAF airfields (Willies 2004; Kirkham 2007; Cole 1998), 23 radar stations (Thorpe 2001), 44 Royal Observer Corps stations (Passmore 2003), 40 coastal guns/batteries, 18 decoy airfields, towns and harbours (Cole 1997; 1999) 42 anti aircraft batteries (Cole 2008), 34 Auxiliary Unit bunkers, 10 barrage balloon sites, 103 anti invasion obstructions (Johns 2002; Foot 2006; John Knevitt Practice 1999), 163 pillboxes (Osborne 1990) 13 D Day embarkation hards (Parkes 2006) and maintenance gridirons (Watts 2000), and 5 prisoner of war camps. (Photograph: US/7PH/GP/LOC213 frame 3054 9 March 1944 English Heritage (NMR) USAAF Photography).

1995-2002, continued in Cornwall until 2004. A total of 679 military sites were recorded and visited principally by local volunteer Alwyn Harvey. The *Cornwall and Scilly National Mapping Programme* provided air photo plots of most of these military sites (Young 2006, and this volume).

This war was different. Much of the county was out of bounds, beaches were mined and, estuaries and cliffs patrolled, and Identity Cards and Ration Cards demanded. Many schools, and hundreds of children, were evacuated to Cornwall from London and the South East. Thousands of anti-aircraft landing obstructions were dug across open moorland close to airfields (Predannack, Portreath, Cleave, Davidstow) and radar stations (Dry Tree, Trelanvean) to prevent attack by glider borne troops. Police records recorded the surprisingly large number of bombs that were dropped across the county, whilst major towns and some private institutions (eg Truro High School at Tregolls House) had air raid shelters. Even working mines were bombed (Botallack), and some had shelters (Sharpe 1992; 2011a). The arrival of tens of thousands of white and mixed-race American troops was a cultural shock to both the people of Cornwall and the troops themselves (Breakell 1990; Acton and Carter 1994; 1995; Richards and Reynolds 1994; Edwards 1995; Hancock 2002). Meanwhile large areas of moorland were brought under the plough, and the Land Army and Italian prisoners of war helped farmers bring in the harvest.

The shadows cast by the war have proved unexpectedly long. Around Truro, Treliske Hospital developed from an American D Day camp, as did local authority industrial estates (Treliske and Gloweth), and Truro FC Football ground. The Polwhele Veterinary Centre was a Heavy Anti-Aircraft battery and camp, the Prisoner of War Camp at Whitecross (St Columb) is now a successful holiday camp as are several other camps across Cornwall, and D Day fuel dumps at Tresillian and Summercourt became garages. Well into the 1960s Cornwall County Council was removing beach defences and redundant military buildings, and claiming the costs back from Whitehall.

Sites remain undiscovered, and yet the general narrative of Cornwall's military history has been dramatically enhanced. The work of protecting the best of what survives has begun. The *Defence Areas Project* (2002-2004) has examined anti-invasion defence works that form coherent and legible groupings and survive well in landscapes largely unchanged from those of 1940/41. The defences of St Michael's Mount and Porthcurno are deemed to be of national importance (Foot 2009). The aircraft dispersal pens at RAF Perranporth (Fletcher and Newman 2002) and selected D Day embarkation hards and maintenance gridirons (Schofield 2001) have now been Scheduled.

Landscape
Peter Herring

Preceding subsections all utilised historic maps, two-dimensional representations of land, or landscape, usually for particular purposes (estate surveys for land management and dispute control, tithe surveys for land evaluation, and ordnance survey mapping for land appraisal and military planning). While they are therefore normally more partial than we might wish them to be, because of that partiality they can also reveal something about motivation, power and exclusion, as well as evidence of chronology (via map regression), changing extents, forms and uses.

Publication of the 1694-6 *Lanhydrock Atlas*'s large-scale, highly-detailed maps of the Robartes scattered holdings enables close study of aspects of Cornwall just before steam transformed mining, accelerating commercial activity and further reinforcing diversification of the economy and specialisation in the workforce (Holden *et al* 2010). The maps illustrate great variety in the pace and form of change. Many barrows, crosses, prehistoric 'castles', etc were either recorded or referred to in field-names, and people then seem to have been aware they lived in a world both ancient and modern. We find 'old chappell', 'old tynn works' and abandoned hamlets and farms: 'the Ruines of houses and gardens' at Treglasta, 'the decay'd house and townplace' at Halwyn. There is also variable time-depth visible in late seventeenth-century field patterns; most had medieval roots, but some were later prehistoric survivals, as at Mulfra, Boskednan, Carfury and elsewhere in West Penwith, and some were very new (and occasionally challenged) incursions into rough ground (as at Callestick and Numphra) (Herring 2010).

The Atlas illustrates variety in farming practice, land use, land holding and the field and boundary patterns formed for and framing them, a variety following and reinforcing the Cornish sub-regions in which communities had developed particular or peculiar ways of working and carrying on, areas likened by some to the French *pays* (eg Fox 1989; Turner 2007, 116). These different ways reflected locally distinct society and identity (Herring forthcoming) and are also made visible in local vernacular architecture, hedging styles, other material culture and made audible in dialects (North and Sharpe 1980).

Most of Cornwall's open fields had already been enclosed by the end of the medieval period, so that Richard Carew in 1603 described strip fields then as rare survivals from a more primitive past (Carew 2004, 66r). His was already a world of individual holdings, of farmers some might consider yeomen, even though most still lived in small hamlets. Their holdings, formerly intermixed through the strip

Fig 31. Smoke drifts north towards the National Trust's eighteenth and nineteenth-century landscape park at Ethy, now subject to a long-term management plan. Dinghies lie stranded on low tide's muds and hikers' cars fill the car park beside the stepping stones over the River Lerryn. Modern people come to the creek-head village of Lerryn for leisure when a century ago they came to the numerous quays to send farm and orchard produce up the distant Fowey River to Lostwithiel or down to Fowey. Local people operated lime kilns and worked in the big house, on local farms and in the extensive woods, oak coppices exploited for charcoal and bark as much as for timber. (Photograph: Peter Herring)

fields, were increasingly consolidated into blocks as individual households made arrangements that best suited efficient farming practice. That still involved the long established convertible husbandry (Herring 2006), itself visible in the proportions of arable, meadow and pasture shown in the Lanhydrock Atlas and in the way most holdings comprised around 10 fields (see Later Medieval, this volume). The Robartes estate still retained a few open fields in the 1690s, as at Trenance (Mullion) and Ballowall (St Just), the latter subdivisions in an inherited prehistoric field pattern. In some places, notably at Predannack Wartha, enclosure was still under way,

with several 'fields' or 'cropping units' containing bundles of open-sided strips, other bundles where the strips had been hedged, and others where all strips had been removed (Herring 2010, 28).

The direction of change in fields and commons followed that established in the later medieval period, from communal and cooperative arrangements and towards individual and commercial or profit-oriented ones. New enclosure (usually of rough ground, but also marsh and woodland) reflected this with farmsteads roughly centrally placed in individually held blocks of fields, still typically around 10 of these in new farms (such as those of around 30 acres established in the 1830s in Altarnun's Pridacoombe Valley; Herring and Giles 2008, 143-7), fewer in smallholdings (usually less than five acres), often close to industrial complexes. Enclosure increased the landlord's return, but reduced the common land available to the farmer, or indeed the household who depended upon it for its household fuel (Herring 1997, 77-83; Herring and Giles 2008; Dudley 2011, 49-55).

Cutting, drying and saving the several types of turf (peat), has been closely studied (Herring 2008c), stimulated in part by survey of sub-rectangular or circular platforms known as turf steads on Bodmin Moor and robins on the Lizard and Goonhilly Downs (*ibid*; Dudley 2011) whose interpretation was thrice misapprehended by earlier archaeologists. They were successively prehistoric settlements (Hencken 1932, 103), medieval charcoal manufacturing sites (Hopkins 1980), and 'peat-drying platforms' (Quinnell 1984), to the amusement of Bodmin Moor farmers interviewed by Tony Blackman. They, like those labourers who had explained the 'miniature earthworks' to CK Croft Andrew when he encountered them on Davidstow Moor, remembered them as stands for temporary ricks of already dried turf destined for use in domestic hearths (Christie and Rose 1987, 183-5; Blackman, above; Herring 2008c).

Several surveys have more or less intensively examined woodlands, enabling better appreciation of the remains of their management (perimeter boundaries, banks, lanes and tracks) and exploitation - coppiced and singled trees, dominated by oaks; charcoal burning platforms; saw pits (Parkes 1997; 1998; 2006; Herring *et al* 1998).

Some woods survive through incorporation into the designed ornamental landscapes of country houses of gentry that has itself received greatly increased archaeological attention. In most cases Cornwall's parks are shown to be evolutionary creations with each major phase producing distinctive patterns of planting and structures and the means by which these were displayed, viewed and enjoyed. English Heritage's Register of Parks and Gardens covered 36 gardens considered of special historic interest. Meanwhile the Cornwall Gardens Trust carefully recorded main features of dozens of parks and gardens (reported in their annual journal). Some have been subjected to more detailed archaeological survey, usually to feed into management plans (e.g. Colson-Stone 1994; Herring *et al* 1998; Vyvyan

2000), and sometimes to inform the planning of interested owners (Phibbs 1994; Fletcher 1996; Herring 1997; Schofield forthcoming ; Keystone 2010; Thomas 1994; 1998d; 1996c; Parkes 2005; 2008a; Williams *et al* 2011). There have also been important reviews of Cornwall's gardens, notably Pett's virtually exhaustive survey (1998), but also McCabe (1988), Pring (1996) and Mowl (2005), the last, beautifully constructed and occasionally controversial, places Cornwall's ornamental landscape in regional and national contexts.

We have already considered the effects of industry and war, or the fear of war, on Cornwall's landscape. The twentieth century saw an acceleration of trends begun in the eighteenth and nineteenth, including the subjective appreciation and consumption of landscape that those parks and gardens enabled. Landscape, including that which was largely artificial, like vast slateworks at Delabole and mines at Minions and Carclaze could and can affect its perceivers by being sublime as well as beautiful, familiar and understandable. They excite feelings of awe and unease as well as creating or reinforcing the senses of place, belonging and identity that affect both local people and interested visitors.

References

Acton, V, and Carter, D, 1994. *Operation Cornwall 1940-1944*, Falmouth (Landfall Publications)

Acton, V, and Carter, D, 1995. *Cornish War and Peace - the road to victory and beyond*, Falmouth (Landfall Publications)

Adams, F, and P, 1984. *Star Castle and its garrison*, Liskeard

Andrew, F, 1995. *History of RAF Perranporth 1941-1945*, unpublished

Anon., 1994. F*almouth's wartime memories. The official commemorative publication for the 50th anniversary of D-Day 6th June 1944*, Falmouth

Ashworth, C, 1990. *Action Stations. 5: military airfields of the Southwest*, Wellingborough

Atkins, 2004. *Bude Canal, Conservation Plan*, Epsom

Barnwell, P S, and Giles, C, 1997. *English farmsteads 1750–1914*, London (RCHME, HMSO)

Barratt, J, 2005. *Battlefield Britain. The Civil War in the South-West*, Barnsley

Barry, J, 1999. Towns and processes of urbanisation in the early modern period, in R Kain, and W Ravenhill, eds *Historical atlas of south-west England*, Exeter, 413-25

Berry, E, 1980. *The Penryn Survey*, Cornwall Buildings Group

Berry, E, 1994. *The Samson Buildings - an assessment of the post-medieval houses and farm buildings on Samson, Isles of Scilly*, Truro (Cornwall Archaeological Unit)

Berry, E, 1998a. *Falmouth Conservation Area appraisal*, Truro (Carrick District Council)

Berry, E, 1998b. *Trerice, Newlyn East*, Gwennap (Eric Berry)

Berry, E, 2006a. *Treludick, Egloskerry, Cornwall; outline historic building analysis*, Truro (Historic Environment Service, Cornwall County Council)

Berry, E, 2006b. *Trerithick Manor, Altarnun, Cornwall; outline historic building analysis*, Truro (Historic Environment Service, Cornwall County Council)

Berry, E, 2008. *Higher Penquite, St. Breward - historic building record*, Truro (Historic Environment Service, Cornwall County Council)

Berry, E, 2009. *Tregarton barns, Goran: historic buildings record*, Truro (Historic Environment Service, Cornwall County Council)

Berry, E, Blackman, T, Buck, C, Cahill, N, Colwill, S, Mattingly, J, Powning, J, and Thomas, N, 2008. *Lostwithiel: 'the fairest of small cities'. Historic characterisation*, Truro (Historic Environment Service, Cornwall County Council)

Berry, E, Buck, C, Nowakowski, J A, Reynolds, A, and Thorpe, C, 1997. *Archaeological investigations at City Hall, Truro, 1996*, Truro (Cornwall Archaeological Unit)

Berry, E, Mattingly, J, and Thomas, N, 2001. *Lower Bore Street, Bodmin, Cornwall - archaeological survey and historical analysis*, Truro (Historic Environment Service, Cornwall County Council)

Berry, E, Parkes, C, and Thomas, N, 2010. *Restormel Manor, Lostwithiel - historic building analysis and landscape survey*, Truro (Historic Environment Projects, Cornwall Council)

Berry, E, and Sturgess, J, forthcoming. *Trerice, Newlyn East, Cornwall: Historic Building Analysis*, Truro (Historic Environment Projects, Cornwall Council)

Berry, E, and Thomas, N, 2008. *St Michael's Mount, Cornwall - historic buildings analysis and watching brief of the summit buildings*, Truro (Historic Environment Service, Cornwall County Council)

Bowden, M, and Brodie, A, 2011. *Defending Scilly*, Swindon (English Heritage)

Brayshay, M, 1999. Morphological development of towns since the Middle Ages, in R Kain, and W Ravenhill, eds, *Historical atlas of south-west England*, Exeter, 426-38

Breakell, B, 1990. *Falmouth at war*, Launceston

Breslin, J, 1998. *Rustic rambles and military marches*, Plymouth

British Waterways, 1999. *Liskeard and Looe Union Canal*, Rugby

Brodie, A, forthcoming, a. Tudor Scilly, *English Heritage Historical Review* 2010

Brodie, A, forthcoming, b. Abraham Tovey (1687-1759) – matross, master gunner and mastermind of Scilly's defences, *Georgian Group*, 19 (2011)

Buck, C, 1999. *Tregantle Fort - an archaeological record during repairs to Tregantle Keep roof*, Truro (Cornwall Archaeological Unit)

Buck, C, 2002. *Devon Great Consols Mine - archaeological assessment*, Truro (Historic Environment Service, Cornwall County Council)

Buck, C, and Berry, E, 1996. *St Just town survey and historic audit*, Truro (Cornwall Archaeological Unit)

Buck, C, and Smith, J, 1995. *Hayle town survey and historic audit*, Truro (Cornwall Archaeological Unit)

Cahill, N, 2003. *Cornwall and Scilly Urban Survey. Historic characterisation for regeneration: Penzance*, Truro (Cornwall County Council)

Cahill, N, 2009. *Penzance Harbour South Pier: historic building analysis*, Penzance (Cahill Partnership)

Cahill, N, and Cornwall Archaeological Unit, 2000. *Hayle historical assessment, Cornwall*, Truro (Cornwall Archaeological Unit) (2 vols)

Cahill Partnership and Cornwall Archaeological Unit, 2002a. *Cornwall Industrial Settlements Initiative: St Agnes,* Truro (Historic Environment Service, Cornwall County Council)

Cahill Partnership and Cornwall Archaeological Unit, 2002b. *Cornwall Industrial Settlements Initiative: Redruth and Plain an Gwarry,* Truro (Historic Environment Service, Cornwall County Council)

Cahill Partnership and Cornwall Archaeological Unit, 2002c. *Cornwall Industrial Settlements Initiative: Chacewater,* Truro (Historic Environment Service, Cornwall County Council)

Cahill Partnership and Cornwall Archaeological Unit, 2002d. *Cornwall Industrial Settlements Initiative: Portreath,* Truro (Historic Environment Service, Cornwall County Council)

Cahill Partnership and Cornwall Archaeological Unit, 2002e. *Cornwall Industrial Settlements Initiative: Pool,* Truro (Historic Environment Service, Cornwall County Council)

Cahill Partnership and Cornwall Archaeological Unit, 2002f. *Cornwall Industrial Settlements Initiative: Looe,* Truro (Historic Environment Service, Cornwall County Council)

Cahill Partnership and Cornwall Archaeological Unit, 2002g. *Cornwall Industrial Settlements Initiative: Delabole,* Truro (Historic Environment Service, Cornwall County Council)

Cahill, N J, and Cornwall Archaeological Unit, 2002h. *Cornwall Industrial Settlements Initiative: St Just,* Truro (Historic Environment Service, Cornwall County Council)

Cahill Partnership and Cornwall Archaeological Unit, 2002i. *Cornwall Industrial Settlements Initiative: Camborne,* Truro (Historic Environment Service, Cornwall County Council)

Cahill Partnership and Cornwall Archaeological Unit, 2002j. *Cornwall Industrial Settlements Initiative: Tuckingmill and Roskear,* Truro (Historic Environment Service, Cornwall County Council)

Cahill Partnership and Historic Environment Service, 2005. *Cornwall Industrial Settlements Initiative: Bugle,* Truro (Historic Environment Service, Cornwall County Council)

Carew, R, 2004. *The Survey of Cornwall, Dev and Cornwall Rec Soc*, NS 47, Exeter

Carpenter, C, 1984. *The cannon of Pendennis and St Mawes Castles,* Plymouth

Cavanagh-Mainwaring, G, 1913. *The Royal Miners. A history of the Stannaries Regiment of Miners, late Cornwall and Devon Royal Garrison Artillery Militia,* London

Chadwyck-Healey, C E H, 1902. *Bellum Civile,* Somerset

Chesher, V M, and Chesher, F J, 1968. *The Cornishman's House*, Truro

Christie, P M, and Rose, P, 1987. Davidstow Moor, Cornwall: the medieval and later sites. Wartime excavations by C K Croft Andrew, 1941-2, *Cornish Archaeol*, **26,** 163-194

Chope, R P, ed, 1967. *Early tours in Devon and Cornwall*, Newton Abbot

Coate, M, 1963. *Cornwall in the Great Civil War and Interregnum, 1642-1660*, Oxford

Cole, R, 1997. *Gear Sands, Perranzabuloe - an archaeological assessment*, Truro (Cornwall Archaeological Unit)

Cole, R, 1998. *Royston Farm, Treligga - a rapid archaeological and historic landscape assessment*, Truro (Cornwall Archaeological Unit)

Cole, R, 1999. *Nare Point, St Keverne - an archaeological and historical assessment*, Truro (Cornwall Archaeological Unit)

Cole, R, 2003. *Cargoll Farm, Newlyn East, Cornwall - archaeological watching brief*, Truro (Historic Environment Service, Cornwall County Council)

Cole, R, 2008. *Falmouth Golf Club - archaeological assessment*, Truro (Historic Environment Service, Cornwall Council)

Colson-Stone Partnership, 1994. *Caerhays Castle, historic landscape survey and restoration plan*, Battersea

Conservation Studio and Cornwall Archaeological Unit, 1999. *St Blazey, Cornwall Industrial Settlements Initiative*, Truro (Cornwall Archaeological Unit)

Corney, M, 2008. *Searchlight engine room, Par Harbour, Par, Cornwall*, Hindon (AC Archaeology)

Cornwall Archaeological Unit, 1997. *The Garrison, St Mary's, Isles of Scilly - a walk around the walls*, Truro (Cornwall Archaeological Unit)

Craze, N, Herring, P, and Kirkham, G, 2006. *Atlantic Coast and Valleys Project - historic environment assessments of farms*, Truro (Historic Environment Service, Cornwall County Council)

Deacon, B, 2009. Methodism in Cornwall, 1743-1900, *www.exeter.ac.uk/cornwall/academic.../ics/.../CornishMethodism.pdf*

Dobinson, C, 1996a. *Twentieth century fortifications in England. Vols 1.1-1.5. Anti-aircraft artillery, 1914-46*, York (CBA)

Dobinson, C, 1996b. *Twentieth century fortifications in England. Vol II Anti-invasion defences of WWII*, York (CBA)

Dobinson, C, 1996c. *Twentieth century fortifications in England. Vol III. Bombing decoys of WWII*, York (CBA)

Dobinson, C, 1996d. *Twentieth century fortifications in England. Vol V. Operation Overlord*, York (CBA)

Dobinson, C, 1996e. *Twentieth century fortifications in England. Vol VI. Coastal artillery, 1900-1956*, York (CBA)

Dobinson, C, 1996f. *Twentieth century fortifications in England. Vol VII.1-VII.2. Acoustics and radar*, York (CBA)

Dobinson, C, 2000a. *Twentieth century fortifications in England. Vol VIII. Civil defence in WWII*, York (CBA)

Dobinson, C, 2000b. *Twentieth century fortifications in England. Vol IX.1-IX.2. Airfield themes*, York (CBA)

Dobinson, C, 2000c. *Twentieth century fortifications in England. Vol X. Airfield defences in WWII*, York (CBA)

Dobinson, C, 2000d. *Twentieth century fortifications in England. Vol XI.1-XI.2. The Cold War*, York (CBA)

Dobinson, C, 2000e. *Fields of deception. Britain's bombing decoys of World War II*, London (English Heritage)

Dorman, J, 1990. The later defences of Falmouth 1895-1956, *Ravelin* Special No 4, Kent Defence Research Group

Douet, J, 1995. *Homes fit for heroes. English barracks 1660-1914*, London (English Heritage)

Dudley, P, 2004. *Whiteford Park, Stoke Climsland, Cornwall - historic landscape survey and management plan*, Truro (Historic Environment Service, Cornwall County Council)

Dudley, P, 2007. *St Agnes Head, New Downs Head, Tubby's Head and Trevellas Coombe, Cornwall - archaeological assessment*, Truro (Historic Environment Service, Cornwall County Council)

Dudley, P, 2011. *Goon, hal, cliff and croft, west Cornwall's rough ground*, Truro (Cornwall Council)

Dyer, M J, and Collings, A J, 2000. *Archaeological monitoring and recording during restoration of Bude Canal sea lock*, Exeter (Exeter Archaeology)

Edwards, M, 1995. *Perran at war. Memories of Perranporth pre-war, wartime and the late 1940s*, Truro

English Heritage, 1995. *The Register of Historic Battlefields* (Stratton 1643 and Braddock Down 1643)

English Heritage, 2002. *Military aircraft crash sites: archaeological guidance on their significance and future management*, London

Evans, D, and Foot, W, 2006. *England's Army Camps 1858-2000*, Swindon (English Heritage)

Exeter Archaeology, 1997. *Archaeological assessment and field evaluation at Superdrug, 13 Boscawen Street, Truro*, Exeter (Exeter Archaeology)

Exeter Archaeology, 2001. *A former Second World War oil depot site at Cremyll Maker-with-Rame, Cornwall , archaeological assessment*, Exeter (Exeter Archaeology)

Fellows, D, 2007. *The Garrison, St Mary's, Isles of Scilly: archaeological evaluation, Research Department Report Series no 2007.69*, Portsmouth (English Heritage)

Fletcher, M, 1996. *Godolphin Gardens*, Exeter (English Heritage)

Fletcher, M, and Newman, P, 2002. *RAF Perranporth, St Agnes, Cornwall: Archaeological Investigation Report Series AI/44/2002*, Exeter (English Heritage)

Foard, G, 2008. *Conflict in the pre-industrial landscape of England: a resource assessment*, Leeds (University of Leeds)

Foot, W, 2006. *Beaches, fields, streets, and hills - the anti-invasion landscapes of England, 1940*, York (CBA)

Foot, W, 2009. *Defence Areas: a national study of Second World War anti-invasion landscapes in England*, York (CBA) (Note: Defence Areas 28 [Porthcurno]; and 74 [St Michael's Mount])

Fox, H, 1989. Peasant farmers, patterns of settlement and pays: transformations in the landscapes of Devon and Cornwall during the later middle ages, in R Higham, ed, *Landscape and townscape in the South West*, Exeter (University of Exeter Press), 41-73

Gamble, B, and the World Heritage Site Bid Team, 2005, *Nomination of the Cornwall and West Devon Mining*

Landscape for inclusion on the World Heritage Site List, Truro (Historic Environment Service, Cornwall County Council)

Gaskell-Brown, C, 1998. *Mount Edgcumbe House and Country Park*, Torpoint

Geophysical Surveys of Bradford (GSB), 1994. *Pendennis Castle: report on geophysical survey 94/32*, Bradford

Gerrard, G A M, 1985. Retallack: a late medieval tin milling complex in the parish of Constantine, and its Cornish context, *Cornish Archaeol*, **24,** 175-182

Gilbert, C S, 1820. *An historical survey of the county of Cornwall, vol II,* Plymouth-Dock

Gilbert, D, 1838. *The parochial history of Cornwall*, London

Gillard, B, 2005a. *Cornwall and Scilly Urban Survey. Historic characterisation for regeneration: Liskeard*, Truro (Historic Environment Service, Cornwall County Council)

Gillard, B, Historic Environment Service, and Cahill Partnership 2004a. *Cornwall Industrial Settlements Initiative: Calstock*, Truro (Historic Environment Service, Cornwall County Council)

Gillard, B, Historic Environment Service, and Cahill Partnership 2004b. *Cornwall Industrial Settlements Initiative: Gunnislake*, Truro (Historic Environment Service, Cornwall County Council)

Gillard, B, Historic Environment Service, and Cahill Partnership 2004c. *Cornwall Industrial Settlements Initiative: Praze an Beeble*, Truro (Historic Environment Service, Cornwall County Council)

Gillard, B, and Newell, K, 2005. *Cornwall and Scilly Urban Survey. Historic characterisation for regeneration: Hayle*, Truro (Cornwall County Council)

Goodwin, J, 1993. Granite Towers on St Mary's, Isles of Scilly, *Cornish Archaeol*, **32,** 128-139

Gossip, J, 2000a. *Pendennis Castle - archaeological watching brief during path alteration*, Truro (Cornwall Archaeological Unit)

Gossip, J, 2000b. *Pendennis Castle, Cornwall - archaeological watching brief during Fire Main Installation - Archive Report*, Truro (Cornwall Archaeological Unit)

Gossip, J, 2001. *The Gannel Estuary, Cornwall - archaeological and historical assessment*, Truro (Historic Environment Service, Cornwall County Council)

Gossip, J, 2002. *11-12 Boscawen Street, Truro, Cornwall - archaeological excavation*, Truro (Historic Environment Service, Cornwall County Council)

Gossip, J, forthcoming. *Excavations in Quay Street, Lostwithiel, Cornish Archaeol*

Guy, A, 1990. A good Man in Falmouth: Captain Philip Melville, Defender of the Pendennis Castle 1796-1811, in A Guy, ed, *The road to Waterloo, The British Army and the struggle against Revolutionary and Napoleonic France 1793-1815*, Stroud, 111-125

Hammond, J, 1897. *A Cornish parish: being an account of St Austell, town, church, district and people*, London

Hancock, P, 2002. *Cornwall at War, 1939-45*, Wellington

Harris, D, 1985. An ancient wall at Pendennis Point, Falmouth, *Cornish Archaeol*, **24,** 183-4

Hartgroves, S, Sharpe, A, and Roberts, C, 1989. *Pendennis Castle and the Headland, Falmouth*, Truro (Cornwall Archaeological Unit)

Heason, D, nd. *St Anthony Battery Magazine. Report on future conservation requirements.* privately printed (copy seen at HES, ref ER382)

Heggie, A, and Lane, M, 1989. *St Anthony Battery*, Bodmin, National Trust Coastal Leaflet

Hencken, H O'N, 1932. *The archaeology of Cornwall and Scilly*, London

Herring, P, 1987a. *Bosigran, Zennor, archaeological assessment*, Truro (Cornwall Archaeological Unit)

Herring, P, 1987b. *Carne, Zennor - an archaeological survey,* Truro (Cornwall Archaeological Unit)

Herring, P, 1989. A folly on Kit Hill, *Cornish Archaeol*, **28,** 252-258

Herring, P, 1992. *WAAF Site, Bridge, Portreath - an archaeological assessment for Kerrier Land Reclamation Scheme*, Truro (Cornwall Archaeological Unit)

Herring, P, 1993. *St Michael's Mount*, Truro (Cornwall Archaeological Unit)

Herring, P, 1995. *Bartinney Hill, Tredinney Common and Carn Grean - an archaeological assessment*, Truro (Cornwall Archaeological Unit)

Herring, P, 1997. *Godolphin, Breage, an archaeological and historical assessment*, Truro (Cornwall Archaeological Unit)

Herring, P, 2005. *Cornwall and Scilly Urban Survey. Historic characterisation for regeneration: Torpoint*, Truro (Cornwall County Council)

Herring, P, 2006. Cornish strip f,ields, in S Turner, ed, *Medieval Devon and Cornwall*, Macclesfield, 44-77

Herring, P, 2008a. Quarrying, in Herring *et al* 2008, 83-100

Herring, P, 2008b. Tamar Valley orchards, in I Rotherham, ed, *Orchards and groves: their history, ecology, culture and archaeology*, Sheffield, 86-95

Herring, P, 2008c. Turf, in Herring *et al* 2008, 117-126

Herring, P, 2010. The Cornish landscape in the Lanhydrock Atlas, in Holden *et al* 2010, 27-40

Herring, P, forthcoming. Multiple identities in Cornwall, in S Pearce, ed, *The Archaeology of south western Britain: recent research*

Herring, P, and Berry, E, 1997. Stonaford, *Cornish Archaeol*, **36,** 151-175

Herring, P, and Giles, C, 2008. Agriculture, in P Herring *et al* 2008, 139-162

Herring, P, and Gillard, B, 2005. *Cornwall and Scilly Urban Survey. Historic characterisation for regeneration: Launceston*, Truro (Cornwall County Council)

Herring, P, and Newell, K, 2005. *Cornwall and Scilly Urban Survey. Historic characterisation for regeneration: Camelford*, Truro (Cornwall County Council)

Herring, P, Parkes, C, Pring, S, Green, E, and Spalding, A, 1998. *Ethy Park, St Winnow - historic landscape survey*, Truro (Cornwall Archaeological Unit)

Herring, P, Sharpe, A, Smith, J and Giles, C, 2008. *Bodmin Moor. an archaeological survey. Volume 2: the industrial and post- medieval landscapes*, Swindon (English Heritage)

Herring, P, and Smith, J R, 1991. *The archaeology of the St Austell china clay area, an archaeological and historical assessment*, Truro (Cornwall County Council)

Herring, P, and Tapper, B, 2006. *Cotehele historic landscape characterisation and scoping survey for historic landscape survey*, Truro (Historic Environment Service, Cornwall County Council)

Herring, P, and Thomas, N, 1990. *The archaeology of Kit Hill*, Truro (Cornwall County Council)

Herring, P, and Thomas, N, 1993. *Stratton Hundred - rapid identification survy*, Truro (Cornwall Archaeological Unit)

Herring, P, Thorpe, C, and Morley, B, 1998. *Pengersick Castle, Breage - an archaeological and historical assessment*, Truro (Cornwall Archaeological Unit)

Herring, P, Thorpe, C, Quinnell, H, Reynolds, A, and Allan, J, 2000. *St Michael's Mount archaeological works 1995-98*, Truro (Cornwall County Council)

Higham, R, ed, 1987. *Security and defence in south-west England before 1800*, Exeter

Hogg, I, 1974. *Coastal defences of England and Wales, 1856-1956*, Newton Abbot

Holden, P, Herring, P, and Padel, O J, 2010. *The Lanhydrock Atlas*, Fowey (Cornwall Editions)

Holmes, R, 1989. *Civil War battles in Cornwall 1642-1646*, Stoke on Trent

Hopkins, J J, 1980. Turf huts in the Lizard district, *Jnl Roy Inst Cornwall*, **8.3**, 247-249

Hunt, I, 1980. Plymouth Sound? The defence of the naval station, *Fort*, **11**, 83-93

Johns, C, 1997a. *Fortress Falmouth - Pendennis Peninsula Fortifications Project 9: excavation and consolidation of guardhouse at Crab Quay Battery phase 1 evaluation and excavation*, Truro (Cornwall Archaeological Unit)

Johns, C, 1997b. *Fortress Falmouth - documentation consultancy report*, Truro (Cornwall Archaeological Unit)

Johns, C, 1997c. *Fortress Falmouth - Pendennis Peninsula Fortifications Project 8 - excavation and recording of Blockhouse long platform phase 1 evaluation excavation*, Truro (Cornwall Archaeological Unit)

Johns, C, 1997d. *Pendennis Castle watching briefs 1994 - 1996*, Truro (Cornwall Archaeological Unit)

Johns, C, 1998a. *St Agnes Head - an archaeological survey*, Truro (Cornwall Archaeological Unit)

Johns, C, 1998b. *Pendennis Castle - upgrading of the electrical installation 1997*, Truro (Cornwall Archaeological Unit)

Johns, C, 1998c. *Pendennis Castle - staff car park, Lower Hornworks car park and footpaths - archaeological watching brief*, Truro (Cornwall Archaeological Unit)

Johns, C, 1998d. *Fortress Falmouth, Pendennis Peninsula fortifications, ERDF funded projects - watching brief 1994-1998*, Truro (Cornwall Archaeological Unit)

Johns, C, 1998e. *Pendennis Castle moat bank repairs 1998 archaeological recording*, Truro (Cornwall Archaeological Unit)

Johns, C, 1998f. *The Lizard Wireless Station (Marconi Bungalow), The Lizard, Cornwall – archaeological survey*, Truro (Cornwall Archaeological Unit)

Johns, C, 1999a. *Pendennis Castle gunpowder store - archaeological recording*, Truro (Cornwall Archaeological Unit)

Johns, C, 1999b. *St Mawes Castle nineteenth and twentieth century defences project 12-PDR Quick Fire Battery*, Truro (Cornwall Archaeological Unit)

Johns, C, 1999c. *St Mawes Castle engine room - archaeological recording*, Truro (Cornwall Archaeological Unit)

Johns, C, 1999d. *Pendennis Castle ravelin battery revetment collapse - archaeological recording*, Truro (Cornwall Archaeological Unit)

Johns, C, 1999e. *Pendennis Castle nineteenth and twentieth century defences project - telephone exchange*, Truro (Cornwall Archaeological Unit)

Johns, C, 1999f. *Pendennis Castle nineteenth and twentieth century defences project - east bastion*, Truro (Cornwall Archaeological Unit)

Johns, C, 1999g. *Pendennis Castle nineteenth and twentieth century defences project - bombproof barracks*, Truro (Cornwall Archaeological Unit)

Johns, C, 1999h. *Pendennis Castle nineteenth and twentieth century defences project - anti-aircraft post*, Truro (Cornwall Archaeological Unit)

Johns, C, 1999i. *Pendennis Castle nineteenth and twentieth century defences project - depression range finder cells*, Truro (Cornwall Archaeological Unit)

Johns, C, 1999j. *Goonhilly Dry Tree site - an archaeological assessment survey*, Truro (Cornwall Archaeological Unit)

Johns, C, 1999k. *Pendennis Castle nineteenth and twentieth century defences project - east bastion*, Truro (Cornwall Archaeological Unit)

Johns, C, 2000. *Fortress Falmouth Pendennis Peninsula fortifications project 9 - Crab Quay Battery phase II conservation works*, Truro (Cornwall Archaeological Unit)

Johns, C, 2000. *Hyperfix navigation site, Bass Point, The Lizard, Cornwall - archaeological recording*, Truro (Cornwall Archaeological Unit)

Johns, C, 2001a. *St Mawes Castle, archaeological recording during repairs January to April 2001*, Truro (Historic Environment Service, Cornwall County Council)

Johns, C, 2001b. *The Hornworks Eastern Traverse, Pendennis Headland, Cornwall - archaeological survey*, Truro (Historic Environment Service, Cornwall County Council)

Johns, C, 2002. *Windmill Farm, Landewednack, CWT Reserve - an archaeological assessment*, Truro (Historic Environment Service, Cornwall County Council)

Johns, C, 2003. *Re-cobbling at Pendennis Castle, watching brief*, Truro (Historic Environment Service, Cornwall County Council)

Johns, C, 2005. *Barrack block refurbishment, Pendennis Castle, Cornwall - watching brief*, Truro (Historic Environment Service, Cornwall County Council)

Johns, C, 2006. *The kennels leat system, Coinagehall Street, Helston: archaeological and historical assessment*, Truro (Historic Environment Service, Cornwall County Council)

Johns, C, 2010. *Steval Point Battery, The Garrison, St Mary's Isles of Scilly*, Truro (Historic Environment Projects, Cornwall Council)

DISCOVERY AND RESEARCH

Johns, C, and Fletcher, M, 2010. *The Garrison, St Mary's Isles of Scilly – Conservation Plan*, Exeter (English Heritage)

Johns, C, Johnson, N, and Sharpe, A, 1992. *Pendennis Headland: historical credential, current condition and future potential of the defences 1540-1956*, Truro (Cornwall Archaeological Unit)

Johns, C, and Johnson, N, 1994. *Pendennis Headland, the Hornworks defences*, Truro (Cornwall Archaeological Unit)

Johns, C, and Sawyer, K, 2005. *Lower Benham Battery, The Garrison, St Mary's Isles of Scilly - archaeological recording*, Truro (Historic Environment Service, Cornwall County Council)

Johns, C, and Sturgess, J, 2005. *Pendennis Castle, Cornwall disabled access and safety improvements - archaeological recording*, Truro (Historic Environment Service, Cornwall County Council)

Johns, C, and Thomas, N, 1995. *Pendennis Headland, the Hornworks defences 2*, Truro (Cornwall Archaeological Unit)

John Knevitt Practice, 1999. *Kennack Sands, The Lizard, Cornwall. structural engineering and geotechnical report*, Bodmin

Jones, A, and Reynolds, A, 1997. *The Central Hotel, Truro, Cornwall: an evaluation and excavation*, Truro (Cornwall Archaeological Unit)

Jones, B V, 2001. *The Manor Tannery, Grampound*, Swindon (English Heritage)

Kenyon, J, 1982. Ordnance and the King's fortifications in 1547-8 (Pendennis and St Mawes Castles), *Archaeologia*, **107**, 165-213

Kenyon, J, 1983. A hitherto unknown, early 17th-century survey of the coastal forts of southern England: a preliminary outline, *Fort*, **11**, pp 35-56

Keystone, 1993. *Star Castle, St Marys, Isles of Scilly Report K435*, Exeter

Keystone, 1999. *The barrack complex at Maker Heights, Maker, Cornwall*, Exeter

Keystone, 2010. *Godolphin, Conservation Management Plan*, Exeter

Kiernat, C, and Johnson, N, 1996. *Pendennis Point*, Truro (Cornwall Archaeological Unit)

Kinross, J, 1999. *The Palmerston forts of the South West: why were they built?* Charlestown

Kirkham, G, 2003a. *Cornwall and Scilly Urban Survey. Historic characterisation for regeneration: Hugh Town*, Truro (Cornwall County Council)

Kirkham, G, 2003b. *Cornwall and Scilly Urban Survey. Historic characterisation for regeneration: Truro*, Truro (Cornwall County Council)

Kirkham, G, 2005b. *Cornwall and Scilly Urban Survey. Historic characterisation for regeneration: Bodmin*, Truro (Cornwall County Council)

Kirkham, G, 2005c. *Cornwall and Scilly Urban Survey. Historic characterisation for regeneration: Falmouth*, Truro (Cornwall County Council)

Kirkham, G, 2007. *HEATH archaeological assessment - Predannack Airfield*, Truro (Historic Environment Service, Cornwall County Council)

Kitchens, F, 1989. The beacon system in Cornwall, *Cornwall Association of Local Historians, News Magazine*, April 1989, 12-16

Kitchens, F, 1990a. The defence of the southern coast of Cornwall against the French Revolution, *Cornwall Association of Local Historians, News Magazine*, April 1990, 13-17

Kitchens, F, 1990b. The defence of the southern coast of Cornwall against the French Revolution, *Cornwall Association of Local Historians, News Magazine*, October 1990, 6-9

Lake, J, Cox, J, and Berry, E, 2001. *Diversity and vitality - the Methodist and Non-Conformist chapels of Cornwall*, Truro (Cornwall County Council)

Linzey, R, 1992. *An analysis of the battery observation post Half Moon Battery, Pendennis Castle, Falmouth*, Portsmouth (English Heritage Architecture and Survey Branch)

Linzey, R, 1994. *Recommendations for increasing the statutory protection to Woolpack and Steval Batteries and associated structures*, Portsmouth (English Heritage Architecture and Survey Branch)

Linzey, R, 1995a. *Harbour defences - observations and historical notes on the evolution of the quick fire batteries, submarine minefields and defence electric lights of Falmouth Harbour*, Portsmouth (English Heritage Architecture and Survey Branch)

Linzey, R, 1995b. *Pendennis Castle, Falmouth. Condition survey*, Portsmouth (English Heritage Architecture and Survey Branch)

Linzey, R, 1995c. *Pendennis Castle, Falmouth - observations and historical notes to accompany the condition survey of the later defences of the castle*, Portsmouth (English Heritage Architecture and Survey Branch)

Linzey, R, 1995d. *St Mawes 12-pdr battery: briefing paper for condition survey, consolidation and interpretation*, Portsmouth (English Heritage Architecture and Survey Branch)

Linzey, R, 1999. *The castles of Pendennis and St Mawes, guidebook*, London (English Heritage)

Linzey, R, 2000a. *Fortress Falmouth volume I, a conservation plan for the historic defences of Falmouth Haven*, Portsmouth (English Heritage)

Linzey, R, 2000b. *Fortress Falmouth volume II, a conservation plan for the historic defences of Falmouth Haven*, Portsmouth (English Heritage)

London, P, 1999. *U-Boat hunters. Cornwall's air war 1916-19*, Truro

Lorigan, C, 2007. *Delabole: the history of the slate quarry and the making of the village community*, Reading (Pengelly Press)

Lowry, B, ed, 1998. *Twentieth century defences in Britain: an introductory guide. Handbook of the Defence of Britain project*, York (Council for British Archaeology)

Macray, W D, 1888. *The history of the rebellion and civil wars in England*, reissued, Oxford (Clarendon Press) in 1992

Margary, H, 1977. *The Old Series Ordnance Survey maps of England and Wales. Vol II. Devon, Cornwall and West Somerset*, Lympne Castle

Mattingly, J, 2009. *Cornwall and the coast: Mousehole and Newlyn,* Chichester

McCabe, H, 1988. *Houses and gardens of Cornwall*, Padstow

McLaren, G, 1999. *Bodmin Town Conservation Area character appraisal,* Bodmin (North Cornwall District Council)

Miles, T, and Saunders, A, 1970. King Charles' Castle, Tresco, Scilly, *Post-Medieval Arch*, **4,** 1-30

Milne, B A, 1885. *Historical record of the 1ˢᵗ Cornwall (Duke of Cornwall's) artillery volunteers*, London

Mowl, T, 2005. *Historic gardens of Cornwall*, Stroud

Newell, K, 2003. *Cornwall and Scilly Urban Survey. Historic characterisation for regeneration: Newquay,* Truro (Cornwall County Council)

Newell, K, 2004a. *Cornwall and Scilly Urban Survey. Historic characterisation for regeneration: Redruth,* Truro (Cornwall County Council)

Newell, K, 2004b. *Cornwall and Scilly Urban Survey. Historic characterisation for regeneration: Camborne*, Truro (Cornwall County Council)

Newell, K, 2005a. *Cornwall and Scilly Urban Survey. Historic characterisation for regeneration: St Ives,* Truro (Cornwall County Council)

Newell, K, 2005b. *Cornwall and Scilly Urban Survey. Historic characterisation for regeneration: Penryn,* Truro (Cornwall County Council)

Nicholas, F, 1996. *The Lizard Lighthouse,* (Nicholas)

North, D J, and Sharpe, A, 1980. *A word-geography of Cornwall*, Redruth (Institute of Cornish Studies)

Nowakowski, J, 1987. *Boswednack Farm, Zennor - an archaeological survey*, Truro (Cornwall Archaeological Unit)

Osborne, J, 1990. *Scillonian War Diary 1914- 18* (2 vols MSS)

Oxford Archaeology, 2003. *Cornish Bridge Project: assessment report,* Oxford

Palmer, J, ed, 2000. *In and around Penzance during Napoleonic times,* Penwith Local History.

Parkes, C, 1990. *Fieldwork in Scilly March 1990 - early batteries on the Garrison, St Mary's*, Truro (Cornwall Archaeological Unit)

Parkes, C, 1997. *An archaeological and historical assessment of Cabilla and Redrice Woods*, Truro (Cornwall Archaeological Unit)

Parkes, C, 1998. *Home Farm, Minster - an archaeological and historical assessment, Truro*, Truro (Cornwall Archaeological Unit)

Parkes, C, 2000. *Fowey Estuary historic audit*, Truro (Cornwall County Council)

Parkes, C, 2005. *Trerice, Newlyn East, Cornwall - archaeological assessment*, Truro (Historic Environment Service, Cornwall County Council)

Parkes, C, 2006. *Turnaware Point, St Just in Roseland - an archaeological assessment*, Truro (Historic Environment Service, Cornwall County Council)

Parkes, C, 2008a. *Trewarthenick Park, Tregoney - archaeological assessment*, Truro (Historic Environment Service, Cornwall County Council)

Parkes, C. 2008b. *The Dodman and St Austell Bay. An archaeological survey for the National Trust of The Dodman and Penare, Lambsowden, Lamledra and Bodrugan*, Truro (Historic Environment Service, Cornwall County Council)

Parkes, C, forthcoming. *Tehidy, Illogan, archaeological and historic landscape assessment*, Truro (Historic Environment Projects, Cornwall Council)

Parr, T, nd. *Padstow defences*, privately printed

Pasfield Oliver, S, 1875. *Pendennis and St Mawes: an historical sketch of two Cornish castles*, reprinted 1985, Redruth

Passmore, A, 2003. *Former Royal Observer Corps headquarters building, Truro, Cornwall: Archaeological Recording Report No. 03.11*, Exeter (Exeter Archaeology)

Payton, P, 1987. *Tregantle and Scraesdon. Their forts and railway,* Redruth

Payton, P, 2005, *The Cornish overseas*, Fowey, Cornwall Editions

Perry, R, and Harradence, H, 2008. *Silvanus Trevail: Cornish architect and entrepreneur,* London

Perry, R, and Schwartz, S, 2001. James Hicks, architect of regeneration in Victorian Redruth, *Jnl Roy Inst Cornwall*, 64-77

Pett, D E, 1998. *Cornwall's parks and gardens*, Penzance (Alison Hodge)

Phibbs, J L, 1994. *Godolphin: a survey of the landscape*, Cirencester (Debois)

Pool, P A S, 1974. *The history of the town and borough of Penzance*, Penzance (Corporation of Penzance)

Pool, P A S, 1975. 'The ancient and present state of St Michael's Mount' by William Borlase, *Cornish Studies*, **3,** 29-47

Pring, S, 1996. *Glorious gardens of Cornwall*, Truro (Cornwall Gardens Trust)

Pye, A, Woodward, F, Exeter Archaeology, and Fortress Study Group SW, 1996. *The historic defences of Plymouth*, Truro (Cornwall County Council)

Quinnell, N, 1978. A sixteenth century outwork to King Charles' Castle Tresco, *Cornish Archaeol*, **17,** 142-3

Quinnell, N, 1984. A note on the turf platforms of Cornwall, in G Smith, Excavations on Goonhilly Down, The Lizard, 1981, *Cornish Archaeol*, **23,** 11-13

Radford, R, 1980. *Restormel Castle*, London (English Heritage)

Ratcliffe, J, 1989. *The archaeology of Scilly: an assessment of the resource and recommendations for its future*, Truro (Cornwall Archaeological Unit)

Ratcliffe, J, 1993. *Fieldwork in Scilly 1991 and 1992*, Truro (Cornwall Archaeological Unit)

Ratcliffe, J, 1997. *Fal Estuary historic audit*, Truro (Cornwall County Council)

Ratcliffe, J, and Johns, C, 2003. *Scilly's archaeological heritage*, Chacewater (Twelveheads)

Ratcliffe, J, and Sharpe, A, 1990. *Fieldwork in Scilly, autumn 1990*, Truro (Cornwall Archaeological Unit)

Reynolds, A, 2000. *Helford Estuary historic audit*, Truro (Cornwall County Council)

Richards, P, and Reynolds, D, 1994. *Fowey at War*, Fowey

Ruddle, E and Thomas, N, 2005. *Mullion Harbour, Cornwall - archaeological and historical assessment*, Truro (Historic Environment Service, Cornwall County Council)

347

DISCOVERY AND RESEARCH

Russell, S, 2002. *Cornwall and Scilly Urban Survey. Historic characterisation for regeneration: Helston,* Truro (Cornwall County Council)

Sage, A, 2003. *Tregantle Fort: archaeological recording,* Exeter (Exeter Archaeology)

Saunders, A, 1962. Harry's Walls, St Marys Scilly: a new interpretation, *Cornish Archaeol,* **1,** 85-89

Saunders, A, 1989. *Fortress Britain: artillery fortification in the British Isles and Ireland,* Liphook (Beaufort Press)

Schofield, J, 2001. D-Day sites in England: an assessment, *Antiquity,* **75,** 77-83

Schofield, J, 2004. *Recent military heritage: a review of progress 1994-2004,* English Heritage website.

Schofield, J, forthcoming. The appearances of Godolphin, in volume edited by D Dawson

Schwartz, P S, 2008. *Voices of the Cornish mining landscape,* Truro (Cornwall County Council)

Shapland, J, 1989. *The memories linger on. A collection of reminiscences of wartime RAF St Eval,* St Eval

Sharpe, A, 1986. *Wheal Coates, St Agnes - an archaeological survey,* Truro (Cornwall Archaeological Unit)

Sharpe, A, 1989a. *Minions: an archaeological survey of the Caradon mining district,* Truro (Cornwall County Council)

Sharpe, A, 1989b. *Pendennis Castle - an account of ye excavations undertaken in ye chemise 1989,* Truro (Cornwall Archaeological Unit)

Sharpe, A, 1990a. *Ballowall, St Just in Penwith, Cornwall. An archaeological assessment,* Truro (Cornwall Archaeological Unit)

Sharpe, A, 1990b. *Pendennis Castle - refurbishment of the fire fighting water main - archaeological watching brief,* Truro (Cornwall Archaeological Unit)

Sharpe, A, 1990c. *Coastal slate quarries - Tintagel to Trebarwith,* Truro (Cornwall Archaeological Unit)

Sharpe, A, 1992. *Taylor's Shaft, EPAL. Archaeological assessment,* Truro (Cornwall Archaeological Unit)

Sharpe, A, 1993. Geevor and Levant - an assessment of their surface archaeology, Truro (Cornwall Archaeological Unit)

Sharpe, A, 1999. *Robinson's Shaft, South Crofty: an archaeological assessment,* Truro (Cornwall Archaeological Unit)

Sharpe A, 2003. *An archaeological assessment of the proposed Dudnance Lane to Station Road development area,* Truro (Historic Environment Service, Cornwall County Council)

Sharpe, A, 2007. *Pool Heartlands, Cornwall - assessment of historic environment assets,* Truro (Historic Environment Service, Cornwall County Council)

Sharpe, A, 2008a. *Carn Praunter (Botallack Stamps), Kenidjack Valley, St. Just in Penwith, Cornwall – archaeological assessment,* Truro (Historic Environment Service, Cornwall County Council)

Sharpe, A, 2008b. *Botallack and Wheal Cock - archaeological assessment,* Truro (Historic Environment Service, Cornwall County Council)

Sharpe, A, 2008c. *Geevor and Levant, Cornwall: historic landscape development,* Truro (Historic Environment Service, Cornwall County Council)

Sharpe, A, 2009. *Structures at Taylor's and Davey's Shafts, Consolidated Mines, Gwennap - archaeological assessment,* Truro (Historic Environment Projects, Cornwall Council)

Sharpe, A, 2011a. *Watching brief during improvements works to the Geevor underground tour,* Truro (Historic Environment Projects, Cornwall Council)

Sharpe, A, 2011b. *St Agnes Beacon, Tubby's Head, Wheal Coates, Chapel Coombe, Charlotte and Towan Moor, St Agnes, Cornwall,* Truro (Historic Environment Projects, Cornwall Council)

Sharpe, A, Lewis, R, Massie, C, and Johnson, N, 1991. *Engine house survey: the mineral tramways project,* Truro (Cornwall Archaeological Unit)

Sharpe, A and Smith, J R, 1989. *The mineral tramways project,* Truro (Cornwall Archaeological Unit)

Sheppard, P, 1975. Maker fortifications, *Old Cornwall,* **8.5,** 236-247

Sheppard, P, 1976. Wringford: a picket post in Rame, *Old Cornwall,* **8.6,** 272-276

Sheppard, P, 1980. *The historic towns of Cornwall: an archaeological survey,* Truro (Cornwall Committee for Rescue Archaeology)

Smith, J R, 1986. *The Kennall Gunpowder Co, Kennall, Vale, Ponsanooth - an archaeological and historical survey,* Truro (Cornwall Trust for Nature Conservation)

Smith J R, 1988. *Luxulyan Valley Project - an archaeological and historical survey,* Truro (Cornwall County Council)

Smith, J R, 1989. *Southdown Quay, Milbrook - proposed Insworke marina village,* Truro (Cornwall Archaeological Unit)

Smith, J R, 1991. *Perran Foundry - an assessment of the historic site and buildings at Perran Foundry, Perran Wharf, Mylor,* Truro (Cornwall Archaeological Unit)

Smith, J R, 1992. *Cornwall's china clay heritage,* Chacewater (Twelveheads Press)

Smith, J R, 1999. *Harvey's Foundry, Hayle, Cornwall - an archaeological assessment,* Truro (Cornwall Archaeological Unit)

Smith, J R, 2008a. *Sky-tips in the St Austell china-clay district, an archaeological assessment,* Truro (Historic Environment Service, Cornwall County Council)

Smith, J R, 2008b. China-clay, in Herring *et al* 2008, 101-116

Smith, J R, 2008c. Transport and communications, in Herring *et al* 2008, 171-180

Smith, J R, Berry, E, Johnson, N, and Thomas, N, 1998. *Charlestown, historical and archaeological assessment,* Truro (Cornwall Archaeological Unit)

Stanier, P, 1985a. *The granite industry of south-west England, 1800-1980: a study in historical geography,* unpublished PhD thesis, University of Southampton

Stanier, P, 1985b. The granite quarrying industry in Devon and Cornwall, part 1, 1800-1910, *Ind Arch Rev,* **7.2,** 171-189

Stanier, P, 1985c. Granite-working in the Cheesewring district of Bodmin Moor, Cornwall, *Jnl Trevithick Soc,* **12,** 36-51

Stanier, P, 1986a. The granite quarrying industry in Devon and Cornwall, part 2, 1910-85, *Ind Arch Rev,* **9.1,** 7-23

Stanier, P, 1986b. John Freeman and the Cornish granite industry, 1840-1965, *Jnl Trevithick Soc,* **13,** 7-35

Stanier, P, 1986c. *The Minions Moor*, St Ives

Stanier, P, 1987. Early mining and water power in the Caradon mining district of east Cornwall, *Jnl Trevithick Soc*, **14**, 32-45

Stanier, P, 1992. Granite quarry cranes of Cornwall and Devon: vanishing industrial archaeology, *Jnl Trevithick Soc*, **19**, 18-31

Stanier, P, 1999. *South West Granite, a history of the granite industry in Cornwall and Devon*, St Austell (Cornish Hillside Publications)

Stengelhofen, J, 1988. *Cornwall's railway heritage*, Chacewater (Twelveheads Press)

Stoyle, M, 1996. Pagans or paragons? Images of the Cornish during the English Civil War, *English Historical Review*, **111**, 299–323

Stoyle, M, 1998. The last refuge of a scoundrel: Sir Richard Grenville and Cornish particularism, *Historical Research*, **71**, 44-49

Stoyle, M, 1999. The dissidence of despair: rebellion and identity in early-modern Cornwall, *Journal of British Studies*, **38**, 423-444

Stoyle, M, 2000a. The Gear Rout: The Cornish Rising of 1648 and the Second Civil War, *Albion*, **32.1**, 37-58

Stoyle, M, 2000b. English 'nationalism', Celtic particularism and the English Civil War, *Historical Journal*, **43.4**, 1113-1128

Stoyle, M, 2002. *West Britons: Cornish identities and the early British state*, Exeter

Stoyle, M, 2005. *Soldiers and strangers: an ethnic history of the English Civil War*, Yale

Stoyle, M, 2008. Afterlife of an army: the old Cornish Tertia, 1643-44, *Cornish Studies*, **16**, 26-47

Sturgess, J, 2000. *California Quarry, Western Blackapit, Cornwall - archaeological assessment*, Truro (Cornwall Archaeological Unit)

Sturgess, J, 2001. *The dry dock, Little Falmouth yacht yard, Flushing, Falmouth, Cornwall - archaeological survey and historical assessment*, Truro (Historic Environment Service, Cornwall County Council)

Sturgess, J, 2004a. *Tintagel Haven slate works, Cornwall - historic building survey*, Truro (Historic Environment Service, Cornwall County Council)

Sturgess, J, 2004b. *Goonhilly satellite earth station, Cornwall - updated archaeological survey*, Truro (Historic Environment Service, Cornwall County Council)

Sturgess, J, 2004c. *Cutmadoc farmhouse and cottage, Lanhydrock, Cornwall - archaeological assessment, building survey and watching briefs*, Truro (Historic Environment Service, Cornwall County Council)

Sturgess, J, 2009. *St Michael's Mount ravelin wall collapse - archaeological watching brief*, Truro (Historic Environment Service, Cornwall County Council)

Sturgess, J, 2010. *St Michael's Mount watch tower and gateway complex - archaeological building survey and evaluation*, Truro (Historic Environment Projects, Cornwall Council)

Sturgess, J, and Berry, E, forthcoming. *Trerice House, Newlyn East*, Truro (Historic Environment Projects, Cornwall Council)

Taylor, J, 2002. *Royal Artillery Barracks, Pendennis Castle, Cornwall: archaeological building recording*, Portsmouth (English Heritage)

Taylor, P, 2001. *The toll-houses of Cornwall*, Newquay (Federation of Old Cornwall Societies)

Taylor, S, 2002. *Baker's Pit - a rapid archaeological and historic landscape assessment*, Truro (Historic Environment Service, Cornwall County Council)

Taylor, S, 2006. *St Mawes Castle caretaker's quarters, Cornwall - archaeological recording*, Truro (Historic Environment Service, Cornwall County Council)

Thomas, C, 1957. Cornish Volunteers in the 18th-century (1745-1783), *Devon and Cornwall Notes and Queries*, **27**, 135-144

Thomas, C, 1958a. Cornish Volunteers in the 18th-century (1794-1802), *Devon and Cornwall Notes and Queries*, **27**, 229-236

Thomas, C, 1958b. Cornish Volunteers in the 18th-century (1794-1802), *Devon and Cornwall Notes and Queries*, **27**, 326-331

Thomas, C, 1959a. Cornish Volunteers in the 18th-century (1794-1802), *Devon and Cornwall Notes and Queries*, **28**, 10-16

Thomas, C, 1959b. Cornish Volunteers in the 19th-century (1803-1808), *Devon and Cornwall Notes and Queries*, **28**, 46-49

Thomas, C, 1959c. Cornish Volunteers in the 19th-century (1803-1808), *Devon and Cornwall Notes and Queries*, **28**, 77-82

Thomas, C, 1960a. Cornish Volunteers in the 19th-century (1803-1808), *Devon and Cornwall Notes and Queries*, **28**, 166-174

Thomas, C, 1960b. The Royal Cornwall Local Militia, and the end of the Napoleonic Volunteers (1808-1836), *Devon and Cornwall Notes and Queries*, **28**, 203-209

Thomas. C, nd. *A short history of the Cornish Volunteers 1745-1956*, unpublished MS

Thomas, C (ed), 1974. *An archaeological survey of the Rame peninsula*. Inst Cornish Studies- Spec Rep **2**

Thomas, C, 1989. The names of the batteries on the Garrison, St Mary's, Isles of Scilly, in M Bowden, D Mackay, and P Topping, eds, *From Cornwall to Caithness, some aspects of British field archaeology*, Brit Arch Repts, Brit Ser, **209**, 254

Thomas, N, 1994. *An archaeological assessment of the National Trust estate at Lanhydrock*, Truro (Cornwall Archaeological Unit)

Thomas, N, 1995. *A desk-based study of Nanny Moore's Bridge, Bude, Cornwall*, Truro (Cornwall Archaeological Unit)

Thomas, N, 1996a. *Mennabroom, St Neot - an archaeological investigation*, Truro (Cornwall Archaeological Unit)

Thomas, N, 1996b. *An archaeological survey of Restormel Castle, Cornwall*, Truro (Cornwall Archaeological Unit)

Thomas, N, 1996c. *Heligan Lower Valley Cornwall - an archaeological assessment*, Truro (Cornwall Archaeological Unit)

Thomas, N, 1997. *Golden Keep, Probus, Cornwall - an archaeological evaluation*, Truro (Cornwall Archaeological Unit)

DISCOVERY AND RESEARCH

Thomas, N, 1998a. *Poley's Bridge, St Tudy - an archaeological and historical assessment*, Truro (Cornwall Archaeological Unit)

Thomas, N, 1998b. *Former kennel complex, Tehidy*, Truro (Cornwall Archaeological Unit)

Thomas, N, 1998c. *Loggans Mill, Hayle - an archaeological and historic buildings assessment*, Truro (Cornwall Archaeological Unit)

Thomas, N, 1998d. *Lanhydrock Park - a survey of an historic landscape*, Truro (Cornwall Archaeological Unit)

Thomas, N, 1999. *St Catherine's Castle, Fowey - an archaeological assessment*, Truro (Cornwall Archaeological Unit)

Thomas, N, 2006. *The former ASC stores, Pendennis Castle, Cornwall - archaeological watching brief*, Truro (Historic Environment Service, Cornwall County Council)

Thomas, N, 2010. *St Michael's Mount watch tower and gateway complex, Cornwall: archaeological building survey and evaluation*, Truro (Historic Environment Projects, Cornwall Council)

Thomas, N, and Buck, C, 1993. *A historical and archaeological investigation of Restormel Castle: an interim study*, Truro (Cornwall Archaeological Unit)

Thomas, N, and Herring, P, 2001. *Gribben Head to Lansallos, Cornwall. An archaeological assessment*, Truro (Historic Environment Service, Cornwall County Council)

Thomas, R. 2003. *Twentieth century military recording project - prisoner of war camps (1939-1948)*, English Heritage

Thompson, H, 1993. *A record of the farm buildings of Gerrans and St Anthony-in-Roseland*, Portscatho

Thorpe, C, 2001. *Bear's Down wind farm, Cornwall - archaeological watching brief July 2001*, Truro (Historic Environment Service, Cornwall County Council)

Todd, A C, 1997. *The search for silver: Cornish miners in Mexico 1845-1947*, Padstow

Truro Buildings Research Group [TBRG], nd [1981]. *Truro: Boscawen Street area*, Truro (Truro Civic Society and Truro Buildings Research Group with University of Exeter Extra-Mural Dept)

Truro Buildings Research Group [TBRG], 1985. *Truro: River Street and its neighbourhood*, Truro (Truro Buildings Research Group with University of Exeter Extra-Mural Dept)

Turner, M, 2000. *Clay country voices*, Stroud

Turner, S, 2007. *Ancient country: the historic character of rural Devon*, Exeter

Unwin, A H, and Thomas, N, 2004. *Rosewastis Mill, St Columb Major, Cornwall - historic building analysis*, Truro (Historic Environment Service, Cornwall County Council)

Vyvyan, C, 1910. Defence of the Helford River, 1643-46, *Jnl Roy Inst Cornwall*, **18.1,** 62-102

Vyvyan, R F A, 2000. *Tregrehan, historic landscape survey - management plan*, Trelowarren

WA Heritage, 2008a. *Wacker Quay engine shed, Antony, Nr. Plymouth, Cornwall*, Salisbury

WA Heritage, 2008b. *Scraesdon Fort, Antony, near Plymouth, Cornwall*, Salisbury

Walker, R, 1989. *Pendennis Castle resistivity survey*, Truro (Cornwall Archaeological Unit)

Watson, S, 1992. *Truro leats survey*, Truro (Carrick District Council)

Watts, M, 2000. *WWII maintenance structure (gridiron) at Mylor yacht harbour, Mylor Churchtown, Falmouth, Cornwall*, Exeter (Exeter Archaeology)

White, H, 2000. *The Duke of Cornwall's Light Infantry*, Stroud

Williams, C, Herring, P, and Tyrrell, S, 2011. *Caerhays Castle*, Constantine

Willies, L, 2004. *Portreath airfield, Cornwall, and the adjacent area - archaeological assessment*, Shrewsbury (Enviros Consulting)

Wilson-North, W R, 1993. Stowe: the country house and garden of the Grenville family, *Cornish Archaeol*, **32,** 112-127

Woodward, F, 1990. *Plymouth's defences, a short history*, Plymouth

Woodward, F, 1998. *Forts or follies? A history of Plymouth's Palmerston forts*, Tiverton

Young, A, 2006. The National Mapping Programme in Cornwall, *Cornish Archaeol*, **45,** 214-15

Young, G, 2002. *Scraesdon Fort, Antony, Cornwall. A photographic survey of the Braithwaite Platform, prior to removal*, Exeter (Exeter Archaeology)

Young, W, 2001. *Cleave*, Redruth